Tropical Ecosystems and Ecological Concepts

Over one third of the earth's terrestrial surface is situated in the tropics, with environments ranging from hot deserts to tropical rain forests. This introductory textbook, aimed at students studying tropical ecology, provides a comprehensive guide to the major tropical biomes and is unique in its balanced coverage of both aquatic and terrestrial systems, and in its international scope. Chapters describe the ecology of deserts, grasslands, savannas, tropical rain forests, lakes, rivers and floodplains, mountains, wetlands, mangroves, coral reefs and tropical islands, with descriptive case studies providing a framework around which ecological concepts are presented. Given the concern about humankind's impact on tropical ecosystems, the volume also considers the human ecological dimension, with coverage of issues such as population growth, urbanisation, agriculture and fisheries, natural resource use and pollution, and global issues such as the conservation of biodiversity, climate change and the concept of ecological sustainability. The text is supported throughout by boxes containing supplementary material on a range of topics and organisms, plus mathematical concepts and calculations, and is enlivened with clear, simple line diagrams, maps and photographs. A cross-referenced glossary, extensive reference system and a comprehensive index are included as further aids to study.

Patrick Osborne is Executive Director of the International Center for Tropical Ecology at the University of Missouri-St. Louis. He has spent most of his professional life studying and teaching tropical ecology and has travelled extensively throughout the tropics during the course of his career. His particular research interests focus on tropical lakes and wetlands. He is co-author of *Freshwater Plants of Papua New Guinea* (1985).

Tropical Ecosystems and Ecological Concepts

Patrick L. Osborne

International Center for Tropical Ecology
University of Missouri-St. Louis

CAMBRIDGE
UNIVERSITY PRESS

PUBLISHED BY THE PRESS SYNDICATE OF THE UNIVERSITY OF CAMBRIDGE
The Pitt Building, Trumpington Street, Cambridge, United Kingdom

CAMBRIDGE UNIVERSITY PRESS
The Edinburgh Building, Cambridge CB2 2RU, UK   http://www.cup.cam.ac.uk
40 West 20th Street, New York, NY 10011-4211, USA   http://www.cup.org
10 Stamford Road, Oakleigh, Melbourne 3166, Australia
Ruiz de Alarcón 13, 28014 Madrid, Spain

First published 2000

Printed in the United Kingdom at the University Press, Cambridge

Typeface Swift Regular 9.5/12.25 pt.   *System* QuarkXPress™ [SE]

A catalogue record for this book is available from the British Library

Library of Congress Cataloguing in Publication data
Osborne, Patrick L.
    Tropical ecosystems and ecological concepts / Patrick L. Osborne.
        p.   cm.
    Includes bibliographical references
    ISBN 0 521 64251 5 – ISBN 0 521 64523 9 (pbk.)
    1. Ecology–Tropics.   I. Title.
    QH84.5.O82   2000
    577′.0913–dc21   99-047853

ISBN 0 521 64251 5 hardback
ISBN 0 521 64523 9 paperback

To Emma and Robbie and their generation

Contents

Preface

The aim of this book is to provide an introduction to tropical ecosystems: to describe their structure and function, organisms that live within them and the main ecological concepts that comprise our understanding of them. The book is intended for students in tropical countries who have completed a university-level introductory biology course and are planning to major in biology, ecology or environmental science.

There has been, over the last 20 years, an explosion of interest in tropical ecology fuelled by concern for the impact we are having on tropical ecosystems and the biodiversity they harbour. The rapid growth in both our numbers and our material aspirations has led to the depletion and degradation of the earth's natural resources. This is not a regional issue but one that should concern all humans irrespective of where they live. Ecology, as the science that underpins the conservation, protection and wise use of natural resources, has become more than a sub-discipline of biology. Its study and application require an appreciation of chemistry, physics, geology and physical geography. The conservation of tropical ecosystems also has a human dimension and, therefore, effective husbandry of natural resources also draws from the social sciences of economics, political science, anthropology, human geography and sociology. This book can provide only an introduction to these broader conservation issues.

Ecology is a huge subject, and even limiting it geographically to the tropics leaves far more material and examples than can be covered in a semester-long course or, indeed, in a book to support such a course. I am acutely aware that much has been omitted from this book, and selecting what to include has presented the biggest challenge in writing it. Despite a bias from my life and work in Africa, Papua New Guinea and Australia, I have striven to present a regionally balanced account.

Many ecology texts focus on terrestrial environments with inadequate coverage of aquatic systems. I have redressed this imbalance with chapters devoted to lakes, coral reefs, mangroves, rivers and wetlands. Life in water differs markedly from that on land and these differences can be effectively used to illustrate ecological concepts and provide some stark examples of how organisms are adapted to their environment.

I wish to thank the following colleagues for reviewing draft chapters: Dr Mary Burgis, United Kingdom; Dr David Dudgeon, University of Hong Kong; Dr Terry Erwin, Smithsonian Institution, Washington DC; Dr Max Finlayson, Environmental Research Institute of the Supervising Scientist, Australia; Dr Geoffrey Humphreys, University of Macquarie, Australia; Dr David Harper, University of Leicester, United Kingdom; Dr Michael Huber, Australia; Dr Greg Leach, Conservation Commission, Northern Territory, Australia; Dr Lance Hill, University of Papua New Guinea; Dr Geoffrey Hope, Australian National University; Dr Robert Meade, United States Geological Survey, Denver, Colorado; Dr David Mitchell, Charles Sturt University, Australia; Dr Stephen Mulkey, University of Florida-Gainesville, United States; Dr Nicholas Polunin, University of Newcastle-upon-Tyne, United Kingdom; Professor Ghillean Prance, Kew Gardens, United Kingdom; Dr Robert Ricklefs, University of Missouri-St. Louis, United States; Dr Ian Thornton, La Trobe University, Australia; Dr Peter Woodall, University of Queensland, Australia; and Dr Truman Young, Fordham University, United States. Any errors remaining, however, are my own. I thank Alan Crowden, Maria Murphy, Susan Tuck and Gillian Maude at Cambridge University Press for their support and care in guiding the manuscript through the production process.

I acknowledge the Birge–Allen Charitable Trust for providing a grant through the International Center for Tropical Ecology at the University of Missouri-St. Louis to cover costs of producing the manuscript and purchasing illustrations.

I also thank my wife, Nancy, for her unfailing love and support. This book is dedicated to our children and the next generation – for they are the curators of our legacy.

Patrick L. Osborne
International Center for Tropical Ecology
University of Missouri-St. Louis
email: posborne@jinx.umsl.edu

Abbreviations and units

nm = nanometre (10^{-9} m)
μm = micrometre (1 μm = 1000 nm)
mm = millimetre (1 mm = 1000 μm)
cm = centimetre (1 cm = 10 mm)
dm = decimetre (1 dm = 10 cm)
m = metre (1 m = 100 cm)
km = kilometre (1 km = 1000 m)
ha = hectare (10000 square metres)
μg = microgram
mg = milligram (1 mg = 1000 μg)
g = gram (1 g = 1000 mg)
kg = kilogram (1 kg = 1000 g)
mL = millilitre
L = litre (1 L = 1000 mL)
t = tonnes (metric; 1 t = 1000 kg)
s = second
min = minute
h = hour
d = day
y = year

% = per cent
‰ = parts per thousand
ppm = parts per million
μM = micromolar
mM = millimolar
M = molar
°C = degrees centigrade
cal = calorie (1 cal = 4.184 J)
J = Joule (kg m^2 s^{-2})
μS = micro-siemens
a.s.l. = above sea level
e.g. = e.g. (*exampli gratia*)
et al. = and others (*et alii*)
i.e. = that is (*id est*)
sp. = species (singular)
spp. = species (plural)
< = less than
> = greater than
± = more or less, approximately

Chapter 1

The tropical environment

1.1 | The tropics

The tropics may be defined as that portion of the earth situated between the Tropics of Cancer (23° 28′N) and Capricorn (23° 28′S). This area includes about 50 million km² of land, with almost half of it in Africa. Other substantial portions lie in Central and South America, southern Asia, northern Australia, with smaller areas in the Pacific Islands. Plant and animal distributions, however, are not constrained by these lines on the globe but are determined by variations in climate, soil type and other features of the environment. However, it is interesting that the distributions of tropical rain forests, mangroves and coral reefs do fall largely between these lines (Figures 8.2, 10.2 and 11.10). Therefore, it is appropriate to use the Tropics of Cancer and Capricorn as guides to the parts of the earth described in this book even though the distribution of tropical plants and animals may not, in some places, extend as far as these lines or, in others, extend north or south of them.

In 1855, Alphonse de Candolle proposed that the boundaries to major plant formations were set by climate. He suggested that the limits to deserts and grasslands were set by moisture, but that the latitudinal arrangement of the other plant formations suggested that temperature was the dominant factor. Köppen (1884, 1931) developed climate maps based on vegetation types. In this way, he was able to produce a climate map of the world even though he had very little climatic data from many parts of it. He assigned to each plant formation the climate that seemed appro-

priate to it. Since his climate map was based on the global distribution of vegetation types, it is not surprising that climate and vegetation maps were similar.

It has subsequently been shown, using independent measures, that the distribution of the world's climatic regions are indeed closely related to vegetation and that Köppen's vegetation-derived climate map has been verified through climatic measures. Figures 1.1 and 1.2 show the relationship between rainfall and vegetation in Africa. Clearly climate plays a major role in determining the global distribution of plants and animals. An explanation of plant and animal distributions also requires an understanding of the theory of plate tectonics. In this chapter, we describe climate in the tropics and the theory of plate tectonics and their role in determining the global distribution of plants and animals.

1.2 | Climate in the tropics

Climatic variations are largely determined by latitude and altitude. In concentrating on tropical latitudes, we have narrowed the latitudinal range but significant climatic shifts can still be related to geographical position. The major climatic factors are temperature (daily and seasonal variations) and rainfall (total rainfall and its seasonal distribution).

1.2.1 Temperature

In contrast to temperate regions of the earth, the most significant climatic feature of the tropics at

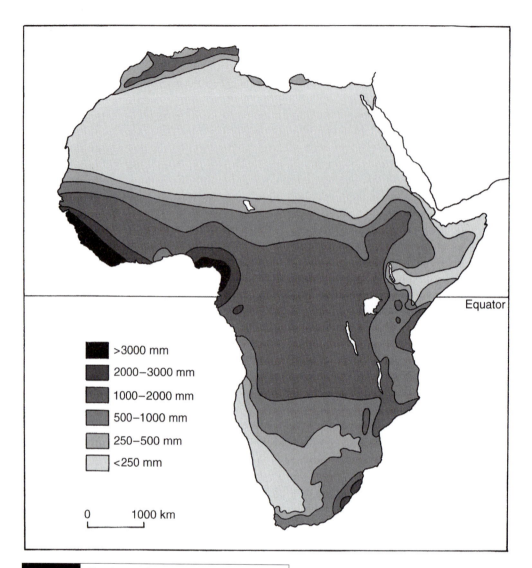

Figure 1.1   Distribution of total annual rainfall in Africa (after Pomeroy and Service 1986 reprinted by permission of Pearson Education Limited, Longman Group Limited).

sea level is the absence of a cold season. The mean annual temperature at sea level usually exceeds 18 °C and seasonal fluctuations in temperature and daily solar radiation are small (Table 1.1). Consequently, seasonality in temperature has less effect on biological activity in the tropics than it has in temperate regions. At higher altitudes in the tropics, diurnal temperature fluctuations can be significant: high during the day and down to, or below, freezing at night (see chapter 9).

Temperatures on the earth's surface follow daily and seasonal cycles; daily because the earth rotates on its axis and seasonal because the earth's axis of rotation is not at right angles to the line joining the earth and sun (Figure 1.3). If it were at right angles, the sun would be overhead at the equator every noon throughout the year. As the earth is tilted, the noon position of the sun moves progressively north after 21 March (**equinox**) and at noon on 21 June (**summer solstice**) it is directly overhead the Tropic of Cancer. The sun then appears to move south, crossing the equator on 23 September (equinox) to be directly over the Tropic of Capricorn at noon on 22 December (**winter solstice**). The solstices are

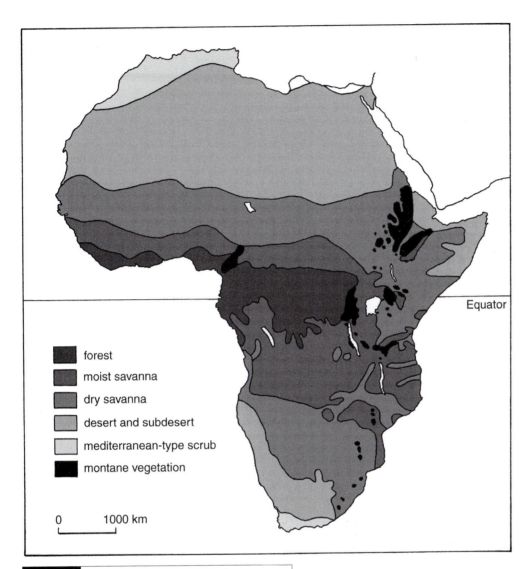

Figure 1.2 Distribution of the main types of vegetation in Africa. Note the relationship between the distribution of rainfall (Figure 1.1) and vegetation type (after Ewer and Hall 1978).

named after the prevailing season in the northern hemisphere. After 21 December, the sun appears to move north again and is directly over the equator at noon on 21 March.

The tropics are hotter than temperate regions because the sun's rays strike almost at right angles near the equator but at an increasingly acute angle towards the poles. Therefore the same amount of radiant heat is concentrated over a smaller area in the tropics than it is nearer the poles (Figure 1.4a). Moreover, near the poles the sun's rays have to pass through a deeper layer of atmosphere and lose more energy by absorption, reflection and scattering. Day-length changes at latitudes away from the equator partially compensate for the reduced heat input (Figure 1.4b), but total annual insolation is still lower at higher latitudes.

As a result of the variations in energy supply with latitude, lower latitudes have more heat, delivered at a more constant rate than higher latitudes. There is a mass transfer of heat away from the equator, towards the poles. This transfer occurs in both the oceans and the atmosphere.

Latitude	Daily max J cm^{-2} d^{-1}	Daily min J cm^{-2} d^{-1}	Maximum/minimum	[(Max − Min) × 100]/Min
0°	3890	3430	1.13	13.4
10°N	3786	3180	1.19	19.1
23°N	4100	2552	1.61	60.7
50°N	4309	878	4.90	390.5

Table 1.1 Annual range of daily solar radiation at the top of the atmosphere at tropical and temperate latitudes.

Notes: Note that, at the equator, the annual maximum solar radiation is only 13% higher than the minimum. This percentage increases sharply outside the tropics and reaches almost 400% at 50°N and S.

Source: List 1971.

Oceanic heat transfer is significant since the heat capacity of water (see Box 2.1) is high, but heat transfer through the atmosphere is more rapid and is mostly responsible for the climatic shifts we observe on a daily basis.

1.2.2 The inter-tropical convergence zone and rainfall

The concentration of radiant heat above the equator warms the air and it expands and rises. As it rises, the air cools and, since cold air holds less moisture, rain falls. The air near the ground is replaced by air from the north and south. The rising air spreads out and falls again at about 30°N and S (see Figure 2.2). In this region, cool, dry air warms as it falls to earth and this explains why deserts are often found at these latitudes (chapter 2).

The rotation of the earth results in the deflection of these northerly and southerly winds so that they blow from the north-east (northern hemisphere) and south-east (southern hemisphere) respectively. This deflection is caused by the **Coriolis** force. The earth rotates from west to east. At the equator, the rate of rotation is faster than it is either to the north or south, since, at the equator, the earth's surface is furthest from the axis of rotation. This force causes oceanic and atmospheric currents to be deflected to the right in the northern hemisphere and to the left in the southern hemisphere.

These winds (north-east (northern hemisphere) and south-east (southern hemisphere)) are known as **trade winds** (they powered the sailing ships that plied the trade between the Orient and Europe) and are renowned for their consistent speed and direction. These winds meet in an equatorial low-pressure trough, warm air ascends and precipitation results. This zone, the **Inter-Tropical Convergence Zone (ITCZ)**, is where mixing of trade winds from the northern and southern hemispheres often results in zones of low atmospheric pressure (depressions) or cyclones.

The ITCZ is not a continuous feature in either time or space. The ITCZ moves north of the equator during the northern summer (June–August) bringing rain to the underlying regions. At the end of the northern summer, the ITCZ migrates south of the equator and these regions have a wet season between November and January. Equatorial regions exhibit a bimodal rainfall pattern, with peak rainfall occurring each time the ITCZ crosses the equator. In other words, there is a seasonal migration of a rain belt that follows the seasonal movement of the sun. At the higher tropical latitudes, a single rainy season occurs following the summer solstice in each hemisphere. Two peaks in the mean annual rainfall are recorded at sites near the equator in response to the passage of the overhead sun at the equinoxes. There are days when ITCZ-generated cloud stretches in an almost unbroken band around the globe, but it is often broken into strips

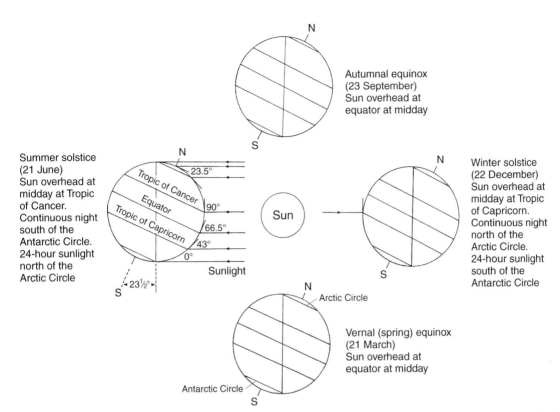

Autumnal equinox
(23 September)
Sun overhead at
equator at midday

Summer solstice
(21 June)
Sun overhead at
midday at Tropic
of Cancer.
Continuous night
south of the
Antarctic Circle.
24-hour sunlight
north of the
Arctic Circle

Tropic of Cancer
Equator
Tropic of Capricorn

23.5°
90°
66.5°
43°
0°
Sunlight

23½°

Sun

Winter solstice
(22 December)
Sun overhead at
midday at Tropic
of Capricorn.
Continuous night
north of the
Arctic Circle.
24-hour sunlight
south of the
Antarctic Circle

Arctic Circle

Vernal (spring) equinox
(21 March)
Sun overhead at
equator at midday

Antarctic Circle

Figure 1.3 Rotation of the earth around the sun. The axis of rotation is tilted at 23° 28′ from the vertical. At the summer solstice (northern hemisphere summer) the sun is overhead at midday at the Tropic of Cancer. At this time of the year, above the Arctic circle, the sun does not set and below the Antarctic circle the sun does not rise. At the winter solstice (northern hemisphere winter), the sun is overhead at midday at the Tropic of Capricorn. At this time of the year, above the Arctic circle, the sun does not rise and below the Antarctic circle the sun does not set. At the autumnal (23 September) and vernal (21 March) equinoxes the sun is directly over the equator at midday (after Pomeroy and Service 1986 reprinted by permission of Pearson Education Limited, Longman Group Limited).

and may disappear entirely. The mean position of the ITCZ in January and July is shown in Figure 1.5.

1.2.3 Monsoons, typhoons and tropical storms

To the north and south of the trade winds, beyond 40 degrees, lie the westerlies. The equatorial westerlies are responsible for the monsoons that occur over West Africa and the Indian subcontinent (Figure 1.5). Land masses heat more rapidly during summer than do the adjacent oceans and, conversely, the land cools more rapidly following the onset of winter. These differential rates of heating and cooling cause seasonal switches in winds. From May to October, air rises over the warm Asian interior and draws in moisture-laden air from the Indian Ocean over the Indian subcontinent (**south-west monsoon**) and air drawn from the Pacific flows over Asia (**south-east monsoon**). From November to April, air sinks over the cold Asian interior resulting in the north-east monsoons. Monsoons also occur in northern Australia and West Africa.

Air converging upon a low-pressure cell (**cyclone**) rises, the air cools, clouds form and rain falls. This contrasts with the warming and drying that occurs in a high-pressure cell (**anticyclone**). In the tropics, cyclones may form a rotating storm known as a **hurricane** or **typhoon**. These storms can be devastating, causing flooding in coastal areas through storm surges and torrential rains. High wind speeds wreak further havoc. In 1991, a typhoon struck the Bay of Bengal and was

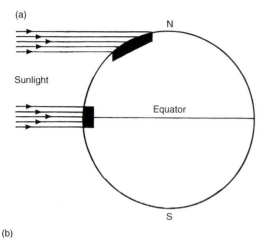

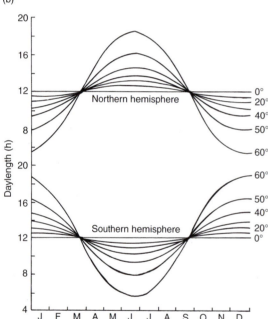

Figure 1.4 (a) Owing to the spherical shape of the earth, solar energy is concentrated over a smaller area in equatorial regions than in polar regions. Distance travelled through the atmosphere is also shorter at the equator. Consequently, tropical regions are warmer than polar regions. (b) Variations in day length throughout the year in relation to latitude in the northern and southern hemispheres.

responsible for 250 000 deaths in Bangladesh. Hurricane Mitch devastated communities in Central America in 1998. These storms not only affect the lives of humans living in their path but also cut a swath through the forests, resulting in the destruction of large trees and providing an opportunity for their replacement with new individuals. This regeneration process plays an important role in maintaining species diversity in tropical forests (see chapter 8).

1.2.4 Rainfall patterns and seasonality

Since land and sea absorb heat at different rates, diurnal and seasonal changes are larger on land than in water. Tropical deserts are hot during the day but they lose their heat rapidly at night by radiation of infra-red energy and by conduction and convection (Figure 1.6). In contrast, tropical rain forests, with their mantle of cloud and vegetation are much cooler by day and retain warmth at night. The vegetation and clouds act as a blanket absorbing and reflecting radiation. Loss of heat by conduction and convection is minimised because the thick forest undergrowth reduces heat gradients and wind speeds (Table 1.2).

Variations in rainfall and humidity are extreme within the tropics and largely determine the suite of organisms that live in a particular region. Some desert areas receive no rainfall, rain forests may be deluged with more than 10 m of rain in a year. The intensity of storms and the total amount of rain falling in heavy storms are considerably higher in the tropics than in temperate areas. Raindrops in tropical downpours are often larger and contain more potential energy and, therefore, more erosive power.

Considerable variation in rainfall can occur within a relatively short distance, especially where the topography is steep and mountainous. Rain may fall in heavy, localised storms and therefore rainfall, even within a small area, may be highly variable and unpredictable (Figure 1.7). The impact of this variability (and indeed the variability itself) is probably greater in areas where water is scarce (see chapter 2). In higher rainfall areas, where variability receives less attention, it is likely that variability is similar to that recorded at higher latitudes.

Rainfall intensity in the tropics is commonly so high that infiltration capacity is exceeded regardless of land management. This leads to water-logging on flat ground or soil erosion on slopes. The ratio run-off : infiltration depends on

(a)

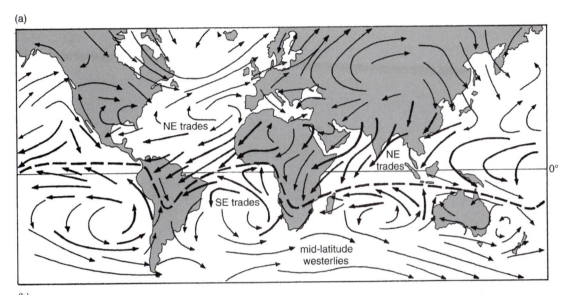

(b)

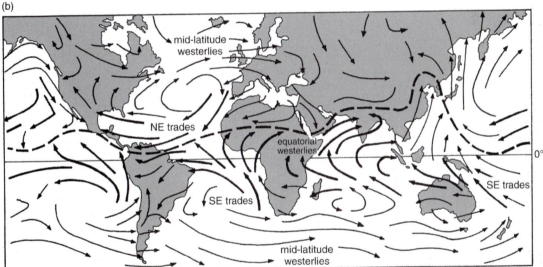

Figure 1.5 Mean surface winds over the earth in (a) January and (b) July showing the approximate position of the Inter-Tropical Convergence Zone (dashed line) (after White *et al.* 1993 with kind permission from Kluwer Academic Publishers).

the rate of precipitation (drizzle or downpour), vegetation cover, soil porosity, litter cover and organic matter content of the soil, soil moisture level and topography.

The decrease in mean annual rainfall at increasing distances from the equator is accompanied by increasing seasonality. The increase in seasonality is linked even more closely with the magnitude of change in day length with increasing latitude (Figure 1.4b). In temperate regions, day length plays a key role in providing organisms with a biological clock. However, within the tropics, seasonality in rainfall has greater impact on the life of tropical organisms. Germination, flowering and fruiting in tropical plants and breeding, feeding and life history strategies in tropical animals are markedly affected by rainfall.

Seasonal movements of animals (migration) are often made in response to food supply which, in turn, fluctuates in abundance with rainfall. The influence of environmental factors on organisms

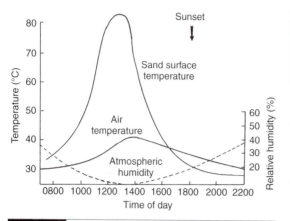

Figure 1.6 Diurnal variations in air and soil surface temperature and humidity recorded in September at Wadi Halfa, Sudan (after Cloudsley-Thompson and Chadwick 1964).

Table 1.2	Mean maximum temperatures and daily temperature range at two heights above the ground in tropical rain forest

	Dry season		Wet season	
Sampling height (m)	0.7	24.0	0.7	24.0
Mean maximum (°C)	29.7	33.9	26.8	30.9
Daily range	5.8	9.9	5.5	9.2

Source: Richards 1952.

Figure 1.7 Localised rainfall on the Chilwa Plain, Malawi (Photo: Patrick Osborne).

and their populations will be discussed in chapters 2, 3 and 4. An important general difference between tropical and temperate environments is that the wet tropics have seasonal rainfall and near constant temperatures, whereas, in temperate areas, rainfall varies less during the year but temperature is markedly seasonal. Climate diagrams provide a convenient way to display temperature and rainfall patterns, and construction and interpretation of these diagrams is described below.

1.2.5 Climate diagrams

A good, comparative way of presenting climatic data is through climate diagrams developed by Walter and Leith (1967). In these figures, seasonal variations in temperature and rainfall are plotted on one diagram (Figure 1.8). The lower curve shows the mean monthly temperature (10 °C intervals on the *y*-axis; the upper curve presents mean monthly rainfall (20 mm intervals on the *y*-axis, except where rainfall exceeds 100 mm when the scale is reduced by 10:1). The area under this reduced scale is conventionally shaded black to indicate very wet periods. The reduced scale serves to keep the diagrams to a manageable size. Periods in which the curve for rainfall falls below that for temperature indicate arid months.

Another important convention in drawing these diagrams is that data from the northern hemisphere are plotted from January to December, those from the southern hemisphere are plotted from July to June. This facilitates visual comparison of diagrams from opposite sides of the equator (Figure 1.9). These diagrams are compiled from mean values and therefore do not provide information on interannual or diurnal variations.

1.2.6 World distribution of tropical climates

Climate not only varies spatially and seasonally but variations also occur from one year to the next. We are gradually beginning to understand some of these variations between years, and significant progress has been made in documenting and predicting the occurrence of one process which has world-wide impact. In the

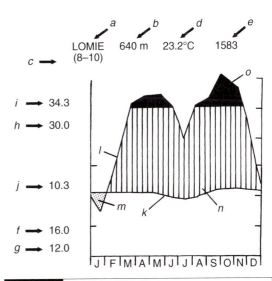

Figure 1.8 Example of a climate diagram for Lomie in Cameroon. The symbols and figures on the diagram have the following meaning: (a) station name; (b) station altitude; (c) number of years of observations (first figure: temperature; second figure: rainfall); (d) mean annual temperature; (e) mean annual rainfall mm; (f) mean daily minimum of coldest month; (g) lowest temperature recorded; (h) mean daily maximum of warmest month; (i) maximum temperature recorded; (j) mean daily temperature range; (k) graph of monthly mean temperatures (scale divisions are 10°C); (l) graph of monthly mean rainfall (scale divisions are 20 mm); (m) drought period; (n) humid period; (o) monthly rainfall greater than 100 mm (scale 1/10 that of rainfall) (after Walter 1971 with kind permission from Gustav Fischer Verlag, Stuttgart 1991 © Spektrum Akademischer Verlag, Heidelberg, Berlin).

1920s, attention was drawn to an oscillation in atmospheric pressure between the east and west sides of the Pacific Ocean. This phenomenon was called the **Southern Oscillation (SO)**. It has now been shown that the SO is related to variations in rainfall and sea surface temperatures in the equatorial eastern Pacific. The irregular occurrence of warmer than usual water off the Peruvian coast has been known there a long time and is locally called **El Niño**. Under normal conditions, the winds and ocean currents of the tropical Pacific travel from east to west, producing a large reservoir of warm water around Indonesia. El Niño is a reversal of winds and ocean currents across the Pacific that usually lasts for a year or two, and occurs typically every four to five years. Recent **El**

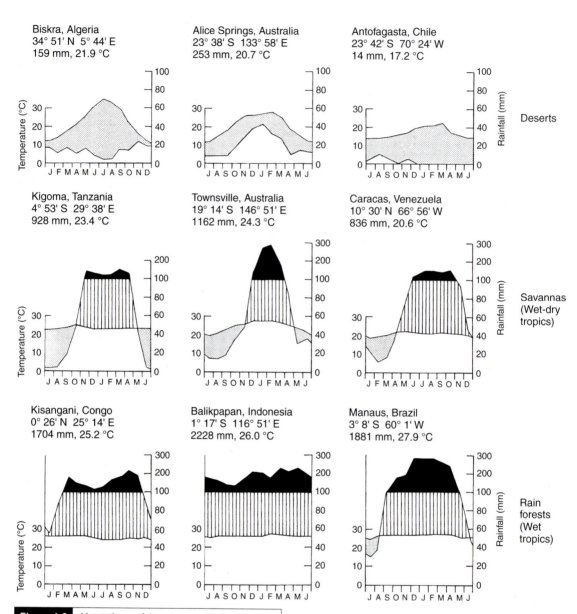

Figure 1.9 Homoclimes of desert, savanna and rain forest regions in Africa, Australia, South-East Asia and South America (after Walter and Leith 1967 with kind permission from Urban and Fischer Verlag).

Niño Southern Oscillation (ENSO) events have occurred in 1972–73, 1976–77, 1982–83, 1992–93 and 1997–98. The impact of these ENSO events is of global significance with common features including droughts in southern Africa, eastern Australia and Brazil, forest fires in Indonesia, storms and wet weather along the American coast from Alaska to Peru and warmer winters in the American mid-west.

The 1982–83 ENSO was one of the strongest this century and regions as far apart as Australia, the Philippines, southern India and southern Africa suffered severe droughts. In East Kalimantan, the impact of the drought was exacerbated when some 3.5 million hectares of forest were destroyed by fires. In both 1991–92 and 1997–98, El Niño struck again with floods, famines and forest fires occurring in regions throughout the tropics. A devastating drought in southern Africa and storms in California were accompanied by drought and food shortages in Brazil. At least a quarter of the maize crop in Zimbabwe and Zambia (Central Africa) was lost.

Cane *et al.* (1994) demonstrated a strong correlation between an El Niño index and both rainfall and maize yield in Zimbabwe. The El Niño index was derived from tiny temperature fluctuations in the Pacific Ocean. Surprisingly, the correlation of this index with maize yield was stronger than that with rainfall. These scientists believe that computer models developed to predict occurrences of ENSO events can be used to predict maize yields up to a year in advance. These computer models will provide farmers with a prediction for the coming growing season before the crops are planted. In El Niño years, this will provide an early warning system which will assist in planning relief efforts designed to minimise the effects of drought-induced famines.

Some researchers warn that El Niño events could become more intense with global warming (the most recent event (1997–98) certainly supports this conclusion; see chapter 14). These events appear to be triggered by a build-up of very warm water in the western Pacific. Therefore, these scientists argue that, the warmer the oceans, the greater the potential for El Niño events to develop.

1.3 Biogeographical regions

Clearly the tropics do not comprise a region of uniform climate. The position of the continental masses, topography, air flows and sea currents combine to produce variations in rainfall, humidity, temperature, wind and the occurrence of tropical storms. Variation in climate together with that in soil type and nutrient status mainly determine the vegetation, and hence the animal communities, an area will support. Tropical vegetation is most luxuriant when: (1) mean annual rainfall is sufficient to avoid water stress in plants but not too high to cause leaching of nutrients from the soil; (2) rainfall is seasonally uniform; (3) temperatures remain warm through-

out the year; (4) soils are sandy loams, rich in organic matter; and (5) the terrain is level with well-drained soils.

Composite cloud-free images of planet earth compiled by the Space Shuttle show variations in features such as ice cover, vegetation type and the depth of oceans. We have been aware of these variations for many years before space travel and have used our knowledge to classify regions of the earth in a variety of ways. One such way is to divide the earth into regions based on the assemblages of plants and animals that occur in each particular region. Six distinct biogeographical regions have been identified (Figure 1.10).

Some species have a distribution that extends over two, three or even more of these regions, but none the less each region can be distinguished by the mix of plants and animals that reside within it. Despite these differences in the species composition of the organisms inhabiting the four biogeographical regions which straddle the tropics, there are some surprising similarities in the flora and fauna of these distant areas. For example, species of the plant family Proteaceae, today, occur in Australia, southern Africa, South America, New Zealand, New Guinea and tropical South-East Asia. Outside of Australia and New Guinea, some species of marsupials occur in South America and one lives in North America. The science known as **biogeography** studies the geographical distribution of plants and animals (both extant and extinct) and draws on geological, geographical and biological knowledge to explain these distribution patterns. Continental drift and the theory of plate tectonics help to explain both the similarities and differences in the distribution of plants and animals over the continents. We will look at salient features of biogeography in chapter 12.

1.3.1 Plate tectonics and continental drift
In 1912, Alfred Wegener, a German geophysicist, suggested that all the continents had once been joined to form a single large land mass which he called **Pangea**. The simplest evidence to support this theory is an examination of the continents on either side of the Atlantic Ocean. It is readily apparent that they could fit neatly together like

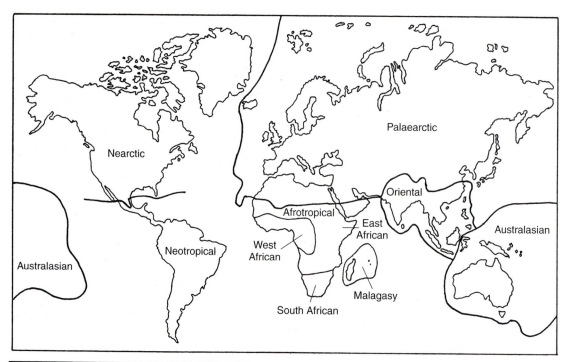

Figure 1.10 The six major biogeographical regions of the world. Each region can be divided into sub-regions and this has been done for the Afrotropical region. Within each region are found distinctive assemblages of plants and animals. Some species are found in more than one region but only a few have a worldwide distribution. Wallace's line lies between the Oriental and Australasian region, bisecting the Indonesian archipelago (after Pomeroy and Service 1986 reprinted by permission of Pearson Education Limited, Longman Group Limited).

pieces of a jig-saw puzzle (Figure 1.11). There is now a wealth of other information drawn from geophysics, geology and biology to support this theory. The change to the present-day distribution of continents has occurred through **continental drift** and the process has been explained by the theory of **plate tectonics**.

The earth's surface is covered by a comparatively rigid layer composed of a **crust** and the uppermost part of the underlying **mantle**. The mantle layer surrounds an iron-rich **core**. The crust and upper mantle is 100 km thick and broken into a number of plates. These plates float on the more fluid lower mantle. At the edges of these plates intense geophysical activity is common. Chains of volcanic mountains mark the edges of the plates and these chains run through all the ocean basins. These chains are known as **mid-ocean ridges**. At these ridges, the adjoining plates are moving slowly apart. As they do so, a rift is created. This releases some of the pressure on the underlying mantle and material is forced up through the rift. This material and the displaced crust form the mid-ocean ridges and earthquakes and volcanic activity are associated with their formation. These ridges create new sea floor through a process known as **sea-floor spreading**. The continents may be carried along with the plates as they move away from the ridge. This is the mechanism of continental drift. The continents may move a few centimetres each year, but, relative to the size of the earth, these changes are very small.

This construction process along the mid-ocean ridges is balanced by a destructive process which occurs at trenches. A trench is formed where an oceanic plate collides with a continental plate. The oceanic plate descends into the mantle because it is denser than the material that makes up the continental plate. This process is known as **subduction**. Subduction also produces earthquakes and volcanic activity. When two oceanic

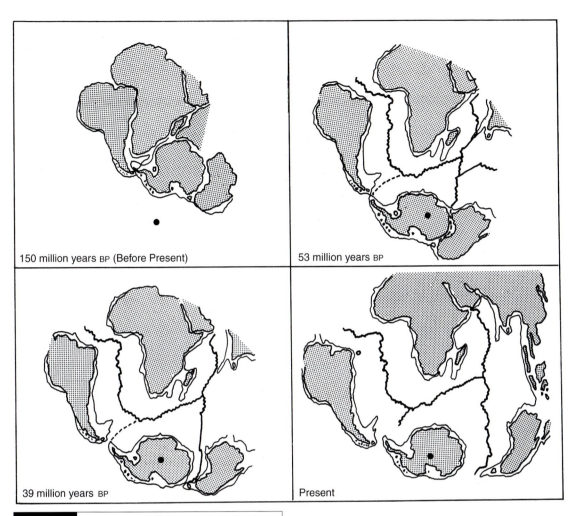

150 million years BP (Before Present)

53 million years BP

39 million years BP

Present

Figure 1.11 Reconstruction of the stages in the break-up of the super continent of Gondwana, showing the separation of the southern continents and the formation of the South Atlantic and Indian Oceans. The thin line around each continent is the limit of water less than 1000 m deep (● = South Pole). Edges of the main tectonic plates are also shown (after Norton and Sclater 1979; copyright by the American Geophysical Union).

plates collide, one dips beneath the other to form a trench, and again earthquake and volcanic activity may occur. Collision of two continental plates results in the formation of fold mountain chains such as the Himalayas which were formed through the collision of India, as it moved northwards, with continental Asia, resulting in the massive uplift of former marine sediments.

In some parts of the world, two plates slide past each other. In these cases, there is neither destruction nor creation of lithosphere. However, in the zone where the two plates are rubbing against each other, a fault develops. Friction between the plates can result in the build up of stress that may be released as an earthquake. Perhaps the most famous **fault boundary** (also known as a **shear boundary**) is the San Andreas Fault in California.

From the information that supports the plate tectonic theory, we know that, in the Cretaceous Period up until 100 million years ago, Antarctica, India, Africa, South America and Australia were all part of a large, southern super-continent called **Gondwana**. Around 100 million years ago, this enormous land mass started to break-up. South America, Africa and India moved north towards their present positions. Australia and Antarctica remained in the same position until about 49 million years ago. Australia then broke away and gradually drifted north to its present position leaving Antarctica behind (Figure 1.11).

The Australian continental plate which includes the island of New Guinea has been isolated from the other plates since the break-up of Gondwana. At this time, the flowering plants and mammals were in the early stages of evolution. This helps to explain why the fauna and flora of Australasia are so distinctive and different from that of, what are today, the nearby islands of the Indonesian Archipelago. Alfred Wallace first demarcated the boundary between the oriental faunal region and the Australasian region with its distinctive marsupials and birds. The boundary between these two regions, known as **Wallace's line**, passes east of Java and Bali (Indonesia) and between Borneo and Sulawesi, extending eastward to the south of Mindanao in the Philippines (Figure 1.10).

1.3.2 Biomes

The word 'desert' conjures up an image of dry expanses of sand with little or no vegetation, of camels and isolated, palm-fringed oases. The image of a rain forest is very different: luxuriant, steamy jungle, trees covered in epiphytes and abundant insect and bird life. Deserts and rain forests are just two examples of **biomes**. Biomes are subdivisions of biogeographical regions that support characteristic forms of plants and animals. Other examples of biomes include grasslands, savannas, deciduous forests and tundra. The distribution of the world's biomes can be related to the prevailing mean annual rainfall and the mean annual temperature (Figure 1.12).

These biomes occur across the boundaries of biogeographical regions: rain forests, for example, are found in the Neotropical, Afrotropical, Oriental and Australasian regions (Figures 1.10, 8.2). In each of these regions, the rain forests bear more than a superficial resemblance in terms of climate, vegetation structure and animal communities, and therefore they share many features in the way the biome functions. However, more detailed study of rain forests, within each of the

biogeographical regions where they are found, soon reveals that the species composition varies markedly not only between regions but also within them. This feature of overall similarity in structure and function but difference in the species composition applies to most of the biomes. This book leans on the similarities that exist within biomes from different regions in order to unravel the major features of their ecology. Readers will need to consult local or regional descriptions for information on the more intricate and specific features of particular biomes or areas within them.

1.3.3 Ecosystems

Rowe (1991) divided the study of ecology into three functional levels: **ecosphere**, **ecosystem** and **environment**. The ecosphere includes the land, ocean, atmosphere, organisms and their interactions: an entire ecological system of planetary proportions. Each organism interacts with the biophysical system that surrounds it and this system was designated the environment by Rowe (1991). In between these two extremes lies the ecosystem consisting of a subdivision of the ecosphere in which organisms interact both with their environment and with each other.

Drawing lines on the globe to divide areas into biogeographical regions is based on the assumption that there are clearly distinguishable borders between adjacent regions. This is generally not the case. Tropical rain forests do not end abruptly on the border with savanna. There is usually some transition from the dense rain forest to the more scattered tree cover exhibited by savannas. Similarly, savannas meld into deserts through zones of decreasing plant cover and a replacement of savanna trees with grasslands and grasslands with plants adapted to even drier conditions. In chapter 2 we will describe environmental factors and investigate ways in which organisms are adapted to the environment and how the environment imposes limits on the growth and reproduction of organisms.

Ecologists, instead of using area to define a unit under study have developed the ecosystem concept. An **ecosystem** is a unit of study in which energy flows from the sun through **autotrophs** to

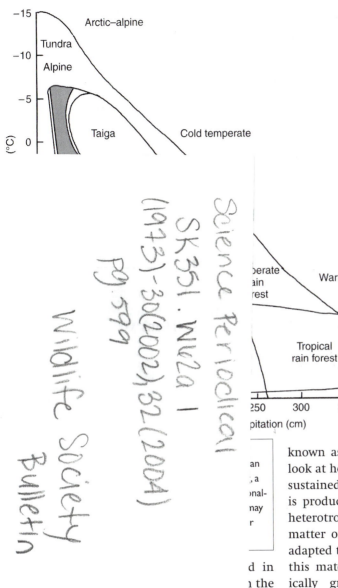

known as **heterotrophs** or **consumers**. We will look at how animal **populations** develop and are sustained in chapter 4. The organic material that is produced by autotrophs and transformed by heterotrophs eventually ends up as dead organic matter or **detritus**. Some organisms are highly adapted to extracting energy and nutrients from this material, and these organisms are ecologically grouped together as **detritivores** or decomposers. These organisms and their way of life will be covered in chapter 10.

material from inorganic materials using an outside source of energy. The majority of these organisms are green plants and fix energy in sunlight through a process known as photosynthesis. We will look at autotrophs and photosynthesis in chapter 3.

The rate at which plants and other green organisms produce organic matter significantly influences the ecology of the organisms that consume this material. These organisms are

In our definition of an ecosystem, we introduced the terms **energy flow** and **nutrient cycling**. These ecological concepts will be covered in chapters 3 and 5. Energy flow in ecosystems obeys the first and second laws of thermodynamics. The first law states that energy can be transformed from one kind to another, but it cannot be created or destroyed. In other words, the energy entering an ecosystem (or an organism) will equal the sum of energy stored in the system and energy lost from the system. The second law states that no process involving an energy transformation will occur spontaneously unless there is a degradation of energy from a concentrated form into a dispersed form.

As we will see, some organisms have the capacity to change energy from light energy (provided as sunlight) into energy-rich chemical compounds (chapter 3). Another example of an energy transfer is the conversion of chemical energy into heat. This occurs, for example, whenever an animal moves by muscle contraction. Because energy is vital to all organisms, it provides ecologists with a common unit of currency with which to compare the importance of organisms living in a particular ecosystem. We can construct energy budgets (chapter 5) in which the energy entering the system must equal the energy that leaves (usually as heat). **Energy flow** can be defined as the flow and dissipation of energy along food chains and webs within an ecosystem.

Ecosystem processes can be studied by measuring energy flow through them and by assessing how nutrients cycle within them. These studies overlook one very obvious feature of ecosystems: even the simplest of ecosystems contains a variety of plants, animals and micro-organisms. Furthermore, a cursory study of any ecosystem will soon reveal that these organisms interact in a wide range of ways with each other. The study of these interactions forms the basis of **community** ecology (chapter 11). How communities change in response to altered environmental conditions will be described in chapter 6 which focuses on tropical rivers.

Ecologists also need to be able to assess, and explain, why there are so many different types of organisms. How did this multiplicity of life come about and how, in the more diverse ecosystems, do so many species live together? These and other questions on biodiversity will be addressed in chapter 8. Ecosystems not only differ from one part of the world to another, but they also change with time. Ecosystem development, in a process known as **succession**, will be covered in chapter 7. How communities are assembled can be studied in the biological colonisation of recently formed habitats, such as barren volcanic islands. How isolated communities, such as those on islands and mountain tops and in lakes, differ from those on continental land masses will be discussed in chapter 12. Environmental factors change with increasing altitude on mountains. How organisms cope with or avoid the influence of these changes will be covered in chapter 9.

Ecology has become a vitally important subject. Its importance has grown with the degree of devastation that the rapidly expanding human population has wrought on the planet: deforestation, soil erosion, land degradation, pollution of the air, soils, freshwaters and seas, depletion of the protective layer of ozone in the upper atmosphere, climate change through the generation of greenhouse gases and an enhanced rate of species extinctions. These are the topics of study for the applied ecologist, and the final chapters (13 and 14) will describe some of these topical issues and what is being, can be and should be done to manage tropical ecosystems in a way which at least strives for ecological sustainability. To be successful in this aim, we will need a thorough understanding of tropical biomes and the ecological concepts and principles that apply to them.

1.4 | Chapter summary

1. The tropics lie between the Tropics of Cancer (23° 28′ N) and Capricorn (23° 28′ S). The most significant climatic feature of the tropics at sea level is the absence of a cold season. The tropics are hotter than temperate areas because the same amount of heat is concentrated over a smaller area in the tropics.

2. The concentration of heat above the equator warms the air, which expands as it rises, then cools and rain falls. Air near the ground is replaced from the north and south. The rising air spreads and falls again at about 30° N and S. The cool, dry air falls to earth and this explains why deserts are often found at these latitudes.

3. The Coriolis force deflects the northerly and southerly equatorial winds into north-easterlies and south-easterlies respectively: the trade winds. The trade winds meet in an equatorial low-pressure trough, called the Inter-Tropical Convergence Zone. The ITCZ lies to the north of the equator during the northern summer and migrates south during the northern winter. The ITCZ brings rain; equatorial regions have two wet seasons, those to the north and south have only one. Considerable spatial and temporal variation in rainfall occurs over the tropics. El Niño–Southern Oscillation events affect interannual climate throughout the Pacific and other parts of the world.

4. The earth can be divided into six biogeographical regions. Each has a distinctive fauna and flora. Biogeography studies the geographical distribution of plants and animals (both extant and extinct) and draws on geological, geographical and biological knowledge to explain these distribution patterns. The theory of plate tectonics helps to explain the global distribution of both plants and animals.

5. Biomes are subdivisions of biogeographical regions that support characteristic forms of plants and animals. The distribution of the world's biomes can be related to the prevailing mean annual rainfall and the mean annual temperature. Biomes within different biogeographical regions often differ markedly in their species composition.

6. Organism, population, community, ecosystem and ecosphere are levels of organisation of ecological structure and functioning from the individual to the global level. An ecosystem is a unit of study in which energy flows from the sun through autotrophs (photosynthetic organisms) to heterotrophs (consumers) and on to decomposers and in which nutrients and materials cycle through the organisms that make up a food web.

Chapter 2

Hot deserts and environmental factors

Desert biomes are found in areas of the world where the average precipitation is below 250 mm per year. The rain fall is often not only sparse but also highly irregular in both time and space. In some deserts, dew deposited during cool nights is the only source of water. During the day, temperatures and evaporation rates are usually very high. In this chapter, we summarise the ecology of three deserts and discover that, while the shortage of water limits the growth of organisms, it has also stimulated the evolution of some remarkable adaptations. Deserts are unfavourable environments and therefore provide a suitable biome to study environmental factors and how they limit the growth and development of organisms.

Deserts predominantly straddle the Tropics of Cancer and Capricorn (Figure 2.1). Here, the air, carried up from the Inter-Tropical Convergence Zone (see section 1.2.2), settles to form high-pressure cells that dominate the climate over these deserts. As the air descends, it warms adiabatically and air temperatures become oppressive (Figure 2.2). Some deserts are situated on the west coast of large continents adjacent to cold ocean currents, others are in the interior of large continents (Louw and Seely 1982). Cloudsley-Thompson (1977) classified the large desert areas of the world into four categories (see Figure 2.1):

1 Subtropical deserts straddle latitudes 30° S or 30° N and result from persistent overlying high atmospheric pressure cells; e.g. Sahara Desert.

2 Cool, coastal deserts: dry air conditions produced by descending high-pressure air masses are exacerbated by the proximity of cold ocean currents. However, the cold ocean currents, while intensifying atmospheric pressure may also bring cool, moist oceanic winds and advective fog; e.g. Namib, Atacama and Baja California Deserts.

3 Rain-shadow deserts: oceanic winds, interrupted by a topographical barrier such as a mountain range, are deflected upwards and cool adiabatically. The relative humidity rises and orographic precipitation occurs on the windward slopes of the mountain range. The air mass loses much of its moisture before it reaches the leeward side of the mountain and, as it descends, it warms through compressional heating (Figure 2.3); e.g. Mojave Desert, Great Basin of North America and part of the Great Australian Desert.

4 Interior continental deserts are dry because of their distance from the sea and the moist air that blows from it; e.g. part of the Great Australian Desert and North American Desert.

2.1 | The Sahara Desert and arid zones of northern Africa

2.1.1 Environment

The Sahara Desert, the largest in the world, stretches from the Atlantic coast of North Africa eastward to the Red Sea and lies between the Mediterranean Sea and the Tropic of Cancer. This vast area (nearly 6 million km²) includes the arid zones north of the Sahara and the very dry Sahara. To the south of the Sahara lies the Sahel,

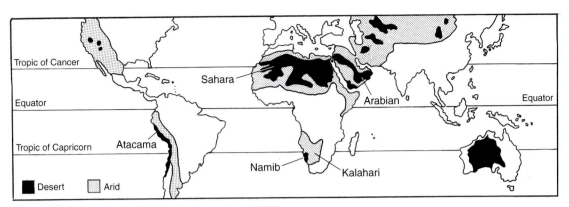

Figure 2.1 The major deserts and arid areas of the world. Note that most of these areas straddle the tropics of Cancer and Capricorn (see Figure 2.2) (after Cloudsley-Thompson 1977).

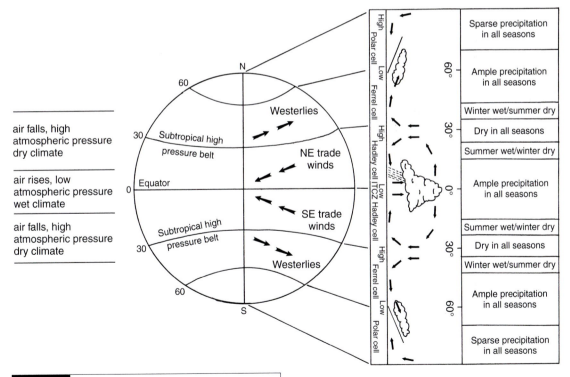

Figure 2.2 Latitudinal air circulation patterns within cells near the equator show how moisture is lost from the trade winds at the equator and therefore the air over 30°N and 30°S is dry. Deserts tend to occur at these latitudes (adapted from Stiling 1996).

Figure 2.3 Precipitation along mountain ranges. The rain shadow downwind of a mountain results because the descending air, already dry, picks up moisture (adapted from Flohn 1969).

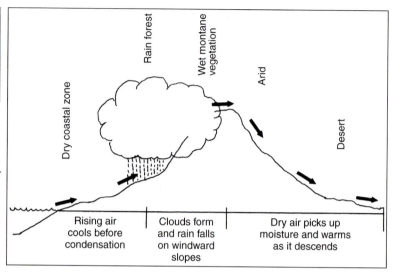

Dry coastal zone | Rain forest | Wet montane vegetation | Arid | Desert

Rising air cools before condensation | Clouds form and rain falls on windward slopes | Dry air picks up moisture and warms as it descends

a transition zone between true desert and savanna vegetation. The very dry regions receive less than 100 mm of rain per year, and in some years no rain falls. Other areas are wetter but still only receive up to 400 mm of rain per year.

The Mediterranean climate of the north gives way to predominantly irregular and sparse rainfall in the southern Sahara and then to more regular, but still low, rainfall of the Sahel. Rainfall generally declines with distance from the coast with a minimum being recorded near the Tropic of Cancer. Higher rainfall is recorded over elevated areas. As with most arid areas in the world, rainfall in the Saharan region is very variable and this variability is not reflected in climate diagrams (see Figures 1.8 and 1.9; Le Houérou 1986). Table 2.1 demonstrates how variable the rainfall in desert regions can be. Note first the wide range between the maximum and minimum annual precipitation. Note, too, that much of the mean annual rainfall may occur in just one day.

The mean annual temperature varies between 18 to 22 °C along the coast, and in the arid zone of the Sahara from 20 to 25 °C (Le Houérou 1986). More important than these mean annual figures are the more extreme values: the mean minimum of the coldest month and the mean maximum of the hottest month. It is these extreme values that curtail the distribution and activities of desert organisms. The mean minimum temperature of the coldest month (January) varies from 10 °C on the coast of Morocco to −2 °C in the arid highlands of Morocco and Algeria. The mean maximum of the hottest month (usually August) is 30 °C along the coast but rises away from the sea to between 35 and 38 °C. In the Sahara, the mean maximum of the hottest month lies between 40

and 45 °C. The highest shade temperature ever measured was recorded at Al Aziziah in Libya: 58 °C.

Humidity declines from 70% near the coast, to 60–65% in the arid zone and 20–40% in the Sahara. The humidity can be markedly lowered by the occurrence of hot winds locally called *sirocco*, *ghibli* and *khamsin*. When these winds blow, air temperatures range from 35 to 45 °C and the humidity falls to between 5 and 15%. These hot, dry winds are particularly harsh on crops and native vegetation (Le Houérou 1986).

Three main land forms are found in the Sahara. Gravel plains occupy about 70% of the surface area, and rock mountains and stony desert pavement less than 10%. The balance, 20%, is sand with dunes up to 300m high. The most important feature of soils in arid areas is their capacity to absorb and store water following rain and to release it to the vegetation afterwards. In this respect, the important soil characteristics include topography, texture, depth and permeability (see section 2.9). The Sahel forms a transition zone between the very dry Sahara Desert to the north and the milder climates to the south. Like many transitions, the boundaries are obscure.

2.1.2 Organisms

The Sahara Desert is floristically poor (by desert standards) and lichens and succulents are rare

Table 2.1 | Extreme precipitation events in African deserts

Location	Maximum annual precipitation (mm)	Minimum annual precipitation (mm)	Maximum rainfall in 24 hours (mm)
Tamanrasset, Algeria	159	6	48
Cairo, Egypt	63	3	44
Gadamis, Libya	79	6	17
Dongola, Sudan	60	0	36
Alexander Bay, S. Africa	95	22	39
Swakopmund, Namibia	29	0	18

Source: Griffiths 1972.

except along the Atlantic coast where fogs provide extra moisture. About 1200 plant species are found in the Sahara and endemism is high (about 20 genera and 200 species) (Le Houérou 1986).

In the central Sahara, significant rain occurs only once every decade or so. Organisms must employ a number of strategies to survive in such an arid environment. One extreme example is provided by the chironomid *Polypedilum vanderplanki*. This insect, as a larva, inhabits small, shallow rock pools in tropical Africa. When these pools dry out, the larva burrows into the sediment where it can survive in a completely dry state. With the next rain, the pool fills, the larva rehydrates and within an hour or so resumes feeding and growth. The larval lifespan is advanced by the time that the pool remains full enough to allow the larva to feed. Eventually the larva pupates and emerges as a non-biting midge. This survival technique, known as **cryptobiosis**, is the persistence of life among desiccated cells in which metabolism has ceased (Cloudsley-Thompson 1994).

Few plants or animals are cryptobiotic. More survive dry conditions in a quiescent state known as **diapause**. This is less drastic than cryptobiosis and involves a state whereby metabolism is reduced to a low level so that little water is lost through respiration. Animals and plants can achieve this by producing resistant eggs and seeds respectively.

Many desert plants are ephemeral and survive dry periods as seeds. Seeds have a very low water content and low metabolic rate, and the seeds of desert annuals are capable of withstanding both high temperature and low humidity. When rain falls, these seeds may germinate rapidly and in some cases the new plants produce seeds within a few weeks. The record for shortness of growing season is probably held by the herb *Boerhaavia repens* which, in the Sahara, takes just 8–10 days from seed germination to seed production. This short life cycle not only ensures that the plant has time to produce seeds (the agents of diapause) before the water runs out, but also ensures that it flowers at a time when insect pollinators are abundant. To facilitate this rapid growth, these plants must have a rapid rate of photosynthesis and they employ the C_4 photosynthetic pathway (see section 3.7).

Owing to the high variability in rainfall in the Sahara, most ephemeral plants are annuals, riding out dry spells as seeds. Perennial ephemerals have to maintain, through the dry period, larger amounts of dormant tissue, in the form of roots, bulbs or corms. Where rainfall is more predictable, the frequency of perennial plants increases (Cloudsley-Thompson and Chadwick 1964).

Animals also utilise diapause. The eggs of tadpole shrimps (*Triops* spp.) survive the hot, dry Saharan summer in a state of diapause. These eggs can tolerate 98 °C for 16 hours when dry. Lethal temperature for adult shrimps is around 40 °C for 2 hours or 34 °C for 24 hours (Cloudsley-Thompson 1991). Diapause also ensures that all the eggs do not hatch when wet by a short rain shower. The shrimps require adequate water in their temporary habitat to ensure that they can develop and reproduce. Diapause provides a mechanism that ensures some eggs are held in reserve.

Belk and Cole (1975) distinguished between **obligatory diapause** which occurs in every generation and is endogenously controlled and **facultative diapause** which is cued by an environmental factor. Obligatory diapause is well suited to an environment in which cyclic change is regular and predictable. Facultative diapause is better suited to an environment which is unpredictable. However, it is likely that organisms utilising diapause as a strategy employ both **endogenous** rhythms (growth regulators, hormones) and **exogenous** (environmental) cues.

Notice that there is an important functional difference between diapause and cryptobiosis. A cryptobiotic organism can alternate between active and dormant phases, advancing its development with each active period. Where seeds or eggs are used to evade harsh conditions (diapause), development (germination or hatching), once started, cannot be reversed.

Human inhabitants have had a major impact on the ecology of the Sahara. Humans have lived in the area for at least several hundred thousand years but, since the beginning of the twentieth century, the human population has increased more than sixfold. Increased areas of cultivation and more intensive methods have led to increased erosion and this has been exacerbated through overgrazing. Further damage to this fragile ecosystem has been wrought through cutting trees and shrubs for firewood.

The large mammals of the Sahara have been severely affected by humans and the growth in the herds of domestic animals. Many of the large animal species disappeared about 100 years ago and those species that remain are rare. Carnivores such as leopard (*Panthera pardus*) and lion (*Panthera leo*) were extinct in the Sahara by the middle of the nineteenth century. Herbivores such as addax (*Addax nasomaculatus*), bubal hartebeest (*Alecelaphus buselaphus*) and oryx (*Oryx dammah*) are now either rare or absent from the Sahara. Some small predators and scavengers have benefited from the increase in domestic animals. Fennec fox (*Vulpes zerda*) and jackal (*Canis aureus*) are still common and hyena (*Hyaena hyaena barbara*) remain in the northern Sahara.

One domesticated animal, the camel (*Camelus dromedarius*), provides a good example of mammalian adaptations to arid environments. They can lose 30% of their total body water over a period of 9 days (Schmidt-Nielsen *et al.* 1957). In the camel, little water is lost from the blood so circulatory efficiency is maintained. Recovery from dehydration is also spectacular. After a 20% loss in body weight, camels can drink enough in 10 minutes to restore their weight. Camels have the capacity to withstand a 6 °C rise in body temperature during the day and to dissipate this stored heat at night. In this way, water loss from evaporative cooling (sweating) is reduced. Body temperature fluctuations are greater when the camel is dehydrated and less when water can be spared for sweating. The camel produces a concentrated urine and very dry faeces. The camel's long legs make locomotion very efficient and reduce heat absorption by holding the body well clear of the ground. Its long neck and legs enable the camel to reach sparse vegetation growing between ground level and 4 m high. The two-toed foot is well padded with fat, providing thermal insulation from the hot sand and fat bodies stored in the hump facilitate heat loss and shield the body from solar radiation.

2.2 | The Namib Desert

2.2.1 Environment

Although the Namib Desert lies just south of the Tropic of Capricorn, it is the most arid part of southern Africa. A cross-section through southern Africa looks like an inverted dish (Figure 2.4). The middle part is slightly depressed, forming the large Kalahari Basin. The Drakensberg Mountains (up to 3000 m high) in the east and the high plateau of Namibia (up to 2000 m) in the west form the edges of the dish. The Namib Desert, a narrow strip of land, lies adjacent to the Atlantic Ocean (Figure 2.5). In summer, the east coast of southern Africa is exposed to easterly trade winds. The trade winds accumulate moisture from the Indian Ocean. As the winds rise on the eastern slopes of the Drakensberg, rain falls. More moisture is lost as the air moves west. The winds blowing up the slopes of the Namibian Plateau in the west do not

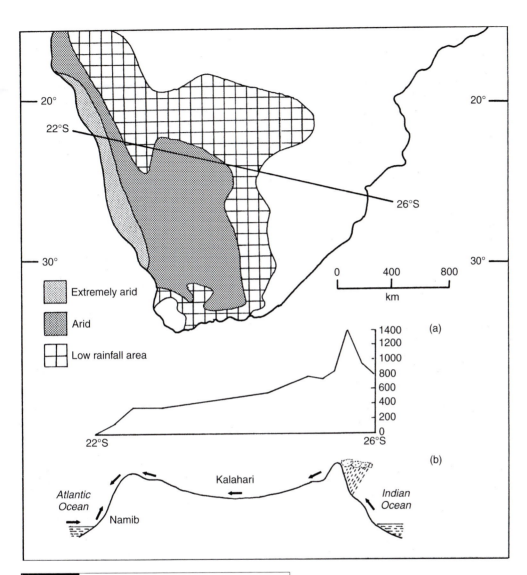

Figure 2.4 Map of southern Africa showing desert and low rainfall areas. (a) Mean annual precipitation (mm) along the transect indicated on the map. The highest rainfall is on the eastern slopes of the Drakensberg. Rainfall declines steadily from the Drakensberg across the Kalahari. The west coast (Namib) is rainless. (b) Cross-section through southern Africa from approximately 22°S in the west to 26°S in the east with the Kalahari Basin in the centre. Arrows indicate prevailing wind direction (mainly from the south-east, except those on the west coast where the winds are south-westerlies) (adapted from McGinnies 1979; Walter 1986 with permission from Elsevier Science).

bring noticeable rain and the Namib is a hot, dry desert.

The central part of the Namib Desert can be divided into three parts: (1) a narrow coastal strip with a mean precipitation between 10 and 25 mm; (2) the outer Namib, about 50 km wide with low, unpredictable rainfall and (3) the inner Namib with annual precipitation of 50 to 100 mm falling mainly in the summer. Although rainfall in this desert is low, air humidity is high, and heavy, wet fogs often blanket the area (Figure 2.6). Water that condenses from these fogs each year is equivalent to 130 mm of rain. This moisture results from a permanent temperature inversion

Figure 2.5 Aerial view of the sand dunes along the Skeleton Coast, north of Walvis Bay, Namibia (Photo: Michael and Patricia Fogden).

in which cold air is overlain by the warm air currents from the east. In deserts with episodic rainfall, individual showers are of greater significance than the yearly mean. For example, in March 1934, 112.9 mm of rain was recorded, 5–10 times the annual mean!

2.2.2 Vegetation

The vegetation of the Namib is surprisingly rich in species. An estimated 5000 species comprise the Namib and adjacent Karoo flora and many of these species are endemic. Lichens are an important component of the Namibian vegetation in the coastal region. They grow best on the leeward side of dunes where they are protected from sandblasting, and survive well here because they are able to absorb water from the moist air. They gradually decline away from the coast as the frequency of fogs decreases.

Soil algae form thin layers on the undersides of translucent, quartz stones that lie on the soil surface. When the stones become wet, water runs down to the algae growing below. Enough light passes through the stones for the algae to photosynthesise. In these organisms, referred to as **poikilohydrous**, water content varies with humidity of the surroundings. They have little ability to control their water content.

Higher plants growing in the Namib have not been shown to be true fog plants and must obtain some water from the soil via their roots. However, the grass, *Stipagrostis sabulicola*, can absorb moisture deposited from fogs. This plant has a very shallow but extensive root system (extending up to 20 m from the above-ground shoot) which enables it to tap water in the sand moistened by condensed fog. The succulent, *Trianthema hereroensis*, can absorb water through its leaves.

Following meagre rain, an ephemeral vegetation may develop consisting of annual species. Habitats where water is available for more prolonged periods are colonised by perennial species, such as the dwarf shrubs *Arthraerua lubnitzia* and

Figure 2.6 Clearing fog bank over sand dunes near Gobabeb, Namib Desert, Namibia. Fog condensation is an important source of moisture for organisms living in the Namib Desert. The dunes in the Namib Desert are among the highest in the world (Photo: Michael and Patricia Fogden).

Zygophyllum stapffii and trees *Acacia erioloba* and *Boscia albitrunca*. In years when ample rain falls, the ephemeral vegetation can be quite luxuriant. Although perennial plants survive by inhabiting moister areas, they still exhibit adaptations to enhance water uptake and storage and reduce loss.

Numerous succulents with developed water storage tissues inhabit the Namib. *Aloe asperifolia* and *Cotyledon orbiculata* have succulent leaves, while *Euphorbia virosa*, *Hoodia* spp. and *Trichocaulon* spp. have stems adapted for water storage. These plants are covered in a thick cuticle which reduces water loss. Some succulents have developed a photosynthetic strategy that allows them to keep their stomata closed during the day and open only at night (CAM photosynthesis, see section 3.7). This significantly reduces water loss by transpiration, but it does result in a reduced rate of photo-synthesis and hence plant growth. Other plants, such as *Adenia pechuellii* and *Kleinia longiflora*, shed their leaves during dry periods.

Perhaps the most unusual plant, endemic to the Namib, is the ancient gymnosperm, *Welwitschia mirabilis* (Figure 2.7). This plant produces only two leaves during its centuries-long life. The two, curling leaves are split longitudinally into strips, on which dew condenses and runs down to the shallow roots. The root tuber projects above the soil and produces reproductive cones most years.

2.2.3 Animals

The fauna of the dry, Namibian dunes is dominated by insects, arachnids and reptiles. Animals are adapted to evade climatic extremes while exploiting the irregular pulses in food and water availability. Most resident dune-dwellers retreat beneath the surface of the sand during hot times of the day. The sand-diving lizard (*Aporosaura anchietae*), uses the sand to warm itself in the early part of the day, but, as sand temperatures

Figure 2.7 Female plant (with cones) of *Welwitschia mirabilis* growing in the Namib Desert. *Welwitschia* is a dioecious (male and female organs are borne on different plants) gymnosperm (Gnetophyta). It is endemic to south-western Africa and most of its moisture comes from fog condensation (Photo: Michael and Patricia Fogden).

approach 40 °C, the lizard adopts a stilt-like walk, with the body held well clear of the hot sand. As it moves across the sand, the animal stops now and then to lift diagonally opposite legs, to allow them to cool. When the temperature rises above 40 °C, the lizard dives beneath the sand. The lizard is usually active twice a day: early- to mid-morning and late afternoon.

The tenebrionid beetle (*Onymacris langi*) also has a bimodal activity regime which allows it to escape the harsh conditions prevailing around midday. Beetles of the genus *Lepidochora* are nocturnal and so avoid high daytime temperatures. This nocturnal activity is controlled by an endogenous rhythm and persists for a few days even in the absence of environmental cues such as light and temperature.

Namib animals make use of condensation from fogs. The side-winding adder (*Bitis peringueyi*) drinks fog droplets that condense on its body. The sand-diving lizard drinks water adhering to dunal vegetation. When water is readily available, this animal may drink as much as 12% of its body weight and store the water in a special intestinal sac. The animal can draw on this store over a number of weeks (Louw and Seely 1982). Some desert insects absorb water from the air between sand grains where the humidity is higher than the open air.

In view of the fluctuating and unpredictability of the food supply, desert animals are typically opportunistic in their feeding behaviour and catholic in their tastes. Feeding specialists are rare. Detritus blown in from outside constitutes a major energy source for animals inhabiting the bare dunes of the Namib Desert. Litter from plants such as *Stipagrostis sabulicola* and the remains of insects are eaten by tenebrionid beetles and termites (*Psammotermes granti*). These insects are, in turn, eaten by predators such as spiders, the noc-

Figure 2.8 The Kuiseb River, Namib Desert, Namibia, on one of the rare days when it was flowing. Note the riverine thickets and the sand dunes behind (Photo: Michael and Patricia Fogden).

turnal golden mole (*Eremitalpa granti namibensis*) and the sand-diving lizard.

Large mammals and birds can move large distances in search of food. When rain triggers the development of ephemeral grasses, large numbers of gemsbok (*Oryx gazella*) move into the Namib to graze. When food availability declines, these animals move to the dry Kuiseb River where a riverine fringe provides shade and food in the form of *Acacia* pods (Figure 2.8). They obtain water by digging holes in the river bed (Kok and Nel 1996).

2.3 | Australian deserts

The most extensive arid area found in the southern hemisphere is in Australia where over 40% of the continent is classed as desert (Figure 2.9). This large, dry area in the centre of the country is characterised by its flatness and mostly lies below 500 m altitude with sites around Lake Eyre 12 m below sea level. This low relief in the arid areas is broken by the MacDonnell and Musgrave Ranges in the centre of the country. Consequently, altitude is insignificant in determining climate; distance inland and latitude are more influential.

Rainfall patterns vary with latitude. In the south, rain falls evenly throughout the year, with some sites recording slightly more rain in winter. Further north, rainfall is higher during the summer than the winter. In all areas, rainfall is low, spatially patchy and highly variable between years. Rainfall variability of inland Australia is 10% or more above the world average for places with the same mean annual rainfall. The Australian arid zone is often well vegetated with rainfall sufficient to produce a 30% ground cover. Barren country and mobile sand dunes, as found in the Sahara, are rare in Australia.

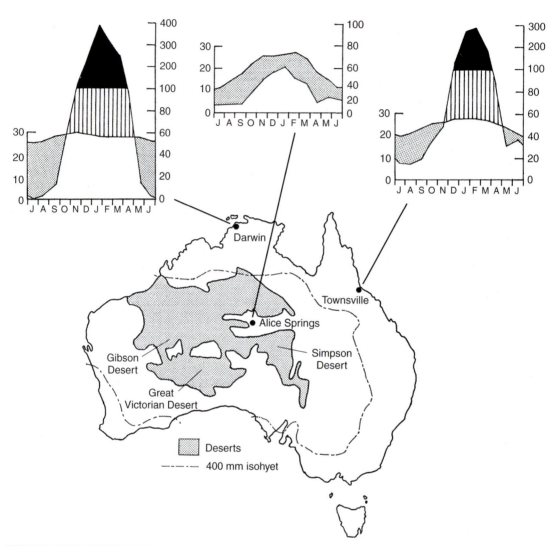

2.3.1 Vegetation

The flora of central Australia contains about 1200 species of which over 40% are endemic to areas receiving less than 250 mm. This rich diversity of plants survives, despite low rainfall and nutrient-poor soils, through two main strategies: drought-evasion and drought-tolerance. The drought-evading, or ephemeral plants, produce dormant seeds which only germinate after rain, the plants grow, reproduce and die. The drought-tolerant plants are perennials and employ a number of strategies to obtain and conserve water.

Five plant associations dominate the arid zone of Australia: *Acacia* shrubland, hummock grassland, low chenopod shrubland, tussock grassland and *Eucalyptus* shrubland. *Acacia* shrubland is dominated by *Acacia aneura* (locally known as mulga). Mulga provides an excellent example of a drought-tolerant species, capable of withstanding severe droughts; many plants live for 100 years or more. Mulga requires heavy summer rain before the trees produce flowers. Further rain is required in the winter for the trees to set seed. The seeds themselves require rain and warm temperatures to germinate and sufficient moisture for seedling establishment.

In an unpredictable, low-rainfall environment, the chance of adequate rain falling in two consecutive summers and the intervening winter is not high. Consequently, mass regeneration only occurs about once in 10 years. Mulga's longevity, and the fact that it lives in an environment where few other plants are able to exist, make this strategy successful. However, with the introduction of cattle and rabbits to Australia, mulga has suffered. Seedlings are particularly vulnerable to grazing when food is scarce, but rabbits will also eat the bark of mature trees, often killing them.

Hummock grasslands are dominated by grasses, locally called spinifex (*Triodia* spp., *Plectrachne* spp.), genera that are endemic to Australia. These grasses branch repeatedly into a large number of culms which intertwine to form a hummock. The rigid leaves of these plants have sharp tips that protect them from grazers. The mature leaf is heavily sclerified and rolled, with the stomata in deep pits on the inside surface of the leaf. While this structure may hinder gas exchange and photosynthesis, it reduces water loss through transpiration. Water loss is further reduced by dense epidermal hairs and a thick, waxy cuticle.

These grasses are perennial and can survive short-term environmental stress. However, following fire, long drought or extreme grazing pressure, the above-ground material dies. The plants recover when conditions improve by growing from meristems buried beneath the soil. Very intense fires may kill the meristems. Intense fires, however, only occur after a good growing season when there is an abundance of fuel (see section 4.1). The plants flower following rain, and seed set occurs when adequate moisture is available. Therefore, even though an intense fire may destroy the plant's capacity to reproduce vegetatively from the underground meristem, these fires usually strike after a good growing season has allowed the seed bank to be replenished. The fire also helps to remove germination inhibitors and the seeds germinate following the next rainfall.

The low shrublands, dominated by species belonging to the family Chenopodiacae, occupy the alkaline and saline soils in the southern half of the arid zone. The saltbush (*Atriplex*) is a perennial that flowers at any time of the year following rain. The seeds remain viable for several years. Germination occurs after wet weather and establishment requires a relatively extended period of wet weather. Black bluebush (*Maireana pyramidata*) flowers most prolifically after autumn or winter rains, but sets seeds only infrequently. The seeds remain viable for only a few months. The timing of seed set means that germination usually occurs in summer. In the rare event of good summer rain, seedling growth is rapid, but, without rain, regeneration does not occur and the seeds die. Consequently, this plant has a more risky reproductive strategy than the saltbush, and in many areas widespread germination has not occurred for more than 50 years.

Tussock grasslands are heavily grazed, and the dominant species forming dense tussocks up to 0.5 m across is *Astrebla pectinata*. *Eucalyptus* shrublands, called mallee, consist of low, spreading trees with multiple stems. This vegetation type occurs on the southern fringes of the arid area, replacing mulga in higher rainfall areas. Large areas are used for grazing, and extensive conversion to croplands (mainly wheat) has occurred in areas where irrigation is feasible.

Although perennial plants dominate the biomass in Australian deserts, ephemeral species bestow the great diversity on the flora. Rain results in the rapid germination, growth, flowering and seed production of a wide range of ephemeral plants. Strictly these should not be called annual plants, as in dry years they may not germinate at all. Ephemerals such as the composite *Helichrysum cassinianum* and the grass *Aristida contorta* only take 2 to 3 months from germination to seed set. These plants do not possess the structural or physiological capacity exhibited by the perennials to withstand drought.

Features of the vegetation in Australian deserts distinguish them from deserts in other parts of the world. Almost all the trees and shrubs are **sclerophylls** (plants with leathery, evergreen leaves). Larger shrubs have phyllodes instead of leaves and where leaves are present they are usually very small. Deciduous, thorny trees, so common in arid areas in other parts of the world are rare in Australia. Large, succulent, rosette plants such as the American *Yucca* and the African *Aloe* are not found in Australia.

2.3.2 Animals

Many arid zone Australian animals are not active during particularly dry periods and survive, through these periods, as an egg or dormant adult. The plague locust (*Chortoicetes terminifera*) has a mechanism to ensure that its eggs hatch at the right time. The eggs must absorb more than twice their weight in water from the soil in which they are buried. In this way, heavy rain is not only a cue for hatching but also ensures that there is an adequate food supply from plants which also respond to the rain.

The desert crab (*Holthuisana transversa*) is widely distributed throughout arid Australia and survives dry periods in humid burrows. Fat reserves built up during wet periods provide maintenance energy whilst underground. This crab has a high tolerance to desiccation and can recover from water loss of up to 40% of total body weight (Greenway undated). This animal can breathe in water using gills and in air by inflating branchial chambers to form lung-like structures.

Most amphibians lose water by evaporation faster than other terrestrial vertebrates. Therefore, few amphibians live in arid areas. However, the Australian water-holding frog (*Cyclorana platycephalus*) survives dry periods by burrowing and being able to extract water from very dry soil (van Beurden undated). As the soil dries, a cocoon is secreted around the frog which significantly reduces water loss. The frog also utilises water stored in the bladder to replace water lost through the skin and other respiratory surfaces. In this condition, the frog can survive for a year or more. This strategy is known as **aestivation**, a process whereby the metabolic rate and body temperature are reduced. The adaptive value is great in endothermic organisms which expend more energy on basal metabolism than do ectothermic animals (see section 2.7.3). Aestivation is similar to **hibernation**, the response exhibited by some temperate organisms to winter.

Marsupials dominate the native mammalian fauna in Australia. Those inhabiting arid regions employ behavioural, physiological and morphological adaptations to maintain water balance and control body temperature. These adaptations are similar to the strategies employed by placental mammals inhabiting deserts elsewhere in the world. Arid zone marsupials are nocturnal or crepuscular and the daytime is spent in burrows or shade. Rock wallabies (*Petrogale rothschildi*) and marsupial cats (*Dasyurus hallucatus*) shelter in caves where temperatures may be 10 °C lower than the outside air. The large red kangaroos (*Macropus rufus*) utilise shade. The hairy-nosed wombat (*Lasiorhinus latifrons*) and the rabbit-eared bandicoot (*Macrotis lagotis*) dig deep burrows which provide excellent protection from overheating with temperatures as much as 20 °C below ambient at a depth of 1 m. In this way, organisms utilise **micro-environments** where the climate is less severe than that recorded by meteorological stations. Ecologists, therefore, need to be careful in assessing the environmental conditions to which organisms are actually exposed. Plants often provide a micro-habitat for other plants and animals.

The majority of arid zone marsupials are solitary or live in pairs. This reduces the impact of the animals on scarce food resources. Euros (*Macropus robustus*) tend to be solitary with a home range often centred on a rocky outcrop. During favourable conditions, this species will roam further afield. The red kangaroo is gregarious and nomadic, an advantage where resources are patchy. A red kangaroo has been recorded 240 km from where it was tagged, whereas a tagged euro was never recorded more than 1 km from its shelter. Emu (*Dromaius novaehollandiae*) have been shown to move up to 500 km in 9 months (Williams 1979).

Marsupials generally have metabolic rates lower than those of similar-sized eutherian mammals. Lower metabolic rates confer two main advantages. Lower energy requirements reduce the amount of food needed and lower energy use reduces heat production which, in turn, reduces the need for evaporative cooling and consequently conserves water. Kangaroo locomotion by hopping is energy efficient and this conserves both food and water.

Kangaroos employ three mechanisms for evaporative cooling: panting, sweating and saliva-spreading. Saliva-spreading is the more unusual of these techniques. A large venous network is present below the skin of the forelimbs and, during periods of heat stress, saliva is spread over this area. Blood flow through the forelimbs increases and heat is lost from the blood through evaporative cooling.

Arid zone marsupials produce a concentrated urine, and, during dehydration, maintain blood plasma volume by withdrawing water from intercellular spaces and the intestinal tract. Body temperatures fluctuate with a relatively low body temperature at the start of the day rising by 2–2.5 °C during the day. In this way less water is required for evaporative cooling. In the rabbit-eared bandicoot, respiratory water loss is reduced by cooling exhaled air. This is probably achieved by a counter-current heat exchange mechanism in its elongated nose.

2.4 | Environmental factors

In this section, we consider limitations on the distribution of organisms incurred through the impact of selected environmental factors: water availability, temperature, salinity and soil nutrients. In chapter 3, the role of light as an environmental factor will be discussed together with photosynthesis. Environmental factors specific to certain habitats will be considered in appropriate chapters: dissolved gases and nutrients, water depth (chapter 5), water flow (chapter 6), low temperature (chapter 9) and wave action and tides (chapters 10 and 11).

2.5 | Water

Living matter is dependent on water, and a review of the properties of this wonderful substance demonstrates why (see Box 2.1). Protoplasm is physiologically active only when its water content is high. If cells dry out, either the physiological

activity of the cells ceases or the cells die. Only a few plants and animals are able to survive in a totally desiccated state (see section 2.1.2).

Terrestrial organisms live in air with a lower water content than their bodies and consequently constantly lose water. Plants lose water by **evapotranspiration**, mostly from stomata but also from all exposed surfaces. Animals lose water through evaporation and in excretory and other waste products. These losses must be replaced through water uptake. Most uptake in plants is through the root system. Animals gain water through drinking, from food and the release of water in the breakdown of organic matter during respiration.

All terrestrial organisms need to maintain a water balance with water uptake both replacing water lost and providing sufficient for growth. Plants and animals living in arid areas show many similar adaptations to maintain a water balance. Setae, hairs and scales that create a boundary layer and reduce air flow over the body surface occur in both plants and animals. This results in a more humid boundary layer which reduces water loss by slowing the rate of diffusion. Stomata in plants and spiracles in insects are similar in that both possess complex passageways that provide resistance to diffusion of water vapour (Cloudsley-Thompson 1977). Water loss in plants and animals may be reduced through the presence of a thick, waxy cuticle. Some desert animals and plants also have special water storage organs or tissues.

Water loss from surfaces can be reduced by having a low surface area to volume ratio. However, gas exchange requires moisture and is facilitated by a large surface area. The ideal gas exchange surface has a large area and is moist and well ventilated: conditions which promote water loss. Therefore, significant water loss occurs through the stomata in plants and from the respiratory surfaces (lungs, trachea, skin) in animals.

2.5.1 Water balance in plants
Some plants are able to withstand significant drying. The water content of lower terrestrial organisms (bacteria, algae, fungi and lichens) varies with the humidity of the surrounding air; they exhibit little control over the water content

Box 2.1 | Water: the wonder chemical

Water (H_2O) has a molecular weight similar to that of hydrogen sulfide (H_2S). At NTP (Normal Temperature and Pressure) water, like hydrogen sulfide, should be a gas. However, the physical properties of these two compounds are very different. The boiling point of water is 100 °C, that of hydrogen sulfide is −61 °C; their respective melting points are 0 °C and −86 °C.

These differences are imparted through the propensity of water to form hydrogen bonds with itself and other compounds. Although the water molecule as a whole is electrically neutral, electrons are shared asymmetrically between the hydrogen and oxygen atoms. Consequently, one side of the water molecule has a small positive charge, the other a small negative charge (dipole). Electrostatic attraction between a positively charged region of one molecule and a negatively charged region of another forms a hydrogen bond. This hydrogen bonding gives water its high boiling and melting points, its high heat of vaporisation (the energy absorbed per gram of water vaporised), its high latent heat of fusion and other properties described below. In essence, water exhibits properties expected of a substance of greater molecular weight.

Water has a high **heat capacity**. A given quantity of water requires a great gain in heat to increase its temperature and it experiences a great loss of heat as it cools. The heat capacity of water (previously known as specific heat) buffers the bodies of organisms against rapid fluctuations in temperature. This property also moderates the temperature changes in moist soils, lakes and oceans. Water's high latent heat of vaporisation provides an effective means of cooling through evapotranspiration in plants and water loss from surfaces in animals (e.g. sweating).

Water is also known as the 'universal solvent' because so many substances readily dissolve in it. Again, this is due to its dipole nature which aids in dissociation of ionic compounds into their constituent ions. As a result, water is the medium in which most biochemical reactions take place. Most chemical compounds (or their constituent building blocks) required by organisms can dissolve in water and this facilitates their absorption.

At a free water surface, water molecules become orientated so that most of the hydrogen bonds point in towards the bulk of the liquid. This confers on the water its remarkably high surface tension (the highest of all common liquids except mercury). Pond skaters use this property in their movement across the surface of ponds. The high viscosity and tensile strength of water are also significant, particularly with regard to the movement of water up plant stems. Water is also unusual in that it has its maximum density at almost 4 °C above its freezing point. Natural water bodies therefore rarely freeze solid, with obvious advantage to aquatic organisms.

Water is of paramount importance to all organisms. Plant cells may contain as much as 90% water and few can survive drying to more than 40% of their normal water content. Most animals cannot survive for more than a few days without access to free water. Plants obtain hydrogen for photosynthesis by splitting water molecules; they use it in support and as their transport medium. Both animals and plants use water in evaporative cooling. Animals use water as a transport medium (blood and lymph) and, in many, it provides the medium for waste disposal (urine). Water is essential in providing a medium for the diffusion of gases across respiratory surfaces. Water is, indeed, a wonderful substance.

of their cells. These organisms are called **poikilohydric**. The cells of such organisms have only a small or no vacuole, so there is little change in volume of the cell contents during drying. The growth rate of these organisms is slow as their physiology is often shut down because of water shortage.

Most mosses, ferns, fern allies and seed plants are **homoiohydric** and maintain the water content of their cells at a high and near constant level. The cells of these plants have a large vacuole which acts as a water store and keeps the surrounding protoplasm hydrated. This strategy of keeping the protoplasm hydrated ensures higher growth rates, but the need to remain hydrated limits the distribution of some of these plants to areas where water is readily available.

Mosses have poorly developed roots and a rudimentary vascular system and therefore rely on low water loss rates (i.e. a humid, damp atmosphere) to maintain their water balance. Ferns have a better water uptake and transportation system but still most are restricted to moist areas. There are, of course, exceptions and some mosses and ferns do grow in deserts. They have an enhanced ability to withstand desiccation through a reduction in cell size and the size of the cell vacuole. In other words, they have assumed a poikilohydric life style. Mosses and ferns are also restricted to damp habitats through the need for free water to effect gamete transfer and fertilisation. The seed plants (gymnosperms and angiosperms), through the development of pollen grains, do not require free water for gamete transfer.

Plants adapted to living in arid regions are called **xerophytes**. Plants adapted to living in water are called **hydrophytes** (see chapters 5 and 6) and those that live in terrestrial environments where water availability is adequate are called **mesophytes**. Xerophytes do not benefit from dry conditions and, in fact, often grow better if the water supply is increased. However, by living in a dry environment they avoid competition from the faster-growing mesophytes.

Among the plants, gymnosperms and angiosperms exhibit the greatest adaptation to terrestrial life with respect to water balance maintenance (Table 2.2). Structural and physiological adaptations have enabled these plants to remain hydrated under even the extremely dry conditions that prevail in some deserts.

Gibson (1998) pointed out that, when analysing plant adaptations to arid conditions, it is important to remember that leaves (or green stems) have not only to be adapted to conserve water, but also to be able to harvest light energy efficiently for photosynthesis (see section 3.5). We are now beginning to appreciate that what might appear to be adaptations to conserve water may, in fact, be directed more towards making photosynthesis more efficient. For example, some desert annuals exhibit **diaheliotropism**, the capacity to track the sun and thereby maximise interception of solar radiation. This is clearly an adaptation to maximise photosynthesis. Other desert plants have leaves that remain vertical. This could be interpreted either as a mechanism to reduce water loss by reducing heat uptake or as a strategy to maximise photosynthesis in the morning when cell water potentials and air humidity are high. Gibson (1998) also suggests that sunken stomata might protect them from contact with dry air, thereby preventing them from closing. In this interpretation, having sunken stomata is viewed as an adaptation to improve carbon dioxide uptake rather than to reduce water loss. Gibson (1998) warns that ecologists should be careful in how they interpret plant structural adaptations and that it should not necessarily be assumed that the primary concern of desert plants is water conservation; carbon fixation, temperature regulation and defence from herbivory are also very important.

2.5.2 Water loss reduction and excretion in animals

Most food contains some water. Water is also released during food breakdown in respiration. For example, every molecule of glucose respired yields six molecules of water. These two sources of water are enough for some terrestrial animals, but others require access to free water for drinking. Water is lost from respiratory surfaces, parts of the body in contact with the air and in urine and faeces. Desert animals produce dry faeces by absorbing water from them in the rectum or

Table 2.2 | Adaptations exhibited by plants and animals inhabiting arid areas

Plants	Animals
Structural and physiological adaptations	*Structural and physiological adaptations*
Low surface area to volume ratio	Possession of an impermeable outer layer, waxy exoskeleton in insects
Leaves reduced to spines or scales	Water reabsorption from faeces
Stems are often fleshy and green (photosynthetic)	Decrease water content in urine (excrete uric acid)
High root to shoot ratio	
High lateral and/or vertical root spread	
Plant covered in a thick, waxy cuticle, impermeable to water	Increased water intake by eating plant tissue with a high water content or by drinking dew
Stomata density low, sunk in pits, surrounded by epidermal hairs	Direct water uptake from the air
Stomata open at night when temperature is low and humidity is high	Survive complete desiccation
CAM photosynthesis for water conservation or C_4 photosynthesis for rapid growth (see section 3.7)	*Behavioural*
	Body orientation to reduce heat uptake during day
Inhibitors in shed leaves to prevent germination of competitors	Reduce water loss by inactivity, finding shade or by going underground
	Nocturnal or crepuscular activity
Life history strategies	
Desert plants are mostly annuals	
Rapid growth rate following germination, to flowering and seed set within a few weeks	
Survive complete desiccation (resurrection plants)	

cloaca. One of the problems animals face, which has not been covered, is the disposal of nitrogenous wastes.

Animals living in freshwater have no difficulty in disposing of nitrogenous wastes. Ammonia, although very toxic, is also very soluble, and therefore these animals simply allow ammonia to diffuse out. Most arthropods, many reptiles and birds and some unusual frogs excrete nitrogenous waste as uric acid. Very little water is required to do this. Mammals produce urea, a highly soluble compound, and therefore this has to be voided in solution with, obviously, some water loss. Desert mammals, however, have kidneys which can produce a concentrated urine to reduce this water loss.

Shantz (1956) classified plants and animals on the basis of four ecological methods by which they met drought conditions (Table 2.3). Organisms may utilise one or more of these strate-

gies to ensure an adequate water supply and survival through a drought.

2.6 | Limiting factors

The most obvious limiting factor in any arid environment is water. Plants in the Namib Desert exhibit a typical response to the removal of a limiting factor. Figure 2.10 compares the biomass of plants in five dunal habitats during a dry (normal) period and after rain. Plant and detrital biomass increased 9-fold on the slipface, 53-fold on the dune slope and almost 3-fold in the interdune valley (Seely and Louw 1980). The marked increase in biomass that occurred after rain demonstrates the importance of water. Furthermore, the dramatic increase in nitrogen content (a measure of the protein content) of the plants is of great significance to the animals that rely on plants for

Table 2.3 Four ecological means by which plants and animals adapt to drought conditions	
Plants	Animals
Drought-escaping Ephemeras which grow during moist seasons and live through dry seasons in the seed stage	Animals that enter arid lands only when moisture is available – largely mobile insects, birds and mammals
Drought-evading Plants which make economical use of limited soil moisture supply through wide spacing, reduced leaf and stem surface	Nocturnal, burrowing animals that do not need to provide water for temperature control
Drought-resisting Succulents that store water and are able to continue growth when soil moisture is not available. Not characteristic of extreme deserts	Animals that resist drought through physiological processes by which they are able to concentrate their urine, lose little water in faeces, stop perspiration, endure dehydration and still remain active – the camel is a fine example
Drought-enduring Drought-dormant plants that aestivate when drought occurs and continue growth when moisture is available. This includes many prominent desert seed plants and also algae, lichens, mosses, and ferns	Animals that aestivate and any invertebrates that recover after desiccation

Source: Shantz 1956.

food. As one might expect, the distribution of animals within the dune ecosystem was found to be very patchy, reflecting the patchiness of the food supply.

Desert rainfall is usually erratic in its seasonal distribution. Therefore the biological significance of average annual rainfall figures in these areas is of limited value. What is far more important is the biological effectiveness or timing of significant rain falls. The mean time interval between rain showers is very important for some plant species. Others are adapted to responding rapidly to the advent of rain, germinating, growing, flowering and setting seed using the moisture from just one rain shower.

Furthermore, desert soils play a role in determining the effectiveness of rainfall. Desert soils are a combination of the erosion products of the underlying rock formed through the action of wind and water and aeolian (wind borne) and fluvial (water borne) deposits. Water supply to plants growing in arid areas is not simply a matter of the quantity of rain – the amount remaining in the soil and available to plants is also important. The amount of water that the soil retains depends upon the soil texture (particle size) and the organic matter content. Sandy soils do not retain water well; clay soils with much smaller particles drain less well (see section 2.9.2). However, in desert areas, water that does not permeate soils, such as those with a high clay content, is more susceptible to evaporation than the water which penetrates deeper into sandy soils. Consequently, following rainfall, the clay soils dry out more quickly than sandy soils. Desert plants with deep roots have access to the water that has penetrated deeper into the sandy soils. In the Sudan, *Acacia tortilis* is found on sandy soils in a zone that has

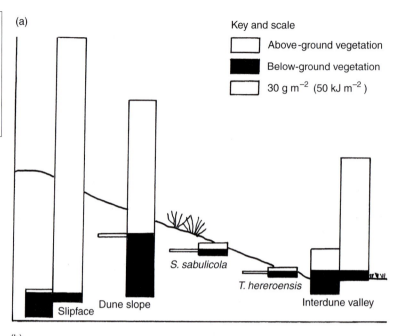

(a)

Figure 2.10 The change in standing biomass of (a) plants and (b) animals from a dry period (left histogram) to a wet period (right histogram) measured on various parts of the Namib dune system (after Seely and Louw 1980 with permission of Academic Press).

Key and scale
☐ Above-ground vegetation
■ Below-ground vegetation
☐ 30 g m^{-2} (50 kJ m^{-2})

S. sabulicola
T. hereroensis
Slipface   Dune slope   Interdune valley

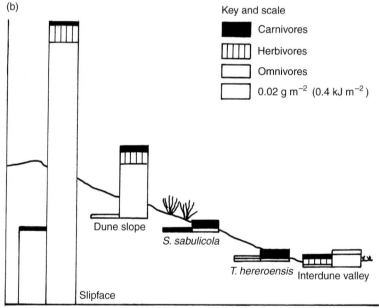

(b)

Key and scale
■ Carnivores
▥ Herbivores
☐ Omnivores
☐ 0.02 g m^{-2} (0.4 kJ m^{-2})

Dune slope
S. sabulicola
T. hereroensis   Interdune valley
Slipface

annual rainfall of 50 to 250 mm. However, this species is restricted to zones with higher rainfall where soils contain more clay. Rocky soils in arid regions often support a shrub and tree vegetation greater than that on nearby fine-textured soils.

In the tropics, rain is the most important of all environmental factors and largely determines the type of vegetation a particular area will support (Figures 1.1 and 1.2). Furthermore, in drier areas

there is a direct relationship between the amount of rainfall and the quantity of plants produced (Figure 2.11). This relationship clearly shows that water supply (rain) is **limiting** the growth of the plants: higher rainfall results in more plant growth. In 1840, Justus Liebig, (see Liebig 1840) an agriculturist, noticed that the growth of a plant was restricted by the factor provided in minimum quantity relative to the needs of the plant. **Liebig's**

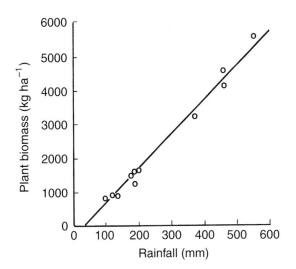

Figure 2.11 Plant biomass (above-ground, dry weight, in kilograms per hectare) in grasslands in Namibia in relation to the annual precipitation (mm) (after Walter 1973 with kind permission from Springer-Verlag GmbH).

law of the minimum states that the development of a population is essentially regulated by the substance occurring in minimal quantity relative to the **requirement** of the population.

Liebig's law is only applicable under steady state conditions. If the supply of a limiting nutrient or substance is enhanced, plant production will increase, and, while this change occurs, there will be no limiting factor. When a steady state of supply and uptake is re-established, the same, or a new factor, may then limit further production. Whether a factor is limiting, can be determined by carrying out an enrichment experiment. If it is hypothesised that water is limiting the growth of desert plants, then provision of water should result in enhanced plant growth. A factor cannot be assumed to be limiting simply because it is present in very small amounts. The supply must be related to the requirements of the plant.

2.7 | Temperature

Most organisms have a narrow temperature range over which activity is possible. Some organisms can exist at very low temperatures for short periods and some bacteria and Cyanobacteria live in hot springs at temperatures approaching 100 °C. Every organism has, for a particular exposure time, an upper and lower lethal temperature. Between these extremes, the rates of metabolic reactions usually increase with temperature and many organisms function most efficiently at temperatures near the upper lethal limit.

Tolerance to temperature in terrestrial organisms is closely linked with the availability of water. Plants and animals living in hot deserts cannot afford, during time of water stress, to cool their bodies by evaporation. The effect of temperature on organisms very much depends upon how they can regulate their body temperature and control heat loss and gain from the environment.

2.7.1 Maintenance of heat balance

All organisms gain heat from, and lose heat to, the environment. They also produce heat internally as a by-product of metabolism. Animals have developed a range of structural, behavioural and physiological adaptations that enable them to regulate their body temperatures and mitigate the effects of temperature extremes. Plants, unlike most animals, are unable to move away from areas of heat stress. Therefore leaves, stems and roots are usually at much the same temperature as the surrounding air or soil. In other words, animals have the capacity to avoid temperature extremes, plants, by and large, have to withstand them or perish.

2.7.2 Plants and temperature

Tropical plants are generally exposed to temperatures that are approximately favourable for growth, above the optimum or lethally high. Some desert plants have to cope with a wide diurnal range of temperatures, and plants near the summits of tropical mountains may be exposed to low or very low temperatures (see chapter 9). We will concentrate here on how plants cope with high temperatures. Plants dissipate heat in three main ways: emission of long-wave radiation, convection and through evaporative cooling in transpiration. Under normal circumstances, most heat is lost through transpiration.

High temperatures in plants usually occur following stomatal closure. The stomata close to reduce the rate of transpiration in order to conserve water. Plants in this situation, therefore, face a combination of thermal and water-deficiency stress. This stress syndrome is commonly experienced by plants existing in hot deserts. Separating the effects of temperature stress from those arising through water shortage is difficult and particularly so in the field. Laboratory experiments have shown that leaf tissue damage results, in most plants, following exposure to 45 °C for as little as 30 minutes.

To avoid heat stress, plant leaves may be covered in dense, white hairs or be pale green to reflect light and reduce heat absorption. Desert plants alter leaf angles through the day, fold leaves or lose them entirely to reduce both heat uptake and water loss. The C_4 photosynthetic strategy (see section 3.7) operates most effectively at higher temperatures and is common in tropical grasses. Some succulents and evergreen sclerophylls have largely forgone transpiration as a mechanism of temperature reduction and have developed metabolic systems that can tolerate high temperatures.

2.7.3 Animals and temperature regulation

Physiologically, it is possible to divide animals into **homeotherms** and **poikilotherms**. Homeotherms have the capacity to regulate their body temperatures within narrow limits, and mammals and birds do this most of the time. Poikilotherms have less control over their body temperature, and mostly rely on external sources of heat to raise it. These two definitions have limitations, as some homeotherms often have body temperatures that fluctuate around the optimum. The camel, for example, is a homeotherm but will, when short of water, allow its body temperature to rise during the day by as much as 6 °C above normal. When the camel has adequate water, diurnal fluctuations in body temperature are much less. Similarly, some poikilotherms maintain a constant body temperature because they live in an environment with a constant temperature regime. Other poikilotherms use behavioural methods and effectively maintain a constant body temperature. The terms 'warm-blooded' and 'cold-blooded' to describe,

respectively, homeotherms and poikilotherms, should be avoided as they are misleading and subjective. So-called cold-blooded organisms may well, at times, have a blood temperature higher than that of warm-blooded organisms.

Another way to distinguish organisms on the basis of their temperature physiology is to use the terms **ectotherms** (animals dependent on the environment as both a heat source and a heat sink) and **endotherms** (animals which exhibit reasonable control over body temperature through independent, internal heat production). These terms are useful and, ecologically, it is important to recognise how the physiological performance of an organism is affected by temperature. Furthermore, organisms have an armoury of mechanisms to regulate their body temperature within physiological limits. Some ectotherms utilise heat generated within their bodies; e.g., many insects generate heat by intense muscular contractions.

Ectotherms metabolise slowly at low temperatures and more quickly as the temperature rises. Endotherms, on the other hand, expend considerable energy in maintaining body temperature at a level which optimises the metabolic rate. They reduce heat loss to the environment by having insulating fur, feathers or subcutaneous fat deposits and can enhance loss through sweating, panting and increasing blood flow through the skin.

2.8 | Salinity

Water normally percolates through the soil but, under the high evaporative conditions prevalent in deserts, there is often a slow upward movement by capillarity. Evaporation of soil water at the soil surface may concentrate the solutes to such an extent that it interferes with water uptake by plants. To understand how this occurs we need to consider the concepts of **water potential** and **osmosis**.

Osmosis is the passive movement of water across a **differentially permeable membrane**. Water, like other molecules, will move from a region of higher energy to one of lower energy. The two most important factors affecting the energy level of water (its water potential) are the substances dissolved in it (solutes) (**osmotic potential**) and the pressures being exerted (**pressure potential**). The addition of solutes to water effectively dilutes the water. This reduces the diffusion rate of water through a membrane. Solutes also interact with water molecules and, in most cases, this further reduces the diffusion rate. When a hydrostatic pressure is applied to water, its energy increases. Water potential (ψ, psi) is the sum of the osmotic potential ($\psi\pi$) and the pressure potential (ψ_p):

$$\psi = \psi\pi + \psi_p$$

Water potential increases with increased pressure or temperature but decreases with the addition of solutes. The water potential of pure water has been arbitrarily set as zero and therefore water solutions have a negative water potential. Water moves from a region of high water potential to one of lower water potential (less negative to more negative). Therefore, the relative water potentials of the soil and the root cells will determine the passive rate of water uptake by the plant.

Soil water potential is a composite measure and defined as:

$$\psi_s = \psi_\pi + \psi_p + \psi_m + \psi_q$$

where: ψ_s is the soil water potential, ψ_m is the **matric potential**, and ψ_q is the **gravitational potential**. ψ_π and ψ_p are defined above.

The matric potential is a measure of the water-retaining capacity of the soil and is affected by soil texture (see section 2.9.5) and soil water content. The force arises from the surface tension of water droplets in the soil pore spaces and forces of adsorption between water molecules and charged particles and surfaces. The matric potential is low in wet soils but increases as the soil dries and may become the dominant force in dry soils. The osmotic potential is determined by the concentration of solutes in the soil water, and its significance increases with salinity. Matric and osmotic potentials are negative. The pressure and gravity potentials relate to hydrostatic pressure and gravity forces respectively and are both positive. These potentials become more significant in saturated soils.

Dry, desert soils will have a strong (negative) matric potential. The salt content of desert soils may also be high, particularly in poorly drained areas. Where this is the case, the osmotic potential will be highly negative. Consequently, dry, saline soils will have a very low (negative) water potential. The ability of such soils to donate water is therefore very low or, conversely, plants may be unable to absorb water from them. Therefore, high salt concentrations in the soil surrounding the root zone of a plant may lead to water stress.

Salinity is a major cause of environmental degradation in arid areas. In Australia, $20\,000\,km^2$ of land is currently salt-affected. This has been caused by clearing forests for crop and livestock production. Plants continuously remove water from the soil. Trees have deeper roots than grasses and herbs, extracting water from deep within the soil. When the trees are removed, less water is used and more enters the deeper layers of the soil causing the water table to rise. In this way, salts in the underground water are deposited in the surface layers of the soil. The water becomes increasingly salty as it rises, dissolving the salt that has accumulated in the subsoil. In dry areas, the water in the subsoil evaporates quickly, leaving the salt behind. Changes in the vegetation quickly follow with the death of deep-rooting plants and their replacement with salt-tolerant species.

Irrigated croplands also face salinity problems. In this case, the rise in the water table is due to poor irrigation practices where more water is applied than can be used by the crop. The excess water percolates through the soil and causes the water table to rise. The excess salinity is harmful to crops because of both the osmotic stress and the toxicity of the salts themselves.

2.9 Soils and nutrients

2.9.1 Soil structure

Soils consist of organic and inorganic matter in three phases: solids, liquids and gases. The solid phase consists in part of inorganic material ranging from fragments of largely unaltered parent rock to mineral grains undergoing

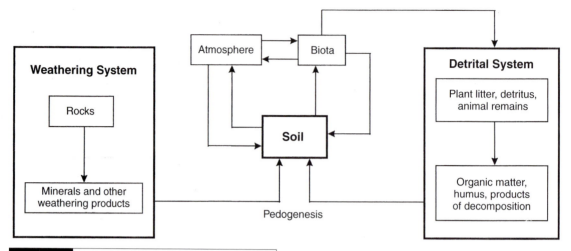

Figure 2.12 Soil formation (pedogenesis) from weathering rocks and minerals and the breakdown of litter and detritus (adapted from White *et al.* 1993 with kind permission from Kluwer Academic Publishers).

weathering and the products of that weathering. The other component of the solid phase is the organic material consisting of plant and animal remains and the products resulting from their decomposition (see chapter 10). In between these solid particles are pore spaces filled with gases and water with solutes. Soil water is not pure, but contains a variety of inorganic and organic substances in solution. These solutes are derived from a variety of sources and provide plant nutrients.

Spaces between soil particles that are not filled with soil water contain air, but the composition often differs from that of the atmosphere, usually with lower oxygen and higher carbon dioxide concentrations. The composition varies depending on the rate of oxygen consumption and carbon dioxide output through respiration by soil organisms and the rate of diffusion from the atmosphere. There is a tendency for these air spaces to become saturated with carbon dioxide, and replenishment of them with oxygen is essential for a healthy soil. This is an important point and it demonstrates that soils are living systems.

Soils arise from weathering of parent rock material and through the deposition of plant and animal remains (Figure 2.12). Some soils are of recent origin and may be only a few centimetres deep, overlying solid rock. Others are old, deep

and highly weathered. The process of soil formation is known as **pedogenesis**. Soil formation occurs through physical, chemical and biological processes. Physical weathering reduces mean particle size, breaking down rocks into their constituent grains. Chemical reactions alter the constituent components of the soil. Soils provide a habitat for many organisms which play significant roles in processing soil particles and providing nutrients in a form that can be taken up by plants. Organisms mix the soil and further modify the soil through the uptake of water and nutrients and the deposition of organic matter as litter. The processes involved in soil formation are clearly interwoven: a reduction in particle size facilitates chemical weathering; organisms aerate the soil and thereby promote chemical weathering.

Differences in soil properties arise through differences in the parent material, climate, topography and vegetation. In dry regions, weathering occurs mostly through mechanical processes such as the impact of wind-blown sand grains on rocks. In more humid environments, chemical weathering is more significant. Weathering reduces particle size and may make soils more susceptible to erosion.

Most soils are composed of several layers. A soil **profile** is a section through the soil from the surface to the underlying parent rock. The uppermost layer consists of fresh and partially decomposed plant and animal remains underlain by organic material in a more advanced stage of decomposition. Beneath this litter layer, is the topsoil (**A-horizon**) or **biomantle**. In many soils, this layer is continuously mixed by burrowing animals (ants, termites, earthworms) in a process known as **bioturbation**. The topsoil may also include aeolian or fluvial deposits derived from soils eroded elsewhere.

In the A-horizon, the products of decomposition enter solution and move downward through the soil. This leaching process results in the transfer of materials, such as soluble salts, clay, iron and aluminium, from this horizon, the **zone of eluviation**, to the next layer, the **zone of illuviation**. The A-horizon, in this way, becomes enriched with the resistant minerals, such as silica, that remain behind. In the **B-horizon**, material leached out from above is deposited and enriches this layer. The **C-horizon** consists of weathered rock or sediment that serves as the parent material which has undergone neither depletion nor enrichment as described above. The thickness of the various horizons is highly variable, and the depths and physical and chemical features of the soil horizons provide significant information on soil fertility. The soil profile also provides a framework against which soils can be compared.

2.9.2 Soil water

As we have seen, soil has particles forming a solid framework with pores in between. If these pores are completely filled with water, the soil is said to be **saturated**. Following precipitation, water infiltrates the soil and gradually percolates deeper, down to the water table. This loss of water will gradually slow down, until it ceases; the soil is then said to be at **field capacity**. The water that percolates through the soil is called **gravitational water**; that which remains at field capacity is called **capillary water**. The field capacity of a soil is the maximum water content the soil can hold permanently. Further loss of water from a soil at field capacity can occur through evaporation and uptake by plants. As water is removed, it becomes more tightly held by the soil particles and it becomes increasingly difficult for plants to fulfil their water requirements.

The water is held in the soil by capillary action and attached to soil colloids by surface forces. It is also held, especially in saline soils, osmotically bound to ions. As the soil dries, the water potential becomes increasingly negative and the capacity for the soil to 'donate' water much reduced. Fine-grained soils, as well as soils rich in colloids and organic matter, store more water than coarse-grained soils such as sands. A high field capacity is advantageous to plants, as the stored water enables them to survive droughts.

If gravitational water persists in the soil, it is likely that the soil will become waterlogged, and the respiration of plant roots and soil organisms will be impeded owing to a lack of air. In areas with high rainfall, the continuous passage of gravitational water will result in the removal of nutrients from the upper soil layers, a process known as **leaching**.

2.9.3 Soil nutrients

Most plants obtain from the soil the water and mineral nutrients that are essential for growth and metabolism. Plants obtain their carbon from atmospheric carbon dioxide and hydrogen and oxygen from water. Oxygen required for respiration comes from the atmosphere. Plants can obtain all the other elements required for healthy growth from the soil. These elements include: phosphorus, potassium, nitrogen, sulfur, calcium, magnesium, iron, sodium, chlorine, iodine, boron, silicon, copper, manganese and zinc. An inadequate supply of any one of these, and some other elements, will affect the growth of the plant and result in reduced growth or a **deficiency disease**. For example, an inadequate supply of magnesium, an integral part of the chlorophyll molecule, may result in chlorosis, a yellowing of the plant owing to a reduced ability to produce chlorophyll.

Most, if not all, plant nutrients are absorbed from the soil solution in ionic form. The common metals are absorbed as cations, and nitrogen, sulfur and phosphorus as ionic oxides. The availability of nutrients in the soil cannot be assessed simply on their concentration in the soil. Plant nutrients occur in the soil in both dissolved and solid forms, and only a tiny fraction of the nutrient supply, at any one time, may be dissolved in the soil water. Most is bound into organic matter, inorganic compounds, or in minerals, and only enters solution slowly through weathering and decomposition. Equilibria exist between the soil solution, the soil colloids and the minerals which may result in replenishment of nutrients in the soil solution which have been taken up by plants. In this way, the soil can provide a continual supply of nutrients. The processes by which nutrients are recycled are described in section 5.13.

2.9.4 Soil organisms

Organisms affect the way a soil develops. Animals burrow in the soil and aid in the breakdown of organic matter through aerating the soil and ingesting particles and egesting faeces. Plants extract soil nutrients and exude organic compounds. Terrestrial organisms add to the organic matter of the soil when they die. Perhaps the most important soil organisms are those involved in the breakdown of this organic matter into its constituent parts. This process is known as decomposition, and is carried out by a range of soil organisms: bacteria, fungi, invertebrates and even some vertebrates. Decomposition is described in chapter 10.

2.9.5 Soil features and classification

Tropical soils are very heterogeneous, and in describing a soil type three main features are used: **texture**, **colour** and **structure**. The texture of a soil is determined by the size of the particles within it, and soils can be classified according to particle size from coarse stones to clays (Table 2.4). In the humid tropics, even temperatures and high rainfall combine to promote leaching, weathering and decomposition. In drier areas, these processes may be impeded by climate. Soil features are also a function of soil age. Soils in tectonically and geomorphologically stable areas are more highly leached and weathered than those found in less stable, volcanic areas where soil formation has occurred more recently (Table 2.5).

Soil colour is measured against standard Munsell colour charts. These charts classify colour along three axes: hue (spectral colour), value (greyness) and chroma (strength of colour). In the humid tropics, soils tend to be reddish or

Table 2.4	Classification of soil types based on particle size (texture)
Particle size (diameter)	Classification
>7.5 cm	Stones
2 mm to 7.5 cm	Gravel
0.2 mm to 2 mm	Coarse sand
0.02 mm to 0.2 mm	Fine sand
0.002 mm to 0.02 mm	Silt
<0.002 mm	Clay

yellowish and this contrasts with the more typical brown soils found in temperate areas. The bright colouration found in some tropical soils is due to enrichment with oxidised iron minerals which remain after intense leaching.

Soil structure refers to the way soil particles are aggregated to form **peds**. Between these peds are structural pores which are created by root penetration, animal burrows and shrinkage of clays during dry weather. Large structural pores facilitate root penetration, animal burrowing and the rapid infiltration of rain water. As structure breaks down, pore size declines, aeration and water percolation are reduced and root penetration becomes more difficult.

2.9.6 Desert soils

Desert soils occur mostly on flat surfaces and are absent from the steeper slopes where bare rock predominates. Soil composition is similar to the parent material from which it was derived and the nutrient status is usually poor. Nutrient supply, after water, may be critical in controlling the growth of desert organisms. Noy-Meir (1974) gave four reasons for this: (1) the rapid growth of plants following rain results in depletion of the soil nutrient pool; (2) the nutrient pool of desert soils is often small; (3) breakdown of plant material and release of the nutrients from it is limited by the lack of water; and (4) nutrients are mainly concentrated on the soil surface because leaching and decomposition rates are so slow. Very little work has been done on the role of soil nutrients in desert ecology. More is known about these cycles in aquatic systems, and therefore we will discuss nutrient cycles in chapter 5.

Table 2.5	Soil classification based on the comprehensive system of the United States Department of Agriculture
Soil order	Description
Entisols	Soils on recent deposits; immature; little or no horizon formation; soils on unconsolidated parent materials such as stabilised dune soils and alluvia.
Vertisols	Soils of tropical and subtropical regions; with high clay content; subject to cracking to great depth when dry; typically associated with savanna grasslands; Black Cotton Soils.
Inceptisols	Soils with weakly developed horizons containing unweathered material; often associated with arctic tundra and mountain areas.
Aridisols	Shallow stony soils of arid climates; high alkalinity and low organic matter content; desert soils.
Mollisols	Soils of the sub-humid temperate grasslands with thick, dark humus-rich A-horizons; high base saturation; prairie and steppe soils.
Spodosols	Soils of cool, humid areas; typically associated with boreal forest; acidic; strongly leached soils; low cation exchange capacity; lacking carbonate minerals.
Alfisols	Soils of humid and sub-humid regions; associated with tropical grasslands; Mediterranean areas and temperate forest; B-horizon enriched with clay washed in from above; moderate to high base saturation.
Ultisols	Strongly leached soils of warm, moist regions; clayey; associated with subtropical, broadleaf forest and monsoon tropical forest.
Oxisols	Deep, highly weathered and leached soils of the humid tropics, red owing to accumulated iron oxides; soils of tropical rain forests; lateritic soils.
Histosols	Dark, organic soils of poorly drained areas; typically acidic and of low fertility; wetland soils.
Andisols	Volcanic ash soils.

Source: Soil Survey Staff 1975; Etherington 1982; Archibold 1995.

Desert soils often have a high sand and low organic matter content and therefore have a low field capacity. The salt content of desert soils may be high, particularly in poorly drained areas. In humid areas with high rainfall, there is a net movement of water and its solutes down the soil profile, and leached minerals accumulate in the subsoil. In arid climates, if the soil has a natural water table or one produced through irrigation, there is a net movement of water up the profile owing to capillarity. Following evaporation, salt accumulates on the soil surface.

2.10 | Environmental factors and plant and animal distributions

Environmental factors, also known as **abiotic** factors, primarily determine whether an organism can survive in a particular environment. Subsequent interactions with other organisms may modify the degree of success of an organism within an area and may even result in its exclusion even though the environment is conducive to its existence (see sections 4.9.4 and 4.10). A number of ecological principles describe how well an organism performs in relation to the supply of resources and under varying environmental conditions. It is in this area of ecology that a sound knowledge of physiology is useful.

2.10.1 Response curves and environmental factors

Shelford, in 1913, recognised that an organism performs best between certain limits of some environmental factors. Above and below these limits, performance is reduced to a point where the organism cannot survive. The relationship

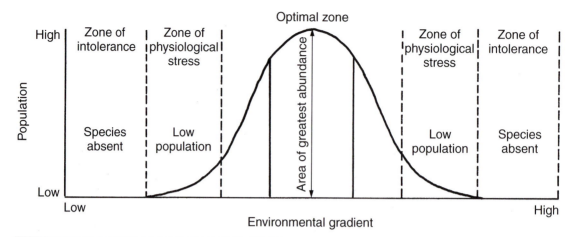

Figure 2.13 A generalised representation of the manner in which the performance of a species is related to the intensity of an environmental condition.

between an organism's performance and an environmental factor often takes the form of a bell-shaped curve (Figure 2.13). Furthermore, within the survival curve, limits for reproduction and growth may be delineated. In other words, towards the extremes, although the organism can survive, its growth or reproductive performance is impaired (**Shelford's law of tolerance**).

This type of response curve is typical for an organism's response to temperature. The rates of biological processes are controlled by enzymes. Each enzyme has an optimum temperature, below and above which the reaction rate slows. At high temperatures the enzyme is denatured (for most enzymes this occurs between 40–50 °C) and the reaction slows dramatically. Some estuarine organisms show a similar optimum response curve to salinity, with growth being impaired by both low and high salinities. Organisms can have a narrow or broad tolerance to a particular environmental factor. If an organism can survive a wide range of temperatures, it is known as **eurythermal**. If it is limited to a narrow range, it is referred to as **stenothermal**. These prefixes (eury-, steno-) can be applied to other environmental factors: **euryhaline** (salinity), **stenohydric** (water). Frequently, the broader the tolerance an organism displays, the lower its overall performance at any one point. In other words, **stenospecies** (specialists) are highly adapted to their narrow range and survive better within it than do **euryspecies** (generalists). Euryspecies have the obvious advantage of a wider choice of places to live.

A second response curve is known as the **saturation response**. Addition of a limiting nutrient to a crop will result in an increased yield. Further additions may increase yield even more. However, above a certain level, no further increase occurs. An excess of this nutrient does not have a negative effect, and the yield remains at a constant high level because some other factor limits growth. Some animals exhibit a sigmoid response curve to the removal of a limiting factor. This occurs in some predators with a strong capacity for learned behaviour (Figure 2.14).

In nature, organisms have to face the whole suite of factors, both biotic and abiotic, that constitute their environment. Whether an organism can survive in a particular area will depend upon the interaction of all the factors that make up the environment. We have seen that desert plants can withstand high temperatures if adequate water is available. However, the maximum temperature at which these plants can grow may be significantly lower if water is scarce.

2.10.2 Response times and acclimation

The impact of adverse environmental conditions on an organism depends on not only the magnitude of the environmental factor but also its duration. Organisms may be able to survive a short period of adverse conditions, but may succumb to

(a)

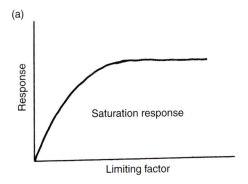

(b)

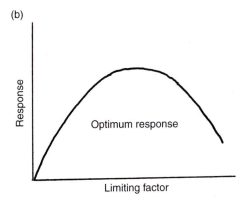

(c)

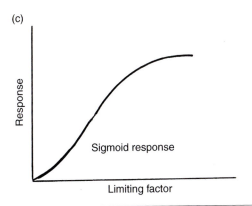

Figure 2.14 Limiting factor response curves. (a) The saturation response curve is the type originally investigated by Liebig. (b) The optimum response curve suggests that the organisms distribution is set by tolerance. (c) A sigmoid response is unusual and exhibited by organisms that can learn behaviour, such as hunting animals (after Colinvaux 1986 with kind permission from John Wiley & Sons).

less adverse conditions, if they persist for a longer time. We have seen that organisms have a range of behavioural and metabolic responses to environmental conditions. Examples include seeking shade and increasing the rate of sweat production in response to high temperature. These behavioural and physiological responses can be made rapidly; they may only involve movement or a change in the rate of a physiological or biochemical process that is already occurring. These rapid responses to environmental conditions do not require any morphological change or initiation of a biochemical pathway.

If you ascend a mountain quickly, you might be stricken by a condition known as altitude sickness. Symptoms include headaches, nausea and tiredness, and the cause is an inadequate supply of oxygen. However, if you remain at high altitude for about a week, your body will have time to manufacture more red blood cells, oxygen transport by your blood will be enhanced and altitude sickness overcome. This type of response, involving a substantial change in body structure or function, is known as **acclimation**. Some birds and mammals living in temperate regions will alternate between a summer and winter plumage. The winter plumage is thicker and often white and therefore provides both extra insulation and camouflage. Animals and plants can also acclimate to seasonal changes by switching between biochemical pathways, with, for example, enzymes that have different temperature optima. This will enhance performance of the organism within the environment to which it is acclimated. The organism will not necessarily perform at its optimum, but will do better than one which has not had time to acclimate.

This capacity for acclimation extends the range of habitats in which an organism can live providing that there is adequate time for the required change in body structure and function. The suitability of any environment will vary over time and space, and acclimation is one way organisms can cope with this variation. Resource availability also varies over time and space, and organisms have developed a range of strategies to cope with this variation as well.

2.10.3 Resource use

We have seen that the life of desert organisms is primarily controlled by water availability, but, for many organisms, food availability also plays a role. Availability of desert resources varies greatly over time and space. There are periods when food and water are abundant, but these periods are usually short-lived and their occurrence unpredictable. Successful desert organisms must be adapted to sequester resources either by being in the right place at the right time or by being able to utilise the meagre resources that are available in one particular place all the time. In other words, desert organisms have developed strategies according to the availability of resources (Shmida *et al.* 1986).

Some organisms are highly adapted to utilising episodically available resources (Figures 2.15 and 2.16). These organisms respond quickly to the advent of rainfall and resource capture is rapid but not particularly efficient. They have a high reproductive rate and a capacity for rapid transition from active to dormant stages of the life cycle. Examples include opportunistic organisms: desert annuals, ephemeral insects, organisms inhabiting temporary ponds and aestivating vertebrates such as desert crabs, frogs and rodents. Desert predators also fit into this category, as their prey can be regarded as a rich resource which is only caught episodically.

Other organisms are adapted to make use of the very poor resources that are always available. These organisms have a high tolerance to drought and temperature extremes, efficient but often slow use of resources and special mechanisms for obtaining and using particular kinds of resources. Examples include xerophytes, succulents, lichens, tenebrionid beetles, termites, some rodents and marsupials and a few large mammals such as the camel and oryx.

Resources may be episodic in time but always available in an area that can be reached by an organism. Utilisation of patchy resources has led to another strategy: mobility. Most of the large desert animals are mobile and travel long distances from one patch of food to another. Plants can also utilise this spatial variation by producing copious seeds to increase the chance of some seeds falling on resource-rich (fertile) ground. Humans adapted to living in deserts (nomads) also utilise this high mobility strategy.

Considering that resources are scarce, there is, surprisingly, significant resource wastage in deserts. This is because either resource patches are too sparse to support a population of resource users, or episodic resource abundance is too unpredictable to allow discovery by potential users. We will discuss issues of resource supply further in section 4.9.4.

2.10.4 Indirect effects of environmental factors

Animals and plants, by living and growing in an environment, alter it. They contribute to the physical structure of the environment, providing surfaces which, in turn, may provide a habitat for other organisms. Plants provide shade for animals; plants remove nutrients from the soil and these are returned to the soil when the plant dies or when it is eaten by an animal and the waste products voided as faeces. Plants also alter the composition of soil by increasing its organic matter content and some plants, in association with bacteria, enrich the soil with nitrogen through nitrogen fixation (see section 5.13.2).

Relationships between environmental factors and population size may not be the result of a direct interaction. For example, the density (see section 4.5) of African buffalo (*Syncerus caffer*) is closely related to rainfall. This relationship is not established directly through water availability to buffalo but through rainfall stimulating grass growth, with grass being the primary food for buffalo. The growth of plants takes place through the process of photosynthesis, and the quantity of material produced is known as primary production. Grasslands and primary production are considered in the next chapter.

2.11 | Desertification or land degradation?

Lamprey (1988) compared the location of the southern border of desert vegetation in western Sudan in 1958 with its location in 1975. He

Figure 2.15 Gravel plains in the Namib–Naukluft National Park, Namib Desert, Namibia before the rains. Tree is a camel thorn (*Acacia erioloba*) (Photo: Michael and Patricia Fogden).

Figure 2.16 Flowers (Fabaceae) blooming on the gravel plains in the Namib–Naukluft National Park, Namib Desert, Namibia after rain (Photo: Michael and Patricia Fogden).

estimated that the boundary had shifted southward by 90–100 km during this period. However, Hellden (1984) could not find field evidence to support this expansion. Nicholson *et al.* (1998) used satellite imagery to detect changes in the boundary of the Sahara Desert between 1980 and 1995. They produced a vegetation index from spectral measurements in the red and near-infrared spectral regions. The red spectral response is inversely related to chlorophyll density. The near-infrared spectral response is directly related to scattering in individual leaves and between leaves in the canopy. A ratio of surface brightness in the red region to that in the infra-red region provides a 'greenness' index that is a measure of the surface covered by vegetation. The data from these spectra provide an estimate of the photosynthetic capacity of the vegetation and this was found to be related to precipitation.

Analysis of these satellite images showed a progressive southward expansion of the Sahara Desert from 1980 to 1984. During this period, the desert area increased by 1 349 000 km². Between 1984 and 1985, there was a retreat in the size of the desert; the desert expanded again in 1987 but showed a further retreat in 1988. What these studies have shown is that desert expansion and contraction can be explained by high inter-annual variations in rainfall and that there does not appear to be a steady southward advance of the Saharan southern boundary.

There is very little evidence to support the contention that major deserts of the world are expanding through some irreversible process of desertification. **Desertification** is the result of human action on a fragile environment and is probably better regarded as a form of **land degradation** rather than some process specific to deserts. The reduction in plant cover, the main symptom of this process, results from clearing of natural vegetation for cultivation, harvesting woody species for fuel and overgrazing. Overgrazing has resulted in the replacement of grasses with less palatable woody species. Total plant cover reduction makes the fragile desert soils more susceptible to erosion by wind and water, cultivation results in reduced soil fertility and irrigation raises soil salinity. This degradation can be reversed through improved land management, but the growth of human populations in some arid areas makes this a challenging task.

The five countries of North Africa now have a population in excess of 100 million people. This has developed from a population of just 8 million 100 years or so ago. The population in the arid areas of this region has been growing at a rate of over 2.5% per year. These larger human populations place an extra burden on a system already under significant ecological stress. We will return to the issue of human population growth and its impact on global ecology in chapters 13 and 14.

2.12 | Chapter summary

1. Tropical deserts vary from very dry and nearly lifeless to those where sufficient moisture enables the existence of well-adapted plants and animals. Regions having less than 25 cm of rainfall per year are generally classed as deserts. Much of the precipitation is evaporated rapidly owing to the high levels of solar radiation.

2. Currently deserts cover an estimated 20–30% of the earth's land area, but expansion of arid areas is occurring through poor land management by humans (overgrazing, excessive use of fire and bad cultivation practices).

3. Water is the basic medium of life. Water has, for

its molecular weight, relatively high boiling and melting points, properties imparted through the propensity of its molecules to form hydrogen bonds. It also has a high heat capacity and many substances dissolve freely in it. For these reasons, and its abundance on the earth, water is an ideal medium for the biological processes occurring within organisms. Terrestrial organisms need to conserve water, and many plants and animals are confined to moist areas because of their limited capacity to reduce water loss.

4. The life of organisms in deserts is controlled by the supply of water and, for many desert animals, a scarcity of food as well. There may be short periods of adequate water and even food abundance. However, the timing of these periods and their duration are usually unpredictable and only a small amount of the primary production is utilised by herbivores. Communities of desert plants and animals are surprisingly species-rich.

5. The development of a population is essentially regulated by the substance occurring in minimal quantity relative to the requirement of the population (Liebig's law of the minimum).

6. For each environmental factor, organisms have an ecological minimum and maximum, with a range in between which represents the tolerance of that organism to that environmental factor (Shelford's law of tolerance). Sub-optimal conditions lead to a reduction in growth and reproduction and an increased chance of mortality.

7. A terrestrial organism's thermal environment is determined by radiation, conduction, convection and evaporation. Diurnal and seasonal temperature fluctuations are greater in terrestrial environments than in aquatic ones. Organisms can be divided into endotherms, which regulate body temperature effectively, and ectotherms, which use less energy but have activity restricted to suitable ambient temperatures.

8. The influence of environmental factors on organisms is reduced through structural, physiological and behavioural adaptations.

9. Environmental factors often interact such that it is difficult to isolate the impact of a single factor.

10. Soils arise from weathering of parent rock material and through the deposition of plant and animal remains (pedogenesis). A soil profile is a section through the soil from the surface to the underlying parent rock. The uppermost soil layer consists of litter and decomposing organic material (biomantle). Within the topsoil (A-horizon), the products of decomposition are leached (zone of eluviation) down to the B-horizon (zone of illuviation). The A-horizon becomes enriched with the resistant minerals, and the B-horizon, below it, enriched with the leachates. The C-horizon consists of the weathered rock or sediment that serves as parent material.

11. If the pores between soil particles are completely filled with water, the soil is said to be saturated. Water that percolates through the soil is called gravitational water. The field capacity of a soil is the maximum water content the soil can hold against gravity.

12. Most plants obtain from the soil the water and mineral nutrients that are essential for growth and metabolism. An inadequate supply of any essential element will affect the growth of the plant and result in a deficiency disease or reduced growth.

13. Soils provide a habitat for many organisms which play significant roles in processing soil particles and providing nutrients in a form that can be taken up by plants.

14. Sessile organisms must be able to survive all seasonal changes in their environment either through adaptation or as resistant propagules. Mobile organisms have the opportunity to select environments within the constraint of their mobility. Annual plants dominate in areas with highly variable rainfall. Perennial plant frequency increases as rainfall becomes more predictable. Desert animals tend to be opportunistic, generalist feeders; specialists are rare.

Chapter 3

Grasslands and primary production

Tropical grasslands, excluding wetlands, cover 15 million km² and, in terms of both land area and biomass, are second only to tropical forests (Leith 1978). Tropical grasslands have been defined as any ecosystem within the tropics in which graminaceous (grass-like) species are a dominant feature of the vegetation (Long and Jones 1992). Thus, by this definition, tropical grasslands include not only purely herbaceous communities, but also the mixed grass and tree communities of savannas.

Tropical grasslands occur where annual rainfall is higher and more predictably distributed throughout the year than that occurring in deserts, and typically occur between equatorial rain forests and hot deserts. Grass-dominated communities occur naturally where soil moisture becomes insufficient to support a closed forest canopy but is adequate for the development of, at least, patchy grass cover. The environmental factors that determine the transition from forest to grassland include precipitation, humidity, soil type, fire frequency, and grazing pressure (Figure 3.1). Distinguishing between the wetter desert areas, grasslands and sparsely treed, open savannas (chapter 4) is difficult and really of little ecological significance. There is a great deal of overlap in both appearance and function of the biotic components that exist in these three systems.

In contrast with the vast treeless expanses of temperate grasslands (prairies in North America, steppes in Eurasia and pampas in South America), tropical grasslands mostly consist of a continuous grass cover with isolated small trees. They have developed under the influence of fire and grazing and form what has come to be called savannas. We will describe this vegetation type in chapter 4. In this chapter, we will look at the role of grasses and other herbaceous plants, with particular reference to how these plants grow, fix carbon dioxide and are adapted to defoliation by grazers.

3.1 | Grass structure and biology

Grasses belong to the family **Poaceae**, and are geographically more widely distributed than most, if not all, plant families. Over 7500 species of grasses in some 600 genera have been recognised, and they grow on all continents and in all climates that support the growth of angiosperms. Before flower production, the grass plant consists of a collection of shoots called **tillers**. Each tiller consists of a leaf blade (lamina) and a leaf sheath which arise from the basal node. The internodes are short and not visible from the outside. In the axil of each leaf, at the node, there is an axillary bud which may grow to form a new tiller. Many grasses have a **ligule**, a membranous structure at the junction of the lamina and the leaf sheath. In some grasses, the base of the lamina is prolonged into two projections known as **auricles** (Figure 3.2).

Grasses have two root systems. The **seminal roots** are highly branched and exploit a large volume of the soil and are particularly important in nutrient uptake. The biomass of the seminal roots is much less than that of the other type of roots, the **adventitious roots**. Adventitious roots arise at the nodes just below the intercalary meristem. In tufted grasses, these roots develop near

Figure 3.1 Large area of grassland in the Markham Valley, Papua New Guinea created following forest removal and maintained by frequent burning (Photo: Office of Environment and Conservation, Papua New Guinea).

ground level, but in some species, such as *Zea mays* (maize), the roots erupt well above ground level and serve a supporting as well as an absorptive function.

Flower formation in grasses occurs through a rapid elongation of the upper internodes, to produce a long flowering stem known as a **culm**. The culm terminates in one of two types of inflorescence: a **spike** which is unbranched or a **panicle** which is branched. Groups of flowers, known as spikelets, are borne on the axis of the spike (rachis) or on the branches of the panicle. The spikelets are usually subtended by a pair of bracts or **glumes**, and each spikelet may consist of one to many flowers. Each floret is protected by another pair of bracts, the **lemma** below and the **palea** above. The floral parts typically consist of three stamens, two styles with feathery stigmas and an ovary with a single ovule (Figure 3.2). Reproductive shoots are adapted to produce seeds

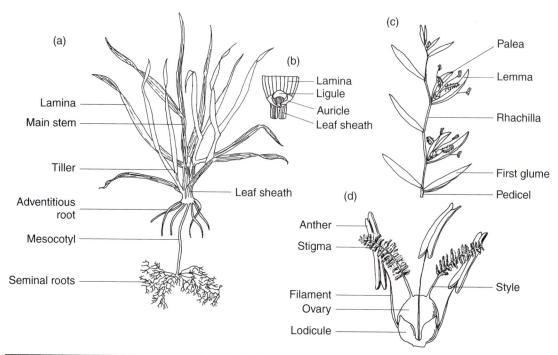

Figure 3.2 (a) Diagram of the structure of a typical grass plant. (b) Leaf base structure. (c) Generalised grass spikelet. (d) Reproductive structures (after Langer 1979; Henty 1969 with permission from Forestry Research Institute, Lae, Papua New Guinea).

rapidly and copious, wind-dispersed seeds are usually produced.

There are three types of life histories found in grasses: **annuals** which complete their life cycle in one year; **biennials** which germinate late in the growing season of one year, and flower and seed in the following year; and **perennials** which continue their growth from year to year. Some perennial grasses reproduce by vegetative **stolons** (shoots which spread along the surface of the ground) and **rhizomes** (shoots which spread within the soil). Stolons and rhizomes have adventitious roots at their nodes and new plants are formed when a stolon or rhizome breaks between two rooted nodes. Perennial grasses live for 4–8 years and new plants arise vegetatively from underground perennating organs. At the end of the growing season, the leaves die back and form a protective layer over the near- or below-ground meristematic tissue.

Plants produce new growth from specialised

and localised tissues known as **meristems**. In most plants, the primary meristems occur at the tips of the shoots and roots. Meristematic tissue is also responsible for adding girth to plants in a process known as secondary growth. However, in grasses, the meristem remains at the base of the plant. Shoot growth is thus initiated upwards. When upper leaves are grazed or burned, grasses regenerate from the meristem that remains near ground level. Modest grazing has been shown to stimulate grass growth, and without it grasslands may develop into lower-quality forage.

Grasses adapted to grazing maintain a high ratio of vegetative to reproductive tissues, and this ensures a high photosynthetic rate and a rapid response to defoliation. Grasses transport some photosynthate to below-ground parts to be used for later growth or stored to initiate growth in the following season. This capacity to relocate resources underground may reduce losses to grazing or fire, and provide a reserve to replace above-ground tissues when lost. This is an important adaptation for small, herbaceous plants subject to grazing and burning. However, not all grasses are herbaceous and small; some of the bamboos are woody and attain a height of over 40 m (see Box 3.1).

Box 3.1 | Giant grasses: bamboos

Bamboos are an important group of useful plants. They belong to the subfamily Bambusoideae in the grass family Poaceae. Representatives are distributed throughout the tropics and subtropics from lowland forests to elevations as high as 4000 m. Worldwide there are some 1300 species of bamboos. Originally, bamboos were separated from herbaceous grasses by having woody culms, three **lodicules**, six stamens and three stigmas but, based on anatomical features and flower structure, some herbaceous grasses are included in the bamboo subfamily.

Some bamboos flower every year, but the majority flower at longer intervals, some as infrequently as once every few decades. In species that bloom at these longer intervals, flowering is gregarious with all plants in the population flowering at much the same time. The longest cycle known in bamboos occurs in *Phyllostachys pubescens*, which forms large monotypic stands, covering approximately 70% of the area of bamboo forests in China (Long and Jones 1992). All plants of the same stock flowered after 120 years regardless of geographic location or climate! A mechanism to account for this synchrony has yet to be proposed. This 'big bang' flowering pattern is called **monocarpy**. The plants may grow for many years and then, over a whole district, flower, fruit and die. Thirty-five years after its introduction from India, *Arundinaria falcata* flowered at the same time in botanic gardens in Algeria, France, Luxembourg and Ireland (Janzen 1976).

Flowering in the bamboo *Melocanna bambusoides* initiates a sequence of ecological events. In its native habitat around the Bay of Bengal, India, this plant produces copious flowers and fruits once every 30–35 years. This abundant supply of fruit fuels a rapid increase in rodent populations which not only destroy grain fields and stored food but also spread human diseases, such as typhus, typhoid and bubonic plague which may reach epidemic proportions. Similar rodent plagues follow the infrequent flowering of *Merostachys* sp. in southern Brazil.

3.2 | Neotropical grasslands

Grasslands and savannas occupy nearly one-fourth of the South American continent. Sarmiento (1992) distinguished, on the basis of soil water availability, three types of savanna grasslands. **Seasonal savanna grasslands** have a dry season lasting between 3–7 months. **Hyperseasonal savannas** occur on poorly drained sites and experience periods of both water shortage and water excess, and the grasses inhabiting them have to be adapted to both drought and inundation. **Semi-seasonal savannas** do not encounter a period of water shortage and the soil remains water-saturated for several months. In this chapter, we will look at the adaptations of grasses inhabiting seasonal savannas; adaptations of floodplain grasses will be described in chapter 6.

3.2.1 Seasonal grasslands

Perennial tussock grasses dominate in seasonal savannas. In most perennial species, the above-ground plants die off during the dry season, but some green leaf area may be maintained and photosynthesis and transpiration may continue at low rates. Highest biomass is attained during the wet season, but growth patterns differ between species. Some species start growing after the first rainfall, or even earlier if they are burned, while other species are less precocious. Most species flower once a year, but some have two or more peaks of growth and flowering and reproductive behaviour can be modified by both burning and grazing.

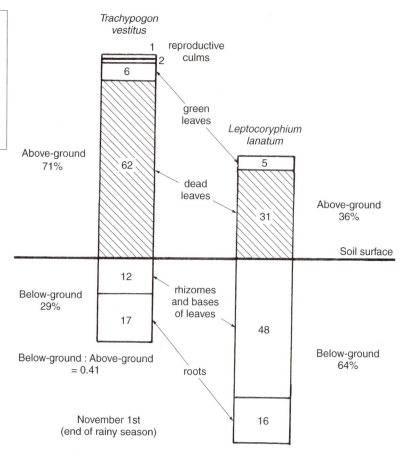

Figure 3.3 Biomass allocation (g dry weight per plant) in the precocious *Leptocoryphium lanatum* and the later sprouting *Trachypogon vestitus* in a seasonal savanna of the Venezuelan *llanos* towards the end of the rainy season (after Sarmiento 1992 with permission from Opulus Press).

Perennial grasses in Venezuelan savannas were classified into four groups based on their periods of flowering and maximal growth (Sarmiento 1983). The first group consists of precocious species that flower at the start of the wet season. These species are highly dependent on fire. In a population of *Sporobolus cubensis*, 7% of the shoots flowered after burning, whereas in a fire-protected population only 0.05% bloomed. *Imperata brasiliensis* will only flower after fire (Sarmiento 1992). The early grasses form the second group, and these species bloom after 2 or 3 months of vegetative growth. The intermediate grasses, which form the third group, bloom during the latter half of the rainy season, and the late grasses, the fourth group, bloom during the final stages of the wet season. The precocious grasses are short and culmless, intermediate grasses are of medium height and late species are the tallest grasses in each community.

A distinctive feature of perennial plants growing in savannas and tropical grasslands is the high proportion of below-ground biomass. Figure 3.3 shows the distribution of live and dead biomass in the precocious *Leptocoryphium lanatum* and the later flowering *Trachypogon vestitus*. These two plants employ different growth strategies. The greater below-ground storage material in *Leptocoryphium lanatum* provides this species with the resources required to initiate its early growth. *Trachypogon vestitus* requires less below-ground material at the start of the growing season because it relies on the new season production which is delayed until adequate soil water is available. The former species, during the growing

Table 3.1 Some major morphological and functional features of tropical savanna grasses and consequences for their survival and ecological success

Morphological and functional features	Ecological consequences
Tussock growth form	
Bud bank close to ground level (protected by old leaves) or below ground	Low mortality from drought and fire
High below-ground to above-ground ratio	Intensive use of water in wet season, water shortage during dry season. Accumulation of below-ground reserves, carbon and nitrogen costs
Evergreen, semi-rest phase	
Carbon assimilation all year	Positive carbon budget
Minimum green leaf area during the dry season	Minimum water losses, accumulation of litter
Low concentration of nutrients	
Low concentration of leaf nitrogen and mineral nutrients	Low rates of net primary production
High C:N, sclerophylly, high specific leaf weight	Low palatability, slow decomposition
Nutrient partitioning	
Decrease in nutrient leaf content with age	Decrease in net primary production
Accumulation of nutrients in below-ground organs	Rapid regrowth after fire or drought
C_4 photosynthetic pathway	
High potential net primary production	High assimilation rate when water and nutrients are not limiting
Gradual fall in conductance with decreasing leaf water potential	Gas exchange at high water stress; low water loss during dry season
Gradual fall in net primary production with decreasing leaf water potential	Positive carbon budget even at very low leaf water potentials
Annual fires	
Consumption of litter	Nutrient loss or recycling
Improved light conditions at ground level	Increase in net primary production
Decreased tillering and plant production	Increase in plant mortality
Induced blooming	Increase in reproductive output

Source: Sarmiento 1992.

season, must replenish its large underground store (Sarmiento 1992).

Neotropical grasses exhibit a range of morphological, phenological and physiological strategies for coping with drought and fire (Table 3.1). The lack of distinctive adaptations to grazing by large herbivores is a major difference between Neotropical grasses and their African counterparts. Tree growth in the central *llanos* of Venezuela is probably impeded by the presence of a hard pan below the soil surface. This hard pan is built up of fine sediments cemented by ferric oxides and prevents penetration by tree roots. However, grasses use water in the upper soil layers through their extensive but shallow root system, and some grass roots penetrate cracks in the hard pan. Annual burning further restricts tree growth, and even fire-resistant species such as *Curatella americana* and *Platycarpum orinocense* are unable to colonise these frequently burned grasslands, as their seedlings are sensitive to burning (San José and Medina 1975).

3.3 | Light as an energy source

Solar energy is transmitted as electromagnetic radiation. All electromagnetic radiation has wave characteristics. Light that reaches the upper atmosphere surrounding the earth has wavelengths extending from high-energy, short-wavelength x-rays at one end of the spectrum to low-energy, long-wavelength radio waves at the other. As light passes through the atmosphere most of the ultraviolet radiation is absorbed, primarily by ozone (O_3). This is just as well, since ultraviolet light, because of its high energy, is damaging to exposed cells and tissues. Therefore the ozone layer in the atmosphere forms an important shield, protecting life on earth from the most damaging wavelengths. The visible spectrum extends between wavelengths of about 400 nm (violet) and 700 nm (red). This wavelength range corresponds to that known as the **photosynthetically active radiation (PAR)**.

Leaves are the photo-receptors of most plants, but in some this function is taken over by green stems. Leaves are also the main site of carbon dioxide uptake. Leaves are arranged on a plant so as to present the largest possible area for carbon dioxide uptake and light interception. To attain this dual aim, leaves need both to have a large surface area and to exploit a large volume of the atmosphere. This is best achieved by having a multi-layered arrangement. Light not absorbed by the uppermost leaves can be utilised by the layers beneath. Plants that grow in low light environments, such as under a forest canopy, receive so little light that there is no point in having a second layer. In fact, letting a little of the light through might allow another plant to develop underneath and subsequently compete with it (Horn 1971). The leaf blade (lamina) is thin so that the diffusion pathway for carbon dioxide is short and also so that adequate light can reach all photosynthetic cells.

The number of leaf layers present in a particular community can be assessed by calculating the **Leaf Area Index (LAI)**: the leaf area (m²) arranged vertically above a square metre of ground. This is a useful measure of canopy density. Leaf Area Indices are highest in forests where light limitation is common and lowest in arid deserts where light rarely limits.

The successful plant is not just the one with the greatest leaf area but the plant that supports the leaves in the best position for light interception. Therefore there is an advantage to being tall, but also a cost in terms of the allocation of resources to structural materials. Herbs and grasses inhabiting grasslands do not have to grow tall, as they are unlikely to be shaded by a competitor. In grasslands, some factor other than light (usually water availability) limits growth. We will see that, in tropical forests, this is not the case and being tall in this habitat is a distinct advantage (chapter 8). Leaves not only must be adapted to maximise light interception, but they also must absorb enough carbon dioxide to sustain carbon fixation rates and play a role in the plant's water balance maintenance. Striking a balance between carbon dioxide uptake and water loss through evapotranspiration is the function of stomata.

3.4 | Carbon dioxide uptake by plants

One of the raw materials for photosynthesis is carbon dioxide. Plants obtain this resource from the atmosphere which only contains about 0.036% of carbon dioxide. Most of the carbon dioxide that enters a plant does so through small, but numerous, pores in the leaves called **stomata**. Once in the sub-stomatal cavities, carbon dioxide diffuses into the chloroplasts of the mesophyll cells where chemical reduction utilising light-generated energy takes place (see section 3.5.1).

3.4.1 Stomata

Stomata are pores formed by a pair of specialised **guard cells**, which are found in the surface of the aerial parts of most higher plants. The guard cells have the capacity to change shape, and in this way can control the stomatal pore size. It is through these pores that most carbon dioxide enters the plant. The pores also provide an avenue for water loss from the plant in a process known as **transpiration**. Transpiration, through evaporative cooling, plays a role in temperature regulation, particularly in tropical plants. Transpiration also facilitates the uptake of water and mineral salts and their movement in the xylem from the soil to all parts of the plant. A plant unable to replace water lost in transpiration must take steps to conserve water.

Terrestrial plants have significantly reduced water loss (and their capacity to take up carbon dioxide) by covering exposed surfaces in a waxy cuticle. Stomata provide the mechanism which enables terrestrial plants to balance the rate of carbon dioxide uptake with the need to conserve water. Since stomata control around 95% of the carbon dioxide and water exchange between the plant and the atmosphere, their importance in regulating the rates of both photosynthesis and transpiration can not be over emphasised. Therefore an appreciation of the environmental factors affecting stomatal function is important in understanding both photosynthesis and transpiration, two processes that are fundamental to a plant's ecological performance.

The guard cells act as the first line of defence against water stress by regulating stomatal pore size, and serve to reconcile the conflicting needs of photosynthetic efficiency and water balance maintenance. Stomatal pore size is directly affected by a complex suite of environmental factors: light quantity and quality, water availability, humidity, carbon dioxide concentration, and temperature. Surprisingly, the first response of stomata to water stress is to open slightly. This opening phase soon passes and, as water stress continues, the stomata progressively close. This response to water stress is related to the osmotic mechanism that controls stomatal function.

Most plants open their stomata during the day and close them at night (C_3 and C_4 plants); the exception to this rule is provided by those plants which photosynthesise using the CAM strategy (see section 3.7). The typical diurnal response of stomata is to open slowly soon after sunrise and to remain open for most of the day. The stomata close rapidly at dark. Some tropical plants exhibit a midday closure. This diurnal rhythm is consistent with the needs of most plants to take up carbon dioxide only during the day and to conserve water at night when photosynthesis can not occur.

Light, carbon dioxide and water (see section 2.5) are the environmental resources required for photosynthesis. We have seen how plants obtain these resources, so we can now look at the photosynthetic process itself.

3.5 | Photosynthesis

Plants accumulate organic matter through photosynthesis, a complicated photochemical and biochemical process, for which the equation for the overall process is:

$$6CO_2 + 6H_2O + \text{solar energy} \rightarrow C_6H_{12}O_6 + 6O_2$$

Although the equation above shows glucose as the primary product of photosynthesis, numerous compounds are produced through a series of biochemical pathways. Photosynthesis consists of two major processes: the **light reaction** in which light energy is used to produce energy-rich compounds, and **carbon dioxide fixation** in which these energy-rich compounds are used to reduce carbon dioxide to energy-rich sugars and other organic compounds.

3.5.1 The light reaction

In the light reaction, radiant energy of particular wavelengths is absorbed by pigments. In eukaryote organisms, the pigments are contained within chloroplasts, whereas, in the photosynthetic bacteria and Cyanobacteria, pigments are associated with cellular membranes. All photosynthetic organisms contain one or more organic pigments capable of absorbing visible radiation which will bring about the light reaction. The three major classes of pigments found in plants and algae are the **chlorophylls**, **carotenoids**, and **phycobilins**.

Chlorophylls give plants their characteristic green colour and chlorophyll *a* is the primary light-absorbing pigment. Absorption of radiant energy by chlorophyll *a* is strongest in the red and blue regions of the spectrum and weakest in the green and yellow regions. Chlorophyll *b* has an absorption spectrum shifted slightly towards the green wavelengths and acts as one of the accessory pigments, absorbing photons that chlorophyll *a* cannot.

In the light reaction, a photon of light is captured by a pigment, resulting in excitation of an electron within the pigment. The excited (energy-enriched) electron is shuttled along an electron transfer chain that drives the synthesis of **Adenosine Tri-Phosphate (ATP)**. The formation of the high-energy phosphate bonds requires an input of energy. Conversely, hydrolysis of these bonds provides energy which can be used in the synthesis of organic molecules or to pump ions across a membrane against a concentration gradient. Hydrolysis of ATP results in the production of Adenosine di-phosphate (ADP).

In the light reaction, the electron stripped from the pigment molecule must be replaced to prevent the pigment from becoming deficient in electrons. The electrons and protons that oxygen-forming photosynthesis uses to form NADPH are obtained from water. In a complex series of reactions, water is split into electrons (used to replace those lost from the pigments), H^+ ions (used to reduce $NADP^+$) and OH^- radicals. The OH^- radicals are reassembled as water and oxygen. Oxygen is, therefore, a by-product of the light reaction. **Nicotinamide adenine dinucleotide phosphate (NADP)** is a co-enzyme that exists in two interconvertible forms: the oxidising agent $NADP^+$ and the reducing agent NADPH.

In this way, the light reaction results in the formation of ATP, production of a strong reducing agent, NADPH, and the evolution of O_2 from splitting a water molecule. The formation of ATP is coupled to the flow of electrons from H_2O to NADP. The energy-rich ATP and the reducing power of NADPH are used in carbon dioxide fixation.

3.5.2 Carbon dioxide fixation

Carbon dioxide fixation occurs in four distinct phases: **carboxylation, reduction, RuBP regeneration**, and **product synthesis**. In carboxylation, carbon dioxide is added to a 5-carbon sugar, ribulose 1,5 biphosphate (RuBP) to form two molecules of phosphoglycerate (PGA), a 3-carbon compound. This reaction is catalysed by the enzyme **ribulose biphosphate decarboxylase (RUBISCO)**. In the reduction phase, PGA is converted to a 3-carbon sugar phosphate using the energy in ATP and the reducing power of NADPH. RuBP is regenerated through a complex series of reactions involving sugar phosphates and a further input of ATP (Figure 3.4).

In the last phase of the carbon fixation process, 3-, 4-, 5-, 6- and 7-carbon compounds provide carbon skeletons for the synthesis of all the carbon compounds (carbohydrates, fats, fatty acids, amino acids and proteins) required by the plant. Note that carbon fixation relies on the ATP and NADPH produced in the light reaction, and carbon fixation ceases once these compounds become unavailable. This occurs very soon after sunset, and therefore it is not sensible to refer to carbon fixation as the 'dark reaction', a term used by many textbooks that is best avoided.

3.6 | Photorespiration

The enzyme that operates in carbon fixation, RUBISCO, can also use oxygen as a substrate. In this process, RUBISCO, initiates the oxidation of RuBP in a process called **photorespiration**. Carbon dioxide is released and, effectively, this process undoes the work of photosynthesis. Photorespiration was not a problem when the early photosynthetic organisms were evolving, since the earth's atmosphere at that time lacked oxygen. As the oxygen concentration in the atmosphere increased through oxygen produced by the early photosynthetic organisms, so rates of photorespiration increased. This means that photorespiration has the capacity to reduce the efficiency of carbon fixation and hence plant growth. Through this process, many plants lose up to 50% of the carbon that could be fixed during photosynthesis. Therefore, this photosynthetic mechanism has been rendered less efficient through enhanced concentrations of one of its waste products: oxygen. Some plants have developed biochemical strategies which reduce the impact of photorespiration, and others have

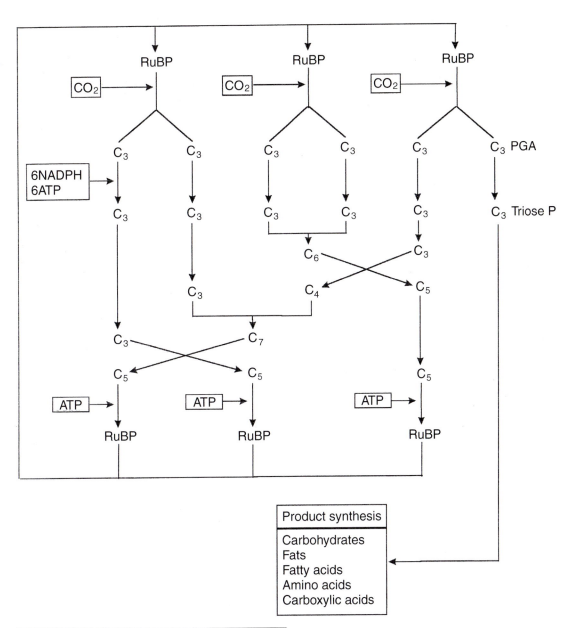

Figure 3.4 Summary of the reactions of photosynthetic carbon dioxide fixation showing the regeneration of RuBP and the production of one 3-carbon compound. The carbon skeletons used in the regeneration of RuBP can also be used in product synthesis (after Hall and Whatley 1967 with permission of Academic Press).

strategies which conserve water and facilitate their growth in arid environments.

3.7 | Photosynthetic strategies

The majority of plants fix carbon dioxide initially as **phosphoglycerate** (PGA), a 3-carbon compound and are therefore referred to as C_3 **plants**. The enzyme system used in this process is ribulose biphosphate decarboxylase (RUBISCO) and the biochemical cycle is known as the **Calvin cycle**. Some plants, notably many tropical grasses, initially combine carbon dioxide with phospho-enol-pyruvate (PEP), into a 4-carbon compound – **oxaloacetate** – using what is known as the C_4 **pathway**. Oxaloacetate is transported deep into the leaves to specialised cells which surround the vascular bundle: the **vascular bundle sheath**. Here, in modified chloroplasts, the carbon dioxide is released from the PEP and re-fixed with RUBISCO. This cycle is known as the **Hatch and Slack cycle**.

A third photosynthetic strategy was first found to occur in plants belonging to the family Crassulaceae and was therefore called **Crassulacean Acid Metabolism (CAM)**. It has since been shown that plants belonging to other families also use this mode of carbon fixation. These plants seem best adapted to very dry conditions. They close their stomata during the day, thereby reducing water loss, but this also reduces their ability to fix carbon dioxide. To enable them to grow, albeit more slowly, the plants open their stomata at night and store carbon dioxide in a temporary fashion. During the day, the stored carbon dioxide is released, and, with the light-generated reducing compounds, fixed in much the same way as in C_3 plants. These pathways are compared in Figure 3.5.

The main disadvantage of the C_3 system is revealed when plants are grown in hot, dry conditions. The weak link lies in photorespiration in which oxygen competes with carbon dioxide for sites on the carbon-fixing enzyme system, RUBISCO. Photorespiration rates are enhanced by high temperatures and high light intensities, conditions prevalent in tropical grasslands.

The advantage of the C_4 pathway lies in the ability of the plant to store carbon dioxide. This allows for a more efficient use of available sunlight, and PEP acts as a scavenger for any carbon dioxide that might not be fixed because of photorespiration. However, the C_4 pathway incurs energy costs because extra work is done in driving the cycle and in moving the organic acids through the mesophyll. Table 3.2 compares features of C_3 and C_4 plants.

Warm conditions stimulate photorespiration, and so the higher the temperature, the greater the depression of photosynthesis. At temperatures below 25 °C, C_3 plants are more successful. C_4 plants are sensitive to cold probably because some of their enzymes work less well at low temperatures. Moreover, the C_4 system requires greater energy inputs, largely to bring about PEP regeneration. Under conditions of high light intensity and high temperature, C_4 plants are more productive than C_3 plants. In Kenya, for example, no C_3 grasses were found growing below 2000 m altitude, and no C_4 grasses were found above 3000 m (see section 9.5.2).

CAM plants grow slowly. However, the CAM strategy enables these plants to colonise very dry areas where water conservation is more important than the competitive advantage conferred through efficient photosynthesis. Some plants inhabiting salt marshes utilise CAM photosynthesis. These plants face a physiological drought as the uptake of water from saline soils is an energy expensive process. Therefore, again these plants need to conserve water and the CAM strategy aids in achieving this.

Surprisingly, a freshwater aquatic plant (*Isoetes howellii*) has been shown to use CAM (Keeley 1988). The advantage gained by this plant, while obviously not from water conservation, is through efficient carbon dioxide uptake. This plant uses a dual strategy of the CAM and C_3 mechanisms. The carbon dioxide concentration in the water declines each morning as all the submerged plants photosynthesise. By mid-morning, photosynthesis is limited by carbon dioxide availability. To avoid this limitation, *Isoetes* uses the CAM mechanism at night to store carbon when it is in plentiful supply. Early in the morning, *Isoetes* fixes

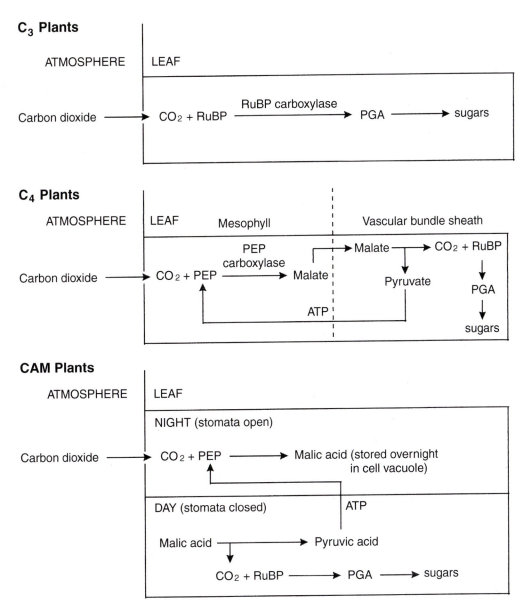

C$_3$ Plants

ATMOSPHERE | LEAF

Carbon dioxide ⟶ CO$_2$ + RuBP ⟶(RuBP carboxylase)⟶ PGA ⟶ sugars

C$_4$ Plants

ATMOSPHERE | LEAF | Mesophyll | Vascular bundle sheath

Carbon dioxide ⟶ CO$_2$ + PEP ⟶(PEP carboxylase)⟶ Malate ⟶ Malate ⟶ CO$_2$ + RuBP

Pyruvate

ATP

PGA

sugars

CAM Plants

ATMOSPHERE | LEAF

NIGHT (stomata open)

Carbon dioxide ⟶ CO$_2$ + PEP ⟶ Malic acid (stored overnight in cell vacuole)

DAY (stomata closed) | ATP

Malic acid ⟶ Pyruvic acid

CO$_2$ + RuBP ⟶ PGA ⟶ sugars

Figure 3.5 Scheme of carbon fixation pathways for the three main photosynthetic plant types C$_3$, C$_4$ and CAM (adapted from Keeley 1988 with kind permission from Blackwell Science).

carbon dioxide by the C$_3$ mechanism. Later in the day, uptake of carbon from the water is minimal, and the plant switches to utilising the carbon stored overnight as malic acid. Cells in the submerged portion of leaves of this plant exhibit this capacity to utilise both CAM and C$_3$ mechanisms, but leaf cells held above the water surface use only the C$_3$ mechanism. With access to atmospheric carbon dioxide, cells no longer face the marked diurnal fluctuations in carbon dioxide availability.

3.8 | Respiration

Organisms require a continual input of new energy to balance losses from metabolism, growth

Table 3.2 The characteristics of C_3 and C_4 plants

	C_4 plants	C_3 plants
Type of plant	Herbaceous, mostly grasses and sedges	Herbs, shrubs or trees
Morphology Leaf characters	Vascular bundle sheath present with cells packed with agranal chloroplasts	No vascular bundle sheath
Physiology Photosynthetic rate	40–80 mg CO_2 dm^{-2} h^{-1} in full sunlight; no light saturation	10–35 mg CO_2 dm^{-2} h^{-1} in full sunlight; light saturation at 10–25% full sunlight
Response to temperature	Growth and photosynthesis optimal at 30–45 °C	Growth and photosynthesis optimal at 10–25 °C
CO_2 compensation point	0–10 ppm CO_2	30–70 ppm CO_2
Sugar transport out of the leaves	Rapid and efficient	Slower and less efficient
Water requirements (g water needed to produce 1 g dry matter)	260–350	400–900
Biochemistry Carbon fixation	C_4 (Hatch–Slack) and C_3 (Calvin) cycles	C_3 pathway only
Photorespiration	Not detected	Present

Source: Black 1971.

and reproduction. All work carried out within a cell involves an expenditure of energy. Photosynthesis produces a wide range of organic compounds that can be used by plants to produce new tissues or to form an energy store. ATP is not a very stable compound and therefore is produced as and when it is required by the plant. Most plants store photosynthate as starch, a very stable compound. When energy is required, the starch is converted to glucose and energy is extracted from the glucose through the process of respiration. In eukaryotes, this process occurs in the mitochondria. Oxygen is utilised and carbon dioxide is a waste product. Plants respire all the time but are only capable of photosynthesis when adequate light is available. Plants must, therefore, lose some weight, albeit a small amount, during the night.

Plants utilise organic matter, through respiration, to release energy. Compounds, in addition to glucose, can be used as respiratory substrates: other carbohydrates, fats and even proteins. Different metabolic pathways are used for the respiration of fats and proteins with more energy per carbon atom released when fats are respired. The overall chemical equation for respiration is the reverse of that given above for photosynthesis. However, the biochemical pathways for photosynthesis and respiration are different and occur within chloroplasts and mitochondria respectively.

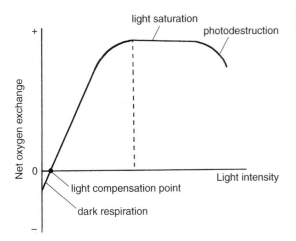

Figure 3.6 A generalised plot of net oxygen production in photosynthesis and consumption in respiration showing the light intensity compensation point and the light intensity at which light saturation occurs.

3.9 Environmental factors and photosynthesis

The rate at which photosynthesis proceeds depends upon a number of internal and external factors. The main internal factors are the structure of the leaf and its chlorophyll content, the concentration of photosynthate within the chloroplasts, enzyme concentrations and the presence of certain nutrients. We are more concerned here with the role of external factors: the quality and quantity of light, temperature and the concentration of carbon dioxide and oxygen in the surrounding atmosphere.

3.9.1 Light intensity and photosynthesis

At low light intensities, usually less than one quarter that of full sunlight, the rate of photosynthesis varies in direct proportion to the light intensity. At higher intensities, the rate of photosynthesis increases more slowly and then levels off at the **light saturation point**. For most plants, photosynthesis becomes light saturated at light intensities well below the maximum they may experience (Figure 3.6). This is largely because the rate of photosynthesis is, at higher light levels, limited by the rate of carbon dioxide supply and

increasing rates of photorespiration. The light intensity, at which carbon fixation by photosynthesis equals that lost by respiration, is known as the **light intensity compensation point**.

Light rarely limits plant growth in tropical grasslands, because light levels usually exceed the saturation point of most plants. However, plants growing beneath a forest canopy may become light limited. The problem faced by shaded plants is to maintain a positive carbon balance. This can be achieved through (1) reducing the rate of respiration; (2) increasing leaf area; and (3) increasing the rate of photosynthesis. Reducing the rate of respiration will lead to slower growth, and this may put the plant at a competitive disadvantage and acerbate the low light conditions as surrounding competitors shade the slower-growing plant further. Some forest plants, known as **sciophytes**, are highly adapted to living in shaded conditions. Similarly, aquatic plants are also adapted to photosynthesise in low light environments. We will look at the role of light in these environments in chapters 5 and 8. Most grasses are sun-loving plants (**heliophytes**) and many tropical grass species are C_4, and therefore highly adapted to both high light intensities and high temperatures.

3.9.2 Temperature and photosynthesis

For most lowland tropical plants, temperature is not generally a major factor in controlling the rate of photosynthesis. Primary production increases with temperature in the cooler parts of the world, including high altitudes in the tropics (see chapter 9). Above about 25 °C, there is little change in the rate of primary production with increasing temperature. High temperatures can reduce photosynthetic rates and, on hot days, rates may be depressed, particularly during the middle of the day. It is difficult to separate the effects of temperature from those of light intensity and water availability. With an adequate water supply, plants can reduce leaf temperatures through evapotranspiration.

3.9.3 Carbon dioxide, oxygen and photosynthesis

Although carbon dioxide is freely available in the atmosphere surrounding the leaves, concentrations can become rate-limiting for photosynthesis. This is because it is the concentration of carbon dioxide at the chloroplasts that is important. To reach the chloroplasts, carbon dioxide has to diffuse through the stomata, the sub-stomatal air spaces, across the cell wall, through the cytoplasm and into the chloroplast. Therefore carbon dioxide supply is determined by these diffusion rates, and this depends on the maintenance of a carbon dioxide diffusion gradient between the outside air and the chloroplasts.

As with light, photosynthesis also has a **carbon dioxide compensation point**. This is defined as the carbon dioxide concentration at which the rate of carbon dioxide uptake by photosynthesis is balanced by carbon dioxide loss through respiration. The carbon dioxide compensation point for most plants is high (around 50 ppm CO_2) owing to the prevalence of photorespiration. In C_4 plants, photorespiration is negligible, and these plants may have a carbon dioxide compensation point as low as 5 ppm CO_2. This means that C_4 plants can maintain a net carbon gain even when the carbon dioxide concentration is very low. If photosynthesis in bright light is limited by the rate of carbon dioxide uptake, then C_4 plants should have an advantage.

The high concentration of oxygen produced through photosynthesis promotes photorespiration. In C_4 plants, highly efficient carbon dioxide scavenging by PEP ensures that any carbon dioxide released through photorespiration is rapidly refixed. This ensures a high growth rate for C_4 plants despite conditions (high light intensity and high temperature) which favour photorespiration.

3.10 | Primary production

Little of the solar energy entering an ecosystem is actually fixed by plants. Energy conversion occurs in photosynthesis and, in ecology, the matter produced is known as **primary production**. Production is measured as a change in biomass per unit time. Energy flow is a unifying concept for studying and comparing the productivity of ecosystems. The first step in analysing energy flow is to quantify the fixation of solar energy through photosynthesis. We will trace the fate of the energy fixed by this process in chapter 5.

In ecology it is important to distinguish between **gross primary production** and **net primary production**. Gross primary production is the total amount of material produced. A portion of the organic matter produced is used by the plants to fulfil their own respiratory needs. What remains is known as net primary production. **Standing crop** is the amount of plant material existing in an area at any one time. Net primary production is ecologically important because it represents the energy available to herbivores. In the drier regions of the tropics, net primary production is often correlated with rainfall.

3.11 | Assessment of grassland primary production

3.11.1 Harvest method

Grassland primary production has most commonly been assessed by measuring the change in plant biomass over a known time interval. Both above-ground and below-ground material needs to be measured. Sampling of above-ground material is carried out by clipping all material in a known area and weighing it after it has been dried. Sampling below-ground material is more difficult and has been ignored in many studies, often resulting in a large underestimate of production. Underground plant parts can be sampled by using a coring device that samples a known volume of soil. The plant parts can be separated from the soil by careful washing, dried and weighed to obtain the below-ground biomass. At the end of the set time interval, the process is repeated to obtain the change in biomass.

To remove the effect of clipping from the estimate, a different set of plots is used for this second assessment (Coupland 1979). To obtain an accurate estimate of net primary production by the harvest method, sequential harvests need to be made at sufficiently frequent intervals. Furthermore, the heterogeneity of grasslands means that many replicate harvests need to be taken to obtain a statistically significant estimate.

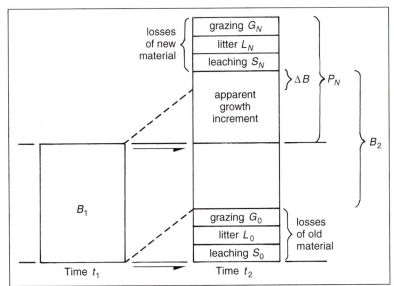

losses of new material
- grazing G_N
- litter L_N
- leaching S_N

apparent growth increment

ΔB

P_N

B_2

B_1

losses of old material
- grazing G_0
- litter L_0
- leaching S_0

Time t_1

Time t_2

Figure 3.7 The components of biomass change with time and their relationship to production (after Chapman 1976 with kind permission from Blackwell Science).

leaching can be split into losses of new and old material (Figure 3.7). The use of this relationship requires estimates of biomass to be made at least twice, but preferably a number of times over the growing season. The net primary production in biomass may be converted to energy using a bomb calorimeter. Measurement of primary production in aquatic ecosystems will be covered in chapter 5.

3.11.2 Losses to grazers

The impact of large herbivores on primary production can be assessed by measuring production in plots accessible to the herbivores and in those from which they have been excluded. Production losses to smaller herbivores are more difficult to estimate and are often ignored. It is difficult to exclude smaller herbivores such as insects without altering the environmental conditions that control photosynthetic rates. These small herbivores can remove a significant amount of the between-harvest primary production. However, these high removal rates only occur in exceptional circumstances, such as when locust populations develop plague proportions. Mostly, loss of live material rarely exceeds 10% of the net primary production. We will look at energy transfers down food chains in more detail in chapter 5. Dead plant material may also be consumed by earthworms, termites, fungi and bacteria. Although herbivores usually consume only a small proportion of primary production, they play a significant role in grassland ecology.

Primary production estimates made using the method described above are usually less than the actual production because losses of plant biomass occur simultaneously with net gain by photosynthesis. Losses occur through material removed by both large and small herbivores (see section 3.12) and through plant material dropping off the plant as litter. Root exudates are another mechanism by which material is lost, and it is also difficult to distinguish between live and dead roots separated from the soil.

The relationship between biomass, time and production is presented below in the standard form of the International Biological Programme (Coupland 1979):

B_1 = Biomass of a plant at time t_1
B_2 = Biomass of a plant at time t_2
ΔB = Change in biomass during the period t_1–t_2. $(B_2 - B_1)$
L = Plant losses by death, shedding and leaching during t_1–t_2.
G = Plant losses by grazing during t_1–t_2.
P_N = Net production by the community during t_1–t_2.

In terms of these symbols:

$$P_N = \Delta B + L + G$$

If ΔB, L, and G can be estimated satisfactorily, P_N can be calculated. Losses to grazing, litter and

Figure 3.8   Impact of excess grazing on grasslands in southern Malawi. The area to the right of the fence has a much higher stocking density of livestock (cattle and goats) than the area to the left (Photo: Patrick Osborne).

3.12 | Effects of grazing on grass growth

Grasses are highly adapted to survive repetitive grazing, and grass growth, with a rapid production of new shoots, may even be stimulated by such treatment. Before the flowering stage is reached, leaf production continues after each defoliation. This can occur because the site of new growth, the meristems, are located near the soil surface, beyond the reach of grazing animals. Even if some meristems are removed, they may be replaced by new tillers. Few plants have such an efficient mechanism of recovery from damage, and this explains why grasses are such an important source of food for animals (Figure 3.8). In fact, grasses flourish only where there are grazers. If grazers are excluded, grasses do not thrive and may be replaced by dicotyledons.

However, maintenance of grasslands by grazing animals depends on grazing intensity. Moderate grazing pressure has been shown to increase palatability of the sward while maintaining high production and ground cover. Grazing involves reduction in leaf area with its effects on tiller development and shoot and root growth. McNaughton (1985) found that over 90% of the above-ground net primary production may be removed by large grazers. The impact of grazing by large herbivores also includes damage from trampling and nutrient enrichment of patches though urine and faeces deposition. Grazing can alter the micro-climate in which the grass grows and also alter the ratio between water infiltration of the soil and runoff. Consequently, overgrazing may result in soil degradation and erosion (Figure 3.9).

Grazing may alter the species composition of the grassland with the replacement of the more palatable species by those that are less so. Grazing also creates a more open canopy, facilitating inva-

Figure 3.9 Degraded savanna–grassland vegetation in south-east Zimbabwe. The vegetation cover is low as a result of the combined effects of drought and overgrazing (Photo: Patrick Osborne).

sion by other plant species and can, therefore, serve to enhance species diversity. Excessive grazing, particularly if it is combined with a high fire frequency, may lead to a reduction in biomass cover, erosion and land degradation (Figure 3.10). Although the large ungulate grazers are the most apparent of the grazers and probably remove the largest proportion of the grass, other consumers should not be ignored. Insects can remove significant amounts of live grass, and dead and decomposing material may also be consumed by termites, earthworms, soil arthropods, bacteria and fungi.

3.13 | Seasonal variation in grassland primary production

Tropical grasslands characteristically exhibit marked seasonal variation in primary production

and the main cause of this is the seasonality in rainfall. San José and Medina (1975) investigated the effects of water availability and fire on grassland production in burned and fire-protected plots in the Venezuelan *llanos*. The dry season ended in April, although some early rain fell in February during the year of this study (1969) (Figure 3.11). Soil water content was highly correlated with rainfall. At the beginning of the dry season, soil water content in the burned plots was higher owing to reduced transpiration activity, since plant cover was less in these plots. With the start of the rains, soils in protected plots remained saturated but those in the burned plots did not, probably because evaporation and run-off were higher in these less well-vegetated plots.

Plant growth in the burned plots began early after the fire, but growth was then restricted until rain fell. Burning near the middle of the dry season increased above-ground biomass by almost 30% (Figure 3.11). Moderate fire stimulated growth of perennial grasses, since they can produce new shoots in a few days and rapid growth occurred

(a)

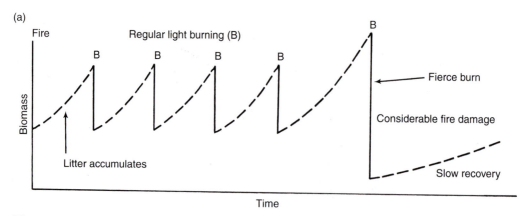

(b)

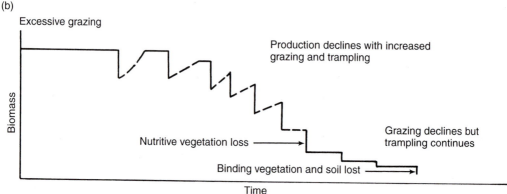

Figure 3.10 (a) In an area of savanna grassland, light burning at short intervals may allow the biomass to build up to roughly the same amount as before. An occasional fire after a more prolonged fire-free period and additional litter accumulation may burn more fiercely than normal. This results in a slower recovery of the vegetation. (b) With excessive grazing, removal of vegetation cover and a breakdown in soil texture eventually leads to the loss of topsoil and degradation of the grassland as a forage provider (after Money 1980 © Evans Brothers Limited).

immediately following the first rainfall. Grasses in unburned plots took longer to respond and never caught-up. San José and Medina (1975) showed that the increase in the above-ground production in the burned plots was due to enhanced growth of a subordinate species, *Axonopus canescens* rather than growth of the dominant *Trachypogon montufari*. Protection from fire increases the amount of litter accumulation, and fire in such a protected, fuel-laden site can be devastating and may initiate invasion of the grassland by dicotyledons.

This marked seasonal variation in grassland production is one reason why so little of the energy available from the sun is actually fixed in photosynthesis. Even though the energy supply in tropical environments varies little, other factors, particularly water supply, preclude full use of the annual energy flux. We will now look at the rates of primary production in terrestrial ecosystems and discuss why they are not particularly efficient in harvesting the available energy.

3.14 | Primary production rates in terrestrial biomes

Terrestrial net primary productivity for the world (excluding wetlands, lakes and rivers) has been estimated to be 110×10^9 tonnes dry weight per year (Table 3.3). The highest rate of terrestrial primary production occurs in tropical rain forests where the combination of strong radiation, warm temperatures and high rainfall provides favourable growing conditions around the year. More

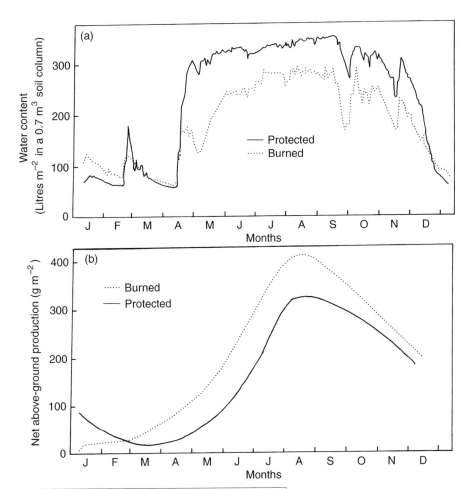

Figure 3.11 (a) Soil water content in a column of 0.7 m³ from the Venezuelan *llanos*. Soil samples were collected down to the maximum root depth from a plot protected from fire and from one which was burnt in the previous December. (b) Net above-ground primary production and leaf area index of the protected and burnt plots (after San José and Medina 1975 with kind permission from Springer-Verlag GmbH and the authors).

than 60% of all production occurs in the tropics. At higher latitudes, plant growth is limited by cooler temperatures and a truncated growing season. Although primary production is ultimately dependent on the incoming energy in solar radiation, clearly this does not alone explain the worldwide distribution of primary production. Tropical and subtropical deserts receive abundant solar radiation, but plants are unable to harvest this energy because their growth is limited by water availability.

There is, however, wide variation and significant overlap in production rates both within and between these ecosystems. Primary production in desert oases can be quite high, and the productivity of the drier savannas approaches that of the wetter desert areas. Furthermore, latitudinal patterns are disrupted in areas, such as central Australia, where water availability limits primary production. For solar radiation to be used efficiently, plants must have access to adequate water and nutrients, an ideal temperature regime and a suitable soil depth, texture and fertility. Solar radiation wastage also occurs through an incomplete canopy cover and the low energy conversion efficiency of photosynthesis. Light interception by plants is low for a variety of reasons. Leaf production may be seasonal, and defoliation occurs through grazing and pest and disease infestations.

Table 3.3 Net annual primary productivity for contrasting terrestrial communities of the world

Ecosystem type	Area (10^6 km^2)	Net primary productivity per unit area (g m^{-2} or t km^{-2}) Range	Mean	World net primary production (10^9 t)
Tropical rain forest	17.0	1000–3500	2200	37.4
Tropical seasonal forest	7.5	1000–2500	1600	12.0
Temperate evergreen forest	5.0	600–2500	1300	6.5
Temperate deciduous forest	7.0	600–2500	1200	8.4
Boreal forest	12.0	400–2000	800	9.6
Woodland and shrubland	8.5	250–1200	700	6.0
Savanna–grasslands	15.0	200–2000	900	13.5
Temperate grasslands	9.0	200–1500	600	5.4
Tundra and alpine	8.0	10–400	140	1.1
Deserts and semi-desert shrub	18.0	10–250	90	1.6
Arid deserts, rock, sand and ice	24.0	0–10	3	0.07
Cultivated land	14.0	100–3500	650	9.1
Total terrestrial	145		848	110

Source: Whittaker 1975.

Primary production, then, is limited by a number of environmental factors and further reduced through the removal of productive tissues by grazers. The environmental factors that limit production may vary through the year. In a tropical grassland, water availability limits during the dry season but nitrogen supply or frequent grazing may constrain productivity during the wet season.

The primary producers (autotrophs) provide all the energy requirements of the secondary producers (heterotrophs). **Secondary productivity** is the rate of production of new biomass by hetero-trophic organisms. These organisms (most bacteria, fungi and animals) derive their energy and matter either directly from plants or indirectly from plants through consumption or decomposition of other heterotrophs. Before we discuss the ecology of this energy flow from primary producers to secondary producers in chapter 5, we need to analyse how animals obtain their food and how their populations are regulated; this is done in the next chapter. We will look at decomposition of dead organic matter by fungi and bacteria in chapter 10.

3.15 | Chapter summary

1. Tropical grasslands occur where annual rainfall is higher and more predictably distributed throughout the year than that occurring in deserts. Soil moisture in grasslands is inadequate to support a closed forest canopy but enough for the development of a patchy or continuous grass cover with a few scattered trees. Grasses are highly adapted to fire and grazing, with meristems close to ground level facilitating rapid growth following defoliation.

2. Plants accumulate organic matter through photosynthesis, a photochemical and biochemical process involving two stages. The light reaction converts light energy to produce two compounds: energy-rich (ATP) and the strong reducing agent (NADPH). These compounds are used in carbon dioxide fixation. Carbon fixation is initiated by the conversion of ribulose biphosphate to phosphoglyceric acid (PGA) in a reaction mediated by the enzyme RUBISCO (C_3 photosynthetic strategy). The rate of this reaction is impeded through a process known as photorespiration in which oxygen competes for sites on RUBISCO.

3. Some plants have developed biochemical strategies that reduce the impact of photorespiration (C_4 plants) and others have a strategy that conserves water (CAM photosynthesis). C_4 plants are adapted to high light intensities and hot, dry conditions and maintain rapid rates of carbon fixation. C_3 plants grow best at temperatures below $25\,^{\circ}C$; CAM plants grow slowly but can survive in arid environments.

4. The main environmental factors controlling photosynthetic rates are light intensity and wavelength, carbon dioxide availability and temperature. Plants utilise light in the 400–700 nm wavelength range. Light acquisition by leaves is more efficient if they are thin and multi-layered on a tree. The light intensity at which the rate of carbon fixation equals that lost by respiration is known as the light intensity compensation point.

5. Carbon dioxide is scarce in the atmosphere (0.036%) and carbon acquisition frequently limits photosynthetic rates. The carbon dioxide concentration at which the rate of carbon fixation equals that lost by respiration is known as the carbon dioxide compensation point.

6. The organic matter produced by photosynthetic organisms is called primary production. Gross primary production is the total amount of material produced; net primary production is that left over after the plant's respiratory needs have been fulfilled. Grassland net primary production can be measured by harvesting above- and below-ground material from a known area over two or more time intervals. Production is measured as a change in biomass per unit area per unit time. Above-ground productivity is usually underestimated because measurements of losses to litter and grazing are difficult to measure.

7. Tropical grasslands are dominated by perennial species which exhibit marked seasonality in growth related to seasonal rainfall patterns. Primary production is also affected by burning and grazing. Annual burning and moderate grazing have been shown to stimulate production.

8. Net primary production represents the energy available to herbivores and detritivores. Much of the net primary production is not grazed and supports the detritus food web.

9. Tropical rain forests are the most productive terrestrial systems where the combination of strong radiation, warm temperatures and high rainfall provides favourable growing conditions. More than 60% of all production occurs in the tropics; at higher latitudes plant growth is limited by cooler temperatures and a shortened growing season. Production in tropical grasslands and deserts is limited by the availability of water.

Chapter 4

Savanna and population dynamics

Savannas cover one-fifth of the land surface of the world and approximately half of the African continent. They are frequently the basis of livestock industries and, in some parts of Africa, the wildlife they support is a central feature of a thriving tourist industry. The savanna areas of Africa (e.g. *miombo* and *mopane* woodlands, Figure 4.1), South America (*campos* in Brazil, *llanos* on the Orinoco River) and Australia (*Eucalyptus–Acacia* savannas) have a long dry, cool season and a short hot, wet season. The resulting vegetation is grassland with scattered trees. The density of trees varies with mean annual rainfall and merges into closed canopy forest in moister regions and into semi-desert in drier areas. There are a number of standard texts describing the ecology of savannas in general (Huntley and Walker 1982; Bourlière 1983; Cole 1986; Walker 1987; Solbrig *et al.* 1996) and those in Africa (Scholes and Walker 1993), South-East Asia (Stott 1984) and the Neotropics (Sarmiento 1984) in particular.

Seasonality is a distinctive feature of savannas, and the plants and animals that inhabit them not only are adapted to survive seasonal extremes, but also may require such variations to do so. In the wet season, soil water content increases and groundwater discharge may occur. Soil moisture often remains high for some time after the end of the rains, and this extends the growing season into the early part of the dry period. Flower and seed production in trees varies considerably, with some plants flowering at the beginning, others in the middle and others at the end of the rainy season.

The dry season, which lasts from 3 to 7 months each year, is the most important factor limiting plant growth. Trees may lose their leaves and new leaves may appear several weeks before the normal start of the rains when the weather is very hot and the soil moisture at its driest. This adaptation may allow trees to take advantage of early showers.

The above-ground shoots of grasses and herbaceous plants die off in the dry season. In perennial species, the dry, above-ground shoots form a protective cover over the soil surface reducing water loss from the soil surrounding the perennating organs. The predominant species of savanna grasses utilise the C_4 photosynthetic pathway (see section 3.7) which, under the prevailing conditions of strong solar radiation, high temperatures and high evaporation rates, is more efficient. Savanna grasses have their growing season during the rains and set seed at the start of the dry season. After setting seed, the above ground parts become moribund. By the end of the dry season, the dry grass burns easily. Fire plays a central role in savanna ecosystems, and most savannas, particularly African ones, may owe their existence more to the impact of fire and large herbivores than to climate.

4.1 | Fire and savanna vegetation

Bush fires are characteristic of all savannas (Figure 4.2). The driest savannas only burn when above-average rainfall has allowed the production of sufficient plant matter as fuel. Savannas in higher rainfall areas only burn after an extended dry

Figure 4.1 Savanna vegetation (*miombo* woodland) near Zomba, Malawi at the end of the wet season (Photo: Patrick Osborne).

season has caused the grass to become tinder dry. Natural fires, resulting from lightning during thunderstorms, are infrequent in comparison with those started by humans. Savanna fires may spread along lines many kilometres long and travel at speeds of up to 5–10 metres per minute. At the ground surface, temperatures as high as 600 °C may be sustained for a short period. Below the surface, the ground is heated by only a few degrees and, while above-ground plant material may be destroyed, that below-ground usually survives.

Much savanna vegetation is maintained through regular burning, and savanna plants exhibit adaptations to fire. Trees and shrubs have a thick and insulating, corky bark and can sprout from underground organs. Crown fires are rare in savanna because tree crowns are held well above the ground and trees are widely separated.

Grasses that sprout after a fire will continue normal growth providing that soil moisture is adequate. The new sprouts may well grow fast as light intensity will be high, the soil surface enriched with nutrients from the ash and daytime soil temperatures may be elevated, favouring C_4 plants. Annual grass species rely on seeds for regeneration. The sharply pointed seeds of the Australian grasses *Themeda australis* (kangaroo grass) and *Heteropogon contortus* possess a hygroscopic mechanism which drills the seeds into the soil. Here, they are protected from lethal fire temperatures. Dormancy of seeds of kangaroo grass is broken when the seed is exposed to fire-generated high temperatures.

New shoots after a fire often wilt or are grazed before they are able to restore below-ground reserves. Consequently, plant species that are not adapted to fire may be replaced by those that have developed some strategy that allows them to cope with frequent fires. Fire frequency determines the length of time that a plant has to recover before the next fire occurs. The slower the rate of

Figure 4.2 Bush fire, Meru National Park, Kenya (Photo: Steve Turner, Oxford Scientific Films).

recovery and the higher the fire frequency the more likely it is for fire to cause changes to the vegetation. Fire-tolerant species that regenerate vegetatively recover more quickly than those that reproduce only by seed. Recovery is markedly affected by the rainfall, drought and intensity of herbivory following the fire.

Much savanna vegetation (species composition and biomass) is maintained through regular burning by humans. Fires are set to improve pastures, to clear land for cultivation and to keep animals, particularly snakes, away from villages.

Fires have a number of indirect effects. The exposed soil surface is more susceptible to drying and, following the onset of the rains, is more easily eroded. The ashes left by the fire can significantly enrich the nutrient content of the soil.

In African savannas, elephants (*Loxodonta africana*) act in concert with fire to convert woodlands into grasslands. Elephants push over trees and, by opening up the canopy, favour grasses. The grasses provide fuel for fires and the fires inhibit tree recruitment by killing tree seedlings.

Table 4.1	Savanna vegetation classification

Savanna woodland
Deciduous and semi-deciduous woodland of tall trees (more than 8 m high) and tall mesophytic grasses (more than 80 cm high); the spacing of the trees more than the diameter of canopy

Savanna parkland
Tall mesophytic grassland (grasses 40–80 cm high) with scattered deciduous trees (less than 8 m high)

Savanna grassland
Tall tropical grassland without trees or shrubs

Low tree and shrub savanna
Communities of widely spaced, low-growing perennial grasses (less than 80 cm high) with abundant annuals and studded with widely spaced, low-growing trees and shrubs often less than 2 m high

Thicket and scrub
Communities of trees and shrubs without stratification

Source: Cole 1963.

At the end of this chapter, we will discuss the complex interrelationships between the savanna environment and the plants and animals that live there.

4.2 | Savannas of the world

The term savanna has been applied to different forms of vegetation in different continents, and several attempts have been made to classify them. One classification scheme works well in both Australasia and Africa where five categories can be distinguished by appearance and species composition (Table 4.1). By contrast, South American savannas generally exhibit a continuum from dense woodland to open grassland with the same species occurring, albeit in different proportions.

Savanna is most widely distributed in tropical Africa where it covers 65% of the continent in a swath surrounding the wet forests of the Congo Basin and into southern West Africa. Sixty per cent of Australia and 45% of South America are savanna. Despite the similarities highlighted at the start of this chapter, the savannas on these three continents, and the smaller patches that occur in India, South-East Asia and on Pacific Islands, support very different faunas and floras.

4.2.1 Neotropical savannas

In tropical America, the term savanna is used for any grassland, with or without trees. In Brazil, savanna is described by a variety of local names on a continuum from dense woodland to open grassland: *cerrado* (dense woodland), *campo cerrado* (open woodland), *campo sujo* (low tree, shrub savanna), *campo limpo* (open grassland). The Pantanal in south-west Brazil, is a moist to wet grassland with a few, scattered trees. The *caatinga* vegetation is woodland dominated by deciduous, thorny xerophytes with few grasses.

In Venezuela, savanna (locally called *llanos*) dominates the landscape on the plains around the Orinoco River. The *llanos* between Venezuela and Colombia covers approximately half a million square kilometres forming the largest, uninterrupted expanse of savanna in the Neotropics north of the equator. The *llanos* consists of treeless grasslands or lightly wooded savanna with *Byrsonima crassifolia*, *Curatella americana* or *Bowdichia virgilioides* dominating. The *llanos* are found at low elevations (up to 300 m), and in poorly drained areas semi-aquatic grasses and the palm *Mauritia flexuosa* may occur.

Cerrado is the most extensive savanna region in South America. The trees characteristic of this savanna (*Kielmeyera* spp. and *Vochysia* spp.) have leaves that are large and leathery. In the drier savannas, trees, such as those belonging to the genus *Caesalpinia*, have small, pinnate leaves. *Curatella americana* trees shed their leaves and produce new ones almost simultaneously so that they are virtually evergreen. The dominant grasses are species of *Andropogon*, *Aristida*, *Paspalum* and *Trachypogon*.

The mammalian fauna of South American savannas comprises a few deer on open grasslands in Brazil, larger populations of the rodent, the capybara (*Hydrochoerus* spp.) in the Pantanal of Brazil and a few predators. As with Australia, the impoverished large herbivore fauna of Neotropical savannas contrasts markedly with that of African savannas, and this difference has intrigued researchers. However, fossil evidence indicates that Neotropical savannas have not always had a depauperate fauna. Throughout the Tertiary Period, the fauna of South American savannas was as diverse as those in Africa today. Diversity peaked in the early Miocene Epoch but declined in the late Miocene and Pliocene Epochs.

The land bridge between north and south America was established in the Pliocene Epoch, and a range of mammals (horses, tapirs, peccaries and deer) moved into the southern continent. Most of these species disappeared in the Pleistocene Epoch probably because grazing degenerated in response to a drier climate. The high diversity of animals in Africa is explained in terms of the long period of environmental stability that this continent has had. The Neotropics, conversely, have undergone great climate change and this could explain their depauperate fauna.

4.2.2 Australasian savannas

Savanna woodland in this region is found in the northernmost part of Australia, into eastern Queensland and along parts of the southern coast of New Guinea. In Australia and New Guinea, savanna woodlands are dominated by *Eucalyptus* species. These trees have drooping, sclerophyllous leaves rich in resins. In the drier areas, some of the grasses (*Aristida contorta* (kerosene grass) and the spinifex species of *Triodia* and *Plectrachne*) are also resinous. *Acacia aneura* (mulga) is often the sole dominant tree in the drier climate of central and southern Queensland. In wetter areas, *Melaleuca*

species may replace eucalypts. Australasian savannas lack the faunal diversity found in African savannas. Many of the grass species in Australia are unpalatable, and sweet grazing is confined to local pockets of *Astrebla* and *Dichanthium* grasslands. The eucalypts and acacias do not provide good browse (Cole 1986; Archibold 1995). In Australia, marsupials are the dominant large, native herbivores.

4.2.3 African savannas

Although the trees that dominate savanna in the three continents are different, there are some similarities between the savanna floras of Australia and Africa. Members of the Proteaceae, an evolutionary old, Gondwana (see section 1.3.1) family, have representatives in both Australia (*Banksia*, *Grevillea* and *Hakea*) and Africa (*Protea* and *Faurea*). Savanna parkland in Africa is characterised by *Acacia*, *Terminalia* and the occasional baobab (*Adansonia digitata*). In Australia, parklands have a similar generic composition with *Acacia*, *Piliostigma* and *Terminalia*. Australia, too, has its own baobab: *Adansonia gregorii*.

Large tracts of savanna woodlands with tall grasses occur throughout Angola, Malawi, Zambia and Zimbabwe where they are referred to as *miombo* woodland. These woodlands of deciduous trees, up to 20 m high, are dominated by species of *Brachystegia*, *Isoberlinia* and *Julbernardia*. In drier areas with poor soils, *mopane* savanna is found with *Colophospermum mopane* and *Acacia* spp. dominant.

North of the Congo Basin, savannas extend across Africa in a broad belt from Senegal in the west to Sudan in the east. This belt has been divided into three zones: the Sahel, the Sudan and the Guinea zone (Figure 4.3). The Sahel in the north, adjacent to the Sahara Desert, is very dry with scattered, short trees. The Sudan zone is densely populated and the vegetation has been severely modified by humans. *Acacia* species dominate in both this and the Sahel zone to the north. In the Guinea zone, trees such as *Burkea africana*, *Anogeissus leiocarpus*, *Lophira lanceolata*, *Isoberlinia* spp. and *Terminalia* spp. grow to a height of 12–15 m above a grass layer dominated by species of *Hyparrhenia*, *Andropogon* and *Pennisetum*.

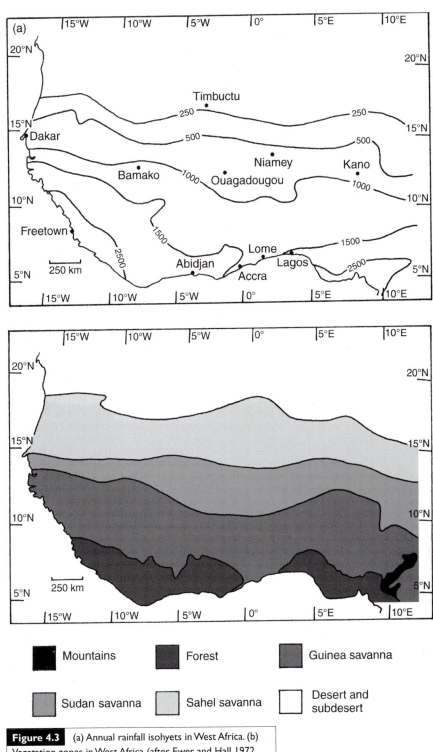

Figure 4.3 (a) Annual rainfall isohyets in West Africa. (b) Vegetation zones in West Africa (after Ewer and Hall 1972 reprinted by permission of Pearson Education Limited, Longman Group Limited).

Figure 4.4 Zebra (*Equus burchelli*) grazing in Hwange National Park, Zimbabwe (Photo: Patrick Osborne).

One distinguishing feature of the African savanna is the enormous diversity of birds and large mammals that exist there. For African savannas, 708 bird species have been recorded. This compares with 521 for Neotropical savannas and only 227 for savanna in Australia (Archibold 1995). Each of these three savanna regions has its own species of a large, flightless bird with long legs: the ostrich (*Struthio camelus*) in Africa, the emu (*Dromaius novaehollandiae*), in Australia and the rhea (*Rhea americana*) in South America.

African savannas support the most spectacular mammalian fauna of all ecosystems and this provides a wonderful setting to discuss the dynamics of biological populations (Figure 4.4). Over 90 species of ungulates and a wide range of large predators have been recorded from African savannas, and one area in particular, the Serengeti, in East Africa, not only has a high diversity of these species but also supports them in enormous numbers. It is for this reason that we

will discuss features of population ecology by drawing on examples from work carried out in the Serengeti.

4.3 | The Serengeti

The best studied savanna–grassland ecosystem in the world is the Serengeti region of East Africa. Ecologists working for many years in this area have been able to piece together interactions between environmental factors, plants, herbivores, carnivores, diseases and humans (Sinclair and Norton-Griffiths 1979, Sinclair and Arcese 1995).

The Serengeti National Park is in northern Tanzania and is one of the largest national parks in the world. The northern extension to the park joined the Tanzanian park with the Masai Mara National Park in Kenya (Figure 4.5). Neither park constitutes an ecological entity as animals migrate to and fro across the borders. Ecologically, the Serengeti ecosystem is best delimited by the movements of the large herds of migratory wilde-

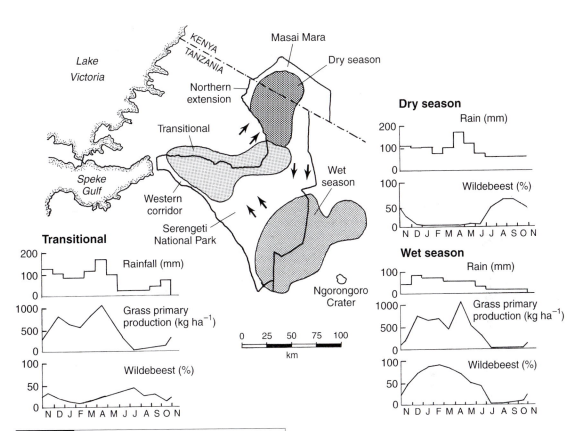

Figure 4.5 Map of the Serengeti–Mara ecosystem showing the boundary of the Serengeti National Park, the Masai Mara National Park and Ngorongoro Crater. The stippled areas show the seasonal ranges occupied by migratory wildebeest. Graphs show the relationship between rainfall, (histograms) grass primary production (food supply) and wildebeest numbers. Wildebeest prefer the short grass plains in the south-east but, as the dry season progresses, leave the plains for the wetter areas in the western corridor. The wildebeest then move north where less seasonal rainfall ensures a greater supply of green grass. Note how the wildebeest return to the short grass plains as soon as the rains come at the end of the year (adapted from Sinclair (1995), with kind permission of University of Chicago Press, © 1995 by the University of Chicago; Delany and Happold 1979 with kind permission of D.C.D. Happold).

beest (*Connochaetes taurinus*) and zebra (*Equus burchelli*), an area that extends beyond the border of the Serengeti and Masai Mara National Parks.

4.3.1 Climate

The Crater Highlands, rising to 3600 m and encompassing the panoramic Ngorongoro Crater, lie to the east of the Serengeti. These highlands cast a rain shadow over the eastern part of the Serengeti (mean annual rainfall of 350 mm) but rainfall increases away from this region to a mean annual rainfall of 1200 mm in the north-west. The average year is divided into a dry season from June to October and a wet season from November to May (although January and February tend to be drier). Rainfall in these grasslands and savanna remains a significant limiting factor and the rain-fall-determined growing season ranges from just 90 days in the south-east to virtually continuous in the north-west. The arid south-eastern area is known as the short-grass plains, the vegetation to the north and west is more lush with tall grasses and scattered trees.

4.3.2 Vegetation

Expansive grasslands occur in the south-east of the Serengeti and scattered patches are found in the western corridor. *Acacia* woodlands form a broad swath through the centre of the region with *Commiphora trothae, Acacia tortilis, A. clavigera, A. senegal* and *A. hockii* dominant. However, there are also extensive woodland areas dominated by *A. drepanolobium,* the whistling thorn tree. Woodland thickets line the banks of rivers. In the north-west Serengeti, broad-leaved trees (*Terminalia mollis* and *Combretum molle*) dominate the woodland with scattered bushes of *Heeria mucronata* and *Grewia bicolor.*

The short grass plains in the south-east of the Serengeti are dominated by the grasses *Digitaria macroblephora* and *Sporobulus* spp. and a sedge *Kyllinga nervosa.* The long-grass plains, towards the centre of the park, are dominated by *Themeda triandra* and *Pennisetum mezianum.* In between these two grass types are the intermediate plains with *Andropogon greenwayi* dominant. The grassland communities are not as distinct as described above and actually form a vegetation continuum varying in species and stature (McNaughton and Banyikwa 1995). Herbivores exert a powerful controlling influence on grassland composition. Grazing intensity is greatest in the *Sporobolus–Digitaria* grasslands that occur on the Serengeti plains and least on grasslands dominated by citronella grass (*Cymbopogon*). Citronella grass has a low palatability imparted through the distasteful chemicals it contains. This strategy, producing distasteful substances known as secondary compounds, is employed by many grasses and other plants to reduce or avoid herbivore attack.

4.4 | Savanna plants and heterogeneity

Savanna vegetation consists of a patchy occurrence of trees in what is otherwise an open grassland. The trees increase the structural complexity of the grassland and this results in greater environmental heterogeneity. The trees create low-light and cooler micro-habitats for colonisation by species preferring such conditions. The trees also provide forage, shade for animals, roosting sites for birds and hence serve to increase faunal diversity (Belsky 1994). The trees further increase heterogeneity by focusing nutrients resulting in higher nutrient concentrations

under the crown of trees than in open areas. This occurs through animals spending time in the shade of the tree and depositing nutrients there in urine and faeces, and through the tree drawing up nutrients from soil horizons deeper than those accessible to grasses. These nutrients are returned to the soil surface when leaves and fruits fall from the plant (Figure 4.6; Belsky and Canham 1994).

How trees affect the productivity of the grass understorey depends on tree density and environmental factors. Trees can reduce herb productivity through competition for light, water and nutrients (Walker 1987). In communities with low tree density, low rainfall and moderate soil fertility, studies have shown that the effect of trees is to increase productivity in the area beneath their crowns (Belsky *et al.* 1993). Tree density affects grass productivity through (1) improved soil fertility and structure beneath the crown; (2) improved water relations of the shaded grasses; and (3) through competition between trees and understorey plants for soil moisture and nutrients. Note that, in the first two of these, trees improve the habitat for grasses, whereas, in the third case, grasses and trees are competitors. Therefore, at low tree density, grass growth is enhanced. As tree density increases, adjacent patches interact as tree crowns shade, and tree roots invade, neighbouring patches. At high tree densities, resources available to the grasses are reduced to limiting levels and grass productivity declines (Belsky and Canham 1994).

The impacts of a tree on the surrounding grassland vary with distance from the tree, and this makes defining the size of the patch difficult (Figure 4.6). Belsky *et al.* (1989, 1993) carried out an intensive study of *Acacia tortilis*-dominated patches in Kenya. They showed that around an isolated tree with a crown radius of approximately 10 m, patches of nutrient-enriched soil were confined to within 15–20 m of trunks. Total incoming solar radiation was reduced by crown interception from 40 m west to 40 m east of the trunks, but significant differences in soil temperature were found only from 20 m east to 20 m west of the trunks. Understorey productivity was significantly elevated as far as 20 m from tree bases. Heterogeneity in savanna vegetation (struc-

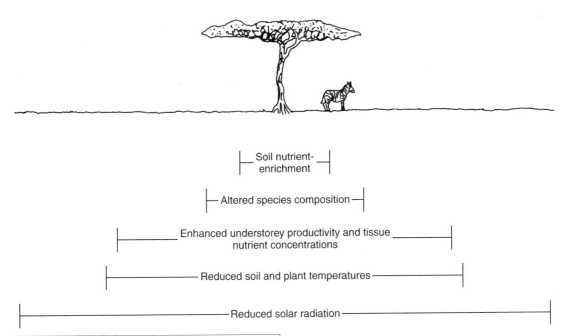

- Soil nutrient-enrichment
- Altered species composition
- Enhanced understorey productivity and tissue nutrient concentrations
- Reduced soil and plant temperatures
- Reduced solar radiation

Figure 4.6 Zones of altered characteristics surrounding an isolated tree, *Acacia tortilis*, in Tsavo National Park, Kenya (after Belsky and Canham 1994 © 1994 American Institute of Biological Sciences).

ture and function) is further enhanced by micro-topographical features and very patchy rainfall. Ridges tend to be drier than the depressions between them, and patchy rainfall markedly affects grassland utilisation by herbivores.

4.5 Animal population dynamics in the Serengeti

Our story of the animal populations begins just before the European discovery of the Serengeti in 1894 when a viral disease, rinderpest, swept through the area. This disease decimated wilde-beest, buffalo (*Syncerus caffer*) and giraffe (*Giraffa camelopardalis*) populations. Rinderpest epidemics recurred until extensive cattle inoculation pro-grammes brought the disease under control in the mid-1960s. Wildebeest, buffalo and giraffe populations increased as a result, reaching large, apparently stable populations (Table 4.2). Although wildebeest and buffalo populations increased following the control of rinderpest, note that zebra populations remained static

throughout the 1960–90 period (Figure 4.7). The massive decline in buffalo numbers from 1975 to 1985 has been attributed to poaching (Sinclair 1995; see section 4.16.1).

The Serengeti supports the largest herds of migrating ungulates in the world. The large her-bivore populations that inhabit the Serengeti have adapted to the rainfall patterns through sea-sonal migrations (Figure 4.5). During the wet season (November to May) the herbivores feed on the more arid plains in the south-east. Wildebeest give birth there, mostly during a three-week period in February. Zebra also give birth on the short-grass plains but do so over a longer period. It is at this time that the protein content of grass is greatest and most readily available to the milk-producing females.

Table 4.2 gives the raw densities of the three migratory species over the whole area that they may utilise. **Density** is defined as numbers per unit area. The densities as calculated for the Serengeti–Mara system as a whole are ecologically rather meaningless, since the area includes the whole range of habitats, some of which are never utilised by these herbivores. These figures are therefore **crude densities**. Of more relevance are the densities that may be achieved when the migratory species are on the short-grass plains

Table 4.2 Estimates of herbivore populations in the Serengeti made from counts carried out between 1985 and 1992

Species	Number	Density in Serengeti–Mara (km^{-2})	Ecological density wet season (km^{-2})
Wildebeest	1.3 million	52.0	250
Zebra	200 000	8.0	38
Thomson's gazelle	440 000	17.6	85
Topi	80 000	3.2	
Buffalo	46 000	1.8	

Notes: Densities (numbers km^{-2}) have been calculated on the assumption that the whole population of the migratory species moves to the short-grass plains in the wet season. This does not happen as some animals remain in the Western Corridor and Northern Extension throughout the year. The area of the Serengeti National Park is 14 763 km^2 but the migratory herbivores also utilise the Serengeti–Mara system with an area of 25 000 km^2. An area of 5200 km^2 has been used to calculate the maximum density of migratory herbivores on the short-grass plains in the wet season (Schaller 1972).
Source: Sinclair and Arcese 1995.

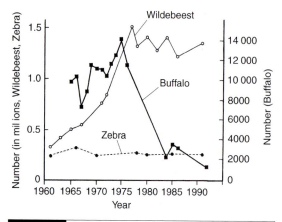

Figure 4.7 Population trends for wildebeest and zebra in the Serengeti from 1961 to 1991 and for the African buffalo population in the northern Serengeti. No censuses were conducted between 1977 and 1983. (adapted from Sinclair (1995), with kind permission from University of Chicago Press, © 1995 by the University of Chicago).

on food supply, the **ecological density**, is more meaningful than the crude density.

Animals, during the wet season, feed on the short grasses growing on the ridge tops. When the ridge tops dry out, zebra and buffalo move down the **catena** and are followed by topi (*Damaliscus korrigum*), wildebeest and Thomson's gazelle. In this **grazing succession**, the larger animals make the grazing at the lower levels more favourable for the smaller animals by removing the coarser material (Bell 1970). The micro-topographical heterogeneity of the catena is an important feature in supporting these large, diverse herds of herbivores (Figure 4.8).

This grazing succession may be initiated through the need for more food by the larger herbivores. Larger species must therefore be unselective and eat abundant lower-quality grass (buffalo), grass stems (zebra) or even woody material (elephants) (Sinclair 1983). To meet these needs, the larger herbivores must move down the catena to maintain high intake rates, leaving scattered remnants behind. The smaller animals can support themselves on these higher-quality remnants. These smaller animals, as ruminants, require nitrogen-rich food to enhance fermentation. This enables them to meet their energy requirements despite having small stomachs and high metabolic rates. Sinclair (1983) concluded

during the wet season. Note that densities here are much higher. They are calculated on the assumption that the entire population migrates to this region. For wildebeest and Thomson's gazelle (*Gazella thomsonii*) this is not unreasonable, as 80–90% of the populations of these animals do congregate on the plains, although zebra are less concentrated (Maddock 1979). In terms of impact

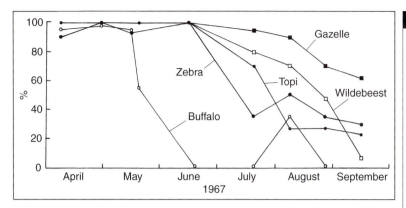

Figure 4.8 The topography of the Serengeti is a series of undulations and grass tends to be longer in the depressions where water accumulates than on the ridges. In the longer grass, some of the grazing animals have difficulty reaching the most nourishing parts of the grass. This figure shows the percentage of the population of different species using short-grass areas (ridge tops) in the Serengeti. (after Bell 1970 with kind permission from Blackwell Science).

Figure 4.9 Wildebeest (*Connochaetes taurinus*) with calf approximately 6 months old in the Northern Extension of the Serengeti National Park, Tanzania (Photo: Patrick Osborne).

almost $400\,\mathrm{g\,m^{-2}}$ (85% of the initial standing crop). This grazing stimulated net primary productivity and McNaughton was able to show that Thomson's gazelle favoured sites previously grazed by wildebeest and that the association with these sites was still evident at the end of the dry season, 6 months later. This has been described as **forage facilitation**, with each herbivore wave facilitating the grazing of subsequent species.

In May–June, the herds move towards Lake Victoria in the west and then north towards the Kenyan border as the dry season progresses (Figures 4.5 and 4.9). This is also the mating season. The migration pattern of the herbivores is important as it permits these large herds to exert a heavy grazing pressure. This pressure is intense but only for a short period, and is followed by a time which allows for plant recovery. Animal populations responded to an adequate food

that, although the larger species get most of the food, they can not completely exclude the smaller animals. In this way herbivore coexistence is achieved through the herbivores being of different size and therefore requiring different amounts and qualities of food. Large herbivores have lower metabolic rates than small herbivores and can therefore survive on lower quality food. This difference provides a mechanism for grasslands to support a greater biodiversity (see chapter 8) of herbivores.

McNaughton (1976) showed that migratory wildebeest reduced green plant biomass by supply and the control of a serious disease with a significant increase in numbers. Before we investigate what factors regulate population numbers, let us look in more detail at how herbivores feed.

4.6 | Herbivores and herbivory

Large herbivores may be divided into those which feed on grass and herbs (**grazers**) and those which feed on woody vegetation (**browsers**). Browsers feed at about head level so different species crop different levels of the trees and shrubs. The giraffe at 5 m tall is the highest browser, and below that there are a range of browsers down to the dikdik (*Rynchotragus kirkii*) only capable of reaching leaves less than a metre from the ground. Some herbivores obtain part of their sustenance from underground plant tissues. Warthog (*Phacochoerus aethiopicus*) primarily graze, but also dig up tubers and roots (Figure 4.10). The elephant is mainly a browser, but will frequently graze and, like the giraffe, can reach leaves, fruits and shoots growing up to 5 m above the ground. If food on a tall tree is out of reach, the elephant may push the tree over (see section 4.17).

Herbivores in the Serengeti can be divided into migratory herds and resident populations. Residence or migratory behaviour is not species-specific; some individuals of species which mostly migrate remain in some localities as resident herds. McNaughton and Banyikwa (1995) recognised two fundamentally different types of grazing behaviour: **sustained-yield grazing** and **rotational-passage grazing**.

Sustained-yield grazing occurs during the wet season when the herbivores occupy a limited area for an extended time. During the dry season, herbivores move rapidly through tall and medium grasslands, but return to areas on which rain has subsequently fallen or in which sufficient soil water moisture remains to regenerate the grasses. This strategy is known as rotational-passage grazing. The transition from one grazing strategy to another is often abrupt. Resident herds employ similar strategies, moving more during the dry season but over less expansive areas than the migrating herbivores.

Figure 4.10　Warthog (*Phacochoerus aethiopicus*) family in Hwange National Park, Zimbabwe (Photo: Patrick Osborne).

Herbivores are faced with a constantly changing mosaic of productivity driven by the irregular and scattered rain showers that occur in the wet season. Grazers in the Serengeti track these rainfall-driven pulses of primary productivity with considerable accuracy (McNaughton 1985). Herbivores arrive in an area of increasing primary productivity soon after rain has stimulated production and leave as the production and biomass decline. In this way, the herbivores utilise the ever-changing, resource-rich islands of primary productivity.

Grazers have a significant impact on grassland composition. The food value of grasses in heavily grazed areas is higher with a greater nitrogen and fibre content. Urination enhances the nitrogen content of plants, and grazers have been shown to select these urine-enriched grass regrowth areas (Day and Detling 1990). There is also evidence that herbivores in the Serengeti may enhance grass production through herbivory by facilitating nutrient cycling (McNaughton *et al.* 1988; Figure 4.11; see section 5.13). McNaughton *et al.* (1997) showed that both nitrogen and sodium were at considerably higher concentrations available to plants in soils of highly grazed sites than in soils of nearby areas where animal density was lower.

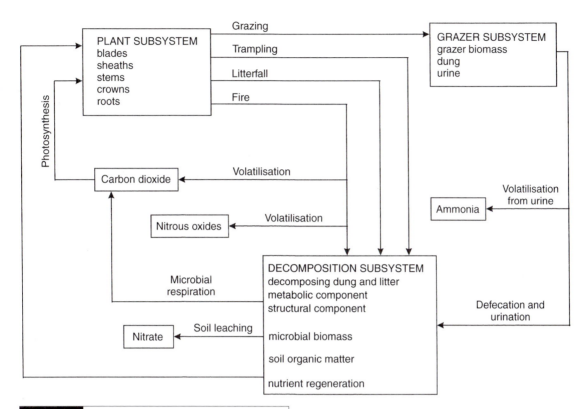

Figure 4.11 Relationships between plant, grazer and decomposition subsystems of the Serengeti grasslands supporting herds of large mammals. The model shows how herbivory enhances nutrient cycling and promotes plant production (after McNaughton *et al.* 1988 © 1988 American Institute of Biological Sciences).

Grazers have also been shown to enhance species diversity (see chapter 8) of the Serengeti grasslands. Areas fenced off to exclude the large herbivores become dominated by a few taller, slower-growing species that invest heavily in stem structure. These taller species shade out the smaller ones. Herbivory, therefore, favours the faster-growing species.

The resident herds represent the principal reservoir of mammalian diversity within the Serengeti. Species include topi, buffalo, hartebeest (*Alcelaphus buselaphus*), impala (*Aepyceros melampus*), waterbuck (*Kobus ellipsiprymnus*), reedbuck (*Redunca redunca*), roan antelope (*Hippotragus equinus*), oribi (*Ourebia ourebi*) and gazelles. They may also include some non-migrating zebra and wildebeest. It has been shown that these resident animals are not uniformly distributed but are concentrated into areas which have been called 'hot spots'. The same hot spots have been shown to be selected year in and year out for two decades or more.

Two reasons have been given to explain why these spots are so favoured. First, the different herbivore species, through their selective grazing, facilitate the foraging of other species. Second, congregation into herds reduces the threat of predation. McNaughton and Banyikwa (1995), however, favour another explanation. Grasses growing on these hot spots were shown to contain greater concentrations of sodium and phosphorus than grasses of the same species and stage of development growing in areas not so heavily utilised by herbivores. Sodium usually occurs in low concentrations in plant tissues but is required by animals, and sodium and phosphorus are particularly important to females during late pregnancy and lactation.

Forage facilitation and protection from

predation may also play a role in attracting herbivores to these areas. However, forage facilitation is more effective if herds follow the shifts in primary productivity that occur with the erratic rainfall. Predation risk is reduced if herds are less predictable and therefore remaining in one area does not, by itself, reduce the threat of predation. Grazing in herds, and particularly in mixed-species herds, does, however, increase the chance of a predator on the prowl being noticed.

Similar work has shown that the migrating herbivores move along a nutritional gradient. The grasses on the south-eastern Serengeti plains in the wet season were shown to be nutritionally superior to those growing elsewhere in the Serengeti. This may well explain why the animals migrate to the more arid regions in the wet season and why calving occurs there at that time.

Before discussing how herbivores reduce competition for food, we need to cover the basic principles of population growth.

4.7 | Principles of population growth

We have described above changes, over time, in the numbers of the different large animals living in the Serengeti. Each of the animal species living in this area could constitute what ecologists call a **population**. The same term is use by plant ecologists and refers to a group of organisms of the same species occupying a particular space at a particular time. This means that individuals belonging to the same population have an opportunity to interbreed.

The population is an important concept in ecology, and ecologists have developed a range of techniques to study populations and how (and why) they change over time. The growth of populations is a function of the **birth rate**, the **death rate** and the number of individuals in the population, as well as the movement of individuals into (**immigration**) and out of (**emigration**) the area. Being able to determine these population parameters has important bearings on the conservation of plant and animal species, biological resource management and the control of weeds and pests.

4.7.1 Estimation of population density

The techniques used to measure population density vary depending on the organism being studied. Static organisms such as trees and sessile animals can simply be counted and the number expressed per unit area to give the density. Mobile animals present more of a challenge. Wildebeest, on the open plains of the Serengeti, can be counted from the air, with photographs of the larger herds being taken and the number in the prints counted later. Relative population densities can be obtained from counts of spoor (tracks) or scats (faecal pellets) along transects of known distance. These measurements will not give actual numbers, but might indicate whether a population has increased or decreased since the last census.

Where a direct count is not possible, a technique known as capture–mark–release and recapture may be used. In this technique, a few individuals in a population are captured and marked in some way. Animals may be tagged, marked with paint or have a band attached to one leg. The way the animal is marked should not make it more susceptible to predation or other cause of mortality. Small mammals and reptiles can be marked by injecting a tiny bar-code label under the skin which can then be read by a hand-held bar-code scanner.

Marked individuals (M) are released back into the population at time T_1 and it is assumed that they become evenly distributed throughout the population. After a certain time interval ($T_2 - T_1$), a second sample (n) is captured. Some of these animals will be marked individuals (R). We can then calculate the total number of animals in the population (N) as:

$$N = nM/R$$

This method assumes that there is no immigration, emigration, deaths or births in the population between T_1 and T_2. Marked individuals must be neither more susceptible to re-capture (trap happy) nor less so through learning to avoid traps.

A very useful technique for studying small populations of large animals is to establish a photographic record of all individuals in the population. This has been done in studies of elephants, lions and primate species. This not only

Table 4.3 | Some features of the two phases in desert locusts (*Schistocerca gregaria*)

	Phase	
	solitaria	*gregaria*
Behaviour		
Tendency to aggregate	absent	present
Mobility	low	high
Activity rhythm	not synchronised	synchronised
Adult flight	nocturnal	diurnal
Physiology		
Food and water reserves at birth	lower	higher
Early mortality of young	higher	lower
Development rate	slower	faster
Instar number	greater	less
Fecundity	more, but smaller eggs	fewer, but larger eggs
Coloration		
Nymph	uniform green	yellow–black pattern
Adult	no changes	changes with maturation and age
Morphology		
Head	smaller	larger
Tegmen	shorter	longer
Hind femur	longer	shorter
Sexual size dimorphism	pronounced	slight

Source: Uvarov 1961.

permits a very accurate census of the population, but also facilitates detailed studies on relationships between individuals within the population.

4.7.2 Population ecology of the locust

The population ecology of locust species provides a good example of how birth rate, death rate and mass movement interact to determine population size and density with, in the case of the locust, potentially devastating consequences. There are three species of locust in tropical Africa: the migratory locust, *Locusta migratoria migratorioides*, the red locust, *Nomadacris septemfasciata* and the desert locust, *Schistocerca gregaria*. All locusts undergo metamorphosis from egg to nymph to adult. The desert locust has been known as a major crop pest for over 3000 years and was one of the plagues of Egypt as described in the Old Testament. All these locusts exist in two phases which are so distinct that taxonomists initially classified each phase as a different species. This made understanding their biology and population dynamics initially extremely difficult. Once it was realised that the locusts alternated between two phases called *gregaria* and *solitaria*, their biology was more easily understood.

When locusts are at low density, they exist in the *solitaria* phase, but as numbers increase there is a transition to the *gregaria* phase. Individuals in the two phases differ markedly in their behaviour, physiology, colouration and morphology (Table 4.3). The stimulus initiating the change in phase from *solitaria* to *gregaria* appears to be an increase in density, which in turn appears to be associated with rainfall affecting the quantity and quality of vegetation.

Almost all the differences between the two phases listed in Table 4.3 confer upon the *gregaria* phase a greater potential to swarm and on the *solitaria* phase a more solitary existence. The differences between the two phases are often not particularly distinct, with a continuum existing with some individuals clearly belonging to one or other phase and others with intermediate characteristics. These observations can be explained, in part, by the fact that there is a developmental sequence with behavioural changes being followed, in turn, by physiological, colour and, finally, morphological changes.

When environmental conditions favour an increase in numbers, there is a trend towards the production of swarming migrants, the *gregaria* phase. Huge population numbers are produced and these fan out and travel long distances, consuming prodigious quantities of food and destroying crops. Evidence suggests that the *gregaria* phase individuals are far more resistant to drought and food shortages than the *solitaria* phase, and the two phases represent a division of labour. *Gregaria* phase individuals are best adapted to conditions that favour high density, movement and opportunism. *Soiltaria* phase individuals are better adapted to a more stable environment and low population density. Dempster (1963) viewed the *gregaria* phase as the dispersal (see section 4.9.3) phase of the species, and the role of this phase as colonisation, a function particularly important in a habitat with patchy, discontinuous resources.

Two features of the population dynamics of the locust are significant. First, the *gregaria* form has the capacity for very rapid population growth, to an extent whereby the food supply in the vicinity can no longer support the population. The density of the population does not remain at these very high levels for long as it is reduced through movement to other areas. Second, population numbers in particular areas are characterised by an enormous range in size, with low populations of the *solitaria* phase and vast populations in the *gregaria* phase. The rapid development of locust swarms is an example of **geometric population growth**.

4.7.3 Geometric and exponential population growth

The most basic feature of a population is its size or **density** (the number of individuals per unit area). Population density is increased by **natality** (birth rate) and **immigration** and decreased by **mortality** (death rate) and **emigration**.

$$\text{Natality} = \frac{\text{number of organisms produced per unit time}}{\text{mean population size}}$$

$$\text{Mortality} = \frac{\text{number of deaths per unit time}}{\text{mean population size}}$$

Populations usually begin with very few organisms, but increase their numbers with time. If a population were to grow continuously, with no limits to its expansion, the increase in number would follow a curve like that in Figure 4.12a. Most species, however, have a distinct breeding season, and therefore their populations grow at that time and then decline until the next breeding time. Such a population grows **geometrically**.

The growth rate (usually expressed as λ) is given by the ratio of a population size in one year $N_{(t+1)}$ to that in the preceding year $N_{(t)}$:

$$\lambda = N_{(t+1)}/N_{(t)}$$

and therefore

$$N_{(t+1)} = N_{(t)}\lambda;$$
$$N_{(t+2)} = N_{(t)}\lambda^2;$$
$$N_{(t+3)} = N_{(t)}\lambda^3 \text{ and so on in a geometric}$$
progression.

Some species do not have a distinct breeding season and their populations grow continuously or **exponentially**. In this case, the population growth rate is the number of organisms added to the population minus the number lost per unit time:

$$\text{Population growth rate } (r) = \frac{\text{numbers produced} - \text{number of deaths}}{\text{mean population in time interval}}$$

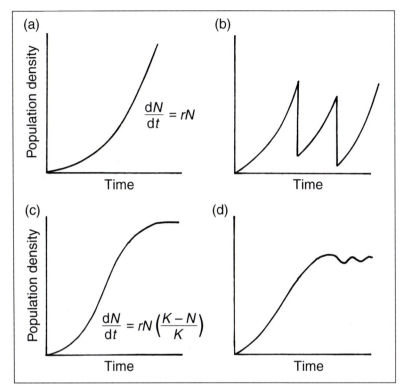

Figure 4.12 Types of population growth curves. (a) Exponential or geometric growth, J-shaped curve. (b) Series of exponential or geometric increases followed by population crashes. (c) Sigmoid or logistic growth curve. (d) Sigmoid growth curve followed by decreasing oscillations around the carrying capacity (K).

On a per capita basis: $r = b - d$ (births – deaths).

The rate of change of the population at any instant of time (dN/dt) is expressed as:

$$\frac{dN}{dt} = rN$$

Integrating this equation gives:

$$N_t = N_0 e^{rt}$$

where

N_t is the number of individuals at the end of a time period (t);

N_0 is the number of individuals at the start of the period;

e is the base of natural logarithms ($= 2.718$);

r is the intrinsic rate of growth.

The equations for geometric and exponential growth are similar with e^r replacing λ. Note that, when a population is not growing, $\lambda = 1$ and $r = 0$. Also note that, for increasing populations, λ is greater than one and r is positive, and, for decreasing populations, λ is less than one (but greater than zero) and r is negative.

Since populations can grow geometrically or exponentially, they have the potential to become enormous in a short time. This type of population growth is known as **J-shaped growth** (Figure 4.12a). However, no population can grow forever and, in the J-shaped form, density increases rapidly until some environmental factor halts growth or density declines through emigration. Often this type of population growth is followed by a catastrophic fall in numbers. This may be caused by the food supply becoming exhausted, by a disease which spreads rapidly through the overcrowded population or by dispersal from the area. Following recovery of the food supply or a reduction in disease prevalence, the population may start to grow again and the process repeated. This results in a violently oscillating population density (Figure 4.12b).

4.7.4 Population growth of the migratory locust

The red locust usually produces one generation per year and is capable of a 100-fold increase in one year. If we assume that, for a population of 1000 individuals, there is a 100-fold increase in the population each year and that the rate does not change with population density, we can calculate the population size for each generation using:

$$N_{t+1} = N_t \lambda$$

Table 4.4 Growth of a hypothetical red locust population from an initial size of 1000 individuals with a growth rate of 100 per individual per generation

Generation	Population size (N_t)
0	1000 (10^3)
1	100000 (10^5) (1000 × 100)
2	10000000 (10^7) (100000 × 100)
3	1000000000 (10^9) (10000000 × 100)
4	100000000000 (10^{11}) (1000000000 × 100)

where:

N_t = population size of reproductive females at generation t

N_{t+1} = population size of females at generation $t+1$

λ = net reproductive rate, or number of female offspring produced per female per generation

In four generations, our hypothetical locust population has grown to a staggering size (Table 4.4). The environment is unable to support such growth indefinitely and the population may either decline as resources become limiting or disperse to new areas.

4.7.5 Logistic population growth

Another type of population growth follows an S-shaped or sigmoid growth form (Figure 4.12c). In this case, the population increases slowly at first, then more rapidly, before slowing to an equilibrium level where the population fluctuates around a maximum. This equilibrium density is termed the **carrying capacity** and is represented by K in the following model (**logistic growth equation**):

$$\frac{dN}{dt} = rN \frac{(K - N)}{K}$$

where r is the intrinsic rate of growth and N is the population size. Note that, as N increases, N/K approaches 1 and the population growth rate keeps falling. When $N = K$, the population growth rate (dN/dt) becomes zero.

This logistic growth model assumes that there is a linear relationship between density and the rate of increase, and that the effect of density on the rate of increase is instantaneous. This latter assumption is rarely met in nature as there is usually a time lag between the birth of a new individual and its own reproduction. Carrying capacity is likely to change both seasonally and from one year to the next and therefore can rarely be regarded as a constant. The logistic growth model also assumes that all individuals reproduce equally and that there is no immigration into or emigration out of the population. Again, these assumptions are rarely met in nature.

4.7.6 Population growth of wildebeest in the Serengeti

Populations can not grow forever. What happens in many populations is that, as the density rises, the population growth rate declines. Density may act, for example, through a reduction in reproductive capacity or through an increase in mortality. Let us track the growth of the wildebeest population in the Serengeti following the control of rinderpest using the logistic growth equation. The population of wildebeest in 1963 was around 250000 and the population levelled off in 1977 at around 1.3 million (Sinclair 1995). Let us assume, then, that the wildebeest carrying capacity of the Serengeti system was 1.3 million. If we assume, that the sex ratio of the wildebeest is 1:1 then, in 1963, the population contained 125000 females. If we further assume a reproductive capacity of 0.85, the number of births in 1963 would be 106250. Let us assume that the mortality rate, for the whole population, was 15%. Therefore, in 1963, 37500 deaths would have occurred.

Therefore:

$r = (b - d)/N = (106250 - 37500)/250000) = 0.28$

Table 4.5 Hypothetical growth in the population of wildebeest in the Serengeti

Year	$(K-N)/K$	rN	dN/dt	N
1963				250000
1964	0.808	70000	56560	306560
1965	0.764	85837	65579	372139
1966	0.714	104199	74398	446537
1967	0.657	125030	82145	528682
1968	0.593	148031	87782	616465
1969	0.526	172610	90793	707258
1970	0.456	198032	90303	797560
1971	0.387	223317	86424	883984
1972	0.320	247516	79205	963189
1973	0.259	269693	69850	1033040
1974	0.205	289251	59296	1092336
1975	0.160	305854	48937	1141273
1976	0.122	319556	38986	1180259
1977	0.092	330472	30403	1210662

Notes: Calculations are based on an assumed carrying capacity (K) of 1300000, an initial population of 250000 in 1963 and a constant annual growth rate of 0.28.

We can use the logistic growth equation as a simple model to chart the increase in the Serengeti wildebeest population (Table 4.5).

In this model, $(K-N)/K$, is a measure of the unutilised habitat that is available to the population. Note that this term declines as the population approaches the assumed carrying capacity of 1300000. The population ceases growth when the carrying capacity is attained (i.e. $N=K$ and $(K-N)/K=0$). dN/dt, the rate of increase in the wildebeest population, is low to begin with, increases to a peak in 1969 and declines thereafter (Figure 4.13). Note that, although the model does follow closely the observed changes in the wildebeest population (Figure 4.7; Sinclair 1995), it is based on assumed birth and death rates, which while probably close to field rates, are not actual measurements. Similar growth trends could be achieved by either reducing the birth and death rates or by increasing them. Therefore, Table 4.5 is not an attempt to validate the model but serves to demonstrate the role of the term $(K-N)/K$.

4.8 | Factors determining population density

We have seen what happened to the size of the wildebeest and buffalo populations following rinderpest control in the Serengeti. An important feature of biological populations is therefore that they change in size, increasing in response to factors such as adequate resources, decreasing owing to, for example, resource limitations or the ravages of disease. By understanding clearly how populations change in size and what factors control these changes, we may be able to manage natural animal populations more effectively. This is particularly important in our efforts to manage wildlife reserves and national parks. To do this we need to understand the process by which new animals are added to the population (recruitment) and how animals are removed from it (mortality).

4.8.1 Reproduction
The number of offspring an individual female may produce throughout her life depends on a

Figure 4.13 (a) Calculated population growth curve for the Serengeti wildebeest. The model is based on an initial population of 250 000 with a constant growth rate (*r*) of 0.28 in a habitat with an assumed carrying capacity (*K*) of 1.3 million. The calculated growth curve has been constructed with the aim to resemble that of the Serengeti wildebeest population but note that the growth rate (*r*) used is not based on actual measurements but derived using a number of assumptions (see text). Note that the mathematically derived curve is smooth and this contrasts with that depicting the field data (Figure 4.7). (b) The change in dN/dt with time of the calculated population growth of the Serengeti wildebeest. Note that, according to this model, population growth reached a maximum in 1969.

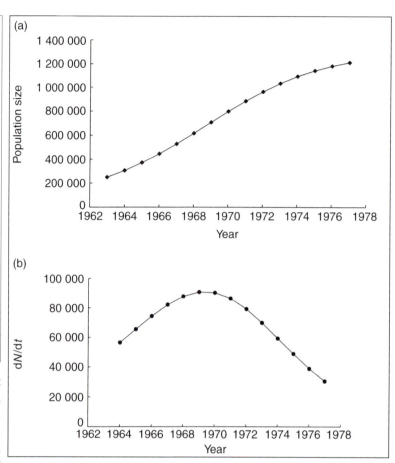

number of factors: age at first reproduction, the **gestation period** (length of pregnancy), number of offspring produced in each litter, interval between successive litters (**calving interval**) and age at which reproduction ceases. These physiological features combine to determine the innate capacity for increase. For example, a female elephant becomes fertile at around 13 years old and the gestation period is 22 months. If an elephant remains fertile until 55 years old, the maximum number of calves that could be produced is around 20. This assumes that the female becomes pregnant again soon after giving birth. This physiological maximum is rarely achieved in nature. The calving interval in elephants has been shown to be usually more than three years, the onset of puberty may be delayed and mean **fecundity** (the number of young produced per female in the population) is therefore much lower than that calculated above.

Organisms, like the elephant, that reproduce more than once in a lifetime are known as **iteroparous** and these contrast with those organisms which employ a once-in-a-lifetime ('big bang') approach (**semelparous**). Some fish, such as salmon, utilise this latter strategy. **Fertility** (the number of eggs or offspring produced) varies enormously between species with most mammals producing one to a few with each cycle but other organisms may produce many millions. This variation in clutch size is accompanied by variation in the size of the offspring. Large offspring are often better competitors and have an improved chance of survival.

Plants employ similar reproductive strategies with some species producing copious, small seeds (e.g. most grasses) while other produce fewer, larger seeds often protected by a thick, woody seed coat (e.g. legumes). Seed production in some plants occurs over a number of months, in others timing ensures that seed production occurs just before the start of an unfavourable season. Annual plants use this latter strategy and the seed may be dispersed during a period in which the adult plant is unable to survive. Some plants are semelparous, flowering once, often in great profusion across their range, and then dying (see section 8.3.2).

Reproductive strategies have developed as a continuum from two extremes: one in which numerous, small (poorly resourced) offspring are produced and the other in which only a few, well-resourced offspring are produced. We will consider these differences further in section 4.13.

4.8.2 Mortality

Animals die from a variety of causes. If food is scarce, animals may die from starvation, or, more likely, succumb to a disease they are unable to resist in their malnourished state. Animals may be killed by predators or die in accidents. Wildebeest have been seen to drown when the herd stampedes across a river. The stampede occurs because the animals feel vulnerable to predators in the riverine thicket and to attack by crocodiles (*Crocodylus niloticus*) when in the water.

Ecologists have distinguished between two types of factors that limit the size of populations: **density-dependent mortality factors** and **density-independent mortality factors**. The death rate per capita is said to be density-dependent if it increases as density increases. Density-independent mortality factors do not vary in their impact as density changes. Density-dependent mortality factors are mainly biotic in nature: disease, competition and predation, whereas density-independent factors are mainly abiotic, mostly related to climate. The term **population regulation** is used when the population size is restricted by a density-dependent factor. That is, a factor that results in a reduced reproductive rate or an increased mortality rate as the population density increases is a regulating factor. **Population limitation** operates when a factor restricts the growth of a population to a level below that which it would attain in the absence of the factor.

4.9 | Density-dependent mortality factors

4.9.1 Food supply

Whether food supply regulates the size of animal populations is a difficult question to answer. One feature of grasslands and savannas (and most terrestrial systems) is the small amount of primary production that is consumed by herbivores. Therefore, it would seem unlikely for food supply to limit the population size of herbivores. However, primary production cannot simply be equated with food; herbivores show clear food preferences and food ingested may not be digested and absorbed (Sinclair 1975).

Studies of wildebeest and buffalo populations in the Serengeti have shown that there are relationships between rainfall and food supply. Sinclair (1977) showed a strong relationship between rainfall and the crude density of African buffaloes in different areas of eastern Africa (Figure 4.14). Sinclair (1979b) showed that dry-season wildebeest mortality was higher during drier years. In wetter years, dry-season mortality was similar to that for the average year. Figure 4.15 shows that dry-season mortality was inversely related to population size, but this figure does not consider interannual variation in rainfall and dry-season food availability. Sinclair et al. (1985) were able to test a relationship proposed by Hilborn and Sinclair (1979) which predicted that (1) the wildebeest population in the Serengeti would stabilise between 1.0 and 1.5 million animals; and (2) dry-season mortality would be density-dependent and sufficient to account for the population stabilisation.

Sinclair et al. (1985) produced a relationship between animal density (expressed as animals per kg green grass per day) and percentage mortality per month during the period of wildebeest population growth (1968–72). The population did stabilise at approximately the level predicted by Hilborn and Sinclair (1979). In 1982 and 1983, dry-season monthly mortality was measured directly. Grass growth was also either measured directly or estimated from rainfall. In both years, the dry-season monthly mortality was above that

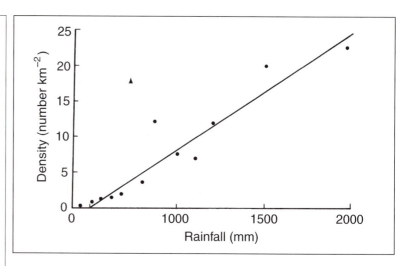

Figure 4.14 The relationship between mean crude density in different areas of eastern Africa and mean annual rainfall. The regression line is for the data excluding that from Lake Manyara (triangle). The buffalo density in the Lake Manyara Park is high compared with other areas with similar rainfall. Lake Manyara Park has extensive wetlands and rich lakeshore grasslands which increase the food availability to the buffalo beyond that produced through rainfall (redrawn from Sinclair (1977), with kind permission of University of Chicago Press, © 1977 by The University of Chicago).

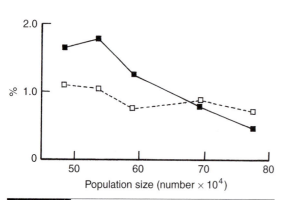

Figure 4.15 The proportion of wildebeest dying per dry-season month (solid squares), compared with the average monthly mortality rate during the year (open squares), plotted against population size (redrawn from Sinclair (1979b), with kind permission of University of Chicago Press, © 1979 by The University of Chicago).

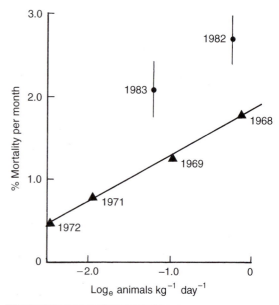

Figure 4.16 Mean dry-season monthly mortality of adult wildebeest plotted against natural logarithm of density (animals per kg green grass per day). Regression line from the years 1968–72 is the model. Vertical lines are 95% confidence limits (after Sinclair et al. 1985 with kind permission from Springer-Verlag).

predicted by the previously derived model. Therefore, mortality was severe enough to prevent continued population increase and this supported prediction (2) above (Figure 4.16).

Coe *et al.* (1976) were able to produce relationships between rainfall, primary production (food supply) and the biomass of herbivores in the drier African savannas. These relationships might be used to predict herbivore carrying capacity of particular savanna areas from rainfall records. However, these relationships, based on mean annual rainfall of some very large wildlife

reserves, probably conceal a great deal of the ecology of the herbivores. Rainfall varies from 400 mm to 1100 mm across the Serengeti and herbivore biomass does not remain in one place but follows the food supply. None the less the relationships developed by Coe *et al.* (1976) do serve to illus-

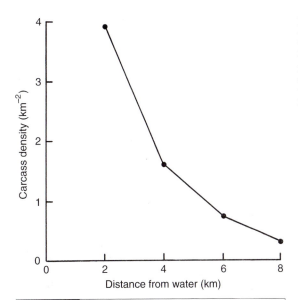

Figure 4.17 Carcass density of elephants at different distances from water. The elephants died during the 1970–71 drought in Tsavo National Park (after Corfield 1973 with kind permission from Blackwell Science).

trate the importance of food supply in determining herbivore biomass.

Dependence on water constrains animals to finding food within a certain distance from surface water. This is particularly true of the hippopotamus (*Hippopotamus amphibius*) which is a nocturnal grazer, spending the day in water. This animal may have to travel great distances each night in order to satisfy its food requirements. Unusually low rainfall in Tsavo National Park, Kenya in 1970–71 provided a disturbance which demonstrated that lack of food for elephant calves and their mothers within reach of water, not the lack of water itself, caused a dramatic increase in elephant mortality. In other words, it was a famine rather than a drought (Figure 4.17; Corfield 1973).

When considering the role of food supply in determining animal populations, the balance between energy gained from the food and the energy expended in obtaining it must be assessed. We will study the construction of an energy budget for animals in section 5.8. If food is both abundant and of a high quality, an animal will need to spend less time and energy feeding. A predator will have greater hunting success when prey species are more abundant. In a more stressful environment, herbivores will need to spend more time feeding and predators more time hunting. The time animals can devote to feeding is reduced by the need to carry out other activities such as territory defence, defence from predator attack and courtship. Under conditions of an inadequate diet, it is not difficult to see how population size may be reduced.

Measurement of the food available is also difficult. Herbivore species have different diets and the same species may vary their diet seasonally. The variety and wide range in size of herbivores present in African savannas also result in very efficient use of food resources (see section 4.9.5).

4.9.2 Disease

Disease is an important regulator of population size. The impact of rinderpest on some herbivores in the Serengeti has already been described. In 1994, 40 lions in the Serengeti died from an outbreak of distemper (Miller 1994). Research into the outbreak of this disease indicated that the virus that caused the disease may have mutated to become more virulent. Another factor, and this is an important point with respect to population ecology, is that the lion population was at a record high when the epidemic hit. The large number of lions in the Serengeti may have made it easier for the disease to pass from animal to animal simply because they were in more frequent contact with each other.

Wild dog (*Lycaon pictus*) populations in the Serengeti and elsewhere in Africa, have also declined, and the cause of this is not clear (Figure 4.18). Burrows (1995) suggested that the death of all packs under study in the Serengeti may have been caused by rabies exacerbated by stress in handling study animals (e.g. when fitting radio-tracking collars). The rabies virus could spread quickly through a pack by saliva exchange during oral social greeting (kissing and nuzzling).

4.9.3 Space

Space is important to both plants and animals. Some animals such as wildebeest and zebra are

Figure 4.18 Lone wild dog (*Lycaon pictus*) on the short-grass plains of the Serengeti National Park, Tanzania. Numbers of wild dog throughout their range have declined in recent years (Photo: Patrick Osborne).

social and live in large herds, others are solitary or live in pairs or small family groups. The area an animal lives in is called its **home range**. In the case of the Serengeti wildebeest, the home range is enormous. Others, such as the resident herbivores, have a much smaller home range. Some animals will defend a part, or all of their home range and this is then known as the animal's **territory**. Territories may be established to defend a food supply, breeding area, nest site or shelter. Territorial animals may expend a considerable amount of time and energy encouraging other animals to leave their territory.

The costs of this territory defence must not be greater than the benefits that accrue. Gill and Wolf (1975a, 1975b) studied territoriality in the African sunbird, *Nectarinia reichenowi*. These birds feed on nectar and will defend a patch of the flowers that produces the nectar. When nectar

production is high everywhere, the birds do not waste their energy defending a territory. However, if the food supply becomes variable, with some patches providing copious nectar and others less productive, territorial defence intensifies. The costs of territorial defence escalate with increasing bird density and, at high bird densities, territoriality is again abandoned because it becomes too expensive. This study concluded that territoriality can be explained in terms of the economic costs and benefits.

As resources in a particular area become limiting, animals can move to new areas. As the wildebeest population grew following the control of rinderpest, herds colonised a larger area of the Serengeti. When locusts swarm, they spread out over very large areas. This process of moving away from a centre of population growth is known as **dispersal**. Most organisms have some mechanism to promote dispersal. For mobile organisms, dispersal is straightforward. Plants and sessile organisms also have a range of techniques to effect dispersal of reproductive propagules, and use agents such as wind, water and animals. We will look at dispersal in more detail in chapter 12.

Dispersal not only reduces the population density of the organism in the source area, but may also serve to increase the geographical distribution of the species. Whether this latter function is achieved will obviously depend on the organism's ability to withstand the environmental conditions prevailing in the new area (see section 2.10). Dispersal should not be confused with the term **dispersion**, which, in ecology, refers to the spatial distribution of the organism.

If a population were spread uniformly over an area, the population density would be the same for the whole area. However, this is very rare in nature, and organisms often are concentrated in certain parts of their range; sparse or absent in others. Three patterns of dispersion (or spatial distribution) of a population over the area it occupies can be recognised. In a **regular** dispersion, the spacing between organisms is approximately equal. Truly regular dispersion is rare but may be seen in colonies of nesting birds in which birds defend small nesting sites.

In a **randomly** dispersed population, there is

an equal chance of any individual occupying any point within the area, and the presence of one individual is not influenced by the position of others. Very few organisms are randomly dispersed because the environment is seldom entirely uniform. Most dispersion patterns in nature show conspicuous **clumping**. These aggregated or contagious dispersions may reflect irregularities in the environment, and organisms, through reproductive enhancement, become concentrated in the more favourable spots.

4.9.4 Competition

In the early stages of recovery of the herbivore populations in the Serengeti, animals expanded the area that they utilised. Animals moved from the Serengeti Plains in the wet season to the Western Corridor in the dry season, with some animals going further afield into the northern region of the Park. As the population expanded further, the number of animals travelling north into the Mara River basin increased. This expansion in the area utilised was probably brought about through competition for food. Even though zebra and gazelle populations did not change during this period, the expansion of the wildebeest population forced these other species to expand their ranges as well.

Interaction between two species that limits the distribution or performance of one or both of them is known as **competition**. Competition occurs when two or more individuals require a common resource that is actually or potentially limiting. Tilman (1982) defined a resource as 'any substance or factor which is consumed by an organism and which can lead to increased growth rates as its availability in the environment is increased.'

Keddy (1989) recognised four types of resources based on the way in which they vary over time (Figure 4.19). Increasing resources are those which increase over the active season of the organism and then suddenly decline. Leaves on a deciduous tree, being fed on by a herbivore, exemplify an increasing resource. Decreasing resources are produced suddenly at the beginning of the season and then gradually decline. Seeds on annual plants may be produced in copious quan-

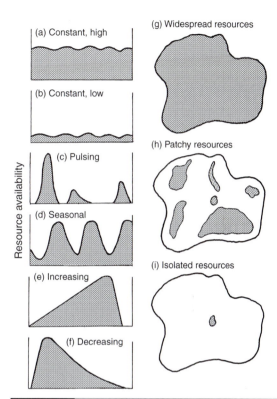

Figure 4.19 Resource availability in time and space.
(a) Resource is available throughout the year at a high level.
(b) Resource is available throughout the year at a low level.
(c) Resource availability is patchy and unpredictable (pulsing).
(d) Resource availability is seasonal and predictable.
(e) Resource availability increases with time.
(f) Resource availability decreases with time.
(g) Resource is available everywhere.
(h) Resource availability is spatially patchy.
(i) Resource availability is isolated (adapted from Keddy 1989 with kind permission from Kluwer Academic Publishers).

tities at the end of the growing season and organisms feeding on these seeds will be faced with a decreasing resource. Pulsing or ephemeral resources increase and then decline rapidly. Deserts receiving irregular rainfall and ephemeral pools provide examples of habitats in which resources occur in pulses. Steadily renewed resources are continuously replenished over long periods and this occurs with leaves and flowers in wet, tropical forests.

Southwood (1977) considered how habitats, and therefore resources, vary in time and space. Over time, resource supply can be regarded as **constant**, **seasonal**, **unpredictable** or **ephemeral**.

With respect to space, resources can have a **continuous** or **patchy** distribution or occur in such an **isolated** location as to make colonisation by an organism unlikely (Figure 4.19). Savanna is an example of a seasonal habitat and resource supply is seasonal for most organisms inhabiting them.

Two forms of competition have been recognised: **Resource competition** occurs when a number of organisms utilise a common resource that is scarce. **Interference competition** occurs when an organism defends a resource, even if the resource is not in short supply. Time and energy expended in this activity affects the competitors adversely. Competition may be **interspecific** (between two or more different species) or **intraspecific** (between individuals of the same species). Plants compete for resources such as light, nutrients and water. Animals compete for food, water, a place to live, or for mates. Responses to competition will obviously differ between plants and animals. Plants are rooted and may respond to competition through growth and secretion of compounds that inhibit the germination or growth of potential competitors.

Animals respond to competition in a number of ways. The population of one species may decline as that of the more successful competitor increases. One species may leave areas where competition is so intense that it is unable to obtain adequate resources. Another strategy is to use resources that are not being utilised. This last strategy leads to a process known as **resource partitioning**.

4.9.5 Resource partitioning in herbivores

One of the interesting features of the African savanna is the variety of large mammals that occupy them. Excluding primates, more than 90 large (over 5 kg body weight) herbivorous mammal species exist in Africa. At least 10 species occur in most wildlife reserves and more than 20 are recorded for the Serengeti. The large herbivores of the African savanna range in size from the dikdik of 3–5 kg to the adult male elephant weighing up to 2.5 tonnes. How does this large variety of herbivores coexist?

In Tarangire National Park, Tanzania, Lamprey

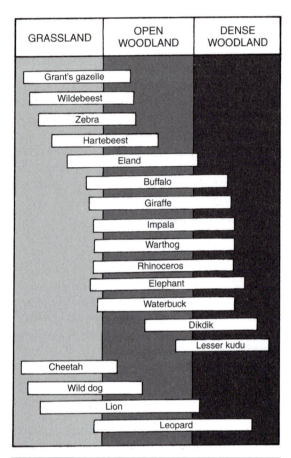

Figure 4.20 Habitat preferences of herbivores and predators in Tarangire Game Reserve, Tanzania (after Lamprey 1963 with kind permission from Blackwell Science).

(1963) studied fourteen large herbivores that lived together even at times when food resources were critically low. He investigated resource use by these herbivores and four of their predators. He recorded habitat preferences (grassland, open woodland, dense woodland) for these species and found that the species could be arranged in a continuum from those favouring grassland to those spending most time in dense woodland (Figure 4.20).

In areas where species showed significant overlap, ecological separation could be explained in terms of seasonal occupation of habitat and food preferences. For example, giraffe obtain much of their food from the tops of trees and therefore, despite having a habitat preference almost identical to impala and buffalo, do not compete for food. Lamprey (1963) also indicated from his study, that impala utilised the vegetation edges or **ecotones** between woodland and grassland. These ecotones supported a richer diversity of herbivores than areas away from the boundaries between woodland and grassland. Impala found these ecotones attractive because they used the woodland for protection, shade and dry season browse, and the grassland for grazing. The majority of herbivores in Tarangire showed some seasonal movement and this would also tend towards resource partitioning.

Small herbivores tend to seek out high-quality food such as shoots, buds and flowers; resources which are widely spaced and which are eaten whole. An animal feeding on these scattered items increases its spacing from other individuals of the same species. Consequently, small animals tend to be solitary or live in pairs. Larger animals feed on more abundant grass, and the fact that an animal does not consume a whole grass clump before moving on allows these animals to live in herds. Jarman (1974) was the first to notice this relationship between body size, type of food eaten and typical size of social group. This relationship is not only important in terms of food supply but also results in different behaviour patterns such as in predator avoidance (see section 4.11.2).

4.10 | Competition theory and the competitive exclusion principle

The competitive exclusion principle states that two species with identical ecological requirements cannot live together in the same place at the same time. Hardin (1960) stated this principle succinctly: 'Complete competitors cannot coexist.' Lotka (1925) and Volterra (1926) derived equations to describe the outcome from competition between two species. These equations are based on the logistic growth curve (section 4.7.5). The growth curves for two species can be written as:

for species 1:
$$dN_1/dt = r_1 N_1 (K_1 - N_1)/K_1$$
for species 2:
$$dN_2/dt = r_2 N_2 (K_2 - N_2)/K_2$$
where:

N_1 = population size of species 1
t = time
r_1 = per capita rate of increase of species 1
K_1 = asymptotic density (carrying capacity) for species 1

and similarly for species 2.

When these species are in competition, the population growth of both species is reduced. This reduction can be included in the above equations by letting the competitive effect of species 2 on species 1 be α and the competitive effect of species 1 on species 2 be β. Hence, for species 1:

$$dN_1/dt = r_1 N_1 (K_1 - N_1 - \alpha N_2)/K_1$$

and for species 2:

$$dN_2/dt = r_2 N_2 (K_2 - N_2 - \beta N_1)/K_2$$

If species 1 attains a population size of K_1, species 2 will have died out. Conversely, species 2 reaching a population size of K_1/α, will spell the demise of species 1. Between these two extremes, an equilibrium may be reached in which both species coexist at population levels described by the line joining K_1 and K_1/α (Figure 4.21a). A similar result can be obtained when expressing the competition in terms of species 2 (Figure 4.21b).

The magnitude of α and β determines the outcome of the competition. There are three possible outcomes: (1) species 1 dies out; (2) species 2 dies out or (3) both species coexist at some lower population size (Figure 4.22). If the species coexist they can do so by achieving either a stable or an unstable equilibrium. These four possible outcomes of competition are best viewed graphically (Figure 4.23).

The Lotka–Volterra competition model is based on the following assumptions: there is no immigration or emigration and no time lags; resources must be limiting; the competition coefficients (α and β) and carrying capacities (K_1 and K_2) must be constants and density dependence must be linear. Further consideration of the

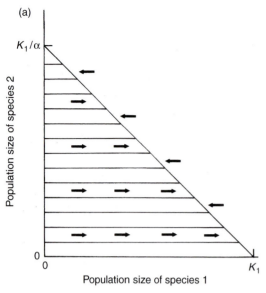

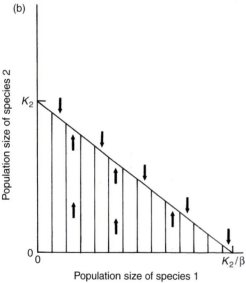

Figure 4.21 (a) Changes in population size of species 1 when competing with species 2. Populations in the hatched area will increase in size and will come to an equilibrium at some point on the diagonal line. (b) Changes in population size of species 2 when competing with species 1. Populations in the shaded area will increase in size and will come to an equilibrium at some point on the diagonal line (after Krebs 1994 adapted by permission of Addison-Wesley Educational Publishers, Inc.).

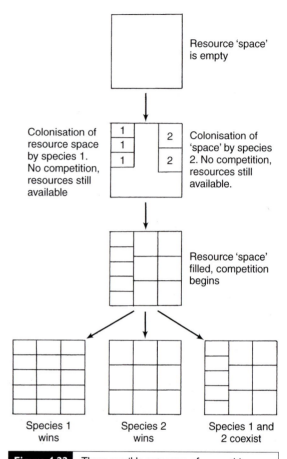

Figure 4.22 Three possible outcomes of competition between two species for finite resources.

competitive exclusion principle led to the development of the niche concept and this is described in chapter 11. However, other factors also regulate herbivore population size and, particularly in the Serengeti, one control mechanism is predation, another is poaching (see section 4.16.1). The Serengeti supports the largest and most diverse populations of mammalian predators in the world.

4.11 | Predation

Predation is another density-dependent factor: the more abundant the prey, the easier they should be to catch. As the prey population decreases, each individual is more difficult to catch and the predator must expend more time and energy hunting.

Large carnivores are a conspicuous feature of

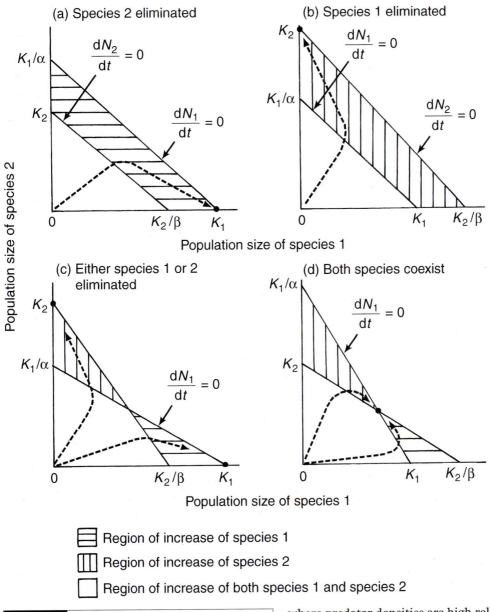

(a) Species 2 eliminated

(b) Species 1 eliminated

(c) Either species 1 or 2 eliminated

(d) Both species coexist

Population size of species 1

▤ Region of increase of species 1

▥ Region of increase of species 2

▢ Region of increase of both species 1 and species 2

Figure 4.23 Four possible outcomes of competition between two species. Dashed arrows indicate direction of change and final equilibrium points are indicated by a black dot (after Krebs 1994 adapted by permission of Addison-Wesley Educational Publishers, Inc.).

African savannas and are frequently observed feeding on herbivore carcasses. This suggests that they may play a significant role in regulating the population size of their prey species. This may be the case in small, highly managed game parks where predator densities are high relative to prey densities. Whether this is the case in an area as expansive as the Serengeti is a challenging research question.

Predators in the Serengeti area include lions (*Panthera leo*), hyenas, leopards (*Panthera pardus*), wild dogs and cheetahs (*Acinonyx jubatus*). In the Serengeti, two predators have been extensively studied: lions (Schaller 1972) and hyenas (Kruuk 1972). The spotted hyena (*Crocuta crocuta*) is the most common carnivore in the Serengeti. The

Table 4.6	The major prey species of lion, hyena, wild dog and cheetah in the Serengeti		
Lion	**Hyena**	**Wild dog**	**Cheetah**
Wildebeest	Wildebeest	Thomson's gazelle	Thomson's gazelle
Zebra	Zebra	Wildebeest	Grant's gazelle
Thomson's gazelle	Thomson's gazelle	Zebra	
Buffalo		Grant's gazelle	
Warthog		Warthog	
Hartebeest			
Topi			

Notes: The species listed accounted for the following percentages of their diet: lions 90% (Scheel and Packer 1995); hyenas 95% (Kruuk 1972); wild dogs 93% (Schaller 1972) and cheetah over 90% (Schaller 1972).

Table 4.7	Summary of hunting characteristics of four Serengeti predators				
	Hunting pack size, territorial behaviour	Hunting time and main habitat	Hunting technique	Chase distance	Scavengers
Lion	Usually small 1–3, territorial behaviour, some nomads	Nocturnal Woodlands	Stalking, concealment, short rush	Short	Yes
Hyena	Variable, large for zebra, small for wildebeest, territorial	Nocturnal Grasslands	Coursing, good stamina	Long	Yes
Wild dog	Usually large, cohesive, no territorial behaviour, home range restricted during denning	Diurnal Woodlands and grasslands	Coursing, high speed, good stamina	Long	Yes
Cheetah	Solitary, not territorial	Diurnal Grasslands	Fast, but brief coursing	Very short	No

major prey species taken by lion, hyena, cheetah and wild dog are listed in Table 4.6, and the hunting strategies employed by these predators also differ (Table 4.7).

Lions in the Serengeti adopt one of two life styles: residents which remain a year or more in one area, and nomads which wander widely, often following the migratory herds (Schaller 1972). Lions are very social animals living together in prides consisting of two to four adult males, several adult females and a number of young and cubs. As lions are not particularly fast and have little stamina, they use stealth to get close to their prey. They often hunt alone but other pride members may be nearby, watching the hunt. Lionesses hunt more than males. Lions also practice communal and co-operative hunting, particularly when stalking larger prey. Small prey animals are knocked down and usually killed with a bite around the neck or head. Larger prey are pulled to the ground after being attacked from behind. When the animal is on its side the lion lunges for the neck or nose and bites. Death usually results from strangulation. In some cases,

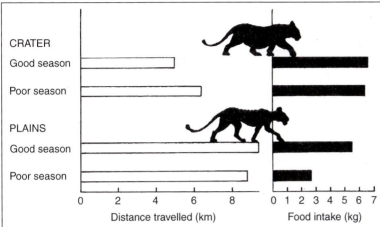

Figure 4.24 Average distance lions travelled per day in each habitat and their average food intake rates (shaded bars) in different seasons (redrawn from Hanby *et al.* (1995), with kind permission of University of Chicago Press, © 1995 by The University of Chicago).

the prey suffocates when the lion clamps its mouth over the prey's nose and holds it shut. Males usually feed before females and adults before cubs. The lions will stay with the kill until it is finished. Prodigious amounts of meat are consumed and may be as high as 25% of body weight (Schaller 1972).

In the Serengeti, seven species accounted for over 90% of the total lion kills observed by Scheel and Packer (1995) (Table 4.6). Lion predation on each prey species changes between seasons, across habitats and from year to year, and most of this variation can be attributed to the annual migrations made by the dominant prey species. The dominant prey species in the wet season is wildebeest, but this switches to gazelle in the dry season. In Ngorongoro Crater, prey biomass is more constant throughout the year, and migrations across the crater floor are much less pronounced than those in the Serengeti. Crater lions had higher rates of food intake than lions living on the Serengeti plains and travelled shorter distances per day to obtain more food (Hanby *et al.* 1995). Cub mortality on the plains is seasonal and higher than that in the crater. Hanby *et al.* (1995) concluded that lions on the plains live a harder life than their crater counterparts: food supplies are more ephemeral, water and den sites are scarcer (Figure 4.24).

Hyenas live in territorial clans of up to eighty animals. Within the clans, females dominate males and each clan has one den site. Hyena cubs may be born at any time of the year but there may be a birth peak during the wet season. The typical litter size is two. Hyenas kill most of their prey themselves but they also scavenge. Hunting behaviour varies depending on the prey. Zebra are hunted by packs of up to twenty-five hyena, whereas wildebeest are chased by only one to three hyena and Thomson's gazelle are usually killed by a solitary animal. Kruuk (1972) found that packs hunting zebra may form before the prey had been sighted. During the wildebeest calving period, hyena concentrate their hunting almost entirely on calves.

The African wild dog is one of the most endangered of the large mammalian predators. They live in packs with pack sizes ranging from 2 to 15 (Burrows 1995). An earlier study (Schaller 1972) recorded a pack size of 32 individuals. The home range of the pack is centred on a den when young are present. Otherwise the pack is very mobile, travelling widely with ranges overlapping with other packs; but packs rarely meet and there is little evidence to suggest that the pack is territorial. The scarcity of packs tends to space them out, and olfactory cues may help to avoid interpack contacts.

The feeding habits of the Serengeti dogs are seasonal with wildebeest dominating the diet during the wet season and Thomson's gazelle dominating when the wildebeest have left the plains in the dry season. Dogs hunt mainly in the morning and evening, leaving the den in single file. Hunting methods vary with prey species. Only one or two dogs chase a gazelle, and speeds may reach over $65\,\mathrm{km\,h^{-1}}$. The gazelle is caught by the side, rump or thigh and pulled down. A bite in the lower abdomen disembowels the prey. When hunting wildebeest, the dogs will single out a calf or yearling and several dogs will be required to pull it to the ground. Adults give pups priority at the kill, a behaviour pattern which contrasts with that of lion and hyena. Hunting success rate is very high.

Cheetah live alone or in small groups of usually less than four individuals. They live at low densities throughout their range; the reasons for which are not clear, particularly in the Serengeti where prey abundance is usually high. Laurenson (1995) confirmed that predation, mainly by lions, was a major cause of cheetah cub mortality, accounting for approximately 73% of deaths between birth and independence. This is an unusual example of a predator having a significant impact on the population size of another predator. The cheetah is an animal built for speed, and is therefore most commonly found in or near open country. In the Serengeti, cheetah range extensively, following the herds of Thomson's gazelle (Schaller 1972).

Out of a total of 261 cheetah kills observed, 91% of them were Thomson's gazelle. The other prey species included Grant's gazelle (*Gazella granti*), wildebeest, impala and hare (*Lepus* spp.) (Schaller 1972). Cheetah hunt alone and mainly during the day with most kills occurring in the morning and late afternoon. Cheetah utilise their great speed (up to 110 km h^{-1}) to close on their prey. When the prey starts to take evasive action, the cheetah has to slow down to follow the twists and turns made by its quarry. When close enough, the cheetah slaps the hind-quarters of the prey to bring it down and the prey is probably killed by suffocation with the cheetah gripping its throat.

Cheetah do not pursue their prey over long distances and the chase rarely exceeds 200–400 m. Cheetah select small fawns because of a very high hunting success rate and prefer to select gazelles in small herds. Selection also depends on prey size and distance from the cheetah. Cheetah feed rapidly probably because other predators frequently appropriate the kill. They have little in the way of defence against lions and hyenas and abandon their kills when threatened.

4.11.1 Resource partitioning and ecological separation in predators

When several predators operate within the same area, it is possible that competition for a limited prey resource might arise. One way this can be avoided is through **resource partitioning** or **ecological separation**. We can see from Tables 4.6 and 4.7 that four predators living in the Serengeti are separated in terms of major prey species, habitat and time of hunting (see also Figure 4.20). They also employ different hunting techniques which may bring about further separation.

Ecological separation is clearly not complete in both space and time. Hyena and lions share similar diets, and cheetah and wild dogs both hunt during the day. These predators often come into conflict, and there is often strong antipathy between them. Schaller (1972) distinguished between predators hunting predators for food and aggressive behaviour. Aggression occurs most often over kills, and lions and hyena steal kills from each other.

Both lion and hyena populations increased in the Serengeti following the elimination of rinderpest. This suggests that enhanced prey populations led to increased recruitment into the populations of these two major predators, and that this limitation was removed through the growth in the populations of those species previously affected by rinderpest.

4.11.2 Anti-predator tactics

Predators are endowed with killing weapons, and possess a range of hunting strategies to catch their prey. However, prey species are not without some tactics of their own which serve to thwart predators. Large herbivores, feeding on open grasslands, where food abundance is adequate for their needs, cannot hide easily from predators. They seek safety in numbers, increasing the chance of a predator being seen. The bulging eyes of these animals give them wide-angle vision, useful for spotting slight movements. Scent is also used. As long as a predator is visible, obviously resting and not hunting, plains animals often ignore it. A more threatening predator is watched carefully (Figure 4.25) and the herd alerted to its presence by snorting and foot-stamping. Plains species are

particularly cautious when entering a thicket where a predator may lie in wait. Wildebeest will stampede through riverine thickets and across a river in such a frenzy that some herd members may be drowned (Schaller 1972).

An approaching predator will usually cause a herd to run a few metres and then turn. This shows that keeping the predator in sight is extremely important to the prey. Once a chase begins, a herd on the run is confusing to a predator, but it also gives the predator a chance to detect the young or infirm animals; wild dogs, in particular, do this. Group defence is used by large herbivores such as buffalo. They will form a defensive circle, making use of their horns and large size.

We have seen that the young of prey species, in particular, are singled out by predators. Wildebeest calves are particularly vulnerable but have a number of adaptations to increase their chances of survival. They can walk within 5–10 minutes of being born and can run with the herd before they are a day old. The very tight synchronisation of calving in this species is another adaptation to reduce predation risks (see section 4.5). Saturation of the food supply will give some of the offspring in each cohort an increased chance of surviving. Sinclair (1977) also noted that, in the Serengeti, the time most wildebeest births occur, 07.30–10.30, is just after the morning hunting period of the main predator, the hyena. This gives the new-borns time to get up to running speed before the evening hunt.

Small herbivores (e.g. duiker (*Sylvicarpa grimmia*), dikdik), because of their food needs (see section 4.9.5) can not form groups. They use cryptic coloration, 'freezing' when alarmed, and hiding during the day to avoid detection. The presence of other individuals is a disadvantage in this strategy. Slightly larger herbivores (e.g. reedbuck) will stand still on seeing a predator but will run a short distance once they see that the predator has detected their presence. Impala execute a behaviour known as 'starburst' if ambushed by a predator. The group explodes in all directions in an attempt to confuse and distract the predator. Floodplain herbivores (e.g. lechwe (*Kobus leche*) and sitatunga (*Tragelaphus spekei*)) will run into the water and submerge completely when threatened.

Small size is a disadvantage when it comes to predation. We have seen that even the largest predators will take small animals when given an opportunity. Therefore an increase in body size is advantageous and the largest herbivores (elephants, rhinoceros (*Diceros bicornis*, *Ceratotherium simum*)) are infrequent targets of predators. However, an increase in body size also leads to greater interspecific competition for food (Sinclair 1983). The catholic tastes of predators also mean that prey species need to be adapted to avoid attack from a range of predators and therefore can not specialise.

4.11.3 Predator–prey relationships

Predation occurs when an organism, the predator, kills another organism, the prey and consumes it. Predation can be a major influence in the dynamics of animal populations. Our understanding of interactions between populations of predators

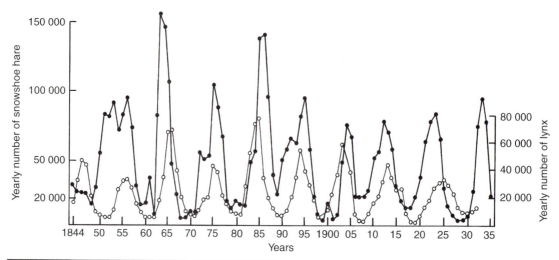

Figure 4.26 Changes in the abundance of the lynx (o) and snowshoe hare (●). The hare population has peaks approximately every 10 years, while the lynx population usually peaks 2 years later. Until 1903, data on hare numbers were based on sales of furs to the Hudson Bay Company, but from 1903 to 1935 data were compiled from replies to questionnaires. Lynx numbers were derived from fur returns until 1911 and then from a variety of sources (after MacLulich 1937).

and prey species initially came from ecosystems that are inherently simpler than those in Africa. The classic example is the North American lynx (*Lynx canadensis*) which preys almost exclusively on the snowshoe hare (*Lepus americanus*). It was noticed that an increase in the snowshoe hare population was followed soon afterwards by an increase in lynx numbers (Figure 4.26). This was first explained in terms of a predator–prey relationship as follows. If the prey population (snowshoe hare) increases, there will be more food for the predator (lynx). As a result the predator population increases. This increase in the predator population means more predation leading to a decline in the prey population size. This, in turn, is followed by a decline in the predator population. Consequently the populations of the predator and prey oscillate, out of phase.

More detailed analysis, however, demonstrated that declines in the snowshoe hare population were related more to their food supply than to heavy predation rates. At times of high snowshoe hare numbers, birth rates declined,

juvenile survivorship decreased, individual body weights and growth rates were low. Although shortage in the food supply may not result in starvation, the loss of body condition may well have made the hares more susceptible to predation. All these factors then combine to produce a collapse in the hare population, which is followed by a collapse in the predator population. In other words, the decline in the hare population was controlled more by food supply than predation (Smith *et al.* 1988).

As with competition, mathematical models were developed by Lotka (1925) and Volterra (1926) to describe predator–prey relationships; their equation for the prey population is:

$$\frac{dN}{dt} = r_1 N - \varepsilon PN$$

where r_1 is the intrinsic growth rate of the prey population, N is the size of the prey population, ε is a constant indicating the ability of the prey to escape predation and P is the size of the predator population. The equation for the predator population is:

$$\frac{dP}{dt} = -r_2 P + \theta NP$$

θ is a measure of the predator's skill in catching prey (Figure 4.27). As with the competition model, this predator–prey model is based on a number of assumptions: there is no immigration or emigration and there are no time lags; the growth of the

(a)

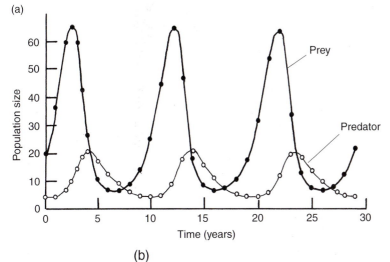

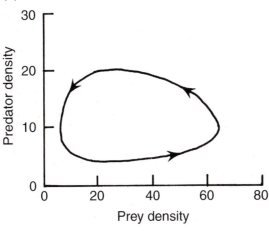

(b)

prey population is limited only by predation; and the predator is a specialist that can only persist if the prey population is present. It is also assumed that individual predators can consume an infinite number of prey and that predator and prey encounter one another randomly in an homogeneous environment.

These simple models provide an approximation of interactions between predator and prey populations in situations where one predator is feeding on one prey species in an environment that varies little between years. Even though the lynx and snowshoe hare show such striking oscillations in density with peaks every 9 to 10 years, it is probably food shortage during the winter that initiates the decline in hare numbers

and predation only plays a secondary role in further reducing the population size.

A distinct relationship between the size of predator and prey populations is even less likely to be found in savannas because of greater inter-annual variation in rainfall which largely determines food supply. Food supply probably exerts an even greater influence on prey populations than predation. Furthermore, Table 4.6 shows that the main predators in the Serengeti are not restricted to single prey species. Both these features would mask relationships between predator and prey numbers. Relationships are further complicated by consideration of other population-controlling factors such as inter- and intra-specific competition and disease.

In the Serengeti, with a population of some 2000–2500 lions and populations of over 2 000 000 prey animals, it would seem unlikely that lions would make a significant impact on the populations of herbivores. However, Sinclair (1995) concluded that the populations of topi, impala, Thomson's gazelle and warthog in the Serengeti may be predator-limited. The Serengeti ratio of 1 lion to 1000 prey animals contrasts with that found by Smuts (1978) in the Kruger National Park, South Africa where the ratio was 1:110. Smuts concluded that lions and the other predators present in the Kruger National Park were largely responsible for a decline in the wildebeest and zebra populations.

There are also some excellent case studies that show the impact predators can have on prey populations. One such example is the impact the predatory fish, the Nile perch (*Lates niloticus*), has had on fish populations in Lake Victoria (Box 5.6). Another example is provided by the ecosystem changes that followed the disappearance of large predators from an island created by the construction of the Panama Canal (Box 4.1).

Box 4.1 | Ecosystem responses to predator removal

The construction of the Panama Canal included the formation of Lake Gatun by damming the Chagres River. Within Lake Gatun, a small island (Barro Colorado Island, BCI) was created. Large predators, such as pumas and jaguars, require a large territory and, at 16 km², BCI is too small to support puma (*Felis concolor*) or jaguar (*Felis onca*) populations; though both these predators were present in the area prior to construction of the canal. A single adult jaguar needs 30–50 km² to maintain itself, and therefore the creation of Lake Gatun brought about the demise of large predators on BCI. This release from predation by large predators resulted in a dramatic increase in the populations of their prey species: agouti (*Dasyprocta* sp.), paca (*Agouti paca*) and coati (*Nasua narica*). Densities of these animals are now 8–20 times greater on BCI than on the nearby mainland.

These prey species subsist on the large seeds of canopy and subcanopy trees. Terborgh (1992) predicted that the increase in their number could be expected to lead to a reduction in the tree density of species that provide them with their seed diet. On islands in Lake Gatun which are even too small to support populations of the major seed predators, the vegetation has changed to one dominated by tree species which produce large seeds. Terborgh (1992) predicted a chain of interactions extending from the carnivores (pumas and jaguars) to the larger seed predators (agouti, paca and coati) and on to the large-seeded trees such as species of *Dipteryx*, *Protium* and *Scheelea*. A decline in trees producing large seeds could be compensated for by an increase in small-seeded trees whose seeds are eaten by mice, rats and tinamous. An increase in these animals could result in an increase in their predators: ocelot, owls and diurnal raptors. The absence of large predators on BCI has resulted in the abnormal abundance of seed-eating mammals and Terborgh (1992) has suggested that this change has the capacity to produce a major upheaval in the composition of species on the island. The full impact of the abundance of seed-eating mammals on the vegetation and fauna of BCI has yet to be fully determined.

4.12 | Density-independent mortality factors

Populations living in harsh environments rarely achieve high densities. In these situations, the population is usually regulated by abiotic factors such as weather, water supply or nutrients. For example, a population of desert plants may thrive following rain. However, if further rain is not forthcoming, the population may dwindle and this population crash will occur irrespective of the density of plants that might have developed. Density-independent factors tend to cause, often marked, shifts in population size, and a significant change in the carrying capacity might result. This contrasts with density-dependent factors that tend to act through natality and mortality rates to cause small fluctuations in population size around the carrying capacity of the area.

4.13 | Reproductive strategies and population growth

You may have noticed that there is a great difference in the way wildebeest and locusts allocate resources to reproduction. A wildebeest female is long-lived, usually produces one calf each year, nurtures it with milk and protects it from predators. The locust, on the other hand, is relatively short-lived, produces many offspring and provides no care to the nymphs. Ecologists, on observing these sorts of differences in reproductive strategies, proposed that organisms could be regarded as adapted to habitats that are either *r*-selecting or *K*-selecting (MacArthur and Wilson 1967; Pianka 1970). The terms, from the logistic growth equation, reflect the population growth strategies of the organisms at these two extremes.

In some environments, organisms exist with a population density close to the carrying capacity (*K*) for much of the year and are said to be subject to *K*-selection. These organisms usually live in an habitat that is either constant or predictably seasonal. Wildebeest provide a good example of a *K*-selected organism. Although, their environment is far from constant, it is predictable enough for them to have developed the strategy of migration to fulfil their food requirements. There is, however, often intense competition between *K*-selected organisms and this affects fecundity and survivorship.

In harsh, variable environments such as deserts, organisms tend to exist at population densities below the carrying capacity but have highly developed techniques to reproduce rapidly when environmental conditions improve. These organisms live in an environment that is either unpredictable or ephemeral. They live comparatively free of competitive pressure and have few strategies to cope with it. Survivorship is determined more by the environment and the ability the organism has to sequester limited resources.

Perennial organisms have to be able to survive the range of conditions that occur with the changing seasons, and therefore there is a tendency for them to be *K*-selected. *r*-selected species, with their need to reproduce rapidly during favourable conditions, tend to live less than one year. *K*-selected organisms concentrate their investment of resources in reproduction, producing fewer and larger offspring and may provide parental care. This contrasts with *r*-selected organisms which produce copious, small offspring with little or no parental care. The characteristics of *r*-selected and *K*-selected organisms are summarised in Table 4.8.

While insects generally would be regarded as *r*-selected and mammals as *K*-selected, there are some animals in both taxonomic groups which exhibit characteristics that make their allocation to one particular end of the *r*–*K* spectrum less clear cut. For example, rabbits are renowned for producing numerous offspring, and some insects, particularly the social insects, have a highly developed system of parental care.

Plants, too, can be arranged along an *r*–*K* continuum but Grime (1979) described a modified system more applicable to plants. Plant distributions are limited by **stresses** such as shortages of light, nutrients, or water and by **disturbances** such as fire, herbivory, pathogens, landslides or soil erosion. When stresses and disturbances are low, dense plant populations may develop. In this case, **competition** will become intense and a

Table 4.8 Summary of features of r-selected and K-selected organisms

	r-selection	K-selection
Climate	Variable and/or unpredictable; uncertain	Constant or predictable; seasonal
Mortality	Often catastrophic, non-directed, density-independent	More directed, density-dependent
Survivorship	Often type III (section 4.14.3; Figure 4.32)	Usually types I and II (section 4.14.3; Figure 4.32)
Population size	Variable in time, non-equilibrium; usually well below carrying capacity of environment; unsaturated communities or portions thereof; ecological vacuums; recolonisation each year	More constant in time, equilibrium; at or near carrying capacity of the environment; saturated communities; no recolonisation necessary
Intra- and inter-specific competition	Variable, often lax	Usually keen
Selection favours	1. Rapid development 2. High r_m (innate capacity to increase) 3. Early reproduction 4. Small body size 5. Simple reproduction	1. Slower development 2. Greater competitive ability, low fecundity 3. Delayed reproduction 4. Larger body size 5. Repeated reproduction
Length of life dispersal powers	Short, usually less than one year good dispersal powers	Longer, usually more than one year poor dispersal powers
Consequence	Productivity	Efficiency

Source: Pianka 1970.

competitive strategy would be advantageous. In harsh environments, **stress-tolerant** plants would tend to replace competitors. In environments that undergo frequent disturbances, plants with a capacity for rapid colonisation would tend to predominate. Grime (1979) therefore recognised three life-history strategies in plants: **competitors (C)**, **ruderals (R)** and **stress-tolerators (S)** (Table 4.9).

Grime suggested that ruderal and stress-tolerators correspond with the extremes of r- and K-selection respectively and that competitors occupy an intermediate position (Figure 4.28). Again we see that these three strategies (C–R–S) represent extremes of specialisation and adaptation, and in between will be many plants experiencing intermediate levels of stress and disturbance. In other words, there is a continuum of habitats from the most disturbed to the most

stressful, with habitats in the centre being the most desirable, but with plants occupying this central position facing the stiffest competition.

4.14 | Population age structure and life tables

4.14.1 Population age structure
Another basic feature of a population is its age structure. This is the number, or proportion, of organisms within the population of different age groups. Teeth, bones, claws (in mammals), scales and otoliths (in fish) often show annual incremental rings which can be used to age the organism in the same way as trees can be aged by counting annual rings. Tooth wear and their eruption sequence can also be used to age some animals. Once the ages of individuals in a

Table 4.9	Some characteristics of competitive, stress-tolerant and ruderal plants		
	Competitive	Stress-tolerant	Ruderal
Morphology			
Life forms	Herbs, shrubs and trees	Lichens, herbs, shrubs and trees	Herbs
Morphology of shoot	High, dense canopy of leaves. Extensive lateral spread above- and below-ground	Extremely wide range of growth forms	Small stature, limited lateral spread
Leaf form	Robust, often mesomorphic	Often small or leathery or needle-like	Various, often mesomorphic
Life-history			
Longevity of established phase	Long or relatively short	Long to very long	Very short
Longevity of leaves and roots	Relatively short	Long	Short
Leaf phenology	Well-defined peaks of leaf production coinciding with period(s) of maximum potential productivity	Evergreens, with various patterns of leaf production	Short phase of leaf production in period of high potential productivity
Phenology of flowering	Flowers usually produced after periods of maximum potential productivity	No general relationship between time of flowering and season	Flowers produced early in the life history
Frequency of flowering	Established plants usually flower each year	Intermittent flowering over a long life history	High frequency of flowering
Proportion of annual production devoted to seeds	Small	Small	Large
Perennation	Dormant buds and seeds	Stress-tolerant leaves and roots	Dormant seeds
Physiology			
Maximum potential relative growth rate	Rapid	Slow	Rapid
Response to stress	Rapid morphogenetic responses	Morphogenetic responses slow and small in magnitude	Rapid curtailment of vegetative growth, diversion of resources into flowering
Photosynthesis and uptake of mineral nutrients	Strongly seasonal, coinciding with continuous period of vegetative growth	Opportunistic, often uncoupled from vegetative growth	Opportunistic, coinciding with vegetative growth

Table 4.9 *(cont.)*

	Competitive	Stress-tolerant	Ruderal
Acclimation of photosynthesis, mineral nutrition and tissue hardiness to seasonal change in temperature, light and water supply	Weakly developed	Strongly developed	Weakly developed
Storage of photosynthate and mineral nutrients	Most photosynthate and mineral nutrients are rapidly incorporated into vegetative structure but a proportion is stored and forms the capital for expansion of growth in the next growing season	Storage systems in leaves, stems and/or roots	Confined to seeds
Other features			
Litter	Copious, often persistent	Sparse, sometimes persistent	Sparse, not usually persistent
Palatability to unspecialised herbivores	Various	Low	Various, often high

Source: Grime 1979.

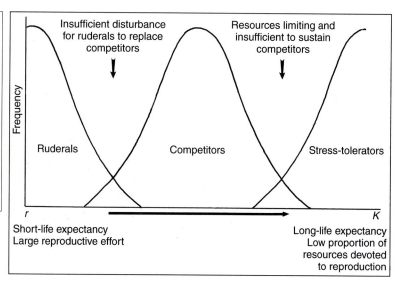

Figure 4.28 Distribution of ruderals, competitors and stress-tolerators along an *r*–*K* continuum. With a high frequency of disturbance, ruderals dominate, but where disturbance is rare and resources are abundant a competitive strategy is advantageous. A stress-tolerant strategy is appropriate where resources are scarce or conditions harsh (after Grime 1979 with kind permission from John Wiley & Sons Limited).

Figure 4.29 Idealised age pyramids for (a) stable, (b) increasing and (c) declining populations. Populations with high proportions of young or old organisms are indicative of increasing and decreasing populations respectively. However, this conclusion will only hold if survivorship is not markedly different between the age classes.

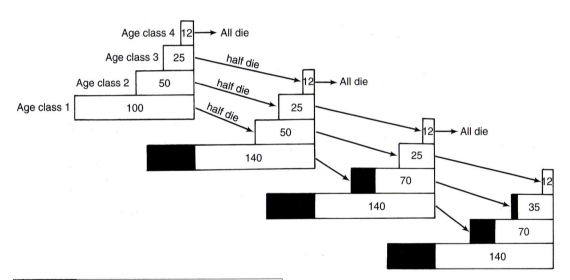

Figure 4.30 Age pyramids for a theoretical bird population showing change in pyramid shape as a result of increased egg survival over four generations. In the model, half the individuals in each age class die (adapted from Whittaker 1975).

population are known, an age pyramid can be constructed.

The age distribution influences both natality and mortality. Usually a population with a very high proportion of young individuals will be increasing, whereas one with more old individuals will be decreasing. In a stable population, the age structure tends to be more even (Figure 4.29).

We will return to an analysis of age pyramids when we consider human populations in chapter 13. Figure 4.30 shows how an age pyramid relates to natality and mortality. In this example, the input to the population is equal to the loss and therefore the population is stable. Consider what would happen to the shape of the pyramid if egg losses were reduced to zero for just one breeding year. Similarly, what would happen if the mortality rate of birds aged 1 and 2 years declined? One way of analysing how populations are changing through time is to construct a life table.

Table 4.10 Life table for tsetse flies (*Glossina morsitans*) in Zimbabwe (see Box 4.3)

Age in days (x)	n_x (number alive at age x)	d_x (number of deaths by age x + 1)	l_x (survivorship at beginning of age class)	L_x (mean number of individuals living in each age class)	m_x (mortality rate per 1000 individuals)	s_x (survival rate)	T_x	e_x (life expectancy)
0	1000	25	1.000	987.5	0.025	0.975	9470.0	94.7
0–10	975	130	0.975	910.0	0.133	0.867	8482.5	87.0
11–20	845	45	0.845	822.5	0.053	0.947	7572.5	89.6
21–30	800	40	0.800	780.0	0.050	0.950	6750.0	84.4
31–40	760	30	0.760	745.0	0.039	0.961	5970.0	78.6
41–50	730	40	0.730	710.0	0.055	0.945	5225.0	71.6
51–60	690	35	0.690	672.5	0.051	0.949	4515.0	65.4
61–70	655	70	0.655	620.0	0.107	0.893	3842.5	58.7
71–80	585	70	0.585	550.0	0.120	0.880	3222.5	55.1
81–90	515	55	0.515	487.5	0.107	0.893	2672.5	51.9
91–100	460	65	0.460	427.5	0.141	0.859	2185.0	47.5
101–110	395	80	0.395	355.0	0.203	0.797	1757.5	44.4
111–120	315	70	0.315	280.0	0.222	0.778	1402.5	44.5
121–130	245	30	0.245	230.0	0.122	0.878	1122.5	45.8
131–140	215	20	0.215	205.0	0.093	0.907	892.5	41.5
141–150	195	45	0.195	172.5	0.231	0.769	687.5	35.2
151–160	150	25	0.150	137.5	0.167	0.833	515.0	34.3
161–170	125	20	0.125	115.0	0.160	0.840	377.5	30.2
171–180	105	10	0.105	100.0	0.095	0.905	262.5	25.0
181–190	95	40	0.095	75.0	0.421	0.579	162.5	17.1
191–200	55	20	0.055	45.0	0.364	0.636	87.5	15.9
201–210	35	15	0.035	27.5	0.429	0.571	42.5	12.1
211–220	20	15	0.020	12.5	0.750	0.250	15	7.5
221–230	5	5	0.005	2.5	1.000	0	2.5	5.0
231–240	0	0	0	0			0	

Source: Data provided by R.J. Phelps, University of Zimbabwe.

4.14.2 Life tables

The life insurance industry uses life tables to calculate premiums based on how long it is likely that a customer of a particular age and sex will continue to live, that is their life expectancy. Life expectancy is of obvious relevance to providers of life insurance, but is not particularly useful to ecologists studying animal populations. Ecologists, however, use life tables to investigate the number of organisms of a particular age in a population and the number, in each age group,

that dies and the mortality rate. It is usual to express the life table as a proportion of the population and this is known as a **cohort**. In Table 4.10 we follow a cohort of 1000 tsetse flies (Boxes 4.2 and 4.3). The first column gives the age interval, and the second the number of flies remaining alive at the start of the next age interval. The column headed d_x shows how many organisms died during the corresponding age interval. L_x gives the average number of individuals living between the two age intervals and is given by:

$$L_x = \int_x^{x+1} l_x \cdot dx$$

but, if the age class is small:

$$L_x = \frac{l_x + l_{(x+1)}}{2}$$

where l_x is the number of individuals in one age class and $(l_{(x+1)})$ is the number of individuals in the following age class. The **mortality rate per age interval** (m_x) is the proportion of individuals of age x dying by age $x+1$ and is given by:

$$m_x = d_x / \text{number alive at age } x$$

The mortality rate per age interval is an **age specific death rate** and is a more useful statistic than the **crude death rate**. The crude death rate is simply the number of individuals dying in a population regardless of age. Population growth is obviously going to be affected more by the death of pre-reproductive and reproductive individuals than it is by the death of post-reproductive individuals. Therefore the age specific death rate is a useful index. It is defined as the quotient of the number of organisms of age x dying in a short interval of time divided by the number of individuals of age x that were alive at the start of that interval of time.

Box 4.2 | The tsetse fly and trypanosomaisis

The tsetse (pronounced tetsee) fly occurs throughout tropical Africa and is the vector of trypanosomaisis (sleeping sickness), a disease endemic to sub-Saharan Africa, that affects cattle and humans. *Trypanosoma* strains also occur in wild game populations. There are over twenty species of tsetse fly belonging to the genus *Glossina*, and, because of their economic significance, they have been subject to intensive scientific study. The adult fly feeds only on blood, sucked from a wide range of reptiles and mammals: crocodiles, antelope, mice, humans and elephants. The fly has a physiological mechanism which rapidly reduces the water content of its blood meal, thereby facilitating flight after each meal.

The life cycle of the fly is rather unusual. Fertilisation of a female occurs only once, and sperm are stored in special glands called spermathecae. At ovulation, a single egg passes into the uterus where it is fertilised. The egg hatches within the uterus and the larva is nourished from a milk gland. During the three larval instars, no excretion takes place and nitrogenous wastes accumulate in the hind gut. The female produces just one well-nourished larva at a time, and soon after the larva is extruded it buries itself and pupates. The pupa hatches into an adult fly. The female will then start to rear another larva using the stored sperm to fertilise the next egg.

Trypanosomiasis is caused by species of *Trypanosoma*, a protozoan. The parasites pass from the blood of an infected mammalian host to the tsetse fly as it feeds. The parasites are carried into the gut where they multiply. They then migrate to the salivary gland where further multiplication occurs. The parasites are injected into another mammalian host along with an anti-coagulant contained in the fly's saliva. The protozoan parasite lives in the blood plasma of humans, causing sleeping sickness. In cattle, another species causes a disease known as *nagana*.

Although antelopes and a range of other African wild animals are infested with trypanosomes, they do not seem to show the same serious ill effects exhibited by humans and cattle. The disease has severely restricted the spread of cattle-ranching in Africa, and has therefore, inadvertently, played an important role in African wildlife conservation.

Table 4.11	Life table of the wildebeest population in Umfolozi Game Reserve, South Africa				
Age in years (x)	l_x (survivors at beginning of age class)	d_x (numbers of deaths in each age class)	m_x (mortality rate per 1000 individuals	b_x (Fertility)	$l_x b_x$ (Number of young born)
0	1000	300	0.30	0.00	0
2	700	130	0.19	0.12	84
4	570	260	0.46	0.92	524
6	310	140	0.45	0.92	285
8	170	30	0.18	0.92	156
10	140	50	0.36	0.92	129
12	90	40	0.44	0.92	83
14	50	30	0.60	0.92	46
16	20	20	1.00	0.92	18
18	10	20		0.00	0
					$\Sigma = 1325$

Source: Attwell 1982.

Let us look at a life table for a wildebeest population, not in the Serengeti, but in Umfolozi Game Reserve in South Africa. In Table 4.11 the cohort size is 1000 wildebeest, the starting population. The life table then follows these 1000 animals through a series of age classes and records the number dying in each age class (d_x). The number surviving into the next age class is obtained by subtracting the number dying during that age class. Of the original 1000 wildebeest, 300 die before the age 2, leaving 700 in the second age class. The proportion dying (m_x) is a quotient of the number dying and the number surviving. This quotient gives the mortality rate in each group. This is an important measure. Notice that, although fewer animals die towards the end of the animal's lifespan, the proportion dying rises. These tables show the age classes where wildebeest are most vulnerable.

4.14.3 Survivorship curves

Both tsetse flies and wildebeest have a poor survival rate in the very early part of their lives (Figure 4.31). In the case of wildebeest this is probably due to high rates of predation. Tsetse flies have a higher survival rate in the middle phase of their life history and early on in their life than do wildebeest.

Three types of survivorship curves have been recognised (Figure 4.32). Type I shows a curve of an organism in which the probability of death is low in early life but increases late in life. This curve is typical of animals which provide significant parental care. The Type III survivorship curve is typical of organisms in which mortality is high during the young stages. Organisms that illustrate this type of survivorship include sessile marine organisms which have a free-swimming larva. Larva mortality is very high, but survivorship improves significantly once larvae manage to settle. In a Type II survivorship curve, age specific mortality remains constant throughout the life of the organism.

4.14.4 Age specific natality

The addition of young to a population is known as **recruitment**. Age specific natality can also be considered using life tables (Table 4.11). The cohort of 1000 wildebeest produced 1325 offspring. Therefore the net reproductive rate (R_0) is 1.325. Each wildebeest therefore, left, on average 1.325 offspring, and we can conclude that this population is expanding. Attwell (1982) showed that a later cohort of the wildebeest population in Umfolozi Game Reserve had a net reproductive rate of 0.773, indicating that, at this time, the

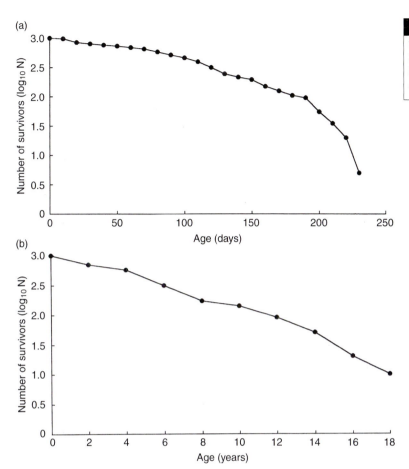

(a)

(b)

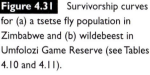

Figure 4.31 Survivorship curves for (a) a tsetse fly population in Zimbabwe and (b) wildebeest in Umfolozi Game Reserve (see Tables 4.10 and 4.11).

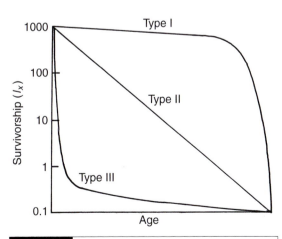

Figure 4.32 Three contrasting survivorship curves of hypothetical populations. Number of survivors is on a logarithmic scale to show the pattern in young organisms more clearly.

population was declining. This example demonstrates that life table analysis has some useful practical applications in managing populations. In a situation where a population is being managed sustainably, hunting pressure could be increased when R_o exceeds one and curtailed whenever it fell below one.

4.15 | Key factor analysis

In animals which have a number of stages to their life history – a feature particularly common among insects – it would be useful to be able to identify the key factors that regulate the population. This can be done quite simply for animals that do not have overlapping generations, that is one discrete generation per year. Key factor analysis assesses the mortality that occurs between each stage of the life cycle. For example, from egg

Box 4.3 | Calculation of the tsetse fly life table

The numbers of flies alive at the end of each age class form the raw data of the life table.
The number of flies dying in each age class is given by:
$d_x = n_x - n_{(x+1)}$
Therefore:
$d_0 = n_0 - n_1 = 1000 - 975 = 25$
$d_1 = n_1 - n_2 = 975 - 845 = 130$
$d_2 = n_2 - n_3 = 845 - 800 = 45$ etc.

The survivorship values (l_x) are given by: l_x / l_0.
Therefore:
$l_0 = l_0/l_0 = 1000/1000 = 1.000$
$l_1 = l_1/l_0 = 975/1000 = 0.975$
$l_2 = l_2/l_0 = 845/1000 = 0.845$ etc.

The mean number of individuals living in each age class (L_x) is given, when the age interval is small, by:
$$L_x = \frac{l_x + l_{(x+1)}}{2}$$
Therefore:
$L_0 = (l_0 + l_1)/2 = (1000 + 975)/2 = 987.5$
$L_1 = (l_1 + l_2)/2 = (975 + 845)/2 = 910$
$L_2 = (l_2 + l_3)/2 = (845 + 800)/2 = 822.5$ etc.

The proportion of individuals of age x dying by age $x + 1$ is given by:
$m_x = d_x/n_x$
Therefore:
$m_0 = d_0/n_0 = 25/1000 = 0.025$
$m_1 = d_1/n_1 = 130/975 = 0.133$
$m_2 = d_2/n_2 = 45/845 = 0.053$ etc.

The survival rate is the proportion of individuals of age x surviving to age $x + 1$ and is given by:
$s_0 = l_1 = 0.975$
$s_1 = l_2/s_0 = 0.845/0.975 = 0.867$
$s_2 = l_3/s_0.s_1 = 0.800/0.975 \times 0.867 = 0.946$
$s_3 = l_4/s_0.s_1.s_2 = 0.760/(0.975 \times 0.867 \times 0.947) = 0.950$ etc.

The life expectancy (e_x) is the expectation of further life of individuals age x.
first calculate:
$$T_x = \sum_{l=0}^{x} Lx$$
$T_0 = (L_0 + L_1 + L_2 + \cdots + L_{22} + L_{23}) = (987.5 + 910 + 822.5 + \cdots + 12.5 + 2.5)/1000$
$T_1 = (L_1 + L_2 + L_3 + \cdots + L_{22} + L_{23}) = (910 + 822.5 + \cdots + 12.5 + 2.5)/1000$
$T_2 = (L_2 + L_3 + L_4 + \cdots + L_{22} + L_{23}) = (822.5 + \cdots + 12.5 + 2.5)/1000$ etc.
T_x has no ecological significance but it facilitates calculation of e_x. Life expectancies are expressed as number of age classes; multiply by age interval (10 days) to convert to days:
$e_x = T_x/n_x$
$e_0 = T_0/n_0 = 9470/1000 = 9.47$
$e_1 = T_1/n_1 = 8482/975 = 8.70$
$e_2 = T_2/n_2 = 7572.5/845 = 8.96$ etc.

to first larval instar, from first larval instar to the second, from larva to pupa and from pupa to adult. This is done by utilising the information in a life table. The number of survivors in each life history stage is tabulated and the first k value calculated:

$$k_1 = \log N_E - \log N_{L1}$$

where: k_1 is the instantaneous mortality coefficient for the first transition stage in the life cycle, from egg to first instar larva; N_E is the number of eggs produced; and N_{L1} is the number of first instar larvae produced. The k-values for the entire life cycle can be summed to give a total generation mortality, K (this symbol should not be confused with the K used to denote carrying capacity).

$$K = k_1 + k_2 + k_3 \cdots + \cdots k_n$$

The k-values can be plotted against time, and the one contributing most to the animal's total mortality can be identified visually. The next stage is to attempt to determine what causes the mortality at each of the stages in which key factors appear to be operating. By plotting k-values against the population density of the life history stage on which they operate it is possible to determine whether the factor is density-dependent or not. This technique is particular useful in studying the population dynamics of insect pests, and can lead to efficient control measures centred on the life history stage most at threat from natural mortality.

4.16 | Conservation of African wildlife

The national parks and wildlife reserves in Africa contain an extraordinary diversity of large mammals and birds. This diversity has an enormous potential to attract tourists and bring in foreign exchange, so desperately needed by many African countries. Protecting and conserving this resource has proved to be an enormous challenge for wildlife ecologists. Regrettably, the main threat to wildlife has been through poaching. However, political interference and inadequate

knowledge about how these ecosystems function have also played a role.

4.16.1 Poaching

A marked increase in human settlement has been documented along the western boundaries of both the Serengeti National Park and the Mara Reserve (Dublin 1986). Similarly, Hanks (1973) showed that dense human populations also surrounded the national parks and reserves in Zimbabwe. These large human populations have resulted from population growth rates as high as 3.5% per annum and from immigration. The increase in population along the Serengeti border has, in recent times, approached 15% per year (Sinclair 1995). This large population on the borders of the Serengeti, coupled with a decline in anti-poaching activities, resulted in an invasion of the northern and western Serengeti by poachers. The rhinoceros (*Diceros bicornis*) population was reduced by 50% in one year (1977). By 1980, the population in the Serengeti was decimated with only the occasional sighting of an animal that had strayed in from Kenya (Sinclair 1995).

The dramatic decline in buffalo numbers (Figure 4.7) from the mid-1970s to the mid-1980s has been attributed to poaching for meat. Some 50% of the elephant population disappeared from the Serengeti between 1984 and 1986. Some of these animals migrated to the Mara Reserve where poaching was less intense, but the other missing animals were probably killed for ivory. The elephant poaching rate slowed when ivory sales were declared illegal in Burundi, and ceased entirely when, in 1989, the world ban on the ivory trade was imposed (Sinclair 1995).

4.16.2 Elephants, humans and the ivory trade

Management of elephant populations in Africa has been fraught with controversy (Figure 4.33). In the 1960s and 1970s ecologists were concerned that elephant populations in national parks were too high and recommended that numbers be reduced (Laws 1970). The expansion of the human population throughout Africa has resulted in the compression of elephant populations into smaller and smaller areas, with consequent increases in

Figure 4.33   Elephant herd in Hwange National Park, Zimbabwe (Photo: Patrick Osborne).

elephant densities. This has had a significant impact on the vegetation within wildlife reserves and national parks. Increased elephant densities during the recovery of herbivore populations from rinderpest in the Serengeti led to drastic declines in tree cover, with some densely wooded areas being changed into savanna and even grasslands, all within the space of twenty years (Lamprey *et al.* 1967). More recently, a savage reduction in elephant numbers in the Serengeti, together with high grazing pressure has brought about a recovery in the woodland vegetation (see section 4.17.1).

Elephant numbers declined in many African countries through poaching for ivory. This led, in 1989, to a comprehensive ban on all international trade in elephant products and a precipitous decline in the price of ivory followed. As a result, elephant poaching has been reduced and ele-

phant populations are recovering. Some countries (particularly Zimbabwe and South Africa) opposed the ban as profits from trade in elephant products were being used to fund wildlife conservation efforts. In these countries, poaching was kept under control and dense elephants populations were converting the savanna woodlands in the game sanctuaries into grasslands. Annual elephant culls had become routine, and entire family herds were culled in an attempt to reduce distress among the elephant population. However, recent research has shown that elephants are able to communicate over great distances using a complex, infrasonic (sound at frequencies inaudible to the human ear) language. Therefore culling programmes may cause significant disturbance in game reserves and changes in elephant behaviour. In 1998, restrictions on trade in ivory were relaxed for countries in Southern Africa. In many parts of Africa, the conflict between local people and wildlife is probably the most serious ecological problem adjacent to nature reserves (see section 14.3).

4.17 | Ecosystem dynamics and ecological models

4.17.1 Ecosystems dynamics

We have seen that a large number of factors interact in determining the size of animal populations: rainfall affects food supply, inter- and intraspecific competition determines how much of the resource the species will be able to utilise and predation, diseases and accidents take their toll.

We have looked at simple models with respect to population growth, competition and predation that, given a particular starting-point, will predict one outcome. The logistic population growth model is an example of such a model and, given the parameters required for the model, it will predict K, the carrying capacity. These models are called **deterministic**. The size of biological populations, as we have seen, is not determined in such a simple way. Rainfall varies from year to year, and there is a chance that, as the population grows, predation rates will increase or reproductive output might decline. If ecological modelling is to be more realistic we need to incorporate into it the **probability** of such events occurring. **Stochastic** models do this.

Let us look at some examples of why it is inadequate to use deterministic models in predicting animal population sizes. If we are to manage wildlife areas in a sustainable fashion, we need to consider the impact of management options. We will do this by describing a model developed to test alternative management policies in the Serengeti (Hilborn *et al.* 1995).

Savanna systems are dynamic and a small perturbation in the system may bring about marked changes in the populations of the dominant species. Furthermore, these changes may have far-reaching repercussions on the rest of the system and have severe implications for resource managers. The cause of these perturbations may be biotic, abiotic or a combination of the two. For example, in the Serengeti, the percentage of lion cubs surviving into their second year was significantly lower between 1966 and 1969 than it was between 1974 and 1977. It has been suggested that this difference was due to shortages of food.

When prey is short, there is no food left for the cubs after the older animals have eaten. This food shortage resulted from low rainfall affecting grass production and, hence, herbivore numbers. A food web for a few of the mammals in the Serengeti is shown in Figure 4.34.

Sinclair (1979a) produced a simple model to demonstrate the chain reaction that reverberated through the Serengeti ecosystem following the control of rinderpest (Figure 4.35). The immediate result was enhanced survival of wildebeest yearlings. The wildebeest population increased from about 250 000 in 1961 to 500 000 in 1967. When the wildebeest leave the plains at the end of the wet season, they move as large herds and remove up to 90% of the initial standing crop. This obviously reduces the quantity of moribund grass at the end of the growing season and the amount of fuel for fires. Furthermore, grazing intensity is often patchy and this may establish a mosaic, with some areas hardly grazed, and therefore fire-prone, interspersed with heavily grazed areas forming fire breaks.

Increased grazing on the plains also led to more herbs, the favoured diet of Grant's gazelle, and this in turn led to more cheetah, the main predator of gazelle. In the woodlands, less grass reduced the frequency of fire and buffalo numbers. The reduction in fire allowed more small trees to survive, which favoured giraffe. The larger population of giraffe caused a decline in large trees. The ecosystem ramifications of controlling one disease were great indeed. Note that this model does not include the effects of elephants (Figure 4.35).

The Serengeti–Mara ecosystem, like many savanna areas throughout the world, has experienced major vegetation changes in its recent history. Lamprey *et al.* (1967) concluded that tree reduction in the Serengeti was caused by an increase in the elephant population, and that the recovery of the woodlands was hindered by fire. Changes in the size of large herbivore populations have significant impacts on the function of ecosystems as a whole. For example, during the period of expansion of the Serengeti wildebeest population, following the control of rinderpest, the prevalence of fire declined in all regions of the Serengeti.

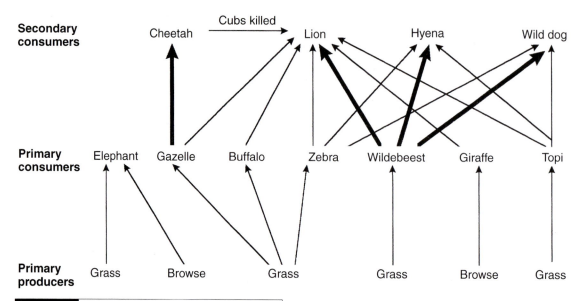

Figure 4.34 A simplified grazing food web based around some of the dominant herbivores and predators found in the Serengeti. Note that there are no natural predators of elephants and that predators consume a variety of herbivores. The food web is far from complete both in terms of the species included and the interconnections between them. The heavy arrows indicate strong predator–prey linkages.

These changes and more recent ones, have been documented by Dublin (1995). She demonstrated that there has been an alternation between open grassland and dense woodland and back to open grassland over the past century. In other words, the vegetation of this region is not stable but may be subject to long-term changes initiated through perturbations. At the start of the twentieth century, early explorers described the Serengeti area as an open grassland with lightly wooded patches. By the 1940s, the area had become densely wooded. In the 1950s, the woodlands began a rapid decline and reverted to grasslands.

Woodlands in the northern Serengeti recovered in the mid-1980s to early 1990s, but the opposite occurred in the Masai Mara to the north, where significant loss of woodland has been documented. The major difference between these two areas at this time was the comparative density of elephants. The Serengeti elephant population declined by 81% from 2460 in 1970 to 467 in 1986.

It is estimated that 1500 were killed by poachers and 400–500 moved into the comparative safety of the Masai Mara (Dublin 1986).

Elephants in high densities can have a pronounced impact on woody vegetation. They eat woody vegetation of all sorts and push over trees and strip the bark from them. In the Masai Mara, elephants opened up passageways through *Croton* thickets. Dense grass swards developed, but herbivores were kept away through fear of predators hidden in the remaining thickets. These passageways, in the dry season, consequently became the opposite of firebreaks and, when they burnt, some of the adjacent trees and shrubs were also destroyed. With each fire, the area of thicket declined. Elephants in the Masai Mara also fed on saplings and this has significantly hindered the rate of woodland recovery. Thus, although fire was necessary to change the vegetation from woodland to grassland, elephants held it in this state. This led Dublin *et al.* (1990) to propose that there are two stable states: woodland and grassland and that the latter is maintained by herbivores.

This contrasts with the conclusion of Lamprey *et al.* (1967): elephants were the primary cause of woodland degradation and fire was responsible for maintaining the area as grassland. Other workers (see Frost and Robertson 1987) have concluded that fire alone is both the cause of woodland loss and the agent responsible for

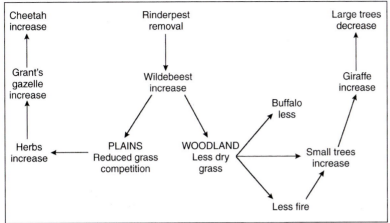

Figure 4.35 The response of various components of the Serengeti ecosystem to rinderpest control (redrawn from Sinclair and Norton-Griffiths (1979), with kind permission of University of Chicago Press, © 1979 by The University of Chicago).

maintaining grasslands. Belsky (1984) from her study, in the Serengeti, on the role of browsers in woodland regeneration, concluded that these animals were found to be as important as fire in reducing the mean height of trees whether or not the plots were also burned.

4.17.2 Ecosystems models

Ecosystem models are clearly required if we are to understand and be able to predict the outcome of interactions such as those between trees, fire, elephants, browsers, grazers and grasses in the Serengeti or elsewhere. Hilborn and Sinclair (1979) produced simulation models to predict herbivore and predator populations in the Serengeti, and Norton-Griffiths (1979) developed a model to investigate the influence of grazing, browsing and fire on vegetation in the Serengeti. These models were developed to aid understanding research results rather than to provide management guidance. Models which address management issues such as the effects of anti-poaching patrols, controlled burning, tourist use and culling programs are also needed.

Hilborn *et al.* (1995), in developing their model, first considered the design criteria: the issues it should address, the evaluation of the performance of management policies and the management actions that should be considered (Table 4.12). The Serengeti ecosystem was divided into 10 areas selected to reflect the annual migratory pattern of wildebeest, zebra and Thomson's gazelle and to include areas in which human

impact on the system was significant. The model was further simplified by considering a year to consist of an 8-month wet season and a 4-month dry season.

The model began in 1960, when serious scientific research into the area was initiated and the eruption of wildebeest populations began. The model consisted of five sub-models: vegetation, ungulates, predators, inside park and outside park. We will only look, in detail, at the construction of part of the vegetation sub-model (grass production) and provide some information of what went into the other sub-models.

The key variables in the vegetation sub-model were:

- $\text{Rain}_{\text{dry:}y}$ = dry season rain in year y in mm
- $\text{Rain}_{\text{wet:}y}$ = wet season rain in year y in mm
- $\text{Grazed}_{y,i}$ = percentage of area grazed in dry season, year y, area i
- $\text{Burned}_{y,i}$ = percentage of area burned in year y, area i
- $\text{Tallgrass}_{y,i}$ = amount of dry season grass in year y, area i (kg ha^{-1})
- $\text{Green}_{y,i}$ = amount of dry season new growth in year y, area i (kg ha^{-1})
- $\text{Woods}_{y,i}$ = percentage of area i that is woodland in year y
- $\text{Cultiv}_{y,i}$ = percentage of area i that is cultivated in year y
- Wild_y = total wildebeest population in year y (in thousands)
- $\text{pburn}_{y,i}$ = the proportion of area i not in cultivation that is burned in year y

The ungulate sub-model considered the migratory species (wildebeest, zebra and Thomson's gazelle) and elephant, buffalo and others ('brown animal': topi, impala, hartebeest). The predator

Table 4.12	Lists of issues to be addressed, performance indicators and management actions to be included in a model to assess management policies in the Serengeti		

Issues	Performance indicators	Management actions
Population changes in humans	Animal population sizes	Poaching control enforcement
Visitor capacity	Tourist numbers	Hotel construction
Adjacent land use	Tourist satisfaction	Livestock vaccination
Hunting and poaching	Revenue to national parks	Burning and fire control
Climate change	Employment	Road construction
Disease outbreak	Vegetation condition	Adjacent land uses
Vegetation change	Illegal harvest	Reintroductions
Population dynamics of	Encroachment on national	Improvement of water supply
herbivores and carnivores	parks land	and other infrastructure
Economics and cash flow	Livestock per family	
International tourism	Local population health care	
Species loss	Household income	

Source: Hilborn *et al.* 1995.

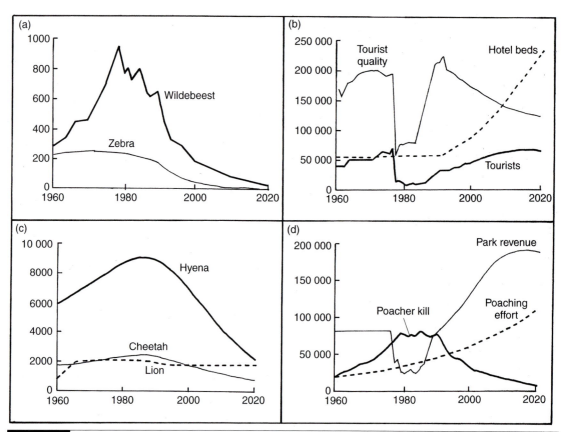

Figure 4.36 Output from a computer model of the Serengeti ecosystem in which current management practices and poaching levels are maintained. (a) Wildebeest and zebra population numbers, both in thousands. (b) Number of tourist nights, number of hotel beds and tourism quality. (c) Numbers of hyena, lion and cheetah. (d) Poacher kills, park revenue and poaching effort (redrawn from Hilborn *et al.* (1995), with kind permission of University of Chicago Press, © 1995 by The University of Chicago).

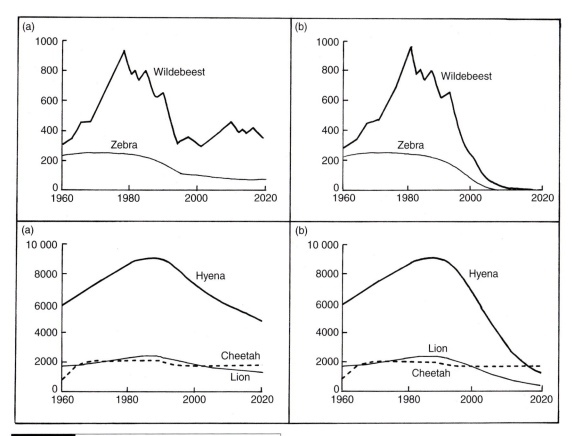

Figure 4.37 Outputs from a computer model of the Serengeti ecosystem in which (a) anti-poaching patrols are increased fivefold and (b) anti-poaching patrols are nearly eliminated. (redrawn from Hilborn et al. (1995), with kind permission of University of Chicago Press, © 1995 by The University of Chicago).

sub-model had two major components: calculation of the number of prey animals killed and the population dynamics of the predator.

The inside park sub-model dealt with tourism and considered issues such as tourist crowding and satisfaction. Tourist satisfaction is driven by the number and diversity of animals seen. For example, tourists will generally rate cheetah as more desirable than wildebeest and therefore the tourist model rates 10000 wildebeest as being equal to one cheetah. The outside park sub-model considered poacher effort and kill, human population growth and changes in land-use. It was this component of the model that really dis-

tinguished this model of a wildlife reserve from previous attempts.

The model was used to explore six scenarios: current management actions maintained, increased anti-poaching patrols, reduced anti-poaching patrols, poor rainfall, human population decline and a repeat of a rinderpest epidemic. Outputs from four of these scenarios are shown in Figures 4.36 and 4.37. Note that in the model, where current management activities were modelled, the increase in animal populations that occurred between 1960 and 1990 is 'predicted' by the model. This is how models can be verified and evaluated; by running them through a period where the results are known. Note, too, the marked fall in predicted hyena populations as predicted wildebeest populations fell in the late 1990s.

Under the scenario of increased anti-poaching patrols, a dramatic reduction in poacher kill results, and this slows down the decline in ungulate populations (Figure 4.37). The converse results if anti-poaching patrols are almost completely disbanded. Note, in this scenario, the greater decline in wildebeest, zebra, lion and hyena populations. A decline in the human population, a situation which could result from the distressingly high incidence of AIDS in this part of Africa (see section 13.6.1), has a similar impact on animal populations as an increase in anti-poaching activities. This clearly illustrates the desperate need to involve people living in and around wildlife reserves in their management and reject the exclusive policies that might have been followed in the past. This model attempts to do so by incorporating the role of humans both as inhabitants of, and visitors to, the area.

4.18 | Chapter summary

1. Savannas are grasslands with scattered trees that cover one-fifth of the land surface of the world and approximately half of the African continent. The savanna areas of Africa, South America and Australia have a long dry, cool season and a short hot, wet season.

2. Seasonality is a distinctive feature of savannas, and the plants and animals that inhabit savannas not only are adapted to survive the seasonal extremes, but also may even require such variations to maintain community structure.

3. Savannas are regularly burnt, and their vegetation structure is maintained through burning. Savanna plants are adapted to fire. Trees and shrubs have a thick and insulating, corky bark and can sprout from underground organs. Grasses sprout after a fire and will continue normal growth providing that soil moisture is adequate.

4. Density is defined as number of organisms per unit area. Estimates of crude density include habitat areas that may never be utilised, whereas ecological density is an expression of the number of organisms per unit area of habitat actually used.

5. Large herbivores may be divided into those which feed on grass and herbs (grazers) and those which feed on woody vegetation (browsers). Herbivores in the Serengeti exhibit a grazing succession in which larger animals make the grazing more favourable for smaller animals by removing coarser material.

6. A population is a group of organisms of the same species occupying a particular space at a particular time. Individuals belonging to the same population have an opportunity to interbreed. Population density is increased by natality (birth rate) and immigration and decreased by mortality (death rate) and emigration.

7. Population growth or decline is geometric if change occurs periodically (seasonally) with the increment proportional to population size. Exponential growth occurs in organisms that breed continuously. If the growth rate of the population varies with population size (logistic growth), the population will attain and remain at its carrying capacity. In logistic growth, the maximum rate of population increase occurs at a density equal to one half the carrying capacity.

8. Dispersal is the tendency for an organism to move away from its birth site. Migration is the periodic movement, to and from a given area, usually along a well-defined route. Dispersion refers to the spatial distribution of individuals within a population.

9. Organisms that reproduce more than once in a lifetime are known as iteroparous. Semelparous organisms only reproduce once in a lifetime. Fertility (the number of eggs produced) varies between species, with most mammals producing one to a few with each cycle, but other organisms may produce many millions. Mean fecundity is the number of young produced per female in the population.

10. The death rate per capita is said to be density-dependent if it increases as density increases. Density-independent mortality factors do not vary in their impact as density changes. Density-dependent mortality factors are mainly biotic: disease, competition and predation. Density-independent factors are mainly abiotic, mostly related to climate.

11. Competition is an interaction between individuals, brought about by a shared requirement for a resource in limited supply, leading to a reduction in the biological success of the competing organisms.

12. Resource competition occurs when a number of organisms utilise a common resource that is scarce. Interference competition occurs when an organism defends a resource, even if the resource is not scarce. Competition may be interspecific (between two or more different species) or intraspecific (between individuals of the same species).

13. The Lotka–Volterra model of predator–prey interactions predicts that predator–prey populations undergo oscillations with fluctuations in predator population size lagging behind those of the prey. The regulatory effects of predators on prey populations are difficult to demonstrate, particularly where predators have a choice of prey species.

14. Animals can be arranged along a continuum from those exhibiting r-selection reproductive traits (small size, early reproduction, once-in-a-lifetime reproduction and production of many, but small, off-spring) to those that are K-selected (large size, late reproduction, repeated reproduction, few, large off-spring and significant parental care). Three life-history strategies have been recognised in plants: competitors (C), ruderals (R) and stress-tolerators (S).

15. Life tables provide a summary of the age-related survivorship of individuals in a population. A static life table is constructed from the age structure of a population at a single moment in time. A cohort life table follows the fate of a group of individuals born at the same time from birth to death of the last individual in the cohort.

16. In animals which have a number of stages to their life history, it is useful to identify key factors that regulate population size. Key factor analysis assesses the mortality that occurs between each stage of the life cycle.

17. Ecosystem models may be either deterministic (change is predetermined) or stochastic in which an element of probability is incorporated into the model.

Chapter 5

Lakes, energy flow and biogeochemical cycling

We have seen that seasonal changes significantly influence ecological processes in grasslands and savannas (chapters 3 and 4). Although the most obvious change in a tropical lake through the year might be a rise and fall in water level, significant seasonal changes also occur beneath the surface of deep lakes which have profound effects on lake ecology. These changes come about through seasonal shifts in water density with depth, resulting from changes in water temperature. The process varies from lake to lake, as examples described below show, but in tropical lakes it commonly consists of an annual alternation of layering or **thermal stratification** of the water column with a period of mixing.

5.1 | Thermal stratification

5.1.1 Theory of thermal stratification in lakes

Although lakes are often called standing waters and appear to be without currents, the water is not motionless. Movements are powered by wind, by water density differences, by inflow and outflow currents, by landslides and earthquakes and by geothermally induced convection currents. While significant mixing to great depths can occur, and often does on an annual basis, some lakes are stratified into layers that never or only rarely mix.

As water temperature increases above 4 °C (the temperature at which it is at its maximum density) there is a progressive decrease in its density (Figure 5.1). As the surface layer of a lake is warmed through insolation (heat from the sun),

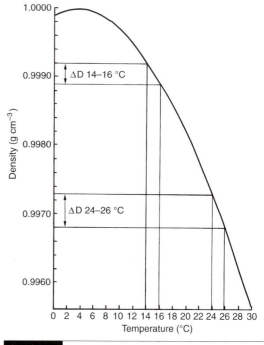

Figure 5.1 The physical relationship between temperature and the density of pure water under one atmosphere of pressure. Maximum density occurs at 3.94 °C. Lines demonstrate that the density differential (ΔD) for a 2 °C change in temperature is greater at higher temperatures (24–26 °C) than it is at lower temperatures (14–16 °C). Therefore, stratification stability is greater per unit change in temperature in warmer waters (adapted from Beadle 1981 reprinted by permission of Pearson Education Limited © Longman Group Limited).

it becomes less dense and floats on the cooler, denser water below. Water is a poor conductor of heat and, although wind may mix the warmer surface waters downwards, in a deep lake, the

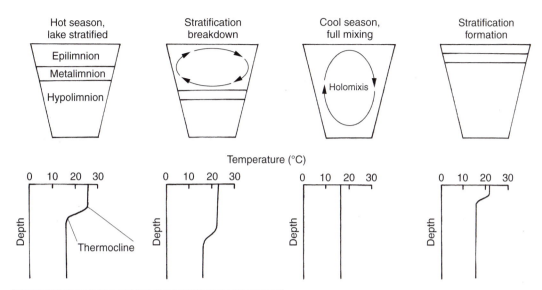

Figure 5.2 Layers of a stratified lake, showing the epilimnion, metalimnion (or thermocline) and hypolimnion and the breakdown of stratification at overturn leading to holomixis. Seasonal temperature-depth profiles are shown.

wind energy is usually inadequate to do this to the bottom of the lake. Consequently, a stable thermal stratification may result. The upper layer, the **epilimnion**, is separated from the lower layer, the **hypolimnion** by the **metalimnion** (Figure 5.2). The metalimnion is characterised by water temperatures declining sharply with depth and this layer is also called the **thermocline**.

Heat is lost from lakes through evaporative cooling, and the rate of this loss increases with higher temperatures and lower vapour and barometric pressures. Therefore, it is the epilimnion that is most subject to significant diurnal heating and cooling and to mixing by winds. Some convection currents occur when surface waters are cooled, become more dense and sink, and these currents can be particularly important in tropical lakes. The depth of the thermocline is related to the strength and duration of these mixing forces.

The hypolimnion is effectively isolated, by the epilimnion, from the supply of oxygen in the atmosphere. In contrast, nutrients, released into solution from the decomposition of organic matter produced in the epilimnion, accumulate in the hypolimnion. Some transfers do occur between the two layers but these are much greater when stratification breaks down.

At the end of a hot season, stratification breakdown may be brought about by cooling at the surface resulting in an increase in water density. This, together with wind-induced turbulence, results in mixing of the water column. This mixing event, which may occur quite rapidly, is known as **overturn**. The water column becomes **isothermal** and nutrients and oxygen evenly distributed with depth. Lakes which exhibit an annual alternation of a stratified water column with one that is mixed, are referred to as **monomictic** (one mixing). Lake Kariba, a man-made lake on the Zambezi River between Zimbabwe and Zambia is an example of a monomictic lake.

5.1.2 Lake Kariba

Kariba dam was closed in December 1958 and a huge lake, 300 km long and over 100 m deep, flooded the Zambezi valley behind it (Figure 5.3). This vast man-made lake provides an informative case study in which to follow the development of an aquatic system from a terrestrial one, and to discuss some of the impacts of thermal stratification on lake ecology in general and nutrient cycling in particular.

When full, Lake Kariba has a maximum depth of about 120 m. Although rainfall on the lake itself is low (400–800 mm year^{-1}), that in the upper

Figure 5.3 Kariba Dam on the Zambezi river between Zimbabwe and Zambia (Photo: Patrick Osborne).

Zambezi is not (800–1600 mm year^{-1}). The annual inflow to the lake is high and amounts to about one-quarter of the volume of the lake. This introduces the concept of a lake's **water residence time**. This is the mean time water remains in a lake and is calculated by dividing the volume of the lake (m^3) by its annual inflow (m^3 year^{-1}). The water residence time for Lake Kariba is approximately 2–3 years. This contrasts with the water residence times of 700 and 1500 years for Lakes Malawi and Tanganyika respectively (see section 5.1.3). The water residence time of man-made lakes is often much less than that of naturally formed lakes.

Mean daily air temperatures in midwinter (June–July) and midsummer (December–January) at Kariba are 17 °C and 28 °C respectively. At the end of winter the temperature of the surface water is around 20 °C and there is little difference in water temperature with depth (**isothermal**). As air temperatures warm with summer, the surface

waters heat up, the water density is reduced and the lake becomes stratified.

As the lake filled in 1959, the terrestrial vegetation was flooded, causing it to die and start to decompose. Measurements made near the dam wall in November 1959 showed marked stratification with a thermocline at about 10 m. Below the thermocline, the water became devoid of oxygen (**anoxic**) and contained free hydrogen sulfide (Figure 5.4). Decomposition of the flooded vegetation consumed oxygen, and hydrogen sulfide and methane were produced from the breakdown of organic matter. Throughout the summer, the depth of the thermocline increased to about 30 m by May. Air temperatures then declined and the density of the surface waters increased, and this, coupled with the onset of south-east winds, resulted in overturn. This brought oxygen to the bottom and the hydrogen sulfide was oxidised. Stratification was re-established in August following a rise in air temperatures and calmer conditions (Beadle 1981).

The rapid deoxygenation and production of copious hydrogen sulfide in the hypolimnion

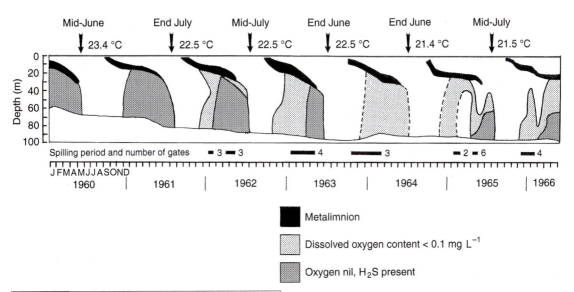

Metalimnion

Dissolved oxygen content < 0.1 mg L^{-1}

Oxygen nil, H$_2$S present

Figure 5.4 The monomictic thermal regime in newly formed Lake Kariba showing the alternation of periods of stratification and deoxygenation of the hypolimnion during the warm and calm season with periods of mixing (overturn) occurring during the cooler and windier season from June/July to September/October. Period of overturn and temperature of homothermal water are indicated for each year. Notice the decline in the extent and duration of deoxygenation as the breakdown of the flooded terrestrial vegetation progressed from 1960 to 1966. Measurements were made at a deep-water station near the dam wall. The increase in water depth records the gradual filling of the lake (filling began in 1958) (after Coche 1968 with kind permission from Director of Department of Research and Specialist Service, Government of Zambia).

caused some concern for managers of the fishery and the hydroelectric power generation. The shallow epilimnion at the onset of stratification limits fish to the surface waters, and high concentrations of hydrogen sulfide in the waters from the hypolimnion passed through the turbines causing corrosion. In the early years of the lake's existence, deoxygenation was due to the decomposition of the flooded terrestrial vegetation (see chapter 10). Decomposition not only consumed oxygen in the hypolimnion but also released nutrients. These nutrients were made available to plants and algae in the euphotic zone at overturn. The **euphotic** zone of a lake extends from the surface to the depth at which only 1% of surface light remains. Effectively, it is the zone in which net photosynthesis is possible (see section

5.2.3). The nutrient-rich, upwelling waters supported dense populations of phytoplankton and led to a condition described as **eutrophic** (see section 5.15). The early years of Lake Kariba were characterised by considerable variation in the numbers and biomass of fish, birds and other organisms. The most spectacular response to these early, nutrient-rich conditions was the explosive growth of the aquatic weed *Salvinia molesta*.

Floating mats of *Salvinia molesta* (see Box 5.1), an alien fern from South America, were first seen on Lake Kariba in May 1959. When the lake first reached its full supply level in 1962, *Salvinia* mats covered about 1000 km² (21.5%) of the lake surface (Mitchell and Rose 1979). The high nutrient content of the lake water, the capacity of *Salvinia* to sequester nutrients and recycle them through the mat and the extensive areas of calm water were largely responsible for its rapid colonisation of the new water body. The area covered by *Salvinia* remained approximately constant from 1962 to 1972. Throughout the early- to mid-1970s, the area covered by *Salvinia* was much less. This decline in the *Salvinia* population has been attributed to the introduction of one of three biological control agents, an aquatic grasshopper, *Paulinia acuminata*. *Paulinia* is a South American species which has a marked preference for feeding on *Salvinia*, particularly its new tissues.

Box 5.1 | *Salvinia molesta* D.S. Mitchell

The South American free-floating fern, *Salvinia molesta* has, since 1930, been spread by humans to lakes in Africa, India, South-East Asia and Australasia. Initially thought to be *Salvinia auriculata*, the plant was described as a new species in 1972. The plant consists of paired, floating leaves attached to a submerged root-like structure which is, in fact, a modified leaf. The upper surface of the exposed leaves is covered in multi-cellular papillae which are water repellent. The papillae bear four hairs that are united at their tips in a bird-cage like structure. The plant is pentaploid and bears sporocarps with sporangia in groups on the branches of the root-like leaves. During the first meiotic division of spore production, genetic incompatibility blocks the formation of spores and as a result the sporangia are nearly all empty, or contain only a few aborted spores. *Salvinia molesta* reproduces entirely by vegetative means: plants breaking up into several viable pieces.

Different growth forms of the plant are produced in response to environmental factors (Figure 5.5). With high concentrations of nutrients and uncrowded conditions, the plants are small with long internodes and the leaves lie flat on the water surface. Plants in this form fragment easily and rapid spread is possible. Under ideal conditions (a good supply of nutrients and temperatures between 25–30 °C), *Salvinia* can double its dry weight in 2–3 days. As the mat develops and the plants become more tightly packed, the internodes shorten, and the leaves increase in size and fold vertically.

Its transition in form and rapid growth rate makes *Salvinia molesta* successful at colonising the open water of lakes. Its ability to form tightly packed mats has made it a very serious aquatic weed in many parts of the world. In the mat form, it blocks waterways, restricting boat movements and hindering fishing. Permanent mats also shade out submerged plants and inhibit phytoplankton production which, in turn, results in reduced levels of dissolved oxygen beneath *Salvinia* mats. Within a lake, *Salvinia* is spread by wind and currents but, between catchments, the main agent of dispersal is humans. The biological control of this weed is described in Box 5.3.

Another factor attributed to the decline in *Salvinia* populations was reduced nutrient availability. The excess nutrients present in the lake following flooding of the terrestrial vegetation gradually declined through their incorporation into the sediments and loss through the outflow. These processes took some time to have an impact on *Salvinia* growth because *Salvinia* is so well adapted to its free-floating existence. The plants retained nutrients which may otherwise have been lost from the water column and, being free-floating, the plants could rise and fall with the frequent changes in the water level of Lake Kariba.

The water in the major inflow to Lake Kariba, the Zambezi River, is nutrient-poor. Nutrients in Lake Kariba derived from the decomposition of terrestrial vegetation were flushed from the lake and were not replaced. Gradually, both biological productivity and the fluctuations in the number and biomass of organisms in Lake Kariba declined. A more diverse aquatic flora became established and competition from these plants may also have played a role in the decline of *Salvinia* populations. Submerged plants such as *Lagarosiphon ilicifolius*, *Ceratophyllum demersum* and *Potamogeton pusillus* probably were able to utilise nutrients regenerated from *Salvinia* decomposition more effectively than the *Salvinia* itself.

5.1.3 Lakes Malawi and Tanganyika

Lake Malawi is the third largest lake in Africa and fills 600 km of the great African Rift Valley to a

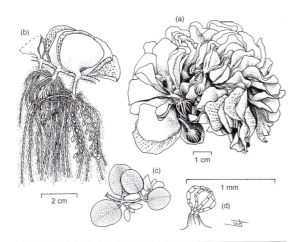

Figure 5.5 *Salvinia molesta*: (a) growth form found in crowded mats; (b) mat form showing the root-like sub-merged leaves with sporocarps; (c) open water growth form; (d) detail of leaf papilla and hair (after Leach and Osborne 1985 with kind permission from Forestry Research Institute, Lae, Papua New Guinea).

maximum depth of nearly 800 m. It is flanked by mountain ranges that fall precipitously into the lake. Lake Tanganyika occupies three basins in the rift valley to the north of Lake Malawi and is larger and considerably deeper (1470 m) than Lake Malawi. Most of its coastline, like that of Malawi's, is precipitous except at the extreme north and south ends of the lake, where the underwater gradient is more moderate (Figure 5.6).

Both these enormous lakes stratify in summer with an overturn in the cooler season in much the same way as Lake Kariba. However, there is one significant difference. Lakes Malawi and Tanganyika are so deep that they have an unmixed layer beneath the hypolimnion (Figure 5.7). This layer is called the **monimolimnion** and is found in **meromictic** lakes. Lakes, such as Lake Kariba, which mix to the bottom each year, are called **holomictic**. Meromictic lakes generally have a monimolimnion of greater density. The

Figure 5.6 A rock promontory on the shores of Lake Malawi near Cape Maclear (Photo: Patrick Osborne).

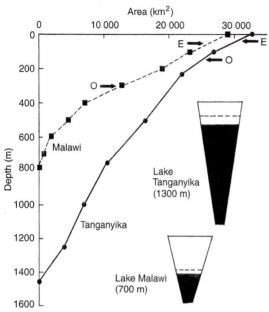

Figure 5.7 Hypsographic (lake depth to lake area) curves for Lakes Tanganyika and Malawi. The mean depths of light penetration (the euphotic zone, E) and the limits of oxygen penetration (O) in each lake are indicated. Profiles of the lakes show the maximum depth to which the water column is mixed each year (dashed line) and the darkened parts of the profiles indicate the permanently unmixed and anoxic deep-water layers. Notice the very small area in both lakes where light can penetrate to the bottom. Note, too, the very large volume of water in both lakes, but particularly Lake Tanganyika, which remains unmixed (adapted from Hecky 1991; Moss 1988 with kind permission from Oxford University Press and Blackwell Science).

enhanced density found in meromictic lakes may be imparted through the accumulation of salts from the sea, mineral springs or from the decomposition products of organic matter entering the layer from the productive layers above.

In the case of Lakes Malawi and Tanganyika, the density difference between the hypolimnion and the monimolimnion is, however, only slight and develops from both lower temperature and higher concentrations of dissolved solids. Only the top 200–300 m mix annually through wind action and temperature-derived density changes. In Lake Malawi, below a depth of approximately 250 m, water temperature is a uniform 22.5 °C. Above 250 m, water temperature varies seasonally

between 24 and 27 °C (Pilskaln and Johnson 1991). Wind is usually unable to mix the entire water column owing to the density difference imparted by the temperature and salinity differences between these upper and lower layers. However, the seasonal rise and fall of the anoxic boundary and the constancy of major ion composition with depth suggest that some mixing has taken place relatively recently.

Because of slow exchange rates between surface and deep waters in Lakes Malawi and Tanganyika, the deep waters are anoxic with high concentrations of CO_2, NH_4–N and H_2S (Figure 5.8; Bootsma and Hecky 1993). Rapid upwelling could have catastrophic effects on fish and other organisms (see Box 5.2). Although there is some evidence that deep mixing does occur in Lake Malawi, it is unlikely that these events represent complete overturns (Eccles 1974). The sediments in Lake Tanganyika possess finely laminated sediments, which suggests that deep mixing (to 400 m) has not occurred in this lake within at least the last 10000 years (Haberyan and Hecky 1987). While complete overturns in these lakes may be rare, fish kills may still occur through localised upwelling (Eccles 1974). These events may pose a threat to fish species, many of which are endemic to just small areas within these lakes (see section 12.6.1).

Concentrations of dissolved oxygen were high in the surface waters of Lake Tanganyika but declined to undetectable levels at the monimolimnion between 100 and 200 m deep (Figure 5.8). The vertical distribution of inorganic nutrients showed strong vertical gradients which reflected the lake's meromixis. Concentrations of dissolved phosphate and inorganic nitrogen (ammonia, nitrite and nitrate) were low in the epilimnion because of uptake by photosynthetic organisms.

Below the euphotic zone, dissolved nitrogen concentrations, as nitrate (NO_3–N), increased. A pronounced minimum in dissolved nitrogen concentrations was recorded at the interface between the oxygenated (oxic) surface waters and the deoxygenated (anoxic) deeper waters. This low nitrogen concentration is probably established through intense microbial activity, converting

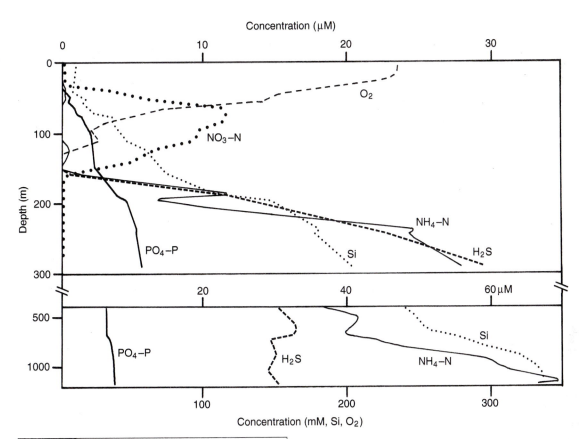

Figure 5.8 Concentration-depth profiles of nitrate (NO$_3$–N), ammonium (NH$_4$–N), phosphate (PO$_4$–P), hydrogen sulfide (H$_2$S) (concentrations in μM); oxygen (O$_2$) and silicon (Si), (concentrations in mM) at a station in the north basin of Lake Tanganyika in April 1975. A different vertical scale is used below 300 m depth and different horizontal scales are used above and below 300 m for H$_2$S, PO$_4$–P and NH$_4$–N. Notice the depletion of the nutrients in the euphotic zone and their accumulation in the unmixed layer below 150 m depth and the switch from NO$_3$–N to NH$_4$–N as the water becomes anoxic (after Hecky et al. 1991 with kind permission from Oxford University Press).

dissolved ammonia, nitrate and nitrite into dissolved nitrogen (N$_2$). These microbial processes are described in section 5.13.2. The higher nutrient levels below the thermocline, and with increasing depth, result from the breakdown of organic matter and regeneration of nutrients from particles descending through the water column.

About one-third of Malawi's shoreline is steep and rocky and two-thirds are gently sloping, sandy beaches or wetlands surrounding the mouths of inflowing rivers. The lake now drains via the Shire River, a tributary of the Zambezi, but previously it drained to east-coast rivers; analysis of the fish species present in the lake indicates affinities with both these east-coast rivers and the Zambezi River system. Lake Malawi has representatives of only 9 of the 14 families found in the Zambezi. Interest in the fish fauna of both Lake Malawi and Tanganyika (and indeed all the African great lakes) has centred on the incredible diversity and high degree of endemicity of species belonging to the Cichlidae (see section 12.6.1).

Lake Malawi is thought to have over 500 cichlid species of which all but 4 are endemic (Lowe-McConnell 1993). Of these many species, about 200 comprise a group which congregate around the algae-covered rocks. These brightly coloured species (locally referred to as *mbuna*) have been assigned to 10 genera and provide a classic example of rapid speciation and trophic radiation. Why and how have so many species developed within, what appears to be, a relatively simple environment? Why are many of these species only found in one lake and often in only one part of the lake? We will attempt to answer these questions in chapter 12.

5.1.4 Lake Lanao

Lake Lanao (8° N, 124° E) is located on Mindanao Island in the Philippines archipelago. The lake has a surface area of 357 km² and a maximum depth of 112 m. The lake was formed behind a larva dam and is probably old as it contains a swarm of endemic fish belonging to the family Cyprinidae. The climate of the area is characterised by a cool, relatively dry period between December and March, with warmer and wetter weather occurring from May to October.

Lake Lanao becomes isothermal each year during the last part of the cool season. At other times the lake is thermally stratified with an unusually deep epilimnion (20–40 m) (Lewis 1978). This great epilimnetic depth precludes mixing of the entire epilimnion by winds. During calm weather, a second or even third thermocline may develop at a depth of 12–25 m. In this way, a two- or three-layered epilimnion is formed. In the upper layer, light penetration enables photosynthesis to occur, but inadequate light penetrates to the lower layer and here decomposition of the organic matter raining down from above occurs. Photosynthesis enriches the upper layer with oxygen while decomposition depletes oxygen in the lower compartment. Similarly, nutrients are assimilated and regenerated in the upper and lower layers respectively.

These epilimnetic layers are disrupted during storms through heat loss from the upper layer, which causes an increase in water density and epilimnetic circulation results. This process is assisted by winds which accompany the stormy weather. Nutrients, which have accumulated in the lower epilimnetic layer, recharge the euphotic zone and photosynthesis is stimulated. Following the storm, stratification is re-established. Consequently, there are repeated episodes of thermocline formation and displacement throughout the stratification period and each results in stimulation of phytoplankton production. This process, called **atelomixis** by Lewis

(1973), enhances primary production in this lake.

Lake Lanao lies 8° N of the equator at an altitude of 701 m a.s.l. and has a maximum depth of 112 m. Lake Kutubu in Papua New Guinea has a similar geographic position in the southern hemisphere: 9° S, 808 m a.s.l. with a maximum depth of 63 m. Despite this similarity in position, the thermal regimes of these two lakes differ, as the next section shows.

5.1.5 Lake Kutubu

If thermoclines are long-lasting, the prolonged rain of nutrients in particulate material from the epilimnion to the hypolimnion, and their infrequent return to the epilimnion, result in nutrient-limited phytoplankton in the epilimnion. This seems to be the case in Lake Kutubu in the Southern Highlands of Papua New Guinea. Lake Kutubu (Figure 5.9) is flanked by high hills along its length and is drained by the Soro River, a tributary of the Kikori River. The lake is approximately 19 km long, 4 km wide at its maximum and has a surface area of 4924 ha. The lake has low phytoplankton populations and very clear water indicative of its nutrient-poor surface waters.

Bayly et al. (1970) described anecdotes that indicated that occasionally a 'turning of the waters' occurs whereby the water in the lake turns red and fish die. From this evidence, they concluded that Lake Kutubu is probably **oligomictic**. Osborne and Totome (1992a) measured seasonal depth profiles of temperature, oxygen, nutrients and other physico-chemical features that usually indicated two distinct layers with a metalimnion between 10 and 25 m deep in a lake with a mean depth of 36 m. The epilimnion was well oxygenated and between 1.6 and 3.3 °C warmer than the anoxic hypolimnion.

A disruption of this thermal stratification was observed in September 1990 (Osborne and Totome 1992a). At one end of the lake, anoxic water bubbled to the surface, the water was cloudy with red particles and asphyxiated fish and prawns floated near the surface. At the other end of the lake, dissolved oxygen concentrations were elevated in the hypolimnion. The normal thermal stratification had been disrupted by the coincidence of cold weather and strong winds blowing

Figure 5.9 Lake Kutubu in the Southern Highlands of Papua New Guinea. Notice the calm water in this oligomictic lake (Photo: Patrick Osborne).

down the length of the lake, resulting in a tilted oxycline and upwelling of hypolimnetic water at one end of the lake. The most obvious feature of this upwelling was the marked discoloration of the water. The red colour was due to the precipitation of ferric oxides and hydroxides which are more soluble in anoxic water but become less so as waters become oxygenated. The upwelling of the hypolimnion brought anoxic water, loaded with dissolved iron, to the surface. Fish and prawns died and iron salts precipitated out as the oxygen concentrations subsequently increased. Aquatic animals survived at the other end of the lake, which provided a refuge. The lake soon returned to its peaceful condition following the onset of calm, warm weather, and water clarity was re-established.

The term **oligomictic**, introduced by Hutchinson and Löffler (1956), refers to tropical lakes of small or moderate area, or of very great depth, or in regions of high humidity, in which a very small temperature difference between surface and bottom is normally sufficient to maintain a stable stratification. Such lakes circulate completely only at rare, irregular intervals when abnormally cold and stormy weather occurs. When deep circulation occurs, deoxygenated water containing considerable amounts of hydrogen sulfide are brought to the surface and mass fish mortality may occur. The upwelling of deep waters may also fertilise the surface waters by greatly increasing the concentration of nutrients such as nitrogen and phosphorus and, as a consequence, phytoplankton blooms, often involving blue-green algae, may develop shortly after such events.

Although some fish and prawns were asphyxiated when stratification breakdown occurred in Lake Kutubu, this does not compare with the devastation wreaked by a similar event in Lake Nyos (Box 5.2).

Box 5.2 | Killer lake: Lake Nyos, Cameroon

In the evening of 21 August 1986, a deadly cloud of gas erupted from Lake Nyos in the Cameroon highlands of West Africa. The gas swept down the valleys north of the lake leaving hundreds of people and livestock dead in its wake. Lake Nyos lies in a volcanic crater some 200 m deep which was formed by a violent volcanic eruption a few hundred years ago. Scientists first assumed that the 1986 disaster was due to the reawakening of the dormant volcano. Further investigation, however, soon revealed the problem was due to an eruption of carbon dioxide that had accumulated, over a long time, in the deep waters of the lake. It is likely that the carbon dioxide came from the interior of the earth, seeping into the lake from below. Water samples collected, from depth, using standard limnological water samplers released so much gas as they were brought to the surface, that they exploded. Further work, using samplers that could be sealed deep in the lake and brought to the laboratory under pressure, revealed that 250 million cubic metres (measured at standard temperature and pressure) of carbon dioxide remained in Lake Nyos after the disaster. Furthermore, analysis showed that carbon dioxide was being added to the lake at a rate of nearly 5 million cubic metres per year. The carbon dioxide probably accumulates in a dense layer of water that does not mix with the water above.

What caused the eruption of carbon dioxide from the lake? A number of causes have been proposed, generally invoking a role for volcanism, if only in the initial provision of carbon dioxide. A simple explanation would be that the gas entered the lake after some kind of volcanic eruption. However, such activity would have disturbed the fine sediment at the bottom of the lake and the water would have remained turbid for some time afterwards, but none of the deep-water samples collected soon after the disaster contained any sediment. Another theory suggested that carbon dioxide-enriched bottom waters, by some mechanism, became unstable. One possible cause of instability could have been a landslide on the steep western shore of the lake.

Freeth (1992) presented the following scenario to explain the event. Water from deep in the lake, enriched with carbon dioxide, rose towards the surface in the north-eastern part of the lake. At this time of the year the prevailing winds are from the north-east and these would push the cool surface waters to the southern part of the lake. Whenever enough of the slightly denser top layer accumulated in one part of the lake, it would eventually become unstable and sink, pushing gassy water from deep in the lake to the surface elsewhere. This rising water released bubbles of gas and these bubbles increased the convective flow, helping to drag upwards more of the gas-laden bottom waters. The release of carbon dioxide is an endothermic reaction and therefore energy is absorbed and both the gas and the water cool down. The rising bubbles expanded as they approached the surface and consequently cooled further. The gas bubbling out of the water and the water itself may have been as much as 10 °C cooler than that in the deep parts of the lake.

Carbon dioxide is more dense than air and therefore the gas spread across the surface of the lake as a cold, toxic layer. The cold surface waters became more dense and sank, pushing more of the gas-laden deep water to the surface resulting in further cooling. The surface waters then sank to greater depths, forcing even more of the CO_2-laden deep waters upwards. This scenario explains why the sediment was not disturbed and also why the lake lost only some of the gases stored in it. The dense carbon dioxide produced then swept down the valleys below Lake Nyos as an asphyxiating cloud resulting in the death of 1700 people. The deep waters in the lake were also rich in ferrous bicarbonate, and, on mixing with the oxygenated surface waters, hydrated ferric oxide precipitated turning the surface waters brown (see section 5.1.5).

5.1.6 High-altitude tropical lakes

Tropical mountains experience marked diurnal changes in air temperatures (see chapter 9). Although lake waters gain and lose heat much more slowly than the air, the diurnal changes in air temperature are often large enough to cause diurnal changes in the thermal behaviour of high-altitude tropical lakes.

Lakes Piunde (Figure 5.10) and Aunde on Mount Wilhelm, Papua New Guinea are above 3500 m altitude. Lake Aunde was isothermal at 09.00 on 29 and 31 March 1969, but exhibited temperature gradients in the evenings of 28 March and 1 April (Figure 5.11). Distinct, but weak, stratification was recorded at 14.30 on 30 March in Lake Piunde. Löffler (1973) concluded that these lakes were transitional between **warm polymictic** (with short periods of lasting stratification) and **cold polymictic** (with almost daily full circulations). It is likely that, during the rainy season, both these lakes circulate frequently, a condition which is further promoted by increased inflow, whereas during the drier season a shift towards warm polymixis occurs.

Chambers *et al.* (1987) conclude that the seven lakes studied by them in the central highlands of Papua New Guinea were probably not deep enough to exhibit permanent stratification, and suggest that they were warm polymictic. These lakes may stratify temporarily, often on a diurnal basis, with surface cooling at night causing partial or complete mixing. Chambers *et al.* (1987) observed a significant inverse relationship between altitude and bottom water temperature in these highland lakes, and Talling (1992) presents a similar relationship for various water bodies in tropical Africa (Figure 5.12).

5.1.7 Shallow lakes

Stable seasonal stratification does not occur in most shallow lakes as the entire water column can

Figure 5.10   Lake Piunde on Mount Wilhelm, Papua New Guinea (Photo: Patrick Osborne).

be heated, and mixing to the bottom can readily occur. However, some shallow lakes do exhibit quite distinct layering established during the day, with mixing occurring at night. Lake George, Uganda, straddling the equator, is only a little over 2 m deep, but strong stratification can occur during the day, with surface water temperatures reaching 35 °C by 17.00 h whilst bottom water temperatures remain at 25 °C. During the night, the water column is mixed both by cooling of the surface waters and by wind. In this way, the thermal regime of this lake, with its equitable

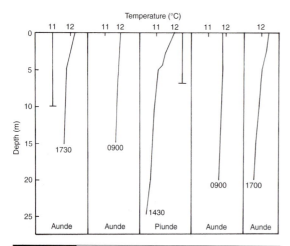

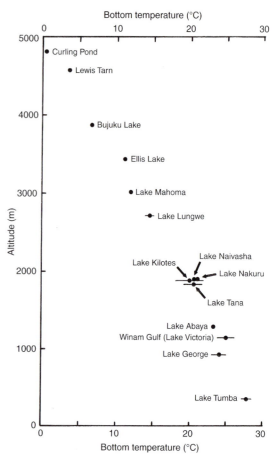

Figure 5.11 Temperature depth profiles in Lakes Aunde and Piunde, two high-altitude lakes (3500 m a.s.l.) on Mount Wilhelm, Papua New Guinea, showing the development of weak thermal stratification during the day and its breakdown overnight (adapted from Löffler 1973 with kind permission from the Regents of the University of Colorado).

climate, is dominated by a daily, rather than an annual, cycle (Ganf 1975).

This marked variation in the daily temperature and light regime found in Lake George is reflected in biological processes (Figure 5.13). Carbon and nitrogen fixation (see section 5.13.2) and oxygen production from photosynthesis were clearly related to solar radiation. Feeding rates in the copepod *Thermocyclops hyalinus* and in two fish (*Sarotherodon niloticus* and *Haplochromis migripinnis*) also exhibited a diurnal pattern. By increasing their intake during the day, these organisms were feeding on phytoplankton enriched with carbon and nitrogen (Moriarty *et al.* 1973; Ganf and Blazka 1974).

5.1.8 Thermal stratification in tropical and temperate lakes

Prevailing climatic conditions (largely determined by latitude and altitude) and lake morphometry are major factors in determining the thermal regimes in lakes. The geographical position of a lake (latitude and altitude) are important determinants of its seasonal circulation pattern. The near-bottom water temperature in lakes is more stable than surface temperatures and its magnitude is closely related to altitude

Figure 5.12 Decrease of near-bottom temperatures with increasing altitude measured in various tropical African water bodies. Bars indicate seasonal ranges (after Talling 1992 with kind permission of Institute de Recherche pour le Développement).

(Figure 5.12). Annual variations in surface water temperature increase with latitude (Figure 5.14), and the amplitude of the variation is a key determinant of the seasonal circulation pattern found in a lake. This annual variation is further reflected in the difference between surface and bottom temperatures of lakes during stratification. When these two temperatures are plotted against latitude, a steep decline in the bottom temperature with latitude is apparent (Figure 5.15). Note, too, the small difference in temperature between the surface and bottom waters in lakes at low latitudes. However, the large change in water density from a small change in temperature at high temperatures results in a surprisingly high density

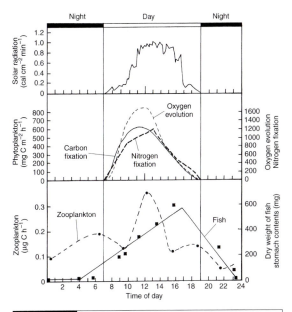

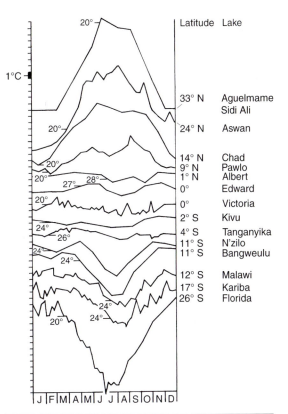

Figure 5.13 Diurnal changes in solar radiation, carbon and nitrogen fixation (nmoles ethylene $m^{-2} h^{-1}$), oxygen evolution (mg O_2 $m^{-2} h^{-1}$) by phytoplankton and ingestion of food by the zooplankton copepod *Thermocyclops hyalinus* and the fish, *Sarotherodon niloticus* in shallow, equatorial Lake George, Uganda (adapted from Burgis 1978 with kind permission from E. Schweizerbart'sche Verlagsbuchhandlung).

Figure 5.14 Annual variation of surface temperature in 14 African lakes arranged by latitude. Successive curves are displaced downwards and the common temperature scale refers to differences only. Absolute values can be located using the single temperature marked on each curve (after Talling 1969 with kind permission form E. Schweizerbart'sche Verlagsbuchhandlung).

differential and imparts stability to the stratification of the lake (Figure 5.1). For this reason, tropical lakes of moderate to great depth are typically monomictic (Lewis 1996).

The small temperature differential found between the surface and bottom waters of near equatorial lakes is interesting in that, in some, the density difference imparted is enough to make a lake in this region oligomictic but others are polymictic. Oligomictic lakes are found at low altitudes where both seasonal and diurnal temperature variations are low; polymictic lakes near the equator are mainly found at mid- to high-altitudes. Hutchinson and Löffler (1956) classified lakes according to their circulation patterns into six categories:
- **Amictic** – perennially ice-covered;
- **Cold monomictic** – one annual turnover, temperatures never greater than 4 °C;
- **Dimictic** – two turnovers per year;
- **Warm monomictic** – one annual turnover, temperatures never less than 4 °C;
- **Oligomictic** – turnovers rare and at irregular intervals; and
- **Polymictic** – frequent or continuous circulation.

Figure 5.16 shows the relationship between the geographical position of a lake and its type of stratification. However, this figure also clearly shows that latitude and altitude alone can not explain the variation in a lake's thermal behaviour, particularly in those lakes that occur within the tropics. Tropical lakes can usually be characterised as warm monomictic, oligomictic or polymictic. Lakes Kariba and Lanao are warm monomictic lakes. Lewis (1973) pointed out that a lake the same size as Lake Lanao but only 40 m deep would be polymictic, whereas a similar lake

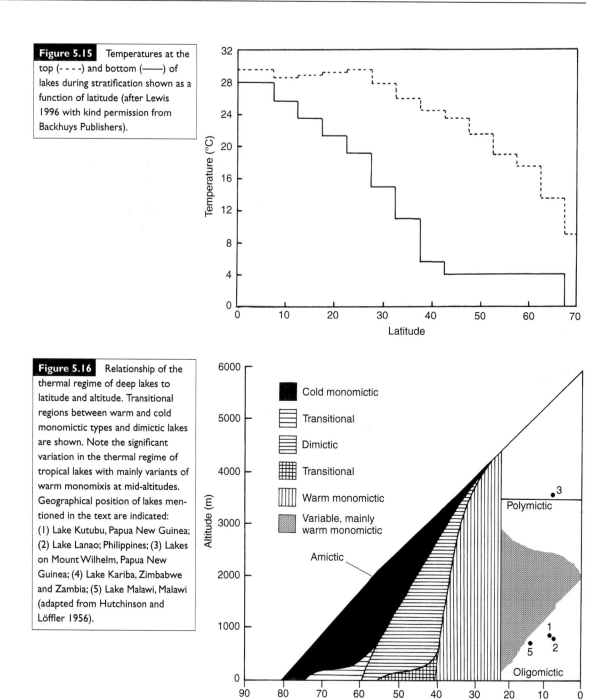

Figure 5.15 Temperatures at the top (- - - -) and bottom (———) of lakes during stratification shown as a function of latitude (after Lewis 1996 with kind permission from Backhuys Publishers).

Figure 5.16 Relationship of the thermal regime of deep lakes to latitude and altitude. Transitional regions between warm and cold monomictic types and dimictic lakes are shown. Note the significant variation in the thermal regime of tropical lakes with mainly variants of warm monomixis at mid-altitudes. Geographical position of lakes mentioned in the text are indicated: (1) Lake Kutubu, Papua New Guinea; (2) Lake Lanao; Philippines; (3) Lakes on Mount Wilhelm, Papua New Guinea; (4) Lake Kariba, Zimbabwe and Zambia; (5) Lake Malawi, Malawi (adapted from Hutchinson and Löffler 1956).

200 m deep would probably not mix completely each year and therefore would be classified as oligomictic. Although Lake Kutubu is only 63 m deep, it is oligomictic because it is so sheltered from the prevailing winds and this contrasts with the more exposed Lake Lanao which is mono-mictic with atelomixis (Lewis 1978; Osborne and Totome 1992a). Clearly the shape of a lake basin (**morphometry**), the topography of the surrounding land and the orientation to the prevailing winds and their speeds are also all important in determining a lake's thermal behaviour.

Not all lakes fit neatly into these categories. Ball and Glucksman (1978) recorded high levels ($7\,mg\,L^{-1}$) of oxygen to a depth of at least 300 m in Lake Wisdom, Papua New Guinea and concluded that the lake appeared to circulate throughout its depth. They speculated that the active volcanic cone, Motmot Island, near the centre of the lake may be causing convection currents through geothermal heating (see Osborne 1995).

5.1.9 Consequences of thermal stratification

It is clear from the descriptions provided above that thermal stratification in lakes has profound effects on the physical, chemical and biological characteristics of these systems. The major consequences of thermal stratification and its breakdown are:

1. The isolation of the hypolimnion from the atmosphere leads to the development of clines in dissolved oxygen and carbon dioxide. Uptake of nutrients by photosynthetic organisms in the surface waters and their regeneration from detrital particles descending into the hypolimnion often results in the establishment of strong chemoclines with depth.

2. Low oxygen concentrations in the hypolimnion may result in release of nutrients such as phosphorus, nitrogen and silica from the sediment into the overlying water column.

3. Stratification restricts (but does not entirely inhibit) the diffusion of nutrients from the often nutrient-enriched hypolimnion to the often nutrient-deficient epilimnion.

4. Inadequate nutrient supply within the epilimnion may result in reduced primary production, leading to a reduction in secondary production. Nutrient limitation may also result in a change in the species composition of the phytoplankton and zooplankton.

5. Stratification may limit the habitat area available to particular organisms.

6. With the breakdown of stratification, nutrients are carried up into the euphotic zone and oxygen transported to the bottom waters. The breakdown in stratification may be marked by an increase in primary production.

7. Very deep lakes may exhibit seasonal cycles of thermal stratification in their surface waters but retain a deep, unmixed, anoxic layer in which nutrient accumulation may occur. This deep layer acts as a nutrient sink and prevents the return of nutrients to the euphotic zone.

8. Shallow, tropical lakes rarely exhibit seasonal stratification but thermal stratification may develop each day and breakdown each night.

Clearly, the ecology of a lake is profoundly affected by the thermal regime that operates within it. This is particularly true in the **pelagic zone** (deep, open water areas), where primary production is almost entirely due to microscopic organisms floating in the euphotic zone. Ecologically, these organisms, referred to as **phytoplankton**, have little control over their vertical or horizontal position in the water column and must obtain their nutrients from the water that surrounds them. They have no contact with the frequently nutrient-rich sediments, and rely on the water movements to replenish nutrients in the euphotic zone.

Whereas phytoplankton may be distributed throughout the surface waters of a lake, some aquatic primary producers, known as **hydrophytes**, are restricted to a narrow depth range within the **littoral zone**, the shallow water areas near the shoreline. Many of the plants that inhabit the littoral zone have roots and therefore do not rely on the water column for their nutrient supply. Other producers include **epiphytic** algae (algae attached to plants, coating them in a green slime) and **benthic** algae (algae living on sediments and rocks). In the next two sections, we will investigate the ecology of the pelagic and littoral zone producers and describe some of the techniques used to study them.

5.2 | Pelagic zone production

5.2.1 Phytoplankton

Phytoplankton consist of a diverse assemblage of microscopic algae ranging in size from 1 μm to 1 mm. Although many species can move independently and others have mechanisms to regulate buoyancy, they have little control over their position in the water column. Most algae are more dense than water and tend to sink, relying on water turbulence to retain them within the euphotic zone. Many species exhibit adaptations that slow the rate of sinking. A large surface area to volume ratio, possession of spines, hairs and other projections and a flattened, disc-shape are ways in which these organisms can retard sinking. Some species possess gas vesicles and store low-density substances such as oils and lipids to enhance buoyancy.

Although phytoplankton sinking below the euphotic zone will perish, there are advantages to sinking slowly within the euphotic zone. The availability of nutrients often increases with depth, and nutrient uptake may be enhanced within these lower layers, which could be advantageous if the phytoplankton is to stand a reasonable chance of being returned, by water turbulence, to the euphotic zone. Photosynthesis in many algae is inhibited by the higher light intensities found in the near-surface waters and, consequently, the highest concentration of algae is often found a metre or so below the surface (see section 5.2.3).

In temperate lakes, a distinct seasonality in the biomass and species composition of the phytoplankton is commonly observed. Growth is negligible during the winter but increases greatly in the spring, with algal populations generally dominated by diatoms. Summer populations are initially dominated by green algae but, later, profuse populations of Cyanobacteria may develop. The shift from diatoms to green algae in many lakes results from silicon depletion, but a reduction in turbulence with the onset of summer stratification may also play a role. The shift from green algae to blue-green algae generally follows nutrient depletion, and the nitrogen-fixing capacity of the blue-greens gives them the advantage when other forms of nitrogen are depleted. A diatom bloom may occur in the autumn following the breakdown of stratification. Although there is great variability in the seasonal succession of phytoplankton biomass and species composition in temperate lakes, the pattern described above is a common one.

Lewis (1978) studied, in detail, the phytoplank-ton dynamics in Lake Lanao (see section 5.1.4). He found that the major environmental factors controlling phytoplankton growth were light and nutrient availability. The overall pattern of species succession in Lake Lanao differed from the common pattern found in temperate lakes. In Lake Lanao, phytoplankton succession occurred as a series of episodes initiated by abrupt changes in abiotic factors, and these changes were more numerous over the year than in most temperate lakes. Growth maxima of diatoms occurred during periods of relatively low light availability and high nutrient availability. Growth pulses of green algae and blue-green algae occurred successively towards the high light and low nutrient end of the spectrum. This successional sequence is similar to that found in the annual algal succession commonly found in temperate lakes but differs in that, in Lake Lanao, the cycle may be repeated in a number of episodes throughout the year. Owing to Lake Lanao's atelomixis (see section 5.1.4), variations in the supply of resources (light and nutrients) are much more irregular in Lake Lanao than in comparable temperate lakes. The phytoplankton community in Lake Lanao is maintained on average in an earlier seasonal condition by the premature termination of successional episodes.

Lewis, W.M. (1986) showed that there was a clear progression in the dominant phytoplankton species in Lake Valencia, Venezuela, and that the changes could be related to the nitrate concentration in the surface waters. With stratification, the concentration of nitrate in the surface waters declined, and euglenophytes, diatoms and chlorophytes were replaced by Cyanobacteria and dinoflagellates. With the breakdown in stratification, surface waters were enriched with nitrate, and euglenophytes and diatoms again dominated the phytoplankton. It should be noted that nitrate availability is only a measure of the thermal stability of the lake and not necessarily the cause of the successional changes.

Melack (1979) recognised three temporal patterns in the seasonal variation of phytoplankton in tropical lakes. He found that most tropical lakes exhibit pronounced seasonal fluctuations that usually correspond with variation in rainfall, river discharges or vertical mixing. A second pattern contrasts markedly with that typical of temperate lakes and the tropical lakes with profound seasonal fluctuations. In this second type of lake, diurnal changes often exceed month to month changes and the same phytoplankton assemblages tend to persist. Two African lakes (Elmenteita and Nakuru) have been shown to exhibit neither a regular seasonal cycle nor a near constant condition, but one in which an abrupt change from one persistent algal assemblage to another persistent condition occurred. The actual cause of the switch in assemblages is not clear, but may be related to an altered water chemistry.

5.2.2 Measurement of aquatic primary productivity

Primary production (see section 3.10) of large aquatic plants can be measured using adaptations of the harvest method described in section 3.11.1. However, a significant amount of primary production in lakes and the sea is carried out by phytoplankton. Since these organisms are short-lived and move with water currents, the harvest method can not be used to measure their primary productivity. The rate of photosynthesis in these organisms can, however, be measured either as the rate of oxygen production or the rate of carbon dioxide uptake.

Oxygen production as a measure of aquatic plant photosynthesis can be used to estimate photosynthetic rates of either aquatic plants or phytoplankton. Replicate samples of the plant or phytoplankton suspension are enclosed in clear bottles (light bottle) and in identical bottles from which light is totally excluded by covering the bottle in black, waterproof tape (dark bottle). The bottles are suspended in the lake at the depth at which the plant material or phytoplankton were collected (see Figure 5.17a). In this way the samples are exposed to light and temperature conditions that are similar to those outside the bottles. Oxygen is produced through photosynthesis in the light bottle and some is also consumed through respiration. In the dark bottle, the initial oxygen concentration is depressed by respiration.

The bottles are incubated in the lake or sea for a set period, usually between 1 and 4 hours. The incubation period should not be too long, as conditions within the bottles will soon deviate significantly from those in the surrounding water, but should be long enough to produce a detectable change in oxygen concentration. When a suitable time has elapsed, the bottles are removed and the oxygen content in them determined (Figure 5.17b). The difference in the oxygen concentration between the light and the dark bottle is a measure of gross primary production. The rate can be expressed as mg O_2 L^{-1} h^{-1} for phytoplankton and as oxygen produced per unit biomass for plants (Figure 5.17c). This method assumes that the rate of respiration is the same in the light and dark bottles and that both photosynthesis and respiration are unaffected by enclosure in the bottles.

In low productivity systems where a long incubation period may be necessary, a more sensitive method measures the uptake of carbon using the radioactive isotope ^{14}C. The ^{14}C is usually added to a phytoplankton sample enclosed in a bottle in the form of $H^{14}CO_3^-$. The amount of labelled carbon added is known and the amount of unlabelled ^{12}C can be obtained from the pH and alkalinity of the sample. The quantity of ^{14}C fixed by the algae can be measured by filtering a sample of the algae and counting the activity in the algae using a scintillation counter. The total quantity of carbon fixed can be calculated from:

$$\text{Total } ^{12}C \text{ assimilated} = \frac{^{14}C \text{ in algae} \times ^{12}C \text{ available}}{^{14}C \text{ introduced}}$$

It has been shown that algae take up ^{14}C at a slower rate than ^{12}C and therefore some workers apply a correction factor to compensate for this. By including a dark bottle, it is possible to account for carbon uptake in the dark. The ^{14}C method measures the amount of carbon that remains in the algae at the end of the incubation period and therefore should be a measure of net production. This, however, assumes that the relative uptake of ^{14}C and ^{12}C is proportional to their respective concentrations in the water. It also assumes that they are respired in the same ratio. What this method actually measures is a rate somewhere between net and gross primary production.

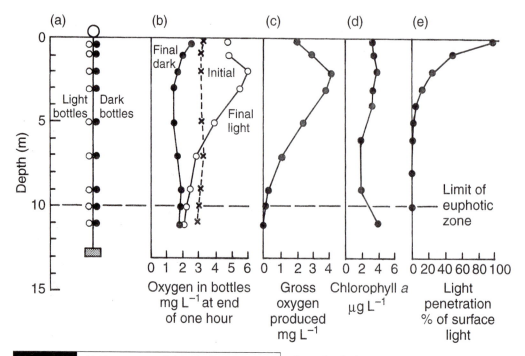

Figure 5.17 (a) Measurement of phytoplankton production in a lake using the light (o) and dark (●) bottle technique. (b) The initial and final oxygen concentrations in the light and dark bottles at the end of the incubation period. (c) Typical curve of gross oxygen production ((light bottle oxygen concentration minus dark bottle oxygen concentration)/incubation time) with depth. (d) Variation in the concentration of chlorophyll *a* (a measure of phytoplankton biomass) with depth. (e) Light penetration as a percentage of sub-surface illumination (after Beadle 1981 reprinted by permission of Pearson Education Limited © Longman Group Limited).

5.2.3 Light availability and photosynthetic depth profiles

Light availability at the surface of a lake will depend upon its geographic position (latitude, surrounding hills) and degree of cloud cover. Some of the light impinging on the water surface will be reflected and the balance penetrates beneath the surface. The depth to which light penetrates depends on the quantities of dissolved substances (water colour) and particulate matter in the water column. Absorption and scattering of the light by the water and suspended particles results in a dwindling of light with depth. This attenuation in the amount of light is exponential with depth, with the green and yellow wavelengths being more strongly absorbed than the blue and red. It is because of this weak absorption of blue light, that lakes with clear, unstained waters appear blue.

A simple way to measure light penetration in lakes is with a **Secchi disc**. This simple instrument consists of a flat, metal disc (usually 20 cm in diameter) painted in alternating black and white quadrants. The disc is weighted and lowered from a boat and the depth at which it just disappears is noted. This is the Secchi disc transparency depth. This crude measure provides a surprisingly good estimate of the depth of a lake's euphotic zone (see section 5.1.2).

It would be reasonable to assume that the exponential decline in light intensity would be paralleled by an exponential decline in the rate of aquatic photosynthesis. However, the most usual distribution of photosynthesis with depth is illustrated in Figure 5.17c. Light of high intensity is detrimental to many algae and therefore lower rates of photosynthesis are often detected near the surface. This is known as **surface photoinhibition** and probably due to high levels of ultraviolet light. Maximum photosynthesis occurs where the light intensity is optimum and this is usually underlain by a zone of near-exponential decline

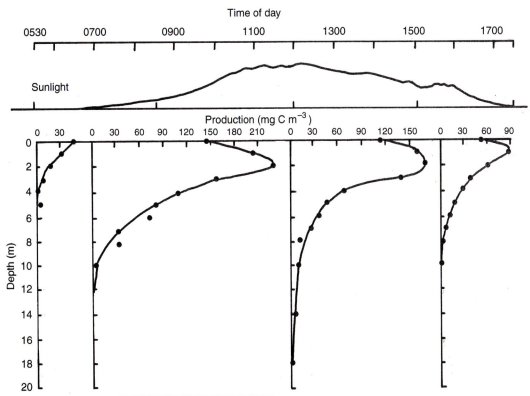

Figure 5.18 Primary production depth profiles measured using the ^{14}C uptake method at four times throughout a day in Lake Lanao, Philippines. The upper figure is a measure of the light intensity from sunrise to sunset (after Lewis 1974 with permission of The Ecological Society of America).

in photosynthesis to the bottom of the euphotic zone. Figure 5.18 shows primary production depth profiles measured in Lake Lanao (see section 5.1.4) at four times during the day. In the early morning, there was no evidence of surface photoinhibition as light intensities were low. However, throughout the rest of the day photosynthetic rates were lower near the surface, with maximum photosynthesis occurring between 1 and 2 m depth (Lewis 1974).

The depth at which maximum rates of photosynthesis occurs and the shape of the photosynthetic depth profiles depend largely upon water transparency. The open waters of many lakes are nutrient-deficient, and phytoplankton populations are limited by the availability of key nutrients, particularly nitrogen and phosphorus. Addition of these nutrients often results in

a number of changes including increased phytoplankton growth (see section 5.15). As phytoplankton densities increase, so the depth of light penetration decreases. In some nutrient-rich lakes, although surface photoinhibition may occur, its effects are masked by rapid light attenuation through self-shading by the dense phytoplankton populations that develop in response to high rates of nutrient supply.

5.3 Littoral zone producers and primary production

5.3.1 Aquatic plants

Aquatic plants (**hydrophytes**) often grow in distinct zones related to water depth. Around Lake Kivu in Central Africa, elephant grass (*Pennisetum purpureum*) grew down to the water's edge (Figure 5.19). The shallow water zone was dominated by the reed *Phragmites mauritianus* and creepers (*Vigna luteola* and *Ipomoea cairica*) covered the damp soil between the bands of *Pennisetum* and *Phragmites*. In the water, to below a metre deep,

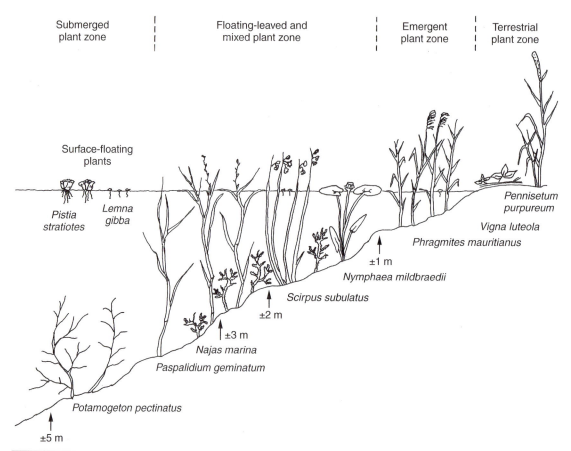

Figure 5.19 Typical zonation of the littoral vegetation in an African lake (after Van der Ben 1959 with kind permission from the Royal Belgian Institute of Natural Sciences, Belgium).

Scirpus subulatus, the aquatic grass *Paspalidium geminatum* and water-lilies (*Nymphaea calintha* and *N. mildbraedii*) grew in mixed stands. Below 3 m deep, two submerged plants (*Najas marina* and *Potamogeton pectinatus*) dominated with *Potamogeton* able to colonise to a depth of almost 5 m. Two free-floating plants (*Pistia stratiotes* and *Lemna gibba*) were not restricted to a particular depth zone but tended to occur in calmer water near the edge of the lake.

In the profile described above, the vegetation changes with depth, and zones dominated by different aquatic plant life-forms are apparent. This is typical of vegetation on gently sloping shorelines of lakes, and four ecological categories of aquatic plants have been recognised. The shallow water is occupied by **emergent plants** rooted in the sediments with emergent vegetative shoots. Typical emergent plants include *Cyperus papyrus* (papyrus), *Phragmites* spp. (reed) and *Typha* spp. (cattail). Floating islands, consisting of mats of vegetation, are common in tropical lakes and wetlands, and these may form when, through erosion of the substrate on which these plants grow, large areas break away and float out into the lake. Emergent plants predominate in many wetlands and will be discussed in more detail in chapter 7.

Next in line are **floating-leaved plants**. These are rather restricted in the range of water depth that they can occupy. Their leaves are buoyant owing to large air spaces in the mesophyll (**aerenchyma**) and are anchored to the sediment by petioles longer than the water depth. The additional length allows for both water turbulence and some change in water level. Leaves of this type of plant often have a waxy cuticle or are hairy so that the surface is kept free of water. The enormous leaves of the famous Amazonian water-lily, *Victoria amazonica,* have numerous small perforations through which water can drain from the surface of the leaf. The leaves of this plant also have very sharp thorns! As the leaves of floating-leaved plants are in contact with the air, absorption of carbon dioxide and oxygen takes place through stomata on the upper surface. Lake sediments are often anaerobic, and rooted plants need to conduct oxygen down from the leaves where it is produced in photosynthesis or absorbed from the atmosphere. These plants have air-filled passages in their petioles to facilitate this gas conduction.

Other rooted plants are adapted to living entirely under water (**submerged plants**) and are capable of colonising deeper water, although water clarity and turbulence tend to restrict these plants to the littoral zone. Many of these submerged plants develop aerial flowering shoots and some are not rooted at all (**free-floating plants**). Free-floating plants are adapted to their watery existence through possession of large intercellular air spaces. As they are unable to access the comparatively nutrient-rich lake sediments, they often have very dissected leaves, providing a large surface area for nutrient uptake. Other free-floating plants have leaves above the surface with roots or root-like structures suspended in the water. Some tropical examples of these plants include the notorious aquatic weeds: *Eichhornia crassipes* and *Salvinia molesta* (see Boxes 5.1 and 5.3).

Box 5.3 | Biological control of *Salvinia molesta*: another alien strikes back

Salvinia molesta (see Box 5.1) is regarded as one of the world's worst aquatic weeds and nowhere has its effects been worse than on the floodplain of the Sepik River in Papua New Guinea. The Sepik River is 1100 km long and, for much of its length, it meanders through an extensive floodplain with numerous ox-bow and depression lakes interconnected by a network of natural and man-made channels. *Salvinia* was probably introduced in the early 1970s; by 1977 it covered 32 km^2 of the floodplain water bodies (Thomas and Room 1986) and spread to infest 500 km^2 of lakes in the lower half of the Sepik floodplain, completely covering half their area. 80 000 people live on the floodplain and are dependent on water for transport to markets, schools and medical facilities and obtain much of their food from fishing and sago (*Metroxylon sagu*) harvesting. The solid mats of *Salvinia* that blocked the waterways of the Sepik constituted a socio-economic as well as an ecological disaster.

Control efforts included physical removal, chemical spraying and construction of barriers to reduce reinvasion of cleared lakes. These early control attempts met with little success as removal was a physically demanding process and the rapid regrowth of the plant was demoralising. Chemical spraying was expensive and reinfestation occurred rapidly. Therefore, proposals for management of this weed centred on finding a biological control agent.

Salvinia molesta is indigenous to southern Brazil and the search for a biological control agent began there. Collections included a beetle that appeared to be *Cyrtobagous singularis*. Intensive study of the feeding behaviour and host-specificity of this beetle began, and it was discovered that the adults feed exclusively on *Salvinia* buds and its larvae tunnel through the buds and rhizomes. A population of these beetles was then released on to a *Salvinia*-infested lake in Queensland, Australia and, within 14 months, it had destroyed 200 ha of the weed. Subsequent investigations showed that the insect responsible for this devastation was a new species: *Cyrtobagous salviniae* (Thomas and Room 1986).

In 1982, the beetle was established on a *Salvinia* mat growing on a lake in the Sepik floodplain (see Figure 5.20). Establishment was slow until it was discovered that the nitrogen content of the *Salvinia* growing in the Sepik was low. To speed up the growth of beetle populations, researchers fertilised the weed with nitrogen! On a nitrogen-enriched *Salvinia* diet, beetle populations developed more rapidly. Destruction of patches of *Salvinia* by the beetle either enhanced nitrogen content in the damaged tissues, or the nitrogen, released as the plant matter decomposed, enriched remaining patches of *Salvinia*. Whatever the cause, once established, beetle populations spread rapidly without further nitrogen applications until only a few plants remained among the marginal vegetation.

With this success, a massive operation began to spread *Salvinia* infested with the beetle to all parts of the Sepik. This was achieved by boat to nearby lakes and by airlifting the weed to central distribution points for the more distant ones. Co-operation from local people resulted in the rapid spread of the beetle throughout the Sepik floodplain, and, by 1985, the beetle had reduced the percentage of water surface covered from 54% to just 0.5% and some 2 million tonnes of weed had been destroyed. Most of the *Salvinia* died and sank in the lakes and there were no indications of any harmful effects from this process. In all cleared lakes, a residual population of beetles on scattered plants remained; an incredible change and enormous benefit to the people living along the Sepik. Regrettably the story does not (yet) have a happy ending. Soon after the control of *Salvinia*, the Sepik was invaded by *Eichhornia crassipes*, another notorious weed. So far three biological control agents have been released in Papua New Guinea to control this noxious plant, but its larger size and its reproduction by seeds make its control more difficult (Figure 5.21).

One important reason for the success of *Salvinia* control lies in careful taxonomy. Populations of *C. salviniae* increase until the food supply runs out, whereas populations of *C. singularis* seem to stop increasing much earlier. This probably explains why earlier attempts in Africa and elsewhere to control *Salvinia* with *C. singularis* met with little success. Notice that the weed and its control agent have both been described as new species (see Box 5.1). Clearly, correct identification of both the weed and its control agent is crucial to successful biological control efforts. Furthermore, any introduction of an alien species also needs careful study before release to ensure that the control agent itself will not become a pest. Unfortunately, this is rarely done, and the consequences of exotic introductions, like *Salvinia* and *Eichhornia*, have often been devastating (see Box 5.6).

The depth to which submerged vegetation can occur is usually limited by light availability and, even in lakes with very clear water, it is rare to find plants growing much below 5 or 6 m. The combined effect of atmospheric and water pressures is the ultimate limitation on the depth to which large aquatic plants can colonise. The air-filled spaces within the plant body collapse under high pressure. In some high altitude lakes, such as Lake Titicaca, Peru (3803 m a.s.l.), aquatic plants can grow to depths of 10–11 m because, at these altitudes, atmospheric pressure is lower. Water depth is clearly an important factor in determining the distribution of aquatic plants, and therefore

Figure 5.20 *Salvinia molesta* infestation on Gerehu Lake, near Port Moresby, Papua New Guinea. The dark patch is a spreading infestation of the mat with the biological control agent *Cyrtobagous salviniae*. This site was used to assess the efficacy of the weevil in controlling the weed in Papua New Guinea (Photo: Patrick Osborne).

water level fluctuations will significantly affect these distributions.

Near the end of the dry season, the sluice gates at Kariba (see section 5.1.2) are opened to make space for the floodwaters from the inflowing rivers during the forthcoming wet season. The fall in lake level has varied from year to year from 3 to 8 m and, along gently shelving shorelines, this has resulted in an alternation of drying and flooding of extensive areas. On exposure, the aquatic vegetation dies and the land becomes covered with grasses such as *Panicum repens*. Herds of large mammals graze the shoreline and deposit their dung.

When the water level rises, the flooded organic matter decomposes releasing nutrients. Water plants such as *Potamogeton pusillus*, *Ceratophyllum demersum* and *Lagarosiphon ilicifolius* soon develop.

Clearly, the annual rise and fall of the lake play a role in nutrient cycling within the lake, but the relative significance of this has not been fully determined. In lakes in which water-level changes occur more frequently or less predictably, exposed shorelines are often barren with inadequate time for the development of either aquatic or terrestrial plants.

5.3.2 Environmental factors and primary production in aquatic ecosystems

Two environmental factors are of overriding importance in determining the level of primary production in aquatic systems: light availability and nutrient supply. Light availability within aquatic systems is a function of latitude (see Figure 1.4b) and water clarity. Schindler (1978) used multiple regression analysis to relate lake variables (e.g. latitude, algal biomass, total phosphorus concentration, the rate of nitrogen and phosphorus supply to the lake, mean depth and water residence time) to rates of phytoplankton production. He did not find a significant relationship between latitude and phytoplankton

Figure 5.21 *Eichhornia crassipes* infestation on Waigani Lake, near Port Moresby, Papua New Guinea (Photo: Patrick Osborne).

productivity nor with nutrient supply to the lake. However, he did find a very significant correlation between annual phytoplankton production and annual phosphorus supply once a simple correction for water renewal time had been applied. He therefore concluded that nutrient supply appears to be an important factor in controlling freshwater production. This result contrasted with an earlier analysis (Brylinsky and Mann 1973; Brylinsky 1980) which demonstrated a significant correlation between latitude and phytoplankton production. This relationship is probably not related to energy variables and Schindler (1978) suggested that this earlier correlation arose through a co-correlation between latitude and nutrient supply.

The nutrient supply to a lake has been shown to be very closely related to features of, and, in particular, human activity within, its catchment area. This close association between a lake and its catchment area has led to the development of the catchment area concept.

5.4 | The catchment area concept

Lakes and ponds are often used as examples of ecosystems because the water's edge forms such a clear boundary – on one side of the boundary your feet remain dry, on the other they get wet! A consideration of the ecological processes within a lake or pond will show, however, that there are numerous and vital interchanges between the lake and its catchment area. Nutrients and soil particles are carried into water bodies from the catchment area by rivers and streams. Organisms produced within the lake may be eaten by terrestrial animals (e.g. piscivorous birds), and this may result in the transfer of nutrients from the lake back to the land. Aquatic insect larvae develop into terrestrial adults and, in some species of chironomids and chaoborids, emergence occurs in dense clouds of insects flying over the lake. The number of these minute insects may be so great that, on the shores of Lake Malawi, they can be collected and made into tasty, protein-rich 'burgers'!

Conversely, Hippopotami (*Hippopotamus amphibius*), massive African amphibious mammals, spend the day wallowing in shallow pools and feed on land at night. They are gregarious animals and often congregate in schools of between 10–20 animals. Five thousand hippos lived around Lake George in Uganda, and an attempt was made to assess nutrient transfers, by these animals, from the land to the water. The nutrient content of hippo faeces was measured and extrapolations were made from analyses of cattle urine. Evidence suggests that there is a continuous passage of food through the gut and the animals spend 10 hours each day on land, so it was possible to deduct this period of excretion from the total. Viner and Smith (1973) showed that the total loss of nitrogen from the lake by outwash was 3400 tonnes per year, and that of phosphorus was 220 tonnes per year. It was calculated that the hippo population contributed 76–99 tonnes of nitrogen (2% of the total lost from the lake) and 15–26 tonnes of phosphorus (about 10% of the washout values). Therefore significant quantities of nutrients, particularly phosphorus, were delivered to the lake by the hippos.

Owing to these interchanges between freshwater ecosystems and the land that surrounds them, the functional unit for studying lakes and rivers is the catchment area or drainage basin. A **catchment area** can be defined as that area of land surface that drains water, sediment and dissolved materials to a common point along a drainage system or river. Drainage basins are isolated from each other by topography, and interactions between them are limited to agents such as mobile organisms and some groundwater transfers. The extent of the catchment and the amount of rain falling on it largely determine the volume of water draining from it. The chemical composition of the rain water is altered as it drains from the catchment, and this depends mostly on the geology of the catchment area and its vegetation cover. The chemical composition of the water and sediments in a lake basin is, therefore, determined by the supply of materials from the catchment area and various chemical, physical and biological processes that take place within the lake itself.

The abiotic components of lakes are inorganic and organic compounds: water, oxygen, carbon dioxide, mineral salts and an enormous variety of organic compounds resulting from the production and decomposition of organic matter. Most of these materials are stored in the sediment at the bottom of the lake, but a small and vital fraction is dissolved in the water. **Allochthonous** particles are those delivered to the lake from the catchment area. These particles may be, for example, the products of erosion or leaves and other parts of terrestrial plants. Chemical precipitation is, in many tropical lakes, an important process of sediment formation and can occur through evaporative concentration as in salt deposition in saline waters (see section 5.14, Box 5.5) or through processes such as the deposition of $CaCO_3$ following an elevation in pH (Figure 5.22).

The addition of biologically derived materials to lake sediments occurs through sedimentation of organic matter and inorganic plant and animal remains (e.g. diatom frustules, mollusc shells, fish bones). Materials produced within the lake are referred to as **autochthonous**. Sediment deposition within a lake may well occur sequentially, producing a stratigraphy that records the historical development of the lake (see section 5.15). In shallow lakes and the littoral regions of deeper lakes, resuspension of sediments may occur, with re-deposition occurring in the deeper parts of the lake, a process known as **sediment focusing**. The supply of allochthonous particles and materials in solution to a lake is closely linked with its hydrology and the hydrological cycle (Box 5.4).

Solar energy (light) and nutrient supply undoubtedly play significant roles in determining the biomass, species composition and distribution of the primary producers in lakes (see section 5.3.2); the biologic, climatic and geologic components involved in the supply of energy and nutrients to a tropical lake are summarised in Figure 5.22. The energy and materials contained within the primary producers provide sustenance for the animals, and links can be drawn to show the flow of energy and materials through **food chains**. Animals rarely rely on just one species for food

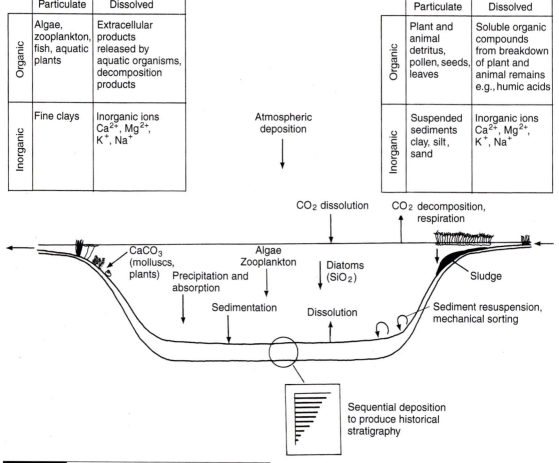

Figure 5.22 Diagram summarising relationships between a lake and its catchment area and the role of organisms and processes in the lake that determine sediment deposition within the lake basin. (adapted from Talling 1992; Oldfield 1977 with kind permission of Arnold Publishers and Institut de Recherche pour le Développement).

and, therefore, these food chains combine to form **food webs**. Food webs are the basis of energy flow in any ecosystem, and it is informative to consider them in terms of energy transfer, but, before doing so, let us consider the organisms that constitute the links in the food chains of tropical lakes.

5.5 | Aquatic consumers

The consumers within lakes belong to a wide range of phyla such as Rotifera, Annelida,

Arthropoda (Crustacea, Insecta), Mollusca and Chordata (fish, amphibians, reptiles, birds and mammals). Herbivores feed on phytoplankton or aquatic plants and include a diverse group of organisms: zooplankton (*Daphnia*), molluscs (*Bulinus*), planktivorous fish (*Tilapia*) and large mammalian grazers such as the hippopotamus. Carnivores feed on herbivores and consumers; examples include predatory fish (*Hydrocynus vittatus*, *Lates niloticus*) and crocodiles (*Crocodylus niloticus*, *Crocodylus porosus*). Ecologically, aquatic consumers have been divided into **zooplankton** (organisms living in the water column and having little or no control over their position), **benthos** (organisms living in, or on the bottom sediments) and **nekton** (larger, free-swimming animals, such as macro-invertebrates, amphibians and fish).

Box 5.4 | The hydrological cycle

The water content of the entire hydrosphere has been estimated to be about 1.5×10^9 km^3. Of this, 97% is found in the oceans and only 0.001% is in the atmosphere. Groundwater ice cap and glaciers account for another 2.3%, leaving only a tiny, but very vital, fraction of a per cent in lakes and rivers. Water enters terrestrial and aquatic ecosystems as precipitation (rain, hail, dew, sleet and snow), with snow and sleet only occurring in the tropics at high altitudes. A number of pathways are taken by the precipitation. Some is intercepted by the vegetation and evaporates from leaves and stems; some flows down the stem to the ground (**stemflow**) and the rest of the precipitation falls directly on the soil surface (Figure 5.23).

The water that reaches the ground either infiltrates the soil or flows along the surface. Surface run-off and ground water flows accumulate in streams and rivers and these carry the water to the oceans. The oceans constitute the major store of water, and the fluxes from them by evaporation and to them through precipitation are the largest in the hydrological cycle. The balance of the cycle is maintained by the flows from the land to the oceans described above. The energy required to drive the hydrological cycle is derived from solar radiation and utilises approximately 15% of the total radiation reaching the outer atmosphere.

The average water molecule stays in the atmosphere for one to two weeks before returning to the earth as some form of precipitation or condensation. The **residence time**, defined as the volume of the water divided by the volume leaving it per unit time, for a water molecule in the ocean is much longer: 300–10 000 years. Precipitation over the land surface exceeds evapotranspiration from terrestrial habitats. The converse is true for the oceans where evaporation exceeds precipitation. The hydrological cycle forms an important link between terrestrial and aquatic systems and is the major driving force behind the flow of materials from the land to rivers and lakes and ultimately the oceans.

The crater lake, Ranu Lamongan (113° 23′ E, 7° 59′ S) is one of several lakes on the lower slopes of the mildly active volcano, Gunung Lamongan, in East Java, Indonesia. It lies at an altitude of 240 m a.s.l. and has a maximum depth of 30 m. Like Lake Kutubu (section 5.1.5), Ranu Lamongan is oligomictic. This lake is one of the few classical study sites for tropical limnology owing to the detailed work carried out by the German Sunda Expedition in 1928 (Ruttner 1931). The lake remained stratified throughout the six weeks of Ruttner's visit, but anecdotal evidence of periodic fish kills suggested to Ruttner that occasional breakdowns in thermal stratification occurred. Green *et al.* (1976) were able to trace the recovery of the lake after such a mixing event which, like that recorded for Lake Kutubu, occurred following the coincidence of cold weather and strong winds.

Green *et al.* (1976) were also able to compare the biology of the lake with that recorded by Ruttner some 45 years earlier.

The species composition of the phytoplankton recorded by Green *et al.* (1976) had changed little from that described by Ruttner (1931) with the diatom genera of *Synedra*, *Nitzschia* and *Melosira* and cyanobacterial species being recorded by both expeditions. However, Ruttner's samples were dominated by Cyanobacteria, whereas *Synedra* dominated samples analysed by Green *et al.* (1976). This change may have been related to the overturn at the beginning of the later study which may have made more nutrients available in the epilimnion and favoured the growth of diatoms. Enhanced water turbulence accompanying the breakdown of stratification would also have favoured diatoms over Cyanobacteria.

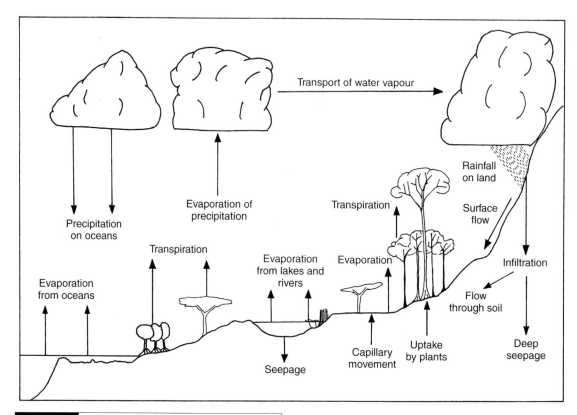

Figure 5.23 The hydrological cycle.

The zooplankton fauna in the lake was dominated by the rotifer *Brachionus caudatus* and the cyclopod *Thermocyclops hyalinus*. Other important rotifers included *Brachionus falcatus* and *Hexarthra insulana*. The ostracod, *Cypria javana*, the cladoceran *Ceriodaphnia cornuta* and two other copepods were recorded in the lake. The carnivorous cyclopod *Mesocyclops leuckarti* was found by Green *et al.* (1976) in low numbers, but they showed that egg production increased three weeks following the overturn. The insect larva, *Chaoborus*, is also carnivorous and makes considerable vertical migrations, ascending towards the surface at night and descending to the bottom at sunrise. These movements are a mechanism to reduce predation on the larvae by fish (see section 5.6).

Green *et al.* (1976) recorded 9 species of fish in the lake, 4 of these are exotic species which have been widely introduced into Indonesian freshwaters: *Oreochromis* (formerly *Tilapia*) *mossambicus*, *Barbus gonionotus*, *Aplocheilus panchax* and *Poecilia*

reticulata. Of these, *Oreochromis mossambicus* and *Barbus gonionotus*, together with the prawn, *Macrobrachium sintangense*, now form the basis of an active fishery. The natural fish fauna only consisted of five species: *Barbus microps*, *Rasbora lateristriata*, the catfish *Clarias batrachus*, *Ophicephalus gachua* and *Monopterus albus*.

The loose meshwork of *Eichhornia* roots that extended some 30 cm below the surface supported an abundance of aquatic organisms (Figure 5.24). Few species of animals fed directly on the submerged roots, but these were the main diet of the water beetle *Hydrophilus bilineatus*, the prawn *Macrobrachium sintangense* and *Barbus gonionotus*. The roots were coated in algae and rich in diatoms, and many animals grazed on this algal lawn. Macro-invertebrates were abundant, attached to or swimming amongst the roots. Carnivorous invertebrates included the isopod *Tachaea lacustris*, the zygopteran larva *Hyphydrus* sp. and dragon-fly larvae. The larvae of two species of mayfly were common among the roots; the main fish predators of these larvae were

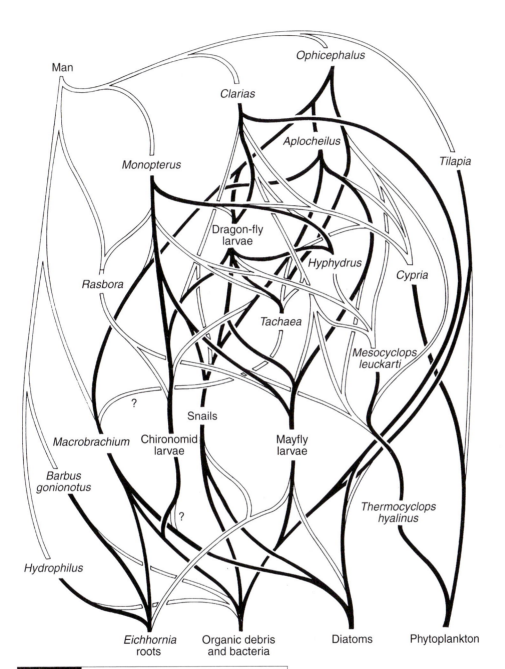

Figure 5.24 A simplified food web for the *Eichhornia* root-mat community in Ranu Lamongan, Indonesia. The diagram is based on gut content analyses of animals caught in or near *Eichhornia* or known to have fed there because of fragments of *Eichhornia* roots in the gut. The link between a consumer and its food is black if the food item was ever recorded as the main contents of the consumer (after Green *et al.* 1976 with kind permission from The Zoological Society of London).

Monopterus albus and young *Clarias*. The people living around the lake constitute the top predator in this food web.

5.6 | The biota of tropical and temperate lakes: a comparison

Lewis (1996) identified four characteristic features of tropical lakes in comparison with temperate counterparts: (1) greater efficiency in producing phytoplankton biomass for a given nutrient supply; (2) an inclination towards nitrogen, rather than phosphorus limitation of primary production; (3) a lower efficiency in passing primary production to the highest trophic levels; and (4) greater non-seasonal variation superimposed on a seasonal cycle. For a given nutrient status, primary production in tropical lakes is generally higher than that of temperate lakes. This difference is primarily due to efficient nutrient cycling combined with higher temperatures and greater stability in solar radiation. Phytoplankton are more often nitrogen-limited in tropical waters since many tropical soils are nitrogen-deficient, and therefore the supply of nitrogen to natural waters in catchments with such soils is low.

In contrast with the high species diversity found in most terrestrial systems in the tropics (see chapter 8), the biota of tropical lakes, except for fish, is generally believed to be no more complex than that found in temperate lakes. Many tropical lakes have endemic fish species, and very high species diversity is found in the fish fauna in Neotropical rivers and the large, rift valley lakes in Africa (see section 12.6.1).

The herbivore communities of tropical lakes are similar in composition to those of temperate lakes, with many species apparently having a cosmopolitan distribution. Tropical lakes differ from their temperate counterparts in the rarity of large zooplankton species. *Daphnia* spp., so common in temperate lakes, are rarely found in large numbers in tropical lakes and, when present, are smaller. Herbivory appears to be no more efficient in tropical plankton communities than it is in temperate ones and there have been few studies to

demonstrate what regulates the size of herbivore populations in tropical lakes.

Lewis (1996) stresses the importance of the carnivorous phantom midge, *Chaoborus*, in suppressing herbivore populations in tropical lakes. The early instars of this insect larva are confined to the bottom mud, but the final stages migrate up through the water column at night and feed on zooplankton. As the larva grows, it devours larger zooplankton species and, therefore, over its larval lifespan it feeds on the entire size spectrum of herbivorous zooplankton. *Chaoborus*, in turn, is fed on by fish and its transparent body (hence its name, phantom midge) and nocturnal migrations are adaptations to reduce predation. *Chaoborus* populations reach only modest abundances when exposed, throughout the water column, to predation. In lakes in which an anoxic hypolimnion develops, *Chaoborus* populations can reach staggering proportions. The anoxic hypolimnion provides the larva with a refuge from fish predation.

Studies in Lake Valencia showed that *Chaoborus* predation powerfully suppressed herbivore numbers. When the lake was stratified, *Chaoborus* became abundant, using the anoxic hypolimnion as a refuge from their fish predators. By making diurnal vertical migrations, up into the epilimnion at night and down again at dawn, *Chaoborus* was able to devour herbivores with relative impunity. Lewis (1996) pointed out that, since tropical lakes develop anoxic hypolimnia more quickly than temperate ones, they are more likely to provide *Chaoborus* with a refuge from its fish predators.

Lewis (1996) also indicated that *Chaoborus* may have two very significant effects on the biota of tropical lakes. First, *Chaoborus* may constrain herbivore populations at levels that are too low to allow efficient harvesting of phytoplankton. This might lead to the development of large phytoplankton populations. Second, the addition of another link in the food chain leading from primary producers (phytoplankton) to fish effectively reduces the energy available to the fish, since each link in the food chain uses some of the energy fixed by the primary producers (see sections 5.7 and 5.8). Effectively, the presence of

Chaoborus could reduce the fish yield from a lake. Indeed, this seems to be the case. *Chaoborus* is absent from Lake Tanganyika (see section 5.1.3) and planktivorous fish are present. Since the food chain is shorter, fish yields are greater in this lake than either Lakes Malawi or Victoria where dense populations of *Chaoborus* occur (Hecky 1984).

The *Chaoborus*–herbivore interactions described above demonstrate that herbivore populations could be either limited by food supply if phytoplankton production was nutrient-limited or suppressed through excessive predation. These two possible controls on the size of herbivore populations are referred to as '**bottom-up**' and '**top-down**' controls respectively. We will look at how these two processes operate in section 5.12. We also noted above that energy availability declines with each link in the food chain, and now need to look at energy flow and food chains in more detail.

5.7 | Food chains and energy flow

When one species feeds upon another, the two species become ecologically linked; these links may form complex **food webs** and may have, in all but the simplest of ecosystems, a myriad of interconnections. The number of interconnections or realised links in a food web divided by the number of possible interactions is a measure of **food web connectance**. Food webs rarely tell a complete story. Species interactions may vary seasonally, and some of the interactions depicted in the web may be strong, others weak. Food preferences may change with age.

The food web illustrated in Fig 5.24, although on first inspection appearing complex, is clearly a simplification of the feeding relationships of the species found associated with the *Eichhornia* mat in Ranu Lamongan. The web does little to indicate the relative importance of components in an animal's diet, and links in the web are unlikely to be of equal importance. Ideally, we need to know the relative contribution, in energy terms, of each of the food items that make up an animal's diet. To achieve this for an entire ecosystem, such as Ranu Lamongan, would be an enormous under-taking, but some significant ecological principles have been established through the analysis of energy flow along food chains.

Energy is defined as the ability to do work, and the behaviour of energy is described by the **laws of thermodynamics** (section 1.3.3). Living organisms expend energy continuously in activities such as movement, growth, respiration and reproduction. Energy expenditure by organisms varies on daily, seasonal and life history time scales. A dormant seed expends less energy than the same seed undergoing germination; a fish avoiding a predator uses more energy than one feeding quietly.

The start of all energy flow within communities is through the energy fixed in photosynthesis as described in chapter 3. The plant material produced may be consumed by herbivores or, after death, by detritivores. Much of the plant material is not consumed and accumulates in the soil or sediments as organic matter (see section 2.9). The fate of the material consumed by animals can be followed through an analysis of food chain energetics.

5.8 | Food chain energetics

By measuring the quantities of energy ingested as food, that lost in excretory products and faeces and that attributable to new growth and respiration, it is possible to construct an energy budget for an animal. This partitioning of energy through an animal can be determined from the following basic equation:

Energy = Energy + Energy lost + Energy lost
content content in respiration in faeces
of food of tissues and urine
ingested produced

The energy content of tissues produced includes that contained in new growth and that required for reproduction (gametes, asexual reproduction).

The allocation of an animal's energy intake can provide some very useful insights into its feeding ecology. This is best done by calculating a series of energetic efficiencies. The first of these is a measure of the animal's efficiency at exploiting food resources:

$$\text{Exploitation efficiency} = \frac{\text{Ingestion of food} \times 100}{\text{Prey production}}$$

Only a proportion of the food ingested is assimilated, the balance is voided as faeces:

$$\text{Assimilation efficiency} = \frac{\text{Assimilation} \times 100}{\text{Ingestion}}$$

The assimilation efficiency is largely a factor of diet. Seed eaters may assimilate as much as 80% of their energy intake, but organisms eating plant material rich in hard-to-digest materials such as cellulose and lignin may only be able to absorb 30–40% of the energy intake. In organisms with a diet of decaying wood, such as termites and millipedes, or soil organic matter (e.g. earthworms) the assimilation efficiency may be as low as 15%. Carnivores have a diet that is more easily digested, and the assimilation efficiencies of predators vary between 60–90%. Faecal production is high in animals with low assimilation efficiencies (herbivores) and low in carnivores with more efficient assimilation.

Some of the energy assimilated is lost in respiration and therefore:

$$\text{Net production efficiency} =$$

$$\frac{\text{Production (growth and reproduction)} \times 100}{\text{Assimilation}}$$

The net production efficiency reflects an animal's life style and physiology. Endotherms (see section 2.7.3) and those that are particularly active have a low net production efficiency (1–10%) because their respiratory demands are so high. Less mobile and ectothermic animals may succeed in converting as much as 75% of their assimilated energy into new tissues. Sedentary aquatic animals which rely on water currents to deliver their food often have particularly high net production efficiencies. We can also calculate the gross production efficiency, a measure of the energy conversion efficiency inclusive of respiratory losses:

$$\text{Gross production efficiency} = \text{Assimilation efficiency} \times \text{Net production efficiency}$$

$$= \frac{\text{Production} \times 100}{\text{Ingestion}}$$

Gross production efficiencies of endotherms such as birds and large mammals usually fall between 1–5%, but may be even less than 1%. Most insects are more efficient (5–15%) and some aquatic animals may have gross production efficiencies as high as 30%. The efficiency with which prey production is converted to consumer production is a measure of ecological efficiency:

$$\text{Ecological efficiency} = \text{Exploitation efficiency} \times \text{Assimilation efficiency} \times \text{Net production efficiency}$$

$$= \frac{\text{Consumer production} \times 100}{\text{Prey production}}$$

Constructing energy budgets for individual animals is informative and provides a basis to explain features of animal behaviour such as the time spent foraging for food. It also provides a mechanism to investigate the allocation of an animal's resources to growth, respiration and reproductive effort. Energy flow through ecosystems can also provide significant insights on how ecosystems function, and Lindeman (1942) developed the trophic level concept.

5.9 | Trophic levels

Energy flow is one way, from the sun to the earth. Only about half of the sun's radiation reaches the earth owing to absorption and reflection by the atmosphere. The amount of radiant energy entering ecosystems is a function of latitude, altitude and weather, particularly cloud cover. The intensity of radiation is lower at higher latitudes and increases with increasing altitude. Intensity is markedly reduced by cloud cover.

There are three major ways in which organisms fix or obtain energy. Organisms that fix the energy from solar radiation into energy-rich organic compounds are called **photosynthetic autotrophs** or primary producers (see chapter 3). A few bacteria are **chemosynthetic autotrophs** and obtain their energy from inorganic chemicals. **Heterotrophs** obtain their energy by eating plants or animals. **Herbivores** eat plants, **carnivores** eat animals and **omnivores** have a mixed diet. This is an example of a **grazing food chain** in which the first component is living plant matter.

Autotrophs constitute the first **trophic level**. Of the energy fixed by these organisms, some is used by them for respiration, growth and reproduction and some is passed on to the next trophic level, herbivores. Some of the energy enters another food chain system, known as the **detritus food chain** (see chapter 10). There is little functional difference between grazing and detrital food chains, and the same organisms may form links in either type of chain. We can analyse a food web by looking at features such as the number of organisms, their biomass and energy content in each trophic level.

5.9.1 Pyramids of number and biomass

Trophic structure may be shown graphically by means of ecological pyramids. There are usually more organisms at the base of a food chain than in the trophic levels above, giving the layers a shape like a pyramid. This is not always the case. For example, numerous insects could be feeding on just one tree, producing an inverted number pyramid. Similarly, small predators which hunt in a pack (e.g. wild dogs) may consume a few large animals, perhaps less than the number of predators in the pack.

If we were to weigh all the insects feeding on the tree described above, we would obtain their **biomass**. If we also were able to weigh the tree, we would discover that the tree had a higher biomass than the insects feeding on it. Similarly, the total biomass of the prey is greater than the biomass of the dogs themselves. Therefore pyramids of biomass are less likely to be inverted than pyramids of number. However, in situations where primary production is very rapid, the standing biomass of autotrophs may be lower than the organisms feeding on it. In this case, the biomass pyramid will be inverted.

5.9.2 Energy pyramids

Energy pyramids are never inverted. These pyramids depict the transfer of energy from one trophic level to the one above, and clearly show

that the amount of energy available to higher trophic levels is significantly less than that available to lower levels. (Figure 5.25). Energy pyramids are constructed on the assumption that energy flows from one trophic level to the next without missing a level. This is often not the case; many organisms have rather catholic tastes, feeding on a range of organisms from different trophic levels. Indeed, feeding patterns may change with an animals age. *Clarias gariepinus*, the African catfish, is an omnivore feeding on phytoplankton (producer trophic level), zooplankton (primary consumer) and other fish (secondary consumers). Indeed, it even feeds on its own kind. The tarpon (Figure 5.26) feeds at two trophic levels and, indeed, humans feed at a number of trophic levels. This variety can make the allocation of organisms to trophic levels difficult. Feeding relationships combine to form very intricate food webs.

Omnivory makes trophic level allocation difficult. If a food species is a carnivore, we need to know the feeding history of all the organisms that the carnivore has eaten before we can allocate it to a trophic level. To construct an energy pyramid, for organisms that feed at several trophic levels, the energy absorbed must be apportioned to one level above each of the levels from which food is derived. This entails an enormous amount of work. Furthermore, there is a tendency for omnivory to become more prevalent at higher trophic levels for two reasons. First, there are more trophic levels for the organism at higher trophic levels to feed on and, second, omnivores typically gain most of their energy from the lowest trophic level on which they feed (Hairston and Hairston 1993).

Decomposer organisms break down organic matter produced at all trophic levels and therefore operate at all levels, but care is needed in allocating these organisms to trophic levels. For example, decomposers breaking down either plant detritus or the undigested remains of plants in animal faeces are, in energy terms, acting at the same trophic level (primary consumers). This again illustrates a limitation of the trophic level concept.

Of the energy fixed by autotrophs, some is used

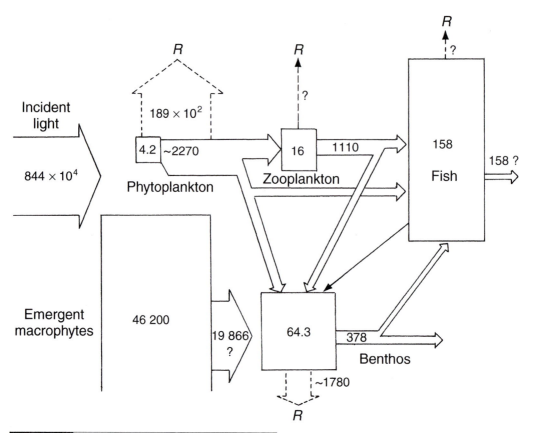

Figure 5.25 Energy flow diagram for Lake Chad, West Africa. Note that the biomass in each of the successive trophic levels (phytoplankton, zooplankton and fish) increases; the biomass pyramid is inverted. The energy flow between these trophic levels shows a progressive decline, with energy lost at each transfer and therefore the energy pyramid is not inverted. Biomass is in kJ m^{-2}, rates of production and respiration (R) are in kJ m^{-2} year^{-1} (adapted from Carmouze et al. 1983 with kind permission from Kluwer Academic Publishers).

to meet their needs and the balance may be assimilated by organisms in the next trophic level, the herbivores. The energy transferred to the second trophic level is either not absorbed by the animal and passed out as faeces or absorbed. The portion that is absorbed may be excreted, used in respiration or assimilated for growth and reproduction. In this way, even less energy, transferred from the producer to the herbivore, is made available to the third trophic level. Energy flow from one trophic level to the next is of considerable ecological inter-est and is assessed by calculating ecological efficiencies. The efficiency of any plant can be calculated from:

$$\text{Efficiency} = \frac{\text{kJ in newly formed plant material} \times 100}{\text{kJ in incident sunlight}}$$

The efficiency of plants varies between species and also with environments, but for land plants it is usually only around 1%, and is even lower for aquatic plants. We have seen that efficiencies can be calculated for individual animals (see section 5.8). Ecological efficiencies can be calculated for each link in a food chain and for the food chain as a whole. As energy is lost at each transfer between trophic levels, ecosystem food chains must have a limited length and, in most ecosystems, it is rare to find more than 3 or 4 trophic levels.

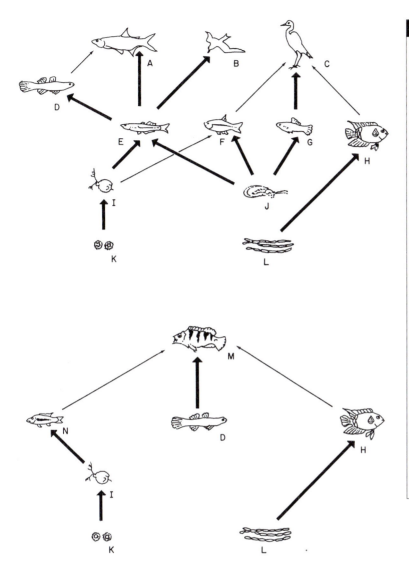

Figure 5.26 Generalised food web of common Gatun Lake populations, contrasting structure before (top) and after (bottom) the introduction of the top predator *Cichla ocellaris*. Thick arrows indicate that the food item is of major importance to the consumer, and thin arrows indicate a minor importance. Key to species: (A) *Tarpon atlanticus*; (B) *Chlidonias niger*; (C) several species of herons and kingfishers; (D) *Gobiomorus dormitor*; (E) *Melaniris chagresi*; (F) Characinidae, including four common species; (G) Poeciliidae, including two common species – one exclusively herbivorous, *Poecilia mexicana* and one exclusively insectivorous, *Gambusia nicaraguagensis*; (H) *Cichlasoma maculicauda*; (I) zooplankton; (J) terrestrial insects; (K) nannophytoplankton; (L) filamentous green algae; (M) adult *Cichla ocellaris*; (N) young *Cichla* (after Zaret and Paine 1973. Reprinted with permission from Zaret, T. M. and Paine, R. T. Species introduction in a tropical lake. *Science* 182, 449–455. Copyright 1973 American Association for the Advancement of Science).

5.10 | Limited length of food chains

The number of trophic levels, or links in the food chain, in ecosystems is typically 3 or 4 and rarely more than 5. Pimm (1982) proposed four hypotheses to explain why food chains are short; these are reviewed below. The hypotheses relate to energy flow, size and design criteria, optimal foraging and the fragility of long chains.

5.10.1 Energy flow

The amount of energy that is made available to the next trophic level is usually a small fraction of that consumed. This is a measure of ecological efficiency (see section 5.8) and varies from 3% in endotherms to nearly 60% in some insects. Most of the energy at one trophic level is lost from the system as heat, and some is not assimilated by the animal. Given such a high rate of energy reduction at each trophic level, there must soon come a time when there is inadequate energy to support another trophic level.

In natural systems where primary production is extremely low, energy flow may impose limits on food chain length. However, if energy is the controlling factor, food chains should increase in length with increasing productivity. Also, food chains made up of energy efficient organisms (e.g. insects and insectivores) should be longer than those with links that include less efficient organisms (e.g. endothermic vertebrates). Neither of these relationships have been demonstrated, and Pimm (1982) concluded that energy can not be the sole factor limiting food chain length.

5.10.2 Size and design criteria

The size of an animal has the potential to limit the length of a food chain. Generally a predator will be larger than its prey, and this places design limits on a species. Increased size also means increased energy requirements. Therefore a larger animal added to the end of a food chain will require a proportionately larger increase in primary productivity to support it. Although larger animals need more energy, their large size enables them to forage over a larger area than smaller animals.

5.10.3 Optimal foraging

Since there is more energy available at lower trophic levels, it has been argued that food chains are surprisingly long (Hutchinson 1959). There is some reason to expect animals to feed at the lowest trophic level where energy is most abundant. In other words, why are not all animals herbivores? While energy availability may be an advantage, competition may force species to utilise other food sources, and herbivores are susceptible to predation. While there are advantages in feeding low in the food chain, there are also advantages in being higher up the chain: the diet of carnivores is more easily assimilated than that of herbivores.

An animal, through its food, needs to fulfil both its energy and nutrient requirements. To do this, the animal can adopt a range of strategies. For example, it can feed for a longer time on poor-quality food, or spend some time looking for rich food resources and less time actually feeding. An animal seeking food (**foraging**) will be more exposed to predators than one hiding in a shelter. So an animal is faced with a series of decisions. Where to look for food? How long to spend feeding in one area before moving on to another? How

long to spend feeding each day? Which type of food to eat?

The optimal foraging theory states that an animal should only remain in an area so long as its net rate of energy gain is above a certain level. The net energy gain can be measured as the amount of energy in the food minus the energy expended in finding, ingesting and digesting it. Food spread is not uniform but occurs in high- or low-density patches. Large food items are usually less common than small food items, but a large food item may give a better return per unit effort. A large prey item may take considerable effort to capture and may require a team effort. In this case, the prey has to be shared with the team. Therefore, social structure also must be factored into the optimal foraging equation.

That an optimal foraging strategy is being used can be demonstrated by comparing the size distribution of prey available to an animal and the size distribution of the prey captured by the predator. If these two size distributions differ, the animal may be exhibiting a selective foraging strategy. Showing, through a study of energetics, that the size selected by the predator is the size that can be caught and eaten with the greatest return in energy leads to the conclusion that an optimal foraging strategy is maximising energy gain.

5.10.4 Fragility of long chains

Long food chains are fragile. Fluctuations at lower levels are magnified at higher levels and top predators suffer most. Therefore, in an environment where fluctuations are common (i.e. an unstable environment), predators must be able to recover from catastrophes. Recovery from environmental perturbation is slower in systems with longer food chains. However, Briand (1983) analysed 40 food webs and was unable to show a difference in the length of food chains from fluctuating environments in comparison with those from more stable environments. None the less, food chains are short and the number of links is usually less than five.

5.10 5 Food chain lengths in different ecosystems

It has been shown that the food chains in the open water communities of lakes are generally longer than those found in terrestrial systems. Typically, terrestrial communities have 3 trophic levels, whereas the pelagic zones in lakes have 4. Hairston and Hairston (1993) suggested the following reasons to explain this difference. Aquatic primary producers are small and unable to retain space. They live in a mobile environment and are selected to be small for buoyancy, rapid nutrient uptake and high reproductive rates. Trees in a forest are adapted to compete for space and being tall is a great advantage (it is also costly, as the tree has to invest in a large trunk which contributes nothing directly to carbon fixation). Trees are long-lived and reproduce slowly.

Aquatic herbivores are generally small as they feed on small algal cells. They usually engulf entire organisms, and most of their food intake is readily assimilated. Terrestrial herbivores vary greatly in size and are selective in the parts of the primary producers they consume. Furthermore, they consume only a small fraction of the net primary production. Competition for space selects for large size and longevity.

Zooplanktivorous fish provide the only suitable prey for larger fish. Predatory fish have to catch their prey with their mouths as their limbs have become modified for propulsion and are not suitable for prey capture and handling. Consequently, these animals experience a strong gape limitation: the maximum prey size that can be captured and consumed is limited by the size of the predator's mouth. Most terrestrial animals have a greater capacity to manipulate food and therefore can handle prey that may be significantly larger than themselves. Terrestrial carnivores generally feed indiscriminately both on other carnivores and the more numerous herbivores.

Clearly, the analysis of food webs is far from simple, and convincing explanations as to why food chains are so short and why they vary in length are not yet available, although, as described above, a number of plausible hypotheses have been proposed. The trophic level concept, as developed by Lindeman (1942), provided a framework that seemed to simplify the study of food webs and was, therefore, attractive to ecologists working on energy flow and feeding relationships. However, energy flow through ecosystems even with only a few species is far from simple, and future food web studies will need to be more detailed if patterns of energy flow are to be explained.

5.11 Food chain efficiencies

It is important to note that energy flows through an ecosystem, it does not cycle. At each transfer, some energy is lost from the system as heat, and some energy may be used, for example, by a fish in swimming or gill ventilation. This energy is, therefore, not available to the next trophic level.

Energy transfer between trophic levels can be assessed by calculating what has been called Lindeman's efficiency (Lindeman 1942):

$$\text{Lindeman's efficiency} = \frac{\text{assimilation at trophic level } n}{\text{assimilation at trophic level } n-1}$$

Lindeman efficiencies have frequently been found to be around 10%. That is, about 10% of the net production of plants ends up as net production in herbivores and about 10% of this makes it way into net production of the third trophic level. This is a very rough approximation and May (1979) noted that it was largely based on studies of food chains in freshwater lakes and laboratory aquaria. Humphreys (1979) studied the relationship between annual production (P) and respiration (R) in natural animal populations. Several interesting features emerged from his study. Production efficiency is significantly lower for herbivores than carnivores and detrital feeders. Biochemical conversion efficiencies for animals eating other animals are likely to be higher than those of animals eating plants. Plants contain a significant amount of material that is difficult to break down.

Humphreys (1979) also showed that: there is no significant correlation between production efficiency and the magnitude of production;

Table 5.1 Mean production efficiency, $P/(P+R)$, for various groups of animals

Group	Mean production efficiency (%)
Insectivores	0.9
Birds	1.3
Small mammal communities	1.5
Other mammals	3.1
Fish and social insects	10.0
Non-insect invertebrates	25.0
Non-social insects	41.0
Non-insect invertebrates	
herbivores	21.0
carnivores	28.0
detritivores	36.0
Non-social insects	
herbivores	39.0
carnivores	47.0
detritivores	56.0

Source: Humphreys 1979.

there is no correlation between production efficiency and animal weight; and habitats (aquatic or terrestrial) do not seem to affect production efficiencies. Table 5.1 shows that homeothermic animals (endotherms) have production efficiencies in the range 1–3%, poikilotherms (ectotherms) in the range 10–40%. In other words, endotherms pay a high price to maintain their body temperatures within narrow limits (see section 2.7.3).

Pimentel *et al.* (1975) assembled estimates of the percentage of plant production that is consumed by animals (Table 5.2). May (1979) pointed out that, by merging Tables 5.1 and 5.2, it can be shown that food chain efficiencies can vary over two or more orders of magnitude from less than 0.1% to more than 10%. Therefore this evidence clearly shows that the 10% rule for energy transfers is rather too general.

5.12 | Food web dynamics

The introduction of four species of fish to Ranu Lamongan did not appear to have a major impact on the species present within the lake (see section

5.5). The lake was studied prior to the introductions by Ruttner (1931) and the fish were probably introduced in 1949. Subsequent work by Green *et al.* (1976) showed remarkably little change in the flora and fauna, although the active fishery within the lake was centred on two of the introduced species. The introduced species were not top predators and this is probably the major reason why so little impact was made. Let us now consider the change that resulted in the food web of a lake to which a voracious top predator was introduced.

In 1967, *Cichla ocellaris* (Cichlidae), a voracious piscivore, was introduced to Gatun Lake in the Panama Canal Zone. *Cichla ocellaris* is native to the Amazon River and its tributaries and was introduced to Lake Gatun because it is both good to eat and an exciting fish to catch. While this fish has indeed provided entertainment and is the only freshwater fish sold for consumption in this area, its introduction had one unforeseen effect. In less than 5 years, the introduction of this predator, which can grow up to 2 kg, led to the elimination of 6 of the 8 common native fish (Zaret and Paine 1973).

The initial introduction of *Cichla* to Gatun Lake

Table 5.2	The percentage of plant production consumed by feeding animal species, for various systems	
Plant	Consumers	Percentage of productivity consumed
Beech trees	Invertebrates	8.0
Oak trees	Invertebrates	10.6
Maple–beech trees	Invertebrates	5.9–6.6
Tulip–poplar trees	Invertebrates	5.6
Grass + forbs	Invertebrates	4–20
Grass + forbs	Invertebrates	<0.5
Alfalfa	Invertebrates	2.5
Grass	Invertebrates	9.6
Aquatic plants	Bivalves	11.0
Aquatic plants	Herbivorous animals	18.9
Algae	Zooplankton	25.0
Phytoplankton	Zooplankton	40.0
Marsh grass	Invertebrates	4.6–7.0
Meadow plants	Invertebrates	14.0
Sedge grass	Invertebrates	8.0

Source: Pimentel et al. 1975.

was made at one end of the lake, and its spread through the lake, surprisingly, occurred as a wave with the leading edge composed of sub-adults. Intense fishing slowed the spread of the fish, and the fish is territorial during the breeding season. Parents remain with their offspring for 2 months or more and breeding occurs for a considerable portion of each year. Consequently, breeding adults tend to remain in one vicinity during this extended breeding period. Immigrants to previously unexploited habitats were mostly immature; this introduced a lag into the rate at which new areas of the lake were colonised. This curious mechanism of population expansion provided Zaret and Paine (1973) an opportunity to compare the food webs in an area where *Cichla* had not yet invaded with one which had a high density of the introduced predator (Figure 5.26).

The predator-free arm of the lake contained a community composed of 14 fish species, with 11 species contributing significantly to the total fish biomass. In contrast, the site with the predator had only 7 species with the biomass dominated by just 2 species: *Cichla ocellaris* and *Cichlasoma maculicauda*. The increase in *Cichlasoma maculicauda* was probably due to a reduction by *Cichla* of the predators that previously fed on *Cichlasoma* fry.

The species most obviously affected were the secondary consumers (*Melaniris*, Characinidae and Poeciliidae). The decrease in numbers of the planktivore *Melaniris* resulted in changes in the zooplankton community. The zooplankter, *Ceriodaphnia* exists in two forms (**cyclomorphosis**), one with pointed extensions of the exoskeleton ('horns') and one without ('unhorned'). The unhorned forms possess a reproductive advantage but are also more susceptible to predation than horned forms. Zaret and Paine (1973) found that unhorned forms of *Ceriodaphnia* predominated in areas where *Melaniris* populations had all but been extinguished through *Cichla* predation.

The tertiary-consumer populations such as tarpon, black terns, kingfishers and herons, dependent on small fish for food, appeared less frequently in the *Cichla* areas of the lake. Zaret and Paine (1973) also noticed an apparent decline in phytoplankton biomass in those areas inhabited by *Cichla*. Thus the introduction of this top predator seems to have produced a **cascade** effect on the trophic levels within Gatun Lake: a large population of top predator leading to lower populations of secondary consumers leading to enhanced populations of zooplankton leading to reduced phytoplankton populations.

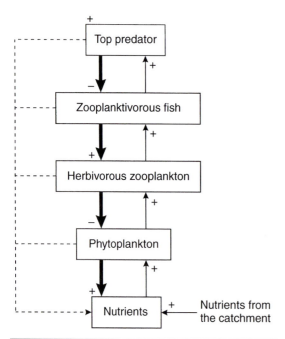

Figure 5.27 A trophic cascade in which top-down influences (large arrows) are stronger than bottom-up (nutrient supply, small arrows) controls. Addition of a top predator will result in a trophic cascade with a decrease in zooplanktivorous fish, an increase in herbivorous zooplankton and a decrease in phytoplankton. Notice that addition of nutrients from the catchment powers the food chain.

5.12.1 Cascade theory

The example described above illustrates that a change in the top carnivore population is transmitted to lower trophic levels through a **trophic cascade**. As the population of the top carnivore rises, so the biomass of the planktivore on which it feeds declines (Figure 5.27). The decline in the biomass of the planktivore is reflected in an increase in herbivore biomass, which, in turn, is reflected in the decline of phytoplankton populations (Carpenter *et al.* 1985).

Productivity at a given trophic level is maximised at an intermediate biomass of its predators. This is because potential productivity at all levels is set by nutrient supply. If a nutrient required by algae is scarce, algal growth will be limited by that nutrient (see section 2.6). The actual productivity depends on the rate at which nutrients are recycled; this is highest when predation intensities at all trophic levels are at intermediate levels. The

control of food web structure and function by top predators is known as '**top-down control**'. Food web structure and function can also be controlled by the rate at which nutrients are supplied; this type of control is referred to as '**bottom-up control**'. The relative merits of these two mechanisms will be debated in section 5.16 but first we need to describe how nutrients cycle within lakes, other ecosystems and, indeed, on a global basis.

5.13 | Biogeochemical cycles

Elements also flow through ecosystems. They are carried into lakes from the surrounding catchment by inflowing waters, by birds, by wind and a range of other mechanisms. They leave the lake by a number of routes: the outflow (if there is one), migration of organisms, or through the capture of aquatic organisms by terrestrial organisms. The important difference between the passage of energy through ecosystems and that of nutrients is that nutrients may cycle many times within the system before being lost from it. There is no mechanism by which energy can cycle. Energy flows through ecosystems but elements may cycle within them.

Ecologically, there are two distinctive types of biogeochemical cycles: those in which the most significant reservoir of the element is the atmosphere (e.g. carbon and nitrogen) and those in which the reservoir is an insoluble compound stored in the soil or sediment (e.g. phosphorus). Cycles with a large gaseous reservoir must be considered on a global basis, as gases are able to diffuse rapidly throughout the atmosphere. Sedimentary cycles are more localised, and the element is often less mobile, locked up in insoluble constituents of rocks and soil particles. Elements with a sedimentary reservoir tend to move from the land to oceanic deposits; the return of significant masses to land requires geological upheavals such as continental uplift and volcanic eruptions forming new land masses.

Many transformations within nutrient cycles are mediated by micro-organisms. These micro-organisms are particularly important in breaking down organic matter into its constituent ele-

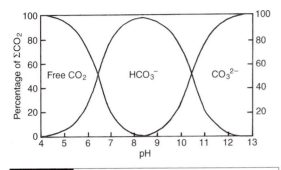

Figure 5.28 Relationship between pH and the relative proportions of total inorganic carbon dioxide (ΣCO_2 and the dissociation products of carbonic acid: bicarbonate (HCO_3^-) and carbonate (CO_3^{2-}) (after Golterman 1969 with kind permission from Blackwell Science).

ments. This organic matter break-down process is known as **decomposition** and will be covered in more detail in chapter 10.

5.13.1 Carbon cycle

The carbon cycle in aquatic systems starts with a physical exchange between the atmosphere and the water. Carbon dioxide is usually only a very small component of the atmosphere, but dangerously high concentrations can accumulate in some situations such as volcanic vents and lakes in volcanic craters (see Box 5.2). Carbon dioxide is soluble in water and the formation of HCO_3^- and CO_3^{2-} greatly increases its solubility:

$$CO_2 + H_2O \Leftrightarrow H_2CO_3$$

$$H_2CO_3 \Leftrightarrow H^+ + HCO_3^- \Leftrightarrow 2H^+ + CO_3^{2-}$$

The concentration of these three carbon species is dependent upon the pH of the water (Figure 5.28). Some of the carbon in the water column may be lost when it precipitates out as insoluble calcium carbonate:

$$Ca^{2+} + CO_3^{2-} \Leftrightarrow CaCO_3$$

The rate at which this deposition takes place is dependent upon the pH and the concentrations of calcium and carbonate ions. Calcium carbonate has a low solubility and under most conditions readily precipitates out. However, water containing a high level of carbon dioxide readily dissolves calcium from its carbonate minerals:

$$CaCO_3 + CO_2 + H_2O \Leftrightarrow Ca^{2+} + 2HCO_3^-$$

Removal of carbon dioxide, as occurs in photosynthesis, shifts the above equilibrium to the left and an accumulation of calcium carbonate results. This process is particularly important in the deposition of marl on aquatic plants and in the formation of the calcium carbonate skeletons in coral reef organisms. We will discuss this latter process in more detail in section 11.2.2.

Photosynthesis and respiration are the two major biological processes that influence the amount of carbon dioxide in natural waters. Once fixed as organic matter, the carbon cycle follows the links in the food chain with, at each stage, some carbon being returned to the water as carbon dioxide through respiration.

Much of the carbon dioxide found in natural waters results from the breakdown of organic matter by bacteria and through that produced in respiration. As photosynthesis requires light, this process is restricted to water depths receiving adequate light (see section 5.2.3). If the lake is stratified and productive, the carbon dioxide concentration in the epilimnion will be depressed through photosynthesis. The organic matter produced in the epilimnion gradually descends into the hypolimnion. Here, photosynthesis is no longer possible and decomposition takes place. Consequently, in the hypolimnion, the oxygen concentration declines and the carbon dioxide concentration rises. The shape of these carbon dioxide and oxygen depth profiles depends on the rates of: (1) interchange of carbon dioxide between the water and atmosphere; (2) photosynthesis; (3) respiration; and (4) the bicarbonate–carbonate system (see Figure 5.29). The vertical profiles that develop are destroyed at turnover. The carbon cycle is summarised in Figure 5.30.

Although it has been stated that the carbon dioxide concentration in the atmosphere is low, its current level is much higher today than it was a century ago. This increase has been attributed to our enhanced use of wood, coal, oil and gas as fuels. It has been suggested that this change in the atmosphere is resulting in significant global warming that could lead to a potentially

(a) Oligotrophic lake

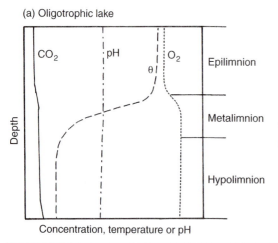

(b) Eutrophic lake

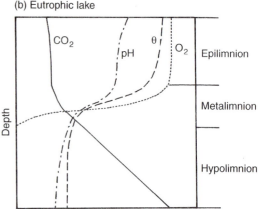

Figure 5.29 Generalised vertical distributions of the inorganic carbon content (ΣCO_2), pH, temperature (θ) and dissolved oxygen (O_2) in stratified lakes: (a) oligotrophic (nutrient-poor); (b) eutrophic (nutrient-rich, see section 5.15). In the eutrophic lake, CO_2 is removed from the epilimnion by dense populations of phytoplankton which have developed in response to the nutrient-rich conditions. Decomposition of the large amounts of organic matter produced in the epilimnion of the eutrophic lake occurs in the hypolimnion resulting in enhanced concentrations of CO_2 and depletion of O_2. In the oligotrophic lake, the O_2 concentration in the epilimnion decreases as the temperature of this layer increases, since the solubility of gases is inversely related to temperature. Oxygen production by phytoplankton is inadequate in the nutrient-poor waters to compensate for this loss. Approximate positions of the epilimnion, metalimnion and hypolimnion are indicated (Figure from Limnology by R.G. Wetzel, © 1975 by Saunders College Publishing, reproduced by permission).

devastating rise in mean sea level and a major alteration in the world's climate (see section 14.4).

5.13.2 Nitrogen cycle

The atmosphere is the major reservoir of molecular nitrogen (N_2) and, in this form, it is inaccessible to most organisms. Molecular nitrogen enters the nitrogen cycle through the process of **nitrogen fixation**, which is only carried out by certain species of bacteria and Cyanobacteria. Nitrogen fixation involves the reduction of molecular nitrogen to ammonia and requires an expenditure of energy supplied as carbohydrate:

$$3CH_2O + 2N_2 + 3H_2O + 4H^+ \rightarrow 3CO_2 + 4NH_4^+$$

The biochemical process is complex and poorly understood. Only a few species of aquatic micro-organisms have the enzyme system needed to fix atmospheric nitrogen and include the photosynthetic bacteria *Azotobacter* spp. and Cyanobacteria such as *Anabaena* spp. and *Aphanizomenon* spp. In most natural waters, the amount of nitrogen entering the system through nitrogen fixation is a small fraction of that derived from other sources.

In terrestrial systems, nitrogen fixation is best known in the symbiotic association between *Rhizobium* spp. and legumes. The *Rhizobium* bacteria are found in root nodules that develop in response to attack of the root hairs of a young legume. The nodules are connected to the plant's vascular system providing the bacteria with access to photosynthetic products which provide the energy required to break the strong bonds in the dinitrogen molecule. In return for the ideal environment and the energy provided to the bacteria, the plant assimilates some of the reduced nitrogen. Some non-legume plants also fix nitrogen through an association with actinomycete bacteria. In some tropical situations, the amount of reduced nitrogen fixed by some free-living bacteria can form a significant component of the nitrogen income to the ecosystem and may be as high as 100 kg ha^{-1} year^{-1}. Indeed, most of the biologically cycled nitrogen can be traced to nitrogen fixation, and its accumulation has occurred over millions of years.

Nitrogen is absorbed by most plants primarily

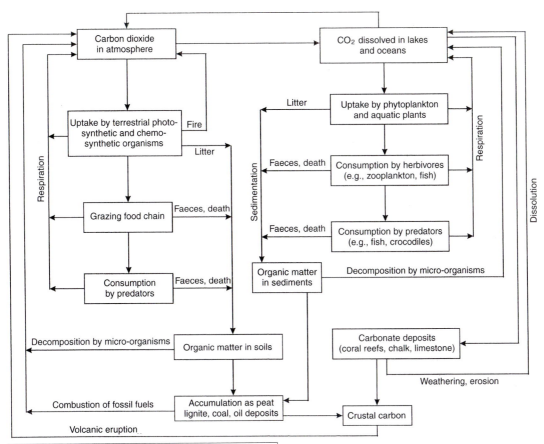

Figure 5.30 The carbon cycle.

as nitrate. Conversion of the ammonia produced through nitrogen fixation to nitrate occurs through **nitrification**. In this process organic and inorganic nitrogenous compounds are converted from a reduced state to a more oxidised state. The production of nitrate from ammonia is a two stage, energy-releasing process and both steps involve nitrifying bacteria. The nitrifying bacteria capable of oxidising NH_4^+ to NO_2^- are mostly *Nitrosomonas* spp. in the soil and *Nitrosococcus* spp. in the sea, but several other genera are capable of this process. Oxidation of nitrite to nitrate is mediated by *Nitrobacter* and *Nitrococcus* species. The overall nitrification reaction requires two moles of oxygen for each oxidation of NH_4^+:

$$NH_4^+ + 2O_2 \rightarrow NO_3^- + H_2O + 2H^+$$

Although oxygen is required for nitrification, these processes will continue in environments with oxygen concentrations as low as 0.3 mg O_2 L^{-1}. In anoxic hypolimnia and lake sediments, the rate of nitrification is zero and NH_4^+ accumulates. Furthermore, under these conditions, the adsorptive capacity of the sediments is reduced and marked release of NH_4^+ from the sediment into the overlying water may occur.

Nitrogen is one of the major constituents of cellular protoplasm and an integral part of amino acids and proteins. It is, therefore, an essential nutrient and its rate of supply can control the productivity of both aquatic and terrestrial systems. Many nitrogen-containing organic compounds are produced by plants and animals, and are released either through excretion or through decomposition when the organism dies. The release of the nitrogen in these organic compounds occurs through **ammonification**: the hydrolysis of proteins to produce amino acids and their oxidation to produce ammonia. In this process, some carbon is oxidised with the

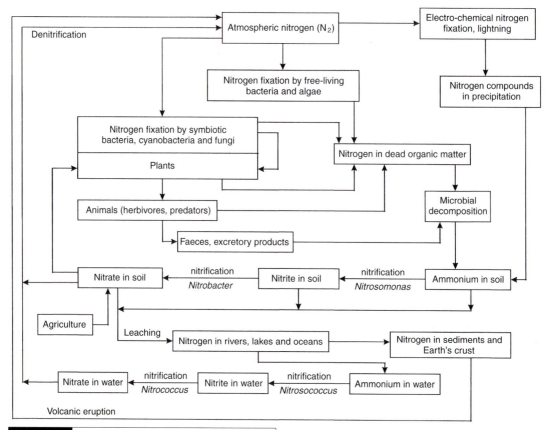

Figure 5.31 The nitrogen cycle.

release of energy, but, unlike nitrification, the energy potential of the nitrogen atom does not change.

We can now see that, through nitrogen fixation, nitrification and the action of organisms, nitrogen occurs in freshwaters in numerous forms: as dissolved molecular nitrogen (the raw material for nitrogen fixation), ammonium (NH_4^+), nitrite (NO_2^-), nitrate (NO_3^-) and in a wide array of nitrogen-containing organic compounds. The major sources of nitrogen include precipitation on the lake surface, inputs from surface groundwater drainage and, as described above, nitrogen fixation. Nitrogen leaves lakes through the outflow, permanent storage in the sediments and through **bacterial denitrification**.

Denitrification is an important process as it is the mechanism by which fixed nitrogen is returned to the atmosphere. The process is one of reduction of oxidised nitrogen as in the following sequence:

$$NO_3^- \rightarrow NO_2^- \rightarrow N_2O \rightarrow N_2$$

These biochemical processes can be assembled to produce a nitrogen cycle (Figure 5.31). The atmosphere is maintained at approximately 80% nitrogen since the rates of nitrogen fixation and denitrification approximately balance.

5.13.3 Sulfur cycle

Sulfur enters lakes in weathering products, from agricultural run-off and in both dry fall-out and precipitation from the atmosphere. As with carbon, the atmospheric sources have been greatly augmented through enhanced industrial activity and currently dominate all other sources of sulfur. The increase in sulfur oxides in the atmosphere has resulted in a decline in the pH of rain (acid rain) in many parts of the world. Like nitrogen, sulfur has a number of oxidation states, the most oxidised and reduced forms being sulfate (SO_4^{2-}) and sulfide (S^{2-}) respectively. The predominant form of sulfur in water is as sulfate but in the decomposition of organic matter, sulfur is mostly released as hydrogen sulfide.

Sulfur is utilised by all living organisms as it is an important constituent of some amino acids. However, the ecological role sulfur plays is perhaps more important than its requirement as a nutrient. Sulfate-reducing bacteria are heterotrophic and anaerobic and use sulfate as a hydrogen acceptor. These bacteria (*Desulfovibrio* spp. and *Desulfomonas* spp.) derive oxygen from sulfate for the oxidation of either organic matter or hydrogen:

$$H_2SO_4 + 2(CH_2O) \rightarrow 2CO_2 + 2H_2O + H_2S$$

$$H_2SO_4 + 4H_2 \rightarrow 4H_2O + H_2S$$

Photosynthetic sulfur bacteria require light as an energy source and use the sulfur in hydrogen sulfide as an electron donor in the reduction of CO_2:

$$CO_2 + 2H_2S \rightarrow (CH_2O) + H_2O + 2S$$

Compare this reaction with that describing the photosynthesis of green plants (see section 3.5). In the above photosynthesis, sulfur takes the place of the oxygen atom in water as an electron donor. The sulfur produced accumulates in the sediments of the lakes unless the overlying water becomes oxygenated in which case the sulfur is oxidised first to sulfite and then to sulfate. Accumulation of hydrogen sulfide in the sediments of lakes and wetlands explains why gases released from them often smell of rotten eggs.

5.13.4 Phosphorus cycle

Phosphorus is a key nutrient and its role in aquatic systems has been intensively studied. The interest in phosphorus stems from its importance in cell metabolism and, ecologically, from its often frequently inadequate supply and the response of lakes when that supply is enhanced. Phosphorus is a major constituent of nucleic acids, ATP, cell membranes and plant cell walls and is deposited in the teeth and bones of animals. Unlike the numerous forms in which

nitrogen occurs, the only significant form of phosphorus dissolved in natural waters is as anions of orthophosphoric acid (H_3PO_4). In waters with a normal pH range, $H_2PO_4^-$ and HPO_4^{2-} predominate. More than 90% of phosphorus is present in a range of dissolved and particulate organic compounds and, as an element, its supply frequently limits algal growth. This is because the supply to demand ratio of phosphorus is often the lowest of all nutrients in natural waters.

Phosphorus enters a lake via precipitation, in solution and as particles in inflowing rivers and in effluents from sewage treatment plants, industries and the surrounding land. It is lost from lakes through the outflow and through either temporary or permanent deposition within the sediments. Mountain lakes, with catchment areas dominated by hard-rock, generally have waters deficient in phosphorus. Lowland lakes, surrounded by areas with deeper soils, are often more phosphorus enriched. Since phosphorus often limits primary production, increased inputs of this element frequently results in an increase in the primary production of a lake. Lakes which receive run-off from cultivated or deforested catchments or phosphorus-rich sewage effluents are often highly productive and this enrichment significantly alters both the biomass and the species composition of the lake's biota (see section 5.15).

Even though aquatic organisms only contain about 1% phosphorus by dry weight, uptake by algae can rapidly deplete the water of its soluble phosphorus. The algae, on death, sink to the bottom taking phosphorus with them and, therefore, exchange of phosphorus between the sediments and the overlying water is, in many lakes, a significant part of phosphorus cycling in lakes. In most lakes, there is a net movement of phosphorus from the water column into the sediments and therefore algal growth, in these lakes, is reliant on a continual supply of phosphorus from the catchment.

Organic matter in the sediments is broken down by decomposers and, in this process, oxygen is consumed. If the supply of oxygen from the water column above the sediment is sufficient to replace that consumed, decomposition continues and the water and surface layers of the sediment remain oxygenated. However, in a stratified lake with an organic-rich sediment, high rates of decomposition may lead to deoxygenation of the hypolimnion. Under these conditions, phosphorus compounds in the sediments are more soluble and phosphorus may be released from the sediments into the hypolimnion. At overturn, the phosphorus-enriched, hypolimnetic water mixes with the epilimnion and enhanced algal growth often results. Therefore, phosphorus cycling within a lake is closely related to the lake's thermal regime (see section 5.1).

Many soils are deficient in phosphorus and its supply in fertilisers is essential if crop production is to be enhanced. Orthophosphate availability to plants is significantly affected by pH and is most readily available to plants growing in soils with a near neutral pH. In acid soils, phosphate ions are precipitated as aluminium and iron compounds and, in alkaline soils, the phosphate ions react with calcium carbonate to produce the relatively insoluble hydroxiapatite ($Ca_5(PO_4)_3(OH)$). Owing to these precipitation reactions, little phosphorus leaches from the soil and therefore even intensive crop farming is often not a major supply of phosphorus to natural waters. This contrasts with the high loss of nitrogen in the drainage water from agricultural fields.

Phosphorus has many applications apart from fertilisers and is used in animal feed supplements, detergents, pesticides and herbicides and in medicines. Most of the mined phosphorus comes from sedimentary deposits of marine origin, but about 5% of the world's phosphate production is from guano – sea bird droppings. The phosphorus cycle differs from that of carbon and nitrogen in that there is no atmospheric reservoir of phosphorus (apart from dust particles). Human activity has played a major role in accelerating the rate at which phosphorus is cycled (Figure 5.32).

5.13.5 Silicon cycle

Silicon is the second most abundant element in the lithosphere and it enters aquatic systems through the weathering of feldspar rocks. The silica (SiO_2) content of river waters tends to be remarkably uniform, but, in lakes, concentrations

frequently exhibit marked variations in seasonal and spatial distribution. Silicon is an essential element for diatoms which produce a cell wall with two, overlapping shells (frustules) composed of silica. Depletion of silica concentrations in the euphotic zone is often clearly associated with the intensive assimilation of silica by diatoms. Diatom growth can, through this requirement for silica, be limited by the supply of this element, and clear relationships between silica supply and diatom growth has been demonstrated in a classic study of a temperate diatom (Lund 1950).

Kilham et al. (1986) demonstrated that blooms of the diatom *Melosira* in Lake Malawi were associated with high concentrations of dissolved silica which occurred following the breakdown of thermal stratification (see section 5.1.3). *Melosira* has a high demand for silica as it typically produces thick-walled frustules, and the growth of this alga rapidly depletes the water of silica unless it is replenished by turbulence or upwelling of silica-enriched bottom waters. The occurrence of the diatom *Stephanodiscus* in Lake Malawi and other African rift valley lakes has been correlated with low dissolved silica and periods of stable stratification. High abundances of *Stephanodiscus* often precede *Melosira* blooms at the beginning of the mixing season when dissolved silica levels are low, and occur again when the *Melosira* bloom has depleted the silica concentrations in the water column. This provides a neat example of the limiting factor concept described in section 2.6.

5.14 | Quantitative aspects of nutrient supply and cycling

In our discussion of nutrient cycles above, we have seen that all nutrients reside in a number of compartments or pools. The cycles consist of a series of interchanges or paths between these compartments, and the concentration of the nutrient within a particular pool may indicate its availability for uptake by plants and animals. While the availability of a nutrient measured as its concentration may be important, consideration must also be given to its **rate of supply** and **rate of uptake** to and from these compartments.

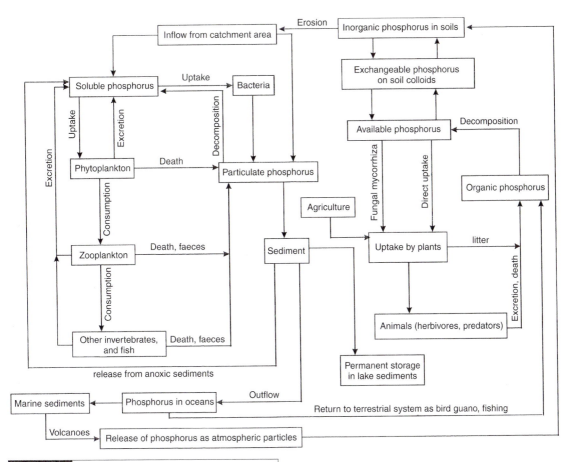

Figure 5.32 The phosphorus cycle.

The rate of movement between compartments is a measure of the **nutrient flux**. To study nutrient fluxes and to understand nutrient cycling within ecosystems, nutrient budgets need to be constructed. This quantitative approach to nutrient cycling can be applied to any ecosystem, and its application to lakes is described below.

The rate of nutrient supply to the water column of lakes occurs through two mechanisms: **external loading** and **internal loading**. External loading is the supply of nutrients from surrounding systems and includes the nutrients which enter the lake, for example, in inflowing waters, as wind-borne material, as leaf litter, or through the action of amphibious animals. Internal loading refers to the release of nutrients from the sediment within the lake. In most cases, there is a net passage of nutrients into the sediments as organ-

isms and other particles settle to the lake bottom. Under certain conditions and through the action of decomposers, nutrients may be released from sediments and made available to organisms growing in the upper parts of the water column. We have described how this occurs in the nitrogen and phosphorus cycles (see sections 5.13.2 and 5.13.4). Nutrients are lost from the water column of a lake through the outflow, through permanent accretion within the sediments and through the loss of organisms (fish migration, fish and aquatic plant harvesting, emergence of insects). Where a lake has no outlet, lying within a closed or **endorheic** basin, evaporation removes pure water and leaves any chemicals brought into the lake behind. Such lakes become saline or sodic lakes (Box 5.5).

When nutrient loads on a lake increase, significant changes in the lake's biota often result. This nutrient enrichment and the suite of mostly

Box 5.5 | Life in saline and sodic lakes

Endorheic lakes in areas with high evaporation rates which receive waters rich in chemicals, soon become saline (enriched with sodium chloride) or sodic (enriched with sodium carbonate). Most such lakes occur in hot, dry environments.

Salt lakes occur on all continents and are, by convention, taken to be lakes with salinities greater than 3 g L^{-1}. The variety of species inhabiting salt lakes declines with increasing salinity and very saline waters contain few species. Nevertheless, a variety of organisms thrive in salt lakes and include bacteria, algae, plants and a wide range of invertebrates and vertebrates (Williams 1995). In highly saline lakes, aquatic plants are absent and the phytoplankton often dominated by one species, the green alga *Dunaliella salina*. In less saline waters, *Dunaliella* is joined by diatoms and Cyanobacteria. The fauna in salt lakes comprises three major groups: **halobionts** (animals living in highly saline waters), **halophiles** (animals adapted to moderately saline waters) and salt-tolerant freshwater species. The animals inhabiting salt lakes either are able to tolerate high body fluid concentrations (**osmoconformers**) or have a strong ability to regulate body fluid concentrations (**osmoregulators**; see section 6.5.1). Salinity is not the only feature to which organisms inhabiting salt lakes must have evolved adaptations. High light intensity, high temperatures, low oxygen concentrations and seasonal or long-term desiccation are other features to which these organisms have to be adapted.

The biota of soda lakes is also depauperate. Lake Nakuru, Kenya, contains no large plants and its phytoplankton community is dominated by just one species of Cyanobacteria: *Spirulina platensis*. This and other soda lakes are incredibly productive, and photosynthetic rates have been shown to approach theoretical upper limits (Talling *et al*. 1973). *Spirulina* is eaten by a calanoid copepod (*Lovenula africana*) and a small cichlid (*Oreochromis alcalicus grahami*). Five species of rotifers and six aquatic insects complete the simple aquatic community. The paucity of aquatic species contrasts with the diversity of birds, and vast numbers of lesser flamingo (*Phoeniconaias minor*) often form a pink, flickering halo around the edge of the lake. These birds are filter feeders, using their beaks to strain algae and other microorganisms from the water. Fish-eating birds (pelicans, cormorants, herons, egrets, grebes and kingfishers) also occur in abundance. These birds have only been attracted to the lake since the introduction of fish to this once fishless lake.

---

adverse changes that accompanies it is known as **eutrophication** (see section 5.15). Eutrophication is caused by an increase in the nutrient supply to a lake, and it has been shown that lake restoration can be effected by reducing the supply of the nutrient that limits primary production. In most lakes, that nutrient is phosphorus. Several loading models have been developed to predict the reduction in phosphorus load required to effect this change (see, for example, Vollenweider 1975).

These models are complicated by the fact that lakes are not static water bodies. Adding a micro-gram of phosphorus to a beaker containing one litre of distilled water would result in a concentration of $1 \mu g$ P L^{-1}. However, if we now have a stream of water flow through the beaker, the phosphorus concentration will be gradually reduced as phosphorus is flushed from the beaker and diluted by the inflow. We can further complicate the system by having a number of inflows, each with a different and variable flow rate and each with a different and variable phosphorus concentration. We can add to our model lake an exchange between the water column and the bottom sediments, a seasonal alternation between periods of stratification and complete mixing, and the role of organisms in addition or removal of phosphorus from the lake. Despite these complexities, a number of mathematical models have been developed which can, with reasonable accuracy, predict the concentration of phosphorus, or other element, in a lake that will result from a change in the elemental loading on the lake.

These models also have been useful in identifying general principles relating to nutrient loads and the resultant nutrient concentration. For example, large lakes are less susceptible to pollution and nutrient enrichment than small lakes because of the effect of dilution. However, this general principle needs to consider the water residence time of a lake. Nutrients and pollutants entering lakes with short renewal times (i.e. high flushing rates) will be removed from the lake more quickly than from lakes with longer renewal times. Nutrients will also tend to be retained longer in lakes that are stratified, since nutrients which enter the hypolimnion may remain there until overturn. This point is particularly relevant to oligomictic lakes which may mix, and then only partially, once every few years. If the water in inflowing streams is significantly cooler than the lake water, materials entering the lake will be deposited in the hypolimnion and, in an oligomictic lake, they will accumulate there until the next mixing event. Osborne and Totome (1992a) found this to be the case in Lake Kutubu (see section 5.1.5).

Few nutrient budgets have been constructed for tropical lakes, and most of our understanding of relationships between nutrient loads and nutrient concentrations comes from studies on temperate lakes. Nutrient budgets have been used to predict the reduction in nutrient load required to effect a recovery from eutrophication. In doing this, the prediction must include nutrient inputs from all external sources and possible nutrient release from nutrient-enriched sediments (internal loading). Nutrient budget construction is not simple and requires extensive sampling (fortnightly or even weekly) of all inflows and the outflow, as well as of sites within the lake at representative depths. It also requires good hydrological information in order to construct a water budget for the lake. Regrettably, few tropical lakes have been studied this intensively. However, many tropical lakes have been subjected to nutrient enrichment and have become eutrophic as a result. Two case studies are presented below.

5.15 | Eutrophication

5.15.1 Lake Victoria

Lake Victoria in Central Africa is the world's second largest lake by area (68 800 km²) but, in comparison with the other great African lakes, it is rather shallow (40 m mean depth, 79 m maximum depth). The catchment area of Lake Victoria differs from that of Lakes Malawi and Tanganyika in being of low relief and therefore amenable to dense human habitation. Limnologists studied Lake Victoria in the 1950s and 1960s and therefore, unlike many tropical lakes, there is a data set against which we can compare the present status of the lake.

The deep waters of Lake Victoria in 1990–91 contained less oxygen than in the 1960s, and anoxia below 45 m depth was frequently encountered when the lake was stratified (October to March). Anoxia now affects up to 50% of the deeper waters for prolonged periods (Hecky 1993). In the early 1960s, such anoxia was infrequent and present only in samples collected near the sediments (Talling 1966). Catastrophic fish kills are now commonly reported and can be related to the widespread anoxia and vertical currents within the lake that occasionally bring this foul water to the surface. In contrast to this deep-water anoxia, the surface waters of the lake are now saturated or supersaturated with oxygen throughout the year. Talling (1966) measured values consistently below saturation. The higher oxygen concentrations in the surface waters have been attributed to a twofold increase in pelagic photosynthesis over the 30 years between 1960 and 1990 (Mugidde 1993). The increase in phytoplankton populations has resulted in a decrease in the depth of the euphotic zone in the lake (Figure 5.33).

The recent and historical studies on Lake

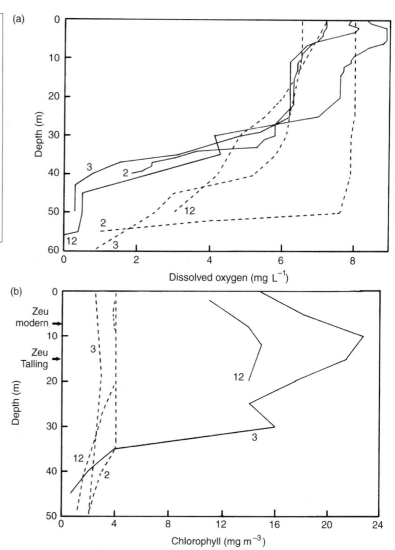

Figure 5.33 (a) Comparison of oxygen depth profiles in Lake Victoria in December (12), February (2) and March (3) in 1960–61 (dashed lines) and in 1989–90 (solid lines). (b) Chlorophyll depth profiles in December, February and March in 1960–61 (dashed lines) and 1989–90 (solid lines). The depth of the euphotic zone (Z_{eu}) in 1960 and 1990 is indicated (after Talling 1966; Hecky 1993 with kind permission from Wiley-VCH Verlag and E. Schweizerbart'sche Verlagsbuchhandlung).

Victoria indicate that sometime between 1960 and 1990 Lake Victoria underwent a limnological transition. The cause and timing of this change are important questions. A fundamental change in the fish community within Lake Victoria started in the 1980s with a population explosion of the introduced Nile perch (*Lates niloticus*) which has decimated the formerly species-rich pelagic haplochromine community (see Box 5.6). However, changes within the lake pre-date the introduction of this voracious predator.

One way of obtaining historical information of ecological changes in lakes is through the analysis of dated sediment cores. If it is assumed that lake sediments are deposited sequentially and that no post-deposition disturbance occurs (reasonable assumptions in sediments collected from deep-water areas), then analysis of sediment layers might provide insight to both the timing and causes of ecological changes within a lake or its catchment area. The study of a lake's ecological history, usually done through the analysis of dated sediment cores, is known as **palaeolimnology**.

Layers of a sediment core collected from a site 55m deep in Lake Victoria were dated and analysed. The core was dated by measuring the ^{137}Cs and ^{210}Pb content in each layer. [137]Cs entered

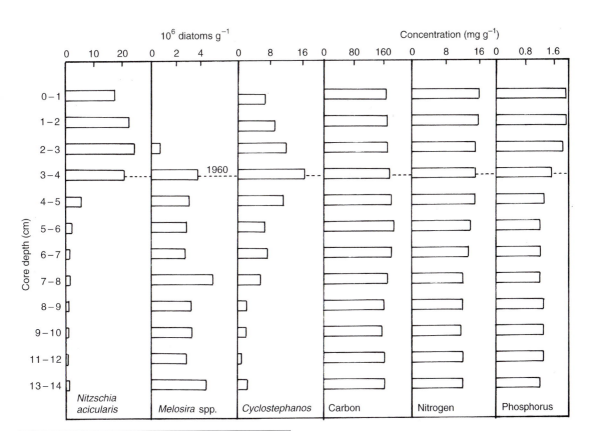

Figure 5.34 Profiles of diatom genera and the carbon, nitrogen and phosphorus content in a sediment core collected from Lake Victoria. The core was 14 cm long and dating using ^{137}Cs indicated that sediments between 3 and 4 cm were laid down around 1960 (dashed line). The ^{210}Pb dating technique suggested that the oldest sediments in the core were deposited around 1800 (after Hecky 1993 with kind permission from E. Schweizerbart'sche Verlagsbuchhandlung).

lake sediments during the period of atmospheric testing of nuclear weapons. The concentration of this fallout product increased when tests began, reached a peak and declined following the implementation of the atmospheric nuclear test ban treaty in 1963. [210]Pb is present in the atmosphere and is a decay product of naturally occurring [238]U. It is washed out of the atmosphere and reaches lake sediments where it decays with a half-life of 22.26 years. Measurement of ^{137}Cs and ^{210}Pb in sediment core sections can be used to date recent lake sediments.

Diatoms produce a silica shell (frustule) which come in a variety of intricately patterned shapes,

features on which diatom taxonomy is based. The frustules are somewhat resistant to destruction and are commonly found in lake sediments. Furthermore, some diatom species are planktonic, others are epiphytic or benthic; some thrive in nutrient-rich waters, others in waters poor in nutrients. From the species composition of the frustules in sediment layers it is often possible to infer features of the lake's ecology at the time the sediments were deposited. For example, the presence of epiphytes would indicate the concurrent presence of aquatic plants and a decline in epiphyte numbers, a decline in aquatic plant cover. Analysis of the diatom frustules within the layers of a sediment core can thus provide an avenue to reconstruct the ecological changes that have occurred within a lake and its catchment area (see Figure 5.22).

The diatom stratigraphy in the sediment core collected from Lake Victoria shows an increase in the sedimentation of the diatom *Cyclostephanos* occurring concurrently with an increased deposition of carbon and nitrogen (Figure 5.34). In the

1960s, phosphorus deposition increased and, by the late 1960s, *Melosira* spp. were largely replaced in the diatom community by *Nitzschia*. *Melosira* is a large, heavily silicified diatom whereas *Nitzschia* has thin-walled frustules and a preference for nutrient-rich conditions. The dated sediment core can also provide an estimate of sedimentation rates and results indicate that sedimentation rates increased from $57 \, \mathrm{g} \, \mathrm{m}^{-2} \, \mathrm{year}^{-1}$ in 1960 to $90 \, \mathrm{g} \, \mathrm{m}^{-2} \, \mathrm{year}^{-1}$ in 1990.

The increase in nitrogen and phosphorus deposition within the sediments was almost certainly due to enhanced clearing and burning of the vegetation surrounding the lake by the rapidly increasing human population. Nitrogen inflows to the lake increased first as natural vegetation in the catchment was removed, and phosphorus inputs were enhanced as soil erosion and burning, to increase soil fertility, became more widespread.

This process of nutrient enrichment and the changes in a lake that result from it is known as **eutrophication**. Eutrophic lakes are usually characterised by dense phytoplankton populations and, hence, poor light penetration, high oxygen concentrations in surface waters and anoxic hypolimnia. An increase in aquatic plants may occur in the early stages of eutrophication, but a decline, particularly of the submerged plants, occurs as phytoplankton densities rise. Floating plants, such as *Eichhornia* and *Salvinia*, may flourish under eutrophic conditions, and the dense mats that develop exclude light from the water column. This prevents oxygen production through phytoplankton photosynthesis (see section 5.2.1), and under the mat the entire water column may become anoxic. In eutrophic lakes, where phytoplankton populations develop, they are commonly dominated by a few species of Cyanobacteria. These characteristics contrast with those of nutrient-poor or **oligotrophic** lakes that typically have clear water and high oxygen concentrations throughout the water column even when it is stratified.

Box 5.6 | An ecological soap opera: Lake Victoria and the Nile perch

Lake Victoria provides one of the most dramatic examples of the damage that can be wreaked through the introduction of exotic fish species to a lake. The Nile perch (*Lates niloticus*), a piscivorous fish, was introduced (despite warnings of the likely adverse impacts, see Fryer 1960) to Lake Victoria around 1960. Its introduction was a misguided effort to enhance fish yields and to provide a sport fishery for tourists. In 1969–70 a lakewide survey found haplochromines in sufficient quantities to support a trawl fishery and a fish-processing plant to convert the catch to fish meal. The enterprise was not a success because in 1980 the fish species composition underwent a dramatic shift (Figure 5.35). Fish biomass in the lake shifted from one dominated by a diverse fauna of haplochromines to one dominated by the introduced Nile perch. The trigger for the sudden eruption in the Nile perch population is not known and was surprising, given that it had persisted for two decades at low density.

At least half of the estimated 400 haplochromine species, are now probably extinct. Goldschmidt *et al.* (1993) suggested that this may well represent the largest extinction event among vertebrates in the twentieth century. It is noteworthy that other East African lakes naturally inhabited by the Nile perch have few haplochromine species, and it may be that the Nile perch has regulated fish diversity in these lakes. The change in the species composition of the Lake Victoria fish catch has had a number of broader ecological and social consequences. The Nile perch has an oily flesh and can not be sun-dried, a method of preservation that works well for haplochromines. The Nile perch flesh can be smoked, but this requires firewood and, even in the 1980s, supplies around most of Lake Victoria were inadequate. This new demand for firewood accelerated the decline of forests in the Lake Victoria catchment, and this deforestation may be one of the causes of increased nutrient loadings on Lake Victoria and its subsequent eutrophication.

The Nile perch is now the basis of a thriving commercial fishery, and its fatty, flaky fillets are refrigerated and sold to local hotels and exported to Europe and Israel (Kaufman 1992). The revenues are far greater than those ever realised by the fishery dependent on the native fish species, but the wealth generated is concentrated in a few entrepreneurs. Local people miss the variety in taste and texture of their previously species-rich catches and, more seriously, face the spectre of malnutrition; an incredible, sad irony in a region which exports 200 000 tonnes of fish protein every year!

The ability of the Nile perch to switch prey enables it to maintain a high population density even when populations of some prey species are low. Its diet now includes not only the dwindling stocks of haplochromines but also a tiny native shrimp and its own kind; the perch is cannibalistic.

The inherent complexity of any ecosystem makes it very difficult to predict the consequences of introducing exotic species. Classic cases of introductions gone wrong include rabbits and prickly pear (*Opuntia* sp.) to Australia, *Salvinia molesta* (see Boxes 5.1 and 5.3) and *Eichhornia crassipes* to many water bodies throughout tropical Africa, Asia and Australasia, the cane toad (*Bufo marinus*) to many Pacific islands, the brown tree snake (*Boiga irregularis*) to Guam and *Mimosa pigra* and water buffalo to northern Australia. In some instances, introductions have improved living conditions for people in the area. The introduction of fish species belonging to the family Cichlidae (*Sarotherodon* spp., *Tilapia* spp.) has boosted fish production in rivers and lakes throughout Asia and in the Sepik River of Papua New Guinea. Proposals for further species introductions, with or without prior research programmes, are still being formulated by international agencies such as FAO (see Turner 1982, and rebuttal by Eccles 1985) and completely unplanned introductions continue. However, we have very little information on the impact of these introductions on the local flora and fauna, and the far-reaching consequences they might have on the sustainable production of these systems. The experience gained from Lake Victoria and other parts of the world, should be enough to suggest that exotic introductions should only be used as a last resort.

Although some nutrient enrichment may initially enhance fish production, eutrophication usually reduces the value of water resources. The water becomes more difficult to filter if it is to be used as a drinking water supply, and the algae, through secretion of organic compounds, may taint the water. Some Cyanobacteria that develop in eutrophic waters release toxins which can be strong enough to kill cattle and sheep that drink the contaminated water. The amenity value of the water body is usually depreciated through eutrophication, and changes in fish species composition that may accompany the process are often undesirable. Whether nutrient enrichment of a water body is perceived as a problem very much depends on the people and their use of it. Some lakes in Asia are fertilised to enhance fish production, whereas catchments of reservoirs built to supply potable water need to be protected to minimise nutrient inputs.

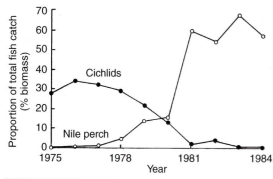

Figure 5.35 Change in the fish catch composition in the Kenyan waters of Lake Victoria following the introduction of the Nile perch. The decline in the cichlid catch is attributed to the rapid growth in the Nile perch population (Miller 1989; reprinted from *Trends in Ecology and Evolution* 4, 56–59, with kind permission from Elseveir Science).

5.15.2 Laguna de Bay

Excessive enrichment of lakes can result in hyper-eutrophication. Laguna de Bay is a large (900 km²) shallow lake on the outskirts of Manila in the Philippines. Over 2 million people live around the lake and use it for fish production, domestic water supply, irrigation, transport, power generation (cooling water), flood control and as a depository for domestic, industrial and agricultural wastes. The lake is drained by the Pasig River which is highly polluted with sewage and industrial effluents from Manila through which it flows to the sea. At the end of the dry season, the level of Laguna de Bay may fall below the level of high tide, resulting in the intrusion of seawater up the Pasig. With this flow reversal, the polluted waters of the Pasig River may enter Laguna de Bay.

The multi-purpose use of the lake has increased food (mainly rice through irrigation) and fish production, generated more power and created employment within the basin. However, these gains have come at the expense of a marked decline in water quality in the lake. The lake has been highly eutrophic for at least 50 years, and algal blooms have occurred regularly during summer. More recently, changes in the biology of the lake have become apparent. Rooted aquatic plants are now almost entirely absent from the lake, yet they were an important part of the ecosystem in the 1960s. Also at that time, at least

23 species of fish were present in the lake, even though several were introduced species (*Cyprinus carpio*, *Oreochromis mossambicus*). Before the development of intensive aquaculture, the local fishery was dependent on the catch of just three species: *Therapon plumbeus* (sliver perch), *Glossogobius giurus* (white goby) and *Arius manilensis* (catfish). Owing to overfishing, the open water fishery collapsed, leading to the economic demise of 13 000 fisherfolk and their families.

Aquaculture was introduced in the early 1970s; it grew at an explosive rate and within a decade one-third of the lake surface was covered in fish-pens. The main cultured species were milkfish (*Chanos chanos*) and tilapia (*Oreochromis mossambicus*). However, for many reasons, both environmental and economic, fish-pen culture has proved not to be sustainable at the very high stocking rates initially used. Conflicts between fisherfolk and fish-pen operators have arisen and, to a certain degree, these have been resolved through enforcement of resource allocation programmes. However, since there is inadequate scientific information on the sustainable fish yield, the allocation of areas to aquaculture and capture fisheries has been somewhat arbitrary.

The major environmental problems confronting the managers of Laguna de Bay are (1) rapid siltation as a result of erosion from the deforested watershed; (2) nutrient enrichment with domestic and agricultural effluents and from fish-pen fertilisers; (3) increasing loads of industrial pollutants; (4) social conflicts between subsistence fisherfolk and commercial fish-pen operators; and (5) rapid human population growth within the basin. These changes have culminated in decreased productivity of the lake, declining harvests of fish and shrimps and more frequent fish kills from anoxia.

5.16 | Aquatic resource management

Freshwater habitats occupy a relatively small portion of the earth's surface, but assume great human ecological significance, particularly in many tropical countries, as a source of drinking water, as a cheap method of waste disposal, as a source of energy (hydroelectric power) and protein food (fish, prawns), as a means of transport and for the aesthetic pleasure they frequently provide. In tropical countries, water bodies are often an important source of food (rice, fish) and home to hosts of a number of serious human parasites (Box 5.7).

The way a lake might be managed will largely depend upon the primary use of the water body. If the water is to be used for domestic water supply, clear, unpolluted water is easier to filter and purify. Consequently, such lakes should have a low nutrient content so that phytoplankton populations are limited. Conversely, a lake which is utilised for fish production, might require nutrient enrichment to promote fish growth. Many lakes, particularly the larger ones, will be put to multiple uses, and management techniques, often involving compromises, are required.

5.16.1 Eutrophication control

The cause of eutrophication is an increase in nutrient loadings (particularly those of phosphorus and nitrogen) on the lake. The enhanced loadings usually stem from altered human activities and management practices within the catchment area. A feature of eutrophication is that the process is, to a certain extent, reversible. By reducing nutrient loadings it has been frequently shown, in temperate lakes at least (see Edmondson 1970; Schindler and Fee 1974), that a eutrophic lake will develop more oligotrophic characteristics. This is frequently possible in lakes where the major nutrient sources can be identified (point sources) and where it is possible to deploy a strategy that reduces nutrient income to the lake. This can be done by diverting effluents with high nutrient concentrations to another, less sensitive, catchment, or by reducing the phosphorus concentration in the effluent. Both techniques are expensive and have rarely been used in tropical lakes.

Nutrients also enter lakes, not at a single point source, but from many diffuse sources dotted throughout the catchment. It is even more difficult to reduce the nutrient income to a lake in which diffuse nutrient sources predominate. For example, nutrients enter Laguna de Bay from sewage treatment plants (point sources) and from activities such as agriculture within the catchment area and the addition of fertilisers to fishpens (diffuse sources). With 2 million people living within the basin, many in informal, squatter communities, the challenge of reducing nutrient loads has social, economic and educational as well as environmental dimensions. Clearly, efforts to improve water quality in this lake and similarly polluted water bodies need to be mounted on a catchment-wide basis and will require significant collaboration between all the stakeholders.

5.16.2 Biomanipulation

Most efforts at reversing eutrophication have centred on reduction in the supply of the key nutrients, nitrogen and phosphorus. Work on temperate lakes, however, has shown that altering food webs through manipulation of consumer populations can also be a useful management tool in restoring the water quality within lakes (see section 5.12.1). This technique of food web manipulation, or biomanipulation as it has become known (Shapiro *et al.* 1975), aims to reduce phytoplankton populations by altering the trophic structure within the lake. If there is an odd number of levels in the dominant food chain (1, 3, 5), the lake will potentially support a large phytoplankton population. On the other hand, if the number of feeding levels is even (2 or 4) algal populations are suppressed. Therefore, addition or removal of top predators could be used to regulate algal populations.

Biomanipulation requires a very sound knowledge of food webs before being used as a management tool. Few tropical lakes have been studied in sufficient detail to permit adequate prediction of the effects of either predator introduction or planktivore removal from lakes. Indeed, predator introductions to tropical Lakes Victoria and Gatun have had disastrous outcomes. Therefore, with our present knowledge of tropical lake ecology, restoration of eutrophic, tropical lakes is probably best tackled by bottom-up rather than top-down control techniques (see section 5.6).

Box 5.7 | Tropical scourge: schistosomiasis

Schistosomiasis, or bilharzia, is a debilitating disease infecting more than 200 million people living in tropical and subtropical regions. The parasite, *Schistosoma* spp., is a trematode flatworm which lives in the blood and produces eggs which are voided from the human host in the urine (*S. haematobium*) or faeces (*S. mansoni, S. japonicum*). S. *mansoni* occurs in South America and the West Indies, with the disease particularly prevalent in Brazil. This species is also found in Africa along with *S. haematobium* and, in some, wetland, rural areas, such as around Lakes Victoria and Chilwa (Malawi) and along the Nile Valley, over 80% of the populace may be infected. *S. japonicum* is found in restricted areas of South-East Asia and infects cattle and rodents as well as humans.

If the eggs are voided into water, they hatch to produce free-swimming miracidia which must find a snail host within about 24 hours. Each bilharzia species has a particular snail as its intermediate host: S. *haematobium* infects *Bulinus*; S. *mansoni* infects *Biomphalaria* and S. *Japonica* infects *Oncomelania*. The miracidium burrows into the snail and multiplication occurs within the snail. Within 1 to 2 months, several thousand cercaria larvae are released. They live for about 48 hours, and in that time must find a human host. The cercaria burrow through the skin, enter the bloodstream and develop into male or female worms. The male has a groove in which, after finding a female, he retains her for life. Eggs are laid in the blood vessels and have a sharp spike with which the capillary walls are lacerated. The eggs enter the bladder or rectum and are voided with either urine or faeces. If eggs enter freshwater, the life cycle is complete.

Control measures include breaking the parasite's life cycle through improved conditions of human sanitation, reducing snail populations through molluscicide application and reducing human contact with waters infested with bilharzia snails. Attempts at reducing the spread of the disease have not been particularly effective, probably because of the large increase in human populations in tropical countries and the dependence of many of these people on infested water bodies for food and water.

5.17 | Chapter summary

1. Tropical lakes of moderate depth may stratify during the hot season into a warm, upper epilimnion and a cooler, hypolimnion separated by a zone of marked temperature change, the thermocline. In these lakes, stratification may break down with the onset of cooler weather and mixing (overturn) occurs once each year (monomixis). Some lakes near the equator are oligomictic and remain stratified for a number of years, with occasional, short-lived, mixing events occurring with the coincidence of cold weather and strong winds.

2. Shallow lakes in the tropics may become thermally stratified during the day with mixing occurring at night (polymixis). High-altitude lakes in the tropics are also often polymictic owing to marked diurnal fluctuations in air temperatures.

3. In a stratified lake, the isolation of the hypolimnion from the atmosphere leads to the development of chemoclines, with concentrations of dissolved oxygen being lower and concentrations of carbon dioxide higher in the hypolimnion than those in the epilimnion. Uptake of nutrients by photosynthetic organisms in the surface waters and their regeneration from detrital particles descending into the hypolimnion often results in the establishment of strong nutrient chemoclines with depth. Low oxygen concentrations in the hypolimnion may result in release of nutrients such as phosphorus, nitrogen and silica from the sediment into the overlying water column.

4. With the breakdown of stratification, nutrients are carried up into the euphotic zone and oxygen transported to the bottom waters. The breakdown in stratification may be marked by an increase in primary production.

5. The primary producers of the open water areas of lakes (the pelagic) are microscopic phytoplankton; production in the littoral zone (shallow water area) is mostly carried out by large plants (hydrophytes). Hydrophytes often grow in distinct zones related to water depth.

6. Phytoplankton primary productivity can be measured either as the rate of oxygen production or the rate of carbon dioxide uptake of populations enclosed in transparent containers suspended *in situ*. Phytoplankton productivity in lakes varies with depth. High light intensities in the surface water result in depressed photosynthetic rates (surface inhibition). Below the depth at which optimum light conditions promote maximum photosynthetic rates, light intensity and the rate of photosynthesis decline exponentially with depth. Light availability (depth of penetration) and nutrient supply are the most important environmental factors controlling primary production in lakes.

7. The functional unit for studying freshwater ecosystems is the catchment area, and the hydrological cycle forms the link between terrestrial and aquatic ecosystems.

8. The number and biomass of organisms at each trophic level can be represented as pyramids of number and biomass respectively. Number pyramids make no allowance for either the size or metabolic rates of the organisms involved. Biomass pyramids may be inverted when the higher metabolic rate of the smaller producer populations may allow development of a greater biomass of their consumers.

9. Energy flow through ecosystems occurs through a multiplicity of pathways (food webs) and consumption, assimilation and production efficiencies determine the relative importance of energy pathways. Organisms can be grouped into trophic levels on the basis of their position in the food chain with regard to the number of energy-transfer steps required to reach that level. The energy available to successive trophic levels declines.

10. Food chains are limited in length and rarely contain more than five links, or trophic levels. Food chains in the open water areas of aquatic systems are generally longer than those found in terrestrial systems.

11. Introduction of a top predator to a lake may result in a trophic cascade with a decline in the population of its prey, an increase in herbivore populations and

a decline in phytoplankton populations. Removal of a top predator has been shown to have the opposite effect.

12. Energy can not be cycled and reused. Nutrients can be recycled. Both energy and matter can be imported into and exported from linked ecosystems. Biogeochemical cycles can be divided into those with the atmosphere as the primary reservoir (e.g. carbon and nitrogen) and those with the soil or sediment as the main reservoir (e.g. phosphorus).

13. Photosynthesis and respiration are the driving forces in the carbon cycle. Concentrations of carbon dioxide in the atmosphere have increased through combustion of fossil fuels and deforestation of large areas of tropical forests. pH plays an important role in the carbon cycle in natural waters and has direct and indirect effects in both aquatic and terrestrial environments.

14. Nitrogen fixation involves the reduction of molecular nitrogen in the atmosphere or dissolved in water to ammonia, and is only carried out by a few species of bacteria and Cyanobacteria. In terrestrial systems, nitrogen fixation occurs in a symbiotic relationship between *Rhizobium* bacteria and legumes. Conversion of ammonia produced by nitrogen fixation to nitrate occurs by nitrification. Nitrate is the primary source of nitrogen for most plants. Nitrogen returns to the atmosphere through denitrification.

15. The predominant form of sulfur in water and soil solutions is as sulfate. Decomposition of organic matter results in the production of hydrogen sulfide. Sulfate-reducing bacteria are heterotrophic and respire anaerobically, using sulfate as a hydrogen acceptor. Photosynthetic bacteria use hydrogen sulfide as an electron donor for the reduction of carbon dioxide.

16. Phosphorus supply often limits algal and plant growth in natural waters. Many soils are deficient in phosphorus, and enhanced crop production often requires the application of phosphorus fertiliser. Unlike nitrogen which is readily leached from soils, phosphorus is not.

17. Nutrient enrichment of lakes, particularly with phosphorus, results in eutrophication, a suite of ecological changes in the lake's biota which includes enhanced phytoplankton production and dominance by Cyanobacteria, an anoxic hypolimnion and decline in submerged plants and the fauna associated with them.

18. Lake management strategies need to optimise multiple-purpose use of the water body and include nutrient budget manipulation, pollution control, disease vector control, introduction or control of exotic species and the biomanipulation of food webs.

Chapter 6

Rivers, floodplains and estuaries
The flood-pulse and river continuum concepts

Rivers differ from standing waters not only in their continuous, unidirectional flow but also in their **longitudinal diversity**. This longitudinal change in riverine features from the headwaters to the mouth contrasts with the horizontal zonation (littoral to pelagic) and vertical stratification so characteristic of deep lakes. Even many large rivers are shallow water bodies and vertical stratification only occurs in slow-flowing, non-turbulent sections and in estuaries (see section 6.5). Some rivers do have deep sections – the lower reaches of the Amazon River, for example, are up to 100 m deep.

Rivers and streams have a one-way, downhill flow, and in these **lotic** (cf. lentic) environments, flow rate is of prime importance in determining the nature of plant and animal communities.

However, many rivers, particularly in the tropics, also have significant interactions with the land lining the main river channel through inundation of this land, the **floodplain**. This lateral water movement, particularly in the lower reaches of many rivers, is frequently of greater ecological significance than the transport of materials and organisms from the upper **catchment** (see Box 6.1). Organisms inhabiting floodplains are subject to an alternation of aquatic and terrestrial phases and exhibit a range of strategies that adapt them to this fluctuating environment. Floodplains play a significant functional role in the nutrient balance and energy flow within the river system, and the relationship between the floodplain and the terrestrial system that lines it is both intimate and complex.

Box 6.1 | Some river terminology

The **discharge** of a river is a measure, at a particular point along its course, of the water flow expressed as volume per unit time and differs from **velocity** which is the speed of flow in a river. The velocity, for a constant discharge, changes with the morphometry of the river channel. The **catchment area** or **drainage basin** of a river is the land area that the river system drains. Catchment areas are separated from each other by a **divide** or **watershed**. In the United States, watershed is used instead of catchment area as defined above. **Stream order** refers to the number of tributaries that have joined the river network. First-order streams have no tributaries, a second-order stream is formed by the junction of two first-order streams and a third-order stream forms through the junction of first- and second-order streams and so on.

The longitudinal profile of a river is generally concave with a steep gradient near the source declining towards the mouth. The steep, fast-flowing upper reaches of the river are called the **rithron**; the lower, flat, slow-flowing stretches, the **potamon** (Figure 6.1). Sediments deposited on the banks of floodplains form **levees**.

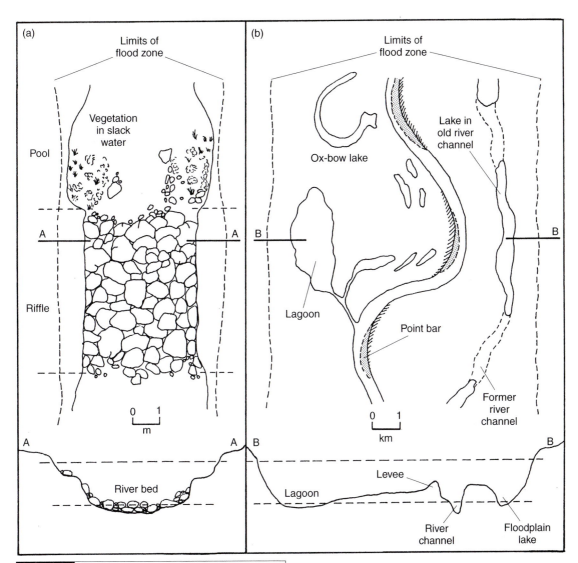

Figure 6.1 Typical cross-sections of a river in (a) the rithron (headwaters) and (b) the potamon (after Welcomme 1983 with permission of the Food and Agricultural Organization of the United Nations).

Most rivers flow to the sea (some discharge into **endorheic** basins in arid areas from which the water evaporates). Mixing of the fresh, riverine water with seawater occurs in the lower reaches of some river channels to form an **estuary** or, in other rivers, mixing occurs some distance out to sea. Rivers which carry a high sediment load may discharge to the sea through a **delta**.

In the tropics, marked seasonal fluctuations in the physical and chemical characteristics of the floodplains contrast with the greater constancy of many tropical lakes. Rivers are open-ended, discharging systems and this contrasts with lake basins which tend to accumulate materials. Rivers are ecologically important as transport agents, scouring the earth, moving loose soils downstream and depositing them on floodplains or into the sea. Rivers also provide channels for migration by aquatic organisms, and along their banks human civilisations flourish.

Humans have interfered with many rivers to such an extent that there are few large ones left in which flow is unregulated. Most major rivers in the world have been regulated through the

Table 6.1 | Physical features of some of the large rivers of the world

River	Length (km)	Discharge ($m^3 s^{-1}$)	Drainage basin area (km^2)	Ratio of discharge:drainage area relative to that of the Murray River
Nile (Africa)	6670	2830	3349000	2.7
Amazon (South America)	6570	200000	6150000	105.4
Mississippi (USA)	5970	15040	3230000	15.1
Mekong (South-East Asia)	4180	14200	811000	56.8
Murray (Australia)	3750	326	1057000	1.0
Fly (Papua New Guinea)	1290	6000	64000	303.9
Purari (Papua New Guinea)	630	2607	33670	251.0

construction of dams, weirs and canals or through a reduction in their discharge through extraction of water for irrigation and provision of domestic and industrial water supplies. The ecology of the Nile, Purari and Amazon Rivers is described below; these very different rivers illustrate some of the ecological concepts that have been developed to explain how riverine systems operate and the impact that humans have had on these systems.

The Nile and Amazon Rivers are both very long, but the Nile drains a relatively dry catchment and, for most of its length, flows through a very dry desert. The hydrology of the Nile has been significantly modified by humans, and these modifications have affected the ecology of the river and the land areas adjacent to it. In contrast, the Purari, in Papua New Guinea, flows through a humid, high-rainfall area, and is a comparatively short but turbulent river with a high discharge. Human impacts on this river are minimal. The Amazon is the largest river in the world and, like the Purari, is also relatively unmodified. The physical features of these three rivers are compared with other large rivers in Table 6.1. Notice the very low relative discharge to drainage basin ratios for the Nile and Murray Rivers which drain very low-rainfall catchments in comparison with those flowing through the wet tropics (Amazon, Mekong and, particularly, the New Guinean rivers).

6.1 | Nile River

The Nile drains 10% of the African continent, and is the only large river on the continent that drains north into the Mediterranean Sea (Figure 6.2). The Nile is closely linked with the human cultures that have lived for millennia along its banks, and is famed for its variable and unpredictable discharge. Aligned south to north, the Nile extends from the equatorial climate around Lake Victoria to the Mediterranean climate at its delta. The river traverses the eastern Sahara Desert, bringing water to an area that would otherwise be uninhabitable. Until recently, over 90% of Egyptians depended on the waters of the Nile, but this direct dependence has declined with industrialisation of the Nile valley (Figure 6.3).

The Nile drains all or parts of 10 sovereign states and therefore allocation of this vital resource has political as well as ecological implications (see Box 6.2). Early Egyptians were made painfully aware of the fickle nature of the river as periods of low river levels were coupled with droughts and famines. The burgeoning human population along the middle and lower reaches of the Nile has increased demands for water and allocation of this limited resource will undoubtedly present difficulties in the future.

The source of the Nile River is considered to be Lake Victoria, but the drainage basin of this great river also includes the rivers that flow into Lakes Victoria, George, Edward and Albert. The Nile is

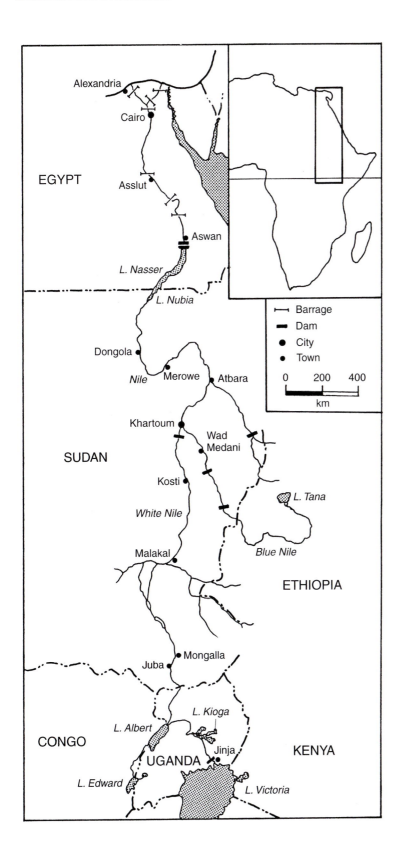

Figure 6.2 Geographic features of the River Nile (adapted from Drake 1997 with kind permission from the National Council for Geographic Education).

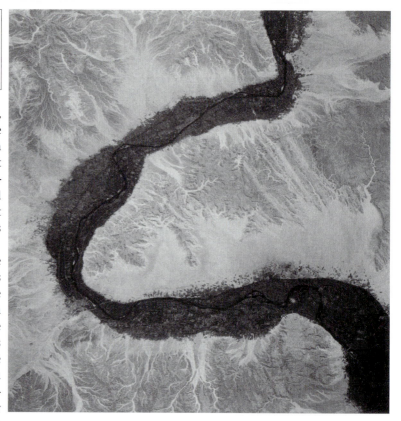

Figure 6.3 Satellite view of the Nile Valley near Luxor, Egypt showing the river and fertile valley flanked by desert (Photo: NASA, Oxford Scientific Films).

the longest river in the world, flowing 6670 km from Lake Victoria to the Mediterranean Sea. Although it is the longest river in the world, its catchment area is relatively small (Table 6.1) and about half of it is dry desert and contributes no water (Rzóska 1978).

Some tributaries join the main stem of the river in its upper reaches, and above Khartoum the river is known as the White Nile. The Blue Nile, draining the highlands of Ethiopia, joins the White Nile at Khartoum. The Atbara River is the only major tributary of the Nile below Khartoum and the simple structure of this river system contrasts with the myriad tributaries that join the Amazon River along its entire length (see section 6.3).

The White Nile descends over 500 m from the East African Plateau to the Sudan plains. The tributary draining from Lake Victoria passes through Lake Kioga and flows over the Murchison Falls into the northern end of Lake Albert. The Nile outflow from Lake Albert is also at the northern end of the lake and the river flows into the Sudan plains and the vast expanse of the sudd wetland. This wetland consists of a mosaic of open water, fringed with papyrus and water courses choked with vegetation.

The Blue Nile leaves Lake Tana, Ethiopia at 1829 m and plunges over Tissisat Falls into a rocky gorge 800 km long and, in parts, 2000 m deep. The river then flows, more sedately, some 800 km across the Sudan Plain to the confluence with the White Nile at Khartoum. The Nile flows through a series of cataracts into Lake Nubia–Nasser formed behind the Aswan High Dam. The total annual discharge from the Nile is, for such a long river, very low by world standards (Table 6.1). The Blue Nile generates 60–70% of this total discharge and the main floods are caused by the summer monsoon rains that fall on the Ethiopian plateau (Dumont 1986). The White Nile contributes around 25% and the balance of the water comes from the Atbara River and the other tributaries. Seasonal fluctuations are marked. River levels rise in June–July and the peak flood occurs in August–September. The river level measured at Khartoum is low from December to June. From July to October, the White Nile flow slows as the silt-laden floodwaters from the Blue Nile cause water to back-up.

The banks of the lower Nile valley have been built up through the annual deposition of silt carried down from the Ethiopian highlands. The silt is rich in nutrients and the fertile soils have been used for millennia for irrigated agriculture. Historically the water quality of the Nile River has been excellent for both irrigation and drinking. The river was little affected by pollution although

Box 6.2 | Water wars or conflict resolution?

While oil has made countries in the Middle East wealthy, water may prove to be the more valuable resource. Water within this arid region already limits agricultural and industrial production, and international competition for control of water supplies is likely to intensify in the future. Rapid human population growth within this region has exacerbated the water shortage. The human population in the region has grown from 60 million in 1950 to 286 million in 1996. It is projected to double again in just 30 years (Drake 1997). The demand for water has also increased through the rapid economic development and rise in living standards brought about, at least in part, by oil revenues. Coupled with this increased demand for water, is a litany of poor water management and water pollution within the area. People living in the upper catchments not only extract precious water, they also use the rivers to carry away their wastes.

The Nile catchment is shared by 10 countries, and the Tigris and Euphrates rivers flow through three countries. Our capacity to alter the flow of these large rivers and to extract large volumes for irrigation and domestic water supplies has given upstream nations the opportunity and power to sequester water, making less available to nations downstream. In such an arid area, this is a formula for conflict and peaceful solutions through sustainable resource allocation and use are urgently needed.

Drake (1997) lists a number of practical solutions: reduce water loss through waste and inefficient methods of water use such as flood irrigation, allocation of water to uses that provide greater returns (e.g. industrial production replacing agriculture), enhanced water storage capacity and interbasin transfers and greater use of solar-powered desalination technology. Education of the public in ways to conserve water and of the need to reduce population growth should be given a high priority.

Political and economic co-operation underlies all these solutions. Ecological solutions to water resource issues must also transcend international boundaries, as each river basin needs to be considered in its entirety. Integrated catchment management is the way forward with nations sharing in the planning and development of water resource projects irrespective of national boundaries. International agreements based on principles of sustainable resource use can be reached which will lead to optimal use of scarce water. Much will depend on political leadership and goodwill and a sound understanding of water resource issues, but motivation should be derived from the fact that co-operation is cheaper than conflict.

deoxygenation has been recorded in the water leaving the Sudd wetland (Talling 1976a). The Nile River itself does not stratify for prolonged periods and water temperature of the river water falls from around 28 °C in the Sudan Nile to between 17–19 °C near Cairo. The headwater lakes of the White Nile exhibit little seasonal variation with temperatures in Lake Victoria only varying between 23 and 27 °C. Further north, greater seasonal variation in temperature occurs and temperatures in Lake Nubia–Nasser range between 16 and 30 °C.

Conductivity is low in the water leaving Lake Victoria but increases as this water mixes with that from Lakes Edward and Albert. Conductivity values in the Blue Nile rise between Lake Tana and Roseires but change little between there and the confluence with the White Nile. In the Delta Lakes conductivity increases markedly through the ingress of seawater and high rates of evaporation. The most significant changes in water quality and aquatic organisms occur in the reservoirs that have been constructed along the Nile and its tributaries.

6.1.1 River regulation

Regulation of the flow of the River Nile dates back to 4000 years BC when the Egyptians developed irrigation techniques. Around that time they also considered diverting flow from the Nile into a depression in the Western Desert to create a reservoir. This reservoir now exists (Lake Qarun) and supplies water to Cairo (Latif 1984). Significant modification of the hydrology of the Nile has occurred over the last 100 years. The first Aswan Dam was built in 1902, but this could not satisfy the needs of the rapidly expanding Egyptian population and work on the Aswan High Dam began in 1959. The reservoir that formed behind the dam (known as Lake Nasser in Egypt and Lake Nubia in Sudan) is over 500 km long with the upstream end extending 148 km into Sudan. The lake has a maximum depth of 130 m and a shoreline length of 9250 km.

Storing water in reservoirs along the Nile significantly alters water quality. The larger sediment particles settle out in the calmer conditions of the reservoir and the same conditions enhance phytoplankton growth. Oxygen is depleted in the deeper layers of thermally stratified reservoirs. Where large phytoplankton populations develop, oxygen supersaturation, from photosynthetically produced oxygen may develop in surface waters. This may lead to the development, diurnally, of significant oxyclines, even in riverine sections both across the river and with depth.

Following construction of the dam, downstream flow was no longer seasonal and variation between years was significantly muted (Figure 6.4). In this way the hydrological regime of the river above the dam is now distinct from that operating below it. The hydrology of the Nile has been further modified through the construction of the Sennar and Roseires Dams on the Blue Nile and the Khashm El Girba Dam on the Atbara River. The now constant flow of approximately 100 million m^3 day^{-1} of water over the Aswan High Dam is less turbid and more saline (Latif 1984; Elewa 1985). The distance of penetration of turbid water into the reservoir has reduced since the lake first filled in 1966 (Figure 6.5). This reduction in the sediment load on the lower Nile has affected the sediment balance of the Nile Delta.

Seasonal changes in the flow regime of the Nile River and the impact of reservoir construction also combine to alter the species composition and biomass of phytoplankton populations. The phytoplankton of Lake Victoria is dominated by Cyanobacteria and diatoms, and the species composition within the lake has changed markedly as the lake has become more productive (see section 5.15.1). Talling (1976b) concluded that few phytoplankton from the headwater lakes survived after their descent to the Sudan plain.

Lake Nasser–Nubia is monomictic (see section 5.1) and an anoxic hypolimnion develops during summer. Radical changes in the biota also occur. The phytoplankton in the upper reaches of the reservoir in March 1976 were dominated by diatoms, but dominance switched to Cyanobacteria nearer the dam wall. In the summer (August 1976), Cyanobacteria dominated throughout the reservoir (Figure 6.6). Consequently, the reservoir provided an inoculum of Cyanobacteria to downstream reaches of the river.

The reservoir has also provided a greater variety of habitats for aquatic plants and Springuel and Murphy (1990) indicated that seven species appear to have colonised the region since the dam was constructed. The reservoir provided a habitat not previously present and plants have not only been able to colonise the reservoir, but also to use it as a 'springboard' to invade suitable habitats upstream. This is another impact of changing a riverine environment into a lacustrine one. The Nile is one of the few major rivers in the world that is so carefully controlled that nearly all its water is utilised. There is some debate as to whether this extensive control is entirely beneficial (see Box 6.3).

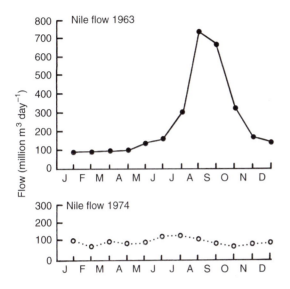

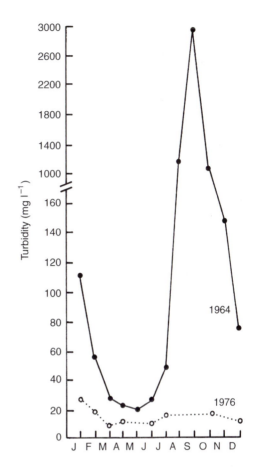

Figure 6.4 Comparison between the monthly average flow rates and turbidity in the lower Nile River before and after the construction of the Aswan High Dam (after Ramadan 1978).

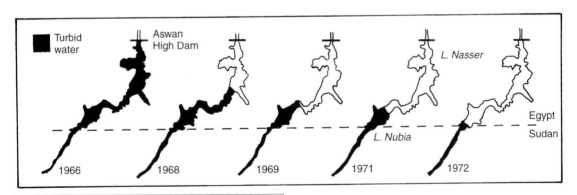

Figure 6.5 Distribution of turbid water in Lake Nasser–Nubia. As the lake filled in 1966, turbid water reached the dam wall, but, as the water level in the reservoir increased, the distance of intrusion by turbid water declined (after Ramadan 1978).

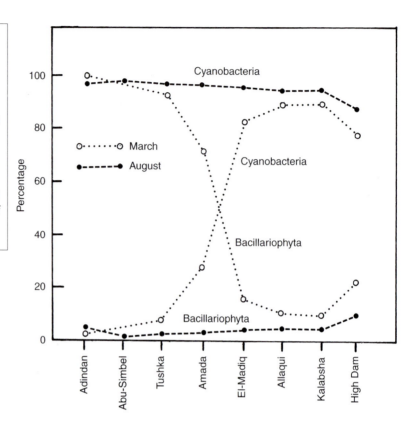

Figure 6.6 Percentage composition of the phytoplankton in Lake Nasser–Nubia in March and August 1976. In the post-flood season (March), diatoms (Bacillariophyta) dominated in the upper reaches of the reservoir, the area most affected by the flood, but a large switch in composition occurred with Cyanobacteria dominant at stations nearer the dam wall. In August (summer) Cyanobacteria dominated throughout the reservoir (after Latif 1984 with kind permission from Elsevier Science).

Box 6.3 | The Aswan High Dam: blessing or curse?

The Aswan High Dam was completed in 1964 with the aim of ensuring a regular water supply to the fertile Nile valley downstream. The reservoir behind the dam was supposed to facilitate complete use of the available water by storing the water that would previously have been lost in floods. The dam would also eliminate damaging flood flows and provide much needed hydroelectricity to fuel the industrialisation of Egypt.

The dam has been controversial from the inception of the project (Rzóska 1976). The lake does provide a more constant supply of water, but losses from the lake surface through evaporation are very high and the water supply to the lower Nile valley has not increased by as much as was hoped. The dam acts a sediment trap, and the sediments that previously built up the rich, alluvial soils of the lower Nile valley now accumulate in the reservoir (Figure 6.5). Farmers now have to apply expensive artificial fertilisers. The detrimental effects extend beyond agriculture; the productive sardine fishery in the Mediterranean, offshore from the Nile Delta, has all but collapsed owing to the loss of the fertilisation of these waters by nutrient-rich sediments.

Other impacts include the loss of many antiquities, drowned as the lake filled. Some of the more spectacular remains at Abu Simbel were saved, but many artefacts of the cultures who lived along the river from the Palaeolithic onwards were lost. The area flooded by the lake was home to some 120000 Nubians, a group of people distinct from both the Egyptians to the north and the Sudanese to the south. They were moved away from the river, with some settling in Sudan and others in Egypt. This social upheaval caused much bitterness.

Not all the news is bad. Hydroelectric power generation has facilitated industrialisation within Egypt and provided employment for the rapidly expanding human population. The extra land available for cultivation has led to increased agricultural productivity. A fishery has been established on Lake Nasser–Nubia which at least replaces some of the protein lost from reduced catches of Mediterranean sardine. However, the construction of this large project and its impacts on the social, economic and ecological environment begs the question: what price for development? This question can only be answered by carrying out detailed environmental impact assessments which carefully balance costs and benefits.

6.2 | Purari River

The Purari River in Papua New Guinea is a short river by world standards (630 km) but it drains a mountainous, high-rainfall and humid catchment and has a high annual discharge of 2607 m³ s⁻¹ with floods in excess of 10 000 m³ s⁻¹ (Petr 1983a). Although the Purari's drainage basin is much smaller than that of the Nile, it has a similar discharge (Table 6.1). The discharge from the Purari is approximately one-quarter of that from the entire Australian continent! The Purari rises in the Bismarck Range of the central cordillera and plunges from the alpine grasslands above 3500 m to the sea through montane forests and highland valleys with rich, fertile soils and dense human populations (Figure 6.7). The river flows on through lowland forests to disgorge into the Gulf of Papua through a mangrove-lined delta. Few people live in the harsh, lowland environment where chronic malaria infections take their toll.

The river flows through a series of climates from the cool, temperate alpine zone with warm days and cold nights (see section 9.1) to the subtropical climate of the highlands and the continuously hot and humid conditions in the lowlands. Rainfall throughout the catchment is high (greater than 2000 mm) and the foothills receive more than 8000 mm per year. The mean annual rainfall on the coast is 3500 mm and most falls between May and October. In the highlands, most rain occurs between December and March. As a result of this seasonal variation in rainfall, floods on the Purari can occur at any time of the year, but the largest ones seem to coincide with the southeasterly wet season (June to September) which brings rain to the middle and lower reaches of the river.

The Purari Delta, 30–50 km wide, has formed through deposition of some of the 90 million m³ of sediment carried by the river during an average year. The water flowing over the lower deltaic plain is brackish, becoming more saline towards the mouth (see section 6.5). The reed *Phragmites karka* grows along the brackish stretches of the delta but is replaced by mangroves, particularly *Sonneratia lanceolata,* as salinity increases. The delta is not a static structure, its morphology is altered through changing rates of sediment deposition and erosion. Erosion can also be severe along the delta margin away from active river mouths where wave attack from the open sea removes material that is not replaced by sediment carried down the river. The delta area is covered by lowland tropical forest, freshwater and brackish wetland vegetation and mangroves. The wetland vegetation slows water velocity and facilitates sediment deposition. Erosion counters this process of sediment accumulation.

6.2.1 Water chemistry

Ionic composition in rivers results largely from the interaction of rain water with the land in the catchment area. Petr (1983b) showed that temperature, conductivity and the concentration of dissolved silica vary with altitude (Table 6.2). Water

Figure 6.7 The Wahgi River, a fast-flowing, turbulent tributary of the Purari River, Papua New Guinea (Photo: Patrick Osborne).

temperature rose from a mean of 11.4 °C for the glacial lakes near the source of the Purari to 24.7 °C near the delta. The rather cool water in the Purari, even along its lowland reaches, results from the rapid fall in altitude and fast flow of the river.

Conductivity increased from around 27 μSiemens cm^{-1} in the upper reaches to over 130 μS cm^{-1} near the delta. Concentrations of dissolved silica also increased downstream to a mean of 23.5 mg L^{-1} between 1000 and 1500 m. Below this altitude range, concentrations decreased and this is probably due to adsorption of silica on to clay particles, since there is little possibility that this reduction can be attributed to algal uptake of silica because the Purari River is too turbid and turbulent for primary production by silica-fixing diatoms.

Similarly, orthophosphate had relatively higher concentrations in the highlands than downstream, again suggesting its adsorption on to clay. Inorganic combined nitrogen ($NH_4-N + NO_2-N + NO_3-N$) increased progressively downstream. These longitudinal gradients are, however, susceptible to abrupt changes, particularly through alterations in the flow regime. Over a three-day period in August 1978, for instance, the Purari River discharge at Wabo increased from 777 m^3 s^{-1} to 4015 m^3 s^{-1} This resulted in decreases in conductivity from 147 μS cm^{-1} to 115 μS cm^{-1} and silica concentration from 17 mg L^{-1} to 9 mg L^{-1}, pre- and post-flood. In this flood, many forest trees were carried downstream and the concentration of suspended solids increased with rising water level. Purari floods also resulted in lower concentrations of calcium, magnesium and sodium owing to dilution by floodwaters.

A distinct plume of sediment-rich river water can be observed as the river water meets the sea. Physico-chemical conditions within one of the channels flowing from the delta and into the open sea were found to change along a longitudinal gradient (Table 6.3). Notice that the impact of the Purari River can be traced a considerable distance offshore.

Table 6.2 Altitudinal gradients of temperature, conductivity and dissolved silica content in streams of the Purari River Basin

Altitude (m)	Temperature (°C)		Conductivity (μSiemens cm^{-1})		SiO$_2$ (mg L^{-1})	
	Range	Mean	Range	Mean	Range	Mean
4000–3500	9.1–14.4	11.4	13–43	27.6	7–13	9.6
3000–2500	12.3–15.6	13.5	12–44	27.0	8–20	14.7
2500–2000	14.7–19.8	17.3	15–62	54.0	9–29	19.0
2000–1500	17.7–22.8	20.1	49–135	72.0	16–33	21.4
1500–1000	20.8–24.9	23.0	69–170	103.0	21–26	23.5
1000–100	21.0–24.6	23.1	86–195	160.0	12–19	15.5
100–20	23.8–26.5	24.7	108–180	136.0	9–24	15.0
10	24.2–26.5	25.0	120–150	136.0	12–16	13.8

Source: Petr 1983b.

Table 6.3 Temperature, Secchi disc transparency (see section 5.2.3) and salinity at four stations from the mouth of the Purari River at Urika to the open sea

	Temperature °C	Secchi disc transparency (cm)	Salinity (‰)
Urika mouth (outside sand bar)	25.7	7	8.5
Open sea, 10 m inside plume	27.8	30	13.0
Open sea, 10 m outside plume	31.0	70	16.0
Open sea, 5 km distant from plume	30.8	95	22.5

Notes: The mean salinity of seawater is around 35‰ so, even 5 km distant from the coast, the sea is diluted by the inflow of freshwater from the Purari River.
Source: Petr 1983c.

We have seen what happened to the ecology of the Nile River following the construction of the Aswan High Dam. Petr (1983a) and his co-workers attempted to predict what would happen to the Purari River downstream of a proposed dam site at Wabo. When a river enters a reservoir, the flow velocity of the water is reduced and, first, coarse, dense sediment particles are deposited as the transport capacity of the water declines. Finer particles are carried further into the reservoir and some may remain in suspension and leave the reservoir in the outflow. It was estimated that the reservoir behind the dam at Wabo would act as an efficient sediment trap and retain over 90% of the sediments entering it. The effects of the reduced sediment content of the water flowing from the dam would include extensive channel erosion in the lower Purari, changes in the sediment balance in the delta and a reduction in the supply of sediments and nutrients to offshore waters in the Gulf of Papua. These changes would probably reduce the extent of mangrove forests in the delta as well as the productivity of the offshore prawn and fishing industry.

6.2.2 Purari fish fauna and food web

The New Guinean freshwater fish fauna, unlike that of the sea that surrounds the island, is not species-rich. The Australasian area lies to the east of Wallace's line (see section 1.3.1) and as a whole

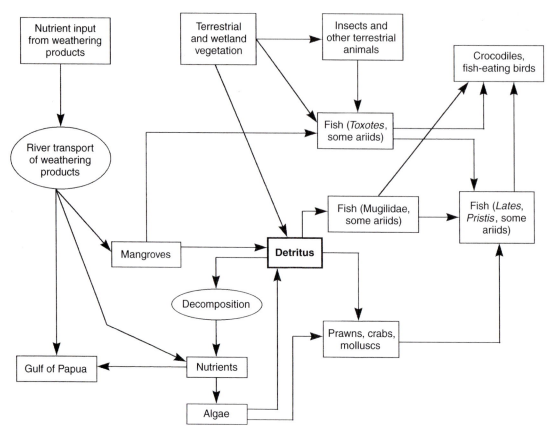

Figure 6.8 Food chain and nutrient flow pathways in the Purari River, Papua New Guinea. The figure shows the importance of detritus and terrestrial plants and animals in the aquatic food chain (after Haines 1983 with kind permission from Kluwer Academic Publishers).

largely lacks 'true' freshwater fish; most species that do inhabit the rivers and lakes are of recent marine origin.

Many of the species in the lower Purari are estuarine (Haines 1983; see section 6.5.1). The fish fauna of the rivers draining to the south in Papua New Guinea is very different to that found in the rivers flowing to the north. For example, in the Sepik River, the largest river flowing to the north, only 29 indigenous fish species have been recorded (Coates 1983) and none of these are found in the more diverse Purari fauna with records of 49 native species (Haines 1983). The fish faunas of each catchment therefore probably represent separate invasions of freshwater by representatives of marine and estuarine families.

As a consequence, each catchment has a unique freshwater fish fauna with a high degree of endemicity. How rivers so close together geographically have such different fish faunas is explained in Box 6.5.

River systems in the humid tropics are often characterised by high sediment loads reflecting intense erosion in the catchment areas. Owing to the high sediment load, light penetration is poor and aquatic primary production low. The animal communities in such systems are consequently dominated by decomposer food chains rather than those based on primary production. The food sources and feeding relationships of the fish faunas of the tropical Pacific follow broadly the patterns discussed by Lowe-McConnell (1975) for all tropical areas. These patterns demonstrate the importance of allochthonous plant material as direct fish food sources and high proportions of insectivorous fish, mud and detrital feeders and predatory fish feeding on these species (Figure 6.8).

Table 6.4 Number and percentage species composition of fish species by trophic niche (feeding category) in four ecological zones in the Purari River, Papua New Guinea

Trophic niche	Purari River		Delta: freshwater		Delta: brackish		Coastal zone	
	Number	%	Number	%	Number	%	Number	%
Omnivores	3	7.5	2	5.6	2	2.9	3	4.8
Fish eaters	6	15.0	7	19.4	15	21.4	14	22.6
Mollusc eaters	0	0	4	11.0	4	5.7	6	9.7
Prawn eaters	12	30.0	14	38.9	20	28.6	15	24.2
Crab eaters	0	0	0	0	11	15.7	6	9.7
Insect eaters	5	12.5	3	8.4	4	5.7	0	0
Fruit eaters	3	7.5	2	5.6	3	4.3	3	4.8
Other plant eaters	3	7.5	0	0	2	2.9	2	3.2
Detritus eaters	8	20.0	4	11.0	9	12.8	13	21.0
Total	40		36		70		62	

Notes: The Purari River zone extends from Hathor Gorge to the top of the delta. The number of species in the coastal zone is probably incomplete.

Source: Haines 1983.

An indication of the relative importance of each pathway is provided by examining the proportions of fish of different feeding habits in the communities of recognisable ecological habitats (Table 6.4).

These data also illustrate two further important points concerning the freshwater fish fauna of tropical Pacific Islands. First, plankton-feeding species are absent owing to the low plankton production in such systems. Second, the fish faunas of the various ecological zones of the Purari are dominated by Ariid catfish, which form 25% of the 49 species listed by Haines (1983). Lakes on the floodplain of these turbid rivers also tend to support animal communities with a high ratio of detritus feeders, since their faunas are derived from the riverine community. Crustaceans, in particular penaeid prawns in estuarine areas and carid prawns such as *Macrobrachium* in the less saline reaches of the Purari Delta, also form an important food resource for fish.

6.3 | Amazon River

The Amazon River is by far the largest river system in the world, its tributaries drain a catchment of some 6.15 million km^2 and it discharges 200 000 $m^3 s^{-1}$ to the sea; some four times that of the Zaire River and ten times that of the Mississippi River (Figure 6.9). The enormous discharge from the Amazon is due not only to its vast drainage basin, but also to the high rainfall that deluges upon it. The Amazon continually transforms its landscape, depositing sediments in one region and eroding them from another.

The source of the Amazon is a trickle at some 4500 m a.s.l. in the snowfields of the Peruvian Andes (Figure 6.10). Technically, using the river length criterion to assign mainstem status, the source of the Amazon is the Apurimac River. However, the early Spanish explorers identified the Marañon River as the source and Brazilians still use this name for the Amazon upriver of the Peru–Brazil border. The Apumirac River becomes the Ucayali River before joining the Marañon upstream of Iquitos. These Andean tributaries cascade through mountain valleys before entering the lowlands through rapids at Menseriche. Even this far from the sea, the river is already large by world standards with a mean annual discharge of 10 000 $m^3 s^{-1}$. Except for the mountainous rim, the Amazon basin is very flat and at elevations less than 200 m a.s.l. The river gradient,

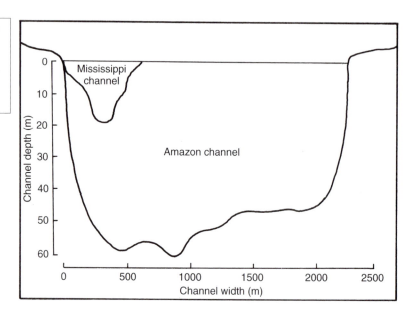

Figure 6.9 Cross-section of the lower Amazon near Óbidos compared with that of the Mississippi River at Vicksburg (after Davis 1964 with permission from Natural History AMNH).

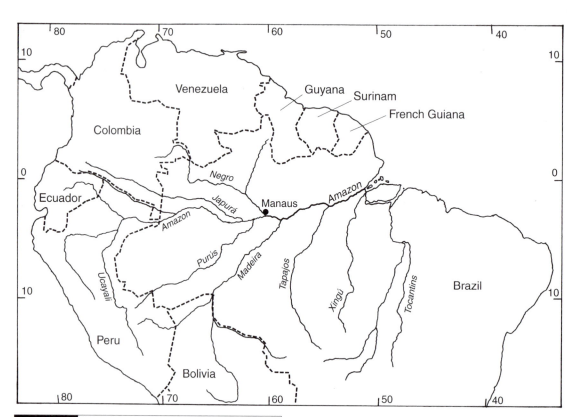

Figure 6.10 Geographical features of the Amazon basin. Only the larger tributaries are shown, but 20 of them are over 1000 km long; note how this compares with the very simple Nile system (see Figure 6.2).

Figure 6.11 Confluence of the Río Negro, a blackwater river, with the Amazon, a turbid, whitewater river. The 'meeting of the waters' occurs a few kilometres downstream of Manaus, Brazil (Photo: Patrick Osborne).

for most of its length between Iquitos, Peru and the Atlantic Ocean, is consequently very gentle, around 2–3 cm km^{-1}. Water temperatures in the upper reaches of the river vary between 5 and 13 °C, but the main river has a remarkably stable temperature regime: 28 ± 1°C.

From Menseriche, the river flows through rain forests with extensive floodplains and flooded forests. Near Manaus, in the great 'meeting of the waters', the turbid River Solimões (as Brazilians call the Amazon from the Peru–Colombia border to its junction with the Negro) joins the dark, clear waters of the Río Negro to form what Brazilians regard as the Amazon (Figure 6.11). The Río Negro, 700 km long, drains a catchment area of 715 000 km^2 and adds around 30 000 m^3 s^{-1} to the mean annual discharge of the Amazon River.

The blackwaters of the Río Negro are rich in humic materials and have low levels of suspended matter since they drain older, more intensively weathered sediments. The water in these rivers is acidic (pH 4.5–5.1) and this contrasts with the nearer neutral pH of the whitewater rivers (pH 6.5–6.9). The streams draining the relatively young Andes are more turbid and suspended solids in the Solimões may be as high as 600 mg L^{-1} (Meade 1985).

Nearly half the annual load of suspended sediment in the Amazon River is derived from the Andes of Peru and most of the other half enters the system via the Madeira River which drains the Bolivian Andes. Sources of water to the Brazilian Amazon, however, show a very different pattern with only 20% and 10% of the total being supplied by the Peruvian and Bolivian headwaters respectively. The remaining 70% of the water enters the Amazon from the low-lying areas of the basin (Meade 1994). Despite its much larger water discharge, the sediment discharge from the Amazon is not significantly greater than that of the much smaller Ganges–Brahmaputra River (Meade 1996). The greater sediment discharge per unit catchment area in the Ganges–Brahmaputra is attributable mostly to tectonism, but the intensive agriculture practised by the dense human population in this basin has also added to the sediment load of this river system. Recent conversions of virgin forest to cattle-grazing pastures have, so far, not caused any discernible increase in the sediment loads of the major Amazonian tributaries (Meade 1996).

Almost all Amazonian water bodies are subjected to varying degrees of water-level fluctuation. River levels may fluctuate seasonally by as much as 13 m, but the average recorded seasonal fluctuation at Manaus is 10–11 m, with the greatest fluctuations occurring in the main river and adjacent floodplain. These floods are regular annual events. When the river level is high, the complex floodplain is inundated but, as the river level falls, the floodplain drains leaving only a few permanent lakes. Melack (1996) found that local runoff contributed 57% of the water budget to Lake Calado, near Manaus, and that the adjacent Solimões River provided only 21%. This seasonal hydrology leads to an alternation between aquatic and terrestrial phases and presents a challenging environment to both the aquatic and terrestrial organisms that inhabit the floodplain.

Plant communities on the Amazonian floodplain may be divided into those which have their main growing period during the aquatic phase and those which respond to dry, terrestrial conditions. When the water level falls, most of the aquatic phase plants dry out or are swept into the main river channel. A few plants may remain, but the main method of recolonisation of the next flood phase is through seeds and spores.

6.3.1 Amazonian river types
Amazonian rivers differ not only in their morphology but also in their physical and chemical properties. Sioli (1984) classified them as follows:

1 Whitewater rivers: turbid waters; pH 6.2–7.2; Secchi disc transparencies 0.1–0.5 m (Río Solimões–Amazon; Río Madeira).

2 Clearwater rivers: more or less transparent, green or olive-green water; pH 4.5–7.8; Secchi disc transparency 1.1–4.3 m (Río Tapajós, Río Xingú). These rivers are typically found under forests.

3 Blackwater rivers: more or less transparent, olive-brown to coffee-brown water; pH 3.8–4.9; Secchi disc transparency 1.3–2.9 m (Río Negro). These rivers drain bleached sand catchments.

These different river types reflect variations in the catchments that they drain. Tributaries that contribute large amounts of sediment from the Andes, such as the Madeira and Apure are distinctly whitewater. Tributaries that contribute large amounts of water and virtually no suspended matter, such as the acidic Negro, are blackwater rivers. The intermediate clearwater rivers are less easy to define (Meade 1994).

6.3.2 Amazonian headwaters
The Amazonian headwaters flow through deep, eroded valleys. The water in the streams in this region is usually clear since little erosion occurs from the forested hillsides. However, landslides occur and subsequent erosion results in turbid waters. In this way the western lowlands of the Amazon basin have become filled with sediment eroded from the Andes.

6.3.3 Small forest streams
Small forest streams in Amazonia are called *igarapés* and they are an important source of allochthonous organic matter (see section 5.4). The streams receive little sunlight (usually less than 10% of the solar radiation that falls on the canopy that shades the stream), therefore there is little autochthonous production, but the often considerable input of allochthonous material supports a diverse food chain almost entirely based on detritus. Water temperatures are usually lower than in the main stem of the river but fluctuate little seasonally ($23 \pm 1\,°C$).

6.3.4 The floodplain
In the lowlands, the Amazonian tributaries develop strong lateral incisions and meander across the floodplain. The meanders form ox-bow lakes as they are cut-off from the main stream and new meanders form as the river finds the path of least resistance. The flat topography of the Amazon Basin and the large seasonal fluctuations in discharge results in an extensive floodplain which is alternately flooded and drained with the

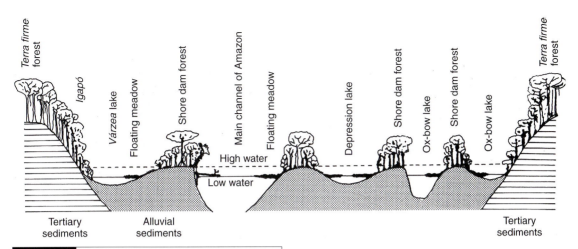

Figure 6.12 Cross-section through the middle Amazonian floodplain (after Sioli 1984 with kind permission from Kluwer Academic Publishers).

annual rise and fall in river level. Floodplain habitats can be differentiated into those that are subjected to an annual dry phase and therefore have distinct terrestrial and aquatic phases and those which are permanently flooded.

Shallow lagoons (*lagos da várzea*), some very large (surface area of up to 2000 km^2) form in depressions on the floodplain (Figure 6.12). When the annual flood inundates the *várzea,* water movement slows and the suspended solids settle. The coarsest particles settle first and form levees, behind which finer particles settle. These lagoons shrink in the low-water period, but some do not dry up completely and form important low-water refuges. The finest particles transported by the river together with organic matter produced within these lakes are deposited in the sediments of these lagoons.

Water chemistry within the *várzea* lakes is influenced by mixing of river water rich in nutrients with a near-neutral pH with the nutrient-poor, acidic waters draining the *terra firme* forests (see section 6.3.5). The water chemistry is further modified through the uptake and release of substances by plants and animals and through sedimentation and decomposition processes occurring within the water column. Superimposed on these processes are those caused by the annual rise and fall in water level. This annual exchange of a large proportion of the water is one of the fundamental differences between floodplain lakes and those less influenced by riverine inputs. Most of the aquatic plants grow in the turbid, whitewater rivers such as the Solimóes River. In the Río Negro, a blackwater river, there is a paucity of aquatic plants as the waters are acidic and nutrient-poor. Most of the plant material produced on the floodplain enters the detritus food chain.

The lakes may stratify thermally (see section 5.1) soon after they fill and may remain stratified throughout the flood season. Decomposition of the flooded vegetation consumes oxygen in the bottom waters. Oxygen production within the water column is low as the water surface is shaded by trees in the flooded forest and by the floating hydrophytes that develop on the water surface. Consequently, oxygen concentrations decline, particularly within the hypolimnion, but low oxygen concentrations are also commonly recorded in near-surface waters. As the high-water season progresses, nutrients accumulate within the hypolimnion. Concentrations of hydrogen sulfide, a product of decomposition and toxic to many organisms, may also increase within the hypolimnion.

During the low-water period, vertical profiles can be quickly destroyed through wind or currents generated by inflowing waters resulting from a rise in river level. Stratification can also be disrupted by sudden drops in air temperature. When this happens, very low oxygen and high hydrogen sulfide concentrations may occur throughout the water column and fish kills may result. However, the plants and animals inhabiting these lakes exhibit a range of adaptations enabling them to survive periods when dissolved oxygen concentrations are low. The shallow water bodies during the low-water period are turbid as the sediments are easily disturbed by wind-generated currents and fish. Some of the sediment may be carried out of the lake into the river as lake level falls, some will settle within the lake. Undisturbed sediments are, therefore rarely found in várzea lakes (Junk 1984).

Aquatic plants growing in várzea lakes have well-developed **aerenchyma**. Aerenchyma is a specialised plant tissue with large air spaces. This provides buoyancy and facilitates gas transport and ensures that adequate oxygen reaches all parts of the plant. Free-floating plants are particularly well adapted to lakes with changing water levels. *Utricularia* spp. and *Ceratophyllum demersum* are submerged free-floating plants, but many other surface-floating species are found in these lakes: *Eichhornia crassipes*, *Pistia stratiotes*, *Salvinia* spp., *Azolla* spp. and *Neptunia oleracea*. Some rooted plants have long petioles attached to surface floating-leaves which can rise and fall with change in lake level. Floating meadows formed by the grasses *Paspalum repens* and *Echinochloa polystachya* (see Box 6.4) develop in the várzea and provide a habitat for large populations of both terrestrial and aquatic invertebrates.

Many of the plant species rooted in the sediment can grow rapidly. This rapid growth allows plants to keep up with rising water levels and this ensures that the exposed parts remain above the water surface. Growth in *Oryza perennis*, for example, may be as much as 20 cm day^{-1} and 3 m month^{-1} (Junk and Howard-Williams 1984). Fast vegetative reproduction is also common in floodplain plants. In this way, plants can colonise habitats exposed by falling water levels (terrestrial plants) and those created as water levels rise (aquatic plants).

Aquatic plants survive the dry season either as reproductive propagules (seeds or spores) or as highly modified terrestrial forms. The terrestrial forms tend to be smaller, with a lower water content and leaves which conserve water and lack aquatic adaptations such as large air spaces. This morphological plasticity is exhibited by plants such as *Neptunia oleracea*, *Ludwigia natans* and *Paspalum repens* (Junk 1984). Junk and Piedade (1994) recorded 387 species of herbaceous plants growing on the Amazon floodplain near Manaus. They attributed this high species diversity (see chapter 8) to the great variety of habitats that exist on a floodplain with a regular flood pulse (see section 6.4.3). In addition to the terrestrial habitats, aquatic ones vary from permanent lakes to temporary pools and wetlands.

The floodplain is a dynamic system with a gradient of stability in habitats from those with highly mobile sediments near the main channel to the more stable ones away from it. The high fertility of the floodplain soils favour plant growth and the seasonal predictability of the flood-pulse allows time for the growth of species adapted to the high- and low-water phases. The alternation of flood and drying phases does not allow time for interspecific competition to develop, and the flood-pulse constrains communities in the early seral stages (see section 7.7). Elimination of the flood-pulse leads to dry areas becoming colonised by forest and permanently wet areas dominated by a few species of aquatic plants.

Many of the fish species in these lakes are air-breathers. In the pirarucú (*Arapaima gigas*) the swim bladder has been modified to carry out the functions of a lung. Many of the catfish use the stomach or intestine for oxygen absorption. The lung-fish (*Lepidosiren paradoxa*) has fully developed lungs. Fish also adapt to periods of low oxygen concentrations by increasing the oxygen carrying capacity of their blood. This can be done by increasing the haemoglobin content and by increasing the red blood cell count.

The biomass of organisms inhabiting the sediments (benthos, see section 5.5) varies with oxygen concentration. During periods of high water, biomass is low because the lakes are stratified and oxygen supply to the sediments is restricted and decomposition uses what little oxygen may be present. Biomass of the benthos is much higher during the dry season when the

Box 6.4 | *Echinochloa polystachya:* Keeping one's head above water

E. polystachya is a perennial C$_4$ grass (see section 3.7) that grows along floodplain rivers from Mexico to Argentina. On the floodplains of the whitewater rivers of central Amazonia this grass forms large monospecific stands and its growth is well-adapted to the annual rise and fall in river levels. During the dry phase, new shoots form at the nodes of old stems and vigorously send down roots. Competitors are excluded by the dense cover of decaying vegetation produced from the plant's growth in the previous season. The young plants grow rapidly as the flood waters rise. Flowering occurs in the middle of the aquatic phase but, even though copious seed production occurs, vegetative propagation is the main mechanism of reproduction in established stands. New stands develop from seeds which are, therefore, important in dispersal and re-establishment of stands destroyed by fire or erosion.

After flowering, the water level falls and growth slows down. The basal portion of the plant starts to rot and exposure of the sediments is the cue for the production of new shoots. If the sediments are not exposed, the old stems may persist for another year with some new shoots developing at the nodes. This species needs the high nutrient status found in whitewater lakes to sustain its rapid growth; plant growth is stunted in lakes with poor nutrient status and the plant is absent from the nutrient-poor blackwater rivers.

The annual net production of this plant (99 t ha^{-1} year^{-1}) is among the highest recorded for any natural communities (Piedade *et al.* 1991). This very productive plant plays a significant role in the carbon budget of these floodplain lakes. It is a major source of food for capybaras (*Hydrochoerus hydrochoeris*), manatees (*Trichechus inunguis*), turtles and herbivorous fish. The plants provide protection to fry and young fish and a substrate for many aquatic invertebrates. The high productivity of *E. polystachya* is remarkable given the environmental conditions under which it grows. Floodplains are unstable environments, alternating between aquatic and terrestrial phases which exert considerable ecological stress on the plants and animals living on them. *E. polystachya* is highly attuned to this variation and, indeed, stands of this grass are replaced by floodplain forests if flooding becomes less protracted or by aquatic plants if the aquatic phase predominates.

organic-rich sediments (food supply) and oxygen availability combine to create an ideal habitat.

Areas exposed during the low-water phase are rapidly colonised by terrestrial plants. Most of these plants develop from seeds; crucial to their success is the capacity to complete their life cycle before the lake basin is re-flooded. Seeds of sedges (*Cyperus* spp.) and grasses (e.g. *Paspalum* spp.) germinate in the wet mud and rapidly cover the exposed shoreline. Copious seeds are produced and agents of seed dispersal include water, wind and animals. Seed dispersal is important since these floodplain habitats are dynamic systems, with seasonally flooded areas either being lost (converted to permanent dry land or to sites of permanent inundation), or created through sediment erosion and deposition.

Trees developing on the floodplain require a dry phase of 2–3 months for seedling establishment. These plants prefer a fluctuating environment, and prolonged inundation (3–4 years) will kill most of them. Most trees lose their leaves during periods of high water which is the period when most produce seeds. Many of these seeds are dispersed by fish. Fish such as (*Colossoma* sp., *Mylossoma* sp.) feed on fruit and seeds are defecated without losing viability (Goulding 1980).

Large mobile animals such as fish, manatees, turtles and large invertebrates exhibit seasonal migration. During the low-water phase, these animals move into the main river channels, where they have to alter feeding and predator-avoidance strategies. In the river channel, the refuges provided by the flooded vegetation in the *várzea* lakes are largely absent. Furthermore, the river lacks the flooded trees and aquatic plants that provide floodplain animals with so much of their food while in the *várzea* lakes.

Many of the aquatic animals inhabiting floodplains lack adequate mobility and are stranded in pools and die once they dry up. Such animals typically have short life cycles and rapid reproduction producing copious offspring with strong dispersal mechanisms (*r*-selected species, see section 4.13). Some aquatic animals survive the dry period as resistant, resting stages in their life cycle.

Rising water levels signal the start of the season when food for aquatic animals becomes more abundant, and fish spawning migrations predominantly occur at this time. Spawning takes place in the tributary rivers flowing out on to the floodplain. The eggs drift downstream and hatch in the *várzea* lakes where the water is still well oxygenated and food is abundant. Plants in the *várzea* lakes provide the fry with some protection, but the spawning fish and fry are harassed by predators that follow the spawning migrants up the tributaries.

6.3.5 Flooded forests

Three distinct forest types associated with the Amazon River and its tributaries can be recognised. *Várzea* forests are those inundated by the comparatively nutrient-rich, turbid whitewaters, whereas *igapó* forests are inundated by the acidic blackwaters that are low in calcium (Figure 6.12). *Terra firme* forests are found above the flood level (see section 8.1.2).

Igapó forests adjacent to the river courses remain flooded for most of the year (Figure 6.13). The vegetation is dominated by twisted trees up to

8 m in height. Species diversity is relatively low on sandy quartz soils, plants are widely dispersed and the canopy is open. On more nutrient-rich, clay soils, species richness increases and the trees are taller (10–12 m) and sufficiently close together to form a closed canopy. With increasing elevation and distance from the river, trees increase in stature (up to 35 m tall). This upper *igapó* forest zone is inundated for 5–6 months up to 5 m deep. Duration and maximum water level decline away from the river and *igapó* forests are replaced by *terra firme* forests. Many of the floodplain trees show distinct annual growth rings because growth is slowed through oxygen stress on the roots when the forest is flooded. Leaf fall is highest in July and is correlated with maximum insolation and water level and may be in response to stress. Decomposition of the leaves is very slow; to achieve 95% decomposition may take as long as 6 years.

6.3.6 The Lower Amazon

The lower Amazon, from below the confluence of the Río Negro and the Solimões to the estuary, flows in a valley 20–100 km wide. The vast quantity of water entering the Atlantic from the Amazon River depresses salinities as far as 150 km offshore. Although there are no saltwater intrusions into the Amazon estuary, tidal bores (*prororocas*) occur and the effect of tides is registered some 900 km from the mouth of the river.

In the Amazon estuary, water-level fluctuations are determined more by tides than seasonal floods. The Brazil current, running north along the Brazilian coast, pushes Amazon water along the coastline, restricting its advance into the open sea. This current also explains why the Amazon has not developed a delta. However, the mouth of the Amazon is filled with many islands, almost all of them of recent alluvial origin. The large island of Marajó divides the mouth into two branches. This island is covered with 2 m of water from January to May.

In the dry season, the lakes recede and the largest of them becomes saline through evaporative concentration. The outer part of the northern mouth contains islands, with creeks invaded daily by the tides. Water along the eastern coasts of

Photo 6.13 *Igapó* forest near the Río Negro upriver from Manaus, Brazil (Photo: Patrick Osborne).

these islands is brackish and they are lined with mangroves (see chapter 10). Inland of these islands are others that are surrounded by freshwater with a lower Amazonian *várzea* vegetation. South of Marajó Island, the Amazon combines with the Río Pará to form an elaborate network of channels and alluvial islands. The water in these channels flows back and forth with the tides and powerful tidal bores develop.

6.3.7 Fish biology and species diversity in the Amazon Basin

The Amazon River has a wide variety of habitats: large open water, riverine habitats, small, shaded, forest streams, permanent and temporary herbaceous wetlands, channels and lakes of various shapes and sizes. This habitat diversity and the temporal variability combine to provide a wide range of environments. The Amazonian fish fauna is, unlike that of the Purari River, incredibly diverse with around 1300 species recorded (Lowe-McConnell 1987). The high diversity has been attributed to the age of the river system, its large size, habitat diversity and the high proportion of the basin at low altitude with comparatively stable or predictable environmental conditions. Changes in the drainage patterns, over geological time, have allowed the exchange of fish species to occur between catchments in a process known as **river capture** (see Box 6.5).

The fish species of the Amazon are very mobile, entering *várzea* lakes with the inundation and returning to the better-oxygenated river water to spawn. After spawning, the fish return to floodplains tributaries to feed. Goulding (1980) distinguished between spawning migrations and low-water upriver movements. He considered that migration evolved as a mechanism to escape predation, with spawning occurring in headwater streams or turbid waters. Upriver movements help to counteract the effect of eggs and fry being washed downstream.

Floodplain fish show seasonality in food uptake rates. Uptake rates are highest as water levels rise and decline with the fall in water level as fish retreat into the main river channel. Detritus is a major constituent in floodplain food webs, with both fine and coarse particulate matter being consumed. During the flood season, fish feed on fruits, seeds, pollen and terrestrial insects that fall from the flooded forest trees.

6.4 | Ecological concepts

6.4.1 Longitudinal zonation

In all three large rivers described above **longitudinal zonation** is apparent not only in physico-chemical features but also in the distribution of organisms. The upper reaches (**rithron**) consist of turbulent stretches flowing over rapids (**riffle** sections) interspersed with calmer, deeper reaches termed **pools** (Figure 6.1). The river bottom in

---

Box 6.5 | Fish biogeography

We have seen that the fish fauna of the Purari River is not very diverse and differs from that of rivers draining adjacent catchments. Conversely, the Amazon has many fish species. How do these differences come about and how do fish species get from one river system to another? Why are some species found in one part of a river and absent from another further upstream? These are the sort of questions fish **biogeographers** strive to answer. Biogeography is covered in chapter 12 but aspects of the biogeography of fish inhabiting rivers are introduced here.

Few fish can travel over land and cross a watershed (the climbing perch, *Anabas testudineus,* from South-East Asia, is capable of migrating over land) but most fish die after even a short time out of water. Therefore, to invade a neighbouring catchment, fish need a hydrological connection. Major geological upheavals can result in a redistribution of watershed boundaries and a fish fauna in one river system may join with one formerly in a separate catchment. This process is known as **river capture**. **River diversion** is another mechanism by which exchange of fish from adjacent catchments can occur. Some fish can migrate along inshore coastal waters from one river system to next. Even freshwater fish can do this if river discharge is so large that salinity of the surface coastal water is depressed. This is probably how some species travelled between rivers, such as the Purari and Fly draining into the Gulf of Papua.

Fish movement within a river system can be restricted by various barriers. Even small waterfalls (1–3 m high) are sufficient to stop upstream movement of many fish. The fish fauna of a river system may then be different above and below such a barrier. A shallow wetland may constitute a barrier to fish that are not able to tolerate low oxygen concentrations. Other barriers to fish movement are less obvious. Some fish will not move into open water where they may be more susceptible to predation, a biological barrier.

Barriers to fish movement may explain why some fish species are present in one river system but not another. Biogeographers also need to explain why some rivers have many fish species and others have few. The diversity of a fish fauna is determined by the balance between the **speciation** (formation of new species by evolution) and the rate of species loss through **extinctions**. We will look at factors that affect the rate of these processes when we discuss biodiversity in chapter 8 and biogeography in chapter 12.

riffles consists of large boulders, rocks and pebbles and aquatic vegetation is sparse. Pools are deeper and contain finer sediment particles, (small stones and sand) and plants may become established in areas of slack water. Dissolved oxygen concentrations are usually high, although during periods of low flow anoxic conditions can develop in poorly flushed pools. In some rivers, the rithron is subject to frequent disturbance from short-lived floods (**spates**).

In the **potamon** zone, the wider and deeper river channel meanders over a floodplain, and sediments consist of fine muds. Aquatic plants grow in profusion in the river channel and on the floodplain. Water temperatures are higher in the potamon and the concentration of dissolved solids increases. Differences in the physical environment between the rithron and potamon are translated into differences in the plants and animals that inhabit the upper and lower reaches of rivers. Some of these riverine organisms exhibit remarkable adaptations to their often physically demanding environment. The boundary between the rithron and potamon is often not distinct and masked by variations in channel morphology and river gradients.

The rithron reaches of streams are often lined and shaded by trees which contribute leaves, branches, flowers, fruits and seeds to the stream. This plant material is an important source of organic matter as the shady conditions limit the amount of in-stream photosynthesis.

Organisms inhabiting the rithron need to have adaptations that enable them to avoid being carried downstream. Plants have strong roots or, in the case of *Torrenticola queenslandica*, a small, flowering plant living in fast-flowing streams in northern Australia and New Guinea, the roots are flat, ribbon-like structures similar to the holdfasts found in marine algae. Stream algae grow attached to rocks. Diatoms and filamentous green algae dominate, but freshwater red algae such as *Batrachospermum* and *Lemanea* are found in shaded forest streams with clear water.

Aquatic insect larvae shelter among the rocks and, where soft sediments occur, invertebrates burrow into them. Current speeds are not uniform across a stream bed or with depth, and stream organisms seek out areas with reduced flow rates. Organisms are generally small and streamlined, offering reduced resistance to flow. Small body size allows organisms to occupy quiet boundary areas where water velocity is much reduced, or to hide in cracks in and between rocks. Some animals have attachment organs such as hooks and suckers, or produce sticky secretions to help them maintain their position. *Simulium* (black fly) larvae spin a sticky silk web to anchor them to the stream bed. The adult black fly in Africa is the vector of the disease causing river blindness. Some caddis-fly larvae construct cases from sand grains which act as ballast, making dislodgement more difficult.

Advantages of living in the rithron include a good oxygen supply, food delivered and excretory products removed by the flow. Many of the animals living in streams are filter feeders, collecting particles carried by the current. Net-spinning caddis-fly larvae collect particles in the net which they then consume. Black fly larvae use fans of fine hairs attached to their heads to filter particles of organic matter.

Fish inhabiting fast-flowing streams may be adapted to grip or cling to the substrate. Adaptations include mouth suckers, ventral friction pads and spines on pectoral fins. Other species are streamlined, strong swimmers and can move against the current. They do this in short bursts dashing from one area of low current to the next. Few species are adequately adapted to survive the rigours of headwater streams, and fish diversity increases downstream. For example, in a stream in Sierra Leone only two species of fish were found in the headwaters 400 m a.s.l. Four species were recorded downstream at 100 m a.s.l. and 16 species were recorded in lowland reaches (Payne 1986). This increase in diversity reflects the increasing variety of habitats and greater availability of food and places to hide.

The potamon is environmentally more complex than the rithron. Current velocities are generally lower and the river bed is of sand or mud. The main river channel may meander across a floodplain and divide and recombine in a series of **anabranches**. At each meander, current velocities are faster along the concave shore and bank erosion occurs here. On the opposite side of the meander sediment may be deposited to form sand bars. Phytoplankton and zooplankton populations develop in the main river channels when flow rates are low. Aquatic plants may grow in profusion. Invertebrate communities are often species-poor, but sediment-dwelling invertebrates such as chironomids may be common. In contrast, fish diversity is often greater. The ecology of the potamon is highly modified in those rivers that have a seasonally inundated floodplain (see section 6.3.4).

Observation of this longitudinal zonation in the physical features and the biological communities that inhabit river sections led to the development of an ecological concept known as the River Continuum Concept.

6.4.2 | River Continuum Concept

The River Continuum Concept (RCC) proposed that the rivers and streams should be viewed as longitudinal systems in which ecosystem processes occurring downstream are affected by what happens upstream (Vannote *et al.* 1980; Minshall *et al.* 1983). The RCC is based on the premise that a gradient of physical conditions exists from the headwater to the mouth of a river. Organisms distribute themselves along this gradient in a way that the downstream organisms capitalise on the inefficiencies of resource use by organisms upstream.

The RCC is based around the concept of stream order (see Box 6.1). Low-order streams often have an irregular flood pattern because they are so strongly influenced by local rainfall. Some annual streams may change from a dry river bed to a raging torrent in just a few hours or less. The response time of larger rivers to rainfall is much longer and changes are often imperceptible. The flood curve of larger rivers is therefore smoother and more predictable. Seasonal climatic changes may take a few weeks or even months to have an impact on the downstream reaches of a river draining a large catchment.

Energy inputs to first-order streams are either **allochthonous** (from terrestrial vegetation) or **autochthonous** (from aquatic primary producers in the stream). This organic matter is processed by heterotrophs and some is carried downstream which provides a further source to organisms living in downstream reaches of the stream. The RCC predicts the relative importance of allochthonous, autochthonous and downstream transport as sources of organic energy, and the community composition of heterotrophs with respect to mechanisms used to harvest the organic matter in different reaches of the stream.

The upper reaches of the stream are small and in a forested catchment, little light penetrates through to the water surface. Consequently, autochthonous production rates are low and the major supply of organic matter is allochthonous as leaves and twigs falling into the water. This organic matter is processed by invertebrates capable of either shredding this coarse material (shredders) or collecting the particles (collectors) as they are carried downstream (Figure 6.14).

As the stream increases in size, the influence of the riverbank trees declines and autochthonous production increases with greater light availability. In this zone, invertebrates which graze on algae replace the shredders but collectors remain an important part of the invertebrate fauna. In the wide expanses of large streams and rivers, allochthonous inputs are of minor significance and within stream primary production is reduced through high water turbidity. Here, the main energy source is the organic matter carried downstream and collectors dominate the invertebrate fauna. Predators form a fourth feeding group and are found in similar proportions from the headwater reaches to the river mouth.

Some environmental factors change along the river continuum. Water temperature tends to increase downstream (see Tables 6.2 and 6.3) and the particle size of the river sediments declines with large boulders present in the upper reaches and fine clays predominating near the river mouth. Shredders utilise coarse particulate organic matter (CPOM) and as they do so reduce the particle size. This promotes the activities of the collectors which can utilise fine particulate organic matter (FPOM) (Figure 6.15).

Changes in the invertebrate fauna are reflected in the fish species that inhabit the upper and lower reaches of streams and rivers. Most

(a)

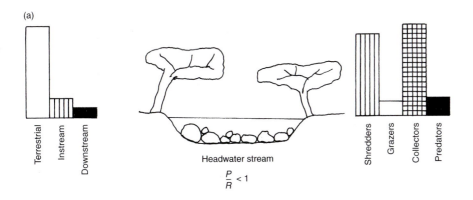

Headwater stream

$$\frac{P}{R} < 1$$

(b)

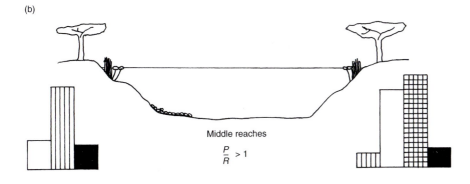

Middle reaches

$$\frac{P}{R} > 1$$

(c)

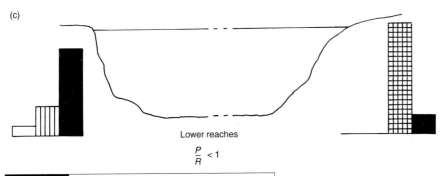

Lower reaches

$$\frac{P}{R} < 1$$

Figure 6.14 Diagram of the River Continuum Concept (RCC) depicting cross-sections of a river channel and riparian vegetation in (a) upper, (b) middle and (c) lower reaches of a river. Particle size of the sediments decreases downstream and river depth increases. The influence of the riparian vegetation on the aquatic system declines downstream. Bar charts on the left indicate relative importance of energy sources as organic matter inputs. Bar charts on the right indicate relative abundances of benthic invertebrates in different feeding groups. Changes in the ratio of gross primary production to community respiration are shown for the upper, middle and lower reaches of the river (adapted from Johnson et al. 1995 with kind permission of American Institute of Biological Sciences).

headwater fish species feed on invertebrates. The middle reaches of the rivers are dominated by invertebrate feeders and piscivores, while planktivorous and filter-feeding fish species occur in the lower reaches.

A major difference exists between rivers in temperate and tropical regions with respect to the timing of organic matter loading. Dudgeon and Bretschko (1996) noted that up to 80% of allochthonous inputs and bank runoff enter temperate streams during a few weeks in autumn

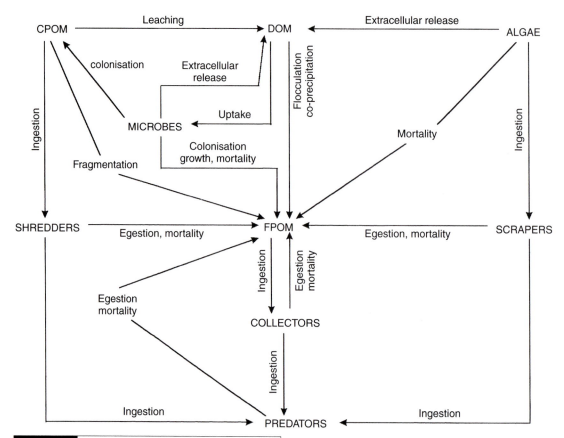

Figure 6.15 A diagram showing the nutrient resource pools, invertebrate functional groups and role of microbes in the processing of organic matter in a stream. CPOM = Coarse Particulate Organic Matter (>1 mm), FPOM = Fine Particulate Organic Matter (1mm > 0.45 μm), DOM = Dissolved Organic Matter (<0.45 μm) (after Cummins 1992 adapted with permission from John Wiley & Sons Limited).

when leaf fall occurs. In tropical Asia, seasonality is less marked, though it may be influenced by the monsoon. Basic information on the longitudinal zonation of environmental conditions and zonation of the fauna in tropical rivers is very patchy, but broad agreement with the predictions of the RCC has been recorded in Lam Tsuen River in Hong Kong (Dudgeon 1984). However, shredders did not constitute as important a part of the fauna in the upper reaches as the RCC predicted. Similarly, in rain-forest streams in Papua New Guinea (Dudgeon 1994) shredders did not exceed 2% of the benthic fauna.

Some river ecologists have questioned the applicability of the RCC to large rivers, particularly those with extensive floodplains (Davies and Walker 1986; Welcomme et al. 1989; Dudgeon and Bretschko 1996). Predictions from the RCC often do not match the field data collected for many tropical rivers. This may be due to short-term sampling programmes, oversimplification of the RCC or the need for significant modification of the concept to make it more generally applicable. Despite these criticisms, the RCC provides a useful framework on which to integrate in-stream and catchment processes and the concept emphasises the close link between rivers and the catchments they drain. This link is particularly intimate in the upper reaches of rivers.

Along the middle reaches of the Amazon River with its extensive floodplain, the longitudinal patterns predicted by the RCC were not readily apparent. It was found that the river could be divided into zones related to the extent of interaction with the floodplain. This observation suggested that the RCC was not applicable to these large, floodplain rivers and led to the development of the Flood-Pulse Concept.

6.4.3 The Flood-Pulse Concept

The RCC was developed from studies of small temperate streams that are permanent and have no component in which the water ceases flow for even short periods. Attempts to extrapolate this concept to rivers in general have therefore met with little success. Many large rivers have extensive floodplains on which river water may stagnate for months. Similarly, reservoirs transform rivers into lakes and the outflow from these reservoirs may have impacts downstream significantly different from those before dam construction (see section 6.4.4).

In river systems with extensive floodplains, interactions between the river and the floodplain may dominate ecosystem function and effectively mask the longitudinal patterns predicted by the RCC. The RCC may be modified to account for short-lived floods in small streams but, as the size of a floodplain increases (usually with increasing river discharge), the frequency of floods decreases and their duration and predictability increases (Junk *et al.* 1989).

The major force controlling biota in these large river–floodplain systems is the predictable pulses that occur in river discharge. These pulses result in an alternation of flooding and drainage of the floodplain and significant lateral transport of organic matter from the floodplain into the river channel. The Flood-Pulse Concept states that the most important hydrological feature of large rivers is the annual flood.

As the water level in the river channel rises, water flows on to the floodplain, bringing with it nutrients and converting the floodplain from a terrestrial system into an aquatic one. Aquatic plants grow rapidly, absorbing nutrients from the sediments and the overlying water. As plants die, the organic matter sinks to the bottom and decomposition begins, effectively transferring nutrients from the sediments to the water column. With a fall in water level, some of the vegetation produced on the floodplain may drain into the main river channel and constitute a significant source of food for riverine organisms (Figure 6.16).

Fish migrate in from the main channel and these migrations are, in many species, associated with breeding. The flooded plant material provides food for juvenile fish. On African floodplain rivers, such as the Kafue in Zambia, crocodiles and hippos spread out over the floodplain during the flood season and elephants and antelope such as waterbuck (*Kobus ellipsiprymnus*) and lechwe (*Kobus leche*) make extensive use of the flooded grasslands (Sheppe and Osborne 1971). As river levels fall, these animals migrate towards the main river channel and their place on the now dry floodplain is taken by a range of large mammals such as zebra, wildebeest and buffalo, less well adapted to wet conditions.

The floodplain is the main source of food for fish and, indeed, floodplain systems are more productive than similar rivers that lack them. The river channel in a floodplain is mainly a route for access to the floodplain which provides feeding areas, spawning and nursery sites. The river is, however, an important refuge area when the floodplain dries.

As the lakes dry at the end of the flood season, the aquatic plants decompose on the exposed sediments and provide a source of nutrients to the terrestrial plants that develop there during the dry season. High rates of primary production are maintained during the dry phase, and most of the nutrients contained within the vegetation are retained on the floodplain when this terrestrial vegetation is flooded. The nutrients are returned to the plants that dominate the aquatic phase. With each flood, nutrients enter the floodplain and the rapid development of the aquatic vegetation ensures that they are mostly retained on the floodplain. Similarly, the rapid replacement of aquatic vegetation by terrestrial species also ensures that nutrients stay on the floodplain.

Nutrient cycling on tropical floodplains is rapid since decomposition is promoted by the high temperatures that prevail throughout the year. During the aquatic phase, decomposition may be slowed by a limited supply of oxygen, but

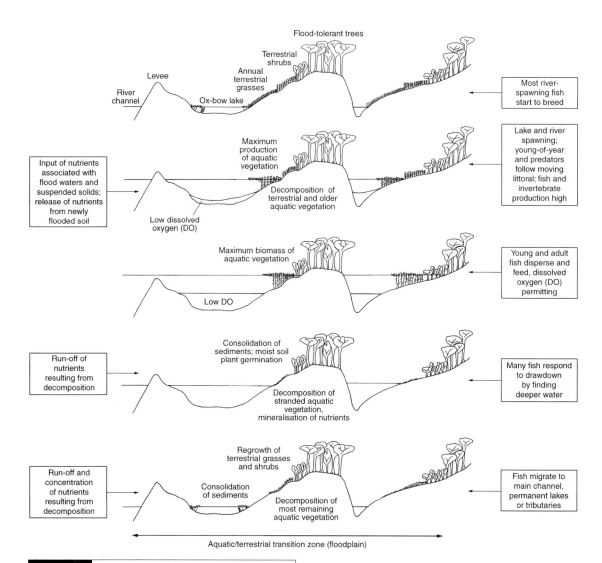

Figure 6.16 The annual migration of the littoral ATTZ (Aquatic/Terrestrial Transition Zone) on the Amazonian floodplain with estimates of annual production (P) in tonnes per hectare per year and biomass (B) in kilograms or tonnes per hectare: (1) phytoplankton (P = 6 t, B = 10–40 kg); (2) annual terrestrial plants (P = 20 t, B = 10 t); (3) perennial grasses (P = up to 100 t, B = 30–80 t); (4) floodplain (várzea) forest (P = 33 t, B = 300–600 t); (5) emergent aquatic plants (P = up to 60 t, B = 3–20 t). Estimates are as dry weight per hectare. Boxes on the right indicate typical stages in the life histories of floodplain fish (adapted from Junk et al. 1989; Bayley 1995 with permission of American Institute of Biological Sciences).

organic matter breakdown occurs rapidly once the material is exposed during the dry phase.

The primary production of the main channel of floodplain rivers is usually only a small fraction of that of the floodplain. Water depth, turbidity, turbulence and strong currents all conspire against primary producers. Aquatic plants may grow along the edge, and in slow-flowing rivers clumps of floating plants such as *Salvinia* spp., *Pistia stratiotes* and *Eichhornia crassipes* may drift slowly downstream.

Timing of the flood is all important. Predictable flood-pulses of moderate duration allow both the aquatic and terrestrial organisms living on them to adapt to what is potentially a stressful system. However, flood-pulses that are unpredictable and of short duration provide inadequate time for aquatic organisms to reproduce on the floodplain. Conversely, extended flooding and a short, dry period will not allow time for terrestrial organisms to complete their life cycle.

The flood-pulse concept has extended the interest of river ecologists to include the lakes, oxbows, wetlands and flooded forests as well as the main river channel. Because of the high rates of organic matter production on the floodplain, the relative importance of organic matter carried by the river from upstream areas, in most tropical floodplain systems, dwindles to insignificance. Biotic diversity is often high on floodplains owing to the rich variety of both aquatic and terrestrial habitats. Junk (1984) considers floodplains to be intermediate between lakes (which tend to accumulate material) and rivers (which transport material downstream). What happens to the ecology of river systems when they are converted into lakes through dam construction has been addressed by the Serial Discontinuity Concept.

6.4.4 Serial Discontinuity Concept

We have seen the significant impact that the construction of the Aswan High Dam has had on the ecology of the River Nile. The lake that forms behind a dam provides a new habitat to be invaded by organisms adapted to lacustrine conditions. The explosive growth, in Lake Kariba, of *Salvinia molesta* and the sardine *Limnothrissa miodon* introduced from Lake Tanganyika bears testament to this (see section 5.1.2). Dams disrupt the longitudinal continuum predicted by the RCC. A dam or weir in the upper reaches of a stream will trap coarse particles and so alter the ratio of coarse-to-fine particulate matter in the water flowing out of the reservoir. A dam further downstream will result in higher water temperatures, alter the flood regime of the downstream reaches and may allow for the development of phytoplankton and zooplankton populations unable to develop in the river before dam construction because of water turbulence and turbidity.

6.4.5 Comparison of the three concepts

Sedell *et al.* (1989) concluded that rivers with constricted, clearly defined channels should follow the linear patterns predicted by the RCC. Rivers which seasonally rise and fall should receive large quantities of organic matter from the floodplain, and this lateral transport should exceed that delivered from upstream. Therefore these rivers will not conform to the continuum concept, but will consist of a sequence of patches with organic matter supply and transport varying with floodplain width and flood magnitude and duration. The flood-pulse concept, with both longitudinal and lateral components, is applicable to these rivers.

Rivers, such as the Nile, which have had their hydrology significantly altered through the construction of weirs, dams and canals will tend to conform to the serial discontinuity concept. However, consider a river that flows through clearly defined channels, enters a reservoir, then flows across an expansive floodplain, through a gorge and into another reservoir before entering the sea. To such a river, components of all three concepts described above will be applicable. The three concepts are based on the assumption that physical conditions control the biological structure of the communities. At the whole-river scale this may be true, but at smaller scales biological interactions might be more important. For example, consider two similar pools along a stretch of river separated by a waterfall. Both contain a similar population of herbivorous fish, but in the downstream pool a voracious predator is also present. The herbivore populations in these two pools are more likely to be affected by the presence or absence of the predator than by small differences in environmental factors arising from the fact that one is further downstream.

Pringle *et al.* (1988) suggested that rivers are organised as a nested hierarchy. Patterns which can be found in lotic systems result from processes operating at different scales. Large-scale processes such as climate and plate tectonics determine patterns in features such as river morphology and the fish species likely to be present. Lower levels of organisation include features such as substrate particle size, light penetration and the biotic communities that develop within a particular reach of the river. The three concepts described above attempt to identify and explain patterns of either a complete river system or at least long stretches of one.

Another way of looking at river systems is to vary the scale, both spatially and temporally, of investigations. While physical features change gradually from the headwaters of a river to its mouth, a more detailed study might reveal patterns that do not fit this gradual change. For example, a gradient in physical features will often exist across a stream bed as well as in the direction of the flow. This variation is not considered by the RCC and only rather superficially by the flood-pulse concept. A significant gradient may extend from the main river channel, where physical features such as flow rate and water turbidity dominate, to the calm waters of an adjacent floodplain lake where biological interactions, such as competition for light and space between species of aquatic plants, are more important.

The analogy of a river as a series of beads on a string has been proposed. Each bead represents a different reach on the river and the string, the connectivity between the upstream beads with those downstream. The three concepts described are not exclusive: application of one concept may be appropriate to a particular reach of a river, and another to one downstream of it. The RCC seems most appropriate to those headwater streams and rivers that arise within forested catchments, with streams well covered by tree canopies, which then flow to more exposed areas where the littoral vegetation is herbaceous and the river remains constrained within its banks. The flood-pulse concept is restricted to the reaches of rivers which have an extensive floodplain and the impacts of the floodplain may be carried downstream. Many rivers today are highly modified systems, and the serial-discontinuity concept provides a framework to describe the impact of dams and other barriers on river ecology. A further change in the physical environment of rivers occurs as they approach the sea, and in these estuarine reaches biological communities develop that are highly adapted to the conditions that prevail.

6.5 | Estuaries

Many tropical rivers have very long and wide estuarine reaches and complete mixing of fresh with saltwater may only take place a considerable distance offshore. Saltwater is denser than freshwater and therefore mixing patterns vary between estuaries and within estuaries with seasons. Estuarine hydrology is complicated by variations in river flow, tidal influences and this layering of freshwater over seawater.

Seawater salinity averages around 35‰ (parts per thousand, every litre of seawater contains 35 g of salt). Freshwater usually has a salinity less than 1‰. For this reason, seawater is denser than freshwater and therefore river water tends to flow out at the surface and seawater enters the estuary at depth. As river water approaches the sea, a salinity gradient of some form develops. Salinity of the water column in an estuary varies with distance from the sea and with depth, with fresher water at the surface and more saline water near the bottom. Down the estuary, water column salinities may take the form of a **wedge of freshwater** overlying a **saltwater wedge** (Figure 6.17).

The distribution of fresh- and salt-water within an estuary will depend on factors such as estuary topography, density differences between the water masses, turbulence and currents, tidal height and the discharge from the river. In some rivers, freshwater discharge is so large that seawater penetration is prevented. In the Amazon, mixing of river water with seawater occurs out at sea and therefore an 'estuary' need not be bounded on two sides by land. Even though mixing occurs out at sea, the Amazon is still a tidal river and tidal impacts can be measured some 600 km from the sea. The Purari River in Papua New Guinea has an extensive delta, and saltwater penetration has been recorded 60 km inland in one of the distributaries (Petr 1983a). If tidal currents are strong, mixing will occur and the water in the estuary will be homogeneous vertically and gradually increase in salinity as the freshwater mixes with seawater.

The relative positions and shapes of these wedges changes with the tides and with varia-

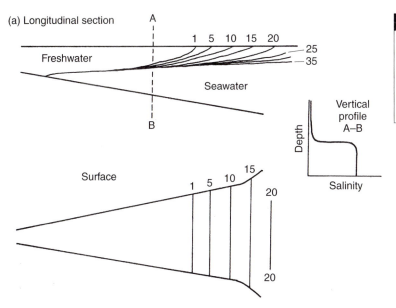

(a) Longitudinal section

(b) Longitudinal section

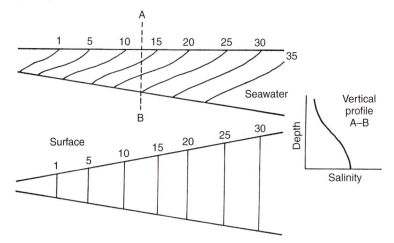

Figure 6.17 Distribution of iso-halines (contours of equal salt concentration) in (a) a salt-wedge estuary with the vertical profile of salt concentrations through A–B and (b) a partially mixed estuary (after Barnes 1974).

tions in river flow rate and turbulence. The salt-water moves up the estuary as the tide rises and recedes once the tide turns. Therefore the zone of mixing is not static, but in rivers with a seasonally constant flow, that discharge into a coastal zone where tidal amplitude is small, variations will be muted. Organisms living in estuaries must either move with the water masses or face exposure to large variations in salinities. Estuarine organisms need to have physiological and ecological strategies to cope with these variations in salinity.

6.5.1 Life in an estuary

Many freshwater and marine species are unable to live in brackish water; some that can are unable to adapt to the frequent changes in salinities that occur within estuaries. Estuaries are not easy places to inhabit and few species have been able to adapt to estuarine conditions. Species that have adapted often thrive there, developing into large, productive populations. Estuaries are also rather simple systems, mainly consisting of a water column and mud flats. The variety of habitats to support diverse communities is, therefore, lacking. None the less, estuaries are often very productive systems.

Nutrients are carried into estuaries from the catchment drained by the river and delivered on a daily basis by the tidal cycle. Dense populations of phytoplankton, seagrasses and mangroves (see chapter 10) develop in response to this rich supply of nutrients. The organic matter so produced is made available to consumers resident in the estuarine muds largely as detritus which is delivered to them by the ebb and flow of the water above them.

Several distinct communities occur in estuaries. Some organisms such as fish are highly mobile and may move into the estuary at high tide and leave as the tide recedes. Some fish species have the capacity to exist in both fresh- and sea-water and will migrate through estuaries to feed or breed in either the sea or the river. Migrants are either **anadromous**, living in the sea and moving through estuaries into rivers to breed, or **catadromous**, feeding in freshwater systems and heading to the sea to breed (see Box 6.6). Planktonic organisms move back and forth with the tide.

Other organisms are permanent residents. Most of these live in or on the surface of the bottom muds. Those that live in burrows are called **infauna**, but many small animals (e.g. ciliates, nematodes, ostracods, coelenterates and rotifers) known as **meiofauna**, live in the spaces between sediment particles. These animals feed on the detritus suspended in the water or deposited on the sediment surface. Some estuarine animals are filter feeders, removing organic matter from the water by filtration through specialised mouth parts. Filter feeders predominate in sediments with a high sand content as fine particles disturbed from muddy deposits tend to clog up their filtration apparatus. Some meiofauna feed on algae and detritus and others are predators or scavengers.

Fish and birds are the main mudflat predators; fish predators operate during high tide and are replaced by birds when the mudflats are exposed at low tide. Estuaries are important staging posts for many migratory wading birds, and huge numbers may congregate during particular seasons. Bird species exploit different prey species, using a variety of techniques and strategies to locate and catch their prey. The length of a bird's bill, for example, determines the depth of penetration into the mud. Birds with short bills are only able to reach animals with shallow burrows. This reduces interspecific competition and is another example of **resource partitioning** (see sections 4.9.5 and 4.11.1).

Organisms that live in estuaries need to be able to cope with salinity changes. Most estuarine organisms evolved from marine species and are **euryhaline** (see section 2.10.1); they can tolerate a wide range of salinities. Maintaining a salt and water balance of body fluids is achieved through **osmoregulation**. Marine organisms tend to have concentrated body fluids and, in the brackish waters of an estuary, absorb water by osmosis. Three main strategies are used by organisms to prevent their body fluids becoming too dilute. The first is to 'run or hide'. Mobile organisms can follow the body of water that matches the osmotic content of their body fluids. Others can hide in burrows or close their shells until the tide returns with more saline water. Barnacles are sessile organisms and, when exposed to extreme salinities, they shut their valves and cease feeding until salinities return to levels they can withstand.

The other two strategies are physiological. Some estuarine organisms simply allow the concentration of their body fluids to fluctuate with the changing salinity of the water that surrounds them. These organisms are called **osmoconformers** and include many of the soft-bodied invertebrates such as polychaete worms. Despite the simplicity of this solution to osmoregulation, these organisms are highly successful and are one reason why estuaries are such productive systems. Other species, **osmoregulators**, are physiologically more sophisticated and maintain the concentration of their body fluids by pumping out excess water and absorbing salts from the environment. These organisms reduce water uptake by having an impermeable layer covering most of their exposed surfaces.

Box 6.6 | Barramundi: migrants with mercury

Barramundi or giant perch (*Lates calcarifer*) is a widely distributed fish found throughout the Indo-West Pacific and is an important food fish for humans. It is biologically interesting both because it is **catadromous** and because individuals from the Lake Murray area of Papua New Guinea have been shown to contain high mercury concentrations, which result from naturally occurring sources within the catchment. For the people living in this area, barramundi is their main source of protein. To study the migratory habits of this fish, Moore and Reynolds (1982) tagged over 6000 fish and released them into the coastal waters around Daru near the mouth of the Fly River and elsewhere within the Gulf of Papua. Subsequent recaptures demonstrated movement of adults from areas throughout the Gulf of Papua to the Daru coastal area during spawning (October to February) and a subsequent return to inland habitats.

On leaving the spawning grounds, the young become distributed throughout the inshore waters near Daru. Major recruitment to the Gulf of Papua and from there to inland areas occurs during the second and third years of life. Three- and four-year-old fish migrate back to coastal waters for spawning, and afterwards return inland, usually to the area from which they originally migrated.

Sorentino (1979) found that the commercial catches of barramundi from Daru at the mouth of the Fly River and in Lake Murray contained unexpectedly high levels of mercury. The mean concentration of mercury for 288 samples from Daru was 0.52 ± 0.34 mg g^{-1} and this is in excess of the World Health Organisation recommended limit of 0.5 mg g^{-1}.

Sorentino (1979) and Kyle and Ghani (1982) showed abnormally high mercury levels in hair from people living around Lake Murray, most of whom consume fish 2–3 times daily. At the time of these studies, there were no agricultural or industrial developments in the Western Province to account for the mercury. Subsequent work has shown that the major source of mercury is the catchment area of the Strickland River (Natural Systems Research 1988) and that the mercury is biologically concentrated in the food chain.

6.6 | Chapter summary

1. Rivers exhibit a longitudinal zonation. Upper reaches of rivers tend to be rocky, turbulent and fast-flowing. Further downstream the river channel is wider and deeper and the flow rate may be slower. In tropical rivers, water temperature increases from the headwaters to the mouth, and there is usually an increase in dissolved and particulate material with distance downstream.

2. Phytoplankton production within rivers is limited by water turbulence and poor light penetration (shading by overhanging trees or high sediment loads). Animals and plants inhabiting rivers exhibit a range of adaptations to avoid being swept downstream or damaged by strong currents.

3. The Nile River has a low discharge and its hydrology has been significantly altered by humans. Rivers in the Amazon Basin reflect the catchments that they drain. Whitewater rivers are turbid draining catchments with tectonically stressed rocks which are still undergoing erosion and weathering. The pH of the water is close to neutral, and conductivity is higher than in blackwater rivers. Blackwater rivers are acidic and stained with humic materials, but carry little suspended material. They drain catchments with sandy soils.

4. The River Continuum Concept provides a framework relating the longitudinal gradient in the physical environment, from the headwaters to the mouth of rivers, to the biological communities that develop along its length. The upper reaches of streams are characterised by low autochthonous production, and organic matter from overhanging trees provides most food and energy to stream invertebrates. The invertebrate community here is dominated by animals capable of handling large particles (shredders) or collecting particles carried by the current (collectors). Further downstream, autochthonous production by algae increases as tree cover declines with increasing stream width. Grazers which feed on algae replace shredders in the invertebrate community. Collectors dominate in the lower reaches where fine particles of organic matter carried downstream are the main energy source. Fish species inhabiting headwater streams mostly feed on invertebrates; the middle reaches are dominated by invertebrate feeders and piscivores whereas planktivores and detritivores dominate the fish communities in the lower reaches.

5. In rivers with extensive floodplains, the alternation of flooding and drainage results in significant transport of organic matter from the floodplain to the river. This lateral transfer of organic matter is often much greater than that provided from upstream sources and therefore the flood-pulse masks the longitudinal patterns predicted by the river continuum concept. Floodplain organisms are highly adapted to this flood-pulse. Primary production is high during the aquatic phase as nutrients are rapidly recycled from the flooded vegetation produced during the terrestrial phase. As water level falls, exposed mud banks are colonised by terrestrial species capable of completing their life cycle before the next flood. Fish utilise the floodplain as nursery grounds, and the young, protected by the vegetation from predators, grow quickly and reach sufficient size to reduce predation losses when water levels eventually fall.

6. Regulation of river flow through the construction of dams, weirs and canals disrupts the longitudinal zonation in rivers. Reservoirs transform riverine environments into lacustrine ones and downstream effects include higher water temperatures, reduced sediment loads and higher phytoplankton and zooplankton populations.

7. Estuaries are the reaches of rivers where fresh river water meets and mixes with seawater. Significant stratification may develop with less dense freshwater overlying layers of more dense saline water. Mixing varies with the hydrology and morphometry of the estuary and may take place well out to sea. Organisms inhabiting estuaries must cope with large variations in salinities. Osmoconformers can withstand changes in the concentration of their body fluids and allow them to vary with the salinity of the water that surrounds them. Osmoregulators exert more control and strive to maintain the concentration of their body fluids within narrow limits. Some species avoid osmotic stress by burrowing in sediments or protecting their tissues by closing their shells.

Chapter 7

Wetlands and succession

7.1 | What are wetlands?

Wetlands have been called the 'kidneys of the earth' (Mitsch and Gosselink 1986) because of the role they play in enhancing the quality of water that flows through them. They have also been referred to as 'mosquito-infested mudholes' (Minter 1991). The RAMSAR convention, held in Ramsar, Iran in 1971 under the auspices of Unesco, defined wetlands as 'areas of marsh, fen, peatland or water, whether natural or artificial, permanent or temporary, with water that is static or flowing, fresh, brackish or salt, including areas of marine water the depth of which at low tide does not exceed six metres'. This is a very broad definition and includes lakes, rivers, floodplains, mangroves and even coral reefs: all systems described in other chapters (Table 7.1).

In this chapter, we describe areas that are either permanently or seasonally flooded with freshwater, comprising a mosaic of vegetation and areas of open, shallow water. Wetlands occupy the transitional zone between permanently wet and deep water bodies and generally dry areas. They exhibit enormous diversity but are characterised by: the presence of water, soils that differ in composition from those that make up the surrounding catchment, and a plant community dominated by **hydrophytes** (water-loving plants). Wetlands occupy approximately 6% of the earth's surface and are important systems in the tropics (Table 7.2).

In this chapter we also consider how ecosystems change over time. Time and spatial scales are important concepts in ecology. Organisms respond to night and day (diurnal changes) and we have discussed the seasonal responses of organisms living in savannas (e.g. wildebeest migration) and have seen how organisms respond to less predictable events such as rainfall in deserts. While diurnal and seasonal changes encompass a degree of predictability, there is also much variation from one day to the next and between years. Some weather events occur periodically every few years (e.g. ENSO events, see section 1.2.6). Other events may have significant, localised ecological impact on an area but return to that same area only after a long time interval (e.g. hurricanes).

Some changes occur over very long time scales. Examples of these include massive geological upheavals, glaciations and large shifts in climate. We need to appreciate these sorts of changes in order to understand, for example, worldwide plant and animal distributions (see section 1.3.1). Other changes, at the global spatial level are occurring over decade-long intervals and we will discuss some of these in chapter 14. What about more local ecosystem changes that occur over intermediate time scales? Changes that occur as a result of interactions between species in a community and the impact they have in altering the environment is the concept considered in this chapter.

Three major categories of tropical, freshwater wetlands (excluding floodplains, see chapter 6) have been recognised and are introduced below: (1) floating sudd communities; (2) permanent and seasonal herbaceous swamps; and (3) swamp forests.

Table 7.1 | Classification of freshwater wetlands according to the RAMSAR Convention

Category	Sub-category
Riverine (6)	
Perennial	Permanent rivers and streams, including waterfalls
	Inland deltas
Temporary	Seasonal and irregular rivers and streams
	Riverine floodplains, including river flats, flooded river basins, seasonally flooded grassland
Lacustrine (5)	
Permanent	Permanent freshwater lakes (>9 ha), including shores subject to seasonal or irregular inundation
	Permanent freshwater ponds
Seasonal	Seasonal freshwater lakes (>9 ha), including floodplain lakes
Palustrine (7)	
Emergent	Permanent freshwater marshes and swamps on inorganic soils, with emergent vegetation whose bases lie below the water table for at least most of the growing season
	Permanent peat-forming freshwater swamps, including tropical upland valley swamps dominated by plants such as *Papyrus* or *Typha*
	Seasonal freshwater marshes on inorganic soil, including sloughs, potholes, seasonally flooded meadows, sedge marshes and dambos
	Peatlands, including acidophilous, ombrogenous (vegetation lying above ground-water level, relying on rain water) or soligenous (receives water from slope run-off) mires covered by moss, herbs or dwarf shrub vegetation, and fens of all types
	Alpine and polar wetlands, including seasonally flooded meadows moistened by temporary waters from snowmelt vegetation
	Volcanic fumaroles continually moistened by condensing water vapour
Forested (6,7,8)	Shrub swamps, including shrub-dominated freshwater marsh, shrub carr and thickets, on inorganic soils
	Freshwater forest, wooded swamps on inorganic soils
	Forested peatlands, including peat swamp forest

Notes: Numbers in brackets refer to chapters in this book dealing with this wetland category.
Source: Bullock 1993.

7.2 | Sudd communities of Lake Naivasha

The term sudd is now used to describe mats of floating vegetation. It was first applied to the massive *Cyperus papyrus* mats that developed in wetlands adjacent to the upper Nile in the Sudan (see section 6.1). Sudd mats form by the rhizomes of *C. papyrus* or the floating stems of *Vossia cuspidata* and *Ludwigia* spp. becoming intertwined. The mat may be further colonised by plants such as *Impatiens* spp., *Aeschynomene* spp., sedges, aquatic grasses and even some normally terrestrial climbers. *Salvinia molesta* (see Box 5.1) and *Eichhornia crassipes* are also very effective at forming complex floating communities and the mats may become so well developed that a person can walk on them.

Table 7.2	Extent of wetlands in the tropical parts of the continents
Continent	Wetland area (km^2)
South America	1 200 000
Asia	350 000
Africa	340 000
Australia	2 000

Source: Bullock 1993.

Lake Naivasha is a shallow lake in Kenya with no outflow (endorheic). It is an unusual natural lake because its water level fluctuates seasonally and, despite having no outfall, it retains freshwater. Gaudet (1977) observed changes that occurred in the littoral vegetation of the lake with the rise and fall of the water level. He found that, as lake levels fell, the exposed mud was colonised by a variety of seedlings. As the lake level rose three vegetation zones could be discerned. A band of *Sphaeranthus suaveolens* (Asteraceae) formed adjacent to the lake. This plant is highly adapted to rising water levels. When submerged, stems lose their leaves below the water surface and develop large chambers filled with air to provide buoyancy. The middle zone was dominated by *Cyperus papyrus*, *C. digitatus* and *C. immensus*. The zone closest to the land was dominated by plants belonging to the Asteraceae (*Conyza* spp., *Gnaphalium* sp.). The final stage in this process was replacement of the vegetation adjacent to the lake by a band of young papyrus plants. Gaudet (1977) showed that this process had occurred four times, producing a series of papyrus reefs. Production of these papyrus bands was correlated with larger cycles of drying and flooding which occurred on the lake at the time of his study.

During the 1980s, the water level in Lake Naivasha declined and large areas of papyrus were cleared for agriculture. A rise in water level in 1988 resulted in the expansion of papyrus, but the wetland was then characterised by more even-aged papyrus plants than that studied by Gaudet in the 1970s (Harper and Mavuti 1996). The sequential stages in the development of shoreline vegetation described by Gaudet (1977) and

repeated in 1988, have been related to seasonal water-level changes.

However, the Lake Naivasha wetland has, over the last two decades, been significantly altered by the introduction of exotic species, nutrient enrichment and swamp clearing for agriculture. Among other changes, these disturbances reduced the area of papyrus swamp and the littoral aquatic vegetation was decimated by the introduced crayfish (*Procambarus clarkii*). Aquatic plants subsequently recovered following the decline in the crayfish population. Notice that with Lake Naivasha we have described two basic kinds of temporal and spatial changes. The first, described by Gaudet (1977), occurred as a reasonably predictable sequence in response to water level fluctuations. The second type of change occurred following ecosystem disturbances by humans: swamp clearing, introduction of alien species and nutrient enrichment. In this chapter we are more concerned with predictable, sequential changes than by those resulting from disturbances. However, following a disturbance, although significantly altered, the ecosystem may subsequently undergo a different series of sequential and predictable changes (e.g. see section 8.14.2). The system may either develop as one similar to that before the disturbance or attain a new stable state.

7.3 | Rooted emergent swamps of Lake Chilwa

Lake Chilwa is a shallow, saline lake situated to the east of the main African Rift Valley in southern Malawi. The lake is surrounded by approximately 600 km^2 of wetlands dominated by *Typha domingensis* (Figure 7.1). The entire lake–wetland system undergoes significant changes in response to lake level fluctuations that have been characterised as catastrophic, seasonal, periodic and long-term (Kalk 1979). The most dramatic (catastrophic) change was the evaporation of this large lake to complete dryness in 1968. Water level changes also occur seasonally with the wet–dry cycle of the regional climate. Periodic changes occur with water levels declining over a few years (recessions) followed by refilling and a period of

Figure 7.1 Lake Chilwa, Malawi showing some of the extensive wetlands that surround this shallow, endorheic lake. The water level of this lake fluctuates, and in 1968 the lake dried up. This photograph, taken in 1978, shows the lake with a particularly high water level; *Typha domingensis* is the dominant plant in this wetland (Photo: Patrick Osborne).

higher mean water levels. Long-term changes relate to geomorphology and significant changes in regional climate and include the formation of the lake from a river and major changes in the size of the lake basin.

Floodplain grasslands occur around the outer periphery of the Lake Chilwa basin. These areas are dry for around 9 months of the year. On acid soils, *Cyperus papyrus* and the tall grasses *Phragmites mauritianus* and *Echinochloa pyramidalis* form the next zone towards the lake. On more alkaline soils, *Vossia cuspidata*, *Cyperus longus* and the legume *Aeschynomene pfundii* grow. The largest area of the Chilwa wetland contains almost pure stands of *Typha domingensis* which ring the area of open water. Swamp transition species such as the grasses *Diplachne fusca* and *Panicum repens* and the sedge *Cyperus laevigatus* may occur together with *Typha* at the landward edge. Free-floating species such as *Pistia stratiotes*, *Ceratophyllum demersum* and *Utricularia* spp. occur on the lake edges of the swamp (Howard-Williams 1979).

The marginal vegetation of Lake Chilwa varies seasonally with water level fluctuations. Few species were present along the landward edge of the *Typha* swamp at the end of the dry season in October. As the water level rose with the onset of the wet season, moist ephemeral species such as *Cyperus esculentus* and *Hibiscus cannabinus* germinated on the wet mud. These plants grew rapidly, flowered and died during the wet season. Flooded areas were colonised by *Panicum repens*, *Nymphaea caerula* and *Utricularia* spp.

In contrast, the distribution of *Typha* was more static. These plants are rooted in an organic-rich clay and grow up to 2–3 m above the water level. Howard-Williams (1979) ascribed the success of *Typha* over *Cyperus papyrus* in the Lake Chilwa basin to the competitive advantage conferred on *Typha* by the high conductivity and alkalinity of the sediments. Emergent swamp plants are often vigorous colonisers and, as we have seen with

Cyperus papyrus in Lake Naivasha, extend rapidly into recently created open areas with a suitable hydrological regime. However, when Lake Chilwa dried up in 1968, *Typha* did not colonise the newly exposed lake bed. The bare mud presented an unfavourable environment with high concentrations of sodium chloride and high temperatures. Furthermore, extensive large cracks developed in the mud making it an unstable substrate for potential plant colonists. Three species were able to grow in this extreme environment: the alkaline grass *Diplachne fusca*, the sedge *Cyperus laevigatus* and *Aeschynomene pfundii*.

Diplachne fusca was particularly successful during this dry phase and colonised over $80\,km^2$ of exposed lake bed. When the lake filled rapidly in 1969, water depth increased by $2\,m$ on the lake side of the *Typha* zone, winds mixed the water column and stirred up the bottom mud making the water turbid and water conductivity increased from 200 to 1500 μSiemens cm^{-1}. These changes caused a sharp decline in the distribution of the lake bed colonists (*Diplachne fusca, Cyperus laevigatus* and *Aeschynomene pfundii*) and once again the margins of the lake were lined with *Typha*.

Clearly, there are distinct seasonal and periodical changes in the wetland vegetation of Lake Chilwa and these can be related to water level changes. However, note that the water level changes are comparatively small ($1\,m$ in most years). This contrasts with the much larger changes in water level that occur on Amazonian floodplains and explains the very different sequence of vegetation changes that accompany the seasonal rise and fall of the Amazon (see section 6.3.4).

Let us now compare differences in the way the two wetlands we have described differ in terms of ecosystem processes such as primary production and nutrient cycling.

7.4 | Freshwater herbaceous wetlands: structure and function

Tropical herbaceous wetlands are usually either dominated by rooted plants such as *Typha domingensis* or *Phragmites karka* or by large floating islands of vegetation. The floating grass meadows on South American floodplains and the *Papyrus-Vossia* islands common in many African wetlands are examples of this latter wetland type. Floating wetlands are structurally and functionally quite different from those dominated by bottom-rooted plants (Howard-Williams and Gaudet 1985; Figure 7.2).

There are significant differences in nutrient cycling between rooted and floating mats in tropical swamps. The inflow to a floating swamp is separated by the mat into 'mat water' surrounding the emergent plant parts and 'swamp water' beneath the mat. Nutrients are absorbed by the plants from the water column. Material breaking away from a floating mat accumulates as a sludge beneath the mat and nutrients need to re-enter the water column before they became available to the mat again. In rooted swamps, nutrients are first incorporated within the sediments and uptake by the plants occurs through extensive root systems.

Although wetlands are regarded as intermediate between terrestrial and aquatic systems, they are best considered to be aquatic systems since the food web within them is largely aquatic. Herbaceous wetlands are vertically layered with an autotrophic layer overlying a heterotrophic one (Figure 7.2). Therefore the wetland food web is split, with primary production largely occurring in the air whilst secondary production and decomposition mostly occur in the water. Because of this spatial separation, there is also a time lag between production of organic matter in the air, its collapse into the water and its subsequent consumption and decomposition there. This temporal and spatial separation is typical of systems in which detritus-based food chains dominate (see chapter 10).

Very little primary production occurs in the water of herbaceous swamps because little photosynthetically active radiation reaches the water surface. The emergent plants in tropical wetlands are often over $2\,m$ tall and grow in dense stands. Furthermore, the water beneath the vegetation is often highly coloured and this reduces the penetration of what little light reaches the water

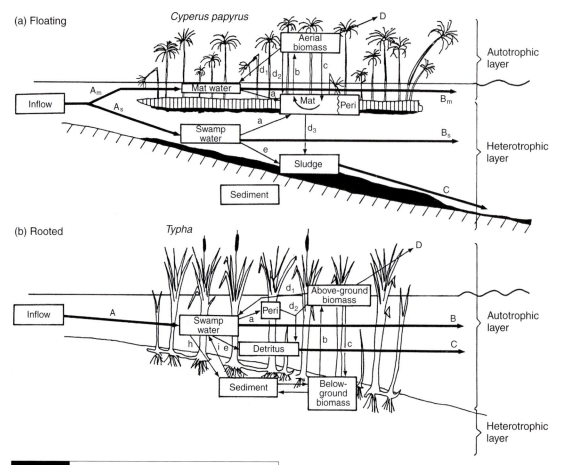

Figure 7.2 Comparison of nutrient pathways in (a) floating papyrus wetland and (b) a rooted *Typha* wetland, showing differences in general structure and the separation of autotrophic and heterotrophic layers. The depth of the autotrophic layer in wetlands with rooted vegetation will not extend to the sediment surface if light penetration through the dense vegetation is inadequate to support photosynthesis. Throughput pathways are labelled with a capital letter and internal nutrient pathways are labelled with a lower-case letter. A = nutrients in inflowing water, subscripts refer to mat (m) and swamp (s); B = nutrients in outflowing water; C = nutrients in outflow of organic matter; D = nutrients lost by grazing, burning or plant harvesting; a = uptake from the water by plants or algae; b = transfer from roots/rhizomes to shoots; c = translocation from shoots to roots/rhizomes; d_1 = transfer from shoots to water (leaching, decomposition); d_2 = transfer from shoots to detritus; d_3 = transfer from floating mat to sludge; e = adsorption from water on to sludge or detritus; h = loss to sediments from swamp water; i = enrichment of water by sediment release; Peri = periphyton (after Howard-Williams and Gaudet 1985 with kind permission from Kluwer Academic Publishers).

surface. Low primary production in the water column, little water movement and high rates of decomposition result in low concentrations of dissolved oxygen.

Despite this low water-column production, wetlands are highly productive ecosystems. Wetland plants have ready access to water, carbon dioxide and nutrients from either the sediment or water column. Nutrient supply to tropical wetlands may be seasonal with higher inputs entering with wet season inflows. Nutrients are absorbed, utilised in photosynthesis and the products translocated to below-ground storage organs such as rhizomes. In many of these plants, stored products are used for vegetative reproduction. Wetland plants are efficient at sequestering nutrients and retaining them and therefore open water areas adjacent to wetlands may only receive a small fraction of the nutrients entering the wetland basin. Many tropical wetland plants

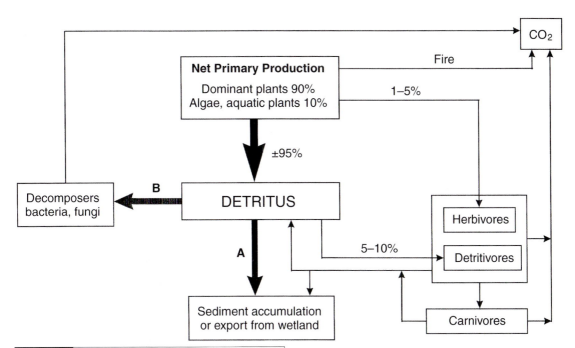

Figure 7.3 Diagram showing the principal energy pathways in an herbaceous wetland. Emergent plants are the dominant primary producers, and submerged plants and algae only contribute around 10%. Little of the total production is grazed by herbivores, and most of the organic matter produced enters the detritus food chain. Depending on the hydrology of the wetland, detritus is either exported or accumulates *in situ* (pathway A). Depending on environmental conditions, particularly oxygen supply, detritus may be broken down by decomposers (pathway B). In tropical wetlands, fire can be responsible for significant losses in organic matter (after Howard-Williams 1977 with kind permission from Malaysian Nature Society).

utilise the efficient C_4 pathway for photosynthesis (see section 3.7).

Few herbivores are adequately adapted to the physically demanding conditions of moving through dense vegetation growing on, at best, a soggy substrate. Lechwe (*Kobus leche*), sitatunga (*Tragelaphus spekei*) and the Nile lechwe (*Ontragus megaceros*) in Africa are large herbivores adapted to grazing in wetlands. Some seed-eating birds also remove primary produce from wetlands. The nutritional quality of wetland plants is poor and many species are rendered unpalatable through the presence of secondary chemical compounds. Therefore very little of the net production is grazed and most forms detritus. We will look at

the fate of that detritus through detrital food chains in chapter 10. Pathways affecting the accumulation of matter in wetland sediments are shown in Figure 7.3. Some nutrients are lost from the system, but *in situ* plant uptake ensures rapid plant growth.

Gross primary production is likely to be higher in tropical wetlands than in temperate ones because of the extended growing season and greater incoming radiation. Respiration rates (and therefore rates of decomposition) are closely related to temperature, and therefore respiration rates are also likely to be higher in tropical wetlands. However, inadequate work has been done on the production and fate of organic matter in tropical wetlands. One major obstacle is the assessment of below-ground production. Many wetland plant species have extensive underground rhizomes or tubers; photosynthate is translocated to these during the growing season and used to initiate growth at the end of any dormant period. These underground stores are less susceptible to losses from grazers and fire. Increase in rhizome biomass may account for 30–90% of shoot production.

Organic matter may accumulate in the sediment as peat (see section 7.5.2), but there are other pathways that preclude this. In tropical wetlands, fire may constitute a major loss of organic matter and energy fixed by primary producers. Howard-Williams and Lenton (1975) estimated that up to 30% of the above-ground vegetation in the herbaceous swamp surrounding Lake Chilwa was burnt annually.

7.5 | Swamp forests

Swamp forests are particularly well developed throughout the flat, lowlands of Malesia, South-East Asia and the Zaire River basin. They are, relative to other tropical forests, species-poor, and the most common genera include *Nauclea*, *Mitragyna*, *Pandanus*, *Phoenix*, *Raphia* and *Uapaca*. *Melaleuca* (paper-bark trees) swamp savanna is characteristic of monsoonal wetlands in tropical Australasia. The trees are scattered with open, grassy areas which become inundated during the wet season and colonised by aquatic plants. Many of the trees growing in swamps have pneumatophores, adventitious (aerial) or stilt roots. The sago palm (*Metroxylon sagu*) is a tall shrub that grows in swampy woodlands in South-East Asia and the tropical Pacific. This palm grows best in shallow swamps with a regular supply of freshwater. The trunk is rich in carbohydrate and is harvested to provide the staple food, sago.

The inundated forests of the Amazon Basin and their links with rivers and floodplains have been described in section 6.3.5.

7.5.1 Swamp forests of Sungai Sebangu, Kalimantan

Indonesia possesses the largest area of tropical, peat-swamp forests with around 6 million ha in Kalimantan. The Sungai (River) Sebangu is a slow-flowing blackwater river (see section 6.3.1) draining a low-lying catchment with vast expanses of peat-swamp forest. The forest vegetation was studied by Page and Rieley (1998) who noted that it changed with distance from the river. The forest adjacent to the river had three canopy layers with trees up to 40 m high. The forest floor consisted of a mosaic of shallow depressions and mounds with the depressions linking to form anastomosing

drainage channels for run-off from the forest. Numerous pneumatophores grew up through the water in these depressions. The mounds were formed by organic matter trapped by the pneumatophores and the buttress or stilt roots of the canopy trees.

From 5 to 6 km from the river there was a gradual transition to lower, denser 'pole forest'. The forest floor in this zone was very uneven with deep pools between hummocks with abundant pneumatophores. There were only two canopy layers, with the upper dominated by *Combretocarpus rotundatus*. Many trees had distorted trunks and small, xeromorphic leaves. The canopy was more open with trees festooned with insectivorous pitcher plants (*Nepenthes* spp.). The abundance of *Nepenthes* may be due to increased light availability below the canopy, but also may be connected with increasing nutrient deficiencies within the peat deposits (see section 7.5.2). There was a dense understorey dominated by *Pandanus* spp.

From 12 to 13 km from the river, pole forest was replaced by dense interior forest with a canopy height up to 45 m. The forest floor had shallow depressions and raised areas formed by tree roots. There were fewer pneumatophores in the depressions of this forest type than in those closer to the river. Epiphytes, lianas and rattans were more common than in the marginal and pole forests, and the main tree species in the canopy were *Agathis* sp., *Casuarina*, *Dactylocladus stenostachys*, *Dipterocarpus* spp., *Palaquium* sp., *Shorea* spp. and *Tristania grandiflora*. All three forest zones grew on a peat substrate. The peat deposits under the forest near the river were up to 6 m deep, but increased to 10 m under pole forest and to between 9–13 m deep under the interior forest.

7.5.2 Peat deposits

Peat is a soil type with a very high organic matter content. In temperate regions, peat deposits are composed mainly of the remains of bryophytes and low herbs. In tropical swamp forests, peat is derived from woody plants and consists mainly of fragments of tree roots, leaves and wood in various stages of decomposition (see section 10.7).

Peat deposits are either **topogenous** or **ombrogenous**. Topogenous peat forms in depressions and plants growing on these deposits are able to extract nutrients from the underlying mineral soil. Topogenous peat accumulation is slower than that in ombrogenous deposits and drainage water from them is less acidic (pH 5.0) and more nutrient-enriched.

The surface of ombrogenous peats is above the surrounding land and the plants that live on these deposits obtain all their nutrients from the peat or directly from rain. In the tropics, this type of peat is typically found behind mangrove forests and deposits may be up to 20 m deep. The peat and its drainage waters are acidic (pH 2.9–3.6) and contain very low levels of the major plant nutrients: nitrogen, phosphorus, potassium, calcium and magnesium. The Sungai Sebangu swamp forest, and similar forests throughout South-East Asia, grow on ombrogenous deposits. These deposits may be lens-shaped, some metres higher at the centre than at the margins. This shape is due to more rapid peat accumulation during the early stages of peat deposition than in the later stages. Anderson (1964) suggested that toxic concentrations of sulfides and sodium found in the clays underlying peat deposits promoted peat accumulation by inhibiting decomposition (organic mater breakdown, see section 10.7).

By analysing the pollen content of these peat deposits we can trace the developmental sequence of the vegetation that grew on them, and, indeed, gave rise to them. Anderson (1964) found that there was an abundance of mangrove pollen at the base of a 13 m long peat profile collected in a swamp forest in northern Borneo. Above this layer, pollen from *Campnosperma coriaceum* and the palms *Cyrtostachys renda* and *Salacca* sp. were found. These plants often grow on the landward side of present-day mangroves. Further up the peat profile (more recent deposition), pollen grains from *Shorea albida* and *Combretocarpus* were found.

This sequence in pollen deposition was very similar to the zonation found in the present-day vegetation. This, therefore, suggests that the zones found in these swamp forests are sequential stages in community development. Anderson (1964) identified four phases in the development of the forests studied by him: (1) colonisation of the coasts by mangroves; (2) replacement of the mangroves by mixed swamp forests and the development of saucer-shaped basins by construction of levees with river-borne alluvium – peat accumulated in the basin and decomposition of it was inhibited by high concentrations of sulfides and sodium; (3) peat accumulation slows down and the deposits are colonised by trees such as *Shorea albida*; (4) the rate of peat accumulation slows down further and the vegetation is a more open, dry forest community.

In this way, vegetation zones vary in their species composition and structure in response to changes in the hydrology of the system owing to peat accumulation. We have seen that zonation is a distinctive feature of wetlands and before looking at wetland change with time let us review wetland zonation.

7.6 | Wetland zonation

We saw that aquatic plant communities may form distinct zones from the shoreline into the deeper water of lakes (see section 5.3.1). We have also seen that in floodplain lakes aquatic plant communities are replaced each year by terrestrial plants when river levels fall and the floodplain dries. These floodplains undergo a repetitive and predictable seasonal cycle of inundation and drying as river levels rise and fall. These floodplains also undergo changes that are not seasonal but, none the less, may follow a predictable sequence with one plant community replacing another in an ecological process called **succession**. Before we look at this ecological process in detail, consider the longer-term changes that have been observed in communities along the Zaire River in Central Africa.

7.6.1 Vegetation sequences in lakes and rivers in the Zaire River system

The sequential development of wetland vegetation in the Zaire River Basin that occurred along a shallow, sheltered shore of a lake differed from that along the river with a seasonal flood regime

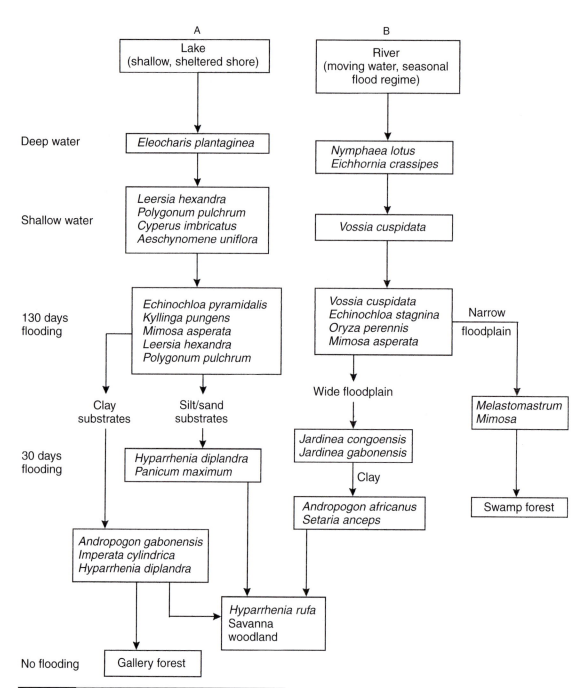

A
Lake
(shallow, sheltered shore)

B
River
(moving water, seasonal
flood regime)

Deep water — *Eleocharis plantaginea*

Nymphaea lotus
Eichhornia crassipes

Shallow water —
Leersia hexandra
Polygonum pulchrum
Cyperus imbricatus
Aeschynomene uniflora

Vossia cuspidata

130 days
flooding
Echinochloa pyramidalis
Kyllinga pungens
Mimosa asperata
Leersia hexandra
Polygonum pulchrum

Vossia cuspidata
Echinochloa stagnina
Oryza perennis
Mimosa asperata

Narrow
floodplain

Clay
substrates

Silt/sand
substrates

Wide floodplain

Melastomastrum
Mimosa

30 days
flooding
Hyparrhenia diplandra
Panicum maximum

Jardinea congoensis
Jardinea gabonensis

Clay

Andropogon africanus
Setaria anceps

Swamp forest

Andropogon gabonensis
Imperata cylindrica
Hyparrhenia diplandra

Hyparrhenia rufa
Savanna
woodland

No flooding — Gallery forest

Figure 7.4 Hydroseres in the Zaire River Basin. Sequence A represents vegetation development from a sheltered shore with a narrow, swampy margin. Sequence B is typical of floodoplain areas adjacent to the river with a pronounced flood regime which results in the elimination of the sudd communities (after Thompson 1985 with kind permission from Kluwer Academic Publishers).

(Figure 7.4). The sedge, *Eleocharis plantaginea*, emerged from the deep water beyond the plants that make up floating sudd islands. Aquatic grasses dominated the floodplain. Higher up the floodplain the grassland that developed depended on the colluvial substrate. With a clay substrate, *Andropogon gabonensis* dominated but was replaced on silt/sand substrates by *Hyparrhenia diplandra*. Above the flood zone, *Hyparrhenia rufa* or gallery forest developed (Denny 1985).

Along the river, the sudd community was absent and *Vossia cuspidata* dominated the aquatic fringe. Further inland on the floodplain, *Vossia* was replaced by a variety of hydrophytic grasses. Above this zone, swamp forest developed along narrow floodplains where the substrate was permanently saturated. *Jardinea* swamp grasslands developed on the more extensive floodplains with illuvial clays and gave way to grasslands dominated by either *Andropogon–Setaria* (colluvial clay substrates) or *Hyparrhenia–Panicum* (silt/sand substrates). *Hyparrhenia rufa* grassland or savanna woodland developed where flooding did not occur.

These sequences can be observed along the transition from open water, across the floodplain to the areas unaffected by flooding. The composition of the vegetation in a particular zone may also change with time. For example, a reduction in flood duration through a change in the hydrological regime may result in the replacement of *Vossia cuspidata*, so well adapted to fluctuating water levels, by species such as *Oryza perennis* which prefer less inundation. A reduction in flood duration could occur through a gradual accumulation of sediment resulting in a rise in the land level relative to the river or lake. These long-term changes in the plant community may be interrupted by a disturbance such as a flood that scours out accumulated sediment. This action creates a habitat more suitable to the plants that made up the early stages in the progression of community replacement. It is these sorts of gradual, non-seasonal changes in the environment and communities that concerns us in this chapter.

7.7 | Wetland succession

As swamps lie between truly aquatic and truly terrestrial systems, a long-term reduction in mean water level should result in a shift in the biological community towards one containing species better adapted to drier conditions. Conversely, a rise in mean water level will tend to favour wetland and aquatic species. However, there are documented cases of long-term stability in wetlands. Rates of wetland succession are regulated by climatic and environmental factors such as water balance, rates of sedimentation and nutrient availability. These changes may be very slow. Some African papyrus swamps, for example, have underlying peat deposits 30 m thick suggesting thousands of years of accumulation. The layers laid down by these wetlands provide an archive of the environmental history of the basin. The layers can be dated using radiometric techniques (^{14}C dating) and changes in the pollen grains found in successive layers provides a picture of changes in both the aquatic and surrounding terrestrial vegetation. These changes in vegetation may be related to long-term changes in climate. Conversely, small, shallow water bodies surrounded by a wetland may progress through to dry land, supporting a community of terrestrial plants within a few years.

There are also examples where wetlands have shifted, through time, to an apparently more aquatic state (see Box 7.1). However, the general direction of wetland succession is a reduction in water level leading to colonisation by plants that prefer a drier regime. Water levels in most tropical wetlands change on a seasonal basis, but in some cases, as we have seen with Lake Chilwa, seasonal fluctuations can be drastic. The lake dried up completely in 1968 and, in the following year, heavy rains resulted in the basin refilling and recovery of the lake ecosystem was rapid. The surrounding *Typha* swamp provided a refuge for fish and other wetland and aquatic organisms (Kalk *et al.* 1979).

However, while these seasonal fluctuations may play a role in determining the rate of successional changes in tropical wetlands, they are not a causal factor. Successional changes in a wetland follow a reduction in the mean water depth. As a lake basin shallows owing to inputs from the catchment and material produced within the lake, the littoral vegetation may gradually invade the lake. As this occurs, the area of open water declines and the lake is transformed into an herbaceous wetland. Further drying of the system may result in the invasion of the basin by terrestrial plants. At an early stage, the emergent aquatic plants are often draped with terrestrial climbers. The vegetation of subsequent stages may include woody plants adapted to rooting in damp soils. This series, of often predictable changes, is known as an **ecological succession** or **hydrosere** and each stage is known as a **sere**.

There are ways wetland succession can be slowed down, interrupted or reversed. Drainage will hasten the replacement of a community dominated by aquatic organisms with one in which terrestrial plants and animals thrive. Nutrient enrichment of wetlands has been implicated as the cause of major changes in the plant community of Waigani Wetland in Papua New Guinea (Box 7.1).

Box 7.1 Waigani Wetland: a hydrosere reversed?

Waigani Wetland comprises a few small, shallow lakes near Port Moresby, Papua New Guinea. The lakes drain into the extensive swamp/river system dominated by the Brown and Laloki Rivers. Waigani Lake is shallow (1–2 m deep) with an open water area of approximately 120 ha; *Phragmites karka*, *Typha domingensis* and *Hanguana malayana* dominate the emergent littoral vegetation. *Oreochromis mossambicus* and *Cyprinus carpio* were introduced to the lake in the 1950s and form the basis of a small but productive fishery. Sewage disposal into the lake began in 1965, and the settling ponds were subsequently enlarged to cater for the rapidly expanding population of Port Moresby.

Major changes in the distribution and abundance of aquatic plants in the Waigani wetland have occurred over the last 50 years. The main lake is now devoid of submerged and floating-leaved plants, but in the late 1960s and early 1970s water-lilies (*Nymphoides indica*, *Nymphaea pubescens* and *Nymphaea dictyophlebia*) dominated the area that is now open water. Aerial photographs taken in 1942 and 1956 both show the central area of Waigani Lake covered by emergent vegetation (Osborne and Leach 1983). The increase in sewage effluent disposal correlates with the decline in floating-leaved plants, and by 1974 only a few small stands remained. By 1978, no floating-leaved plants could be found in the main lake and their decline in Waigani Lake was accompanied by a regression of the surrounding reedswamp. This decline in the area of the emergent reedswamp has continued (Osborne and Totome 1992b). *Salvinia molesta* infested this wetland in 1980, but biological control measures were successful (see Box 5.3). In 1990, *Eichhornia crassipes* invaded the wetland, and by 1992 half of the main lake was covered with a dense mat (Figure 5.21 Osborne and Totome 1992b).

Osborne and Polunin (1986) collected short sediment cores and were able to reconstruct the ecological history of the lake (see section 5.15.1). The lowest sections of their sediment cores had low nitrogen and phosphorus concentrations, undetectable levels of remnant plant pigments and high densities of epiphytic diatom frustules. These characteristics are indicative of an emergent wetland with areas of open water with aquatic plants, the habitat depicted in the aerial photographs taken in 1942 and 1956. Following this phase, nitrogen and phosphorus concentrations in the sediments increased and indicate the onset of sewage disposal into the lake. Further nutrient enrichment with the expansion of the sewage system in the 1970s resulted in higher nutrient deposition in the sediments; at around this time the switch from emergent vegetation to one dominated by floating-leaved plants occurred. The subsequent increase in the area of open water was detected in the cores through the declining density of *Nymphoides indica* seeds and the increasing concentration of frustules of the planktonic diatom *Cyclotella meneghiniana*. Osborne and Polunin (1986) argued that, although an increase in water level is an obvious cause of what they characterised as a partial reversal of the hydrosere, it can not explain all the vegetation changes observed. The timing of changes in the features measured suggested nutrient enrichment was as likely to have played a significant role, but the effects of changes in water level could not be ruled out.

7.8 Ecological succession

All ecosystems change with time. Some of these changes are seasonal: the rise and fall of a river and the effects on the adjacent floodplain (see section 6.4.3); the seasonal migration of animals (see section 4.5) and the stratification and mixing events in lakes (see section 5.1). Other changes that occur are more long-term, progressive and not cyclical (see section 4.17). One such process is **ecological succession**.

Succession is traditionally divided into primary and secondary; autogenic and allogenic. **Primary succession** occurs on bare sites and eventually leads to the development on the site of a **climax** community. Such successions occur on sand dunes, volcanic mud flows and newly formed islands (see chapter 12). The first organisms to colonise an area in the process of primary succession are called **pioneer species**. **Secondary succession** takes place on land that has previously supported vegetation such as abandoned gardens, or follows a forest fire or even the changes that take place after the death and collapse of a large forest tree (see section 8.14). Succession occurs whenever a habitat is created or modified. The habitat can be small, such as a pool in a depression created by an elephant footprint or, indeed, a lump of elephant dung.

Autogenic succession is one that is directed from within the ecosystem itself. This term particularly refers to habitat changes brought about by the biota, as, for example, when soil accumulates organic matter and nutrients. If this soil enrichment promotes the next community replacement then the succession is said to be autogenic. The rate of autogenesis is largely determined by the balance between plant production and the rates of consumption and decomposition of plant products. **Allogenic** succession is succession driven by forces outside the ecosystem. For example, the progressive fall in the water table of a wetland owing to stream down-cutting leads to a succession of plant communities suited to progressively drier habitats. The communities themselves may have had no influence on the critical habitat changes. The conceptual differences between autogenic and allogenic successions are significant. In the former, plants and animals are the genesis of change; in the latter, they merely respond to changing climate or geography.

Ecological succession is defined as a process of directional change in the vegetation and animal life of a particular area possibly leading to a more stable community which is referred to as the **climax**. A **sere** is one stage in an ecological succession and a **climax** community is capable of perpetuation under the prevailing climatic and edaphic conditions. A **hydrosere** (**hydrarch succession**) is a successional sequence resulting in the change of open water communities to those of a wetland through to dry land communities. Successions on dry sites, such as sand dunes or bare rock, which become progressively moister, form a **xerosere** (**xerarch succession**).

7.9 Community development and assembly

Let us trace the steps and changes in community structure that might occur in a primary succession as a community of organisms colonise a barren area. The first step is the arrival of propagules such as seeds, spores or vegetative reproductive structures. Typically *r*-selected species (see section 4.13) are the first to arrive since they have strong dispersal powers. The next hurdle to overcome is **establishment**, and many of the propagules that reach the site are unable to develop. Establishment requires the correct suite of environmental factors necessary for seed or spore germination as well as the availability of resources required for growth and reproduction. Environmental conditions in areas not previously colonised are often harsh, and the successful early colonisers are species exhibiting adaptations that enable them to tolerate the stressful environment.

These early colonisers are plants such as mosses and xerophytic grasses or lichens. Autotrophs have to become established before the site can be invaded by heterotrophic organisms (animals and decomposers). This is one **rule of community assembly**. The colonisers or pioneers produce organic matter, break down rock particles and start to produce soil with greater water-holding capacity. Plants produce shade and add organic matter to the soil, and animals and microorganisms are integral parts of nutrient cycles. In other words, these organisms make the environment more hospitable. This facilitates invasion by other species. However, as more species arrive, competition becomes more intense and the community that develops does so in response to a balance between **environmental facilitation** and **competition**. The species that survive towards the end of a successional sequence are those species which are good competitors (see sections 4.13) and this is another rule of community assembly. Some species are adept at inhibiting the development of others. Some plants produce chemicals that inhibit the germination of seeds from other species; others are good at sequestering resources. Animals may alter the species composition through grazing or facilitate plant propagation through pollination and seed dispersal (see section 4.6).

The progression from colonisation to climax might take centuries, such as when the climax community is a forest. The successional process is rarely smooth and may frequently be disrupted by a disturbance such as a fire, hurricane or volcanic eruption. Disturbance effectively initiates another succession leading to, assuming the same environmental conditions, the same climax. We will look at the role of disturbance in succession in chapter 8 where the changes that take place in a forest will be described. The process of gap-filling provides a good example of secondary succession (see section 8.14). In chapter 8 we will also consider characteristics of climax communities.

7.10 | Wetland loss and conservation

7.10.1 Herbaceous wetlands

Herbaceous wetlands serve some important ecological functions. Wetlands play an important role in modifying the hydrology and reducing flood flows. They act like a sponge during periods of high water inflow, absorbing water and releasing it more slowly than the flood input. The hydrology of the outflow is often more constant, and this has significant implications for downstream ecosystems. Wetland plants retain sediments and so reduce bank erosion. Wetlands also have a high capacity to absorb and retain nutrients and pollutants, and therefore may enhance downstream water quality.

Wetlands are biologically diverse and are important ecosystems not only to resident plants and animals, but also to the vast numbers of migratory waders and other waterbirds that use them as staging posts. Millions of birds (swans, ducks, geese, terns) breed in the vast Arctic wetlands of North America and northern Eurasia. The summer there is short, and the birds use these productive wetlands while it lasts and then fly south. Some species travel as far south as Australia, South Africa and southern South America and they utilise wetlands along the way. The Mississippi flyway forms a major flight path for many of these birds. Therefore wetland conservation must take into account the importance of these wetlands which may only be used by many birds for just a few weeks each year.

For millennia, people have lived alongside wetlands and benefited from the wide range of resources they provide. Wetland productivity is high, and humans have utilised them for crop production, for grazing during the dry season and as fishing grounds when flooded (see Box 7.2). In many landlocked, tropical countries, wetlands provide an important source of fish protein. In Zambia, over 50% of fish production is from freshwater wetlands (Harper and Mavuti 1996). Many wetlands in the tropics have been converted into productive aquaculture ponds.

7.10.2 Swamp forests

Tropical swamp forests have been harvested for the commercially valuable timber they contain and cleared for agriculture. The forests form important habitat for many animals, for example, South-East Asian swamp forests harbour the endangered Sumatran rhinoceros (*Dicerorhinus sumatrensis*) and the proboscis monkey (*Nasalis larvatus*). The peat and timber constitute significant carbon stores, and their degradation converts these systems from carbon sinks into carbon sources (see section 14.4.1). The forests provide a hydrological buffer, reducing flow rates and the impact of floods and, in coastal systems, reducing saltwater intrusions. The forests provide local communities with food, fuel, timber and other products such as rattan canes (Page and Rieley 1998).

Box 7.2 | Exploitation of wetland plants

While in temperate regions, many wetlands have been drained to produce arable land, in the tropics, vast areas have been landscaped to form wetlands for rice cultivation. Rice is now the staple diet of more than half the world's population; well over 1 million km^2 of the earth's surface are devoted to rice cultivation and around 90% is wet paddy rice. In many tropical countries, rice cultivation is coupled with aquaculture of fish, prawns, insects and snails. This productive coupling is further enhanced by allowing ducks or cattle to graze on rice stubble once the grain has been harvested. The wastes from these animals, often a source of nutrient enrichment leading to eutrophication, constitute a valuable fertiliser for the next crop. Rice cultivation is also enhanced by introducing organisms that can fix nitrogen (see section 5.13.2). The aquatic fern, *Azolla pinnata*, grows in association with a cyanobacterium (*Anabaena azollae*) that can fix nitrogen as effectively as the bacteria found associated with legumes.

Many other wetland plants provide a source of food. Taro (*Colocasia esculenta*), water-chestnut (*Trapa natans*), *Ipomoea aquatica*, watercress (*Nasturtium officinale*) and lotus (*Nelumbo nucifera*) are all wetland plants that are either harvested from the wild or cultivated. *Cyperus esculentus* produces edible tubers and *C. papyrus* was the initial source of fibre for paper-making. Sago-palm is a good source of carbohydrate and is the staple food of people living in the lowland swamps of New Guinea. The plant also provides leaves for thatching. In Brazil, the burity palm (*Mauritia vinifera*) is cultivated for a product similar to sago.

Where trees are not readily available, wetland plants (e.g. papyrus in the sudd of Sudan and *Scirpus tatora* around Lake Titicaca) are used to make boats. *Typha*, because of its high productivity, can be a serious weed in rice paddies. However, it is also a very useful plant: it provides, grazing for livestock and material for thatching and weaving, and the rhizome is rich in starch and can be dried and ground into a flour.

Despite their importance, wetlands are among the most impacted and degraded of all ecosystems. In developed countries, many wetlands have been lost. In Ohio, USA, over 80% of wetlands have been drained or destroyed in the last 200 years (Mitsch *et al.* 1994). Wetland loss has occurred because wetland soils are usually very fertile and, with drainage, provide good agricultural land; their flat topography also makes them ideal areas for urban developments. River regulation either results in wetlands being drowned when reservoirs fill, or reduces the areas downstream that are seasonally flooded (floodplain wetlands).

Starting in the 1980s, wetlands have received increasing attention from conservation agencies. This has come about through the realisation of the importance of wetlands locally, regionally and globally (Mitsch 1994). Wise use of wetlands is a key component of the RAMSAR Convention. In 1987, the United States Environment Protection Agency developed a goal of 'no net loss' of wetlands. This programme is designed to reduce the rate of wetland destruction and, where it can not be avoided, to encourage developers to create wetlands to replace those lost. Implementation of this programme has been thwarted by the difficulty to define clearly what constitutes a wetland and to delineate its boundaries. Furthermore, while techniques to create wetlands are improving through intensive research, we are still unable to guarantee that a constructed wetland will carry out the same functions as effectively as a natural wetland.

7.11 | Chapter summary

1. Wetlands are characterised by: the presence of water, soils that differ in composition from those that make up the surrounding catchment and a plant community dominated by hydrophytes (water-loving plants). Herbaceous wetland plants either grow in dense floating mats (sudd) or in mono-dominant rooted stands. Deep peat deposits may accumulate beneath swamp forests and may contain a record of the vegetation development at the site.

2. Wetlands lie between terrestrial and aquatic systems, but the food webs within them are largely aquatic. Wetland food webs are split, with primary production largely occurring in the air whilst secondary production and decomposition mostly occurs in the water.

3. Aquatic primary production in swamps is low because little photosynthetically active radiation reaches the water surface. Wetland plants are highly productive and efficient at sequestering nutrients, and many tropical wetland plants utilise the C_4 pathway for photosynthesis. Little plant material produced in wetlands is consumed by animals; most of it dies and slowly decomposes in the water and flooded soils. In tropical wetlands, fire may well constitute a major loss of organic matter.

4. Aquatic plant communities may form distinct zones, related to water depth, from the shoreline into the deeper water of lakes and rivers. Wetland vegetation may undergo long-term changes that may follow a predictable sequence with one plant community replacing another in an ecological process called succession.

5. Succession is traditionally divided into primary and secondary; autogenic and allogenic. Primary successions occur on bare sites (sand dunes, volcanic mud flows and newly formed islands) and lead from first colonisation to occupation of the site by a climax community. Secondary successions replace a previous community following a disturbance; examples include invasion of abandoned fields and the forest that replaces one destroyed by fire or hurricanes. Autogenic succession is one that is directed from within the ecosystem itself with habitat changes brought about by the biota. Allogenic succession is driven by forces outside the ecosystem.

6. Stages in a succession are called seres. Early seral communities are known as pioneer communities and the succession is said to end with a climax community. Pioneer species alter the environment in a way that may facilitate the invasion of other species.

7. Primary succession follows some rules of community assembly. Autotrophs must become established before heterotrophs. The community that develops on a particular site is determined by the chance arrival of a propagule, the suitability of the environment, competition between and within species and the intensity of inhibitory processes.

8. Wetlands reduce flood flows, trap sediments and nutrients and enhance downstream water quality.

Many wetlands have been drained and destroyed, with severe consequences for the organisms that rely upon them. Human use of wetlands includes water supply, food resources, building materials, energy sources (peat) and recreation.

Chapter 8

Tropical rain forests and biodiversity

Tropical rain forests: 'the greatest celebration of life on earth'

Norman Myers

Lowland tropical rain forests are the world's most species-rich terrestrial communities. Gentry and Dodson (1987) tabulated all the vascular plant species in 0.1 ha sites in a wet forest in western Ecuador. The forests in which they worked had been studied for many years and they are floristically among the best known in the Neotropics. Consequently, they were able to identify all plants to species. One of their wet forest samples was, at the time, by far the most species-rich ever recorded. In only 0.1 ha, they recorded 33 ferns and fern allies, 1 gymnosperm, 77 monocotyledons and 254 dicotyledons: 365 species of vascular plants! Over a third of the species were epiphytes. Gentry and Dodson (1987) concluded that their survey puts tropical rain forests in a class by themselves as the earth's most species-rich terrestrial vegetation. If their sample of wet forest is typical, then these forests are so diverse that they would still be the most species-rich plant communities even if all tree species were excluded from the analysis. Valencia *et al.* (1994) recorded 473 tree species with a diameter at breast height of 5 cm or more in a hectare of Ecuadorian forest. On the basis of these and other studies, it has been estimated that about two-thirds of the estimated 250 000 plant species in the world, occur in tropical forests (Myers 1980). Yet the tropical forests occupy only 7% of the earth's surface.

Erwin (1983) analysed the insects living in the crown of *Luehea seemannii* trees growing in a seasonal tropical forest in Panama. He sprayed the tree canopy with an insecticide and collected the insects falling from it on sheets spread out beneath the tree. Sampled over 3 seasons, 19 trees yielded 955 species of beetles. In the 15 km² of the La Selva Reserve in Costa Rica, it is estimated that there are around 4000 species of moths. These records of high numbers of species found in just one species of tree or in small areas have led to estimates of the number of undescribed insect species in tropical forests ranging from 5 million to 30 million (May 1992). Some biologists think the total may be as high as 60 million. At present, scientists have described and named about 1.75 million species.

Tropical forests may provide a home to 90% of the world's insects. Bird communities in tropical forests are also tremendously diverse relative to those of temperate forests. Blake *et al.* (1990) recorded over 400 bird species within a 15 km² rain-forest site in Costa Rica, and more species have been reported from Costa Rica than from all of North America (Stiles *et al.* 1989).

Gentry (1988) indicated that the upper Amazonian forests may generally have the most diverse floral and faunal assemblages of any in the world. He based this conclusion on the fact that patterns of tree species richness measured by him parallel those of birds, butterflies, reptiles, amphibians and mammals. Gentry concluded that this concentration of diversity in upper Amazonia should warrant special focus on conserving remnants of these rapidly disappearing ecosystems. Indeed, the high diversity exhibited by tropical rain forests in all parts of the world, coupled with the rate at which they are being destroyed, has put rain forests high on the agenda of international conservation agencies. In this

Figure 8.1   Rain forest in Ducke Reserve near Manaus, Brazil (Photo: Patrick Osborne).

chapter, we look at rain-forest ecology and attempt to explain how these diverse systems came about, what mechanisms operate to maintain such high diversity and how diversity can be measured, and conclude with a discussion of applied aspects of rain-forest conservation and deforestation.

Forests are dominated by woody plants (trees, shrubs, herbs and climbers); grasses (apart from bamboos, see Box 3.1) are virtually absent. The trees in a forest form a continuous, layered canopy cover; this continuity distinguishes this vegetation from that of savannas and is also the reason for the paucity of grasses (Figure 8.1). Tropical forests vary in both species composition and appearance with variations in climate, water availability, soils and altitude. Distinct forest formations and features of their habitat are summarised in Table 8.1. Swamp forests, montane forests and mangrove forests, are discussed in chapters 7, 9 and 10 respectively.

8.1 | Biogeography of rain forests

The most significant biological feature of tropical rain forests is their extreme species richness. The number of tree species is high with no species dominating; this diversity of trees provides a complex framework within which a myriad of animal species live. The structure and appearance (**physiognomy**) of tree species are similar in rain forests throughout the world. However, in terms of species composition, the forests of South America differ greatly from those of South-East Asia and both these differ from those found in central and west Africa.

Although most rain forests are very diverse, there are exceptions. Malaysian forests are dominated by Dipterocarpaceae, and some forests in the West Indies are different in that they are dominated by just one species: *Mora excelsa*. South American forests have an abundance of Fabaceae (legumes). Palms are largely absent from African rain forests, but they are abundant in the rain forests of South America. Forests dominated by a single species also occur in Uganda and Congo

Table 8.1 | Formations of tropical moist forests

Forest formation	Climate	Soil water and soils	Elevation
Monsoon forest	Seasonally dry	Strong annual water shortage	Lowland to mid-altitudes
Semi-evergreen rain forest	Seasonally dry	Slight annual water shortage	Lowland to mid-altitudes
Lowland evergreen rain forest	Wet, with no dry period	Soils always moist, mainly oxisols and ultisols	Lowlands
Lower-montane rain forest	Wet, with no distinct dry season	Soils always moist, mainly oxisols and ultisols	1200–1500 m
Upper-montane rain forest	Wet, cold, with frequent mists	Soils always moist, mainly oxisols and ultisols	1500–3000 m
Subalpine forest	Wet, cold, with frequent mists	Soils always moist, mainly oxisols and ultisols	3000 m to tree-line
Mangrove forest; brackish water forest	Variable, seasonally dry or ever-wet	High water table, salt or brackish water	1–2 m a.s.l.
Peat swamp forest	Variable, seasonally dry or ever-wet	High water table, freshwater, oligotrophic peats	Mostly lowlands
Freshwater swamp forest	Variable, seasonally dry or ever-wet	High water table, permanently wet, eutrophic soils	Mostly lowlands
Freshwater periodic swamp forest	Seasonally dry	Periodically high water table	Mostly lowlands

Source: Whitmore 1993.

(*Cynometra alexandri* forests) and Guyana (*Eperua falcata* forests).

The largest area of rain forest is found in the Amazon basin, but extensive areas occur in Indo-Malaysia, Indonesia, Melanesia and in West Africa and the Congo Basin (Figure 8.2). The Neotropical rain forests constitute about 50% of the world's tropical forests and occur in Amazonia, along the Pacific coasts of northern Ecuador, Colombia and north into central America. A formerly large area along the eastern seaboard of Brazil has been severely degraded through deforestation and only remnant patches remain. Small patches of forests remain in the Caribbean. African rain forests are centred on the Congo Basin but extend along the southern coast of west Africa. There are patches of remnant rain forest areas along the east coast of Madagascar (see section 8.18.1).

The forests in South-East Asia and the Pacific Islands account for 30% of the world's tropical forests but they are very fragmented being dis-

persed throughout the islands of Indonesia, the Philippines, New Guinea and the Solomons. On the Asian mainland, drier deciduous forests separate the rain forests of the Malay peninsula, Burma and Thailand from those along the coasts of Cambodia and Vietnam. A narrow strip of forest extends from Cape York peninsula in northern Australia to near the southern border of Queensland; a southerly extent which is similar to that of rain forests in Brazil. Other small patches occur in south-west Sri Lanka and along the Western Ghats of India.

8.1.1 Rain-forest climate

Tropical rain forest is a term coined by Schimper (1903) to describe the forests of the ever-wet tropics where there is no, or only minimal, seasonal water shortage. These forests occur in areas with over 2000 mm of rain per year, an average humidity of 80% and no, or only a very short, dry season. A month with only 100 mm of rain is considered to

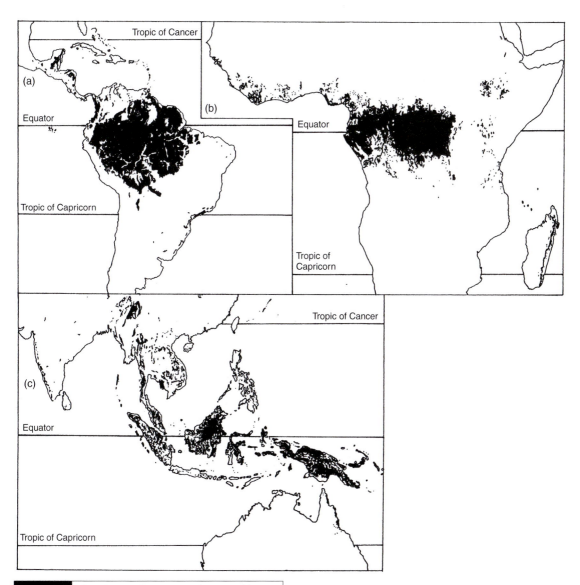

Figure 8.2 Distribution of tropical rain forests in (a) Central and South America, (b) Africa and (c) South-East Asia and Australasia (after World Conservation Monitoring Centre 1992 with kind permission from Kluwer Academic Publishers).

be relatively dry. Bogor, in Indonesia, for example, has a mean annual rainfall in excess of 4000 mm, with 450 mm falling in the wettest month and 230 mm in the driest. The rain usually falls in the middle of the day, in short, heavy downpours, after which the sun shines again. Radiation levels are high and leaves exposed to the direct rays of the sun may heat up by several degrees above the already high air temperature. Consequently, despite the high humidity, the surface of the leaves can be exposed to large saturation deficits. So even in these very wet regions, canopy leaves may be exposed to extreme dryness for a few hours each day. Mean monthly temperatures do not fall much below 25 °C and rarely exceed 35 °C. Seasonal variations are smaller than diurnal variations which may be as much as 10 °C.

Plants growing in the shade beneath the canopy live in a very different environment. The micro-climate prevailing here is more equable. Variations in air temperature are small (both diurnally and seasonally) and the air always humid. The relative humidity at tree-top level can vary from 100% at night to around 60% when the sun is shining. Humidity within the forest remains more constant at around 80%. Canopy trees receive about 5 hours of bright sunlight each day, but the light intensity reaching the forest floor is low: 0.1–1% of the full sunlight to which the canopy leaves are exposed. As light passes through the canopy, wavelengths are absorbed and reflected to varying extents. Therefore the quality of light reaching the forest floor is substantially different from that impinging on the canopy. We will look at micro-climate within a forest in section 8.10.

Below the forest canopy, carbon dioxide concentrations are higher than at tree-top level and its supply is unlikely to limit subcanopy photosynthesis. The elevated carbon dioxide concentration within the canopy is due mainly to rapid decomposition of litter on the forest floor.

8.1.2 The Amazon rain forest

The rain forests of the Amazon Basin cover approximately 5.8×10^6 km^2 (Salati and Vose 1984) and this vast area is dominated by the Amazon River (see section 6.3). Amazonia lies within the humid tropics and its climate is influenced by the seasonal migration of the ITCZ (see section 1.2.2). From April to July, the ITCZ moves north across Amazonia and brings heavy rainfall to northern Amazonia. In June–July, drier conditions develop in the central equatorial region, and in August the circulation pattern reverses. The wettest parts of the basin, with annual totals more than 3000 mm, lie in the west central part of the basin. South, central Amazonia receives more than 2500 mm and even in most of the remaining area annual rainfall is still high: 1500–2500 mm. Variations in solar radiation are low, and mean annual temperatures within Amazonia range between 23–27 °C. The mean daily range throughout the region is generally less than 10 °C.

The combination of high temperatures and rainfall in Amazonia encourages luxuriant plant growth and the lowlands are largely covered by tropical forest. The Amazonian flora is very rich, but it is difficult to give a precise number of species it contains as our knowledge of it is so incomplete. At least 1 million species of plants and animals (10–20% of the world's flora and fauna) are estimated to live in Amazonia.

Forest types in the Amazon are often separated into *varzéa* forests, which are inundated with river water in the wet season and grow on fertile, alluvial soils, and the *terra firme* forests which include all the forest types that are not inundated. This dichotomy is an oversimplification, and great variation in climate, topography and forest types can be found in what at first glance appears to be a rather uniform expanse of lowland rain forest. The *terra firme* forest comprises mainly evergreen trees and represents the climax vegetation for most of Amazonia. This forest type is dense, with emergent trees commonly rising to 45 m, and occasionally to 60 m, but a continuous canopy forms some 25–35 m above the ground. The tree flora in Central Amazonia is dominated by legumes (Fabaceae) which may comprise up to 60% of the tree species. Other well-represented families include: Moraceae, Lecythidaceae, Sapotaceae, Rosaceae, Meliaceae, Palmaceae and Vochysiaceae. In drier areas, the forest intergrades into semi-deciduous and deciduous forests. The *varzéa* wetlands contain both woody and herbaceous plants; the ecology of flooded forests and wetlands is discussed in chapters 6 and 7.

8.2 | Vegetation structure of tropical rain forests

8.2.1 Trees

Tropical rain forests may be stratified with two or three tree layers, a shrub layer and a herb layer. The tallest trees (45–50 m high) in the rain forest are known as **emergents**. Their canopies grow above those of most other trees. These emergents form a discontinuous layer and, as they no longer need to compete for light, they may have wide, spreading canopies, often more than 20 m in diameter. The middle-storey trees form the 'roof' of the rain forest with the crowns forming a continuous canopy 25–35 m above the ground. Tree crowns in this layer are smaller and more rounded, but branches will extend into any available space.

The trees in the bottom layer form a dense, closely packed layer with variously shaped crowns. The trees in this layer reach heights of 10–15 m and the crowns are often narrow in proportion to their height, an adaptation that enables them to take advantage of low light intensities. Tree trunks are typically straight and slender. Owing to competition for sunlight, this layer is discontinuous, becoming dense only where there are breaks in the upper canopy and little light penetrates to the forest floor.

The bark of forest trees is usually thin, since there is little need for protection against either fire or cold. Branching mostly occurs near the crown. This growth form ensures that a tree can grow tall quickly and support its canopy of leaves in sunlight. Competition for sunlight in such dense forest is intense, and this means that tree canopies are often small and cauliflower-shaped.

The leaves of the trees are typically dark-green and leathery with shiny upper surfaces. Many species have leaves with extended points known as **drip-tips** which, together with the shiny upper surface, help water drain from the surface of the leaf. Roots of some trees only penetrate the upper soil layers, and therefore extra support for these tall trees is often provided by very large **buttress** roots.

Buttress roots are randomly distributed around the base of the trunk because they are formed on the lateral roots which grow early in the life of the tree before it is subjected to mechanical stress. However, in older trees, longer buttresses are generally found on the side of the trunk pointing towards the prevailing wind; those on the other side are often taller. This occurs through the asymmetry of forces acting on the tree. The tension on the windward side of the trunk is transmitted out towards the end of the buttress, away from the tree. On the leeward side, forces are transmitted to the soil near the trunk (see Ennos 1993).

8.2.2 Epihytes and lianas

Scattered throughout the vegetation layers of the tropical rain forest is a luxuriant abundance of epiphytes and lianas (Figure 8.3). These plants further enhance the complexity of the living framework providing even more habitats for a phenomenal variety of animals. Epiphytes are plants that grow on the surface of other plants, but, unlike parasitic plants, they do not seem to obtain nourishment from their supporting plant (**phorophyte**). There is some evidence that epiphytes harm their host plant, but it has yet to be demonstrated that there is a transfer of nutrients from phorophytes to epiphytes. However, epiphytes may deprive phorophytes of nutrients by intercepting organic matter, throughfall and rain that would otherwise reach the soil and become available to the supporting plant. This process, referred to as **nutrient piracy** by Richards (1996), may be particularly important in forests growing on nutrient-deficient soils.

Lianas are woody, rope-like climbers with flexible stems up to 30 cm in diameter. These rope-like plants attach themselves to trees by various means. Some lianas, such as rattans (*Calamus* spp.), have numerous, sharp spines which provide purchase, preventing the liana from slipping from the tree. Other climbers have adventitious roots which fasten them to the bark of the supporting tree. These climbers often grow spirally around the tree trunk.

Epiphytes and lianas have, through their growth form, solved the problem of obtaining adequate light by using trees to support them in the sunlight. The elevated position of the epiphytes, however, while ensuring the provision of adequate light, cuts them off from the soil and its supply of water and nutrients. These plants, then, exhibit many adaptations to obtain sufficient water and nutrients.

Spongy roots trap moisture, and epiphytes are also either adapted to withstand desiccation or have a high water storage capacity. Many orchids have leaf tubers, and other orchids and bromeliads have succulent leaves. Roots of epiphytes may serve only as organs of attachment; water is absorbed by the leaves. In bromeliads, water absorption occurs through special scales at the base of the leaves. Epiphytes, such as the bird's-nest fern (*Asplenium nidus*) has a leaf arrangement that traps falling plant debris and in this way

Figure 8.3 Epiphytes (mistletoe (*Phorodendron* sp.) and a bromeliad) growing in the canopy of a yos tree (*Spium* sp.) in cloud forest in Costa Rica (Photo: Michael and Patricia Fogden).

accumulates a humus-rich soil which not only provides nutrients but also has a high water-retaining capacity.

Some epiphytes have CAM photosynthesis (see section 3.7) whereby carbon dioxide absorption occurs at night and the stomata close during the day. This reduces water loss from transpiration, a process that is slower when temperature is low and humidity high (i.e. conditions that prevail during the night). Some epiphytes have the capacity to switch from C_3 to CAM photosynthesis depending on conditions, and some even carry out both processes in different parts of the plant at the same time (Benzing 1990). Microscopic algae and mosses, known as **epiphylls**, grow on leaves in wetter rain forests.

Perhaps the most impressive epiphytes are the 'strangling trees', the best known of which are some figs (*Ficus* spp.). These plants germinate as epiphytes and send out a long root while shoot growth is restricted. Once the root reaches the ground, shoot growth accelerates. Roots surround the supporting tree and effectively strangle it by preventing any further secondary growth. The roots of the epiphyte unite to form a trunk which bears a broad crown, and eventually the supporting tree dies and is replaced by the epiphyte, which now, of course, no longer retains the appearance of its epiphytic start in life.

8.2.3 Profile diagrams

One way to display the vegetation structure of a rain forest is through a profile diagram. These diagrams are produced through meticulous mapping, on graph paper, the vegetation in a plot (usually 7.5 m deep and 60 m long). An example of a profile diagram is given in Figure 8.4. The profile diagram should reveal the following information (Jacobs 1988):

1 the height of the trees;

2 the shape and size of the crowns;

3 the height and shape of the trunks and the direction of the main branches;

4 the larger buttresses;

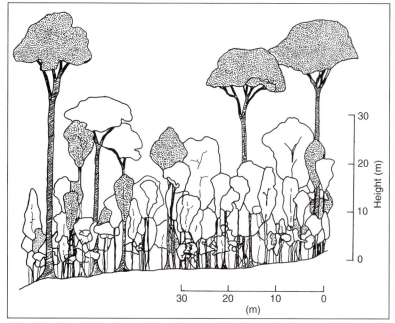

contrast with the marked seasonality in leaf development, leaf loss and growth found in deciduous trees living in temperate climates. In rain forests, competition between plants is intense, and therefore attaining large size is advantageous and continuous ideal growing conditions would suggest that growth should be continuous. Furthermore, the constant environment provides few, if any, distinct environmental cues. Indeed some rain forest trees do appear to grow all the time (e.g. *Macaranga tanarius*), but most rain forest trees exhibit intermittent shoot growth and distinct periods for flowering and fruiting.

8.3.1 Leaf production, survival and loss

Trees with continuously growing shoots lose leaves sporadically, rather than continuously. Trees that grow intermittently, producing leaves in flushes, exhibit three patterns of leaf fall. Some trees are **deciduous**, shedding leaves before bud break, to leave the crown bare, even if only for a few days. In other species, leaf fall occurs at about the same time as bud break; these species are called **leaf exchangers**. Other species are **evergreen**, with leaf fall occurring after bud break. The lifespan of leaves on evergreen rain forest trees probably varies from around 18 months to several years; it is only less than 1 year in those trees which are deciduous annually.

Leaf production and loss varies widely between species and even individual trees growing within the same forest. Indeed, leaf loss and production may occur at different times on

5 distances between the trees;

6 the area of each crown in projection;

7 the trees belonging to one species, and their relative size;

8 the larger lianas and larger plants in the undergrowth;

9 the lower limit of the crowns of the emergents;

10 the effects of previous damage.

From a good profile diagram and its accompanying field notes, it should be possible to derive:

1 the diameter of each tree;

2 the basal area of large trees in the plot;

3 the relation between tree diameter and height;

4 the volume of stems;

5 the volume of crowns;

6 the stage of development of certain tree species;

7 the density of the canopy at various heights.

8.3 | Phenology and reproduction of tropical forest trees

Phenology is the study of leaf, flower and fruit production and other events which seem to be related to climate. Evergreen tropical forest trees

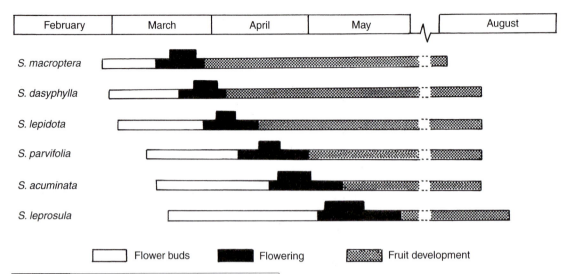

branches on the same tree. In forests where annual dry seasons are distinct, seasonal changes in the trees become more pronounced. In the seasonal tropical forest of Guanacaste in Costa Rica, Reich and Borchert (1984) found that leaf flushing and flowering were controlled by tree water status. At dry sites, leaves were lost early in the dry season and bud break occurred following heavy rain. At wetter sites, trees remained evergreen or exchanged leaves.

Seasonal events are not restricted to seasonal sites. In a 9-year study of 46 species of trees in the aseasonal rain forest at Ulu Gombak, Malaysia, it was found that there were two leaf flushes each year: February–April and September–October. The main peak of leaf growth came at the driest time of the year and most trees flowered annually during the February–April leaf flush (Medway 1972). At La Selva, Costa Rica the forest, as a whole, is evergreen, but around 8% of the trees are deciduous. Mean annual rainfall at La Selva exceeds 4000 mm with no month having a mean rainfall less than 200 mm. However, there are two drier periods, and leaf flushing reaches a major peak early in the first dry season (February) with a smaller flush occurring in the second (September) (Frankie *et al.* 1974).

8.3.2 Flowering and fruiting

Flowering is notoriously unpredictable and sporadic in many forest trees. It is not uncommon to find individuals of the same species flowering and fruiting at the same time, or even for a single tree to be bearing flowers on one branch and fruits on another. Malaysian dipterocarps, however, are fascinating in that they do not flower and fruit each year but, when they do, they do so gregariously (also known as **mast fruiting**). Individuals of the same species, over a wide area, blossom, and subsequently fruit, simultaneously. In Sarawak and Brunei most individuals in many dipterocarp genera (e.g. *Cotyleobium*, *Dipterocarpus*, *Dryobalanops*, *Hopea*, *Shorea* and *Vatica*) fruit synchronously over vast areas (Ashton 1964; Medway 1972). This occurs at intervals of 8–13 years and is triggered either by dry weather (Poore 1968) or by 2–3 nights when temperatures drop 2 °C below normal during El Niño years (see section 1.2.6).

Chan and Appanah (1980) recorded a flowering sequence in six species of *Shorea* over a 10-week period (Figure 8.5). This staggered flowering reduces competition for the thrips that pollinate the flowers of these species. Furthermore, the synchronous seed dispersal that occurs as a result of this synchronous pollination ensures that some seeds survive predation. Gentry (1974) showed that a similar sequential pattern of flowering occurs each year in sympatric species of *Arrabidaea* in Central America.

A few rain-forest trees are **monocarpic**, they flower once and die soon after the fruit has ripened. *Spathelia excelsa* is a slender, unbranched tree found in central Amazonia. After a few years, it produces an enormous panicle of flowers, fruits and the apical meristem then ceases growth and the tree dies. Many bamboos in seasonal tropical and temperate regions grow vegetatively for perhaps as long as a century, and then flower, fruit and die (see Box 3.1). Some monocarpic species flower gregariously. The biological significance of monocarpy is unclear, but Foster (1977) suggested that the death of the parent tree creates a gap in the canopy which promotes the growth of juvenile plants that germinate from the copious seeds produced.

Cauliflory (flowers that develop on older branches or the trunk) is more common in tropical trees than those found in temperate forests. Cauliferous trees are generally short and grow below the canopy; most of them are either bat-pollinated or have their seeds dispersed by bats. The flowers developing on the stem can be reached easily by bats. The Asian durian (*Durio* spp.), which bears a fruit with a rich, pungent smell, is a notable exception. The genus *Durio* includes over 25 species of trees up to 40 m in height. The fruit may reach 30 cm in length and is covered in heavy, sharp spines. Corner (1964) graphically described the competition that occurs during the fruiting season between elephants, tapirs, deer, rhinos, bears, squirrels and primates. All these animals are important dispersers of the seeds, and the large, heavily protected fruit would not be dispersed far without their intervention. Many trees have developed large, nutritionally rich seeds that can provide the seedling with enough reserves to become established once germination is underway. We will look at the role of animal-mediated seed dispersal in more detail in section 8.7.3.

The vegetation structure of tropical rain forests is clearly dominated by large trees, which contrasts with the vegetation types that we have studied so far. Savanna vegetation is a mosaic of scattered trees, woodlands and open grasslands. Deserts have few trees and a high preponderance of annual plants. Observations along these lines led to the development of the life-form concept.

8.4 | Life-form concept of plants

The growth form of a plant is an adaptive response to its environment. Plants can be classified with respect to their growth form and the composition of growth form types related to habitat. In this way, we can compare the growth form composition of plants in the three terrestrial biomes covered so far: deserts, savannas and rain forests. The most widely used growth form system is that proposed by Raunkiaer (1934) based on the position, relative to the ground, of the perennating tissues. In this scheme, five life-forms were recognised, relating to the degree of protection given to the perennating organs (Figure 8.6):

1 **Phanerophytes** support their buds on the tips of branches where they are exposed to climatic extremes; trees and tall shrubs;

2 **Chamaephytes** grow close to the ground; small shrubs and herbs;

3 **Hemicryptophytes** die back at the end of the growing season and the buds are protected by the withered leaves and soil;

4 **Cryptophytes** regenerate from buds, bulbs and rhizomes that are completely buried in soil;

5 **Therophytes** are annual plants that regenerate from seed each year.

Analysis of plant forms found in particular biomes provides a **botanical spectrum**; Figure 8.7 provides spectra for tropical rain forests, savannas and deserts. These spectra clearly show the decreasing importance of annual plants (therophytes) as the environment ameliorates from deserts through savannas to rain forests. They also show the dominance of phanerophytes (large plants with buds exposed to the environment) in rain forests where buds require little protection. Note too, that cryptophytes and hemicryptophytes are important components of savanna vegetation. The protection afforded to the perennating organs by the soil is one adaptation to fire exhibited by these plants.

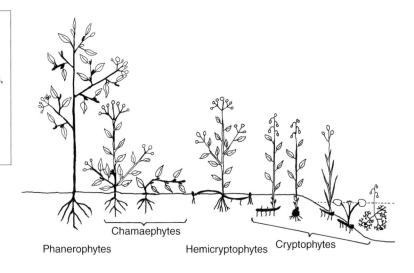

Figure 8.6 Raunkiaer's life-form classification of plants based on the position of the perennating organ. The shaded parts of the plants remain during unfavourable seasons, those unshaded die back. Therophytes, which persist only as seeds are omitted (after Raunkiaer 1934 with kind permission from Oxford University Press).

Phanerophytes

Chamaephytes

Hemicryptophytes

Cryptophytes

8.5 | Rain-forest animals

Animal life in tropical rain forests exhibits the greatest taxonomic variety of any biome. However, animal biomass, particularly of herbivores, may be lower than that in savanna. Like the trees, the animal communities are stratified: the emergents are inhabited mostly by birds and insects which may live out their whole lives without leaving the canopy. The species diversity is most obvious among birds: the abundance of fruits, seeds, buds, nectar and insects has allowed birds to become specialist feeders. This is particularly true in South America which is sometimes called the bird continent. Although fruits form an important component of the diet, frugivorous birds supplement their diet with protein-rich insects.

Mammals, other than bats and primates, are poorly represented in rain forests and are primarily arboreal. More than half the mammals inhabit the crowns of trees and possess a prehensile tail. In the Neotropics, sloths (*Choloepus*, *Bradypus*) are examples of tree-crown herbivores. Rain forest insect diversity is incredible, but data are scarce and few detailed studies of insects and other rain forest invertebrates have been undertaken.

In section 8.1, examples of the large number of species found in rain forests were presented. Explanations of how so many different animal species coexist have centred on partitioning of resources in both space and time (Figure 8.8). The forest is three dimensional, and Slud (1960) noted that the forest layers at La Selva in Costa Rica were occupied by different bird species. Canopy birds included the wholly or partly frugivorous toucans, cotingas and parrots, whereas woodpeckers, trogons, jacamars, humming-birds and antbirds were mostly found below the canopy. Vultures, swifts and hawks flew above the canopy, and curassows, tinamous and wrens remained on or near the forest floor.

We have seen that the species composition of plants and animals in rain forests in different parts of the world differs. However, similarities exist because species within the three land areas (South America, Africa and Asia) have evolved similar responses to the environment in which they live. This is known as **convergent evolution**.

8.6 | Convergent evolution

Although the mammals in African and Neotropical rain forests have different evolutionary origins, counterparts within each display some remarkable morphological similarities (Figure 8.9). Long periods of isolation, following the break-up of Gondwana (see section 1.3.1), have led to the production of unique life-forms. However, through a process known as **evolutionary convergence**, organisms living under similar

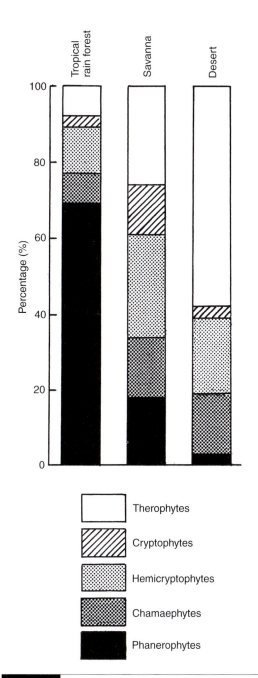

Figure 8.7 Proportional distribution of different life-forms (as classified by Raunkiaer 1934) in tropical rain forest, savanna and desert (adapted from Archibold 1995 with kind permission from Kluwer Academic Press).

environmental conditions have solved common problems through similar adaptations, despite a distinctive historical origin. The hornbills of Africa and the toucans in South America feed on canopy fruits and have developed, in isolation, beaks remarkably similar in structure.

Many flowering plants have evolved as climbers, and this capacity has evolved in many different families with the necessary climbing and attachment structures developing from different structures. None the less, these structures have a superficial similarity and are referred to as being **analogous** (similar in form and function but not derived from equivalent structures with a common evolutionary ancestor). What these observations indicate is that the adaptations of organisms to their environment follow certain rules relating structure to function. Structures which have a common evolutionary history are referred to as **homologous**.

8.7 | Plant–animal interactions

Animals and plants have developed, through **evolution** and **co-evolution** (See section 8.8), intricate relationships; in some cases these relationships are offensive or defensive and in others they are **mutualistic** with both the plant and animal benefiting.

8.7.1 Herbivory

Although animals eating plants do not face the challenge of having to catch their food, they none the less do have to overcome other obstacles. Plant material has a very different chemical composition from that of animals, and therefore a significant amount of the food taken in by herbivores is not readily assimilated (see section 5.8). Their food also often contains large quantities of chemical defences produced by plants to make them less attractive to herbivores. Plant matter is rich in carbon but relatively deficient in nitrogen and protein. Furthermore, only a few organisms (some bacteria and many fungi) have enzymes capable of breaking down cellulose and lignin. Therefore, in what may appear to be a copious

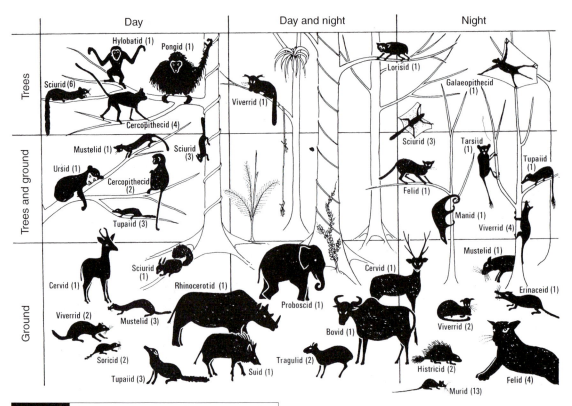

Figure 8.8 Space–time partitioning of resource use in the non-flying mammals of the lowland rain forest in Sabah, Indonesia (after Whitmore 1993 with kind permission from Oxford University Press).

amount of food, only a small part of it is actually available to herbivores.

Herbivores that feed on leaves effectively reduce the surface area available to the plant for photosynthesis. This is one obvious cost to the plant. Another cost, which is increasingly being considered in studies of herbivory, is the manufacture of defence compounds. Some of these compounds are present in the plant all the time, while the production of others is induced by herbivore attack. Janzen (1983) pointed out that herbivory is much broader than leaf eating and must include, for example, the losses to the plant incurred by herbivores that suck phloem and xylem fluids, eat buds, flowers and fruits and drink nectar.

Herbivory on leaves is not the only way in which animals diminish the performance of plants. A leaf roller may destroy much more of a leaf and reduce photosynthetic production more than a herbivore that takes a bite. A herbivore that attacks the shoot tip with the meristem may impede plant growth more than one that attacks leaves.

Many tropical forest herbivores are restricted to feeding on just a few species (**stenophagous**). Even **euryphagous** species such as the tapir are still selective. A captive tapir (*Tapirus bairdii*) in Costa Rica rejected the foliage of at least 55% out of 381 species of deciduous forest plants offered to it (Janzen 1983). Therefore, species richness of herbivores in a forest is likely to be, at least in part, dependent on the species richness of the plants. Furthermore, stenophagous herbivores face a challenge in finding their next meal in a diverse forest.

Seeds generally provide a more nutritionally-rich food source. Seed predators have been grouped by Janzen (1983) into those that eat developing embryos, those that eat nearly mature seeds, and those that act as post-dispersal seed predators. In terms of plant resources lost, predation of young embryos is the mildest because the

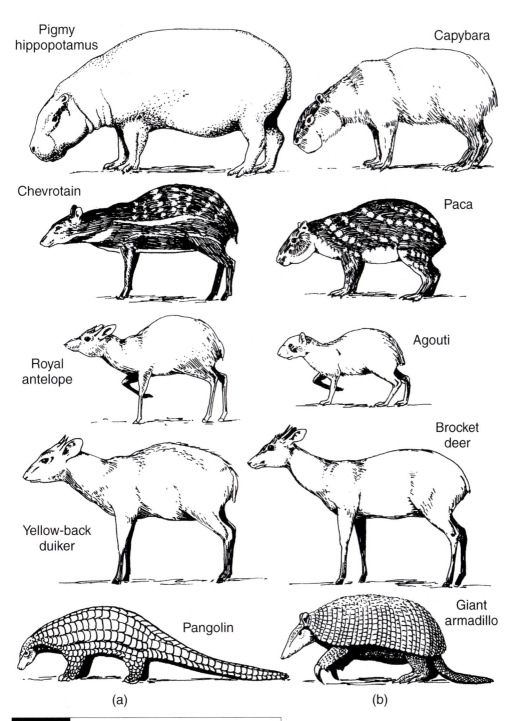

(a)   (b)

Figure 8.9 Convergent evolution in morphology among unrelated African (left) and Neotropical (right) rain-forest mammals. Members of each pair are drawn to the same scale (after Bourlière 1973 with kind permission from the Smithsonian Institution Press).

parent plant has invested little in the fruit and seed at this stage. Predators on full-sized seeds have to deal with a wide array of secondary defensive compounds which are largely absent in the developing embryos. Pre-dispersal predation reduces the size of the final seed crop, and seed predation may be the driving selective pressure behind the reproductive strategies of mast fruiting and long intervals between flowering events (see section 8.3.2).

Post-dispersal seed predators have to deal with the same array of chemical defences as pre-dispersal predators, but may also have to deal with a much harder seed coat. The location of dispersed seeds is much more diffuse, and therefore predators on them will generally have to spend more time foraging. Herbivory costs should also include the plant resources allocated to attract pollinators and seed dispersers.

8.7.2 Pollination

Rain forest trees are rarely wind-pollinated because the high species diversity gives little chance for pollen to be carried from an anther on one individual to a receptive stigma of the same species. Furthermore, frequent rain, humidity and low, subcanopy wind speeds are conditions not conducive to promoting wind pollination. It has been suggested that pioneer species such as *Cecropia* and *Musanga* (see section 8.14) are wind-pollinated. Trees of both genera often grow in nearly pure stands and therefore wind pollination might be effective (Richards 1996). Rain forest plants have developed pollination techniques which ensure a much greater chance of success. They rely on well-developed co-evolutionary relationships with animals: insects, bats, birds and even mammals.

Most plants bloom in the dry season and provide nectar for insects and birds. In some cases, the insects are opportunistic feeders, gathering nectar from as many as 20 species. More interesting are the highly specific relationships that have evolved between a pollinator and a plant. Some orchids utilise complex mechanisms such as deception and mimicry to ensure pollination. The solitary wasp, *Blastophaga psenes,* pollinates

the fig, *Ficus carica,* as it deposits eggs in the sterile ovaries of specialised gall flowers (Wiebes 1979; see Box 8.1).

Bat-pollinated flowers open at night and have a thick, viscid nectar, a musty smell, and are usually white or cream. *Parkia* flowers are suspended below the leaves on long stalks, providing easy access for the bats. Similarly, the bat-pollinated durian (*Durio* sp.) produces easy-to-reach flowers on leafless stems (cauliferous). Bird-pollinated flowers are robust like bat-pollinated flowers but, unlike the latter, they are brightly coloured: red, orange or yellow. The nectar is watery with a low sugar content. Humming-birds (Trochilidae) pollinate flowers such as *Heliconia* in the Neotropics. In Africa and Asia humming-birds are not native and here bird pollination is carried out by sun-birds (Nectariniidae) and honey-eaters (Meliphagidae) respectively. In Madagascar, lemurs (see Box 8.2) are important in pollinating plants and the same seems to be true of bush-babies and night-apes of continental Africa.

8.7.3 Seed dispersal

Dispersal is the mechanism that allows offspring to escape from the immediate environment of the parent. This allows offspring to develop away from the competition of the established parent and also provides a mechanism by which the range of the species can be expanded. The seeds of many forest tree species are nutrient-rich since they must either remain dormant and viable in the soil for a long time or must provide sufficient nutrition to allow the seedling to establish in a poor light climate. Therefore, these seeds may provide a rich food source for many animals.

Many tropical rain forest plants have seeds and fruits that are attractive to animals. Fruits attractive to birds tend to be brightly coloured, whereas in those eaten by bats, odour is the main attractant. Many seeds eaten by animals are regurgitated or pass through the digestive tract unharmed, and the percentage germination is often higher as a result of their passage through the gut. However, some animals are particularly destructive of the seeds consumed. Janzen (1981) found that a tapir destroyed 78% of guanacaste (*Enterolobium cyclocarpum*) seeds and all of carao (*Cassia grandis*) seeds fed to it. Some animals (e.g. agoutis (*Dasyprocta*)) hoard seeds and some in the cache may germinate before they are eaten. In the flooded forests of Amazonia, fish are important agents of seed dispersal (Goulding 1980).

8.7.4 Mutualism

Leaf-cutting ants depend on the growth of a fungus that they cultivate in gardens supplied with pieces of leaves brought into the colony by worker ants. The adult ants have a catholic diet, feeding on nectar, other insects and scavenging. The larvae, however, feed exclusively on the tips of fungal hyphae. The fungi depend on the ants for the provision of suitable leaf material and on dispersal to new colonies.

Some epiphytes have developed special cavities in which ants live. These so-called ant plants (*Myrmecodia*, *Hydnophytum*) provide the ants with a place to live and in return receive nutrients from the ants. Through radioactive labelling experiments, it has been established that ants bring nutrients into the special cavities in the tubers of the ant plants and that these nutrients are, indeed, absorbed by the plants. This co-operation between ants and ant plants (and leaf-cutting ants and their fungal gardens) are examples of **mutualisms**. Mutualists benefit each other, and such interactions are common and widespread in rain forests. For example, most rooting plants have mutualistic fungi associated with their roots (see section 8.17.1), many flowering plants depend upon animals for pollination (see section 8.7.2) and effective seed dispersal (see section 8.7.3). In some cases these relationships are **facultative** (both partners benefit from the relationship but are not entirely dependent upon it), whereas, in others, the association is **obligate** and essential for one or both partners.

There is a great diversity in mutualistic relationships, but most can be classified into three types: trophic, defensive or dispersive. **Trophic mutualisms** are those interactions between two species that involve obtaining energy and nutrients. Examples include the mycorrhizal relation-

ships between fungi and plants, between nitrogen-fixing bacteria and legumes, and between cellulose digesting bacteria and their ruminant hosts. The bull's horn acacia (*Acacia cornigera*) grows in the savannas of Central America and has a close, mutualistic relationship with the ant *Pseudomyrmex ferruginea*. The plant has hollow thorns which the ant uses as nesting sites and its sugar-secreting nectaries provide food for the ants. The ants defend the plant against attack from herbivorous insects and protect the *Acacia* from competitors by snipping off shoots that enter the canopy of the host tree. This is an example of a **defensive mutualism** which also has a trophic component (Janzen 1967a).

Dispersive mutualisms mostly involve pollination and seed dispersal by animals. Most of the flowers offer nectar, pollen or both as a reward for the service the animal provides in carrying the pollen from the anthers of one plant to the receptive style of another. Many different kinds of animals have developed close relationships with flowering plants; these close, mutualistic relationships have arisen through a process known as co-evolution.

8.8 Co-evolution

Many forest-dwelling animals owe an element of their survival to a mutualistic association with a particular plant. In other cases, the relationship is less friendly. In either case, these close relationships between plants and animals have arisen through a process known as **co-evolution**. Co-evolution refers to the evolutionary change that occurs when two populations interact. If the relationship is antagonistic, as it is between predators and their prey, the two species become entangled in a struggle of adaptations, by the predator to enhance prey capture, and by the prey to avoid capture. In the more benign, mutualistic relationships, adaptations strive to promote the interaction between the two species.

Box 8.1 | Figs and wasps: reproduction in concert

The flowers of figs are borne inside the developing fruit and are protected by a mass of interlocking scales which from a barrier at the single entrance. Each species of fig produces three types of flower: male, female and gall flowers. The male flowers produce pollen, the female flowers set the seeds and the gall flowers are sterile and provide an incubator for the next generation of wasps.

The male wasps, maturing within the gall flowers, emerge first. The males are blind and have only rudimentary wings. They inseminate the female wasps which remain inside their gall flowers. This function complete, the males die. The females, already pregnant, then emerge. At the same time, the male flowers ripen and the anthers become covered in pollen. The female wasp must pass over the male flowers on her way out of the gall flower. The female wasp flies to another fig tree of the same species with flowers ready to mature. She enters a fig and probes the various types of flowers, searching for the gall flowers in which to lay her eggs, one egg in each flower. Female flowers are anatomically different from gall flowers and the female wasp can detect this difference and does not lay eggs in female flowers. However, in probing the female flower, pollen is deposited on the style and the female flower is fertilised. Gall flowers have shorter styles and the female wasp easily reaches the ovary and lays an egg there.

Figs mature throughout the year and therefore provide a copious supply of nourishing fruits to a wide range of forest animals: birds, bats, monkeys and squirrels. These animals also provide a service to the fig: seed dispersal. The seeds pass through the animal's gut unharmed and are deposited, together with nutrient-rich faeces, on the forest floor or high in the branches of trees. The seeds that germinate on tree branches send down a root. Once this root is established, the fig begins to grow, sending up a leafy shoot and developing more roots. Eventually the trunk of the host tree is entirely encased in a tangle of roots from the fig. The crown of the strangler fig spreads out above the host plant and the host tree eventually dies. (Not all species of figs (*Ficus*) are stranglers, many are rain forest trees and some are pollinated by other animals such as bats.)

8.9 | Productivity and nutrient cycling in forests

Although tropical soils are generally regarded to be highly leached, acidic and nutrient-poor, there is considerable variation between soils supporting tropical rain forest formations. The warm temperatures and copious rainfall found in the humid tropics promote soil weathering, and therefore minerals are continuously leached from the upper layers. These environmental conditions, also promote rapid breakdown of litter by decomposers. These weathering and recycling processes often result in the development of deep, but nutrient-poor soils. However there are many exceptions. The *várzea* forests in the Amazon basin grow on relatively nutrient-rich soils that are replenished each year by flooding. Rain forests in some parts of the world (*e.g.* Indonesia and Papua New Guinea) grow on rich, volcanic soils. In such areas, forests have been converted to intensive agriculture (oil-palm, coconut) since the soils are so nutrient-rich.

Another oft-stated tenet is that most of the nutrients in tropical rain forests are tied up in the above-ground biomass. Figure 8.10 shows that there is considerable variation in the distribution

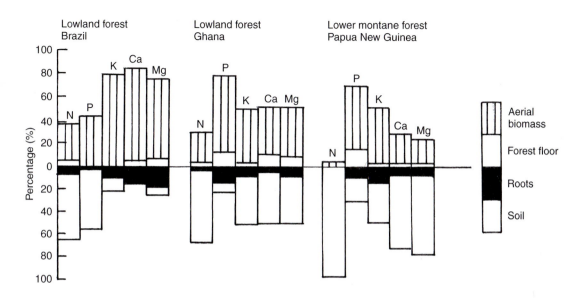

Forest	Biomass tonnes ha^{-1}	Nitrogen kg ha^{-1}	Phosphorus kg ha^{-1}	Potassium kg ha^{-1}	Calcium kg ha^{-1}	Magnesium kg ha^{-1}
Lowland forest Brazil	473	7 540	140	550	530	290
Lowland forest Ghana	287	6 870	170	1 590	5 790	740
Lower montane forest Papua New Guinea	350	20 200	69	1 290	5 510	957

Figure 8.10 Distribution of inorganic nutrients above- and below-ground in various tropical rain forests with biomass of the vegetation (after Whitmore 1984 with kind permission from Oxford University Press).

of nutrients between the above-ground litter and below-ground compartments. In the Brazilian lowland forest studied, most of the calcium, magnesium and potassium were found to be in the above-ground biomass but nitrogen and phosphorus were more evenly distributed between the above-ground and below-ground compartments. Notice, too, the variation between sites and the very high concentration of nitrogen in the volcanic soils at the New Guinea site.

Edwards (1982) studied major nutrient pathways in a lower montane forest in Papua New Guinea and recorded a large increase in nutrient concentrations in rain water as it passed through the canopy (throughfall). Water also reaches the ground as stemflow and this water is also enriched with nutrients. Nutrients incorporated in the vegetation are recycled to the soil through litterfall. Edwards (1982) measured the nutrient flow in this pathway by collecting the fine litter in mesh litter traps of known area. The fine litter consisted of leaves, flowers, fruits and small twigs. The contribution of large branches and tree trunks to nutrients in the litter compartment is more difficult to measure but may exceed that of the fine litter component.

As the litter decomposes, the nutrients contained within it enter the soil compartment and become available for uptake by the vegetation or are lost to lower soil layers or forest streams through leaching. The soil layer may also be enriched with nutrients though the breakdown of soil minerals. Nutrients are lost from the system through leaching, erosion and, particularly nitrogen and sulfur, through burning. The loss of these elements to the atmosphere may not be particularly important as return, with the next rainfall, is likely to be rapid.

Vitousek (1984) recognised that nutrient cycling within tropical forests may be efficient because either (1) the nutrients are retained within the plant through efficient reabsorption from senescing parts and because more carbon is fixed per unit of nutrient in the trees or (2) nutrients released from the tree are rapidly taken up by the roots, mycorrhizae and decomposers and, hence, retained within the forest and not leached from the soil. Vitousek (1984) analysed patterns of nutrient cycling from 62 tropical forests and clearly demonstrated that there were significant differences in nutrient cycling patterns between them. Therefore, it is unwise to generalise about nutrient cycling in tropical rain forests. He did, however, find that phosphorus appears to be cycled very efficiently within tropical rain-forest trees and that litterfall in these forests is phosphorus limited.

The productivity of rain forests seems to depend upon mechanisms that keep the nutrients in organic components so that they are not leached out of the inorganic phase by the abundant rainfall. With constantly high temperatures and high rainfall, rain forest soils are often well weathered, with minerals almost being continuously leached. However, these environmental conditions promote the breakdown of organic matter by decomposers, and therefore nutrients are recycled rapidly. Numerous organisms are involved in this organic matter breakdown. Termites, hidden in their underground colonies, break down the wood. Close associations between the roots of trees and fungi (mycorrhiza) ensure that nutrients released through decomposition are rapidly absorbed by the trees (see section 8.17.1). This rapid recycling ensures that loss of nutrients through leaching is minimised.

If the rain forest is cleared and the wood removed or burned, rapid leaching of the soil nutrient store may occur and, if so, the soil tends not to support crops without significant inputs of fertilisers. If the cleared patch is left, reforestation may occur but usually with fewer species than the original forest. Furthermore, this secondary growth is often not as luxuriant as primary forest. Deforestation, coupled with annual burning, often results in conversion of the forest to herbaceous systems dominated by species such as *Imperata cylindrica* and *Pteridium aquilinum*.

8.10 | Micro-climates and resource acquisition

Tropical rain forests occur in regions in which seasonal climatic fluctuations are small. However, daily temperatures at the canopy level, rise during the day and fall at night. Beneath the canopy, temperature variations are much reduced, and near the forest floor diurnal temperatures may even be constant. Longman and Jeník (1987) divided a tall, forest canopy tree into five micro-climatic zones (Figure 8.11).

The temperature within forests is usually 7–10 °C less than that outside. Significant diurnal variations in temperature occur even within the forest, but these fluctuations are much greater within clearings and gaps (Figure 8.12 and see section 8.14). It is only at the limit of the rain-forest distribution that rainfall becomes important as dry periods of more than 1 month duration may alter the species composition of the forest with true rain forest species being replaced by those which can tolerate rain-free periods (see section 8.16).

Below the forest canopy, carbon dioxide concentrations are enriched through decomposition of the litter on the forest floor. Carbon dioxide use in photosynthesis near the ground is, however, limited by light availability. Therefore, during the day the vertical profile of carbon dioxide concentrations exhibits depressed levels in the canopy and enhanced levels below the canopy.

Near the equator, the effective day length for trees emerging above the main canopy is approximately 12 hours. It is less for trees in the forest and for those growing on steep slopes. Canopy trees experience about 5 hours of bright sunlight each day, but plants at ground level receive only about 1% of this light (Figure 8.13). The light that reaches the forest floor is of three types: (1) uninterrupted shafts of light, passing between the leaves producing sunflecks which move as the earth moves with respect to the sun; (2) light

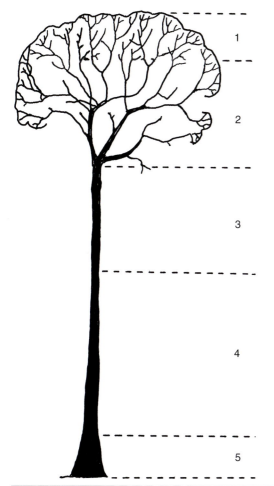

Figure 8.11 Five micro-climatic zones of a forest tree: (1) top of the crown, exposed to weather and full sunlight, with micro-epiphytes; (2) the protected part of the crown, dominant zone of epiphytes, colonising the spreading branches within the canopy; (3) upper part of the trunk, driest micro-habitat colonised by crust-forming lichens; (4) lower part of the trunk, moister with luxuriant growth of mosses and large lichens; (5) the buttresses at the base of the trunk, with moist, shaded cavities filled with abundant mosses (after Longman and Jeník 1987 reprinted by permission of Pearson Education Limited).

to satisfy their photosynthetic light requirements. As the light passes through the forest canopy, reflection and absorption alter the light quality (wavelength composition). Plants growing beneath the canopy have had to adapt to both the quality and quantity of the light falling on their leaves. This change in the quality of the light may play an important role in stimulating the germination of seeds and in sapling growth following the creation of a gap in the forest (see section 8.14). A gap in the canopy results in a higher proportion of far-red light reaching the ground and this change could be registered by a plant through its phytochrome system.

This variety in micro-climate beneath the forest canopy provides a range of habitats, which is one reason given to explain the enormous diversity that exists within lowland tropical rain forests. We will discuss other factors which may be important in allowing so many species to coexist in section 8.12, but first we need to be clear on what biological diversity is (or biodiversity as it has popularly become known) and how we measure and assess it. We will also describe efforts to conserve these systems and why this is so necessary.

8.11 | Biological diversity

Biological diversity refers to the variety of life forms: the different plants, animals and micro-organisms, the genes they contain and the ecosystems they form. This rich diversity is the product of hundreds of millions of years of evolution. Biological diversity, at its most basic level, is the total number of species present. Although studies of **species diversity** have tended to concentrate on plants and animals, organisms belonging to other kingdoms (Fungi, Protista and Prokaryota) should not be ignored.

Species diversity encompasses the range of ecological adaptations exhibited by species to a particular environment. Biological diversity also includes the genetic variation within species, both that contained in populations that are geographically separated and those individuals within a single population. This diversity is referred to as

passing through holes in the canopy; (3) light reflected from leaf and branch surfaces, or transmitted through one or more leaves.

In a Malaysian rain forest, 50% of the light energy used by plants on the forest floor arrives as sun flecks, 6% passes through holes in the canopy and 44% is reflected or transmitted light (Mabberley 1992). Many plants rely on sun flecks

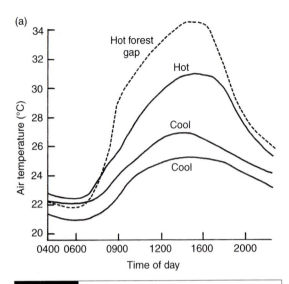

Figure 8.12 (a) Mean daily fluctuations of the air temperature during the hot and cool seasons in Surinam at 1.5 m above the forest floor. Also shown is the mean daily fluctuation in air temperature during the hottest season at 1.5 m in a forest gap. (b) Mean daily fluctuation in soil temperature in a forest in Surinam, at 2 cm depth during the dry season inside the forest (solid line), in a small gap (dashed line) and in a large gap (dotted line) and at 75 cm depth in large gap (horizontal line) (after Schultz 1960).

Figure 8.13 Intensity of light penetrating through the leaves of a tropical forest at various heights above the forest floor (after Kira 1978 with kind permission from Cambridge University Press).

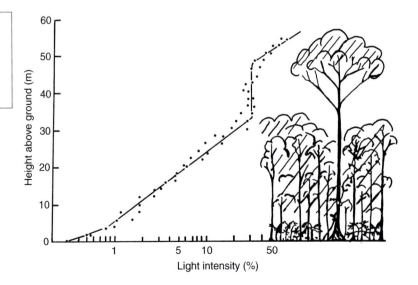

genetic diversity and it provides organisms with the capacity to change and evolve, to maintain reproductive fitness and to develop resistance to diseases. Diversity studies also include a third level: **ecosystem diversity**. This provides an assessment of the variety of habitats available and the ecological functions that they perform. The presence of diverse communities plays an important role in the way ecosystems function. Ecosystems and the organisms they support provide **ecological services**. Nutrients cycle within ecosystems and organisms are essential components of these cycles; note, particularly, the role organisms play in nitrogen fixation, nitrification and denitrification (see section 5.13.2).

8.11.1 Genetic diversity

Genetic diversity refers to the variation of genes within species. This includes variation between distinct populations of the same species and genetic variations within a population. New genetic variation is produced in populations of organisms that can reproduce sexually by recombination and in all individuals through gene and chromosome **mutations**. The pool of genetic variation present in an interbreeding population is shaped by natural selection. Selection leads to certain genetic attributes being preferred and results in changes in the frequency of genes in the **gene pool**.

8.11.2 Species diversity

Species diversity refers to the variety of species. Aspects of species diversity can be measured in a number of ways. Most of these ways can be classified into three groups of measurement: **species richness**, **species abundance**, and **taxonomic** or **phylogenetic diversity**. Tropical rain forests (and coral reefs) support many species of plants and animals, while only comparatively few occur in deserts and tundra. That ecological communities do not contain the same number of species is readily apparent, but how do we assess these differences? The simplest measure of diversity is to count the number of species in a defined area. This gives us a measure known as **species richness**, but it treats rare species and common species as equals.

The number of individuals of each species, their biomass and their energy consumption also need to be considered to obtain a measure of the **relative importance** of each species. These two measures, species richness and relative importance have been combined into a concept known as **species diversity**. Species diversity not only increases with additional species but also with increasing equality of the importance of the species considered. This concept can be illustrated by considering the data in Table 8.2.

On a walk through Community B, a person would have a greater chance of encountering new species than they would in Community A, where most of the organisms belong to one species. Intuitively, therefore, Community B would be considered to be more diverse than community A. However, both these communities would also be regarded as rather unusual. Most communities have a species composition somewhere between the mono-dominance of Community A and the evenness of Community B. Biomathematicians have developed indices which vary both with the number of species (**richness**) and the relative importance (**evenness**). One such measure is the Shannon–Weaver index (H):

$$H = - \sum_{i=1}^{s} (p_i)(\log_e p_i)$$

where p_i is the proportion of the total importance measure (e.g. biomass) accounted for by the species, and s is the total number of species. The Shannon–Weaver index is highest (for a given number of species) when the distribution of importance is perfectly even.

Whittaker (1972) distinguished three types of species diversity. **α-diversity** is the diversity of species within a habitat or community; **β-diversity** is a measure of the rate of change of species along a gradient from one habitat to another; and **γ-diversity** is the richness of species in a range of communities in a location or from one location to another on a geographical or landscape scale. Alpha and gamma diversities effectively measure the same thing and differ only in that the first applies to homogeneous, and the second to heterogeneous, species assemblages. β-diversity is the ratio of the γ-diversity of a region

Species	Community A	Community B	Community C
Table 8.2	The species composition of three hypothetical communities		
1	90	10	40
2	2	10	25
3	1	10	15
4	1	10	8
5	1	10	5
6	1	10	2
7	1	10	2
8	1	10	1
9	1	10	1
10	1	10	1

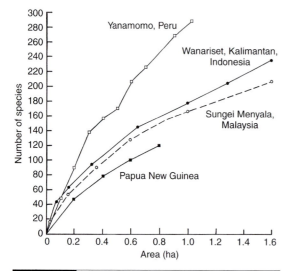

Figure 8.14 Species area curves for tropical lowland rain forests (adapted from Whitmore 1984; Gentry 1988 with kind permission from Oxford University Press).

to the mean α-diversity of the habitats within the region.

8.11.3 Species area curves

If the number of rain-forest plant species recorded in increasing, contiguous, sampling areas is plotted against the area, the curve obtained is initially steep, then rises more gradually, before levelling off as the newly recorded species decline. These curves show graphically the high diversity of rain forests with, initially, each new individual plant sampled having a high chance of being a species not recorded in previous plots. Frequently,

a large area has to be surveyed before it can be concluded that most species have been encountered. Figure 8.14 shows the number of tree species of 0.1 m in diameter or larger on small plots. The number of species varies from just 100 ha^{-1} in Papua New Guinea to a staggering, 300 ha^{-1} in Peru (see section 8.1). Notice that all the curves in Figure 8.14 have not levelled off, indicating that additional species were still being encountered with increasing plot size.

Species richness generally declines with increasing altitude and the canopy height also declines. Ashton (1964) demonstrated very clearly the effect of altitude on species richness within the family Dipterocarpaceae in a study in Brunei extending from sea level to 1700 m a.s.l. (Figure 8.15). The same decline in diversity with altitude has been shown for birds in Costa Rica (Figure 8.16). The concentration of species at lower altitudes has significant implications in terms of biodiversity conservation since lowland and mid-altitude forests are often those under most threat from deforestation for timber extraction and agricultural plantations (see section 8.18).

The high species richness of tropical forests has a number of biological implications which are central to our understanding of how these systems function. Jacobs (1988) described these implications and his ideas are synthesised below:

1 The number of tree species per hectare in lowland tropical rain forests ranges between 80 and 350 and the total number of vascular plant species may be 3 times as high. The large number of species and the dominance by biomass of the trees implies a long tenure in one place and a slow rate of forest regeneration or extension.

2 This species richness and the resultant long distances between individuals of the same species, prevents massive outbreaks of pests and diseases and requires long distances to be bridged for cross-pollination to occur.

3 Almost all rain-forest trees are dependent on animals for pollination and seed dispersal.

4 Rain-forest destruction will endanger a greater number of species per unit area than destruction of any other vegetation type.

Since many species are highly localised within tropical rain forests, there is a high degree of **endemism**. Endemic species are confined to a certain region and do not occur outside that region (see chapter 12). Biodiversity conservation efforts should be directed towards areas which both are species-rich and contain many endemics.

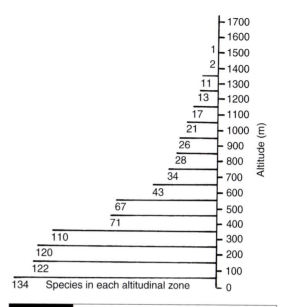

Figure 8.15 Species richness as a function of altitude in the family Dipterocarpaceae in Brunei (data from Ashton 1964).

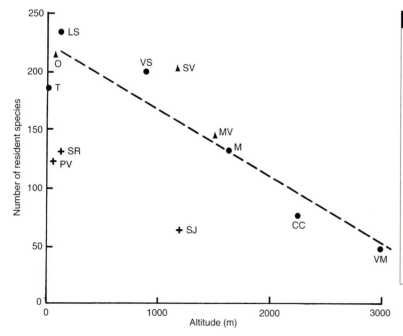

Figure 8.16 Number of resident land bird species at various altitudes in Costa Rica. The localities are: LS = Finca La Selva; O = Osa Peninsula; VS = Virgin del Socorro; SV = San Vito; MV = Monteverde; M = Muñeco; CC = Cerro Chompipe; VM = Villa Mills; SR = Santa Rosa National Park; PV Palo Verde; SJ = San José; T = Tortuguero National Park. (● Localities on Caribbean slope or continental divide; + Humid localities on Pacific slope; ▲ Dry localities on Pacific slope) (redrawn from Stiles (1983), with kind permission of University of Chicago Press, © 1983 by The University of Chicago).

| **Table 8.3** | Hypothesis to explain high species diversity in the tropics |

Non-equilibrium hypothesis
Time – the tropics are older and more stable, hence tropical communities have had more time to develop

Equilibrium hypotheses
I. Speciation rates are higher in the tropics
    1. Tropical populations are more sedentary, facilitating geographical isolation
    2. Evolution proceeds faster owing to:
    2a. a larger number of generations per year;
    2b. greater productivity, leading to greater turnover of populations, hence increased selection;
    2c. greater importance of biological factors in the tropics, thereby enhancing selection.
II. Extinction rates are lower in the tropics
    1. Competition is less stringent in the tropics owing to:
    1a. presence of more resources;
    1b. increased spatial heterogeneity;
    1c. predators exercise increased control over competing populations.
    2. The tropics provide more stable environments, allowing smaller populations to persist, because:
    2a. the physical environment is more constant;
    2b. biological communities are more completely integrated, thereby enhancing the stability of the ecosystem.

Source: Ricklefs 1973.

8.12 | Why are rain forests so diverse?

Rain forests are perhaps rivalled only by some coral reef communities for the great diversity of life that they support. Much debate has focused on the problem of how to account for the coexistence of so many species in tropical ecosystems such as rain forests and coral reefs. Many biologists initially viewed tropical communities as relatively stable systems (MacArthur 1972, Orians 1969) and hence tropical communities have had more time to develop. The stability–diversity hypothesis proposes that systems with more species are inherently stable because any one species in a diverse community is less important than a species in a simpler system. Tropical forests are actually not as stable as they might first appear, and counter to this non-equilibrium hypothesis are a number of equilibrium hypotheses (Table 8.3).

The absence of disturbance, niche diversification and low extinction rates were all proposed as ways to explain the accumulation of many species in tropical forest ecosystems. Climate change has converted rain forest to savanna, and violent events such as hurricanes, landslides and volcanic eruptions can destroy large tracts of forest. Connell (1978) argued that disturbance at some intermediate level acts to maintain high diversity by delaying competitive exclusion (see section 4.10). Such intermediate disturbance may also reduce diversity through local extinctions which can only be balanced by immigration.

8.13 | Latitudinal gradients and species diversity

In 1878, Wallace noticed the tendency for tropical regions to be more species-rich than those at higher latitudes. A number of hypotheses have been proposed to explain this relationship of species diversity to latitudinal gradients and Currie (1991) provided the following review:

1 Time: diversity increases with time because it is a product of evolution, a process which proceeds more rapidly in tropical and stable environments (e.g. those unaffected by sequential glaciations). Over geological time, tropical regions have had a much more stable climate than temperate zones.

2 Spatial heterogeneity: as the physical environment becomes more diverse, so does the biota.

3 Competition: interspecific competition is increased in the tropics, reducing niche size and hence increasing the number of niches (see section 11.7.1). Natural selection at higher latitudes is controlled mainly by physical factors, whereas biological competition becomes more important in the natural selection process in systems nearer the equator.

4 Predation: the greater number of predators and parasites in the tropics reduces the size of prey populations, which, in turn, reduces interspecific competition and allows the addition of new species, both predators and prey. Many tropical species are rare, existing in low population densities.

5 Climatic stability and **favourable environments**: environments that are stable have a more constant supply of resources and provide favourable conditions for many species that are unable to survive in temperate regions. Favourable climatic conditions permit more species.

6 Productivity: productivity is greater in the tropics, and the more energy available to the system the greater will be the diversity. The longer growing season in the tropics permits greater environmental partitioning and hence greater coexistence of species. The correlation between species diversity and productivity is, however, not strong and some areas with intermediate productivity support diverse communities.

7 Disturbance: moderate disturbance retards competitive exclusion and enhances diversity. When disturbances are low, species of low competitive advantage are lost; frequent disturbances results in the loss of highly competitive species.

These determinants of biodiversity may operate together as shown in Figure 8.17. In the ultimate analysis, Whitmore (1984) concluded that a region contains only those plant species which immigration and evolution, plus survival, have enabled to be present. Historical mechanisms (geological and evolutionary) are therefore important. Plate tectonics (see section 1.3.1) and plant migrations have played a part in, for example, the intermingling of floral elements from Gondwana and Laurasia. This intermingling of species has certainly contributed to the species richness of the forests in Malesia.

Kohyama (1993) has proposed that tree species can coexist because they vary in size. Competition for light is one-sided, with larger individuals affecting smaller individuals but not the other way round. Tree species can be segregated by height, with different species occupying different layers of the forest. Trees can **trade-off**, across species, mature height for survival, reproduction or regenerative ability. Variation in tree size structure is brought about through the spatial and temporal variation that occurs due to the opening and closing of gaps.

Tropical forests are rich in species for a number of reasons, and not only because they occur in areas which have had a very long history of stable climate. Short-term disturbances also play a role. The forest canopy provides a large number of spatial and temporal niches; this habitat richness is enhanced through, and thrives from, numerous interactions between plants and animals. Coexistence is tolerated through specialisation, a decrease in niche breadth. We will discuss the concept of the niche in chapter 11. Coupled with this increase in diversity with decreasing latitude, it has been observed that there is a tendency for the latitudinal ranges of species to decline with decreasing latitude. This ecological principle is known as **Rapoport's rule**.

Tropical forests undergo a dynamic process of rejuvenation following a disturbance which creates a gap in the forest canopy. The gap is filled, first by species adapted to the different environmental conditions prevailing within the gap, and then by species adapted to the conditions that result following growth of the gap colonisers. In this way, the forest communities comprise a mosaic of a seemingly everchanging mix of species, and moderate disturbance prevents

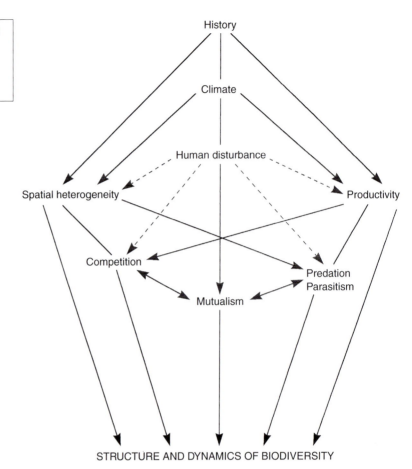

Figure 8.17 Factors interacting to determine the structure and diversity of a tropical rain forest (adapted from Barbault 1992 Copyright MASSON Paris, 1992).

History

Climate

Human disturbance

Spatial heterogeneity

Productivity

Competition

Predation
Parasitism

Mutualism

STRUCTURE AND DYNAMICS OF BIODIVERSITY

competitive exclusion on a local scale, resulting in high diversity. Let us look in more detail at the process by which forest gaps are created and filled.

8.14 | Gap theory

Local species composition of lowland rain forest is, in large measure, altered by the creation of a gap in the forest canopy, and this composition changes as the gap is subsequently filled through regrowth of the vegetation. This process of regeneration or succession has been the subject of detailed study. The various stages in the process add to the complexity of the forest which consists of a patchwork of gaps, regenerating forest and mature forest.

Uhl and Jordan (1984) studied the regeneration of the vegetation on a forest plot in the upper Río Negro region of the Amazon Basin. The plot (0.09 ha) was cleared and burned and the recolonisation process followed for 5 years. In the first year, the plot was dominated by herbaceous plants and then by *Cecropia ficifolia*. In the third year, tree mortality exceeded recruitment because the *C. ficifolia* trees died nearly in unison. In the fourth year, tree density increased markedly as forest species colonised the space vacated by *C. ficifolia*. The canopy became dominated by *Vismia japurensis* and *V. lauriformis*. By the fifth year, the cleared space was filled and there were only 0.07 recruits per m² during year five; 95% of the trees present at the end of year four survived through the fifth year. Of the 56 tree species that had colonised the site, over half were primary forest species and these were most common in the understorey. Litter production increased from 39 g m^{-2} in year one to 825 g m^{-2} in year five.

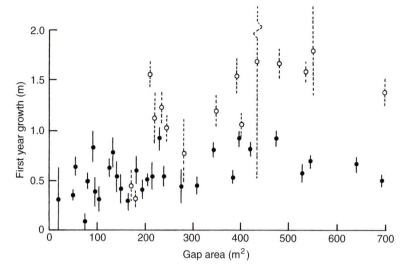

Figure 8.18 Height growth of pioneer (o) and primary species (●) versus gap area at 30 sites on Barro Colorado Island, Panama. The data represent the mean ± one standard error of the first year's recorded growth in height (after Brokaw 1985 with permission of The Ecological Society of America).

Nutrient loss from the site was greatest in years one and two but by the fifth year, losses were similar to those from undisturbed forest.

Brokaw (1985) studied forest regeneration in 30 gaps ranging in size from 20 to 705 m² in tropical forest on Barro Colorado Island (BCI) in Panama. BCI is situated in Gatun Lake and is covered in tropical moist forest ranging from old second-growth (approximately 100 years old) to structurally mature, old-growth forest at least 300 years old. Mean annual rainfall on the island is 2750 mm and there is a distinct dry season from mid-December to early May during which some trees are leafless. In this study, trees were classified as pioneers whose saplings are typically found only in gaps, and primary species which are found either as suppressed stems in the understorey of mature forest or as faster-growing stems where they were exposed in gaps.

In most of the gaps studied by Brokaw (1985), stem densities rose rapidly following gap creation, reached a peak, and declined within 3 to 6 years. This pattern was particularly marked in some large gaps where pioneer species attained high densities but then experienced heavy mortality. In these large gaps, the mean rate of growth (measured as increase in tree height) was greater for pioneers than for primary species. Light is more available in large gaps, and root competition from bordering trees is likely to be less intense. These conditions favour germination of light- or heat-

sensitive pioneer seeds. Pioneer species grew less well, or not at all, in small gaps, and these gaps were filled by primary species (Figure 8.18). Within 3 to 6 years, gaps were filled through colonisation and growth; this created shade which probably resulted in reduced recruitment of both pioneer and primary species. This study showed that gaps of different sizes and stages of regrowth are an important source of heterogeneity in the composition and dynamics within this tropical forest.

Let us now look in more detail at how gaps are created, the environmental conditions that prevail within them and how these change as the gap fills, and compare the biology of the tree species that initially fill the gap with those that follow these early colonisers.

8.14.1 Gap creation and environmental conditions in gaps

The collapse of a canopy tree will eventually occur following the death of the tree; a tree with a large crown (20 m in diameter) will create a gap in the forest (sometimes called a **chablis**) some 400–600 m² in area. Many trees are destroyed during storms and by lightning strikes, landslides, hurricanes, fires and earthquakes. The size of the gap created varies from small holes formed from the fall of a single branch to vast areas following forest devastation by fire or powerful storm.

Light intensity and light duration are greater in gaps. Soil and air temperatures are usually higher in gaps than in the surrounding forest. Humidity in gaps is lower and evaporation from the soil is higher. However, soil moisture, a few centimetres below the surface, may be higher than that in the forest because of reduced root uptake in the gap. Treefall litter and debris provide nutrient enrichment to the soils in gaps. There are, however, complex gradients from the centre of the gap to the unmodified forest surrounding it. Gap micro-climates will vary greatly depending on the size of the gap, and conditions will change as regrowth occurs within the gap.

8.14.2 Gap filling and forest succession

The species that first fill a gap are known as **pioneer** species. Pioneers are species whose seeds can only germinate in gaps in the forest canopy in which sunlight reaches the ground for at least part of the day. These species are not found growing in the understorey of a mature forest, but their seeds lie dormant in the seed bank. The seeds are stimulated to germinate by higher light intensities and higher temperatures.

The west African pioneer tree species *Musanga cecropioides* is an extreme light demander. Its seeds will lie dormant in the shaded forest soil for many years. Following the creation of a gap, numerous seeds germinate and the plants grow rapidly in the bright sunshine penetrating the gap. In South America, pioneer species include *Ochroma lagopus* (balsa), *Cedrela* and the distinctive *Cecropia*. *Macaranga* is a common pioneer in South-East Asia. All these trees share one characteristic: rapid growth rates. *Ochroma lagopus* can grow to over 5 m tall in a year. Pioneer species are light-demanders, shade intolerant and comparatively short-lived.

Seedlings of the emergent trees are **heliophytes** (sun-loving plants) and are unable to mature and flower in the shaded conditions of the forest floor. It is only when a gap is created by the collapse of an old tree that sunlight penetrates to the ground and an emergent is able to reach maturity. Species that thrive in gaps may do so through the timely arrival of a propagule or through the germination of a seed lying dormant in the soil. This store of dormant seeds is known as a **seed bank**.

Other species, known as **climax species**, require shade when young and persist as saplings with little net growth. When a gap is created in their vicinity they are well-placed to fill it and respond rapidly to the new environmental conditions. These seedlings are said to be **released**. Some species of such trees have long-lived seedlings which are released with no or only a small increase in light. These species (e.g. *Parinari* spp.) grow slowly and typically have dense, dark timber. Other species (e.g. *Anisoptera thurifera*, *Entandrophragma* spp.) have seedlings which do not persist for long and are only released following a substantial increase in light.

The seedlings of these climax species may develop below the canopy of pioneer species, and, as the pioneer canopy breaks up with the death of the short-lived trees, these climax species accelerate their growth and succession proceeds with the replacement of the pioneer species by climax species. **Sciophytes** (shade-tolerant or shade-loving plants) develop on the forest floor once the canopy has closed. Some texts refer to these species as secondary species, but this term should be avoided as it can easily be confused with 'secondary forest' which refers to a forest in which regrowth has taken place following destruction of the primary forest. Secondary forests are often less diverse than primary forests and may have only 1 or 2 species per hectare. Given time and little disturbance, the pioneer species in secondary forests decline and are replaced by climax species, effectively converting the secondary forest to a community similar to that of primary forest. The differences between pioneer and climax species are summarised in Table 8.4.

8.15 | Patch dynamics

Forests can be considered to be a mosaic of patches of different ages produced by disturbances of different magnitude, with forest regeneration being influenced by a range of biotic and abiotic factors. Budowski (1965) recognised four successional stages in the development of a mature forest community from a pioneer forest (Table 8.5).

8.15.1 Disturbance regimes

The theory of patch dynamics was first applied to marine, intertidal communities on rocks, where

Table 8.4	Characteristic features of pioneer and climax forest trees	
Feature	Pioneer trees	Climax species
Seed biology	Seeds only germinate in canopy gaps with ground receiving some full sunlight; copious, small seeds produced continuously from early in life; dispersed by animals or wind; dormant seeds usually abundant in forest soil (seed bank)	Seeds germinate under forest canopy; fewer, large seeds produced annually or less frequently; seed dispersal variable including gravity; dormancy often absent; seed bank usually absent
Seedling growth	Seedling photosynthetic rate is high; carbon dioxide compensation point is high	Seedling photosynthetic rate lower; carbon dioxide compensation point usually low
Tree growth	Height growth is rapid; growth is indeterminate with no resting buds	Height growth slower; growth is determinate with resting buds
Roots	Rooting is superficial	Rooting may be deep
Leaves	Leaves short-lived, one generation present (high turnover), susceptible to herbivory; often lack chemical defences	Leaves long-lived, several generations present (slow turnover), low susceptibility to herbivory, chemical defences often present
Wood	Wood is usually pale, of low density and non-siliceous	Often dark, high density, sometimes siliceous
Light requirements	Plants can not survive in shade and young pioneer plants are rarely found under a closed forest canopy	Plants survive in shade and young climax plants are often found under a closed forest canopy
Geographical range and phenotype plasticity	Wide ecological range and high phenotypic plasticity	Often narrow ecological range and low phenotypic plasticity

Source: Swaine and Whitmore 1988.

waves create bare patches on rocks otherwise covered in dense growths of plants and sessile animals. The bare patches were colonised by species which have a high reproductive capacity, rapid growth and short maturation time. These species were subsequently replaced by species which were slower colonisers but superior competitors. This community replacement process can be disrupted by some **disturbance**. A disturbance is any event that changes the community structure, resource availability or physical environment. In forests, disturbance can occur through large-scale events such as fires, floods, hurricanes, droughts or more localised incidents such as a branch falling from a tree creating a gap in the canopy. The response of the community to a disturbance will vary with magnitude of the disturbance and the frequency with which the disturbance is repeated.

In Papua New Guinea, cyclones, earthquakes, volcanic eruptions and fire devastate large tracts of forests creating enormous gaps (Johns 1986). Consequently, forests in this frequently disturbed environment are dominated by shade-intolerant species. In Borneo and Surinam, catastrophic destruction of forests is rare and in these forests shade-tolerant species are more widespread (Whitmore 1989). Species-rich forests will develop in areas where disturbance magnitude and frequency are moderate (Connell 1978). In such a forest there will always be patches of forest with pioneer species, patches with a mix of pioneer and

Table 8.5 Comparison of successional stages in the development of mature forest from a pioneer community, with particular reference to Neotropical forests

	Pioneer	Early secondary	Late secondary	Climax
Community age	1–3 years	5–15 years	20–50 years	>100 years
Canopy height	5–8 m	12–20 m	20–30 m	30–60 m
Number of woody species	1–5	1–10	30–60	>100
Floristic composition of dominants	Euphorbiaceae, *Cecropia*, *Ochroma*, *Trema*	*Ochroma*, *Cecropia*, *Trema*, *Heliocarpus* most frequent	Diverse, many Meliacae, Bombacaceae, Tiliaceae	Very diverse
Natural distribution of dominants	Very wide	Very wide	Wide, includes drier areas	Usually restricted, endemics frequent
Number of strata	1, very dense	2, well-differentiated	3, increasingly difficult to discern with age	4–5, difficult to discern
Upper canopy	Homogeneous, dense	Arranged in whorls, branching, thin horizontal crowns	Heterogeneous, includes very wide crowns	Many variable shapes of crowns
Lower stratum	Dense, tangled	Dense, large herbaceous species frequent	Relatively scarce	Scarce
Growth	Very fast	Very fast	Dominants fast, others slow	Slow or very slow
Lifespan of dominants	Very short, less than 10 years	Short, 10–25 years	Usually 40–100 years, some more	Very long, 100–1000 years or more
Shade tolerance of dominants	Very intolerant	Very intolerant	Tolerant as juveniles, later intolerant	Tolerant, except in adult stage
Regeneration of dominants	Very scarce	Practically absent	Absent or abundant, large mortality in early years	Abundant
Seed dispersal agents of dominants	Birds, bats, wind	Wind, birds, bats	Principally wind	Gravity, mammals, birds
Size of seeds or fruits dispersed	Small	Small	Small to medium	Large
Seed viability	Long, latent in soil	Long, latent in soil	Short to medium	Short
Wood and stem size of dominants	Very light, small diameters	Very light, diameters below 60 cm	Light to medium hard, some very large stems	Hard and heavy, large stems
Leaves of dominants	Evergreen	Evergreen	Many deciduous	Evergreen
Epiphytes	Absent	Few	Many, but few species	Many species
Vines, lianas	Abundant, herbaceous but few species	Abundant, herbaceous, few species	Abundant, but few of them large	Abundant, with some very large, woody species
Shrubs	Many, but few species	Relatively abundant but few species	Few	Few, but many species
Grasses	Abundant	Scarce to abundant	Scarce	Scarce

Source: Budowski 1965.

climax species and patches dominated by climax species.

Hubbell *et al.* (1999) in a 15–year detailed study of a 50 ha forest plot on Barro Colorado Island, Panama, concluded that seed and seedling shortage might be the main cause of high forest diversity. They counted 1.3 million seeds collected in seed traps over 10 years and found that only a few of the 314 adult trees in their plot delivered seed to more than half the traps. The majority of adult trees had no seedlings in the 2000 metre square plots surveyed. This recruitment limitation effectively means that forest gaps are not necessarily colonised by the best competitors but rather by the species that happens to have a seed or seedling in the vicinity. In this way weaker species may be promoted. This study was carried out in a forest which has a relatively mild disturbance regime. Further studies are required to see if recruitment limitation and its role in diversity has wider application.

8.16 | Tropical deciduous forests and ecotones

Deciduous seasonal rain forest on the island of Trinidad in the Caribbean consists of two layers: an upper one of scattered trees up to 20 m tall and a lower one of trees between 3–10 m high. Over two-thirds of the trees in the upper storey are deciduous, losing their leaves every dry season. In contrast, the understorey trees are almost all evergreen. Buttressed trees are absent and some of the trees have thorns. Lianes are not commonly found and epiphytes are rare or absent (Richards 1996).

Nearly all the trees in rain forests are evergreen. Deciduous species are less able to compete with evergreens under conditions in which water is always available. However, this dominance is altered at the margins of tropical rain forests where the dry season is more extended, and in places such as India, Burma, Indochina, East Africa, Northern Australia and parts of the Caribbean and South America where a monsoon climate exists. The climate in regions of deciduous forest is drier than those with tropical rain forests with rainfall averaging 1000–2000 mm per year and falling within a distinct wet season of some 6–9 months duration.

The trees in deciduous forests lose most of their leaves during the short, dry season. These forests have a much simpler structure, with usually only one layer of trees and a greater predominance of shrubs and herbs. Not all the tree species are deciduous and a few retain leaves throughout the dry season. Along river banks, where there is usually ample soil moisture, leaf loss is reduced. A few hardy evergreens are found and these usually have small, leathery leaves which are often highly toxic to herbivores.

More marked seasonality in climate is reflected in more distinct phenology. Many deciduous forest trees flower as the dry season ends. Water loss by transpiration through flowers is slight and flowering therefore has little impact on the tree's water balance. By flowering at the start of the rains, trees are able to allocate resources in the wet season to the production of leaves, fruits and seeds. Fire is a factor in the ecology of deciduous forests, and during the dry season these forests are susceptible to burning. The trees, unlike those in the rain forests, have adapted to fire by having thick bark with deep fissures, which insulate the growing tissues beneath.

Tropical deciduous forests are even more threatened than the more intensively studied rain forests. Deciduous forests occupy land that is easily cleared to produce prime crop and cattle farms. These areas are among the most heavily exploited of the world's biomes and in Central America they have been reduced to less than 10 per cent of the original cover (Lerdau *et al.* 1991).

8.16.1 Ecotones

The transition from one tropical plant formation (evergreen rain forest to deciduous forest; deciduous forest to savanna) is not necessarily marked by a distinct or abrupt boundary. The transition may consist of a gradual replacement of species along an environmental gradient or a mosaic of different plant communities. These transitional zones are known as **ecotones** and will be discussed in chapter 9.

8.17 | Low-diversity tropical rain forests

Tropical rain forests do not always have a high diversity of tree species. In some cases, most of the trees in the canopy belong to a single species. Such single-dominant forests are not particularly rare and are found in each of the three main regions of the world where rain forests occur. *Gilbertiodendron dewevrei* forest covers large areas of the Congo Basin. This dominant tree in the Fabaceae family (subfamily: Caesalpinioideae), grows to a height of 35–40 m and may make up 90% of the large trees in the forest (Richards 1996).

Over 80% of the canopy trees in a forest in Trinidad were *Mora excelsa* (Beard 1946). In this forest, *M. excelsa* trees formed a continuous, level and closed canopy, distinguishing it from more diverse forests with emergent trees giving the canopy an uneven appearance. *Mora* forests in Guyana occur on floodplains and sites with impeded drainage. Wallaba forest, also in Guyana, is dominated by *Eperua falcata* and is characteristically found on 'white sands' (podsols). Anderson (1961) showed that a rain forest in Sarawak was dominated (75%) by *Shorea albida* (Dipterocarpaceae). The heath forests of Borneo are also found on sandy podsolic soils and are dominated by species in the family Dipterocarpaceae.

Single-dominant forests chiefly occur either (1) on sites liable to flooding or with impeded drainage or (2) on white sands (Richards 1996). Connell and Lowman (1989) identified two types of single dominant forests. In the first type, the dominant tree persists beyond one generation, and in the second it does not. These workers suggested that, in forests with a persistent dominant, the species may achieve its dominance either through colonisation of a large patch, or through a gradual replacement of the existing residents.

8.17.1 Mycorrhizal associations
Connell and Lowman (1989) proposed that mono-dominant trees may have an advantage over competitors through possession of a symbiotic association with a fungus known as an ectomyc-

orrhizal association (EM). Most mono-dominant species have an EM association. However, most tropical tree species in the Neotropics and Africa have an internal, endomycorrhizal association, also known as a vesicular–arbuscular mycorrhizal association (VAM). Surface growing EM are found on the roots of many dipterocarps and trees in the legume subfamily Caesalpinioideae. The hyphae of both fungal types extend through the soil, greatly increasing the surface area for nutrient uptake, and largely take over the role of root hairs. The hyphae concentrate around decomposing organic matter and therefore this fungi–plant relationship provides a capacity for very tight nutrient cycling, with the nutrients from plant litter being almost directly returned to the plant. The host plant thus gains an enhanced nutrient-uptake capacity. In return for this, the plant provides the fungi with energy-rich carbohydrates.

Characteristics of an EM association include greater host specificity, greater protection to the host tree from both natural enemies and deleterious physical factors, and an enhanced ability to secure nutrients in organic and inorganic form before they become available to a VAM association. There is also some evidence that EM may be able to utilise protein nitrogen directly. These characteristics bestow a competitive advantage on those trees with an EM over those with a VAM. This hypothesis needs to be tested but, in forests where the VAM type is more common, most tree species are associated with the same set of fungal species and therefore may be nearly equivalent in their competitive ability of securing resources, particularly nutrients.

8.18. | Deforestation and the loss of biodiversity

8.18.1 Deforestation in Madagascar
The large island of Madagascar, 400 km east of Africa, is one of the biologically richest and most fascinating areas on earth. Over 8000 endemic species of flowering plants have been identified and most of these are concentrated in the rain forests along the east coast. Many of the plants and animals living in these forests are endan-

gered, and numerous habitats throughout the country have been degraded since the arrival of humans 1500 to 2000 years ago (see Box 8.2). Some notable species have become extinct, the most famous of these being the Dodo (*Raphus cucullatus*).

Before human colonisation, forest is thought to have covered much of eastern Madagascar including most of the eastern coast (Green and Sussman 1990). Maps based on aerial photographs taken in 1950 and satellite imagery recorded in 1972/73 and 1984/85 show marked declines in the extent of these rain forests. The original extent of the eastern rain forests at colonisation was 11.2 million ha; by 1950 only 7.6 million ha remained. By 1985, this had been reduced to 3.8 million ha or approximately 34% of that which originally existed. In the period between 1950 and 1985, deforestation proceeded at an average rate of 111 000 ha (1.5%) per year (Figure 8.19).

This deforestation can be related to human population densities and topography. Deforestation of flat areas took place first and was followed by tree removal from steeper and steeper slopes. Large forest tracts on low slopes, however, remain in the north, whereas in the south such lands have been cleared. This dichotomy is associated with differences in human population densities. Green and Sussman (1990) showed that significantly more forest has been destroyed in regions of higher population density than in those of lower density, especially on less steep slopes. In areas of high population densities, deforestation rates have fallen since 1973, which can be attributed to a diminishing pool of accessible forest. In these areas, forest only remains on the steepest slopes.

The consequences of deforestation are manifold. First, there is a loss of habitat area. Second, there is a process known as habitat fragmentation by which forest patches become isolated, forming small islands in a grassland sea (see chapter 12). This habitat destruction is having a profound influence on the rate at which species are lost through extinction. Although tropical rain forests cover only 7% of the land surface of the earth, they probably contain at least half the world's species.

8.18.2 Deforestation in Costa Rica

Sader and Joyce (1988) traced the decline in forest area in Costa Rica from 1940 to 1983. In 1940, 67% of primary forest remained and this percentage of forest area declined as follows: 1950, 56%; 1961, 45%; 1977, 32%. In 1983, only 17% of the original, primary forests remained. They found that, in the early part of the study period, deforestation occurred predominantly in tropical dry and moist forest zones. In the 1960s, tropical and premontane moist forests were affected and, by 1983, only the less accessible high-rainfall zones in rugged terrain retained relatively undisturbed forest. Road development, providing access to forests, was an important agent of change in all periods of this study.

8.18.3 Reasons for deforestation

There are a number of reasons why rain-forest deforestation is occurring at such an alarming pace. Population pressures are great in many countries which still retain tracts of primary rain forest. Transmigration of landless people and urban poor into sparsely settled areas is being actively encouraged in areas of the Amazon Basin and also from the Indonesian Island of Java to the western half of New Guinea (Irian Jaya). Rain-forest trees are being harvested through both clear-felling and selective logging operations (Figure 8.20).

Cattle pasture is the land-use replacing almost all forest felled in the Amazonian region of Brazil. Small farmers may plant some annual crops such as rice, maize and manioc (cassava) for a few years following forest clearance and then establish pastures. The cattle pastures become degraded over the course of a decade or two through weed invasions and forest regrowth. Pasture degradation results from the loss of soil fertility through erosion and leaching and from fixation of phosphorus in forms unavailable to plants. Fearnside (1986) noted that the types of vegetation developing on degraded and abandoned pastures vary widely in different parts of Amazonia. However, secondary vegetation growth is slower in those abandoned pastures that have been subject to intensive use.

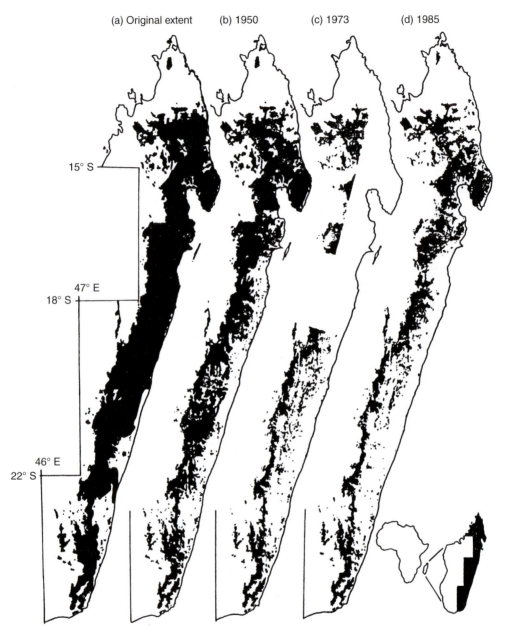

Figure 8.19 Distribution maps of rain forest in eastern Madagascar: (a) before human colonisation when forest is thought to have covered much of the area; (b) 1950 (based on vegetation maps); (c) 1973 (based on incomplete aerial photography); and (d) 1985 (based on Landsat images) (Redrawn with permission from Green, G. M. and Sussman, R. W. Deforestation history of the eastern rain forests of Madagascar from satellite images. *Science* 248, 212–215. Copyright 1990 American Association for the Advancement of Science).

8.18.4 Shifting agriculture

Shifting agriculture is a widespread form of land use within tropical rain forests and is a major cause of deforestation (Figure 8.21). Shifting agriculture involves a cycle of forest clearing, litter burning (hence slash-and-burn agriculture), cropping and forest recovery. This type of farming is practised almost entirely by small farmers and large machinery is not used. Consequently soil

Figure 8.20 Logging road in the Gogol Valley, Papua New Guinea. This area was clear-felled in the 1980s to produce wood chips for paper manufacture (Photo: Office of Environment and Conservation, Papua New Guinea).

damage is slight, and usually little erosion occurs as crops and weeds rapidly colonise the bare soil. Once abandoned, small clearings surrounded by primary forest undergo succession and forest development may take place. However, the sustainability of this type of agriculture depends on the time between crops (the length of fallow periods), the size of plots and their proximity to primary forest. The length of the fallow period required for the forest to re-establish varies greatly, but often exceeds 20 years particularly if the land has been used for a number of years. The enhanced pressure on land resources through human population growth in many tropical countries precludes such long fallow periods and plots mostly have time only to develop secondary growth communities before cultivation is repeated.

Excessively short, fallow periods may lead to a reduction in the regeneration capacity of the forest and grassland communities may become established. Frequent burning of these grasslands may serve to perpetuate their existence.

8.19 | Rain-forest conservation

Tropical rain forests deserve special environmental attention because they constitute the most biologically diverse terrestrial ecosystems. A consequence of the high diversity found in tropical rain forests is that many species occur at very low densities. In some forests a few species are common and many are rare but, in others, no species stand out as more common than others. The low density of tree species means that many species are threatened with extinction through deforestation.

Many of the habitats in tropical rain forest occur in patches and these patches are not stable through time. This patchiness results from variations in the soil types, topography, climate and from the degree and frequency of disturbance. Many species are highly localised in

Figure 8.21 A new garden clearing in the rain forest on the eastern foothills of the Andes in Ecuador (Photo: Michael and Patricia Fogden).

their distribution and occur in only one region. In part this is because many species are rare and do not spread very far.

8.19.1 Keystone species.

Rain-forest species have evolved a number of complex, interspecific relationships: mutualisms. We will see in the chapter on coral reefs, that reef organisms have also formed many similar, beneficial, interspecific alliances. Because of this high degree of interdependence, the elimination of a single species may cause the demise of many other species. Species whose elimination would cause such extinction cascades have been called **keystone species** (Paine 1969). Priority must be given to the conservation of such species. Bond (1993) defined keystone species as those which have a disproportionate effect on the persistence of all other species and grouped such species into categories (Table 8.6).

Walker (1992) recognised that all species are not equal and distinguished between 'drivers' and 'passengers'. Removal of a driver (= keystone) species causes a cascade with significant loss of either species or ecosystem function or both. Conversely, the loss of few passenger species has little effect. In species-rich communities, there are likely to be many passengers and a high degree of **ecological redundancy**. Given our poor knowledge of tropical systems and the species they contain, it has been suggested that the best way to conserve species is to ensure that ecosystems continue to have the same structure and function (Walker 1995). Loss of one species from a diverse system may not have much effect on ecosystem function. However, further loss of species may eventually impair ecosystem performance. Loss of a keystone species may significantly alter ecosystem function. Redundancy is beneficial as it enhances **ecosystem resilience**: the capacity to recover from a disturbance. Therefore redundant species should not be regarded as disposable. Functional groups with little or no redundancy (that is, those that are ecologically significant)

Table 8.6 A classification of types of keystone species

Type	Primary mode of action	Examples
Predators	Suppress competitors	Marine: otters, sea urchins Terrestrial: size-selective seed predators
Herbivores	Suppress competitors	Elephants, rabbits
Pathogens, parasites	Suppress predators, herbivores, competitors	Myxomatosis, tsetse fly
Competitors	Suppress competitors	(1) Successional replacement, e.g. forest trees (2) Weedy species excluding seedlings of long-lived species
Mutualists	Effective reproduction	(1) Plant resources on which key mutualists depend (2) Pollinators (3) Dispersers
Earth movers	Physical disturbance	(1) Rabbits, termitaria (2) Hippo altering hydrology
System processors	Rates of nutrient transfer	(1) Nitrogen fixers (2) Mycorrhiza (3) Decomposers
Abiotic agents	Physical disturbance especially that causing mortality	(1) Fire, frost (2) Plants which alter the fire regime

Source: Bond 1993.

should, however, be made a priority by biodiversity conservation programmes.

8.19.2 Flagship species

Conservation agencies have, particularly in the past, concentrated efforts on the conservation of certain species that attract strong public sentiment. These species are known as **flagship species** and examples include the tiger, panda, African elephant and many of the marine mammals. Currently, conservation efforts are much more directed towards the conservation of habitats, which makes much more sense as this conserves not only the attractive species but also all the organisms that live with it. Conservation of the flagship species of lemurs (see Box 8.2) in Madagascar can only be successful if the few remaining patches of rain forest (see section 8.18.1) are conserved. Therefore, efforts need to be directed towards conservation of the rain forests in their entirety, rather than be centred on, for

example, the breeding biology of the lemurs that inhabit the forests.

8.19.3 Habitat conservation

Disturbance and the subsequent succession that follows such events reduce the threat of extinction for some species (those that tolerate or even thrive through periods of habitat change) while others are threatened by it. Disturbance should not, therefore, be regarded as bad; it plays an essential role in maintaining forest diversity. However, too much disturbance will result in either the replacement of mature forest with secondary forest or deforestation; too little disturbance will reduce forest diversity through preventing the germination and growth of pioneer species and the species in subsequent successional stages.

Efforts to conserve rain forests face an uphill struggle because the features described above (species in low densities, patchiness, endemism,

Box 8.2 | The lemurs of Madagascar

Madagascar, an 'island continent' has been isolated from mainland Africa and Asia for at least 50 million years and probably much longer. With an area of almost 600 000 km², Madagascar is the fourth largest island in the world, and its separation from Africa has resulted in Madagascar's plants and animals developing in isolation. It has been estimated that 85% of all plant and animal species found there are **endemic**. Among the more interesting animals living on the island are the 30 or more species of lemur. The lemurs are a group of primates that are now restricted to Madagascar and the Comoro Islands.

Extant lemurs are classified into five families: Cheirogaleidae (the dwarf lemurs), Megaladapidae, Lemuridae, Indriidae and the monospecific family Daubentoniidae (aye-aye) (Mittermeier *et al.* 1994). The best known of the lemur species is *Lemur catta*, the ring-tailed lemur. This is the only surviving semi-terrestrial (as opposed to arboreal), diurnal lemur in Madagascar. It is easily recognised by its distinctive banded tail. Most of the lemurs are nocturnal and therefore difficult subjects to study. The aye-aye (*Daubentonia madagascariensis*) is, perhaps, the most curious of the lemurs. It has a unique dental formula and continuously growing incisors, a fact which initially led zoologists to classify it with the rodents. It has very large ears used to locate insect larvae in dead wood and a skeleton-like, extremely long middle finger which it uses to extract larvae from holes in the wood.

Since the arrival of humans on Madagascar, eight genera and at least fifteen species of lemur have become extinct. This represents a third of all known species. The major threat to remaining lemur species is habitat destruction. Some hunting and live capture occurs. The main reason for hunting is for food and therefore the larger lemurs are more threatened. Of the 50 taxa (including subspecies) recognised by Mittermeier *et al.* (1994) only 14 were considered to be at 'low risk' of extinction. The magnificent lemur fauna is undoubtedly under some threat, but it also provides a powerful focus for conservation efforts. These curious animals have attracted international attention which has caused a switch in Madagascan economic policy with more emphasis being placed on tourism. Lemur conservation may provide the impetus to conserve the remnants of tropical forests in Madagascar. In this context the lemurs constitute an important conservation 'flagship' group.

mutualistic inter-dependencies and disturbance patterns) combine to dictate that reserves, by necessity, need to be large. Large reserves are likely to contain more species, more patches and more endemics than smaller reserves. In large reserves, disturbances may occur in one part of the reserve and not others. Conservation of a greater number of tree species will support more of the species on which, through mutualism, they depend. Furthermore, to ensure comprehensive conservation of rain forests and the species they contain, a world-wide system of reserves needs to be established (see section 14.3).

8.19.4 Forest fragmentation

The Bogor Botanical Garden, established in 1817, occupies 86 ha in one of the wettest areas of west Java, Indonesia. The heavily wooded area is dominated by tall trees, and until 1936 the forest was continuous with that to the east of the reserve. Destruction of the surrounding forest left the botanical garden isolated with, today, the nearest remaining forest patch being some 5 km away. Diamond *et al.* (1987) demonstrated that, out of the 62 bird species breeding in the Bogor Botanical Garden from 1932 to 1952, 20 had disappeared by 1980–85. A further 4 species had very small populations and the populations of 5 more had declined noticeably. Of the 20 species that vanished from the Garden, all are either now absent or rare in the area surrounding Bogor. Diamond *et al.* (1987) concluded that the most important cause of species decline was a small population in a fluctuating environment. The disappearance of sources of colonisation from the surroundings compounded the impact of the small habitat size.

This process of forest fragmentation (the replacement of large areas of native forest with other ecosystems leaving isolated forest patches) not only leaves the organisms that remain within them a smaller habitat, but also exposes them to environmental conditions, particularly at the forest edges, that differ from those deeper within the forest. These edge effects are the result of interactions between the two adjacent ecosystems resulting in changed biotic and abiotic conditions. Murcia (1995) identified three types of edge effects on forest fragments: (1) abiotic effects, involving changes in the environmental conditions; (2) direct biological effects which involve changes in the abundance and distribution of species; and (3) indirect biological effects involving changes in species interactions such as predation, brood parasitism, competition, herbivory, pollination and seed dispersal. The environment within a forest tends to be cooler, moister and more uniform than adjacent grasslands or pastures. The differences in micro-climate between the two sides of the edge create an environmental gradient which might extend as much as 50 m into the forest.

The creation of an edge increases the incident light and this promotes plant growth. Trees within the forest may respond through increased growth rates, but the trees also become more susceptible to wind throw, fire and colonisation by fast-growing vines and creepers. Tree species composition can also be altered through edge effects, with some species benefiting from the environmental changes and others declining. Similar responses have been noticed for animals, with some species showing a preference for the edge and others avoiding it. These changes in plant and animal communities at the edge of forests interact to produce a cascade of indirect effects. Enhanced plant growth at the forest edge may attract herbivorous insects which, in turn, may attract insectivorous birds which nest on the edge and come to the attention of nest predators.

In 1979, the Biological Dynamics of Forest Fragmentation Project (BDFFP) was initiated in Brazil with the aim of investigating the relationship between the size of a forest fragment and both the stability and species carrying capacity of that forest fragment. The forest being studied is mature, *terra firme*, evergreen, tropical moist forest. Study areas range in size from 1 to 200 ha, and include isolated patches and areas within undisturbed forest. Three 1000 ha areas within undisturbed forest were also studied. The isolated reserves are separated from adjacent forest by corridors ranging between 100 and 700 m long (Bierregaard *et al.* 1992).

Powell and Powell (1987) sampled 15 species of euglossine bees in continuous forest, in the isolated reserves (1, 10 and 100 ha) and in the 100 m clearing that separated the 10 ha isolate from the adjacent forest. Euglossine bees are important pollinators of species in as many as 30 plant families; many orchid species are only pollinated by one particular bee species. The Powells found declines in visitation rates by male bees in all forest isolates. Male bees of four species adapted to deep forest conditions did not cross the 100 m clearing that separated the reserve from continuous forest. Absence of these bees may be expected to decrease pollination rates in some plant species, and this study indicates that a mosaic of forest fragments surrounded by treeless pastures will not support populations of some of these bee species.

As forest was felled around a reserve, birds found sanctuary in the remnant patch of forest. After isolation, capture rates increased markedly in the newly isolated fragments. This indicated both increased activity of the birds in the small reserve as well as increased bird densities

(Bierregaard and Lovejoy 1988, 1989). These elevated numbers, which were inversely correlated with fragment size, persisted for approximately 200 days, after which bird numbers in the reserves fell sharply to below pre-isolation levels. The rate and extent of this collapse in the bird populations was greater in smaller reserves than in the larger ones. Forest fragmentation effects on bird populations were significantly reduced if a forest corridor some 100–300 m wide, connecting the fragment to undisturbed forest, was retained.

8.19.5 Arguments for rain forest conservation

Efforts are being made (and with some success) to redress perceptions of the balance between the value of the timber that can be harvested from a forest and the value of leaving the forest in tact. Various programmes (debt-for-nature swaps; integrated conservation and resource utilisation schemes) have been instituted in some countries, but they need to be expanded to ensure that forest species are conserved in all parts of the world.

It has been argued that rain-forest species have a right to exist regardless of whether they are useful to humans. Ethical arguments also apply to the conservation of the human cultures that have developed within rain-forest systems. Strong,

pragmatic reasons also exist. Myers (1988) has pointed out the numerous economic and human health benefits from foods and pharmaceuticals that have accrued from plants and animals indigenous to rain forests. Rain-forest destruction is likely to have a major impact on global climate and this could result in a major upheaval in the structure and distribution of human societies (see section 14.4).

Another argument for conserving rain forests has been based on the low potential of these areas for sustainable agriculture owing to the poor nutrient status of rain-forest soils. Slash-and-burn agriculture results in a rapid loss of nutrients from the soil (Jordan 1986). While these losses may be compensated by inputs from decomposition of the former vegetation and ash, the nutrients, particularly phosphorus, may not be readily available to the crops planted. Native pioneer species invading a former crop field do not seem to suffer from the same inability to obtain nutrients, and readily develop on abandoned sites. Whether a forest succession will lead to producing a forest similar to that existing prior to deforestation has not been established, but such a process may take 100 years or more (Saldarriaga 1986).

8.20 | Chapter summary

1 Tropical rain forests are the most species-rich terrestrial environments. Large areas of rain forest are found in the Amazon basin, Indo-Malaysia, Indonesia, Melanesia and the Zaïre Basin. They occur in the wet tropics where there is no, or only minimal, seasonal water shortage. Mean monthly temperatures do not fall much below 25 °C and rarely exceed 35 °C. Radiation levels are high, the air always humid and seasonal temperature variations are usually less than diurnal variations which may be as much as 10 °C. Plants growing in the shade beneath the canopy live in a more equable micro-climate.

2. Tropical rain forests may be stratified with two or three tree layers, a shrub layer and a herb layer. The tallest trees (45–50 m high) in the rain forest are known as emergents. The middle-storey trees form a continuous canopy 25–35 m above the ground. Tree

crowns in this layer are smaller and more rounded. The trees in the bottom layer form a dense, closely packed layer with variously shaped crowns. Rain-forest trees may be festooned with epiphytes and lianas. Plants provide a complex living framework of habitats for a phenomenal variety of animals.

3. Phenology is the study of leaf, flower and fruit production and other events which seem to be related to climate. Flowering, fruiting, leaf fall and renewal appear to occur throughout the year in evergreen tropical forest trees. Some tropical forest trees are deciduous, shedding leaves well before bud break. In other species, leaf fall occurs at about the same time as bud break (leaf exchangers). Other species are evergreen, with leaf fall occurring after bud break. Some species, including many dipterocarps, flower and fruit intermittently (not every year) and gregariously (mast fruit-

ing). A few rain-forest trees are monocarpic, flowering once and dying soon after the fruit has ripened.

4. Plants can be classified with respect to their growth form. Raunkiaer's classification is based on the position, relative to the ground, of the perennating organs. The spectrum of growth forms within a particular flora is related to climate.

5. Through evolutionary convergence, organisms living under similar environmental conditions have solved common problems through similar adaptations, despite different historical origins. Rain-forest plants and animals have developed, through evolution and co-evolution, intricate offensive and defensive relationships. Other plant–animal interactions are mutualistic.

6. Many soils supporting tropical rain forests are highly leached, acidic and nutrient-poor, but there is considerable variation both globally and locally. The warm temperatures and copious rainfall promote soil weathering, leaching and rapid litter decomposition.

7. Species diversity refers to the variety of species and can be assessed as: α-diversity, the diversity of species within a habitat or community; β-diversity, the rate of change of species along a gradient from one habitat to another; and γ-diversity, the richness of species in a range of communities in a location or from one location to another on a geographical scale.

8. Species richness in tropical forests generally decreases with increasing altitude, and on a global basis, species diversity decreases with increasing latitude. Tropical communities may be more diverse than temperate communities because they are older and have had more time to accumulate species. Other theories suggest that high diversity in the tropics is due to climatic stability, resource availability (particularly energy), and a moderate intensity and frequency of disturbance.

9. Gaps are created in the forest canopy through the death of a tree and through events such as landslides and hurricanes. Pioneer species colonise big canopy gaps. These species require high light intensities for germination, are fast growing and comparatively short-lived. Climax species usually germinate beneath the canopy and their seedlings are shade tolerant. As the pioneer species die, the small gaps created are filled by climax species.

10. Some rain forests are dominated by just one species. The dominant trees may have an advantage over competitors through possession of an ectomycorrhizal association (EM). Most tropical tree species in the Neotropics and Africa have a vesicular–arbuscular mycorrhizal association (VAM). Advantages of an EM association include greater host specificity, greater protection to the host tree from natural enemies and an enhanced ability to secure nutrients in both organic and inorganic form.

11. Tropical forests are being destroyed through logging activities and to make way for agriculture. Destruction of these diverse systems is having a profound influence on the rate at which species are lost through extinction. Although the forests cover only 7% of the land surface of the earth they contain at least half the world's species.

12. Forest fragmentation not only leaves the organisms that remain within them a smaller habitat, but also exposes them to stressful environmental conditions, particularly at the forest edges, that differ from those deeper within the forest. Edge effects include: (1) abiotic effects (changes in environmental conditions); (2) direct biological effects (changes in the abundance and distribution of species); and (3) indirect biological effects (changes in species interactions such as predation, brood parasitism, competition, herbivory, pollination and seed dispersal).

13. Keystone species have a disproportionate effect on the persistence of other species. Conservation agencies have, in the past, concentrated efforts on species that attract strong public sentiment (flagship species). Today, efforts to conserve biodiversity are focused more on habitat protection.

14. Reasons for conserving rain forests include the goods and services that these systems provide, the poor agriculture potential of many rain-forest soils and ethical and aesthetic considerations.

Chapter 9

Mountains, zonation and community gradients

Tropical mountains experience 'summer every day and winter every night'.

(Hedberg 1964)

9.1 | Tropical mountains

Organisms living on high mountains anywhere in the world experience environmental conditions peculiar to high altitudes. Decreased atmospheric pressure, lower temperatures, lower oxygen tensions, greater exposure to wind and to ultraviolet light all affect the plants and animals inhabiting high-altitude areas. The thin atmosphere at high elevations facilitates rapid dissipation of heat, and this leads to large disparities in temperatures between sun and shade environments and between night and day temperatures. This last feature is particularly true of mountains in the tropics which experience large temperature differentials between night and day giving rise to the quote at the start of this chapter.

Environmental conditions on mountains change with altitude. In general, temperature falls with increasing altitude and the lapse rate is defined as the fall in temperature per 100 m increase in altitude. The **lapse rate** varies with cloudiness, rainfall, humidity and wind speed and direction. On tropical mountains, environmental factors vary little seasonally, and wide diurnal temperature range accommodates a vegetation that grows slowly and shows little sign of seasonality in reproductive activity. These environmental trends are reflected in changes in the structure and species composition of the vegetation. The lowland tropical flora is replaced by a montane flora in which some of the genera and even species are also found in temperate regions. On some tropical mountains, distinct zones can be detected, the most obvious being the tree-line which occurs between 3000 and 3900 m. Other changes in plant and animal communities are, like the environmental conditions, more gradual. These features contrast markedly with the life histories of organisms that live on mountains in the temperate regions where climate is distinctly seasonal and diurnal variations are more muted (Figure 9.1).

9.2 | Zonation on tropical mountains

The basic pattern of vegetation zonation on tropical mountains differs from that found on mountains in temperate regions. Tropical mountains lack the boreal coniferous forests and the deciduous, broad-leaved forests found on temperate mountains, instead evergreen broad-leaved forests or tropical coniferous forests are found. On ascending a mountain in the tropics, lowland rain forest is replaced first by lower montane forest and then by upper montane forest. Trees in upper montane forests are shorter with a distinctive crooked structure and are usually covered in mosses, ferns and other epiphytes, giving rise to the name moss forest. Leaf size on trees declines with increasing altitude. Above the forests, grasslands predominate in the tropical-alpine zone. On many tropical mountains there is a distinct belt where low clouds persist and this has an important influence on the vegetation.

Montane soils also change with altitude. On steep slopes, soils tend to be skeletal, shallow and

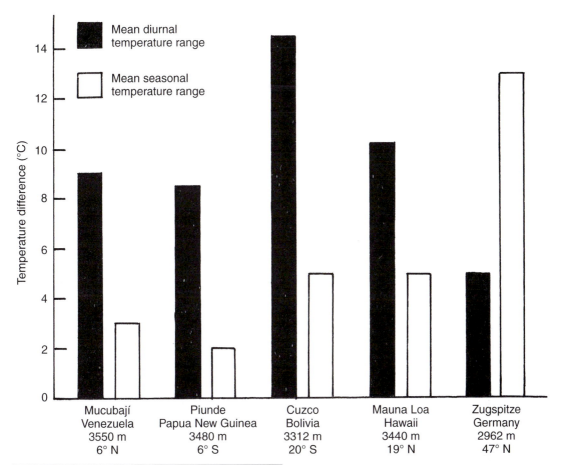

Figure 9.1 Mean diurnal and seasonal temperature ranges for four tropical and one temperate mountain. Note the large diurnal range on the tropical mountains and the large seasonal range recorded on Zugspitze, Germany (47° N) (after Rundel 1994).

rocky. Low temperatures and high soil moisture inhibit microbial decomposition and therefore organic matter content is high and peat accumulates in valleys and depressions.

9.3 | Vegetation zonation on Mount Wilhelm, Papua New Guinea

The mountains in New Guinea provide good examples of altitude zonation since many of them rise precipitously from sea level to over 4000 m (Figure 9.2). Two peaks in Irian Jaya have glaciers

and permanent snowfields and from the summit of these high, icy mountains it is possible to look out over the steamy, lowland rain forest to the muddy waters of the Arafura Sea. Above the altitude to which human cultivation extends, the mountains are covered in forest to the treeline, above which alpine grasslands occur. Traces of Pleistocene glaciation are well preserved on mountains extending above 3550 m, the altitude of the Pleistocene snowline. Glaciers in Papua New Guinea receded 12 000 years ago and by about 9000 years ago all mountains on this side of the island were ice free. The glaciers in Irian Jaya are currently in recession, a probable symptom of global warming (see Box 9.1).

A research station was established on Mount Wilhelm, the highest mountain in Papua New Guinea, in 1965 and the ecology of this area is comparatively well known. Rainfall on Mount Wilhelm has a single maximum during the

Figure 9.2 Mount Wilhelm, Papua New Guinea showing vegetation zonation. A few remnants of lower-montane forest can be seen near the Kegsugl airstrip, but most has been cleared for gardens. Gardening occurs up to 2700 m, and above this elevation undisturbed mid- and upper-montane forest is shown. The treeline is at around 3900 m, above which the vegetation is montane grassland (Photo: Office of Environment and Conservation, Papua New Guinea).

summer, but, even during the driest winter months, more than 70 mm of rain has been recorded. Snow may fall on the highest peaks at any time of the year but rarely persists through a day. Although this mountain has one of the wettest high-altitude climates in the tropics, short periods of water deficit may occur; over 20 consecutive dry days have been recorded (Sarmiento 1986). During the wet season, most days are cloudy with steady rain and thick fog (Figure 9.3). Radiant energy input may be as low as 13% of total possible solar radiation. During the dry season, nights and mornings have clear skies and cloud accumulation may occur in the afternoon leading to light rain. On clear days, up to 95% of total possible radiation may reach the ground. Mean

minimum temperatures on Mount Wilhelm are 3–4 °C warmer than those recorded at similar altitudes on mountains in the Andes, East Africa and Hawaii. The continental position of mountains in the Andes and East Africa may explain the cooler temperatures recorded there, but this explanation can not be used for mountains on the Hawaiian Islands. Heavy cloud cover and high humidity may also be important in keeping minimum temperatures elevated on Mount Wilhelm, but limited climatic data preclude a definitive explanation (Rundel 1994).

The montane zone on Mount Wilhelm (4509 m), is geologically young and formed by uplift associated with the northern movement of the Australian plate, following the break-up of Gondwana (see section 1.3.1). Plant communities on the mountain have been divided into several distinctive forest types by Johns (1982) from which this account is taken (Table 9.1, Figure 9.4). Mixed broadleaf forests occur throughout the whole range but vary considerably in species composition. The mixed lower-montane forests differ markedly from the lowland rain forests. The

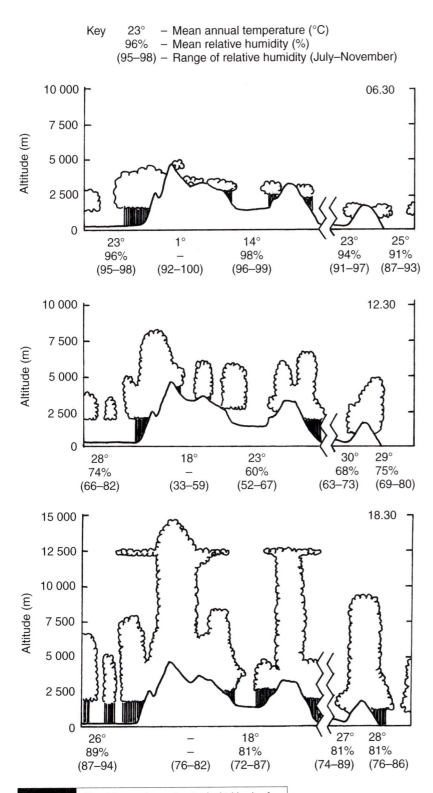

Key
23° – Mean annual temperature (°C)
96% – Mean relative humidity (%)
(95–98) – Range of relative humidity (July–November)

Figure 9.3 The daily weather regime in the highlands of Papua New Guinea showing an increase in cloud cover during a typical day at 06.30, 12.30 and 18.30 (after Brookfield 1964).

Zone	Formation type	Major genera
Table 9.1 Major tree genera of the lower-, mid- and upper-montane forests on Mount Wilhelm, Papua New Guinea		
Sub-alpine zone 3200 m	Upper montane	*Dacrycarpus, Olearia, Rhododendron, Schefflera, Pittosporum, Elaeocarpus, Amaracarpus*
Montane zone 2700–3000 m	Mid montane	*Nothofagus, Dryadodaphne, Podocarpus, Phyllocladus, Dacrydium, Falcatifolium, Elaeocarpus*
Lower montane zone 1500–2000 m	Lower montane	*Elmerrillia, Castanopsis, Lithocarpus, Araucaria, Agathis, Podocarpus, Elaeocarpus, Syzygium, Gnetum*
Lowland zone 300–1000 m	Lowland tropical rain forest	

Source: Johns 1982.

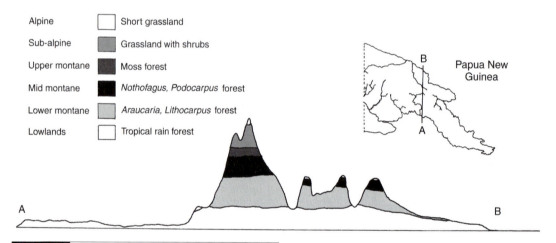

Figure 9.4 North–South cross-section of Papua New Guinea through Mount Wilhelm, showing the gross altitudinal zonation of the major vegetation types. Note that vegetation zones with altitude vary quite significantly between sites depending on local topography and climate. In some areas on the same mountain, zones may be entirely absent (after Johns 1982 with kind permission from Kluwer Academic Publishers).

frequency of palms, lianas and trees with buttress roots is much reduced and tree ferns and mosses are uncommon. The canopy of the forest, 20–25 m high, is composed of broadleaf species and species composition varies markedly throughout this zone.

At altitudes above 600 m, ridge-top forests are dominated by *Castanopsis* and species of oaks in the genus *Lithocarpus*. The mixed **mid-montane** forests are characterised by more conifers (*Podocarpus, Dacrycarpus* and *Papuacedrus*) than the lower-montane forests. *Nothofagus*-dominated forests are common throughout this zone. The **upper-montane forests** (also called mossy forests, montane cloud forests and cloud forests) on Mount Wilhelm are dominated by *Elaeocarpus azaleifolius* and *Podocarpus pilgeri*. This forest, extending up to 3300 m, is richer in species than the **sub-alpine forest** at higher altitudes (Figure 9.5). Most trees are crooked and stunted in growth; the understorey is dense and composed mainly of tree saplings. The forest floor is covered with tangled tree roots, fallen trunks and other forest debris.

The sub-alpine zone comprises a mosaic of forest, grassland and bogs and fens. The forest in this zone has a closed canopy at about 10 m with numerous emergents to 15 m in height. Many of

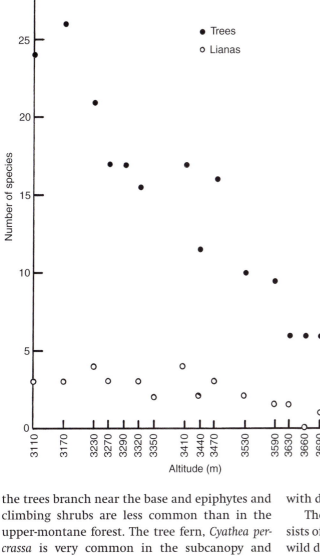

Figure 9.5 Relationship between altitude and number of tree and liana species on Mount Wilhelm, Papua New Guinea (after Wade and McVean 1969 with kind permission from the Research School of Pacific and Asian Studies, Australian National University).

the trees branch near the base and epiphytes and climbing shrubs are less common than in the upper-montane forest. The tree fern, *Cyathea percrassa* is very common in the subcanopy and bryophytes can completely cover the ground (Figure 9.6). At higher altitudes, up to the forest limits, the forest is dominated by Ericaceae (*Rhododendron* and *Dimorphanthera*). The epiphytic fern *Hymenophyllum* is common, lianas are rare and dense shrub and fern thickets dominated by *Gleichenia* are widespread. The uppermost, **alpine zone**, on Mount Wilhelm is dominated by grasslands with scattered shrubs and small trees to 4100 m. Above this altitude, short, alpine grassland (*Festuca papuana* and *Poa callosa*) is associated

with dwarf shrubs such as *Leucopogon suaveolens*.

The vertebrate fauna on Mount Wilhelm consists of several marsupials, rodents, an introduced wild dog, some frogs and a wide selection of birds dominated by honeycreepers. The ring-tailed possum (*Pseudocheirus cupreus*) and the pygmy possum (*Cercartetus caudatus*) are common in the sub-alpine forests and their skeletons have been found as high as 3960 m (Wade and McVean 1969). Other marsupials include the cuscus (*Phalanger vestitus*), the sugar glider (*Petaurus breviceps*) and the tree-kangaroo (*Dendrolagus* sp.). Wade and McVean (1969) reported seeing the bandicoot (*Peroryctes longicauda*) frequently during the daytime in the sub-alpine grasslands where it

Figure 9.6 Tree ferns (*Cyathea percrassa*) in a montane grassland on Mount Wilhelm, Papua New Guinea. Note the margin of the upper-montane forest in the background (Photo: Office of Environment and Conservation, Papua New Guinea).

forms a dense network of runs between grass tussocks. Wild dogs (*Canis* sp.) roam in small packs and feed on bandicoots, rats and possums. They establish lairs in rocky outcrops near the subalpine forests.

About 20 species of birds are common residents (seasonal or permanent) on the mountain above 3350 m. Ten of these species are frugivorous or nectar-feeders. Nectar-eating birds are known to be attracted by the colour red, and species of *Rhododendron*, *Dimorphanthera* and *Vaccinium* produce red flowers with long floral tubes, which suggests that these plants are bird-pollinated. All eight species of *Rhododendron* recorded by Wade and McVean (1969) found growing above 3000 m had red flowers, whereas below this altitude white or pale-pink flowers predominated. Wade and McVean (1969) suggested that the lower-altitude species are moth-pollinated. We know very little about the invertebrates on Mount Wilhelm and,

indeed, this ignorance applies to most tropical mountains.

Fire affects most tropical mountain communities and recovery is slow in these high-elevation forests. Corlett (1987) studied the process of vegetation recovery following fires by reconstructing the recent vegetation history on Mount Wilhelm between 3300 m to the treeline at 3900–4000 m from analysis of pollen and charcoal in short peat cores. Two volcanic tephra layers in the cores were dated at 300 and 1200 years old. The pollen record in the 1200-year-old layer showed that non-forest vegetation was confined to waterlogged areas and that human impact was negligible. Local forest clearance probably started 700 years ago, but a major clearance episode was recorded around the 300-year-old tephra fall. Fires, lit by people, were almost certainly the cause of this forest destruction. Corlett (1987) coupled this information with a comparison of the vegetation recorded in photographs taken 20 years previously with the vegetation present at the time of his study to produce the successional sequence shown in Figure 9.7.

While a single fire killed shrubs down to the ground and allowed invasion by grasses, recovery occurred within about 20 years in the absence of further fires. As invasion of the grassland by shrubs occurred through resprouting and seed germination rather than through an expansion of the forest margin, recovery was patchy. With repeated burning, the grasslands are maintained with the species composition dependent on fire frequency. Fire control leads to the development of secondary forest (see section 8.14.2).

Janzen (1973) recorded very low plant regeneration rates following an intense fire on the steep southern slope of Cerro Asuncion (3300 m) in Costa Rica. Before the fire, shrubs formed a dense and undulating closed canopy ranging from 1–3 m in height. Three years after the fire there were still numerous patches of bare ground covered in cinders and burned wood. The dead stems of many plants remained standing and branches lying on the ground were still intact. The low rates of decomposition were linked to the low temperatures prevailing and to the absence of the larger decomposer organisms such as ants, ter-

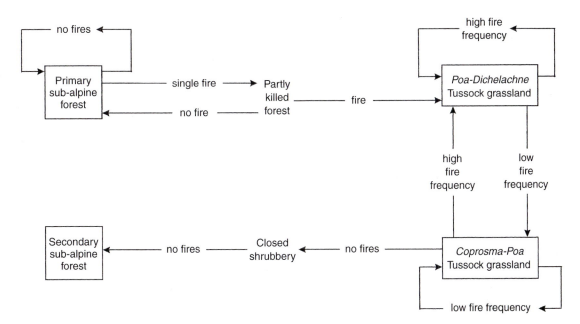

Figure 9.7 Probable successional sequence of vegetation changes following fire on Mount Wilhelm, Papua New Guinea (after Corlett 1987; Copyrighted 1987 by the Association for Tropical Biology, P. O Box 1897, Lawrence, KS 66044-8897. Reprinted by permission).

mites and wood-boring beetles (see chapter 10). The low rates of plant regeneration mean that animal community biomass is constrained.

9.4 | Altitude zonation in Venezuela

Venezuela lies between the equator and 12° N and the vegetation can be zoned both in terms of distance from the coast and altitude. The northern part of the country is exposed to strong trade winds between November and March and these winds bring rain to highland areas. The lowlands have a distinct dry season, lasting 5 months. The annual rainfall rises from 150 mm on the coastal islands in the north to more than 3500 mm in the south. In the mountainous regions, rainfall increases up to cloud level. Rainfall, at altitudes above the cloud level, decreases. Temperature declines by approximately 0.5 °C per 100 m increase in altitude. As air masses rise up the mountains, condensation occurs owing to cooling, clouds develop and rain falls. In this region, cloud or mist forests dominate. The trees in these forests are heavily festooned in epiphytes: mosses, ferns, bromeliads and other plants. The inner valleys in the Andes mountains are in a rain shadow and are very dry.

Temperatures at high altitudes (3600 m) on the mountains in Venezuela fluctuate diurnally from 10 °C during the day to below freezing at night. The plants that survive in this zone are thus exposed to diurnal freezing and thawing. The decrease in soil temperatures with altitude causes the lateral spread of roots of the plants. Consequently, the vegetation at these altitudes becomes sparse and eventually, about 100 m below the snowline, the ground is devoid of plants.

Micro-climates can result in a breakdown in zonation patterns. At an altitude of approximately 4200 m in the Venezuelan Andes where the mean annual temperature is only 2 °C, small stands of the tree *Polylepis sericea* grow. These stands develop on east- or west-facing talus (scree) slopes consisting of large boulders. These trees have roots extending to a depth of 1.5 m. During the day, radiation warms up the air nearest the ground and the cold air between the boulders flows out at the lower end of the talus and warmer air is drawn in between the boulders at the upper end of the talus.

Box 9.1 | Meltdown: tropical glaciers and global warming

A number of mountains in the tropics are high enough for glaciers to form on them. Studies of three glaciers on Indonesian Mount Jaya have shown that the glaciers are retreating. The extent of three glaciers (Meren, Northwall firn and Carstensz) was first recorded in 1936. Scientists have used aerial photographs and maps to show that the glaciers have shrunk by some 16 km^2 and in 1995 only 3 km^2 remain. The rate at which the glaciers are receding also seems to have accelerated from around 30 m per year in 1936 to 45 m per year in 1995. At this rate the Meren glacier may soon disappear entirely (Goss 1995).

On Mount Kenya a similarly dramatic retreat of glaciers has been recorded. During the 88 years between 1899 and 1987, the overall loss of glacial area amounted to about 75% of the 1899 area, an annual loss rate of 0.8% per year. From 1963 to 1987, an area reduction of almost 40% was observed at the considerably more rapid rate of 1.6% per year (Hastenrath and Kruss 1992).

Global warming is the most likely cause. This dramatic indication of climate change has significant implications for the altitude zonation described above. As the climate warms, it is likely that human activity will extend to higher altitudes and the elevation of the treeline may increase. Efforts to conserve biological diversity on tropical mountains will need to consider the effects of this global warming trend. Furthermore, warmer conditions in highland areas may result in the spread of malaria-carrying mosquitoes. This debilitating disease may then infect people lacking the immunity found in people living in coastal areas where the disease is currently endemic. Clearly, global warming will have profound and far-reaching effects (see section 14.4).

9.5 | Plant and animal ecophysiology: examples from Mount Kenya

The mountains in East Africa form an archipelago of isolated islands and this isolation has led to a high degree of endemism in plants found growing near their summits (see chapter 12). These Afro-alpine ecosystems are renowned for their unusual plant growth forms, and the presence of tree-like species far above the tree-line demonstrates the success of these unusual plants. Some of the most striking plants are the giant rosette plants in the genera *Lobelia* and *Senecio* (Figure 9.8).

Mount Kenya is an isolated extinct strato-volcano located on the equator with the summit at 5195 m. The mountain is surrounded by a dry plateau and provides a strong contrast with the very wet slopes of Mount Wilhelm. Like many tropical mountains, rainfall varies with altitude and slope aspect. South-east slopes are wetter than those facing north-west. Mean annual rainfall increases to a maximum of 2500 mm within the altitude range of 2200–3200 m. Above 3200 m, rainfall declines and the summit receives around 850 mm each year. North-west slopes only receive about half as much rainfall. Above 4200 m, a combination of low rainfall and increased frost frequencies result in extensive bare areas (alpine deserts). The difference in rainfall is reflected in the vegetation zones on Mount Kenya. Note how the montane forest extends to lower altitudes on the south-east slopes where rainfall is higher (Figure 9.9).

Relative humidity on Mount Kenya fluctuates with temperature and cloud cover. In bright sunlight, humidity was as low as 20% (measured 26 cm above the ground) but values increased to between 58–71% as cloud cover increased (Coe

Figure 9.8 *Senecio keniodendron* on Mount Kenya (Photo: David W. Breed, Oxford Scientific Films).

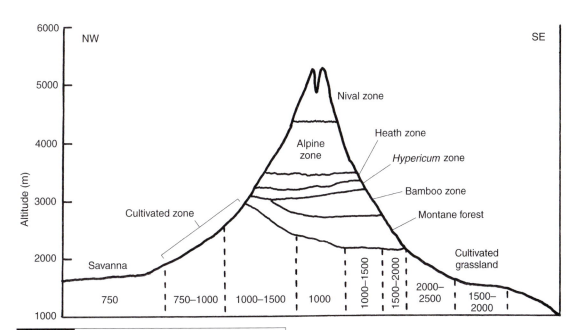

Figure 9.9 Vegetation zones on Mount Kenya. Rainfall (in mm) over the north-west and south-east slopes are indicated. Note the higher rainfall on the south-eastern slopes and the corresponding lower altitude limit of motane forest on these slopes (after Thompson 1966; with kind permission from the Royal Meteorological Society).

1969). Changes in humidity can be rapid. The thinner atmosphere at higher altitudes results in less heating of the air from solar radiation. The other effect of this is more intense insolation at ground level, and particularly the high intensity of ultraviolet light. Many tropical mountain plants have leathery, hairy or heavily pigmented leaves to protect them from UV tissue damage. *Senecio keniodendron*, for example, has large woolly leaves which open during the day to reflect radiation, whilst at night they close, insulating the growing shoot and preventing the plant from freezing. On tropical mountains, plants have to be adapted to withstand freezing conditions at night and intense radiation during the day.

9.5.1 Cold tolerance in Afro-alpine plants

Plants growing on these mountains have to be tolerant to frost and be able to delay cooling through efficient insulation. Furthermore, the plants have to be able to survive rapid thawing of frozen organs as the temperature rises rapidly after sunrise. One of the major problems faced by plants living in environments where temperatures fall below freezing is how to maintain water flow through the stem. Once a leaf thaws, it begins to transpire and exert a pull on the water column in the stem tissues. If the water in the stem tissues or the soil is still frozen, air bubbles may form within the water-conducting tissues and lead to the collapse of the water transport system (Beck 1994). One solution to this problem is to use stored water until water flow is restored, another is to delay the heating of leaves following sunrise.

Plants withstand cold climates through two strategies: **freezing avoidance** and **freezing tolerance**. Freezing avoidance can be achieved through **insulation** of plant organs and reducing heat loss from radiation. Leaf and inflorescence buds are susceptible to freezing damage and, since growth occurs throughout the year, tropical alpine plants do not produce resting buds. In *Senecio keniodendron*, around 80 young leaves are tightly appressed around the central bud. At maturity, they separate from the cone, become green and begin to photosynthesise. At night or during cold weather, the leaves fold up to form a 'night-bud' around the central cone and so insulate the developing leaves

and the central bud (Beck 1994). It has been shown that if the adult leaves are removed or immobilised to prevent the formation of the night-bud, the young, unprotected leaves wilt and die (Smith 1974). The damage may have been done through rapid thawing rather than by freezing, since the leaves did not exhibit necroses typical of freezing damage. The growth form of tussock grasses may have evolved to insulate the younger tissues in the centre of the tussock.

Freezing can also be avoided through accumulation, within the plant, of matter with a high **heat capacity** and high **heat of fusion** (see Box 2.1). *Lobelia keniensis* has a hollow stalk which contains up to 5 litres of a mucilaginous fluid and it has been suggested that this reservoir provides protection against freezing (an antifreeze) or drought (Hedberg 1964; Coe 1967). Krog *et al.* (1979) suggested that a similar fluid found in *Lobelia telekii* is a nucleating agent that prevents supercooling. Young and Robe (1986) demonstrated that the reservoir in *L. keniensis* prevents freezing of the leaf bud (with its sensitive meristem) and that the mucilaginous substance is neither an antifreeze nor a nucleating agent. This substance is a pectin that probably protects the reservoir from evaporating in the dry atmosphere on Mount Kenya.

The outer leaves of Afro-alpine plants do freeze on particularly cold nights and therefore these leaves must have mechanisms that prevent or reduce freezing damage. Freezing can damage cells through: (1) water expansion during ice formation and subsequent crystal growth causing tissue disruption; (2) shrinkage of cells and the damage caused by water loss through ice formation; and (3) the increased concentration of solutes leading to osmotic shock. Uncharged organic compounds, such as carbohydrates and amino acids, through their capacity to form hydrogen bonds with membrane components, can provide membranes with some protection from freezing. *Lobelia* spp. growing in temperatures below freezing have been shown to accumulate photosynthate as sucrose – up to 38% of the leaf's dry weight – and it is believed that this acts as a **cryoprotectant** (antifreeze) in Afro-alpine plants. When these plants are grown under non-

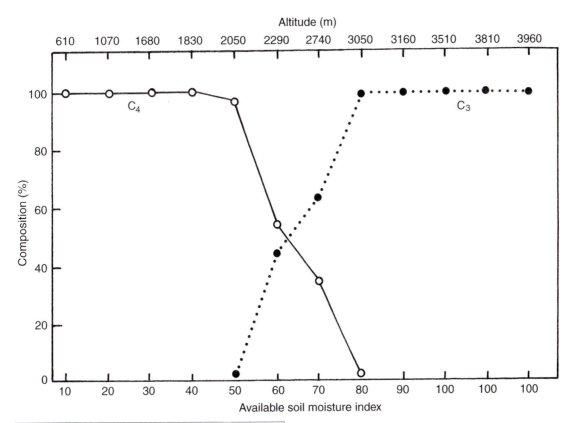

Figure 9.10 Percentage of grass species which have C_3 or C_4 photosynthetic strategies along an altitudinal transect in Kenya (after Tieszen et al. 1979 with kind permission from Springer-Verlag).

freezing conditions, photosynthate accumulates as starch, which supports the contention that the sucrose is being used as a cryoprotectant.

Low temperature is not the only factor that may limit plant growth on high mountains. African montane soils are often thin and, owing to the repeated thawing and cooling, **solifluction** is an added stress. On freezing nights, ice crystals form in saturated soils and the soil is pushed up by the expanding ice crystals. The crystals melt the next morning and the soil drops back. This repetitive, diurnal, churning of the soil (solifluction) prevents seedling establishment and can create alpine deserts even in areas where plants could otherwise grow (Hedberg 1964). Higher plants tend to grow around boulders which provide a more stable soil environment.

High-altitude zones are frequently very dry areas with both low rainfall and a very dry atmosphere and, therefore, humidity may limit plant growth more than frost and low temperatures. The alpine desert on Mount Kilimanjaro extends to lower altitudes on the drier western side than it does on the wetter south-eastern slopes (Beck et al. 1983). Changes in environmental conditions with increasing altitude are also reflected in the photosynthetic strategy plants use to fix carbon.

9.5.2 Zonation of C_3 and C_4 grasses in Kenya and the Hawaiian Islands

More than 500 species of grasses (Family: Poaceae) are found in Kenya. Tieszen et al. (1979) sampled along a transect from the arid, Kenyan lowlands to the top of Mount Kenya. A floristic analysis showed that the low-altitude grasslands were dominated by C_4 grasses, whereas at higher altitudes nearly all the grasses were of the C_3 photosynthetic type (see section 3.7). In the open grasslands, there were no C_3 species below 2000 m and no C_4 species above 3000 m (Figure 9.10).

Young and Young (1983) analysed the area of overlap and found that C_4 plants were found in drier micro-sites and C_3 plants in moister sites.

Rundel (1980) showed a similar distribution of grasses with altitude on the Hawaiian Islands. C_4 grasses dominated both species composition and coverage up to 1000 m but C_3 species were dominant at altitudes above 1400 m. The elevational transition was particularly marked by the degree of coverage. Virtually 100% of the grass cover up to 1000 m was provided by C_4 species with a transition to over 95% dominance by C_3 plants occurring between 1000 and 1400 m. This transition zone corresponds with a low monthly mean minimum temperature of approximately 9 °C and a mean maximum temperature for the warmest month of about 21 °C. The sharp transition between C_4 and C_3 dominance suggests that physiological factors affecting the competitive ability of each photosynthetic strategy are important. Rundel (1980) concluded that the distribution of C_3 and C_4 grasses along environmental gradients resulted from a complex interaction of temperature, precipitation and shade and that his study supported that by Tieszen *et al.* (1979) for Kenya.

Primary production (see section 3.10) of grasses in the tropical alpine zone has not been well studied. The environmental conditions, frosts at night, high insolation in the morning and cloud cover in the afternoon, are not conducive to stimulating high production. However, conditions for growth occur throughout the year, which distinguishes this environment from that found in arctic–alpine regions where plants are exposed to continuously cold conditions during the harsh winter followed by a short summer growing season. On tropical mountains, plant biomass tends to be concentrated in the leaves and not the roots. This differs from perennial arctic–alpine plants which accumulate biomass below-ground and use the stored resources to initiate growth in the spring (see section 3.2.1). Plants on tropical mountains face a harsh, fluctuating environment every day and night and there is, therefore, little point in accumulating material below-ground. Hnatiuk (1994) has also suggested that the perpetually cool soil on tropical mountains restricts root development. However, the

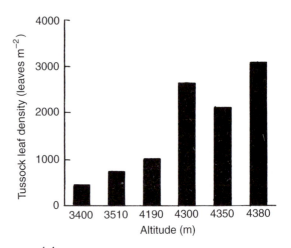

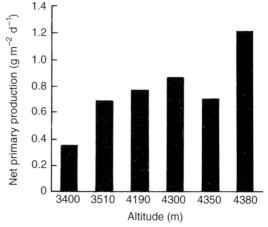

Figure 9.11 (a) Density and (b) productivity of tussock grassland growing on Mount Wilhelm, Papua New Guinea against altitude. The dominant species, *Deschampsia klossii*, is probably a cool-adapted species attempting to invade lower-altitude, warmer sites (after Hnatiuk 1994).

vegetation on the dry side of Mount Kenya includes numerous geophytes, and this may be due to seasonality in rainfall (G. Hope personal communication).

Figure 9.11 shows that leaf density and productivity of tussock grassland growing on Mount Wilhelm increases with altitude. This suggests that the dominant species, *Deschampsia klossii*, is a cool-adapted species attempting to invade lower-altitude, warmer sites. Mean leaf length of this species declines with altitude. Leaf length is controlled by cell length, not by the number of cells, and, as mean temperatures decline, so does cell elongation (Hnatiuk 1994).

Other factors apart from climate affect the vegetation on Mount Kenya. Mulkey *et al.* (1984) noted that predation by elephants on *Senecio keniodendron* was altering the alpine plant community at some sites on Mount Kenya. Elephants were splitting open the trunks and feeding on the central pith, causing extensive damage at some sites, particularly at the lower elevational limit of *Senecio*. The pith of this plant is richer in protein than the leaves and therefore is a good source of protein for elephants. The pith might also provide a supply of mineral nutrients. Mulkey *et al.* (1984) concluded that it is unlikely that *Senecio keniodendron* was in danger of extinction because it grows at elevations above 4100 m where elephants do not feed. However, it is possible that *Senecio* genotypes adapted to lower elevations may be lost in valleys subject to heavy feeding pressure by elephants.

Bamboo (*Arundinaria alpina*) occurs in mono-dominant stands on the wet lower slopes of Mount Kenya and is replaced by *Podocarpus latifolius* in drier areas (Young 1996). Bamboo plants flower synchronously and die back, allowing *Podocarpus* and other species to develop. Reinvasion by bamboo may occur, and the dynamics of this vegetation community may be more related to natural history than to climate.

9.5.3 Micro-climates and animal life

Atmospheric pressure falls with increasing altitude and the partial pressure of oxygen declines by about half every 5500 m rise in altitude. Although the proportion of oxygen in the air remains at around 21%, the total amount available for uptake is less. This low oxygen availability results in a suite of symptoms in humans (headache, nausea and breathing difficulties) known as **mountain** or **altitude sickness**. The initial response to counter this oxygen shortage in humans is an increase in heart and respiration rates. However, after spending a few days at altitude, the number of red blood cells increases and this is followed by an increase in capillary density supplying key organs. As these slower changes take place, heart and respiratory rates decline. This process of physiological response to environmental change is known as **acclimation**. On Mount Kenya, vertebrate life is probably not

limited by oxygen availability, and zebra herds can be seen at over 4300 m (Coe 1969). Food supply and temperature are probably more significant in limiting vertebrate altitude range.

In preceding sections we have described features of **macro-climate** and how it changes with altitude. However, of more significance to animals inhabiting tropical mountains is the **micro-climate** that surrounds the space in which they live. Some small mammals survive in the Afro-alpine zone by constructing burrows. The burrows do not have to be very deep as the nightly frost only penetrates a few centimetres into the soil. The groove-toothed rat (*Otomys orestes*) burrows in soft earth or through the vegetation mats below *Festuca* tussocks. Above 4000 m where the ground is rocky, these rodents burrow into the leaf girdles of *Senecio keniodendron*. The temperature in all these constructed micro-habitats remains above freezing even though the outside air temperature may be as low as $-10\,^{\circ}\text{C}$. Other rodents (*Lophuromys aquilus, Dendromus insignis*) do not appear to make their own burrows but utilise those dug by groove-toothed rats (Coe 1969).

A few species of shrew have been recorded from the Afro-alpine zone and it is surprising that these small mammals survive at such high altitudes (Coe 1969). Their small body size makes them susceptible to low temperatures, and a shrew caught in a live trap will not survive freezing temperatures for much more than an hour. These animals may not spend long foraging outside their burrows, since the ready availability of litter and soil arthropods make food collecting comparatively easy. Giant molerats (*Tachyoryctes rex*) construct prodigious mounds up to 6 m across with burrows extending 50 m from the mound and over 1 m deep. These animals use a chamber as a latrine where they defecate, urinate and store decaying vegetable matter. The heat generated is quite considerable and the rats build grass nests in adjacent chambers.

The alpine duiker (*Sylvicapra grimmia altivalis*) is largely diurnal and avoids the colder night temperature (as well as predators) by lying up in dense vegetation. Eland, buffalo and elephant have all been recorded as high as the base of the main peaks, but probably only in passing from one forest patch to another (Coe 1969). The mountain hyrax (*Procavia johnstoni mackinderi*) is larger than the lowland subspecies and has unusually dark and long fur. These animals sleep clumped together in rocky outcrops, sharing body heat and protected from the night air by the rock hollows. At sunrise they bask in the sun, presenting maximum surface area to the sun's rays, and their body temperature may increase by as much as 6 °C. The leopard (*Panthera pardus*) feeds on hyrax and small antelope and may play a part in controlling prey populations.

The alpine meadow lizard (*Algyroides alleni*) and the small lizard (*Mabuya irregularis*) select rocky outcrop homes carefully. Large rocks take longer to heat up but also retain the heat for longer, whereas smaller rocks heat up and cool down more rapidly. These lizards choose rocks around 20 cm thick under which the temperature remained constant at around 5 °C. These animals are only active during the warmer part of the day.

The activity period for Afro-alpine insects is short and most of them are **cryptozoic**, living in the litter and upper soil layers. The most important micro-habitat for invertebrates is provided by the vegetation. *Festuca* tussocks can be divided into three zones: an outer dry zone with spreading leaves; an inner area of compacted grass stems; and a very wet lower basal disc from which new shoots arise. Temperature fluctuated by as much as 13 °C in the two outer zones, but around the basal disc temperature only varied between 6 and 8 °C (Coe 1969). Even within these tiny habitats, conditions vary diurnally and organisms living in them respond accordingly as the following examples show.

Lepidopteran larvae (*Gorgopis* sp., *Metarctia* sp.) construct silken tubes which run between the grass stems from the basal to the outer leaves, that is, from the less variable temperatures of the basal disc to the more variable conditions that prevail on the leaves. The larvae have small spines which help them in migrating up and down these tubes as air temperatures change. In the morning and late afternoon they are found between the outer leaves, while during the hotter parts of the day and at night they move towards the leaf bases.

Some flies (Order: Diptera) also show interesting diurnal movements within grass tussocks. At sunset, they congregate on the ends of the leaves and remain there if the temperature does not fall below freezing. If it does, the flies, too cold to seek shelter, simply release their grip on the leaf and free fall into the interstices of the tussock. The next day they climb slowly to the tip of the leaf, and bask there awhile before flying away.

9.6 | Mountain zonation

The above descriptions of tropical mountains clearly indicate changes in the environment and biological communities with altitude. On ascending a tropical mountain, temperature and evaporation rates fall, moisture availability increases and may then decline. Lowland forest is replaced by sub-montane forest which usually has only two layers and reduced species diversity. The temperatures experienced by montane forests obviously depend on altitude and latitude. Montane forests are usually continuously drenched in rain or mists. The very humid conditions encourage the growth of epiphytes, mosses, liverworts and ferns. The filmy ferns (Hymenophyllaceae) are especially characteristic. These ferns are so dependent on moisture that they roll up their leaves if relative humidity falls much below 100% (Table 9.2).

The higher one goes, the cooler it is because the atmosphere is thinner. It is cold on high mountains partly for this reason and partly because there is less height of atmosphere to prevent the mountain surface from losing heat by radiation. As the average temperature in mountainous regions falls by 0.5 °C for each 100 m increase in altitude, even near the equator, there is an upper altitudinal limit above which plants can not grow. In the tropics, growth limits in this region are set by the extreme temperatures, the wide diurnal range in temperatures, low or even negative rates of net primary production and an inability to reproduce.

Warm air, meeting a mountain range, is forced upwards and it cools as it rises. This cooling process is known **adiabatic cooling**. Air, as it rises

Table 9.2 | General characteristics of structure and physiognomy of the montane vegetation

Characteristic	Lowland rain forest	Lower montane	Mid montane	Upper montane
Mean height:				
canopy	25–45 m	30–40 m	20–30 m	18–20 m
emergents	60–80 m	70–80 m	to 30 m	to 25 m
Stratification	3–4 layers	Diffuse	Diffuse	1 or 2 layers
Buttress roots	Frequent and large	Common	Rare	Absent
Surface roots	Rare	Rare to common	Common	Abundant
Stilt roots	Rare	Absent to rare	Common to abundant	Absent to rare
Cauliflory	Frequent	Rare	Rare	Absent
Drip tips on leaves	Frequent	Occasional to frequent	Rare	Absent
Lianas	Frequent	Common	Rare	Absent
Lichens, mosses	Rare	Rare	Abundant	Abundant
Tree ferns	Absent	Present	Occasional to common	Abundant
Palms	Abundant	Common	Absent	Absent
Epiphytes	Abundant	Occasional to abundant	Abundant	Abundant

Source: Grubb 1977; Johns 1982; Whitmore 1993.

up the side of a mountain, expands and, in doing so, does work. The energy for this comes from heat and, therefore, the air cools. The rate at which dry (i.e. unsaturated) air cools when rising adiabatically is known as the dry adiabatic lapse rate and is $9.8\,°C\,km^{-1}$. However, if the air is condensing moisture as it cools, the energy release of the latent heat of vaporisation moderates the adiabatic cooling. Therefore the moist adiabatic lapse rate is less than the dry rate and usually around $5\,°C\,km^{-1}$.

Desert mountains cool faster with elevation than mountains in moist regions. As the air cools, it becomes supersaturated and rain falls. The windward side of a mountain, up to around 3000 m is, therefore, usually wetter and has a more luxuriant vegetation cover than its leeward slopes. Furthermore, on the leeward side of a mountain the air is drier, and so the descending air warms at a higher adiabatic rate and valleys on this side tend to be warmer than those on the windward side. Mountains on the equator receive sun on all sides (but mainly in the morning as cloud cover often increases as the day progresses) but aspect differences increase with latitude. The adiabatic cooling rate on a moist mountain (say $5\,°C\,km^{-1}$) is very similar to the cooling that occurs in approximately 200 km of latitude.

Clearly, then, a number of environmental factors change with altitude. Which of these factors are responsible for the altitudinal zonation that is observed on tropical mountains? Why are some boundaries between zones distinct, whereas others are less clear? These are difficult questions to answer because possible causative environmental factors change in unison. The treeline altitude may be set by the decrease in rainfall above the cloud level, by an increase in frosts, by low air or soil temperatures, by changes in soil type or by a combination of these and other factors.

Walter (1973) suggested that soil temperature is of great importance in determining the treeline. On equatorial mountains, diurnal temperature fluctuations are greater than seasonal changes. Hence, temperature variations are short-lived and do not have time to penetrate deeply into the soil. Roots and germinating seeds are, therefore, exposed to more constant soil temperatures. In shady areas, the soil temperature at a depth of 30 cm is usually constant and approximates to the mean annual air temperature. Therefore, measuring soil temperature at a depth of approximately 30 cm provides a quick estimate of the mean annual air temperature at sites above the cloud level on tropical mountains.

The temperature requirements for root growth of tropical montane tree species have been poorly studied. However, the optimum temperatures for enzymes responsible for protein synthesis in roots are well above freezing. The soil temperature at the treeline in Venezuela is around 7–8 °C and this coincides closely with estimates of the temperature requirements for seed germination and root growth. On subtropical mountains, seasonal temperature variations are much greater and soil temperatures in the summer are considerably warmer than the mean annual temperature. On these mountains the treeline occurs at a higher altitude.

The altitudinal limits of particular vegetation formations vary greatly. Large mountain masses tend to be warmer at comparable altitudes than isolated mountains. This is known as the **Massenerhebung effect**. Extensive, upland areas present a large land surface for heating by radiation. Therefore, altitudinal limits are higher on taller, more massive mountains than on smaller mountains and outlying ridges. On mainland New Guinea, the upper limit of lower-montane rain forest can be as high as 3900 m and as low as 1800 m. On many of the offshore islands, the limit is at 700 m (Grubb 1977). We can now look at how ecologists have come to perceive biological communities and how they change along environmental gradients.

9.7 | Variation in plant and animal communities

We have seen that the structure and species composition of forests on tropical mountains change with altitude and that eventually forest gives way to alpine vegetation and then to barren peaks. Within each altitude zone, many species coexist to form a biological community. A **community** can be defined as populations of plants, animals and micro-organisms living together within a defined spatial area. There are some problems with this definition as some species, such as migratory birds, utilise areas that may be separated by great distances. Such bird species belong to communities in two very different parts of the world. Similarly, some animals have both aquatic and terrestrial stages in their life cycle and, therefore, are integral parts of both aquatic and terrestrial communities.

Within each community, energy flows and nutrients cycle and the rates of these processes are largely controlled by environmental factors. These ecosystem processes influence the growth of populations, and this determines the relative abundances of the species that make up the community. Consequently, the concept of a community is more than an assemblage of species in a particular area: it also includes the interactions that occur between them and with the environment. Examples of biological interactions include competition and predation (chapter 4), nutrient cycling (chapter 5), mutualism (chapters 8 and 11) and parasitism. We have looked at how communities change with time (chapter 7) and how forest communities respond when a canopy gap is created (chapter 8). In this chapter, we look at how community composition varies with spatial change in the environment.

A community has been viewed as a superorganism with an integrity analogous to that of cells in an organism (Allee *et al.* 1949). This is the **holistic** or **unitary** view of a community and one championed by Clements (1916). He regarded the community to be a highly integrated unit that operated very much within itself with little interaction with surrounding communities – a **closed community**. According to his concept, each community was a distinct entity with easily observable boundaries, called **ecotones** (Figure 9.12). The species composition of each community was highly predictable (**deterministic**), as were processes such as succession that operated within them. Certainly some communities do have a sharp boundary, particularly where environmental change is marked, such

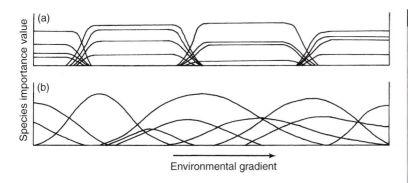

Environmental gradient

Figure 9.12 Community change along environmental gradients. (a) Communities with distinct species composition separated by ecotones where environmental conditions change sharply. These communities are referred to as closed communities and correspond to the Clementsian concept of the community. (b) Gradual community change along an environmental gradient leading to open communities with no distinct boundaries; the individualistic concept of Gleason (after Whittaker 1975).

as at the treeline on mountains or at the edge of a lake.

Gleason (1926) viewed communities very differently – as unique assemblages of species that had come together through chance (**stochastically**). His **individualistic** concept of communities invoked a lack of interspecific organisation with species composition being determined by the chance arrival of propagules, by abiotic factors and then by interspecific interactions (competition, predation, mutualism, parasitism). Gleason perceived the community as having no distinct boundaries – an **open community**. He perceived communities as changing gradually along an environmental gradient. In his view, species gradually and independently replace one another along a **continuum**.

These contrasting views are compared in Figure 9.12, and both have some validity in nature. Abrupt changes in environmental conditions are frequently accompanied by abrupt changes in species composition, and distinct communities are readily apparent. In other situations, environmental conditions change gradually, and alterations in community species composition are similarly gradual with boundaries between communities difficult to detect. Changes in animal communities are often coupled with changes in plant communities.

Environmental factors and biological competition are important in determining the ways that plant and animal communities change along gradients. First, environmental conditions will determine which species are able to colonise and reproduce within a particular area, and hence maintain a population there. Once this has been determined, competition with the other organisms in the area will act to refine community composition. These are basic **rules of community assembly**. Some ecologists view a community as being inevitable and predictable: a particular area will support a particular community and, even after disturbance, the 'designated' community will re-form. Other ecologists believe that chance plays an important role in determining the species mix within a community.

The role of competition in determining the structure of plant communities differs from the way it acts on animal communities. Plant propagule dispersion is largely a matter of chance and, once a seed germinates, the plant is literally rooted to the spot. The plant must be able to survive the full range of environmental conditions to which it is exposed and compete successfully with all species in the community or perish. In contrast, most animals are able to avoid harsh environmental conditions by moving to areas where more suitable conditions prevail. We will look at the role of competition in determining community structure in more detail in chapter 11.

The distribution of plants and animals on mountain tops needs to be set in an historical context. Glacial episodes have resulted in lowering the altitude of the treeline and, during these periods, the opportunity for interchange of species between mountain tops was enhanced. Mountain summits are habitats isolated from each other by the surrounding lowlands. We will look at how this isolation affects species composition in chapter 12.

9.8 | Chapter summary

1. Mean temperatures on tropical mountains commonly decrease by around 0.5–0.6 °C per 100 m increase in elevation. There is little seasonal variation in temperature on tropical mountains since day length is more constant than it is in temperate regions and therefore prolonged periods of below-freezing temperatures do not occur. The tropical mountain climate differs from that in the adjacent lowlands, principally through the lower temperatures that prevail throughout the year and the wide range in diurnal temperatures. Large mountain masses tend to be warmer at comparable altitudes and latitudes than isolated mountains (Massenerhebung effect).

2. Seasonal drought is common on many tropical mountains and rainfall generally decreases with increasing altitude. Trade winds can create distinct climatic differences between the leeward and windward slopes. The thin soils on steeper slopes have a low water-holding capacity, whereas organic-rich deposits in the valleys are usually waterlogged.

3. Tropical mountains lack the boreal coniferous forests and the deciduous, broad-leaved forests found on temperate mountains, but instead evergreen broad-leaved forests or tropical coniferous forests are found. With increasing altitude, lowland forest is replaced, in turn by lower-montane and upper-montane forests. Grasslands replace forests above the treeline.

4. Organisms living at high altitude in the tropics have morphological, physiological and life history adaptations to low mean temperature, little seasonal variation in temperature, diurnal freeze–thaw cycles and high exposure to ultraviolet light. Change in morphology and physiology by organisms in response to altered environmental conditions occurs through a process known as acclimation. Species richness declines with altitude and C_3 grasses tend to replace C_4 grasses at higher altitudes.

5. Biological communities consist of populations of interacting species. These interactions, together with environmental conditions, determine the rates of energy flow and nutrient cycling and, through competition, the relative abundances of the species that constitute the community. Communities are not normally units with distinct boundaries, species composition alters gradually with changes in the environment. However, where environmental change occurs over a short distance, two communities may be separated by a short, intermediate zone known as an ecotone.

Chapter 10

Mangroves, seagrasses and decomposition

Mangroves occur between the sea and the land and line approximately 75% of tropical coasts. The term mangrove refers to both the plant community found in this saline, intertidal zone as well as the constituent tree and shrub species that grow there (Figure 10.1). Even though mangroves include plants from many different genera and families, they exhibit numerous similarities in appearance, physiology, reproduction and adaptation to habitat. This provides another example of **convergent evolution** (see section 8.6). Attempts to define a mangrove as a particular type of plant without reference to its habitat has always been unsatisfactory because many mangrove adaptations such as stilt roots and pneumatophores are found in plants growing in areas other than the coastal zone. If one accepts the view that mangroves (the habitat) are tidal forests (Schimper 1903), then one can define a mangrove (the plant) as any woody species that grows in these forests (Mepham and Mepham 1984). It should be noted that this will include species that grow well outside the coastal zone, and, indeed, few mangrove plants are confined exclusively to the tidal zone.

There are two main centres of mangrove diversity. The more diverse eastern group (East Africa, India, South-East Asia, Australasia and the Western Pacific) has around 40 species with peak diversity in Northern Australia and Papua New Guinea (Fig 10.2). The western group (West Africa, South America, the Caribbean, Florida, Central America and the Pacific coasts of North and South America) is far less diverse with only eight species (Tomlinson 1986). No mangrove species is pantropical in its distribution but five species in the eastern group can be found from East Africa to the Pacific. *Avicennia marina* has both wide longitudinal and latitudinal range but this species probably should be sub-divided taxonomically. Wide-ranging species in the western group include *Avicennia germinans*, *Laguncularia racemosa* and *Rhizophora mangle*. Mangroves are best developed in areas with high rainfall and runoff, and grow particularly well along the banks of estuaries. For example, mangrove diversity is higher (18 species) along the wetter Queensland coast of Australia than it is along the arid west Australian coast at the same latitude where only four species occur (Tomlinson 1986).

With increasing latitude, the number of species decreases but the distribution of these plants extends into the subtropical and warm temperate regions, where the water temperature is greater than 24 °C in the warmest month and where rainfall exceeds 1250 mm. The effect on mangrove distribution of the cold Humboldt current which flows north along the west coast of South America can be clearly seen in Figure 10.2. Mangroves on the Peruvian coast only extend to 3° S whereas on the Atlantic coast of Brazil, mangroves can be found south of the Tropic of Capricorn. Mangroves flourish where the air temperature in the coldest month does not fall below 20 °C but *Avicennia marina* can survive winter temperatures as low as 10 °C in New Zealand.

Most mangroves do not tolerate high-energy localities; this may be due to substrate instability and the inability of seedlings to become established. Mangroves prefer a muddy habitat, but can

Figure 10.1 Mangroves with prop roots growing on the southern coast of Papua New Guinea (Photo: Office of Environment and Conservation, Papua New Guinea).

be found growing on sandy soils and coral islands. Extensive mangrove stands are found lining the estuaries of large rivers that flow into shallow seas, such as the Ganges–Brahmaputra (Bangladesh), the Mekong Delta (Vietnam) and the Fly, Kikori and Purari Rivers which drain southern Papua New Guinea. In probably all mangroves, the distribution patterns of plant species are greatly influenced by salinity levels. In low-rainfall areas, salinity levels can exceed tolerance levels and salt pans may develop landward of mangroves. Most mangroves can grow in freshwater and their absence from such conditions is probably not due to an obligate requirement for sodium chloride but more likely results from their low ability to withstand interspecific competition.

Mangroves inhabit a changeable environment. With each high tide the sea inundates the roots and lower portions of mangrove stems. At low tide, the sediment may be completely exposed or, if the mangrove occurs along an estuary, the roots may be bathed in freshwater. Tidal range varies from place to place and also with the relative positions of the earth, moon and sun. The range is at a maximum at new and full moon (**spring tides**) and at a minimum (**neap tides**) in between full and new moon; spring tides are highest at the equinox.

Mangroves and the seagrass beds that often occur seaward of them are ecologically significant because they act as filters, removing soil and terrestrial organic matter that flows into them from the adjacent land. They provide a habitat for a wide variety of fish, marine invertebrates, insects and birds. Mangroves and seagrasses are also significant producers of dead organic matter (**detritus**) that contributes to offshore productivity. The production and subsequent fate of this detritus is the focus of this chapter, but first we need to appreciate the ecological characteristics of the plants and animals that live at this interface between land and sea. As mangrove forests are most diverse in Australia and New Guinea, we will use these to illustrate their ecological features.

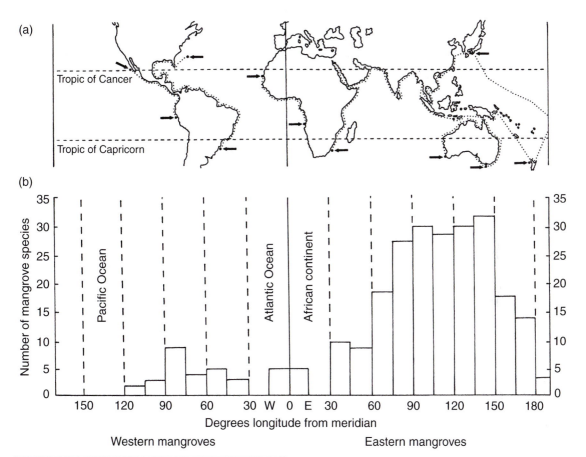

Figure 10.2 (a) Global distribution of mangroves. Arrows indicate latitudinal extremes of mangroves on large land masses. Mangroves occur on islands in South-East Asia and the Pacific but are not mapped. (b) Histogram of the approximate number of mangrove species per 15° of longitude. The floristic richness of the eastern group with peak diversity centred on Australasia and South-East Asia is clearly shown (after Tomlinson 1986).

10.1 Mangroves of Australia and New Guinea

Mangrove generic diversity is centred on the archipelagos of Indonesia and New Guinea and the north and east coasts of Australia. The mangrove flora of New Guinea is composed of 13 genera and 37 obligate (found only in mangrove habitat) species of woody dicotyledons together with 5 to 6 other obligates such as species of *Nypa*, *Acrosticum* and *Acanthus*. Furthermore, some of the largest extant stands of mangroves world-wide are found around the coasts of New Guinea. The 37 species of obligate mangrove trees in New Guinea include representatives of all genera currently found in Australia and South-East Asia except for the South-East Asian genus *Kandelia*.

10.1.1 Mangrove zonation

That mangroves occur in distinct, often monospecific zones, is often obvious. In New Guinea, the tidal zone of mangroves is dominated by species of *Rhizophora*, *Avicennia*, *Bruguiera*, *Xylocarpus* and *Sonneratia*. *Ceriops tagal* occurs in shallow water, often on a stony substrate. Several species (*Sonneratia alba*, *Cynometra ramiflora*, *Lumnitzera littorea* and *Excoecaria agallocha*) are restricted to the zone inundated by spring tides. *Bruguiera gymnorhiza*, *Aegiceras corniculatum* and *Scyphiphora hydrophyllacea* are found on the banks of tidal streams.

Avicennia marina is a widespread, pan-tropical species, probably because of its ability to withstand low temperatures. Together with *Sonneratia alba*, it is often the first to colonise newly exposed sediments and dominates the seaward zone. *Rhizophora stylosa*, with its well-developed prop roots, often dominates the next zone. Behind the *Rhizophora* zone, where tidal inundation may only occur during spring tides and evaporation results in elevated salt concentrations, grow mangroves such as *Ceriops tagal*.

The species that develop further inland depend largely on rainfall and drainage patterns. In high-rainfall areas with poor drainage, a freshwater wetland may form, and in New Guinea such a habitat may be colonised by *Excoecaria agallocha*. In areas with lower rainfall or marked seasonality, strongly saline soils may develop to form a salt pan without vegetation or a salt marsh sparsely colonised by succulent herbs and salt-tolerant mangrove species such as *Ceriops tagal*. Mangroves also line the banks of the large rivers that flow into the Gulf of Papua. Here, zones correspond to salinity levels, but mangroves extend as far as the upper tidal influence where freshwater predominates throughout the year.

Marked zonation occurs in mangrove communities subjected to environmental gradients and these gradients are usually related to the transition from salt to brackish to freshwater. Zonation patterns are most obviously associated with water depth. In flat areas, zonation patterns are difficult to detect, but, even in areas with a barely perceptible slope, some zonation is usually present. Mean water depth controls the seaward limit of mangroves, but the duration of inundation is probably more important than water depth in determining landward zones.

Mangrove zonation has been used to suggest that succession is occurring, zonation in space being equated with zonation in time. However, Johnstone (1983) pointed out there is no true mangrove climax, as continual progression of the shoreline ultimately leads to the establishment of a terrestrial vegetation climax, not one dependent on inundation by seawater. Mangroves on the seaward edge alter the nature of the substratum and the rate of sediment accretion and, as a con-

sequence, are themselves replaced by other species in a successional process (see sections 7.7 and 7.8). On stable shorelines where the rate of accretion is low, mangrove zones are often compressed into a relatively narrow fringe between the sea and land. In actively accreting areas, mangrove vegetation may be more extensive with wider zones.

Zones subjected to differing degrees of saltwater inundation have been divided into five major classes: (1) areas inundated by all high tides, few species can grow here but *Rhizophora mucronata* may do so; (2) areas inundated by all medium high tides, *Avicennia* spp. and *Rhizophora mucronata* grow well here; (3) areas inundated by all normal high tides where all mangroves thrive; (4) areas inundated by spring tides, where *Bruguiera* spp. and *Ceriops* spp. do well in this drier habitat; and (5) areas only inundated by exceptionally high tides. Factors which play a role in the distribution of mangroves include not only the degree of inundation but also salinity (a function of inundation regime, rainfall and freshwater inputs), substrate type and the dispersal of reproductive propagules through coastal water movements and currents.

10.2 | Ecological adaptations of mangroves

Owing to the large spatial and temporal variation in the physical and chemical factors found in mangrove-dominated environments, the biological communities display some remarkable adaptations to this harsh environment. These adaptations include modifications to plant structure, physiology (salt tolerance) and reproduction.

10.2.1 Plant structure

Mangrove soils are highly saline and may be anoxic just a few millimetres below the surface. Mangrove root penetration is shallow, but extensive lateral spreading provides support. Radiating from these lateral or **cable roots** are anchor roots. Fine **nutritive roots** are responsible for nutrient uptake (Figure 10.3). Many species also produce stilt and buttress roots to improve anchorage in

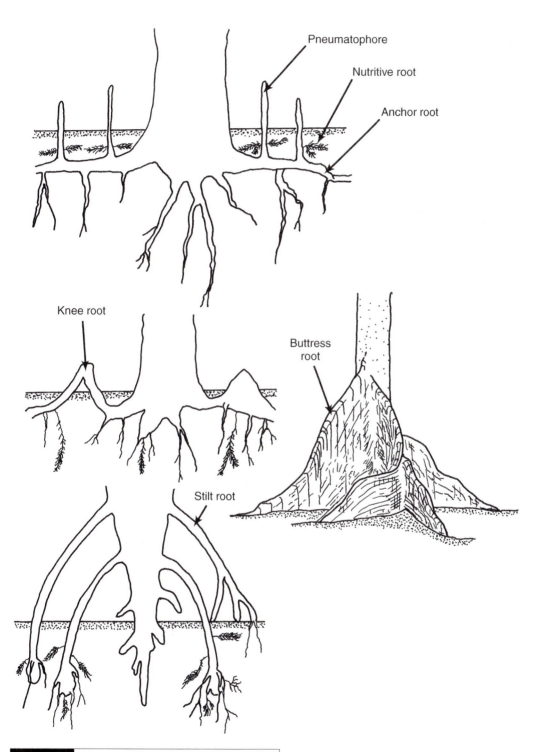

Figure 10.3 Major morphological root types found in mangroves (after Hutchings and Saenger 1987 with kind permission from the University of Queensland Press).

Figure 10.4 Stilt roots of mangroves (*Rhizophora* sp.) near Galley Reach, Papua New Guinea (Photo: Patrick Osborne).

the often unstable, almost fluid mud (Figure 10.4). Even so, mangroves are highly susceptible to storm damage and high winds and hurricanes frequently devastate large areas of them.

As the sediments are anoxic, in some mangroves (e.g. *Bruguiera* spp.), the roots produce 'knees' at intervals which stick out above the sediment surface (Figure 10.3). These 'knees' are covered in **lenticels** which draw in air. When the lenticels are covered by the incoming tide, the pressure in air spaces beneath them declines as oxygen is used in respiration. On re-exposure to air, the negative pressure serves to draw air into the root, thereby replenishing the oxygen supply. Lenticels are also found on the trunks of many species. The density and distribution of lenticels up the main trunk may be related to factors such as tidal height and nature of the substratum. Oxygen supply to the roots of some species is increased by **pneumatophores** (breathing tubes). Mangroves rooted in anoxic sediments can not survive if the lenticels or pneumatophores become blocked. This explains why mangroves are very susceptible to oil spills.

Species which lack pneumatophores such as *Aegialites* may grow with the main cable roots above the surface, or grow in better-drained substrata where oxygen availability is higher. In areas where sediment deposition is rapid, pneumatophores may continue to grow upwards. Species of *Avicennia* and *Sonneratia* which colonise rapidly accreting shorelines, produce upwardly-growing pneumatophores. In species where the lenticels are carried on prop or stilt roots such as *Rhizophora*, extra arches of prop roots are formed as sediments accumulate.

The leaves of most mangroves have a thick, waxy cuticle to reduce water loss. *Avicennia* leaves are covered in white hairs which trap a layer of air close to the leaf surface and retard water loss, as well as acting as a heat reflector. Stomata are generally restricted to the lower leaf surface and in many species are sunk in pits. Mangrove leaves may have a well-developed **hypodermal** layer between the epidermis and spongy mesophyll to store water (succulence). With these adaptations, water loss through evapotranspiration is minimised.

10.2.2 Salinity

Mangroves are members of terrestrial plant families that have adapted to conditions of high salinity, low oxygen and poor nutrient availability in the soil, strong wind and wave action and an unstable substrate. The main advantage to growing in this environment stems from reduced biological competition (see section 4.9.4). Few plant species have the physiological mechanisms to cope with high soil salinities (see section 2.8). The main problem is obtaining adequate freshwater to replace that lost through evapotranspiration. Water availability depends on the frequency and volume of the tidal exchange, rainfall (quantity and seasonal distribution) and rates of evapotranspiration. Mangrove leaves exhibit xeromorphic adaptations (thick cuticle, sunken stomata, thick epidermis and hairs) and these help to minimise water loss.

Mangroves have adopted three main strategies to maintain water balance in this saline environment. Some mangroves (*Rhizophora*, *Ceriops*, *Bruguiera* and *Osbornia*) have physiological mechanisms that preclude salt uptake (**salt excluders**); other species allow the salt to enter the plant, but have effective methods of getting rid of excess salt (**salt excretors**). The third mechanism is **salt tolerance**. Mangroves may utilise all three strategies, but predominant use of one of them means that mangroves can be classified as excluders, excretors or tolerators. Exclusion of 80–90% of the salt in seawater has been demonstrated in species of *Rhizophora*, *Sonneratia*, *Ceriops*, *Avicennia*, *Osbornia*, *Bruguiera*, *Excoecaria*, *Aegiceras*, *Aegialites* and *Acrosticum* (Scholander 1968). Presumably these plants possess some ultra-filtration technique in the roots.

Salt secretion occurs via specialised salt glands in the leaves of *Avicennia*, *Sonneratia*, *Aegiceras*, *Aegialites*, *Acanthus* and *Laguncularia*. Salt-secreting glands in *Aegiceras* consist of cells packed with mitochondria and connected by fine threads of cytoplasm to the basal cell, salt being secreted through a small slit on to the cuticle.

Accumulated salt is washed off by rain. How the salt pump works in moving salt to the gland for removal is not fully understood. Tolerance of salt accumulation has been shown to occur in species of *Excoecaria*, *Lumnitzera*, *Avicennia*, *Osbornia*, *Rhizophora*, *Sonneratia* and *Xylocarpus*. The site of accumulation varies in different species, but generally includes older leaves and the bark of stem and roots. In species that shed their leaves annually, leaf storage of salt may represent an important mechanism for salt disposal.

10.2.3 Mangrove reproduction

Most species possess small, sticky pollen grains; pollination agents include bees (*Aegiceras*, *Cynometra*), bats (*Sonneratia*) and sunbirds (*Bruguiera*). Tomlinson *et al.* (1979) noted that the large-flowered *Bruguiera gymnorhiza* in Australia tends to be bird-pollinated, whilst the smaller-flowered *Bruguiera parviflora* and *Bruguiera cylindrica* are pollinated by butterflies. The fruits and seedlings of mangroves float and this is the main mechanism of dispersal.

Species of *Rhizophora*, *Bruguiera*, *Ceriops*, *Kandelia*, *Avicennia* and *Aegiceras* reproduce by **vivipary** (Tomlinson 1986). Vivipary is defined as the precocious and continuous growth of offspring whilst still attached to the maternal plant (see Elmqvist and Cox 1996); the fertilised seeds germinate whilst still attached to the parent plant. Young *Rhizophora* plants produce long, spear-shaped stems and roots and may remain attached to the parent for up to three years. If the young plant falls off at low tide it spears the sediment and rapidly produces roots with sufficient growth after just two days to ensure seedling establishment. When the young plant falls into the sea, it floats horizontally in seawater but turns vertically with the roots pointing downwards when in brackish water. The young plant rapidly develops roots on contacting the sediment and its advanced stage of development serves to increase its chances of surviving in a physically demanding environment.

True vivipary has not been recorded in many plants but has been observed in some species of seagrasses, freshwater sedges and plants growing on mudflats. **Pseudovivipary** (asexual production of offspring on the parent plant) is found in plants growing in arctic, alpine or arid habitats (Elmqvist and Cox 1996). The occurrence of true vivipary in unrelated angiosperm families suggests independent evolutionary origins – viviparous mangroves, for example, are placed in four families. True vivipary is most prevalent among plants in tropical, shallow, marine habitats (mangroves and seagrass beds) and it improves the chance of seedling establishment in what are effectively patchy environments. In mangroves and seagrass beds, the parental patch is often large and there is little opportunity for seedling establishment in the vast inhospitable areas that surround these patches. Therefore the loss of dispersal ability that accompanies vivipary is not disadvantageous. Seed dormancy and seeds adapted for dispersal (by wind, animals or other agents) confer advantages of dispersal in both time and space. In tropical marine habitats, no significant advantage is conferred by dispersal either in time (the environment tends towards aseasonality) or in space (the chance of finding a patch better than the parental one is small).

Not all mangroves are viviparous but they do all produce large seeds and fruits. The food reserve in the large seed provides the seedling with energy to help it through the early stages of establishment.

10.3 | Mangrove animals

Mangroves provide a physical habitat for both terrestrial and marine animals. MacNae (1968) identified five micro-habitats in mangrove forests: (1) the tree canopy; (2) water-filled holes in trees; (3) the soil surface; (4) the soil; and (5) permanent and temporary pools. In contrast to mangrove plants, the aquatic animal community is dominated by members of essentially marine families which have become adapted to variable salinities, turbid conditions and to feeding directly or indirectly on materials from mangrove trees, the dominant primary producers. Some terrestrial animals utilise mangroves as an extension of their usual habitats, visiting them for short periods.

Dense monospecific mangrove stands may provide a useful food supply (e.g. nectar) at certain times and the abundance of marine animals attracts terrestrial species that feed on them. However, the poor supply of freshwater and high concentrations of salt and secondary products, such as tannins in mangrove leaves, do not make them attractive as food for many animals.

10.3.1 Terrestrial invertebrates

Insects and spiders dominate the terrestrial invertebrate fauna found in mangroves. Mosquitoes and midges are readily apparent in many mangroves and can make working in them thoroughly unpleasant, and, in areas where malaria and dengue fever are endemic, life-threatening. A wide variety of insects have been found to eat, mine and gall the leaves of different mangrove species, with up to one fifth of the leaf material being removed by herbivores while the leaves are still attached to the tree (Johnstone 1981). Two species of insects, *Cleora injectaria* and *Poecilips fallax* defoliate *Rhizophora* trees in Thailand (Fortes 1988). The damage may affect leaf survival and hence carbon flow into the detrital food chains. This direct herbivore activity may, through destruction of photosynthetically active tissues, reduce the reproductive capacity of the plants. Reproductive capacity may also be reduced as resources are diverted from flower and fruit production into defence and new leaf production.

10.3.2 Birds, reptiles and mammals

Birds are conspicuous in mangroves but rarely occur in high densities and most are only occasional visitors. The low diversity of foraging surfaces has been suggested as the reason for the low utilisation of this habitat by birds. Over 200 bird species have been recorded in mangroves in Australia and Papua New Guinea, but only around a dozen are restricted to this habitat. Fish-eating birds such as the mangrove kingfisher (*Halcyon chloris*) are at the top of the mangrove food web. Other mangrove specialists include honey-eaters, flycatchers and warblers. Honey-eaters visit the flowers of *Bruguiera gymnorhiza* and may also be attracted to the shoots of *Rhizophora stylosa* by the

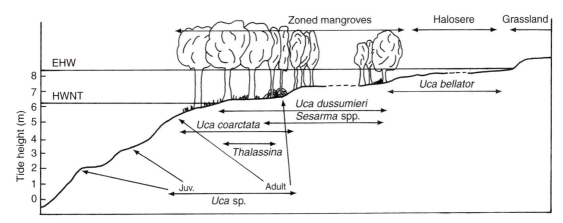

Figure 10.5 Distribution pattern of mangroves and mangrove crabs at St. Lawrence in Queensland, Australia. EHW = Extreme High Water; HWNT = High Water Neap Tide (after MacNae 1966).

sugary substance secreted from the stipules (Tomlinson *et al.* 1979).

In Australia, saltwater crocodiles (*Crocodylus porosus*) enter mangroves with the rising tide to feed on crabs, prawns and fish. However, they rarely use mangroves for breeding, preferring the vegetation that lines estuaries above the extent of mangroves. Other reptiles found in mangroves include terrestrial and sea snakes (*Ephalophis* sp., *Enhydris* sp.), monitor lizards (*Varanus* spp.) and water dragons (*Lophognathus temporalis*). Flying foxes (*Pteropus* sp.) roost in mangroves and, although they forage over great distances, do feed on mangrove flowers as well. Flying fox colonies attract pythons (*Liasis* sp.) which feed on them. Other mammals found in mangroves include monkeys, rats and, in Australasia, bandicoots and possums.

10.3.3 Sediment fauna

A large proportion of the mangrove fauna burrows into the soft sediments, feeding either on the organic matter and associated micro-organisms or algae that grow on the sediment surface. This benthic fauna includes hermit, mud and fiddler crabs. Crab distribution within mangroves is determined by sediment particle size, organic matter content and the suitability of the substrate for burrow formation (Crane 1975). Within

species, differential distribution of size classes may be related to the ability to withstand desiccation, with smaller individuals (having a larger surface to volume ratio) occurring lower in the intertidal zone than larger individuals.

At low tide when the sediment surface is exposed, fiddler crabs emerge from their burrows to feed on algae and litter particles. A male fiddler crab is easily recognised because one of its claws is enlarged and colourful and is used to attract females and defend its territory from intruding males. Different species are found in different mangrove zones and burrow distribution frequently follows a regular or near regular spatial distribution (Figure 10.5).

Mangroves provide important nursery areas for commercial fish, crab and prawn species. The mud crab, *Scylla serrata*, is a large species of commercial and subsistence importance throughout the Indo-West Pacific. It lives in burrows, but, unlike the fiddler crabs, feeds on molluscs and smaller crabs which are crushed with powerful mouthparts or the enlarged chelae. Crabs may make up around 80% of the macro-faunal biomass, and they play a very important role in processing mangrove litter. Their burrowing aerates the sediment, influences soil texture and changes the micro-topography of the forest floor.

The mud lobster, *Thalassina*, is another widespread species which constructs large mounds around the burrow entrance. The burrows extend below the water table, and a pool of water lies at the bottom of the burrow for respiration and/or filter feeding. *Thalassina* mounds form micro-habitats for ferns and other plants since they provide a small, elevated area above high-tide level. These burrows provide a habitat for polychaete worms and are also used as refuges by crabs belonging to the genus *Sesarma*.

In the Gulf of Papua, penaeid prawns spawn in the open sea and the larval stages develop in the plankton. They are brought inshore on currents and the juvenile prawns settle on the bottom in estuaries and deltas. Here they feed on detritus, washed out of the mangroves that line the Gulf, and grow rapidly. Once mature, the prawns migrate out to sea to spawn. There seems to be little seasonality in breeding, and recruitment into the nursery areas occurs throughout the year. Return to the open sea spawning grounds often occurs after heavy rain (Frusher 1983).

The molluscan fauna of mangroves is diverse. Mud-creeping gastropods such as the turret shell (*Telescopium telescopium*) graze on algae on mudflats. Bivalves, such as *Geloina coaxans* and *Anadara granosa*, filter feed on suspended particulate matter in the water, and smaller littorinids graze on algae growing on the trunks and leaf surfaces of the mangrove trees. Most fish come and go with the tides, but some unusual ones remain exposed to the air at low tide (see Box 10.1).

Box 10.1 | Mud-skippers: life on the edge

Mud-skippers are well adapted to alternating periods of submersion in water and exposure to air. When submerged these fish swim like any normal fish, but they are highly modified for activity on the exposed mud surface during low tide. Their eyes are set in turrets on the head and are extremely mobile, providing a wide-angle view for both prey (terrestrial arthropods, crabs, molluscs and other marine invertebrates) and predator location. The eyes are moistened by blinking and protected from desiccation by a modified cornea. The upper half of the eye has more rods, while the lower half is richer in cones. Rods enhance vision in poor light and cones are used in colour vision. The upper half of the eye is used to locate prey and predators, whilst the lower half monitors the territorial display of rivals and suitors.

The skeleton and musculature of mud-skippers are modified so that the pectoral fins can be used as crutches to lift the anterior portion of the body off the ground and swing it forward, followed by setting down on the pelvic fins before swinging the pectoral fins forward again. The fish can also move by a rapid skipping motion (hence their common name). The skipping movement is achieved by bending the tail sidewards and digging the tail fin into the sediment. A rapid straightening of the tail propels the fish explosively forward. This skipping movement is used to escape from danger. In the water, the mud-skipper can skim across the surface, rather like a flying fish. Each flight is preceded by a short burst of swimming during which the momentum for the flight is generated.

In water, these fish respire using gills. On land, they gulp air into the buccal cavity, where it is mixed with trapped water. The modified epidermis at the back and sides of the buccal cavity serves as a respiratory surface. Like mangrove crabs, mud-skippers make burrows which provide a refuge from predators and also a source of water. The burrows are also important in reproduction with the female being attracted into the male's burrow by an elaborate courtship dance. Mating occurs in the burrow. Mud-skippers are probably not related to the fish which first colonised land, but studies of their adaptations have indicated how this process may have occurred.

10.4 | Mangrove productivity

Mangrove communities are highly productive communities with rates comparable to many terrestrial forest communities (Lugo and Snedaker 1974). They form an important source of organic matter for food chains both within the mangroves and in neighbouring estuarine and coastal areas. Some of the primary production is stored in roots, trunks and branches ultimately being utilised by decomposers that often follow in the wake of boring teredinid molluscs. Some primary production is consumed by insect herbivores, whilst some is used by detrital feeders following leaf and bud scale dehiscence. Reproductive structures are eaten by some fish, and, in New Guinea, by the freshwater turtle, *Carettochelys insculpta*.

Litter fall can be a valuable indicator of mangrove productivity and of the energy and materials that may be exported to adjacent coastal waters. Gill and Tomlinson (1971) showed that leaf, flower and fruit production in *Rhizophora mangle* occurred throughout the year. Peak rates of leaf growth and fall were observed in summer. Litter production has been estimated for *Avicennia* in Australia at 1.2–1.5 kg dry weight m^{-2} $year^{-1}$ (Briggs 1977) and for *Rhizophora mangle* along the Atlantic coast from 0.5 kg dry weight m^{-2} $year^{-1}$ (Golley *et al.* 1962) to 0.9 kg dry weight m^{-2} $year^{-1}$ (Heald and Odum 1970). In tropical Queensland, litter production was estimated to be as high as 2.8 kg dry weight m^{-2} $year^{-1}$ (Bunt 1982) but most values have been around 0.5 kg dry weight m^{-2} $year^{-1}$ (Hutchings and Saenger 1987).

For *Avicennia germinans* growing in Guyana, total litter production amounted to 1.8 kg dry weight m^{-2} $year^{-1}$ with leaves contributing 61% of the biomass, followed by fruits (25%), flowers (9%) and woody material (5%) (Chale 1996). Chale concluded that seasonal litter production was affected more by the inflowing rivers draining the Amazon Basin than by local rainfall. In an Australian mangrove dominated by *Avicennia marina*, litter production over two years varied from 831 to 921 g m^{-2} $year^{-1}$ (Mackey and Smail 1995). Leaf fall was seasonal with a maximum in the wet, summer season and wood fall correlated with periods of high wind. The litter consisted of leaves (47%), reproductive parts (30%) and wood (23%).

Bunt (1995), in a continent-wide survey of Australian mangroves, found that the most productive species in terms of litter fall was *Rhizophora stylosa* with a mean yield of 965 g m^{-2} $year^{-1}$. However, he found that litter production varied substantially from site to site and even between litter baskets at the same site. He recorded litter falls as high as 2369 g m^{-2} $year^{-1}$ for *R. stylosa* and 1598 g m^{-2} $year^{-1}$ and 1290 g m^{-2} $year^{-1}$ for *Avicennia marina* and *Ceriops tagal* respectively. He concluded that the capacity for litter production at individual sites depended heavily on local controls such as salinity regime, nutrient inputs and substrate characteristics as well as regional climate.

The majority of studies on mangrove productivity and litter fall have been short-term, usually 1 year. Day *et al.* (1996) assessed above-ground net primary production in a Mexican mangrove over 7 years. The mean annual leaf fall pattern was found to be bimodal with a higher peak at the end of the dry season and a lower peak during the rainy season. Annual above-ground net primary production ranged from 319 to 759 g dry weight m^{-2} $year^{-1}$ and significant variability was detected between years. Litter fall was inversely related to soil salinity. During the dry season, low soil moisture, low tides and high evapotranspiration rates impose water stress on mangroves that enhances both leaf senescence and litter fall. Seventy-four per cent of the total litter fall variability over the 7-year study period was explained by three factors: changes in average soil salinity, minimum temperature in the cold season and minimum rainfall in the dry season. Flower and fruit fall were greatest during the wet season. Day *et al.* (1996) concluded that mangroves would seem to allocate more energy to growth during the wet season when soil salinities are low. Leaf fall during this period is reduced to facilitate high rates of photosynthesis.

Seasonal variation in primary production is known for several species. Saenger and Moverley (1985) measured seasonal leaf production in nine species of mangroves in Queensland and showed the existence of five classes. Species such as *Aegialites annulata* were practically non-seasonal, whilst species such as *Ceriops* were shown to have slight seasonal increases in leaf production during the summer. Highly seasonal leaf production but non-seasonal leaf loss were characteristic of *Aegialites corniculatum* and *Osbornia octodonta*. Bimodal patterns, with minimum leaf production and fall occurring during the flowering season, were recorded in *Avicennia marina*. Highly seasonal species such as *Xylocarpus australasicus* exhibited maximum leaf loss immediately before maximum new leaf production.

Tidal regime, salt balance (rainfall) and nutrient supply are the main factors controlling mangrove productivity. Tidal exchange is important in transporting oxygen and nutrients to the root system and also in removing toxic sulfides and reducing the salt content of the soil water. Salt balance affects the transpiration rate which is controlled by stomatal aperture size. When stressed by water shortage, stomata close and the rate at which carbon dioxide can be absorbed from the atmosphere is reduced. Nutrients enter mangroves with each tide and are also brought in with freshwater drainage from adjacent terrestrial systems.

10.5 | Seagrasses

Seagrasses are the only angiosperms that are completely marine and are a prominent feature of the intertidal zone along tropical coasts. These plants have submerged flowers, and reproduction, including pollination, occurs underwater. Flowers are typically small and inconspicuous, and pollen is carried from the anther to the stigma by water currents. Pollen is thread-like or released in long strands. Seed dispersal occurs either through water currents or by animals that browse on seagrasses. Seagrasses have a well-developed underground stem (rhizome) connecting the erect shoots and anchoring the plant. Leaves are generally strap-like, supple and tough and able to withstand wave action (Figure 10.6).

These plants do not belong to the grass family (Poaceae) and their distribution closely parallels

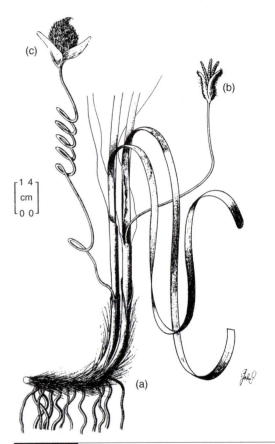

Figure 10.6 Plant structure of the seagrass *Enhalus acoroides*. (a) Habit. (b) Female inflorescence. (c) Fruit (after Brouns 1986 with kind permission of Science in New Guinea).

that of mangroves. The Indo-Pacific flora comprises seven genera in two families: Hydrocharitaceae (*Enhalus*, *Halophila*, *Thalassia*) and Cymodoceaceae: (*Cymodocea*, *Halodule*, *Syringodium* and *Thalassodendron*); it is in this region that seagrass diversity is highest. Four genera grow in the Caribbean and Central America: *Halodule*, *Halophila*, *Syringodium* and *Thalassia*. Note that although four genera are common to both the Indo-Pacific and western-hemisphere floras (pantropical), there are no species in common between these two areas.

Seagrasses provide habitat and food to a variety of fish, invertebrates (molluscs, crustaceans, echinoderms), turtles and dugongs. **Epiphytes** (diatoms, crustose red algae, filamentous green algae) and **epifauna** (such as foraminiferans, hydroids, amphipods) form a thick, felt-like covering on older seagrass leaves. Swimming in amongst the leaves will be copepods, isopods, shrimps, small cephalopods and fish. Polychaetes and echinoderms burrow in the organic-rich sand and asteroids (starfish), holothurians (sea cucumbers) and gastropods such as *Strombus* and *Conus* move about on the sediment surface in seagrass beds.

Seagrass meadows are highly productive systems. Older leaves, in particular, are densely coated in epiphytes, often with a biomass equal to that of the leaves they infest. Therefore carbon is not only fixed by the seagrass plants but also by these epiphytes, phytoplankton and benthic algae. All components of the system must be measured to assess the importance of this habitat as a source of organic matter. Typically net primary production of seagrass beds is 500–1000 g C m^{-2} year^{-1} and, since these plants are not particularly palatable, like mangrove litter, much of the material they produce is fated to become detritus. Marine invertebrates and marine fish have not adapted well to feeding directly on seagrasses, but sea urchins (*Tripneustes* spp., *Echinothrix* spp.) do feed on these plants, although their main food is probably the epiphytes rather than the leaves on which they grow. Some parrot-fish feed on seagrass leaves and many fish such as surgeon-fish, puffers and snappers utilise seagrass beds as nursery areas. Generally, however, utilisation of seagrasses by invertebrates and fish for food is minimal. Some animals associated with this habitat are detritivores, such as sea cucumbers.

In contrast, marine vertebrates that reinvaded the sea from the land have metabolic pathways that facilitate feeding on seagrasses. Dugongs (*Dugong dugon*) feed almost exclusively on seagrasses, only grazing algae when seagrasses are scarce. Dugongs dig up and eat the entire plant, leaving a swathe of destruction. Dugong populations have declined through overexploitation, but occur throughout the Indo-Pacific from East Africa, throughout South-East Asia to tropical Australasia.

These animals consume prodigious quantities of seagrasses and therefore have to forage over large areas. Preen and Marsh (1995) recorded a large decline in the dugong population in Hervey Bay (Queensland, Australia) when two floods and a cyclone destroyed more than 1000 km^2 of seagrass beds. Dugong mortality was highest some 6–8 months after the floods, and recovered corpses were emaciated as a result of starvation. Some dugongs travelled up to 900 km before dying. Three related species of manatees (*Trichechus* spp.) occur around the eastern and western shores of the Atlantic. The sea-turtle (*Chelonias mydas*) also feeds extensively in seagrass beds but, unlike the dugong, this animal only grazes above-ground leaves. Turtles select young leaves that are not heavily infested with algae and bacteria.

Predators also feed in seagrass beds. Stingrays, such as *Dasyatis americana* in the Caribbean and *Taeniura lymma* in the Indo-Pacific, excavate holes in the sand as they hunt for molluscs. These rays have a whip-like tail with sharp barbs and can inject a potent toxin into a foot of anyone unfortunate enough to tread on one buried in the sand. Some carnivorous fish migrate into seagrass beds at night and feed on invertebrates associated with seagrasses. Plant material that is not consumed within the seagrass beds may either be exported with the tides or undergo decomposition.

10.6 | Coastal vegetation and organic matter export

At any time during the breakdown process, organic matter can be transported out of the mangrove or seagrass bed and into the coastal waters. Many studies have stressed the importance of organic matter export from these systems to the productivity of offshore waters. Whether the litter is retained within the mangrove or exported much depends on litter buoyancy and tidal influences. Steinke *et al.* (1983) showed that leaves of *Rhizophora gymnorhiza* were more buoyant than those of *Avicennia marina*. *Bruguiera* leaves have large air spaces and are covered with a thick cuticle on both sides which impedes water inflow. *Avicennia* leaves only have a thick cuticle on the upper surface and therefore water may enter more easily through the lower surface leading to rapid waterlogging.

Lugo and Snedaker (1974) suggested that tidal amplitude and litter accumulation were inversely correlated. Mangrove sediments appear to be kept clear of litter, but this could be as much due to efficient removal by crabs to their underground burrows as to tidal export. Certainly, however, significant quantities of the buoyant litter and organic matter are exported, and the waters adjacent to mangroves are frequently rich in both dissolved and particulate organic matter. How much organic matter is exported and in what form? What is the fate of the organic matter?

To determine the movement of organic matter between mangroves and offshore waters requires **mass balance** studies. Through these measurements, the fate of organic matter produced in the mangrove can be apportioned between consumption *in situ*, decomposition *in situ* and export (**outwelling**) in particulate or dissolved forms. These measurements are not easy to make. Transport in the water is bi-directional as particles flow out on the ebb tide and back in on the flood tide. Organic matter can leave as large pieces (branches, trunks), smaller plant parts (leaves, twigs, flowers), as tiny particles or in solution. Twilley (1985) showed that up to 75% of all carbon exchanged between *Avicennia* mangroves in Florida and the adjacent estuary was in the dissolved form. Dissolved organic carbon may provide a significant and readily utilisable carbon source to offshore heterotrophs. Organic matter can also leave when organisms depart. Animals that spend their larval stages in mangroves and then migrate offshore as adults, may represent an important component of organic matter export from mangroves (Lee 1995).

Slim *et al.* (1996) made a distinction between the inner parts of mangroves and those parts that line the sea. They found that litter exported from the mangrove consisted mostly of leaves from species occurring along the seaward fringe. Furthermore, seagrass litter was also found in this fringe but not further into the mangrove. In other words, litter import and export was impeded by the physical structure of the forest. They con-

cluded that the inner parts of the mangrove forest operated more as a closed system with organic matter produced there being recycled there. Conversely, the seaward mangrove fringe was more open, with significant interchange of materials occurring between mangroves, seagrass beds and the sea. The timing of litter removal from the mangrove varied between the two sites. Mangroves adjacent to the sea were inundated with each high tide and removal occurred on a daily basis. Further inland, litter removal was greater on spring tides and accumulation on the sediment occurred during intervals between spring tides.

Some of the litter may be consumed by animals, such as fiddler (*Uca* spp.), xanthid (*Eurytium* spp.) and sesarmid (*Sesarma* spp.) crabs. McIvor and Smith (1995) demonstrated that these herbivorous crabs were significant consumers of mangrove leaves in Australia. In contrast, carnivorous xanthid and deposit-feeding ocypodid crabs dominated the crab fauna in the southwestern Florida mangrove studied by these authors, and crab herbivory on mangrove leaves was not detected. This suggests that mangrove leaf litter processing in the Indo-Pacific may differ fundamentally from that in the Caribbean. In the Indo-Pacific, herbivory by crabs is important, whereas in the Caribbean detrital pathways may dominate.

Most mangrove organic matter is probably decomposed by micro-organisms (bacteria and fungi) that live in prodigious numbers in the sediment. Accurate estimates of bacterial densities have rarely been made and both temporal and spatial variation is very high. Alongi (1994) quoted bacterial densities in sediments from northeastern Australian mangroves ranging from 0.2 to 35.9×10^{10} cells g^{-1}. These bacteria provide essential food for heterotrophs (protists and invertebrates) that constitute the detrital food web. However, Alongi (1994) pointed out that most bacteria remain unconsumed and die naturally with the next generation of bacteria consuming their remains. Populations of bacteria in these tropical sediments are ultimately controlled by inputs of dissolved and particulate organic matter. These micro-organisms utilise this organic matter and in doing so alter its chemical and physical properties in a process called **decomposition**. This process is a vital one and is an integral part of all nutrient cycles (see section 5.13).

10.7 | Decomposition

Decomposition is the term given to the process of breaking down organic matter into its constituent inorganic components. The major input to this process is **litter** (dead leaves, branches, twigs, flowers and fruits) but also includes animal parts (shed skin, hair, feathers), corpses, waste products, plant exudates, animal secretions, belowground inputs (roots and root exudates) and organic matter carried in from outside the system.

Decomposition is a staged process in which a **resource** (detritus, organic matter) is broken down through a combination of physical, chemical and biological processes. Each stage results in a change in resource quantity and quality and may ultimately lead to the complete removal of carbon or **mineralisation**. Resource quality is a function of the carbon and energy content, the nutrient content and the presence of compounds, known as **modifiers**, that impede microbial attack. The physical breakdown process is simply a reduction in the particle size of the organic matter. In the marine environment, wave action is one important agent in this process. In mangroves, fiddler crabs physically break down large particles into smaller ones during feeding. A decrease in the particle size enhances the rate of biological decomposition. This reduction in particle size is known as **comminution**.

Particles of organic matter are colonised by a variety of micro-organisms (bacteria and fungi) which secrete enzymes that degrade complex organic molecules into simpler ones that can then be absorbed by the microbes. This process is known as **catabolism**. The organisms that feed on detritus eventually die and their remains become detritus which, in turn, are acted upon by other decomposers. Note that there is, thus, a recycling of matter between the detritus and decomposer compartments and that this recycling process is not found in the plant–herbivore system we discussed in chapters 3 and 4. Herbivores and their associated predators are only able to use organic matter fixed by photosynthesis once. However, recycling within decomposition has limits as, with each cycle, carbon is lost from the system as carbon dioxide. Matter may also be lost from the original detrital resource through formation of volatile or soluble compounds. Catabolism results in a changed chemical composition of the resource material.

Any soluble compounds present or produced in the organic matter are susceptible to a third loss process: **leaching**. Leachate loss is influenced by both comminution and catabolism, and compounds in the leachate may be subjected to further decomposition. This decomposition model is summarised in Figure 10.7. Decomposition performs two major ecosystem functions: mineralisation of essential elements which can then be recycled (see section 5.13) and the formation of soil organic matter (see section 2.9). Elements retained within the soil organic matter are said to be **immobilised**. Note that immobilisation inevitably accompanies mineralisation. Some of the carbon in detritus being decomposed by bacteria is respired to carbon dioxide (mineralised) and some is reconstituted into bacterial tissue (immobilisation). Immobilisation is primarily brought about by plants incorporating mineralised elements into organic matter through nutrient uptake and photosynthetic fixation. Immobilisation and mineralisation occur repeatedly as elements cycle in an ecosystem.

A compound that is rendered soluble by catabolism could either be lost from the particle through leaching or absorbed by a microbe, reconstituting it as a particle. Therefore, we can visualise decomposition as a cascade, with the three processes (comminution, leaching and catabolism) occurring repetitively until the detritus has been entirely mineralised (all carbon removed). Obviously the three processes operate simultaneously and each may affect the rate of the other two. For example, particle size reduction may enhance access of catabolic enzymes and catabolism will facilitate leaching. The relative

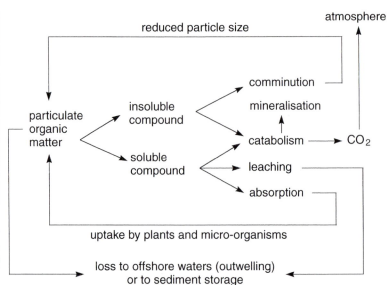

Figure 10.7 A simplified model of a decomposition cascade whereby a resource is broken down by catabolism, comminution and leaching. Through these processes the resource may be mineralised, resynthesised into microbe tissues, stored in the sediment as humus or exported as particulate or soluble material. A suite of environmental and biotic factors control the rates of the breakdown process.

importance of these three processes varies with environmental factors and the suite of organisms present.

Let us follow the fate of a leaf falling from a mangrove to the sediment below. First soluble compounds such as reducing sugars will be leached from the leaf; this may occur quite rapidly if the leaf falls into the water or on to moist soil. This loss will be accelerated if some comminution occurs first. Some enzymes in the leaf may continue to work, breaking down complex molecules, into substances that are more susceptible to leaching. Microbial colonisation of the leaf may be rapid, with fungal spores, algae and invertebrates appearing on the leaf surface within a few hours under moist conditions. These early colonisers utilise the easily mobilised sugars and starches as their respiratory substrate. After about a week, the leaf may be covered in a microbial slime. However, if the tannin content of the leaf is high, this microbial colonisation may be delayed until tannins have leached from the leaf. Many mangrove leaves contain compounds which deter herbivores and decomposers.

As decomposition proceeds, the quality of the litter changes. The concentrations of **labile** (easy to break down) organic compounds decline and more **refractory** materials, such as cellulose, lignin and cutin, remain. As this change occurs, so the suite of micro-organisms changes with the early colonisers being replaced by organisms equipped with enzyme systems that can attack the remaining, more recalcitrant compounds. Decomposition now proceeds more slowly, hin-

dered by the slow penetration of fungal hyphae through lignified cell walls and the scarcity of labile compounds. There is, thus, a natural succession of decomposing organisms, which progressively colonise the resource as the chemical nature of the resource changes. Most decomposers are specialists, equipped with enzymes that will only digest certain compounds. Therefore, decomposition occurs as a series of successive invasions by organisms, as the resource quality changes.

Many studies have shown that litter-feeding animals (**detritivores**) are dependent upon microbial colonisation, relying for their energy supply more on the bacteria and fungi on the litter than on the energy within the litter itself. However, as the litter is ingested and passes through the gut, mechanical breakdown occurs and the partially digested particles egested as faeces are more susceptible to subsequent microbial attack. Other animals (**microbivores**) feed specifically on the microbes that grow on the detritus without actually ingesting it. These animals include protozoans and nematodes feeding on bacteria, and a variety of insects, nematodes and other invertebrates that feed on fungi.

Many detritivores do not have the enzyme systems required to break down cellulose. They rely on bacteria and protozoans which can produce these enzymes (cellulases). In some cases, the bacteria and protozoans live permanently in the animal's gut in an obligate mutualism (see section 8.7.4). Other detritivores make use of cellulases produced by organisms established on detritus. Ship-worms (actually these are bivalve molluscs) such as *Lyrodus pedicellatus* and *Teredo bartschi* bore into wood with a rasping valve. The tunnel created is lined with calcium carbonate and these animals play a major role in wood decomposition both through their own activity and through increasing the surface area of wood available for fungal attack. It has been shown that these animals have special Deshayes glands which contain symbiotic bacteria that can not only digest cellulase but also fix nitrogen (see section 5.13.2). The shellfish, in return for providing a conducive environment and energy supply to the bacterium, gets its carbon source digested along with a nitrogen supplement.

Mangrove bark, with its high tannin concentration, protects the underlying wood from attack by wood borers, fungi and bacteria. However, marine fungi and bacteria soon colonise mangrove wood if the bark is removed or damaged. These organisms then facilitate colonisation by wood borers, which, in turn, provide avenues for further attack by micro-organisms. Borer attack seems to be enhanced by nutrient availability, but it is not known whether this is due to direct nutrient uptake by the shipworms or by the bacterial symbionts that they harbour (Kohlmeyer *et al.* 1995).

Faust and Gulledge (1996) showed that floating detritus, with microbes and associated meiofauna, acted as a platform that rose in the morning and settled back to the sediment at night. At daybreak, algae associated with detritus begin photosynthesis and generate oxygen bubbles. The bubbles adhere to the detritus, make it more buoyant and carry it towards the surface. Nutrient-enriched dinoflagellate resting cysts carried on the detritus re-enter the water column and form new dinoflagellate populations. Near the water surface, algal cells are exposed to warmer temperatures and higher light intensities, conditions which promote their growth. Bacteria also grow well, and the detritus harbours a diverse group of meiofauna (nematodes, ciliates and crustaceans) which feed on the algae and bacteria. In this way, floating detritus acts as a vehicle that, each day, transports benthic microbial communities into the surface waters where micro-organism productivity is enhanced. At sunset, detrital aggregates sink to the bottom. These aggregates contain dinoflagellates which now produce resting stages in the colder, nutrient-enriched waters overlying the sediments. These floating platforms are sites of active algal production and bacterial decomposition and provide food for a diverse heterotrophic community.

10.8 | Decomposition rates and environmental factors

Litter breakdown rates can be estimated by enclosing litter in mesh bags which permit colonisation of the litter by various organisms but retain most of the litter. These bags can be filled, weighed and placed in the field. At regular intervals the bags are removed and reweighed to trace weight loss. The mesh size of the bags is critical – it determines what organisms can invade the bag – and, as some loss from the bags of undecomposed material occurs, actual decomposition rates are likely to be slower than those measured.

Decomposer communities have been classified by size into micro-flora (bacteria and fungi) and micro-, meso- and macro-fauna. The major role of the micro-fauna and meso-fauna lies in regulating micro-flora populations and reworking the faeces produced by larger animals. The animals in these size classes do not have a significant impact on comminution. The macro-fauna can attack plant and animal remains and is responsible for the physical breakdown of large particles of organic matter. With prior knowledge of the structure of the microbial community and careful selection of litter-bag mesh sizes, it is possible to assess the role in decomposition of each of the four size classes.

The rate of decomposition may be limited by colonisation of the resource by suitable organisms, resource quality and environmental factors. Resource quality is largely a measure of the nutritional value of the litter, but could also include a measure of its physical suitability for colonisation (surface properties, texture). The rate of decomposition is particularly influenced by temperature, oxygen supply and the nutritional status of the resource.

Since decomposition involves biochemical reactions controlled by enzymes, temperature plays a fundamental role in controlling the rate of organic matter breakdown. Mackey and Smail (1996) measured decomposition rates (as weight loss in litter-bags) in a subtropical mangrove. They found that rates were higher at sites near the sea (greater inundation) and during summer. In tropical mangroves, decomposers will rarely be limited by low temperature, but, in subtropical mangrove forests, decomposition may be faster during the summer. Therefore decomposition in higher latitude mangroves may exhibit greater seasonality.

Oxygen supply is also important in determining the rate of decomposition, particularly in aquatic sediments. As decomposition proceeds, oxygen is consumed through respiration by the decomposer organisms. If oxygen supply is adequate, aerobic respiration is favoured, if not, less efficient fermentation occurs. Most tropical coastal waters are well oxygenated and, therefore, oxygen supply probably does not limit decomposition. However, the continuous supply of organic matter to the sediments within a mangrove forest and the rapid rates of decomposition by the bacteria and fungi that reside within them, can produce anoxic sediments just a few millimetres below the surface.

In this oxygen-free environment live a variety of bacteria equipped with different forms of anaerobic respiration: denitrifiers, sulfate-reducers and methane producers. These organisms are responsible for the smell that emanates from disturbed mangrove sediments. Breakdown of organic matter by these organisms is less efficient than that carried out by aerobes and, therefore, organic matter accumulation may be greater where oxygen supply is limited. Peat accumulates where the rate of organic matter supply exceeds that of organic matter breakdown and export.

The supply of essential nutrient elements (e.g. nitrogen, phosphorus, potassium, calcium) may limit the growth of decomposer organisms. Such limitation may affect not only the rate at which these organisms function but also the composition of the decomposer community. Carbon to nitrogen ratios provide an indication of the biodegradability of a resource, as the small proportion of nitrogen in plant material often limits the rate of its breakdown.

When the C:N ratio is higher than 25:1, carbon is respired and nitrogen is incorporated into the proteins of the decomposer organism. Under conditions of excess nitrogen (C:N less than 25:1), nitrogen is lost as ammonia. Consequently, addition of organic matter to sediments and soils may result in a decline in the nitrogen content of the substrate. Ratios between carbon and nutrient elements may not provide an index of biodegradability if some nutrient not considered is limiting or if an inhibitory substance is present in the resource.

Plants produce a myriad of compounds to defend their tissues from attack by animals and micro-organisms. Some of these compounds remain effective after the plant part has fallen from the plant. These chemical components that affect decomposer growth are known as **modifiers** or **secondary plant products**. Despite these compounds, the input of litter to mangrove systems provides an energy resource for a variety of organisms: bacteria, Fungi, Protista and invertebrates. This input forms the basis of a detritus food chain.

10.9 | Detritus food chains

Organisms forming links in detrital food chains may be classified as **necrotrophs** (kill their food resources), **biotrophs** (exploit living hosts) and **saprotrophs** (utilise dead material). Many of the benthic organisms feed on bacteria which enrich the protein content of the organic matter by decomposing refractory materials over time. In this way, these organisms obtain a significant amount of their energy from the bacteria that adhere to detrital particles and not directly from the detritus. Therefore, technically, they should not be classed as detritivores. However, since detritus is the source of energy, it seems reasonable to refer in this way to the organisms that rely on it and constitute a detritus food web.

Analysis of the carbon isotope composition of food sources and gut contents provides a way to identify the carbon source of the food that makes up an animal's diet. Primary producers such as phytoplankton and seagrasses fix carbon in different ratios of ^{12}C and ^{13}C and by determining these ratios, food sources can be inferred. Using this technique, Fry and Parker (1979) were able to show that estuarine prawns were feeding on seagrass detritus rather than that derived from phytoplankton. Ambler *et al.* (1994) studied the detrital food web in a Belizean mangrove and found that the detritus did not show a strong signal from the major suppliers: red mangrove, seagrass and dominant intertidal alga and probably reflected subtidal and dinoflagellate sources. They recommended that a more definitive analysis would involve multiple stable isotopes and especially those of sulfur which might discriminate more clearly between algal and mangrove detritus. There is little change in carbon stable-isotopic composition through the food chains, and this can therefore help to reveal sources, while the number of trophic steps can be indicated by nitrogen stable isotopes. Isotope stable data need to be interpreted with some caution but they have proved a useful supplement to our understanding of food webs.

In the organic-rich mangrove sediments, bacterial growth is rapid and controlled largely by nutrient supply and environmental conditions and not by detritivore grazing. Bacteria in mangrove sediments are important not only in providing food for other organisms, but also in mineralising organic matter. Alongi (1994) reviewed the role of bacteria in nutrient cycling in coastal ecosystems and stressed that bacteria provide a trophic link in the benthic food web, recycling nutrients with great efficiency that leads to retention within the ecosystem. He concluded that microbial communities in tropical soils and sediments are responsible for a very large share of the energy and nutrient fluxes through these systems. Therefore, any restoration

of degraded mangrove habitats will require stimulation of bacterial growth to facilitate efficient nutrient recycling and conservation.

10.10 | Decomposition in other tropical systems

Swift *et al.* (1979) provide a summary of decomposition processes in major ecosystems types. Tropical rain forests (chapter 8) are evergreen, and litter input continues throughout the year. Decomposition is not limited by temperature or water availability, and carbon dioxide evolution from the litter and soil layer shows little temporal variation. Animal decomposers occur not only on the forest floor, but also in the tree canopies, and considerable decomposition may occur before the organic matter reaches the forest floor. Termites are abundant and comminution rates are high. Some leaves from tropical forest trees contain high concentrations of tannin, and decay in these leaves is slowed. Microbial biomass, particularly of fungi, is large, and turnover rates are high owing to the constant high temperatures and moisture content.

Savannas differ from rain forest areas in that they experience a distinct dry season (chapter 4). Litter input to savanna soils follows the seasonal growth of the plants and microbial activity, limited by moisture availability during the dry season, peaks during the wet season. The soil fauna is dominated by termites. Operating within galleries of soil, these animals do not seem to be limited by water shortage during the dry season and forage throughout the year. Termites and dung beetles facilitate decomposition through their burrowing activities and microbial biomass is high. Decomposition is rapid during the wet season.

In tropical lakes, the rate of decomposition may be hindered by oxygen supply. Organic matter is produced in the epilimnion of a stratified lake (chapter 5) and settles out into the hypolimnion. In this lower layer, oxygen input is prevented by the little mixing that occurs between it and the overlying waters in contact with the atmosphere. As decomposition proceeds, oxygen is consumed and organic matter break-down may slow as oxygen availability declines. Bacteria and fungi colonise senescent phytoplankton cells as they sink through the water column. The cell, with its complement of micro-organisms, settles on the sediment, and it is here that decomposition may be limited by oxygen supply. Organic enrichment of the sediment may result. In the littoral zone, aquatic plant detritus may accumulate in the sediment faster than it is being broken down and lead to peat deposits.

10.11 | Coastal zone management

Mangroves supply humans with a number of natural products and ecological services. Products include: firewood, charcoal, tannin, dyes, poisons, timber and thatching for house construction and food (fish, shellfish and crustaceans). Many marine species of fish and Crustacea that are important in both subsistence and commercial fisheries utilise mangroves and seagrass beds as breeding and nursery areas. Mangroves and seagrass beds also provide coastal protection from tidal erosion and act as sediment traps, reducing the sediment load of inflowing waters. Organic matter export from mangroves and seagrass beds enhances offshore productivity, and coastal waters adjacent to these ecosystems are more productive as fisheries than other coastal zones.

Overexploitation of mangroves has led to significant declines in their area in recent decades. In Indonesia, more than 2000 km^2 of mangroves produce 250 000 m^3 of wood chips each year and, in Sabah, over 1200 km^2 (40% of the total mangrove area) were set aside for wood-chip production (Fortes 1988). Particularly in South-East Asia, large areas of mangroves have been cleared and excavated to produce prawn, crab and fish culture ponds. In Singapore these areas have been further converted into urban developments.

In many tropical countries, coastal settlements and towns grow faster than the infrastructure required to handle human wastes. Although mangroves have a capacity to absorb nutrients from wastewaters, and, indeed, even benefit from them (Clough et al. 1983), excessive loads can further stress mangrove plants and animals already having to cope with anaerobic sediments. While anaerobic sediments may trap heavy metals and pesticides, our understanding of how these substances might cycle through mangrove food chains is inadequate and further study is required before mangroves are used as waste-disposal sites. Mangroves and seagrass beds are very effective traps for oil slicks. When the oil tanker Showa Maru ran aground in the Malacca Straits in 1975, crude oil spilled from it and killed vast areas of mangroves along the east coast of Sumatra.

Rapid human population growth along tropical coasts and the destruction of mangrove and seagrass habitats has spurred the development of Integrated Coastal Zone Management (ICZM) techniques. Conflicts among human needs, sustainable resource use and coastal zone conservation can only be resolved through careful planning at a regional level. ICZM aims to maximise sustainable use of coastal resources while, at the same time, both maintaining high biodiversity and conserving critical habitats. Successful management requires scientific information (research), planning (at all levels, particularly local community), education and fair and enforceable legislation.

10.12 | Chapter summary

1. Mangroves line approximately 75% of tropical coastlines and extend into the subtropical and warm temperate regions where water temperature is greater than 24 °C in the warmest month and where rainfall exceeds 1250 mm.

2. There are two main centres of mangrove diversity. The eastern group (East Africa, India, South-East Asia, Australasia and the Western Pacific) has around 40 species with peak diversity in Northern Australia and New Guinea. The western group (West Africa, North and South America and the Caribbean) is less diverse with only 8 species.

3. Marked zonation occurs in mangrove communities subjected to environmental gradients, and these gradients are usually related to the transition from salt to freshwater. Zonation patterns are most obviously associated with water depth and tidal regime.

4. Mangrove soils are usually anaerobic. Mangroves have been classified as salt excluders (restrict salt entry into the roots), salt excretors (allow salt to enter and excrete the excess from special glands on the leaves) or salt tolerators. Mangrove roots have lenticels and pneumatophores to facilitate oxygen uptake. A thick cuticle on mangrove leaves serves to reduce water loss. Many species have stilt and buttress roots to improve anchorage in unstable sediments.

5. Some mangrove and seagrass genera are viviparous. Non-viviparous mangroves produce large seeds and fruits, and this food reserve provides the seedling with energy to help it through the early stages of establishment.

6. Mangroves provide a physical habitat for both terrestrial and marine animals and in contrast to mangrove plants, the aquatic animal community is dominated by marine families which have become adapted to variable salinities, turbid conditions and to feeding directly or indirectly on materials from mangrove trees. Many of the terrestrial animals that utilise mangroves, do so only for short periods.

7. Mangrove communities are highly productive with rates comparable to many terrestrial forest communities, and they provide an important source of organic matter for food chains both within the mangroves themselves and, through outwelling, to adjacent estuarine and coastal areas.

8. Seagrasses are marine angiosperms. The Indo-Pacific flora comprises 7 genera in 2 families; the Caribbean and Central America has 4 genera. Seagrasses provide habitat and food to a variety of fish, invertebrates, turtles, manatees and dugongs. Epiphytes and epifauna form a thick, felt-like covering on older seagrass leaves. Seagrass meadows are highly productive systems. Plant material that is not consumed within seagrass beds may be either exported with the tides or undergo decomposition.

9. Decomposition is the breakdown of organic matter into its constituent inorganic compounds and is a combination of three separate processes: comminution (particle size reduction), leaching (loss of soluble compounds) and catabolism (metabolic breakdown). Rates of these processes are controlled by the suite of organisms present, the resource quality and environmental factors (principally temperature, water availability and oxygen supply).

10. Decomposition occurs through successive colonisations by decomposers as the composition of the substrate is altered by previous colonists. Decomposers and detritivores have no control over rates of resource supply. They exist in a 'donor-driven' environment. Nitrogen supply in the substrate often limits the rate of decomposition of plant detritus. Only a few detritivores produce the enzyme cellulase and those lacking this enzyme may form alliances with those that do.

11. Mangroves are used by humans to supply: firewood, charcoal, tannin, dyes, poisons, timber and thatching for house construction and food. Overexploitation of mangroves has led to significant declines in their area in recent decades.

Chapter 11

Coral reefs and community ecology

11.1 | Coral reef communities

11.1.1 Long-spined black sea urchin

In 1983, the population of the long-spined black sea urchin (*Diadema antillarum*) suffered massive mortality (see section 4.7), apparently from disease, throughout the Caribbean Sea and tropical western Atlantic. Other species of echinoderms were not harmed and therefore the pathogen was probably species-specific. *Diadema* populations were drastically reduced by 87–100% in Barbados, 97–100% in Curaçao and 98–100% in Jamaica (Hughes 1994). This die-off of one species led to some profound changes in the species composition of organisms living within coral reef communities in the Caribbean.

Diadema is a major herbivore on Caribbean reefs and, in Jamaica, the dramatic reduction in the population of this herbivore was followed by large increases in algal biomass on many reefs. Coral cover declined to very low levels, as these light-requiring organisms were shaded by algae. The two dominant corals *Acropora palmata* and *A. cervicornis* were virtually eliminated. Algae reduced coral cover by overgrowing corals and prevented coral recruitment by pre-empting space on the reef. Small corals were particularly sensitive. Coral cover was reduced from nearly 50% to only 2–3% on one reef near Jamaica. Some of this reduction was caused by damage from Hurricane Allen that swept over the area in 1980, but many of the surviving corals were smothered in algae. Algae can not settle on live coral and, therefore, the abundance of dead coral resulting from the

hurricane facilitated the expansion of algal populations.

The three-spot damselfish (*Stegastes planifrons*) defends a small territory or algal garden and is so aggressive that it even keeps away larger fish and sea urchins. These fish 'weed' out large algae and corals from their territory and so husband the growth of filamentous algae, their preferred diet. The biomass of algae within the damselfish territory is approximately ten times higher than that outside. Three years after the demise of *Diadema* populations, algal biomass was 5 and 50 times greater inside and outside damselfish territories respectively.

Before the urchin die-off, the heavily grazed algal communities outside damselfish territories were dominated by crustose coralline algae and calcified species such as *Halimeda*. Foliose species formed a dense algal turf within the damselfish territories. Following the *Diadema* crash, damselfish continued to defend and tend their gardens, but the algal community outside their territories switched to one dominated by large, foliose and erect, calcified species such as *Dictyota*, *Padina* and *Halimeda* (Hughes 1994).

Three years after the *Diadema* mortality, populations had not recovered. The smaller populations exhibited a bimodal distribution indicating that the population was made up of some individuals that had survived the mass mortality and a few recruits. By 1994, individuals were large and well fed with well-developed gonads, but the population density remained low. Surprisingly, no changes in the population densities of other echinoderm species living in association with *Diadema* were detected 3 years after the mass mortality.

Numbers of herbivorous fish also remained low, probably because of overfishing. Indeed, it is probable that the large populations of *Diadema* that developed in the early 1980s may have done so in response to declining populations of herbivorous fish through overfishing. On reefs with higher populations of herbivorous fish and lower fishing intensity, algal biomass peaked 6 months after the urchin die-off and then declined steadily. Densities of less conspicuous herbivores such as gastropods, polychaete worms and crustaceans may have increased but not to an extent that could have a significant impact on algal populations. Clearly the reduction in the population density of *Diadema* had profound effects on the coral reef communities in the Caribbean.

11.1.2 Crown-of-thorns starfish

Acanthaster planci is a large starfish (up to 60 cm in diameter) with sixteen arms that feeds on hard corals by everting its stomach, spreading membranes over the coral, and digesting the living tissue within the coral skeleton (Figure 11.1). It also feeds on molluscs and echinoderms but corals form the bulk of its diet. On reefs off the coast of Panama, *Acanthaster* feeds on non-branching corals and avoids the more abundant *Pocillopora* species which coexist with crustaceans that protect the coral from starfish attack.

This starfish is usually recorded in small numbers ($5-6\,\mathrm{km}^{-2}$) on most reefs throughout the Indian Ocean and tropical Pacific. Episodically, huge populations of these predators have developed on reefs in the Pacific and large areas of reef have been devastated by them. In some cases, densities as high as 260 per hectare have been recorded on the Great Barrier Reef with coral cover declining from 30–50% to 6–8%. This starfish is normally nocturnal, hiding during the day, but when large populations develop it feeds during the day as well (Engelhardt and Lassig 1996).

The cause of these outbreaks is not clear, but possibilities include the reduction in the number of *Acanthaster* predators (particularly the giant triton, *Charonia tritonis*), reef degradation from nutrient enrichment, hurricane damage, changes

Figure 11.1 Crown-of-thorns starfish (*Acanthaster planci*) (Photo: Laurence Gould, Oxford Scientific Films).

in salinity or some combination of these. Population control through triton predation has been largely discounted because these predators are rare and often only half the starfish is eaten. The half not consumed can escape and regenerate lost limbs which become functional in about 2 months. The triton only consumes around 1 adult starfish a week and also feeds on other prey and therefore is unlikely to have much impact on *Acanthaster* populations. However, declining numbers of fish (from overfishing) that feed on starfish larvae may allow increased larval settlement.

Another theory proposes that destruction of reefs by blasting and dredging caused these outbreaks. Reef destruction provides larvae of *Acanthaster* with settlement surfaces that are free of filter-feeders, the main larval predators.

Decreased larval mortalities in these areas may result in the development of a concentrated population which forms the nucleus for an infestation. Corals recently killed by adult starfish provide excellent settling areas for larvae and this fuels the explosive population growth. A third theory suggests that nutrient enrichment increases larval food supply, resulting in mass settlement of starfish larvae.

We are really not sure what causes these outbreaks, but scientists are focusing on nutrient enrichment and predator removal as likely causes. Outbreaks not only occur but also disappear, seemingly without explanation and may be a natural and integral way in which coral reefs function. Over time reefs recover from these infestations. However, if the frequency of infestations is being enhanced through human activities such as nutrient disposal and overfishing, this capacity for recovery may be exceeded. This may lead to a permanent loss of coral cover and a decline in the diversity of fish and other animals dependent on corals.

11.1.3 Symbioses among reef species

Coral reefs also abound with examples of both competitive and co-operative interactions between species. Some damselfish aggressively defend small patches of algal turf, chasing away fish many times larger than themselves. Competition for space and light is intense and reef organisms compete for these resources in a number of ways. Some corals are fast-growing, producing branches that shade out competitors. Other species are even more aggressive. On contact with another coral, they extrude filaments that digest away their neighbour. Many corals have stinging cells which are discharged on contact with potential space-invaders. Some of the voracious predators on corals include sea urchins, snails, worms and fish.

There are also many examples of organisms interacting in more peaceful, mutually satisfying ways. Large, non-territorial fish such as wrasses, groupers and parrot-fish congregate at specific sites known as cleaning stations. Here, these large fish have ectoparasites and dead tissue removed by cleaner fish. The cleaners do a thorough job,

even entering the mouth and cleaning between the teeth of the much larger fish!

Fish, such as clown fish, and shrimps will seek shelter from predators by lurking amongst the tentacles of anemones or the spines of sea urchins. The tentacles of the anemone contain stinging cells with a poison capable of killing fish. By living in amongst the tentacles, the clown fish is protected from its predators. You may well ask why does the clown fish not get stung? The anemone stinging cells are triggered when touched. However, the anemone has a mechanism to ensure that one tentacle touching another does not cause stinging cells to fire. It does this by recognising its own body through the specific composition of its mucous covering. The brightly coloured clown fish coats itself in this mucous and thereby avoids being stung because the anemone believes that the fish is a part of its own body! In return for its protection from predators, the clown fish attracts food for the anemone. Clown fish predators who get too close to the anemone are stung and devoured by it. Clown fish have even been observed bringing food to the anemone and feeding it.

Clearly, biotic interactions on coral reefs are extraordinarily intricate. Indeed, as we will see below, the entire reef structure arises from a close association between animals and algae. Community ecology is concerned with questions such as: how and why are such intricate relationships maintained? How do these systems respond to disturbance? Why are they so many species? What determines the relative number of plants, herbivores and carnivores? Before we attempt to answer these questions, let us consider the biology of the organisms that are responsible for building reefs.

11.2 | Coral biology

Coral reefs are impressive and complex biological constructions. They are among the most diverse and productive communities on earth. The organisms primarily responsible for building modern reefs are **hermatypic** corals, belonging to a group called the Scleractinia or stony corals. Hermatypic corals contain **zooxanthellae** (see section 11.2.1) whereas **ahermatypic** corals do not. Corals are cnidarians within the Class Anthozoa, animals closely related to sea anemones. They are radially symmetrical, capture prey with stinging cells known as **nematocysts** and are permanently attached to a solid substrate (sessile) (Figure 11.2).

The corals are made up of tiny organisms called **polyps**. A polyp has a body wall only two cells thick: the epidermis on the outside and the gastrodermis lining the gut cavity (**gastroderm**) on the inside. The two layers are separated by a cell-free, gelatinous layer called the **mesoglea** (Figure 11.2). The gut cavity opens to the exterior only through a mouth that is surrounded by tentacles. The polyps secrete a protective calcium carbonate skeleton. The skeletal wall around each polyp is called the **coralite**. Coral growth is indeterminate with no indication of senescence, and some corals may live for centuries and produce a skeleton 5–10 m across.

Corals can be found in the deep sea as well as on temperate and tropical shores but the reef-building or hermatypic corals are only found in tropical (and some subtropical) waters. Reef corals require water temperatures that never fall below 18 °C, clear, clean water with moderately high salinities, and sunlight.

11.2.1 Coral nutrition

Why do these animals require sunlight? Living symbiotically within the cells of all reef-building corals are photosynthetic algae. These algae are dinoflagellates and, like all other photosynthetic organisms, require light. The algae, known as **zooxanthellae**, are essential to the existence of coral reefs and occur in such profusion that they provide most of the colour seen in corals. Zooxanthellae provide the corals with photosynthate and in return receive protection, access to light and nutrients in excretory products from the coral. The most widely distributed species of zooxanthellae is *Symbiodinium microadraticum*, but many other species of algal symbionts are found and even those in closely related coral species are often different species. These unicellular algae live, photosynthesise and reproduce inside the

cells of the coral animal. These algal symbionts are not only found in hermatypic corals. Soft corals, sponges and many molluscs, most notably the giant clams (*Tridacna* spp.) have algal partners. In clams, the algae live outside the cells of the mantle but the relationship between the two organisms is still, none the less, intimate.

Many reef-building corals grow at a wide range of depths, so the quantity and quality of light available to them also varies. Near the surface, with high light intensities, corals may obtain all the energy and carbon they need from the algae. At greater depths or in less clear water, the algae will not be able to contribute as much and the host may have to capture food from the surrounding water to satisfy its carbon and energy requirements. The mechanism by which carbon fixed by zooxanthellae is transferred to the coral remains unclear.

Corals also gain oxygen from their symbionts and avoid the necessity of excreting many of their cellular wastes. The alga benefits from this relationship through living in a nutrient-enriched environment. The waters bathing coral reefs are notoriously deficient in some of the primary nutrients, particularly nitrogen and phosphorus. Despite being bathed in nutrient-poor waters, coral reefs sustain high rates of primary production. They are able to achieve this because of the large volume of water that flows over the reef with each tide and, more importantly, the large investment reef organisms have made in symbiotic relationships. Inorganic nutrients, such as nitrogen and phosphorus, dissolved in the water, are not available to most animals, but those with algal symbionts can access this nutrient supply. Water replenishment occurs with each tide and with each tide small amounts of nutrients are washed over the reef. Corals, with their algal symbionts, are well adapted to absorbing these nutrients even though the concentrations are very low. Once absorbed, symbiosis and other close biological relationships ensure effective recycling and retention of the nutrients by the reef system.

Carbon fixed by zooxanthellae has three possible fates. It may be (1) used to produce new zooxanthellae, (2) respired by the alga or (3) translocated to the coral polyps. The coral uses the

(a)

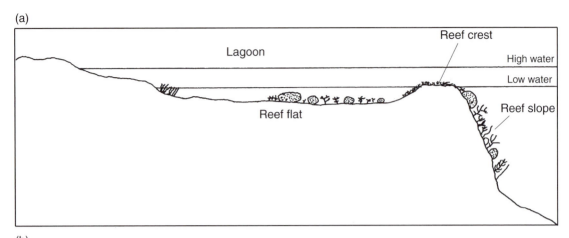

(b)

Figure 11.2 (a) Cross-section of a fringing reef. (b) Corals growing on a fringing reef.

carbon for its own growth, respiration and mucous and gamete production (see section 11.2.3). Some of the fixed carbon is incorporated into the calcium carbonate skeleton (see section 11.2.2).

The zooxanthellae obtain carbon dioxide from that dissolved in the seawater and from that produced by polyp respiration. During the day, photosynthetic uptake of carbon dioxide will exceed that produced by respiration. Therefore carbon uptake from the sea is necessary if the high rates of photosynthesis are to be sustained. It has been assumed that zooxanthellae employ the C_3 photosynthetic strategy (see section 3.7). However, there is some evidence that these algae may use a C_4 pathway as some of the enzymes as well as the early products of this pathway have been detected in extracts of zooxanthellae.

The primary factor affecting the rate of carbon fixation by zooxanthellae is light. In the very clear waters that prevail over most coral reefs, zooxanthellae are able to maintain a positive carbon balance at depths of over 100 m. As light intensity declines with depth, corals respond by reducing light-dependence and increasing their capacity to capture food. Polyp and zooxanthellae densities both decrease with lower light availability. Carbon budgets reveal that there is a high flux of carbon from zooxanthellae to the coral and on to other reef organisms. As depth increases and light availability diminishes, so the flux of carbon declines. In shallow water, corals are phototrophs but, in deeper waters, they switch to greater reliance on heterotrophic nutrition and, where light is inadequate, the corals become obligate heterotrophs.

Light availability may also influence coral morphology in much the same way as it does tree shape (see section 8.2.1). Deepwater, **shade corals**

(c)

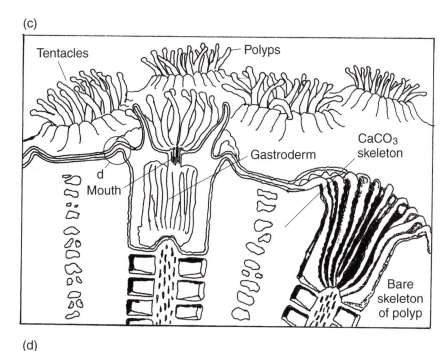

(d)

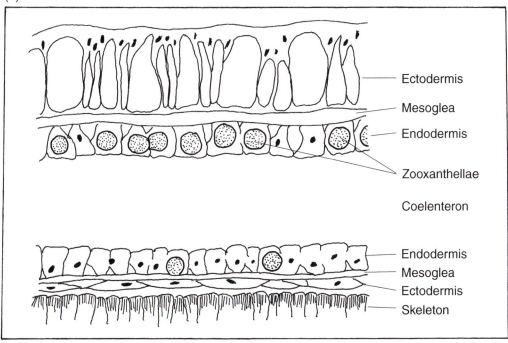

Figure 11.2 (*cont.*) (c) Cross-section through a coral colony showing the structure of the coral polyps within the calcium carbonate skeleton. (d) Cross-section through coral polyp cell layers and their relationship with the skeleton. Note the zooxanthellae in the endodermis (adapted from Castro and Huber 1992; Barnes and Chalker 1990).

grow as flat, horizontal plates, whereas those growing near the surface (**sun corals**) tend to have a more vertical orientation with multiple layers.

Even where light availability is high, corals are unable to rely entirely on zooxanthellae for their nutrition. Carbon translocated from zooxanthellae to corals has a low nitrogen content and has been described as 'junk food' by Falkowski *et al.* (1984). Corals, therefore, do need to supplement their diet, and the nitrogen probably comes from consumption of zooplankton prey. The relative importance of autotrophy versus heterotrophy remains largely unresolved. Dubinsky and Jokiel (1994) argued that, under low light conditions, corals have to supplement zooxanthellae carbon supply with heterotrophic predation on zooplankton. Under high light conditions, although corals receive an adequate supply of carbon from their zooxanthellae, they need to capture zooplankton to supplement their nitrogen uptake. Notice that nutrients obtained by predation are available first to the coral, whereas those absorbed by the zooxanthellae lead first to enhanced algal growth. Each of the symbionts operates to fulfil its needs first and only supports its partner with waste products or compounds that accumulate in excess of their immediate needs.

Coral reefs, with their enormous surface area and numerous polyps constitute a 'wall of mouths' and act as vast filters, trapping particles delivered with each tide. Coral polyps are well equipped to capture food. Corals with large polyps feed on small fish and zooplankton. Species with smaller polyps use cilia to collect plankton and detritus. Prey is captured by the nematocysts borne on the tentacles of the polyps. Some corals also capture prey by mucous entrapment. The prey, once constrained by the sticky mucous, is moved to the mouth by cilia. The food enters the gastrovascular cavity where digestion occurs. Corals tend to feed at night when zooplankton move to the surface to feed and withdraw their tentacles during the day to avoid predation. It was initially thought, based on daytime sampling, that zooplankton populations were too small to provide a significant source of food for corals. However, samples collected at night often contain much higher concentrations of zooplankton.

Minute bacterioplankton, as well as phytoplankton, also provide food for filter feeders on coral reefs. The bacterioplankton utilise organic matter, such as mucous, secreted by coral organisms as a respiratory substrate. In this way, dissolved organic matter is converted into particulate organic matter, and made accessible again to filter feeders.

Clearly, there is a great need to unravel the biochemistry of the symbiotic partners if we are to understand how coral reefs grow. What is clear is that the success of coral reefs hangs on the close relationship between corals and their algal co-habitants (see Box 11.1). This symbiotic relationship is also key to the process by which corals build their massive skeletons, an energy-demanding process known as **calcification**. Without access to the vast quantity of energy in sunlight, corals would not be able to construct such elaborate homes.

11.2.2 Calcification

The skeletons of stony corals are made of calcium carbonate (with some magnesium and strontium) secreted by the polyps as aragonite. Coral deposition of calcium carbonate is very significant and may account for as much as 50% of the total calcium transported into the sea each year by rivers (Smith 1978). The exact mechanism by which these elaborate skeletons are built is unclear but involves removal of calcium from seawater and its combination with carbon dioxide produced from respiration and bicarbonate in seawater. The rate at which the coral skeleton is laid down is strongly influenced by the amount of light available and, clearly, there is a direct link between photosynthesis by the zooxanthellae and **calcification**.

In all cases, photosynthesis by the algae results in increased rates of calcification by the coral host. This is known as light-enhanced calcification. Calcification also occurs at night, albeit at a slower rate. Coral reefs are not entirely constructed by hermatypic corals. A large contribution of calcium carbonate comes from coralline algae, hard, lime-encrusted red and green algae, calcareous hydrozoans, foraminifera, mollusc shells, sea urchin tests and spines and the calcareous remains of other reef animals.

Calcium is the third most abundant cation and bicarbonate the third most abundant anion in seawater. Inorganic carbon is present in seawater as a complex equilibrium that is linked to carbon dioxide solubility and pH (see Figure 5.28). As carbon dioxide dissolves in seawater, the equilibrium shifts to oppose further dissolution of carbon dioxide. The pH of seawater bathing coral reefs is largely controlled by this carbonate equilibrium. This equilibrium is disturbed by photosynthetic removal of carbon dioxide (which causes the pH to rise) and respiratory release of CO_2 (which causes the pH to fall). Precipitation of calcium carbonate occurs when the solubility product of the calcium and carbonate ions is exceeded:

$$H_2O + CO_2 \text{ (aq)} \Leftrightarrow H_2CO_3 \Leftrightarrow H^+ + HCO_3^- \Leftrightarrow 2H^+ + CO_3^{2-}$$

$$H_2O \Leftrightarrow H^+ + OH^-$$

The photosynthetic removal of CO_2 displaces the carbonate equilibrium in seawater; increasing both the pH and the carbonate concentration. As a result, calcium carbonate is precipitated. Calcium carbonate precipitation creates hydrogen ions which oppose further precipitation:

$$Ca^{2+} + H_2O + CO_2 \Leftrightarrow CaCO_3 + 2H^+$$

Some algae can use HCO_3^- as a carbon source for photosynthesis. The bicarbonate is converted, inside the cell, to carbon dioxide in a reaction catalysed by the enzyme carbonic anhydrase. Uptake of HCO_3^- either requires simultaneous uptake of a hydrogen ion or the neutralisation of the hydroxide ion produced when carbon dioxide is released (Barnes and Chalker 1990). Neutralisation of the hydroxide could be achieved by supplying another HCO_3^- ion to calcification.

For each carbon atom incorporated into photosynthate, one carbon atom is added to the calcified skeleton. However, it has been shown that carbon fixation by photosynthesis occurs 4–8 times faster than that fixed by calcification. Calcification is enhanced in those organisms which isolate the site of this process from the surrounding seawater. Scleractinian corals and coralline algae all do this and these organisms are the most important reef builders. These organisms must either have some mechanism to remove or neutralise protons (H^+) created at the site of calcification or a mechanism to prevent the protons reaching the calcification site. The proton may be neutralised with ammonia, produced through the breakdown of urea which would also provide carbon dioxide for skeletal carbonate.

Calcareous algae on coral reefs either deposit aragonite externally or calcite inside the cells. Important calcite depositors include coralline algae such as *Lithothamnion*. The brown alga, *Padina*, deposits aragonite needles in concentric bands. In *Halimeda*, calcification occurs in compartments formed by a network of filaments. The process occurs, like that in corals, outside the organism but isolated from seawater.

Reefs have only developed in tropical seas because high temperatures are required to lay down calcium carbonate at a rate greater than that lost by erosion. The optimum temperature for calcification is between 26 and 27 °C. The rate of calcification slows dramatically when the temperature either falls below 23 °C or rises above 29 °C. Seasonal changes in the rate of calcification produce banding patterns in some of the more massive brain corals. These can be used to age the coral in much the same way as dendrochronologists count the annual rings found in large trees. Furthermore, the banding patterns can also be used to infer interannual differences in the environment.

11.2.3 Coral reproduction

Corals reproduce both sexually and asexually. Asexual reproduction occurs through colony expansion followed by **fragmentation**. Coral fragments which land on a suitable substrate grow into a new clonal colony. This type of reproduction is particularly common in branching corals such as species of *Acropora* that are more susceptible to breakage than the more massive colonial forms. Sexual reproduction involves the production and release of gametes (sperm and egg). The zygote formed following fertilisation, develops into a free-floating larva that facilitates coral dispersal.

Box 11.1: Coral bleaching: when the marriage breaks down

The intimate relationship between corals and their algal partners may break down and when this happens zooxanthellae are expelled from the corals which lose their colour and become bleached. Many reefs throughout the world exhibit annual bleaching when water temperatures rise but rapid recovery may follow. However, particularly severe outbreaks occurred in the Caribbean in 1987 and 1988. The algal symbionts can recolonise the corals, but the longer a coral has to fend entirely for itself the less likely recovery will occur. In 1987, an outbreak of bleaching on reefs off the Cayman Islands in the Caribbean was monitored (Ghiold 1990). Twenty-eight of the 43 species of stony corals were affected, as were several species of sponges that also have zooxanthellae. Many of the bleached colonies had difficulty capturing prey and were only able to feed properly once they had recovered their algal partners. Some corals recovered within a few weeks but others took 2–3 months. Those that died were quickly smothered by algae. Significant bleaching also occurred in widely separate parts of the world from mid-1997 and throughout 1998, a period during which a particularly strong ENSO event occurred (see section 1.2.6).

The cause of bleaching is unclear but seems to be linked with environmental stress: high temperature, prolonged darkness, excessive exposure to ultraviolet light, low salinities or severe weather. Under stressful conditions the coral may be either unable to provide its algal partner with adequate nutrients or it may release substances harmful to the alga. Most corals and their algal symbionts function best within a narrow temperature range, and many tropical marine organisms live dangerously close to the maximum temperature they can tolerate. Therefore, even a small rise in temperature may be enough to cause coral bleaching.

In the eastern Pacific, where corals have been most severely affected by mass bleaching, prolonged sea warming that accompanied both the 1982–83 and 1997–98 ENSO events may have been the primary cause. Hoegh-Guldberg et al. (1996) concluded that elevated sea temperature was the main cause of bleaching but high solar irradiance (especially ultraviolet wavelengths), possible acting in concert with temperature, may also play a role. If coral bleaching is related to only slightly warmer than normal waters, then global warming could bring devastation to tropical coral reefs.

A spectacular reproductive display is exhibited by those corals which **mass spawn**, a synchronous release of gametes, often by more than one species. Species of polychaete worms, molluscs and echinoderms also have mass spawning events. In these events, corals from one or more species release their eggs and sperm at the same time. This impressive display of reproduction occurs in genera such as *Montipora*, *Platygyra*, *Favia* and *Favites*. Mass spawning increases the chance of cross fertilisation occurring, but dilution of gametes in large volumes of sea water can be a major obstacle to zygote formation and fertilisation is often far less than 100%. Synchronous release of gametes is clearly important and corals and other mass-spawning organisms have developed a range of adaptations to enhance the chance of fertilisation. Environmental factors that have been identified as providing spawning cues include variation in temperature and day length, tidal cycle and moonlight. Less predictable cues include plankton blooms and storm events (Babcock 1995).

Mobile organisms that mass spawn often form

massive aggregations before releasing gametes. Vast numbers of sperm may be produced. The crown-of-thorns starfish, *Acanthaster planci*, can release more than 100 g of spermatozoa in a single ejaculation. This large sperm production and the fact that the sperm can survive for relatively long periods in sea water ensured fertilisation rates of over 30% even when male and female were 60 m apart. Eggs may release species-specific sperm attractants and this reduces the chance of gamete wastage through hybridisation and the production of non-viable zygotes. In some hermaphroditic corals, gamete bundles consisting of a lipid-rich egg and sperm are released and float to the surface where the bundle breaks, releasing the sperm close to eggs from other individuals.

On the Great Barrier Reef off Australia, mass spawning occurs in which over 130 species participate. For each species, spawning is restricted to just one or two nights but the entire process may last five days. Spawning occurs around sunset in the week following full moons in October and November (spring). The timing is highly predictable, occurring at the same hour on the same lunar day each year. Up to 30 species have been recorded as spawning on the same night and large slicks of gametes and zygotes form on the sea surface. The lunar cycle seems to be the key environmental cue for gamete formation with the trigger for gamete release being the onset of darkness. Releasing gametes at night probably reduces predation by planktivorous fish and release during a neap tide reduces gamete dilution. With so many species involved it is not surprising that some hybridisation occurs especially between closely related species.

The zygote that forms when the egg and sperm fuse, develops into a **planula larva** which attaches itself to a suitable substrate and grows into a new colony. Some species of coral, such as those of *Acropora*, brood their larvae after eggs are fertilised in a brood chamber. The zygotes are released from the coral and the larvae float to the surface, disperse and eventually settle to form a new colony.

11.3 | Coral reefs

Coral reefs are important land builders in tropical areas forming islands and extending continental shorelines. They occur as three general types: **fringing reefs**, **barrier reefs** and **atolls**. Fringing reefs line the shores of tropical coasts whereas barrier reefs are further offshore and separated from the land by a lagoon. The Great Barrier Reef is by far the largest reef system, bordering some 2000 km of Australia's north-east coast. However, extensive barrier and fringing reefs also occur around the islands of Indonesia, the Philippines, New Guinea and throughout the South Pacific. Major reefs are also found in the Red Sea, Indian Ocean, around the Caribbean islands and along the tropical coasts of Central and South America.

Fringing reefs develop along rocky coastlines throughout the tropics (Figure 11.3). They exhibit several zones related to water depth and degree of exposure to wave action. The **reef crest** is exposed at low tide and may be subjected to severe wave action. Coral rubble tends to accumulate on the fore reef and a **reef flat** extends from the fore reef to the shore. The reef flat is shallow and much of it may be exposed at low tide. Being close to the shore, the reef flat is susceptible to impacts from the inflow of freshwater and sediments. Coral outcrops occur, but most of the bottom may be sand with algae, seagrasses and soft corals. The reef slope may have spurs that extend seaward with sandy canyons between them (see Figure 11.2). The reef slope can be nearly vertical and supports a diverse and dense cover of corals.

Barrier reefs also parallel the coastline, but are usually found further out to sea and may be as far as 100 km offshore. A deep lagoon lies between the barrier reef and the shore (which may be lined by a fringing reef). The barrier consists of a **back reef slope**, reef flat and **fore reef slope**. The fore reef is exposed to the waves rolling in from the open ocean and corals thrive in this environment. On the more protected back reef slope, sediment deposition occurs and coral development is often poorer. Seagrasses, algae, soft corals and coral outcrops grow on the reef flat. Sand and coral debris may accumulate here to form islands (cays). The

Figure 11.3 Fringing coral reefs line one of the Solomon Islands (Photo: Patrick Osborne).

Great Barrier Reef off Australia is not a single reef but a complex system of numerous reefs, islands and lagoons.

Atolls are ring-shaped reefs formed following the subsidence of volcanic islands. Darwin, whilst the naturalist aboard HMS *Beagle* in the 1830s, proposed a mechanism to explain how atolls form. The essential features of this theory are still accepted today. Volcanoes erupting from the seabed form new islands (see chapter 12) which become colonised by coral larvae produced on reefs in the region. In this way, a reef fringing the island is formed. The volcanic island subsides slowly under its own weight and that of the developing reef. The reef, through its growth, may be able to remain in the sunlit surface waters even after the volcanic island has sunk beneath the waves (Figures 11.4 and 11.5). Each atoll rests on what may be a thick layer of dead coral. Drilling on Enewetak Atoll in the Pacific Ocean (site of hydrogen bomb tests by the United States) revealed over 1400 m of shallow-water reef

deposits overlying volcanic basalts. Atolls separate a central lagoon from the open ocean and distinct habitats are formed on the lagoon and seaward faces of the atoll. The circular reef may be cut by deep channels and sand islands may be present.

The dependence of corals on photosynthesis is reflected in their depth distribution. Some small, fragile corals can grow at depths as great as 150 m but most species thrive at depths less than 25 m. Between 50 and 20 m depth, corals growing in clear waters receive adequate light but are protected from the adverse effects of waves. **Coral zonation** is also influenced by wind direction and degree of protection from wave action. In areas where wind direction varies little throughout the year (such as areas subject to trade winds), there is a well-marked windward **reef front**. The front consists of rugged spurs or buttresses separated by deep grooves, a morphology that serves to dissipate wave energy. The grooves form surge channels and material carried down the grooves with each departing waves erodes the coral face. This zone is dominated by massive corals and encrusting coralline algae. Many of the larger predatory reef fish (sharks, barracudas) patrol this area

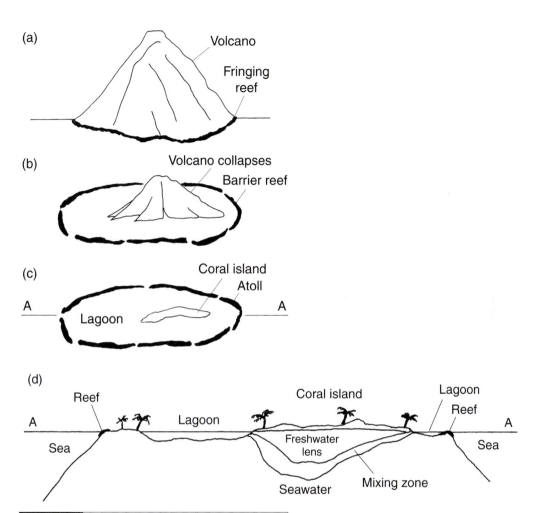

(a) Volcano
Fringing reef

(b) Volcano collapses
Barrier reef

(c) Coral island
Atoll
A   A
Lagoon

(d)
Reef   Coral island   Lagoon
A   Lagoon   Reef
                                                    A
Sea   Freshwater   Sea
                         lens
                                    Mixing zone
            Seawater

Figure 11.4   The development of an atoll. (a) A fringing reef surrounding a volcanic island develops into (b) a barrier reef as the island collapses. The complete submergence of the island leaves an atoll (c) consisting of a central lagoon with a coral island surrounded by a living coral reef. (d) Cross-section through an atoll showing barrier reef and coral island. Rain falling on the island filters through the coral sand and accumulates as a layer overlying the denser seawater. This freshwater lens can be accessed via shallow wells and provides water for people living on atolls (after Commonwealth Science Council 1986).

seeking the smaller fish that hide in crevices and caves in the reef face.

The reef front lies between the **reef slope** (towards the open ocean) and the **windward reef flat**. The reef front may level out to form a platform at around 18 m, a feature that is thought to be a relic formed in the Pleistocene when mean sea level was much lower than it is now. The windward reef front is surmounted by a low, jagged algal ridge, formed by crustose coralline red algae, adapted to survive battering from waves.

A sand island may separate the windward and **leeward reef flats**. The reef flats are barely covered with water at low tide and a wide array of algae, corals, crustaceans, molluscs, echinoderms, holothurians and fish live in the pools on the reef flat. Inside the reef flat is the lagoon. In the Caribbean, lagoon depth usually varies between 5 and 15 m, whereas, in the Indo-Pacific, lagoon depth varies with the size of the atoll and may be over 50 m deep. In the tranquil conditions within the lagoon, vast coral colonies of genera such as *Porites* and *Acropora* are able to develop. Branching forms extend several metres from the bottom, and spread out to capture sunlight and food.

Figure 11.5 Fringing coral reef on an atoll (Korea Island, Kiribati) (Photo: Patrick Osborne).

11.4 | Coral reef algae

Four forms of coral reef algae can be identified: **phytoplankton**, **micro-filamentous algae** (Chlorophyta (green algae), Rhodophyta (red), Cyanobacteria (blue-green)), **coralline algae** (mainly Rhodophyta but also some Chlorophyta and Phaeophyta (brown)) and **macroalgae** (Chlorophyta, Phaeophyta and Rhodophyta). Algae on coral reefs are not clearly zoned, which contrasts with the often distinct bands of macroalgae found on rocky, temperate coasts. The complex physical structure of coral reefs provides a diversity of micro-habitats and the algal flora of coral reefs is usually species-rich.

The coralline algae are unlike most other marine algae which are either unicellular, filamentous or leathery and strap-like. The coralline algae have calcite crystals embedded in their cells and are rigid and hard and they play a significant role in the formation and ecology of coral reefs. This hard outer crust protects these algae from wave damage and makes then less attractive to herbivores. These tough algae are able to colonise parts of coral reefs most exposed to storms and strong currents and they flourish where herbivory is most intense. As with corals, there are costs associated with calcification. It is an energy-demanding process and growth of these algae is often very slow.

In contrast with the coralline algae, the filamentous algae that make up the algal turf that coats exposed reef surfaces, grow incredibly fast. However, intense grazing keeps their biomass in check. Coralline algae avoid being smothered by these turf algae by continuously losing and renewing an outer layer, the **epithallium**. In this way, any would be colonisers are sloughed off with the epithallium. Grazing also helps to keep the coralline algae free of colonists.

Nitrogen and phosphorus are the nutrients most likely to limit algal growth on coral reefs. Concentrations of both elements are typically very low in the coastal waters surrounding coral reefs and retention of these nutrients by the reef ecosystem is high. Nitrogen fixation by Cyanobacteria (see section 5.13.2) may account for 20–40% of the annual nitrogen budget on coral reefs. Light plays a role in determining the depth distribution of algae through both the quantity of light reaching each depth and its quality (wavelength) (see section 5.2.3).

Grazing intensity is a major determinant of algal abundance on coral reefs. Coralline algae are more resistant to grazing and therefore survive well in areas where grazing intensity is high. Turf algae thrive where herbivory and nutrient availability are low. If nutrient concentrations increase, turf algae are replaced by macroalgae. Despite the low biomass of algae on coral reefs, these organisms are responsible for very high rates of primary production which derive from high rates of nutrient cycling. This high nutrient turnover is due to intense herbivory which may remove over 5% of the total algal biomass each day. Utilisation of algal turf biomass may exceed 35% of the standing crop each day. In a thorough study of the territorial jewel damselfish (*Plectroglyphidodon lacrymatus*), Polunin (1988) showed that this fish consumed more than 70% of the net primary production within its territory. As light, at least in the surface waters, is not limiting, coral reef algae clearly facilitate the transfer of this abundant source of energy to the next trophic level.

11.5 | Coral reef herbivores

A great abundance and vast array of animals live in association with corals. Food webs on coral

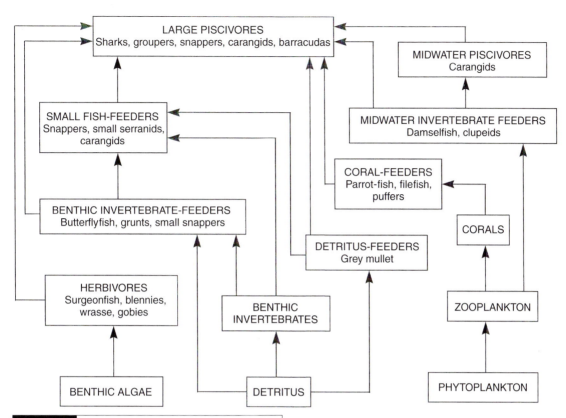

Figure 11.6 Trophic relationships among coral reef fish. Many coral reef animals are omnivores and feed at several trophic levels (after Lowe-McConnell 1987).

reefs are very complex and all trophic levels are represented. Figure 11.6 shows a simple food web of selected coral reef fish. Notice that there are up to five trophic levels (see section 5.9) with the large predators (sharks, barracudas and groupers) at the top of the food chain. In this section, however, we will concentrate on the role of herbivores in shaping coral reef communities.

The major herbivores on reef systems in the Pacific are fish but some of the larger invertebrates such as sea urchins, molluscs and crustaceans can also have a significant impact on algal biomass. In the Caribbean, echinoids are important grazers. We saw at the start of this chapter the changes that followed the demise of one herbivore, the sea urchin, in the Caribbean. Herbivores on coral reefs play a crucial role in maintaining coral populations by preventing them from being smothered by fast-growing algae.

Numerous experiments have demonstrated that coral substrates protected from herbivores are rapidly covered in a higher biomass of algae than those to which grazers have access. Lewis, S. M. (1986) found that exclusion of herbivorous fish (mainly surgeon-fish and parrot-fish) from the barrier reef off the coast of Belize resulted in a rapid and dramatic shift in the algal community. After just 10 weeks of reduced herbivory, an increase in macroalgae (*Padina*, *Dictyota* and *Gelidiella*) and a decrease in the abundance of algal turfs, crustose coralline algae and the coral *Porites astreoides* was recorded. Coral mortality occurred through colonies being overgrown by large algae. Lewis, S. M. (1986) concluded that herbivory appears to maintain a tropical benthic assemblage dominated by algal turf and crustose coralline algae through suppression of macroalgae. The turf species appear to be herbivore-tolerant, but even these species responded to reduced herbivory through increased species

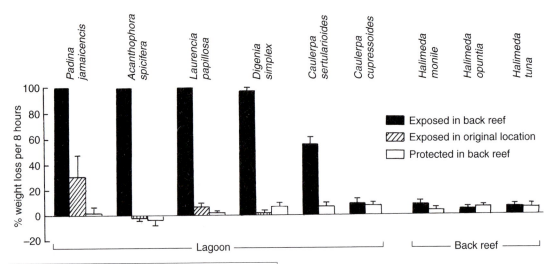

Figure 11.7 The susceptibility of nine algae to herbivory on a coral reef in Belize. Three treatments were set up to test algal susceptibility to grazing. (a) Algae were transplanted into the back reef and exposed to herbivore grazing. (b) Algae were transplanted back to their original location (to ensure that any observed differences were not due to transplanting). (c) Algae were transplanted into the back reef but protected by cages from herbivores. Histograms show the percentage weight loss to herbivores during an 8-hour exposure period. Four species from the lagoon, where grazing pressure is low, were highly susceptible to herbivores and showed 100% weight loss when exposed in the back reef. Notice that the algae growing on the back reef, where herbivory is intense, were not susceptible to grazing and weight loss was less than 10% (after Lewis 1985 with kind permission from Springer-Verlag).

abundances and altered morphology and reproductive status.

Lewis (1985) also showed that algal species transplanted from habitats with low grazing intensity are highly susceptible to grazing. Algae occurring in habitats with high herbivore densities are species highly resistant to grazing. Furthermore, two major components of the herbivore fauna (surgeon-fish and parrot-fish), preferentially grazed different plant species (Figure 11.7). Many algae have mechanisms to deter grazers. Strategies include production of secondary compounds that are toxic or unpalatable, calcification, rapid growth to replace tissues lost through grazing and growth in habitats inaccessible to herbivores.

Halimeda spp. are heavily calcified and have been shown to contain secondary compounds that may deter grazers. However, other algal species that also exhibit morphological and potential chemical defences were shown to be highly susceptible to grazing. The powerful jaws and dentition of parrot-fish may render ineffective any morphological defences. These plants, however, were not grazed by two surgeon-fish which have a much more delicate jaw structure and dentition.

Fish inhabiting coral reefs comprise the most diverse vertebrate faunas known. Some locations in the south-west Pacific may support up to 2000 fish species and within a local habitat it may be possible to view up to 100 species in a single dive. The biomass of fish on coral reefs is also high ranging between 300 and 2000 kg ha^{-1} (Montgomery 1990). These fish not only play a significant role through herbivory, but may also be responsible for transporting large quantities of nutrients between sites on the reef. Planktivorous damselfish (*Chromis* spp.) feed in the waters off the reef during the day and deposit nutrients, as faeces, in their nocturnal shelters on the reef. Reef fish, such as grunts (*Haemulon* spp.) that feed at night in adjacent seagrass beds, also deposit nutrient-rich faeces on the reef during the day.

Herbivory occurs throughout the day and night, with animals actively feeding at different times of the day. A dive on a coral reef at night will reveal a very different suite of animals to that seen

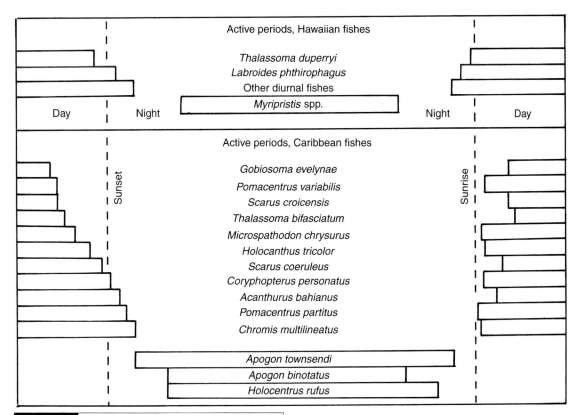

Figure 11.8 Relationship between changes in light level and the activity of fish on Hawaiian and Caribbean coral reefs (after Montgomery 1990 with kind permission of Elsevier Science).

during the day and feeding activity is, in many herbivores, closely regulated by light intensity (Figure 11.8). Around sunset, diurnal feeders leave the reef and seek their nocturnal shelters and a quiet period lasting around 20 minutes ensues until the nocturnal feeders appear. On a reef in Papua New Guinea, this quiet period was stimulated prematurely by a late afternoon total eclipse of the sun. At the end of the eclipse, the diurnal species reappeared (N. Polunin, personal communication). At sunrise, a quiet period occurs after the nocturnal species have retired and before the emergence of the diurnal fish. The nocturnal species tend to be predators and move off the reef at night whereas the diurnal species include herbivores, carnivores and mixed-feeders.

The life cycle of most coral reef fish is divided into two phases. The adults live in close association with the reef, often remaining at the same site for all their lives. Larvae spend from a few days to three months in the open ocean before settling on a reef. In most species, fertilisation of eggs and sperm occurs following their release into the water column, but others lay eggs in nests or are mouth-brooders. Reef fish are **iteroparous** (see section 4.8.1) and their offspring are dispersed over large areas and may colonise reefs far from where they were spawned. Larvae do not depend solely on currents for their dispersal; some have been shown to be fast swimmers with considerable stamina and capable of detecting, probably by sound, a reef 1 km away (Paine 1997).

Reef fish are long-lived (many species live for 10–15 years and some even longer) and therefore reproductive effort is spread over time as well as space. Larval mortality is extremely high and therefore small differences in pre-settling larval mortality will greatly affect the supply of settling larvae. Communities of reef fish are assembled as a result of larval settlement which, because of extensive larval dispersal, may have been produced by adults breeding elsewhere. Therefore coral reef fish recruitment varies in time and space and is not necessarily closely related to local reproductive activity.

Reef fish exist as a series of sub-populations occupying separate reef patches but are connected through the export and recruitment of larvae. Each reef supports a **metapopulation**, a series of partially isolated populations with some level of regular or intermittent migration and gene flow among them. If a population in one area dies out, recolonisation can occur through recruits produced from populations in other areas. Because of this larval interchange, little genetic variation has been detected in reef fish over large areas. For example, no significant genetic difference has been detected in samples of a damselfish collected from Hawaiian reefs 2500 km apart. Greater genetic structure has been detected in reef fish that lack a pelagic larval stage (see Sale *et al.* 1994).

Until recently, coral reef fish communities were thought to be maintained by competition for some limiting resource. In the early 1980s, ecologists realised that sub-populations were limited by the supply of larvae rather than a shortage of resources. Removal of all adult damselfish from a reef off Australia did not enhance recruitment and survival of recruits was not related to density. These results indicate that competition for resources was not occurring (Doherty 1983). Caley (1993) suggested that a variety of post-recruitment processes, notably predation, can modify patterns of species richness and abundance. Increases in the mean species richness and total abundance of non-piscivorous fish were recorded on reefs subjected to periodic removal of predators in comparison with reefs with predators. This experiment demonstrated that recruitment patterns can be disrupted by the action of predators.

Coral reefs are clearly highly diverse and dynamic assemblages. What generates and maintains such high species richness is the subject of the next section.

11.6 | Coral reef biogeography and biodiversity

Populations of coral reef organisms are inherently variable in both time and space. The reefs themselves are distributed in patches across the tropical oceans and they are also patchy on a small, habitat, scale. They are also changeable environments. Fundamental change is brought about simply by coral growth, through violent tropical storms and other disturbances, and, as we have seen, by massive swings in the population size of key organisms such as sea urchins and crown-of-thorns starfish.

The development of coral reefs and their magnificent diversity has been brought about through the ability of their constituent organisms to adapt to change. As in lakes, significant environmental gradients are linked to water depth and corals have exploited these gradients through adaptation and specialisation. This has led to diversification. With diversification, competition has increased, forcing further diversification and specialisation. The key to success has been through the evolutionary fine-tuning of symbiotic relationships between organisms capable of tapping the sun's energy (zooxanthellae) with organisms (the corals and other animals) which can obtain nutrients from a system notoriously poor in dissolved nutrients.

Temperature is probably the dominant factor that controls the geographical extent and distribution of corals and there is a positive correlation between diversity and mean sea surface temperature. Coral reefs are usually absent from coastal areas where cold, nutrient-rich waters upwell (e.g. the Peruvian coast). This is probably due to water temperature, but the effect of nutrients can not be discounted since coral growth is also adversely affected by elevated nutrient concentrations (see section 11.8.3).

On a local scale, coral species diversity is often related to water depth. Diversity is low near the surface and increases to a maximum between 15 and 30 m in depth. Below 30 m, diversity usually decreases. However, the reef environment is very heterogeneous and species composition and diver-

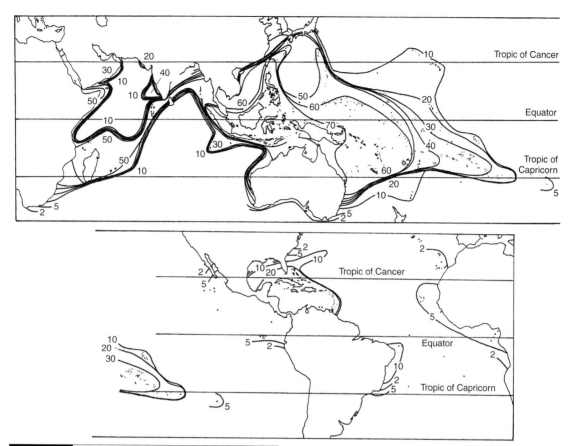

Figure 11.9 Coral generic richness, represented by contour lines. Contours enclose areas with the same approximate number of genera (after Veron 1995 © J.E.N. Veron and the Australian Institute of Marine Science, with kind permission of Cornell University Press and University of New South Wales Press).

sity can not be explained simply by gradients in the physical environment. Micro-habitat conditions and interactions between species are also clearly important (Huston 1985). Competition for space and resources is intense and a small change in community structure (*e.g.* elimination or addition of one species, see sections 11.1.1 and 11.1.2) can have profound effects.

The numbers and taxonomic diversity of animals associated with coral reefs is usually extremely great. Approximately 6000 species of anthozoans exist, all of them are marine. The coral reefs of the Indo-West Pacific are particularly diverse, much more so than those found in the Atlantic and Caribbean. The highest species diver-

sity occurs along the coral reefs of the central and western Pacific around the archipelagos of Indonesia, New Guinea and the Philippines. In this region, 78 genera and approximately 700 species of coral have been identified. The Atlantic Ocean is less speciose with the most diverse reefs being in the Caribbean (24 genera and around 100 species) (Veron 1995; Fraser and Currie 1996; Figure 11.9).

Coral reef diversity decreases with increasing latitude as well as with distance to the east within the Pacific Ocean; diversity is highest at the western, equatorial boundaries of the Pacific, Indian and Atlantic Oceans. Jokiel and Martinelli (1992) have explained this pattern in terms of oceanic currents. Strong and persistent westerly currents dominate surface circulation at tropical latitudes. According to this **vortex model**, these currents carry larvae to the western edges of the oceans at a rate that exceeds dispersal in the opposite direction. Therefore species tend to accumu-

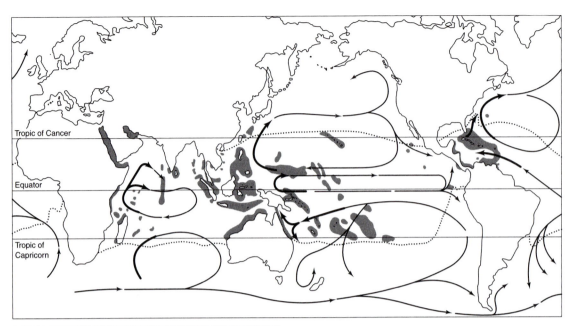

Figure 11.10 Global distribution of coral reefs (dark shading) and the major surface ocean currents. Coral reefs are predominantly distributed on the western margins of the oceans where favourable currents (emphasised by the thicker arrows) deliver clean, nutrient-poor water and disperse larvae from the tropics into higher latitudes. The dotted line shows the 20°C isotherm (after Wilkinson and Buddemeier 1994 with kind permission from IUCN, Gland, Switzerland).

late on the western sides of each of the major tropical oceans (Figure 11.10).

Recent taxonomic work on a range of coral reef animals has revealed a ubiquity of **sibling species** (closely related and very similar but distinct species). Therefore actual reef diversity may be 3 to 5 times greater than previously recognised. Observable differences (colour, shape, size) among sibling species are often small. Occurrence of these sibling species has significant bearing on explanations of coral diversity and its maintenance. Connell (1978) concluded that most corals have broad ranges of distribution and therefore are not habitat specialists. However, with the recent greater taxonomic discrimination, what was formerly recognised as one species is now regarded as several and indicates greater habitat specialisation (Knowlton and Jackson 1994).

A number of theories have been proposed to explain the global distribution of species found living on coral reefs in different parts of the world. A summary of explanations for observed patterns follows (McClanahan and Obura 1996; Fraser and Currie 1996):

1 The origin–dispersal hypothesis states that the areas of high species diversity represent areas of species origination and that species diversity decreases away from these centres.

2 The vicariance hypothesis stresses the importance of barriers to dispersal and isolation in creating new species.

3 Environmental stability leads to high species richness since fewer species can tolerate varying environments.

4 The stress hypothesis maintains that environmental factors (such as cold temperatures) that increase mortality and species extinction will control the abundance of species over both geological and ecological time. Fewer species are physiologically equipped to tolerate stressful environments.

5 The productivity hypothesis contends that high benthic or planktonic primary productivity will support large numbers of species and prevent them from going extinct. Partitioning the available energy among species could restrict community richness. Competition and predation may affect the number of species that can coexist (niche partitioning, see section 11.7.1).

6 The frequency and extent of disturbance may regulate species richness through preventing competitive exclusion.

7 Historical factors such as glaciations and changes in sea level, dispersal and speciation rates may determine species richness.

The applicability of these hypotheses to coral reefs was tested by Fraser and Currie (1996) who found that coral species richness is related most strongly to energy supply. These authors found little evidence to support the other hypotheses, including the hypotheses that disturbance or environmental stability are important controls of diversity. They did find a relationship between coral richness and up-current island density that is consistent with the vicariance model of speciation and dispersal. However, Fraser and Currie (1996) looked at diversity on a large, global scale.

Connell (1978) proposed that at a local scale high levels of diversity are maintained by disturbances that are intermediate in frequency and intensity. Lower diversity results if disturbances are either (1) too frequent or too infrequent or (2) too intense or too weak. For example, Dollar and Tribble (1993) showed that recovery from storm damage to a reef off Hawaii was delayed by repeated intermediate intensity storm events. Furthermore, Rogers (1993) concluded that the effect of disturbances will vary with water depth, life history characteristics and morphologies of the dominant species, and the confounding effects of additional human or natural stresses. Connell *et al.* (1997) showed that the abundance of corals at the Great Barrier Reef site studied by them can largely be explained in terms of the types and scales of disturbances to which each was exposed.

The hypotheses listed above are not mutually exclusive and all may combine to produce the observed global distributions of coral organisms. That so many hypotheses have been proposed is testament to the complexity of these coral-dominated systems and the challenges we face in understanding how organisms interact with each other and their environment. These, and other issues, are being tackled by community ecologists.

11.7 | Community ecology

Organisms do not live in isolation but are linked to other organisms through ecological processes such as food chains and nutrient cycles and through interactions such as mutualism and competition. These associations of organisms and their interactions form the basis of **ecological communities**. Species interactions operating within communities determine energy flow rates, nutrient cycling rates and the relative abundances of the species that constitute the community. Some ecologists have considered a community to include all populations in a habitat. However, much of our knowledge of how communities function has been derived from studies of assemblages of closely related or ecologically similar species such as herbivorous fish, corals, birds or plants. Few studies have even attempted the massive undertaking of detailing all interactions of all species living in one habitat.

We have considered how communities change along spatial gradients (see section 9.7). A simple measure of community structure is the number of species it contains. Why coral reefs and rain forests have so many species is one of the challenging questions community ecologists have tried to answer. We discussed species diversity in chapter 8 as it applies to tropical rain forests, and have seen in section 11.6 that many of the mechanisms used to explain how so many species coexist in a rain forest apply equally well to coral reefs. Therefore, it would seem sensible to look for unifying concepts that might explain how biological communities arise, how they operate and how they change through time. We have looked at how a community might change through time (succession) in chapter 7 and also the changes in community structure that occur following the creation of a gap in a rain forest (see section 8.14).

We have seen in this chapter that interactions between coral reef species are complex and often intimate. We have also seen that removal of just one species from the myriad that occur on a reef can have profound effects on the species that remain. A primary objective of community ecology is to explain the distribution and abundances of species within a habitat and relate these to environmental factors and biological processes (e.g. growth rates, competition, mutualism). We also need to understand both the causes and consequences of shifts in community structure, for example, from a system dominated by corals to one dominated by macroalgae. The **niche concept**, developed by Charles Elton in 1927 and refined by Hutchinson (1957), has provided a theoretical framework that links the number of species in a community to competition for the resources available.

11.7.1 Concept of the niche

In chapter 4 (see section 4.10), we discussed the concept of **competitive exclusion** which states that if two species are using the same resources then one species will out compete the other. Competitive exclusion requires time to occur and therefore is unlikely to be achieved either in environments that never reach equilibrium and are occupied by colonising species or in fluctuating environments that alter the competitive interactions before a conclusion (*e.g.* extinction of one of the competing species) can be reached.

Superficially, a coral reef environment may exhibit little seasonal fluctuation and supports numerous species that seem to be competing for limited resources. It would seem to be an ideal place for ecological competitions to be played out to ultimate conclusions: a reduction in species diversity. How then do so many species survive on a coral reef and yet appear to share similar resources? It has been suggested that each species living within a community, despite the apparent similarity, actually have slightly different resource requirements and take advantage of the variability of resource supply in both time and space.

In chapter 4 we saw how resources vary in both time and space (Figure 4.19). A uniform rate of resource supply would favour those species able to tolerate the lowest resource levels. Species coexistence is promoted in a situation where resource supply is not uniform or where an equilibrium is never attained. We now realise that the coral reef environment is not temporally and spatially uniform. Changes in water temperature, salinity,

turbidity, currents and waves may be quite dramatic. Biotic changes, too, can be pronounced as we have seen in mass spawning events, coral bleaching and population eruptions and declines.

Competition between species that have very similar resource requirements may result in one species succumbing to the other. If however, one of these species altered its resource requirements, even slightly, coexistence might become possible. Each species has a range of environmental conditions within which it can survive (see Figure 2.13) and each requires an adequate supply of resources such as food and space. This suite of environmental ranges and resource requirements determines the **ecological niche** for each species. The ecological niche is not a particular place but represents the relationship of a species to all aspects of its environment, including its interactions with other species. It describes the species role in the community (Elton 1927) and, as it includes many variables (e.g. temperature, humidity, food supply, nesting requirements): it is **multidimensional** (Hutchinson 1957; Figure 11.11).

Each species has a suite of environmental features that delineate the habitat in which it can exist without interference from other organisms. The role of the species in this 'space' is its **fundamental niche**. However, other organisms, particularly competitors and predators confine species to a resource space that is smaller than their fundamental niche. Ecologists refer to this reduced resource space as the **realised niche** of a species. Because so many environmental factors contribute to defining a niche, it is unlikely that we will ever completely determine the niche of an organism. However, by focusing on environmental and biotic factors that seem to matter (limiting factors, food supply) we can use the niche concept to gain some insight into how communities function.

A community is made up of coexisting species occupying niches along gradients of resource supply and environmental condition. Some animals are **generalists** and have a wide ecological tolerance (**eury-species**) and can utilise a wide range of foods. Others are **specialists**, confined to particular habitats or feeding on only one

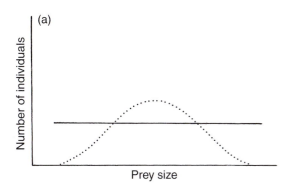

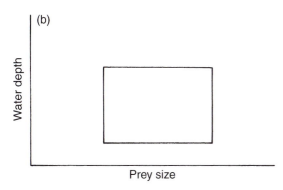

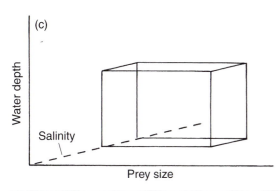

Figure 11.11 Hypothetical diagrams to illustrate the concept of a multidimensional niche. (a) This figure shows the size of prey taken by a fish and delineates the niche in one dimension. (b) By adding a second dimension, water depth, the niche is represented by an area. (c) A third dimension, salinity, produces a three-dimensional niche, represented here as a volume. To describe the fish's niche completely would require *n*-dimensions, where *n* is the number of resources and factors that affect the species (from *General Ecology, 1st edition* by Krohne © 1998. Adapted with permission of Brooks/Cole Publishing, a division of Thomson Learning).

species (**stenospecies**). These specialists, although perhaps limited in where and how they can live, are very good at doing so in the environment to which they are so well adapted. Under these specific conditions, specialists will out-compete generalists. Generalists and specialists can be distinguished by measuring **niche breadth** (see Figure 11.12).

Consider two species that feed on the same prey. If the resource-utilisation curves are widely separated, then prey species of intermediate size are not being utilised (Figure 11.13a). To take advantage of this wasted resource, Species A could extend its ability to handle larger prey and Species B could adapt to give it access to smaller prey individuals. This might result in some overlap in prey size taken by both species. If this overlap is too great (Figure 11.13b) competition might lead to exclusion of the weaker competitor or evolution of altered feeding capabilities again leading to the situation portrayed in Figure 11.13c. Coral reef fish provide a good example of how species have **partitioned resources** in this way to maximise resource utilisation. Through a process known as **character displacement**, two similar species can diverge and adapt in ways that allow them to utilise resources more effectively. We will discuss this process in more detail in chapter 12.

In diverse communities such as those found on coral reefs, there is a good chance that species will be utilising a part of the resource spectrum in common. The degree of niche overlap provides an indication of the strength of competition between the two species. We can use the niche concept to look at how these diverse communities might be assembled and also to develop theories to explain how so many species can coexist.

11.7.2 Community assembly theory

How do communities develop? Are there any **rules of assembly**? Let us build a community using the concepts of niche breadth and niche overlap. Start with a community of just two species arranged along a resource gradient such as light intensity or prey size (Figure 11.14a). As there is no overlap between these species, they will not be competing for this resource. Our simple community could change by these original organisms adapting to

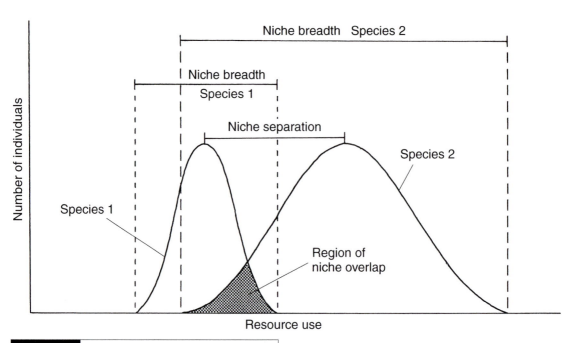

Figure 11.12 Terminology used to describe features of a niche. Each curve describes the resource use, in one dimension, of two species. The degree of niche overlap is a measure of the intensity of competition between Species 1 and Species 2. Niche breadth provides an indication of the degree of specialisation in resource use (from *General Ecology, 1st edition* by Krohne © 1998. Adapted with permission of Brooks/Cole Publishing, a division of Thomson Learning).

Figure 11.13 Hypothetical resource utilisation curves for two species. (a) There is no overlap in resource use and part of the resource is not being used. Both species could benefit by altering their food resource use and evolve towards the situation shown in (c). (b) Significant overlap in resource use indicates intense competition. One species may be driven to seek alternative feeding sites, driven to extinction or, over many generations, the species could evolve feeding differences and, again, move towards the situation shown in (c). (c) There is only a little overlap in resource utilisation and both species should be able to coexist (after Krebs 1994; adapted by permission of Addison-Wesley Educational Publishers, Inc.).

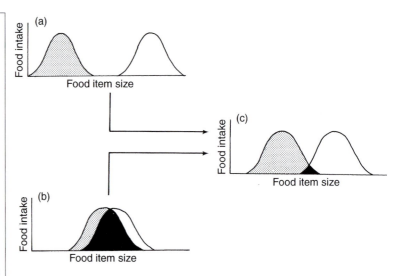

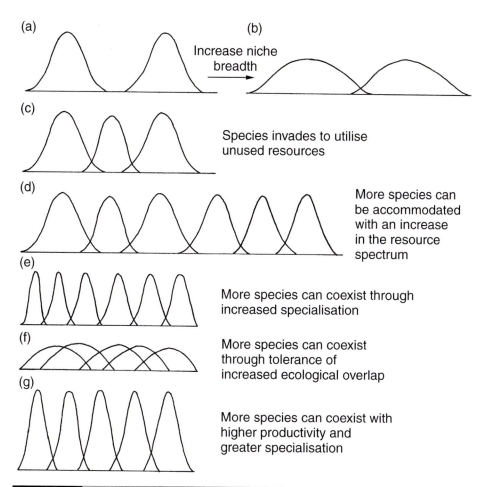

(a)

(b)

Increase niche
breadth
→

(c)

Species invades to utilise
unused resources

(d)

More species can
be accommodated
with an increase
in the resource
spectrum

(e)

More species can coexist through
increased specialisation

(f)

More species can coexist
through tolerance of
increased ecological overlap

(g)

More species can coexist with
higher productivity and
greater specialisation

Figure 11.14 Hypothetical resource utilisation curves showing how curves can be arranged along a resource gradient and altered to accommodate more species. The height and breadth of the resource curves indicate productivity and degree of specialisation respectively.

increase their respective niche breadths (through character displacement) and even include some niche overlap (Figure 11.14b). A gap in the resource use spectrum also provides an opportunity for invasion of the community by a third species (Figure 11.14c). To persist in the community the new arrival must either out-compete its nearest rivals, or be sufficiently different in its resource requirements so that competitive exclusion does not occur. Of course, the new arrival could win a competitive battle and exclude one of the original species.

More species could be added by increasing the variety of resources available (Figure 11.14d) or by decreasing the niche breadth of species in the community (Figure 11.14e). Our resource base could also support a more diverse community if species were able to tolerate greater niche overlap (Figure 11.14f). Notice that the productivity of each species (portrayed as the height of each resource utilisation curve) declines with increased niche overlap. Notice, too, that the niche concept pits competitive exclusion against resource partitioning and the outcome indicates the number of species that can persist in a community.

The niche concept can not only be used to explain the number of species in a community, but also links the evolution of new species to the environment and resource supply. We will look at the process of community development and **speciation** in chapter 12.

Table 11.1 The three most important hazards facing coral reefs and their main effects, as determined by participants at a scientific meeting held in Miami, Florida in 1993

Hazard	Sources	Main effects
Overfishing		**Direct:** population declines; loss of fish diversity; habitat damage from destructive methods **Indirect:** population increases in prey species (e.g. urchins) leading to bioerosion, reduced coral survival, algal overgrowth
Sedimentation	Land clearing, dredging, shipping activity (propwash)	Reduced light penetration; energy cost to corals from sediment clearance; reduced settlement success and early survival of corals; reduced diversity
Nutrient enrichment	Agriculture, sewage, land clearing	Algal overgrowth of benthic organisms leading to loss of cover and diversity; reduced coral recruitment, settlement and survival

Source: Roberts 1993.

11.8 | Coral reef management and conservation

Coral reefs are restricted to a narrow range of environmental conditions and are very sensitive to change in those conditions. Consequently conservation of coral reefs requires maintenance of clear, nutrient-poor water and adequate protection from storms and hurricanes. In 1993, 125 reef scientists met in Miami, Florida to discuss the environmental health of coral reefs throughout the world. They identified three main hazards and their impact on coral reefs (Table 11.1) and these are discussed below.

11.8.1 Overfishing and resource conservation

As human populations along tropical coastlines have increased, so, too, has the fishing effort. As a result, reef fish populations have decreased in some areas of the world. Some fishing techniques, such as dynamite fishing and using poisons, are particularly destructive and have been declared illegal in many countries with coral reefs. These techniques not only damage the reef, but also kill indiscriminately and many fish killed may not be harvested. Other reef products, such as corals and molluscs for the jewellery and curio trade, have,

on some reefs been overexploited. For example, in the Philippines, the ornamental coral trade has led to significant, although localised, reef damage.

Restriction of fishing activity through creation of protected areas has been shown to enhance fish populations, particularly of those species favoured by fishermen. For example, in 1974 a small reserve was established off Sumilon Island in the Philippines. Eight years later, overall fish abundances were double those found in adjacent areas open to fishing (Alcala 1988). When the area was reopened to fishing in 1984, total fish densities in the reserve area fell by 25% and densities of the highly desired species such as snappers and emperors declined by 94%. The size structure of fish populations can also be altered by fishing intensity (Figure 11.15). How we might manage coral reefs so that fish production might be sustainable requires a thorough understanding of how populations of reef fish are sustained.

Populations of marine organisms are typically much more open than their terrestrial counterparts. In many marine species, fertilisation occurs in the ocean and the resultant larva is pelagic and may be carried long distances by currents. This dispersal process connects reef areas that may be separated by expanses of open ocean. Furthermore, through this inter-connectivity,

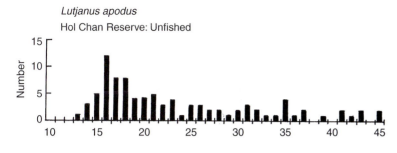

Lutjanus apodus
Hol Chan Reserve: Unfished

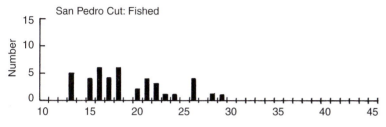

San Pedro Cut: Fished

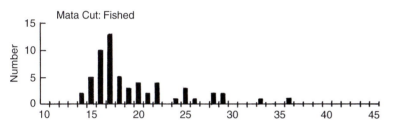

Mata Cut: Fished

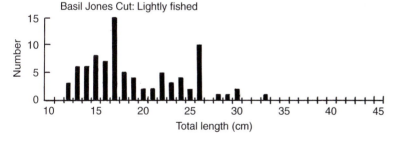

Basil Jones Cut: Lightly fished

Total length (cm)

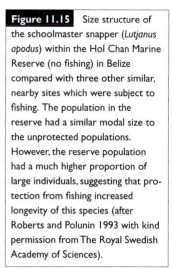

Figure 11.15 Size structure of the schoolmaster snapper (*Lutjanus apodus*) within the Hol Chan Marine Reserve (no fishing) in Belize compared with three other similar, nearby sites which were subject to fishing. The population in the reserve had a similar modal size to the unprotected populations. However, the reserve population had a much higher proportion of large individuals, suggesting that protection from fishing increased longevity of this species (after Roberts and Polunin 1993 with kind permission from The Royal Swedish Academy of Sciences).

population size and community structure at one site may be strongly affected by processes occurring elsewhere (Roberts 1997). Factors determining the abundance and size/age structure of populations of reef fish are illustrated in Figure 11.16.

This open structure has significant implications for the way coral reefs might be managed since sites that are copiously supplied with larvae from upstream reef areas are likely to be more resilient to human disturbance (e.g. overfishing) than places that are more of a source of larvae than a sink. Furthermore, it is possible that, by establishing a patchwork of protected areas and

fishing grounds, spawning stock within the protected areas may produce enough recruits to sustain populations within fished areas (Roberts and Polunin 1993). The existence of a larval dispersal stage allows adult fish reproducing within a protected area to contribute to stocking fishing grounds outside the reserve. In a similar way, a coral reef area could be managed on a temporal basis by rotating areas through an alternating cycle of protection and exploitation. Reserves should have the effect of preventing regional extinction of exploited fish species that occur in metapopulations (see section 11.5).

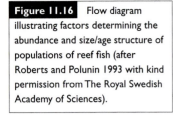

Figure 11.16 Flow diagram illustrating factors determining the abundance and size/age structure of populations of reef fish (after Roberts and Polunin 1993 with kind permission from The Royal Swedish Academy of Sciences).

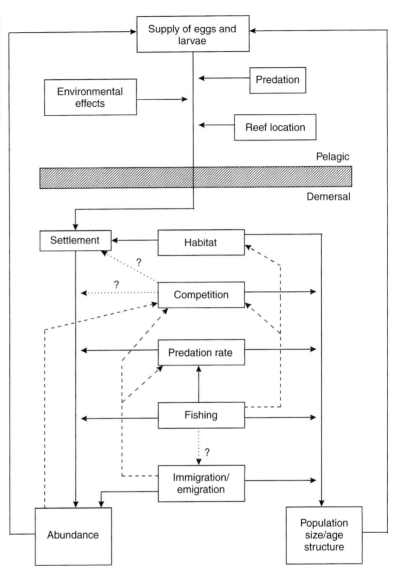

11.8.2 Sedimentation

Human developments along the coasts which parallel coral reefs often result in increased inputs of

Marine resource management raises political and social, as well as scientific issues. We know that the spatial scale for effective reef management needs to be greater than a single reef patch and may extend over tens or even thousands of square kilometres. Therefore, in places such as the Caribbean and South-East Asian archipelagos, reserves for effective management may well extend over international boundaries.

freshwater laden with sediments, nutrients and pollutants. Extensive deforestation in coastal areas has led to enhanced sediment loads on coral reefs carried to them by rivers draining these degraded areas. Corals may be harmed by sediment through burial, leaving them in darkness and without adequate oxygen. In less severe cases, sediments entering coral lagoons reduce water clarity directly while nutrient-rich effluents do so indirectly through stimulating algal growth. In both cases, the light on which the corals depend is reduced. Sediments can also affect corals by settling directly on their polyps and coral species differ in their ability to remove sediments, depending on particle size. Fine particles are removed by cilia, larger ones can be moved by tentacles. Coral diversity and cover can be severely reduced in areas receiving high sediment loads as those species with poor sediment removal capabilities succumb.

11.8.3 Nutrient enrichment and pollution

Nutrient enrichment of the waters surrounding coral reefs can result in eutrophication (see section 5.15). Phytoplankton populations are stimulated by the additional nutrients and these may reduce light penetration to the reef. Usual sources of nutrients causing eutrophication are from agricultural run-off and sewage effluents from coastal towns. Sewage effluents are also rich in organic matter which provides a respiratory substrate for oxygen-consuming bacteria. The resultant low oxygen concentrations may suffocate corals or they may be killed from the hydrogen sulfide that some of these bacteria release. The delicate nutrient balance between corals and their zooxanthellae may be disrupted and the reefs may become smothered in macroalgae.

Zooxanthellae in corals are usually nitrogen-limited, but excess photosynthetic products are donated to their coral partner. With nutrient enrichment, nitrogen limitation is removed and the zooxanthellae are able to utilise all their carbon themselves to enhance their own biomass and translocate less photosynthate to the coral. Calcification rates decline. Zooxanthellae are able to scavenge nutrients from nutrient-deficient waters more effectively than macroalgae. Nutrient enrichment removes this competitive advantage that zooxanthellae have over macroalgae and opens the reef up to invasion by faster-growing seaweeds.

Sewage disposal into Kaneohe Bay in Hawaii resulted in proliferation of the green 'bubble alga' *Dictyosphaeria cavernosa* until it all but carpeted the floor of the bay. This alga smothered corals and phytoplankton populations multiplied, further shading out corals. The reef recovered some of its former glory when the sewage effluent was diverted offshore, away from the reefs. Nutrient levels and phytoplankton populations declined and water clarity improved. The community structure switched away from one dominated by the green bubble alga to a coral-dominated reef community. However, recent surveys have indicated that the rate of recovery has slowed, possibly in response to enhanced nutrient inputs from a range of diffuse sources such as cesspools, boats and land run-off (Hunter and Evans 1995).

Coral reefs are particularly sensitive to pollution. Since most corals release gametes into the water, pollutants may suppress reproductive success. Furthermore, since most corals mass spawn, coral recruitment could be severely affected by pollutants entering the system during a mass-spawning event. The impact of enhanced sediment loads is often compounded by input of agricultural pollutants (fertilisers, pesticides and herbicides) applied to crops grown in the coastal zone.

Tributyl tin is added to paints for boats as an anti-fouling agent. It has been found that compounds leaching from these paints are harmful to reef organisms. Similarly, leakage of oils and fuels from boats and spills from oil tankers can be extremely damaging to reefs. The effect of dispersants used in clean-up operations may be more harmful to corals than the oil itself.

11.8.4 Conservation and tourism

Coral reefs attract tourists. Damage to reefs occurs directly through boat anchors, trampling by swimmers and enhanced exploitation of reef resources for the curio trade. However, the main impact of tourism probably occurs through the indirect effects of coastal zone developments and infrastructure required to support the tourist trade. The tourist trade is strongest in the Caribbean, but, in South-East Asia and the Pacific, activities associated with tourism are increasingly being cited as a major cause of reef degradation.

11.9 | Chapter summary

1. Coral reefs are amongst the most biologically diverse and productive of all natural ecosystems. A strong capacity to absorb nutrients from the nutrient-poor waters in which they generally grow coupled with rapid and efficient nutrient cycling are the main reasons for their high productivity. Retention of nutrients by coral reef organisms is facilitated by close mutualistic associations.

2. The true reef-building corals (hermatypic) deposit a calcium carbonate skeleton (calcification) and have symbiotic algae (zooxanthellae) within their tissues. The algae process waste products from the coral and provide the coral with some of its carbon requirements. The corals also obtain nourishment by catching zooplankton with stinging cells known as nematocysts. This zooplankton food provides an important source of nitrogen for corals.

3. Corals reproduce asexually by fragmentation and sexually through gametes released into the water column. Synchronous release of gametes (mass spawning), often from more than one species, occurs.

4. Coral reefs are tropical, coastal water ecosystems, largely restricted to areas between latitudes 30° N and 30° S. Reefs occur as fringing reefs (adjacent to the coastline), barrier reefs (separated from the land by a lagoon) and as atolls (ring-shaped reefs developed following the subsidence of a volcano).

5. Coral reef algae are responsible for the very high rates of primary production on reefs and their abundance is largely limited by intense herbivory. Nitrogen fixation by Cyanobacteria may account for significant nitrogen income to coral reefs.

6. A diverse array of animals live in association with corals. Reef fish are either diurnal or nocturnal and there is an almost complete exchange of species between day and night. In most reef fish, the larval stage is planktonic and settlement may occur on a reef distant from the spawning site. The supply of larvae may limit coral reef fish abundance.

7. Coral reef diversity decreases with increasing latitude, and reefs in the Indo-Pacific are more species-rich than those in the Atlantic. On a global scale, species richness has been related to energy supply and the direction of ocean currents. Diversity also tends to be higher at sites subject to intermediate levels of disturbance.

8. The resources and environmental conditions required by each species delineate its ecological or fundamental niche. In the presence of competitors, the fundamental niche size is reduced to the realised niche. Species can coexist by not competing for the same resources (occupying different niches). Diverse communities can be assembled by reducing the niche breadth of each species (specialisation) or by increasing the tolerance of each species to niche overlap by similar species. More species may also be able to coexist if the variety of resources is increased or if more resources are available (higher productivity).

9. Coral reefs are being degraded through over-fishing and reduced water quality from enhanced sediment deposition, nutrient enrichment and pollution.

Chapter 12

Isolated habitats and biogeography
Islands in the sea, air and land

12.1 | Island ecosystems

Islands are generally defined as relatively small areas of land surrounded by water. This geographic situation results in a degree of biological isolation – it is more difficult for terrestrial organisms to colonise small islands which lie distant from the nearest large land mass. Other habitats of similar types are also isolated from each other. Mountain tops form 'islands in the air' surrounded by a 'sea' of lowland which may form, for some species, a barrier as difficult to cross as an expanse of sea is for many terrestrial organisms. Similarly, lakes are watery 'islands' surrounded by land, and movement of aquatic species from one lake to another is hindered by this land barrier. Organisms that inhabit distinctly patchy habitats, such as rotting logs or dung, also face the challenge of moving from one island habitat to another. Rotting logs and dung piles are special islands in that the resources they provide dwindle with time and therefore these are not only isolated habitats, but also temporary.

The biological communities of islands, lakes and mountain tops, therefore, share a degree of biological isolation as a common characteristic, and these habitats have provided natural laboratories for studies of **biogeography** and **evolution**. There are a number of reasons for studying the biogeography of islands and isolated habitats. One reason is to discover how biological communities on islands develop, and this requires detailed studies of dispersal strategies, population establishment, competition within the community and loss of species from the community through extinction. Another reason for studying islands is to investigate what determines how many species, and which ones, form island communities. Over much longer time periods, it is interesting to observe how island communities have evolved and adapted to the environment; how species have diversified to fill ecological niches occupied elsewhere by species that have not colonised the island. Although this chapter concentrates on islands surrounded by sea to develop biogeographical concepts, examples from other isolated habitats will also be described. We start by describing the development of biological communities on an island that was cleansed of life by a massive volcanic eruption.

12.2 | Krakatau

On 27 August 1883, a massive explosion, that was heard from Perth, Australia to Colombo, Sri Lanka, occurred on the Indonesian island of Krakatau. This was one of the greatest volcanic explosions ever recorded and the eruption produced devastating tsunamis (marine pressure waves). The largest killer wave wiped out 165 coastal villages, killed over 36 000 people and, in some places, penetrated 11 km inland. Sea level changes were recorded in New Zealand, Alaska and the English Channel, and the cloud of volcanic dust rose 40 km into the atmosphere. The atmospheric particles lowered the earth's average annual temperature by about 0.5 °C and spectacular sunsets were seen in many parts of the world – even the moon appeared blue!

As a result of the eruption, two-thirds of the island of Krakatau, originally 11 km long, disappeared, leaving behind half the Rakata volcano (as the island of Rakata) and a submerged caldera 200 m deep (Figure 12.1). Ash layers and pumice up to 75 m thick covered Rakata and the neighbouring islands of Sertung and Panjang which were considerably enlarged by the pumice and ash fallout (see Thornton 1996). Rakata, with an area of 17 km² and elevation of 780 m, is the largest remaining island fragment of the original Krakatau. Subsequent eruptions produced another island named Anak Krakatau (Figure 12.2).

It is generally believed that no plant or animal on the islands survived this cataclysm. Some biologists have argued that roots, seeds, spores or some soil organisms may have survived, others believe that sterilisation of the island was complete. This issue was hotly debated and Thornton (1996) reviews the controversy which can not now be resolved – it is very difficult to prove the absence of survivors, particularly since recolonisation occurred rapidly.

In May 1884 (9 months after the eruption), the only sign of life found was a solitary spider. However, in 1886, a botanical expedition found 2 mosses and 26 species of vascular plants (11 ferns and fern allies, 10 dicotyledons, 5 monocotyledons), and, by 1888, spiders, flies, bugs, beetles, butterflies and the monitor lizard (*Varanus salvator*) were recorded (see Thornton 1984). By 1897, 14 years after the eruption, 3 bryophytes and 64 species of vascular plants were found, and at low to middle elevations dense grasslands had replaced the ferns that previously covered the slopes. Beaches had a well-developed strand flora with an *Ipomoea pes-caprae* association in front of a narrow belt of coastal woodland with *Barringtonia asiatica*, *Casuarina equisetifolia* and *Terminalia catappa*.

In 1908, woodlands of *Ficus* spp. and *Macaranga tanarius* had formed, and savanna vegetation with grasslands dominated by *Saccharum spontaneum* and occasional forest trees was observed. Between 300 and 400 m altitude, luxuriant woodland was found, and the shrub *Cyrtandra sulcata* was recorded for the first time. The first systematic survey of animals was also made in 1908. Two species of land molluscs, 13 non-migrant land birds and many spiders and centipedes were recorded. No mammals, snakes or earthworms were found, and the only reptiles recorded were the monitor lizard and the common house gecko (*Hemidactylus frenatus*). A python was seen in 1911, and the black rat (*Rattus rattus*) became established with the first longer-term human settlement in 1917. Two species of fruit-bat and two species of earthworms were collected between 1919 and 1922, and in 1924 the saltwater crocodile was recorded and two species of skinks (*Lygosoma atrocostatum* and *Mabuya multifasciata*) were now very common.

As the woodlands developed into closed forests, many of the plants associated with the fern and grass communities were replaced by forest species. The forest canopy provided new habitats for colonising species and, by 1934, 271 higher plants were present on the islands. In 1951, mixed forests of *Macaranga tanarius*, *Neonauclea calycina* and *Ficus* species (together with their pollinating wasps, see Box 8.1) extended up to 500 m above sea level. At the summit, the previously dominant shrub, *Cyrtandra sulcata*, was declining and being replaced by *Schefflera polybotrya*.

Four main vegetation communities on Rakata are now recognised: (1) a coastal *Barringtonia asiatica* and *Terminalia catappa* community, with *Ipomoea pes-caprae*, and *Casuarina*; (2) secondary lowland rain forests dominated by *Neonauclea calycina*; (3) from about 500 m elevation, moss forest with several large *Ficus* species; and (4) near the summit, a shrub woodland dominated by *Schefflera polybotrya* but with a few larger trees (Thornton 1984). The vegetation now supports a diverse array of animals: 20 bats, 38 species of resident birds, 8 reptiles, 16 land molluscs, 47 butterflies, more than 500 hymenopterans and over 100 ant species.

This process of community reassembly provides an excellent example of a primary succession (see section 7.8). On lowland Rakata, successional stages included: (1) Cyanobacteria and ferns; (2) grassland; (3) *Macaranga–Ficus fulva*

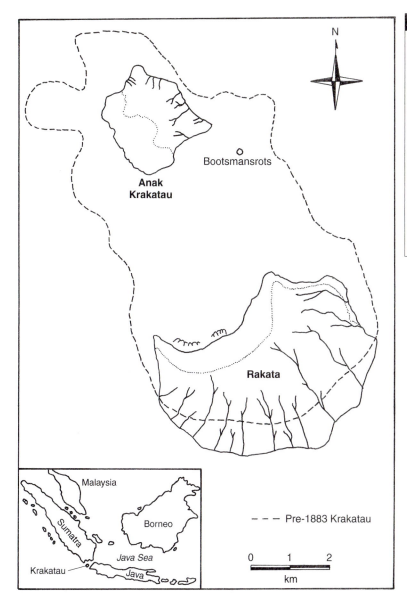

Figure 12.1 The Krakatau Islands are situated in the Sunda Strait between the islands of Sumatra and Java. Before the catastrophic volcanic eruption in 1883, the original Krakatau was considerably larger in area (dotted line) than the present configuration of islands (solid line). Anak Krakatau emerged from beneath the sea in 1930 (adapted with permission of the publishers from *The diversity of life* by E. O. Wilson, Cambridge, MA: The Belknap Press of Harvard University Press, Copyright © 1992 by E. O. Wilson).

forest; and (4) *Neonauclea* closed canopy forest. As the vegetation changed, so did animal communities. Some species, such as butterflies (skippers and lycaenids) associated with grasslands were lost and many forest inhabitants such as wood-boring beetles, fruit bats and frugivorous birds colonised. Of more relevance to this chapter, the study of Krakatau provides insights into how islands become colonised and how communities are assembled (see section 11.7).

The first stage in the colonisation process is **dispersal**: getting to the island. How do organisms get to new areas? What characteristics do successful plant and animal colonists have in common? What processes take place following colonisation? Islands, because of their varying degree of isolation from continents, provide useful sites to study the process of dispersal, but it must not be forgotten that this process occurs across continents as well.

Figure 12.2 Anak Krakatau volcano erupting, 20 October 1981 (Photo: Dieter and Mary Plage, Oxford Scientific Films).

12.3 | Dispersal

Three years after the Krakatau eruption, 60% of the plants that had colonised the barren island had wind-dispersed seeds; the rest were those with seeds that could survive floating in seawater (sea-dispersed). A decade later, the flora was comprised of 44% wind-dispersed, 47% sea-dispersed and 9% animal dispersed (Figure 12.3). By 1908, animal dispersed plants had significantly increased and continued to do so. In 1934 distribution in dispersal agents had altered to 48% wind, 22% sea, 27% animal and 3% human (see Thornton 1984).

Wind also played a dominant role in the early colonisation of the island by animals. The early colonisation fauna lacked ant species with apterous (wingless) females, wingless tenebrionids and

spiders that lacked the capacity to disperse by ballooning. A survey in 1933 (50 years after the eruption) estimated that 92% of the animals on the island could have been carried there by wind. Invertebrates such as earthworms, millipedes, mites, molluscs and insects could reach the island by **rafting**, being carried there on objects such as floating trees. Soil organisms could arrive in soil attached to floating tree roots. The first oligochaete to be recorded on the island was one that lives, not in the soil, but in decaying tree trunks. The nine species of termites found on the island all nest in trees or decaying wood, not in soil or on the ground. In other words, there is a **disharmony** in the distribution of animal species on the island in comparison with the fauna in the source areas (Thornton 1996). Flight, aided by wind currents, was the most likely means of arrival of many butterflies, moths, wasps, bees and winged ants.

Plants with seeds that are animal-dispersed obviously require animals to make the trip from the mainland to the island. This is more likely to occur if fruit-bearing trees are on the island, as these will attract animals. A positive feedback therefore exists: fruiting plants attract animal dispersers which bring in more seeds which grow into trees that attract more dispersers. As the plant community became more diverse, specialist animals were able to colonise the islands. The pink-necked green pigeon arrived in the first 25 years. This bird feeds exclusively on figs but is more of a seed predator than a disperser. The imperial pigeon, a specialist frugivore, arrived on the island by 1919. This bird is a specialist frugivore and effective disperser as it does not digest seeds (Figure 12.4).

Many species of fruit bats forage over great distances, but early colonisation of the islands was precluded by the absence of fruit-bearing forest trees. *Cynopterus sphinx* (a dog-faced fruit bat) was first recorded on the islands in 1919, by which time an extensive stand of *Cyrtandra sulcata* had developed. *C. sulcata* produces white berries that are eaten by both bats and birds. Effective seed dispersal by animals that feed on fruits requires extended retention of seeds in the gut. Shilton *et al.* (1999) showed that Old World fruit-bats, in

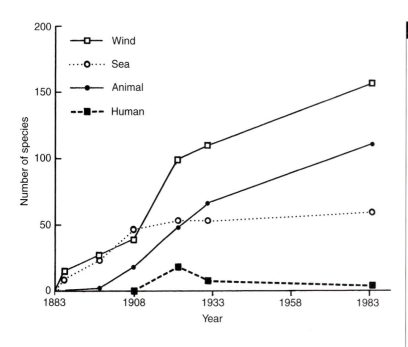

Figure 12.3 Dispersal mode spectra of vascular plants on Rakata at successive survey periods. Surveys made in the periods 1920–24, 1929–34 and 1979–89 are grouped and the data plotted at the mid-point of these periods. Note: (1) how the presence of sea-dispersed plants levelled out after 1924; and (2) the increase in wind-dispersed plants between 1908 and 1924, which was largely due to the arrival and colonisation of species adapted to the more shady conditions provided by the developing forest canopy (adapted from Thornton 1996; Whittaker *et al.* 1992. Reprinted by permission of the publishers from *Krakatau* by Ian Thornton, Cambridge, MA: Harvard University Press, Copyright © 1996 by the President and Fellows of Harvard College).

captivity, may retain seeds for up to 12 hours with the seeds remaining viable when eventually voided. If this retention also applies to bats in the wild, then bats have the potential to disperse small seeds hundreds of kilometres. Previously, it was thought that bats only retained seeds for around 30 minutes (see Shilton *et al.* 1999 for a review).

Plants have evolved a wide array of seed-dispersal techniques, using a variety of agents (animals (attached to them or ingested by them), wind and water). Apart from animals that can fly or are small enough to be carried on wind currents, animals can only reach islands either by swimming or rafting. The chances that a raft will reach a small, distant island are indeed small. However, island colonisation needs to be set against the age of some islands. The recolonisation of Krakatau is very recent, and it lies close to islands supporting populations of potential colonists. The chances of colonists arriving at small islands in the middle of the Pacific Ocean are minuscule. However, some of these islands are ancient. The Galapagos Islands, for example, are around 3 million years old, and an immigration rate of just one plant species arriving every 8000 years would be sufficient to account for the present island flora. Set in this time context, the chance of island colonisation by dispersal is more acceptable.

Diamond (1974) studied birds on the islands to the north of New Guinea. This island arc is part of the so-called Pacific ring-of-fire, an area of intense volcanic activity. Island communities in this area are in varying stages of recovery from volcanic devastation. Diamond suggested that some birds, which he called **supertramps**, are equipped with strong dispersal capabilities and have developed a life history strategy adapted to rapid colonisation of recently devastated islands. According to this theory, these birds breed rapidly, a process facilitated by the lack of competitors, and soon the population reaches and even exceeds the carrying capacity (see section 4.7.5) of the island. At this time, surplus individuals leave and seek out new islands. Diamond suggested that, as an island community recovers, other birds with lesser dispersal powers invade and these superior competitors displace the supertramp species. By this time, however, the supertramp will have dispersed numerous emigrants to search for recently devastated islands. These islands provide a natural laboratory for biogeographical studies and further work is required to understand the complex population ecology of species that utilise them.

The **barrier** to colonisation of islands is clearly

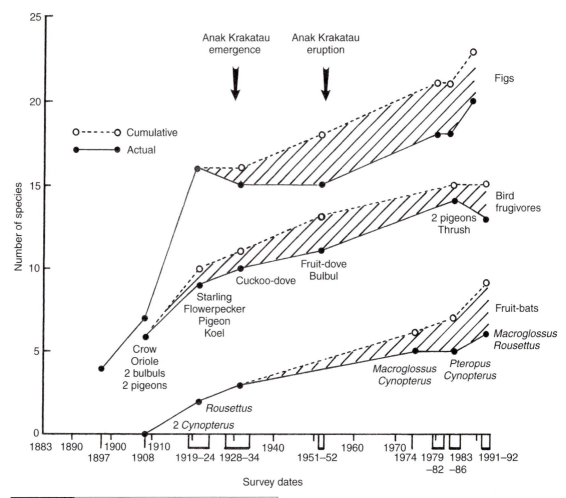

Figure 12.4 Colonisation of the Krakataus by figs (*Ficus* spp.), avian frugivores (indicated at date of first record by common name) and fruit-bats (by generic name), from 1883 to 1992. Actual line plots the number of species recorded during each survey period, and the cumulative line is the number of species recorded by each survey plus those recorded previously and not seen during a particular survey (after Thornton 1996. Reprinted by permission of the publishers from *Krakatau* by Ian Thornton, Cambridge, MA: Harvard University Press, Copyright © 1996 by the President and Fellows of Harvard College. Modified from I.W.B. Thornton et al. (1992) *GeoJournal* 28(2)).

the water that surrounds them, and only organisms (or their propagules) capable of crossing the expanse of sea have a chance of succeeding. Other habitats are surrounded by barriers. Land forms a barrier to range expansion of many aquatic species; those that have a terrestrial stage in their life cycle are exceptions and use this terrestrial stage to disperse and colonise distant water bodies. Organisms inhabiting mountain tops may be isolated by an invisible barrier of unsuitable environmental conditions that exist in the lowlands that surround them. Similarly, lowland species may be unable to spread across mountain ranges because of the environmental conditions that prevail at higher altitude.

Janzen (1967b) concluded that, since the tropics, in general, have a more equitable temperature regime than temperate regions, tropical organisms at a particular site are not exposed to, and therefore not adapted to, a wide range of temperatures. Therefore, there is a higher probability that a lowland, tropical organism will experience an unbearable combination of environmental conditions in attempting to cross a mountain

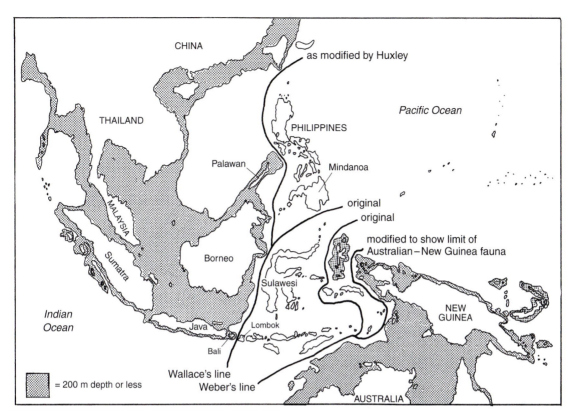

Figure 12.5 Map showing biogeographical lines separating the Oriental and Australasian provinces. Shading indicates shallow water (200 m or less). The islands to the west of Wallace's line were, when sea level was lower, once connected to Asia (after Carlquist 1974, courtesy of the American Museum of Natural History).

range, than will a similar organism living in a more temperate (and more seasonal) climate. Janzen (1967b) concluded that barriers involving gradients in temperature or rainfall are more effective in preventing dispersal in the tropics. For organisms living in predictable environments, a small change in the environment will constitute a significant barrier to dispersal. Many tropical species have very restricted distributions and this, at least in part, may be explained by their inability to cross barriers of even apparently minor differences in environmental conditions.

Barriers to dispersal are neither necessarily fully effective nor permanent. Changes in climate and sea and lake levels may allow organisms to cross areas formerly barred to them or, indeed, create new barriers. For example, sea levels were much lower during the Pleistocene Epoch and until the start of the Holocene Epoch; what today is the island of New Guinea was connected to Australia by a broad land bridge. This land bridge explains some of the similarities in the fauna and flora between Australia and New Guinea. For example, the cassowary, a flightless bird, occurs both in northern Queensland and in New Guinea, and some marsupials are shared between these two areas. Compare these similarities with the stark differences in the mammals either side of Wallace's line (Figure 12.5); the islands of Borneo and Sulawesi are separated by a deep trench, and no land bridge formed between these islands during the Pleistocene Epoch. The land bridge between North and South America (what is now Central America) formed when these two continents drifted together in the Pliocene Epoch, some 6 million years ago. This land bridge facilitated an exchange of mammals between the two continents and resulted in the invasion of South America by the more competitive mammals of North America.

Understanding dispersal mechanisms is

fundamental to our understanding of bio-geography and how biological communities become established. However, dispersal ability is only the first requirement for island colonisation, a suitable habitat must also be available.

12.4 | Colonisation and community assembly

As more species colonised the island of Krakatau, so the importance of dispersal ability declined. What became increasingly important was an organism's capacity to survive and reproduce on the island, particularly in the face of increasing competition for space and resources. The range of some species has been curtailed. For example, *Casuarina equisetifolia* is intolerant of shade and is now restricted to a cliff face where there are no species competing for sunlight. Whittaker and Flenley (1982) predicted that the flora on the island would continue to diversify with the addition of primary forest species (*K*-strategists, see section 4.13). Some loss of secondary forest species (*r*-strategists) would occur as the forest progressed through successional stages. This process may take a long time as the *K*-strategists must overcome fierce competition from the established *r*-strategists. *K*-strategists (primary forest species) are also generally poor dispersers.

Whittaker and Flenley (1982) assessed immigration and extinction rates from the rate of increase of observed species number. They suggested that the arrival of new species on Krakatau reached a peak in 1922 when canopy formation was just beginning to occur, and that many species were brought in by birds utilising the developing forest. Notice that, in the 1920s, the curves of actual number of species of plants and frugivorous birds begin to diverge from the cumulative number (Figure 12.4). The difference between these curves is a measure of species turn-over and indicates that some species are being lost from the island. Notice, too, that the immigration peaks for plants coincide well with that for birds. This suggests that the immigration rates of these two groups were mutually linked: more plant species provide a more diverse habitat for more

birds which, in turn, deliver even more plant species to the island. We can see how the plant and animal communities are intertwined by considering colonisation of the island by fig species.

A fig tree can grow on an island if its seed is brought to the island by one of its dispersers and deposited in a suitable habitat for germination and establishment. However, the fig will be unable to propagate itself if its own fig wasp species is not there to pollinate its flowers (see Box 8.1). The fig also requires frugivores for seed dispersal. Colonisation of the island by figs may take place through repeated immigration, but effective establishment of the island will only be achieved following colonisation by the fig wasp pollinator and bird and bat seed dispersers (see Figure 12.4).

Island communities are clearly not assembled randomly. There is obviously an element of chance involved in a species reaching an island and also in reaching it at a time of community development that allows it to become established on the island. However, there are also some rules of **community assembly** that act to determine community composition. Certain species facilitate the invasion of others, and successful colonists tend to have special attributes: an ability to disperse, rapid reproductive capacity, and ecological flexibility which enables them to change their resource requirements and fit into vacant or underexploited niches on the island. Social animals will tend to arrive on an island *en masse*, and establishing a breeding colony will not be a problem. Solitary animals are more likely to arrive alone, and finding a mate will require at least another invasion.

Diamond (1975a) proposed a set of community assembly rules. Species which are very similar to each other can not coexist. Consider two species with similar resource requirements, one of which is established on the island and the other is not. When a propagule with similar resource requirements arrives on the island, the species will either be prevented from establishment through competition or it will colonise successfully and lead to the demise (extirpation) of the species that had arrived earlier. A species that relies, in any way, on another species can only colonise after the species on which it relies has done so.

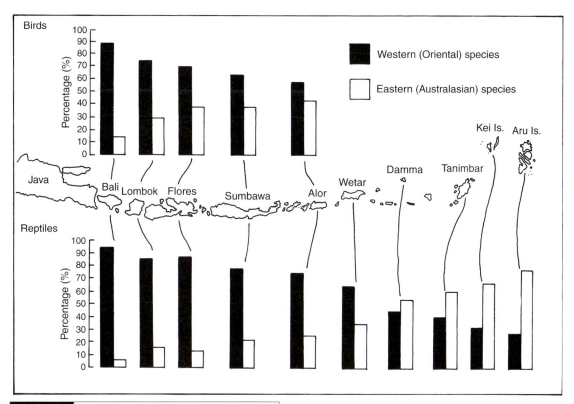

Figure 12.6 For animals with strong dispersal capabilities, such as birds and reptiles, Wallace's line is not so much a barrier (as it is for most mammals) but a filter. Note that the percentages of eastern species decrease westward, and those of western species decrease eastward (after Carlquist 1974, courtesy of the American Museum of Natural History).

The communities that develop on islands are often different from those on the adjacent mainland. These differences arise because some organisms are unable to reach the island and, therefore, there is often **disharmony** between the island fauna and flora and that of the mainland. Disharmony is greatest on small, oceanic islands isolated from the mainland by wide expanses of sea. Conversely, continental islands have a fauna and flora very similar to that of the adjacent continent. For example, the fauna and flora of Sri Lanka is very similar to that of southern India. The distribution of conifer genera in the Pacific illustrates this concept well. *Agathis* and *Araucaria* have heavy seeds and have not been able to colonise Fiji and New Caledonia. Another conifer genus, *Podocarpus*, with much lighter seeds, has colonised islands as far east as Tonga.

Where there is a marked difference in species composition between two areas, biogeographers draw **lines** to delineate **biogeographic provinces**. The most famous of these lines is that drawn by Alfred Wallace which bears his name. **Wallace's line** separates Borneo from Sulawesi and Bali from Lombok. Huxley modified the line to divide Palawan from the rest of the Philippine archipelago (Figure 12.5). The line represents a sharp boundary in the distribution of some mammals. Placental mammals are present on islands to the west of the line but largely absent from those to the east (bats, rats and introduced placentals excepted). The eastern islands support a diverse marsupial fauna which is absent on the islands to the west of the line (see section 1.3.1). For animals with better dispersal capabilities than mammals (birds and reptiles), Wallace's line represents more of a filter than a boundary (Figure 12.6).

The number of species that occur on islands decreases with the distance from the source. For example, the number of genera in a weevil family on islands in the Pacific decline with distance

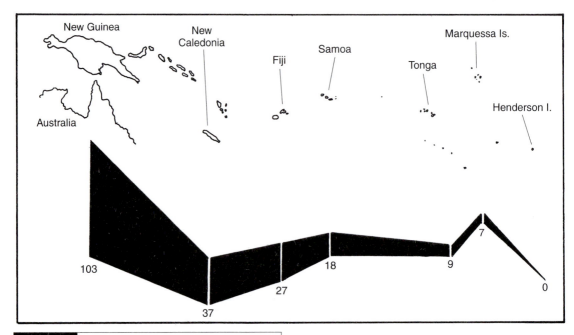

Figure 12.7 The number of genera in a weevil family (Cryptorhynchidae) declines progressively on islands more distant from the source area (New Guinea). The marked taper on this filter is exacerbated by island size as the more distant islands also happen to be smaller (adapted from Carlquist 1974, courtesy of the American Museum of Natural History).

from the source on New Guinea (Figure 12.7). Only weevils capable of colonising islands along the chain will be able to disperse to the most distant island. This phenomenon has been called a **filter** or **filter bridge**. The funnel-shaped filter is probably caused not only by distance from the source, but also because the more distant islands also happen to be the smallest. Some organisms reach distant islands by overcoming enormous odds through chance combinations of favourable circumstances (e.g. unusually strong, dry winds). This is known as the **sweepstakes** dispersal route. In other cases colonisation is facilitated by island **stepping-stones**, islands which provide a habitat for a plant or animal to establish and disperse from there to more distant islands.

As communities on small, isolated islands are usually less diverse than those that develop on larger islands or continents, competition between the species that are present on islands may be less intense. This may allow a species to expand its ecological niche (see section 11.7.1) in a process known as **ecological release**. Cox and Ricklefs (1977) studied bird communities in nine distinctive habitats in central Panama (continental location) and on the Caribbean islands of Trinidad, Jamaica, St Lucia and St Kitts. They demonstrated that ecological release in these bird communities involved both an increase in within-habitat abundance and an expansion of the range of habitats occupied (Table 12.1).

As the community on Krakatau develops, it would seem that, at some stage, a balance in the number of species would be achieved: immigration of new species being balanced by extinctions of established species. The equilibrium reached is also likely to be related to the size of the island, its distance from the mainland, the diversity of habitats available and the supply of potential colonists from source areas. This equilibrium is the basis of the theory of island biogeography.

12.5 | Island biogeography

The theory of island biogeography as proposed by MacArthur and Wilson (1967) produced an important conceptual model to explain features of island communities. They noticed that islands

			Number of bird species observed (regional diversity)	Average number of species per habitat (local diversity)	Habitats per species	Relative abundance per species per habitat (density)	Relative abundance per species
Locality	Area km²	Number of bird species					
Panama	1554	296	135	30.2	2.01	2.95	5.93
Trinidad	4828	205	106	28.2	2.35	3.31	7.78
Jamaica	11525	68	56	21.4	3.43	4.97	17.05
St Lucia	603	42	33	15.2	4.15	5.77	23.95
St Kitts	168	21	20	11.9	5.35	5.88	31.45

Table 12.1 Relative abundance and habitat distribution of resident land birds in five tropical localities

Notes: Panama, in central America, represents a continental site, Trinidad is an island close to the South American continent. The other sites are more isolated Caribbean islands of decreasing size. Note the decline in the number of bird species with the decline in area, with the exception of Panama (continental) and Trinidad which is situated close to the South American mainland. The number of species observed is based on 10 counting periods of 20 minutes in each of 9 habitats at each locality. Notice that almost all the birds on St Kitts were recorded by this census method, but only 45% of the birds recorded for Panama were observed. The relative abundance of each species in each habitat was obtained from the number of counting periods in which the species was seen (maximum 10); this times the number of habitats per species gives the relative abundance of all species.
Source: Cox and Ricklefs 1977.

have low species diversity in comparison with the nearest continental land masses, a diversity that declines with distance away from the land masses. They also noted that biodiversity was greater on large islands than small ones.

Their theory states that the rate of arrival of new species to an island (immigration) gradually declines as an initially barren island is colonised. This occurs because species with good dispersal abilities will colonise the island soon after it is formed, mainland species with lesser dispersal capabilities will take longer to arrive. As colonisation proceeds, the number of species remaining as potential new colonists on the mainland will decline. Immigration continues, but the new arrivals do not enhance island species diversity if the species is already established on the island. When all mainland species have arrived, the immigration rate of new species is zero. Immigration rate, the number of new immigrant species per year plotted against the number of species on the island, declines as a concave curve (Figure 12.8a). The average rate of immigration declines because organisms with strong dispersal powers colonise islands first, leaving behind, in

the source area, species with weaker dispersal strategies.

As more species arrive on the island conditions change. The population size of some of the earlier immigrants may decline as a result of these changed conditions or from competition with the new arrivals. Species that have been able to colonise may also, as time goes by, be lost from the island. This may occur by chance or through competition for space or resources. Early immigrants to islands may have faced a barren and harsh environment (particularly those that arrived on Krakatau soon after the eruption), but competition from other species for resources would be low, simply because few species were present on the island. As species are added and niches (see section 11.7.1) are filled, so competition increases. The number of species becoming extinct increases from zero and rises progressively more steeply as the number of species on the island increases (more species, more competition, more chance for species to go extinct) (Figure 12.8b).

Extinction, in the theory of island biogeography, differs from extinction in the

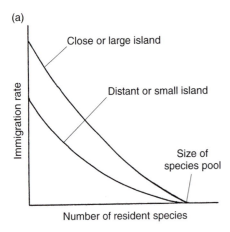

(a)

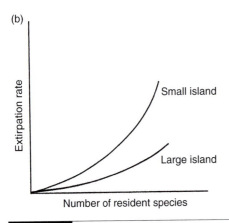

(b)

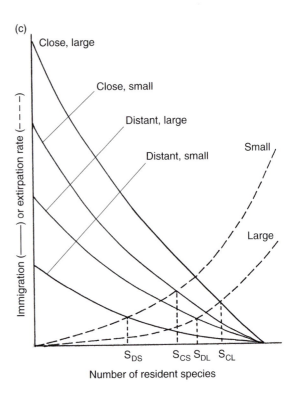

(c)

Figure 12.8 The MacArthur and Wilson equilibrium model of the biota on an island. (a) The rate of species immigration on to an island, plotted against the number of resident species on the island. (b) The rate of species extirpation on an island, plotted against the number of resident species on the island. (c) The balance between immigration and extirpation on small and large islands and on islands close to and distant from the mainland source. The equilibrium number of species (S) on an island is predicted by the intersect between the curves of the rate of immigration and the rate of extirpation. (DS = distant, small, DL = distant, large, CS = close, small, CL = close, large) (adapted from MacArthur, R. H. and Wilson, E. O.; *Theory of island biogeography*, Copyright © 1967 by Princeton University Press, with permission from Princeton University Press).

evolutionary sense. Island biogeographers regard a species as extinct if it no longer occurs on a particular island; populations of the species, however, may remain on the mainland and re-immigration to the island is possible. Extinction to the evolutionary biologist is the complete demise of the species, world-wide (see section 12.7). Some ecologists recommend using **extirpation** to refer to the loss of a species from an area, to distinguish it from extinction, the irreplaceable loss of a species.

Immigration and extinction curves differ depending on the distance of the island from the mainland and the size of the island. Immigration rates will be higher on islands close to the source of potential colonists (the mainland). Extinction rates are likely to be higher on small islands than large islands. Populations are likely to be smaller and habitats less diverse on small islands and therefore extinction rates will be higher (Figure 12.8c). We have seen that the colonisation of Krakatau was not as smooth as the curves depicted in Figure 12.8. For example, closure of the forest canopy on Krakatau produced an upsurge in colonisation rates.

A dynamic equilibrium number of species will

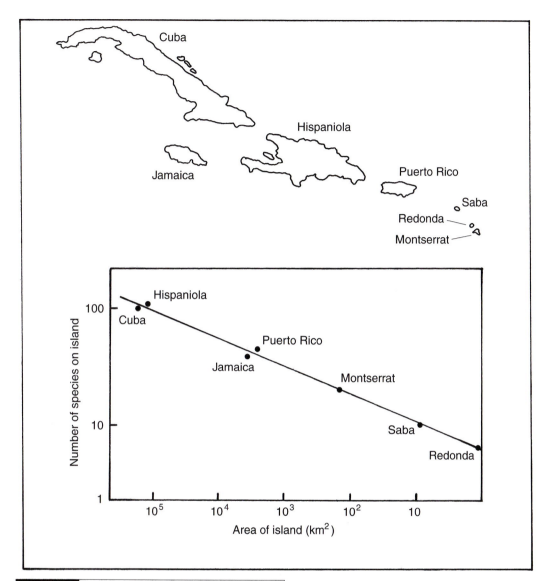

Figure 12.9 The number of species of reptiles and amphibians on seven Caribbean islands plotted against island size (after MacArthur and Wilson 1967; Wilson 1992. Adapted with permission of the publishers from *The diversity of life* by E. O. Wilson, Cambridge, MA: The Belknap Press of Harvard University Press, Copyright © 1992 by E. O. Wilson).

be reached when the number of new immigrants is balanced by the number going extinct. The equilibrium number is thus maintained, over time, by a predictable 'turnover rate' of species. MacArthur and Wilson (1967) showed that the number of species an island would support was related to the area of the island by:

$$S = cA^z$$

where: S is the number of species in a given taxon on the island at equilibrium; c is a constant representing the number of species on an island of unit area; A is the area of the island; and z is a constant measuring the slope of the line relating S and A. The **species–area relationship** for the amphibian and reptile fauna of seven Caribbean islands is shown in Figure 12.9. Note that larger islands have more species than smaller islands. The rate of colonisation is also a function of an island's size since larger islands present larger targets for potential colonists than do smaller islands. Repeated immigration by species already on the island may prevent a species from becoming extinct that, in the absence of this immigration, might otherwise do so. This is known as the **rescue effect**.

Consider an island that is formed either through severance of a land bridge or through the creation of a lake. The flora and fauna on the island, all things being equal, should, to begin with, be as diverse as that of the nearby mainland. The number of species on the island is likely to be higher than that predicted by the species–area relationship. Therefore, it is likely that the rate of extinction will exceed the rate of colonisation and the number of species will decline. This process is known as **biotic relaxation**. Barro Colorado Island, Panama was formed when Gatun Lake was flooded during construction of the Panama Canal. By comparing the bird fauna on the island (15.6 km²) with the nearby mainland, it can be shown that, through biotic relaxation, around 50 species have been lost from the island (see also Box 4.1).

Note that the theory of island biogeography treats all species equally. However, we have seen that the arrival of certain species on Krakatau either facilitated the colonisation of others or led to the demise of close competitors or those that could not survive in the altered environment. Any biogeographic study of island communities must also consider that at any one time the community will consist of a mix of permanent residents, temporary residents (migratory birds that spend part of the year on the island) and transitory individuals that may use the island as a resting place or establish a short-lived colony on the island. Island surveys must consider the balance between these elements. If the majority of species are permanent residents, then the odd temporary or transitory record will have little influence on the study and the time of sampling will be unimportant. However, if a biodiversity survey is carried out when numerous migrants are present, the results will be elevated and it may be erroneously concluded that the island is more diverse than would be expected. This point might be particularly important when making comparisons between species counts made at different times of the year.

The theory of island biogeography was tested experimentally by Simberloff and Wilson (1970) on islands in the Florida Keys. After producing a detailed inventory of the insects on a number of very small mangrove islands (11–25 m in diameter), they completely enclosed each island in a frame covered with plastic sheets and fumigated it to remove all arthropods. They then monitored the recolonisation of these islands and found that the number of arthropod species on each island returned to the original level in about 6 months (Figure 12.10). Species accumulated more slowly and achieved lower equilibrium numbers on the more isolated islands. Species continued to colonise and disappear from the islands, but the number of insect species on each island did not change significantly. Interestingly, the return to the original level of insect diversity was achieved even though only 25–30% of the original species had recolonised the islands within one year: the species composition was very different to that on the islands before defaunation.

An increase in island size is likely to be accompanied by an increase in habitat diversity. Larger islands may therefore support more species not simply because of their larger size but also because they have greater habitat heterogeneity. Therefore the MacArthur–Wilson model can be modified to include a consideration of habitat diversity. One measure of habitat diversity is island altitude. High islands are likely to support more species than low-lying islands of a similar size. Buckley (1982) has shown that incorporating a consideration of habitat diversity into the island biogeography model provides significantly better predictions of actual species richness than the simpler island area–distance model.

Some predictions of the theory of island biogeography have been validated. It has been shown that islands support a constant number of species and also that the species composition changes with time (turnover). However, rates of colonisation have not been clearly related to distance from the source population and, furthermore, extinction rates have not been related to island size. Dispersal rates are very difficult to measure and Simberloff (1976) concluded that, until these rates can be measured, the theory of island bio-

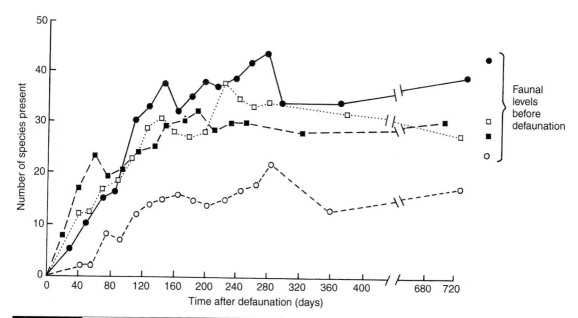

Figure 12.10 Colonisation curves of four small mangrove islands in the Florida Keys following complete removal of all animals (defaunation). Faunal levels before defaunation are indicated (after Simberloff and Wilson 1970 with permission of The Ecological Society of America).

geography should be considered to be a hypothesis. This theory has been applied to the design of nature reserves (see section 14.3.4) but, because of some of the uncertainties surrounding the theory, this application stimulated a vigorous debate in the scientific literature.

The colonisation of an island is likely to go through a series of phases. When both the number of species and their population densities are low, interaction between species will be minimal (**non-interactive phase**). As populations grow and the communities diversify, so biological interactions such as competition and predation increase (**interactive phase**). This then leads to a species sorting process (**assortative phase**). The final phase, in this time sequence, encompasses the changes that come about through evolution.

12.6 | Speciation

Charles Darwin visited islands in the Pacific during his voyage around the world on HMS *Beagle*

from 1832 to 1836. At about the same time, Alfred Wallace (1878) was working on islands in South-East Asia. The fascinating fauna and flora of these tropical islands led these men to lay the foundations to modern evolutionary theory. Species compositions on islands develop through **colonisation** (in ecological time) and through **speciation** (in evolutionary time). These processes are balanced by **extirpation** and **extinction** respectively. We have already considered the processes of colonisation and extirpation, and now turn our attention to the evolutionary processes of speciation and extinction.

Through evolution, populations adapt through genetic responses to environmental changes. When a population has undergone so much genetic change that it is no longer capable of interbreeding with all the individuals that originally constituted the species, a new species can be considered to have formed. This is the process of **speciation**. Speciation is normally a very slow process, and occurs through minute genetic changes accumulating over hundreds or thousands of generations. (Speciation can occur more rapidly in some organisms, particularly some of the lower plants, through polyploidy, in which chromosomes divide unequally but still produce fertile offspring.) Before we consider how speciation takes place, let us consider fish populations in Lake Malawi, one of the largest lakes in the world.

12.6.1 Lake Malawi: evolution laboratory

The African Great Lakes harbour the world's richest lacustrine fish faunas, in which the family Cichlidae provides an incredible example of **adaptive radiation** (Figure 12.11). Lake Malawi has over 500 fish species and most are **endemic** (only found in one region) to the lake. The entire fish fauna of Europe contains less than 200 species! Morphologically, the fish are rather similar but their life styles are very diverse. Some graze algae on rock faces, others are planktivorous or predators (piscivores, snail-crushers and insectivores). Some species feed on fish scales, and a few species of *Lipochromis* are paedophages. One species has a large mouth, thick rubbery lips and outward-pointed anterior teeth: these fish take the head of a mouth-brooding female and suck out the eggs or young!

The most diverse fish assemblages are the brightly coloured cichlids locally known as 'mbuna' with some 200 + species and numerous colour morphs. Mbuna live close to rocks and each community consists of endemics to the locality plus some more widely distributed species. Each rocky area has a distinct community, an 'island' surrounded by an open water barrier. Over 40 species may occur in each community with up to 14 individuals m^{-2} of rock face (Lowe-McConnell 1996). Some species move in and out of the community daily or seasonally and species translocated from one community to another have been able to establish populations in the already very complex communities at their new site (see section 11.7.1).

Male mbuna are territorial and breeding occurs throughout the year. Cichlids are mouth-brooders, the young, when threatened, enter the female's mouth and remain there until the danger has passed. The young, produced from a few large eggs (K-strategists), hide in rock crevices when released by the brooding female and probably spend their entire lives in the same area. Compare this life history with that of coral reef fish, in which the eggs and larvae are pelagic and disperse widely (see section 11.5).

How are so many species able to coexist in what appears to be a rather simple environment? How did so many species come into being? The first question can be answered in terms of the niche concept (see section 11.7.1). Resources are partitioned (see section 4.11.1) by depth, food source and substrate and most species are restricted to a small habitat (**stenotopic**). Mbuna are also opportunistic feeders and can switch from algal grazers to feed on zooplankton and other invertebrates. The second question introduces the concept of speciation.

12.6.2 Speciation and the species concept

New species arise through the evolutionary process of speciation, but first we need to consider what constitutes a species. The **biological species concept** defines a **species** as a group of interbreeding natural populations which is reproductively isolated from other such groups. It is, however, difficult to prove that two populations are reproductively isolated and species are, therefore, generally distinguished by morphological differences and not by whether they can or cannot interbreed to produce fertile offspring. The biological species concept is not readily applicable to those organisms that only reproduce asexually or those that do form fertile, natural hybrids (e.g. many plants) or even exchange genetic material through genetic introgression.

Many biologists today have adopted the **phylogenetic species concept** in which a species is defined as the smallest diagnosable cluster of individual organisms within which a parental pattern of descent can be discerned (see Cracraft 1983). The classification of organisms, under this scheme, should reflect relationships among species or higher taxa and is based on the presumption that they represent evolutionary pathways. Each group is regarded as **monophyletic**, containing all and only the descendants of a common ancestor. Each member of the group is more closely related than those outside it. Perhaps, what is most important to appreciate is that species are not immutable, they change, they deviate to give rise to new species and they go extinct.

Speciation can occur through an interbreeding population becoming separated by a

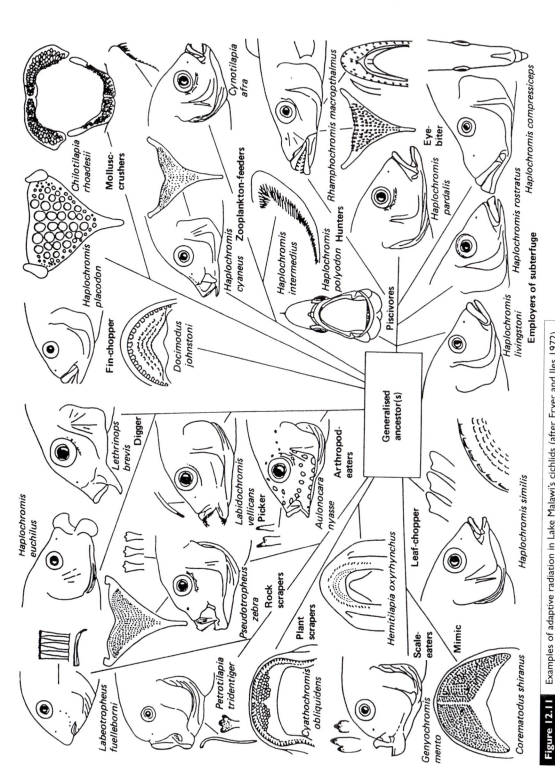

Figure 12.11   Examples of adaptive radiation in Lake Malawi's cichlids (after Fryer and Iles 1972).

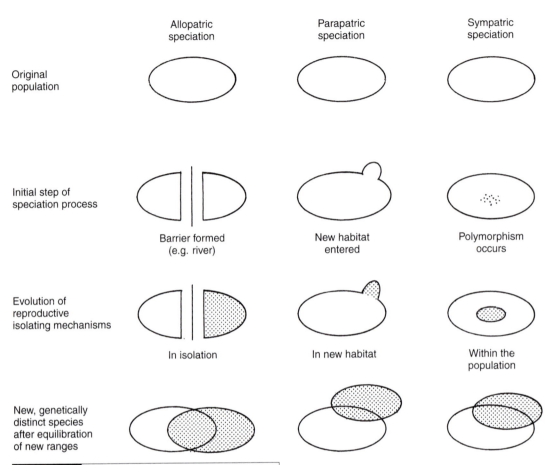

Figure 12.12 Three general hypotheses of speciation, of which allopatric speciation is probably the most common (after Tamarin 1993).

barrier that prevents the members of each sub-population from interbreeding. As there is no gene flow between the two sub-populations, they may diverge both genetically and morphologically. Divergence may occur to such an extent that members of each sub-population may not be able to interbreed even if their populations were reunited. The two populations have become **reproductively isolated** and effectively form two separate species. Speciation occurring through geographical isolation is known as **allopatric speciation** (Figure 12.12). In **sympatric speciation**, the incipient species may live together, but gene flow between them is restricted through some genetic mechanism. In sympatric speciation, the barrier between sub-populations is not

physical, but genetic. **Parapatric speciation** also occurs through polymorphism within a population. A fourth mechanism of speciation occurs through **genetic drift** in a small **founder** population. In this process, a small population, a few colonists on an island, for example, undergoes rapid genetic change owing to its small, unrepresentative gene pool. Each generation may exaggerate the differences (genetic drift) and the founder population gradually diverges from members in the parent population.

On islands, speciation and adaptive radiation may occur rapidly because the small founder populations colonise a habitat deficient in competitors. The original colonists breed, adapt and, over many generations, speciate, giving rise to closely related species that have adapted to utilise the full spectrum of resources available. Examples of adaptive radiation are readily apparent in isolated communities (islands, lakes) where colonisation has occurred by chance and a restricted taxonomic group evolves to fill the niches available. The mbuna of Lake Malawi, Darwin's finches on the Galapagos Islands and lobelias of the Hawaiian Islands are all excellent examples of this process. However, this should not be taken to suggest that adaptive radiation does not occur in non-isolated, mainland habitats.

The gradual separation of two species through competition for a limited resource is known as **character displacement**. Ground finches (*Geospiza* spp.) on the Galapagos Islands illustrate this process particularly well. Beak morphology provides a measure of the food resources being utilised by these birds, and is, therefore, an indicator of competitive interaction. When three species of these birds occur together on an island (sympatry), there is no overlap in their beak morphology, measured as beak depth. However, on islands where only one or just two of these species occur, beak dimensions extend into the range normally occupied by the species that is absent (see Figure 12.13). Coexistence of these species is thus facilitated by differentiation in beak morphology (and, hence, food resource utilisation), but this differentiation only develops under competitive pressure.

The Lake Malawi mbuna life style is conducive to allopatric speciation (Lowe-McConnell 1996). Parental care in habitat-restricted mbuna tends to keep individuals of the same species (**conspecifics**) together. Rocky promontories are separated by barriers of sand or the swampy margins around inflowing streams. Each isolated rocky outcrop supports a fish assemblage which differs from the communities on rocks elsewhere in the lake and gene flow between these isolated populations is extremely low or absent. It would seem that intralacustrine, micro-allopatric speciation has given rise to the diverse mbuna fauna. The degree of endemicity within each community has been related to the distance between habitats and the nearest similar habitat. Habitats close together permit greater gene flow than those further apart.

The speed with which new colour forms develop (a precursor of speciation) is supported by strong evidence that the southern arm of Lake Malawi dried up 200 years ago when lake level dropped by 150 m (Owen *et al.* 1990). This arm now contains rocky shore communities with endemic colour forms which have developed since the lake level rose. In summary, high mbuna diversity is related to this capacity for rapid change but other factors have also been important: (1) biogeographical restriction of fish to particular rocky habitats (barriers); (2) changing lake levels leading to isolation and reunification of populations; (3) the capacity to vary diet; and (4) the ability to adapt to new environments.

Biogeographic barriers facilitate allopatric speciation and lead to high frequencies of **endemism**. Myers (1997) points out that endemism is a nested hierarchy with all organisms endemic to the earth. Biogeographic barriers operate on a range of spatial scales to produce endemics that are highly restricted (mbuna species found only on one rocky outcrop) or species that are more widespread but none the less still have a constrained distribution.

Endemism on islands can be maintained through either poor dispersal ability or failure to colonise. Myers (1994) concluded that, while dispersal provides the vehicle for immigration, the key to colonisation is largely determined by ecological factors. The degree of endemism in a particular area is influenced by its isolation and environmental stability. Oceanic islands and mountain tops are isolated habitats and are rich in endemic species.

What is interesting is that, although the species in each of the three Great African Lakes (Malawi, Tanganyika and Victoria) are different and have evolved in isolation, they exhibit a high degree of **convergent evolution** (Table 12.2). Distinct species in each lake have evolved similar morphological or behavioural characteristics independently to solve a similar ecological problem such as feeding. We saw in chapter 5 that the introduction of the Nile perch to Lake Victoria resulted in the extinction of numerous species of native fish. In the next section we look at extinction and how the rate of this process has varied through geological time and relate this to the current high rate of species loss.

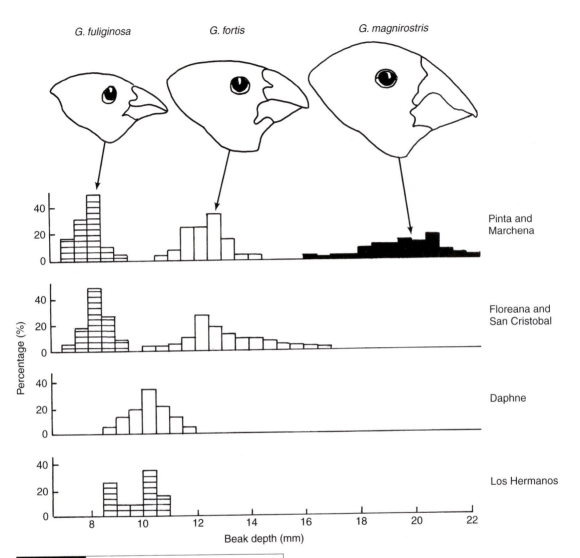

Figure 12.13 Percentages of individuals with beaks of different depths in three species of ground finches (*Geospiza* spp.) on islands in the Galapagos Archipelago. Note the increase in beak depth in *G. fortis* on Floreana and San Cristobal Islands where *G. magnirostris* is absent and the altered beak size distributions of *G. fortis* and *G. fuliginosa* on Daphne and Los Hermanos Islands respectively (after Lack 1947; Ricklefs 1997 with kind permission from Peter Lack and Cambridge University Press).

12.7 | Extinction

Extinction is a natural process. Species disappear when mortality exceeds the rate of production of new individuals for a period long enough to reduce the population size to zero (**demographic failure**). Extinction can also occur through **genetic swamping** in which extensive inter-breeding introgression leads to the absorption of one species into the gene pool of a related species. It has been estimated that some 4 billion different plant and animal species have lived on earth and the vast majority of these have gone extinct. Estimates of the number of species living on earth today (extant species) vary from 5 to 50 million, but we probably live at a time when there are more species on earth than at any time in the past. The diversity of life has been increasing ever since living organisms first evolved, but the fossil record indicates that this increase in diversity has not

Table 12.2	Examples of convergent evolution in three African lakes		
Characteristic	Lake Tanganyika	Lake Malawi	Lake Victoria
Algae-feeding rock scrapers	*Tropheus* spp.	*Pseudotropheus* spp.	*Neochromis nigricans*
Invertebrate-pickers with forceps teeth	*Tanganicodus irsacae*	*Labidochromis vellicans*	*Paralabidochromis victoriae*
Invertebrate-eaters with fleshy-lobed lips	*Lobochilotes labiatus*	*Haplochromis euchilus*	*Paralabidochromis chilotes*
Mollusc-crushers with massive pharyngeal bones	*Lamprologus tretocephalus*	*Haplochromis placodon*	*Labrochromis* spp.

Notes: Each lake supports distinct species or genera which have evolved similar morphological or behavioural characteristics independently to solve a similar ecological problem such as feeding.
Source: Lowe-McConnell 1987.

been steady. At least five **mass extinction** events have been identified from the fossil record. These extinctions occurred at the end of the Ordovician, Devonian, Permian, Triassic and Cretaceous Periods. Scientists recognise that we are currently recording a sixth mass extinction event, one that is being largely caused by overexploitation of natural resources by humans (see section 14.2).

Most previous extinctions have occurred through natural, environmental changes. Environmental changes can either be gradual, such as the retreat of the ice sheet at the end of an ice age, or quite dramatic, such as the impact of a hurricane or volcanic eruption. It has been proposed that extinction of the dinosaurs was brought about by a very dramatic event: the collision of an asteroid with the earth that caused the onset of prolonged darkness as smoke and dust filled the atmosphere. The demise of the dinosaurs was followed by mammalian ascendancy.

The current rate of extinctions is much greater than the rate of speciation and there is strong evidence to show that the rate of extinctions is increasing. Between 1600 and 1900, there were 75 known extinctions of birds or mammals; a rate of 1 species per 4 years. This century, 75 more species of birds or mammals have gone extinct (a threefold increase in the annual rate). It has been estimated that more than a tenth of the world's plant species are heading towards extinction. The IUCN Red List of Threatened Plants, published in 1998 by the World Conservation Union, lists 33 798 plant species as threatened. This list took botanists from all over the world 20 years to compile. Even so, it is probably far from complete, and many threatened plants from poorly studied and species-rich parts of the world, such as Brazil and central Africa, will not have been included.

Some species are more vulnerable to extinction than others. Large animals, especially top predators, are particularly prone to extinction. They require a large resource base and generally have a low reproductive rate and, if they are predators, often occur in small populations. Organisms high up the food chain are more susceptible to pollutants that are concentrated through bioaccumulation. Plants and animals that have specialised habitat requirements may face extinction if the habitat to which they are so well adapted is destroyed. Animals and plants adapted to live in a variety of habitats or a broad range of environmental conditions are more likely to survive through periods of environmental change. Other extinction-prone traits include restriction to a small geographic range, poor dispersal capabilities and a requirement for more than one area or habitat to complete their life cycle.

High rates of species extinctions have also been recorded in island habitats. Most bird extinctions have occurred on islands (see Table 12.3). Many species on islands are endemics and

Table 12.3	Recorded extinctions of various groups of terrestrial organisms since 1600		
Taxon	Continental	Island	Per cent of species
Mammals	30	51	2.1
Birds	21	90	1.3
Reptiles	1	20	0.3
Amphibians	2	0	0.01
Fish	22	1	0.1
Invertebrates	49	48	0.01
Vascular plants	245	139	0.2

Source: Primack 1998. Many more species have presumably gone extinct without being recorded by biologists.

Table 12.4	Causes of historical extinctions of birds in island and continental regions	
Cause	Continents	Oceanic Islands
Hunting	61.5%	14.9%
Predation		41.8%
Competition		6.7%
Disease		5.6%
Genetic swamping		0.7%
Weather		0.4%
Habitat disturbance	23.1%	19.4%
Unknown	15.4%	10.4%
Number of species	11	92
Number of subspecies	2	83
Total number of taxa	13	175

Source: Primack 1998.

therefore extirpation and extinction are, in the special case of endemics, the same. While predators on islands have been shown to be a significant cause of extinction, they are also very susceptible to extinction since their numbers must be substantially lower than those of their prey species (Table 12.4). Consequently, islands often contain a depauperate predator community in comparison with a similar area on the mainland.

Enhanced rates of extinctions correlate closely with human colonisation. The megafauna of Australia was decimated following human colonisation of the continent some 50 000 years ago. However, the extinction of some of the large, Australian animals may have been brought about by factors such as climate change, and it is difficult to attribute their loss definitively to

excessive hunting by humans. In the more recent human colonisations of islands, particularly in the Pacific Ocean, the demise of plants and animals can be more clearly attributed to human activities, and in particular, the introduction of exotic species.

We have seen that through adaptive radiation, island communities of closely related species have evolved from perhaps, just one colonisation event many years ago. Evolution on islands may have taken place in the absence of the natural selection that disease, predation and competition imposed on the evolution of mainland populations. For example, many birds on islands increased in size and lost their ability to fly. These are characteristics that make a bird prone to predators. However, if predation is not a threat, then large size may confer distinct survival and reproductive advantages. Populations that have evolved in a predator-free environment have no need for anti-predator defences and suffer decimation when they encounter one. Numerous examples abound of the impact of exotic (introduced) species on island fauna and flora, including large continental islands such as Australia.

12.8 | Exotic species on islands

Box 5.6 describes the impact of the introduction of the Nile perch on the fish communities in Lake Victoria. There are numerous similar examples of adverse impacts of exotic species on the native fauna of islands. Sheep, goats, pigs and rats were often introduced to islands by sailors in the eighteenth century to provide a source of fresh meat

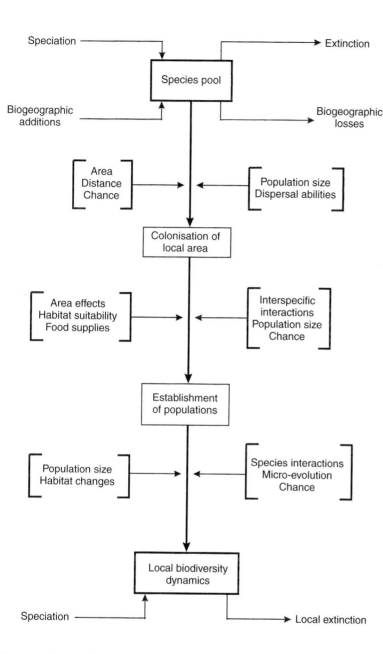

Figure 12.14 Community dynamics through the processes of colonisation, establishment, speciation and extinction and some of the major factors that control these processes. This figure includes both space and time dimensions, and the rates and scales at which the various processes occur may differ markedly. For example, colonisation may occur within a few days or months, whereas speciation, even through micro-evolution, may take many years (adapted from Wiens 1989; Barbault and Sastrapradja 1995).

the next time a ship called. Rats easily kill flightless birds which are often common elements of island faunas. Grazing animals will eat the more palatable species first and these species may often not be well adapted to grazing pressure. Introduced rats and cats have been implicated as the agents for extinction of five birds in New Zealand. On Guam in the western Pacific, the exotic brown tree-snake (*Boiga irregularis*) has devastated the island's birds. The snake was introduced to the island during the Second World War; three birds are now extinct with three more on the verge of extinction.

The Hawaiian Island chain stretches across 2500 km of the tropical Pacific. The largest island of Hawaii is also the most recent, being formed through volcanic activity less than one million years ago. Kauai, at the western end of the chain, is the oldest of the large islands; erupted from the sea-bed between 4 and 5 million years ago. The islands support a very rich flora and fauna, with many endemic species. There were 98 species of birds endemic to the Hawaiian Islands before the arrival of humans in *c.* AD 400. The Polynesian colonists brought with them domestic animals (dog, pig) and introduced a rat. Through habitat destruction for agriculture and increased predation, about half the endemic bird fauna was extinct by the time Europeans arrived in 1778. The introduction of domestic cats and many exotic birds with European colonisation further devastated the bird fauna. The exotic birds brought with them two diseases – avian pox and avian malaria (avian malaria is spread in Hawaii by an introduced mosquito) – and both these are a further threat to the native birds that remain. Few native birds now survive in the lowland forests on the Hawaiian Islands and about 30 species are now listed as endangered.

Why are island faunas more susceptible to predation by exotic species than those on continents? Habitats on continents tend to be larger and more heterogeneous than those on islands, and therefore continents will provide more refuges for prey species. Predators on continents are unlikely to drive their prey to extinction because of prey switching: once one prey species becomes rare, predators can switch to alternative prey. On islands, with their simpler faunas, predators have fewer options. Island organisms have also evolved under reduced competition and in the absence of many pests and diseases. Competition, predators, diseases and pests have all played a significant role in natural selection of the species that thrive on continents. The introduction of exotic species and diseases to islands and the arrival of humans have been the two major causes of species loss on islands.

The observation of enhanced rates of species loss from islands has prompted significant study into changes in species composition following habitat fragmentation. The application of the theory of island biogeography to remnant habitat patches and protected areas has been controversial and we will review some of the issues in chapter 14.

We have discussed features of ecological communities in a number of chapters. In chapter 7, we discussed how communities change with time. In chapters 8 and 11 we looked at diverse communities, how they are assembled and how numerous species can coexist. In this chapter we have seen how new communities can form through colonisation of new areas. Figure 12.14 provides a summary of the main processes involved in community dynamics and some of the factors that control them.

12.9 | Chapter summary

1. Larger islands have more habitats and support more species. The number of species on an island is determined by a balance between immigration of new species, establishment of populations on the island and the continued existence or demise (extirpation) of those populations. Species richness on islands declines with remoteness from major land masses (species source). Newly formed islands may lack species because inadequate time has passed for colonisation.

2. The relative proportions of different taxa often differ on islands from those on adjacent land masses (disharmony), with species with strong dispersal powers disproportionately dominating island communities. Islands are isolated habitats with the sea that surrounds them forming a colonisation barrier for many species.

3. The isolation of islands has promoted the formation of new species through adaptive radiation and speciation. Speciation occurring through geographical isolation is known as allopatric speciation. In sympatric speciation, the incipient species may live together, but gene flow between them is restricted through some genetic mechanism. Parapatric speciation occurs through polymorphism within a population. Speciation can also occur through genetic drift in a small founder population. The gradual separation of two species through competition for a limited resource is known as character displacement.

4. Evolution on islands (or in lakes) can lead to endemism. Endemism is more likely on remote islands and within groups with poorer dispersal powers. Extinction is a natural process. Extinction occurs through demographic failure or genetic swamping. Island populations are more susceptible to extinction because they are often endemic to the island, occur in small populations and are unable to defend themselves effectively from exotic predators and humans.

Chapter 13

Cities and human ecology

Every human being represents hands to work, and not just another mouth to feed.

Former President of the United States, George H. Bush (see section 13.3).

The earth is finite. Its ability to absorb wastes and destructive effluent is finite. Its ability to provide food and energy is finite. Its ability to provide for growing numbers of people is finite. And we are fast approaching many of the earth's limits.

The World's Scientists' Warning to Humanity (see Ehrlich and Ehrlich 1998)

13.1 | Jakarta, Indonesia

Over 20 million people live in the metropolitan area of Jakarta and the central city has a human population density of around 12500 people km^{-2} (Hadiwinoto and Leitman 1994). Jakarta is the government, industrial, commercial and transport hub for the Indonesian archipelago, and, although per capita income in the metropolitan area is much higher than the national average, nearly 1.5 million people in Jakarta live below the poverty line. The poor are concentrated in unplanned slums with inadequate water supplies and waste disposal systems. The population of Jakarta grew at an annual rate of 3.8% from 1980 to 1990. This rapid growth was due to natural increase (more births than deaths) and to the movement of people from rural areas to the city in search of jobs.

The rapid growth in the human population that has occurred in Jakarta, coupled with rapid economic development, has exerted significant stress on the environment. Major problems include those linked to the hydrological cycle (see Box 5.4), solid waste disposal, hazardous waste management and air pollution. The hydrological cycle has been affected through saline intrusion resulting from overextraction of ground water and reduced recharge. Surface waters in Jakarta are heavily polluted with domestic- and industrial-waste waters, and marine waters and sediments in Jakarta Bay have high concentrations of heavy metals. Economic growth has led to increased road traffic and the resultant congestion has adversely affected air quality.

Poor environmental quality has impaired human health. Waterborne diseases such as typhoid, diarrhoea and cholera increase in frequency with distance downstream in the metropolitan area. In 1998, poor air quality in the city was further impaired through smoke from forest fires that were lit to clear land for agriculture. Owing to the dry conditions resulting from the 1998 El Niño event (see section 1.2.6), these fires burned out of control and large areas of South-East Asia were covered in thick smog. Chronic poor air quality in urban areas largely results from the combustion of fossil fuels and is a major cause of respiratory ailments such as asthma.

Most large cities throughout the tropical world experience problems similar to those described above for Jakarta (Figure 13.1). Human populations are becoming more concentrated through a process known as **urbanisation** and it has been estimated that, world-wide, each week 1 million people move from rural areas into cities (Figure 13.2). In developed countries, 80% of the

Figure 13.1 Manila, the capital city of the Philippines. Metropolitan Manila has a population of over 10 million and is experiencing many of the environmental and social problems associated with most large cities in South-East Asia: rapid population growth, air and water pollution, traffic congestion and inadequate waste disposal facilities (Photo: Patrick Osborne).

population now live in cities, and this contrasts with only 30% in developing countries, but this lower proportion is increasing rapidly. In 1950, no Asian city had more than 8 million people. By 1970, the populations of Beijing and Shanghai reached this size and, by 1990, were joined by Calcutta, Bombay, Seoul, Tianjin, Jakarta, Delhi and Manila (Sanderson and Tan 1996). Cities in other parts of the world have shown similar rapid growth.

These large cities require enormous imports of food, water and other materials to support their large populations. Wastes generated within cities have to be removed. These material imports and waste exports exert an ecological stress on the surrounding ecosystems that produce the imports and receive the waste products. Appropriation of these ecosystem goods and services extends the environmental impact of a city far beyond its

Figure 13.2 Crowded housing in Manila, the Philippines. The provision of adequate housing has not been able to keep pace with the rapid growth in the human population of urban areas through migration of people from rural areas (Photo: Patrick Osborne).

urban boundary. The extent of this influence has been referred to as the **ecological footprint** of a city (Folke *et al.* 1997).

How did these massive human conglomerates arise? What are some of the ecological impacts of these cities? How have humans modified landscapes in both urban and rural settlements? Why has the human population grown so large? What are some of the consequences of this rapid expansion in the human population and how might these be ameliorated? To answer some of these questions and explain why humans have been so successful (assuming that population size is a measure of success) we need to review briefly the evolution of human societies.

13.2 | Evolution of human societies

Around 5 to 8 million years ago, hominids split away from the other primates, and evolved (probably somewhere in East Africa) into what is now the sole surviving hominid species: *Homo sapiens sapiens*. Our early ancestors were ape-like, and a significant step in the evolution of early humans was the development of **bipedalism** (walking on two feet). Bipedalism freed the hands and this, together with an increase in brain size, facilitated the development of tool use. Bipedalism is an energy-efficient mode of locomotion and it also decreased the amount of heat absorbed by reducing the surface area of body exposed to the sun.

Early humans survived in the African savanna as hunters and gatherers and competed with a diverse array of other animals. These early hominids had several advantages over their competitors. They had an effective social organisation, a strong capacity to learn, store and pass on information to successive generations and, through possession of an opposable thumb, fine manipulative skills. Social cohesion enabled co-operative hunting, food-sharing and defence. Intelligence led to the capacity to envision a tool and its use prior to its manufacture.

In the early Palaeolithic (500000–1000000 years ago), humans developed tools and learnt to manage fire. Tool-making and fire management enabled these early hominids to expand the range of plants and animals they could harvest for food and other uses. These early societies depended on a sound knowledge of their environment, and were indeed the first ecologists (although maybe not the first conservationists). The development of strong communication skills (language) strengthened social co-operation and facilitated intergenerational transfer of knowledge.

Modern humans (*Homo sapiens sapiens*) appeared around 100000 years ago and migrated out of Africa into the Middle East and Europe. In Europe, modern humans, for a while, coexisted with Neanderthals (*Homo sapiens neanderthalensis*). We do not know whether it was competition for resources or direct warfare that eventually led to the extinction of Neanderthals. By 50000 years ago, humans had colonised Australia and subsequently spread even to small islands throughout the Pacific Ocean. They moved into North America, probably by crossing the Bering Straits, at least 12000 years ago.

It is only in the last 10000 years, following the end of the last ice age, that human societies became more settled and began to domesticate plants and animals and to make more sophisticated tools. The last ice age gave way to a warmer, moister climate and a switch from grasslands to forests. The change in vegetation may have resulted in fewer large mammals, which had probably provided the major source of food for humans. These changes may have forced humans to consider other techniques of food production: **domestication** of plants and animals. The process of establishing settlements may not have occurred abruptly, but may have come about through repetitive use of a number of particular sites, with humans remaining at one site until plants bore fruit before moving on. Agriculture appears to have emerged independently in several parts of the world.

By 5000 years ago, civilisations in the then fertile crescent of the Middle East and Egyptian Nile valley had established cities in the Bronze Age, and around 3000 years ago this led into the Iron Age. It was during the Iron Age that humans began to have a major impact on the environment. Forests were cleared more efficiently and pastures could be converted into arable lands, and these activities significantly altered landscapes around settlements. During this period of enhanced agricultural activity, a drier climate developed and the productivity of these thriving farming areas in the Middle East declined. One school of thought believes that the drier climate that followed this early agricultural period can be directly attributed to poor land husbandry by these early farmers. Other historians attribute it to natural climate change.

There is also a similar debate as to the cause of the extinction of many large mammals in the Quaternary Period. The loss of large mammals from Australia and North and South America follows human colonisation of these continents. Over 75% of large mammal species became extinct soon after human settlement. This was probably caused by humans through the development of efficient co-operative hunting and indirectly through habitat destruction. However, significant climate changes that occurred during this period may have contributed to this decline.

There is increasing evidence accumulating from ecological and archaeological studies that the role humans have played, through the ages, in causing significant environmental degradation has been underestimated. Three to four thousand years ago, the large herds of pastoralists in Africa and the Middle East were probably responsible for significant land degradation through overgrazing and erosion, possibly even leading to increased aridity. In more recent times, significant environmental degradation can be linked both with the expansion of the Roman Empire through Europe and the colonisation of the North American continent. Human activity in the developed world has converted natural ecosystems to highly modified agricultural landscapes with reduced species diversity.

A similar process of landscape modification is occurring or has occurred in many tropical countries through slash-and-burn agriculture, deforestation, conversion of forests to cattle pastures and plantations and the construction of elaborate terraces and drainage systems for rice cultivation (Figure 13.3). In switching from a hunter–gatherer to a more settled existence, humans changed from an organism that har-

Figure 13.3. The Banaue rice terraces, northern Luzon, the Philippines. The rice terraces were created over 2000 years by the Ifugao people using only hand tools (Photo: Patrick Osborne).

vested a variety of plants and animals in much the same way as many other omnivorous animals, to one with a powerful capacity to alter landscapes and the environment. Some hunter–gatherer societies still exist in remote parts of the world, and our understanding of how early societies operated has been enriched through study of these extant groups.

13.2.1 Hunter–gatherer society

The Pawaia live in the Purari River valley of Papua New Guinea (see section 6.2). They occupy a settlement for a number of years and then abandon it and move to a new area. Nearly all routine daily activities are directed towards food gathering, preparation and consumption (Toft 1983). The Pawaia live largely on food gathered from the lowland rain forests that surround their settlements and fish from streams. Sago (*Metroxylon sagu*) provides their staple food and is supplemented by some cultivated plants (plantains, taro, cassava, yam and sweet potato). Gardening is of secondary importance and is practiced using a **slash-and-burn** technique. Men help women clear an area of vegetation and burn the piles if it is not too wet to do so. A variety of crops are planted on the cleared ground. The women are responsible for maintaining the gardens, but input is minimal and the produce only serves to supplement sago on which these people depend.

Men go on short hunting trips that may last 2–3

days. On these trips, bandicoots, lizards, birds and grubs are sought. On more extended expeditions, introduced wild pigs and cassowaries are hunted. Hunting methods include trapping, tracking with dogs and shooting (traditionally with bow and arrow or spear but now guns are also used).

The Pawaia have a sound ecological knowledge of their environment and a taxonomy of the plants and animals in the rain forest based on how they use these organisms. Superficially, it would appear that the Pawaia live in harmony with nature, extracting from the forest all resources they require to fulfil their needs and leaving little trace of their exploits. This is largely only so because their population density has been restricted through high mortality rates, with life expectancy curtailed through the rigours of their life style, diseases, particularly malaria, and high rates of infant mortality.

In other parts of the world, rapid human population growth has been achieved through technological revolutions that have reduced mortality rates and enhanced production of resources, particularly food, which has sustained this dramatic population growth. Let us review, briefly, some of the developments that have allowed the human population to grow so rapidly, particularly over the last century.

13.3 | World population growth

The development of agricultural settlements, some 10 000 years ago, helped the world population grow from less than 10 million to around 150 million 2000 years ago. In the next millennium, the population grew to 350 million. In the fourteenth century, human populations were decimated in Europe and Asia by bubonic plague, a disease spread by fleas on rats. In the following centuries, until the industrial revolution in the nineteenth century, human population growth was relatively slow (Figure 13.4).

The industrial revolution was accompanied by a significant reduction in the mortality rate which led to growth of the human population from approximately 1 billion (a thousand millions) in 1850 to 2 billion in 1930 and to over 6

billion in 2000. The population in 1985 was estimated to be growing at a rate of three people every second, and it has been predicted that the human population in 2030 will be 9.5 billion (McNeely *et al.* 1995). The mortality rate has declined through a more assured food supply and medical advances which have enabled people to live longer. Human fertility is currently falling (see section 13.6.2), but world population is still increasing by about 80 million people per year, down from 90 million per year in 1990.

Today, patterns of human population growth vary regionally. In Europe and North America, human population growth has slowed through falling birth rates and increased longevity has resulted in an age distribution that differs markedly from those found in developing nations (Figure 13.5). The change that has taken place in Europe and North America has been characterised as a **demographic transition**. In this process, human populations first grow very rapidly through enhanced food availability and a rise in life expectancy resulting from better health care and nutrition. Initially birth rates remain high and therefore rapid population growth occurs. In the countries of Europe and North America, social changes which accompanied the demographic transition, have reduced birth rates. People have opted for smaller families and utilise birth control to ensure this. In some of these countries, the population growth is below that required to sustain the population at its current level.

This demographic transition is underway in many countries in South-East Asia where people have moved from rural areas to cities. This migration was stimulated by employment opportunities, and the resultant increased wealth of urban populations has led to a desire for smaller families and the capacity to provide offspring with a better education and an even more comfortable life style. People living in rural areas needed large families to provide adequate labour, and children were also needed to care for their elderly parents. Urbanisation not only decreased infant mortality and therefore reduced the need to produce large families, but also brought with it social programmes which provided care to the elderly.

We can divide the human populations in the

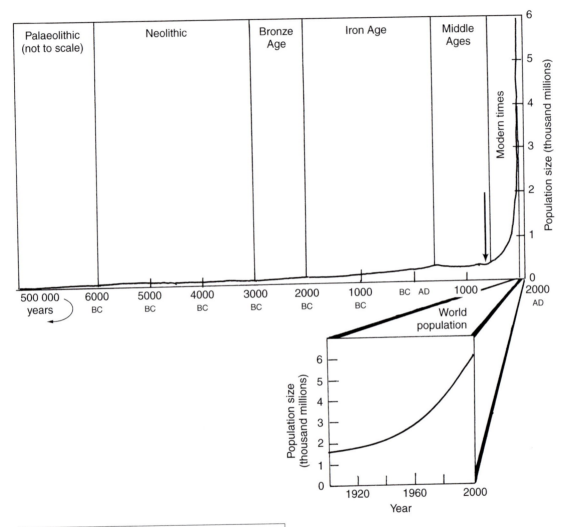

Figure 13.4 Growth in the human population over the last five hundred thousand years. Note that, for most of this period, population growth was slow, but around 1830 a period of very rapid growth began (after Trewartha 1969 with kind permission from John Wiley & Sons Inc.)

countries listed in Table 13.1 into three groups based on their level of fertility (the average number of children produced by a woman) between 1985 and 1989. The low fertility populations include those of China, North and South Korea, Sri Lanka and Thailand. Countries with populations with medium fertility include India, Indonesia, Malaysia, Burma, the Philippines and Vietnam. The remaining countries listed in Table 13.1 all had populations with high fertility during the late 1980s. Figure 13.6 shows how the popula-

tion growth in these three groups has changed through the latter half of the twentieth century. Note that countries with low fertility populations in 1985–89 had the highest population growth in the period 1950–54. Conversely, those countries with populations with high fertility in the 1980s had the lowest population growth in the 1950s. We can see the reason behind this demographic transition or cross-over if we study the age structure of human populations in countries with differing fertility rates.

The age structure (see section 4.14) of the human population in China is undergoing a change, with a reduction in the number of children below the age of 15 (Figure 13.5). Notice, however, that there is still much of the population

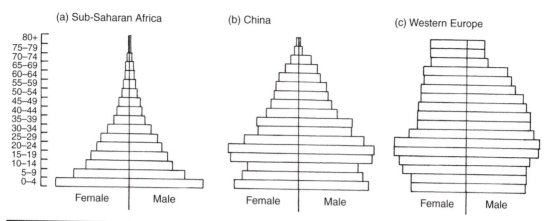

(a) Sub-Saharan Africa   (b) China   (c) Western Europe

Figure 13.5 Age pyramids for the human populations of Sub-Saharan Africa, China and Western Europe. In Sub-Saharan Africa, high birth and death rates have shaped the pyramid into one with a broad base and narrow apex. Declining birth rates over the past 20 years in China have created a smaller population of children, but this narrow base is surmounted by a large proportion of women of child-bearing age. The population of Western Europe has a high proportion of elderly people. Note the larger proportion of elderly women in comparison with men in Europe (after Pearce 1998b with kind permission of New Scientist – *Inside Science* no. 112).

between the ages of 15 and forty, when female fertility is highest. As fertility declines, the proportion of women of reproductive age in the population increases. This results in an increase in the birth rate (see section 4.7) and this, in turn, impedes the decline in the rate at which the population grows. This explains why changes in population growth rate occur slowly. This factor is known as **population momentum**. Consider an example from Bangladesh. Even if Bangladeshi women averaged around 2.1 births (replacement rate level of fertility) over their reproductive life span from 1990 and 2030, the population would still grow but by 62% instead of the predicted 74%. Effectively, this means that around 80% of the population growth projected for Bangladesh between 1990 and 2030 is inevitable.

In Sub-Saharan Africa, the base of the pyramid (Figure 13.5) is broad and the proportion of old people is much less than those for the populations in China and Western Europe. The population in Sub-Saharan Africa is growing rapidly with a high proportion of children and this places stress on the provision of health and education. The small proportion of elderly people in Sub-Saharan Africa suggests high mortality rates and a lower life expectancy. Notice that the population in Africa will continue to grow rapidly even if replacement rate fertility was achieved today because the large number of children will, in a few years, enter their reproductive years.

The demographic transition has not occurred in many developing countries where large families are still very much the norm. This is particularly true of Sub-Saharan Africa where much-improved health care has significantly reduced mortality, but birth rates remain high and there is little incentive to reduce them. In Kenya, the population growth rate exceeded 4% in the 1980s although it has since declined. There is a lag in time between a reduction in fertility and a significant reduction in the population since the fertility rate must be multiplied by the number of women of child-bearing age in the population.

The Western European population has many old people and this brings with it stresses to the social services provided by governments to the elderly in most of these countries. The proportion of people in the productive phase of life (workers) is small in comparison with those that are no longer economically productive (retired workers). This demographic structure reduces national economic performance and some politicians in Europe are concerned how this may impact the political status of European nations. We can see that the demographic transition has not started

| Table 13.1 | Human population sizes in selected Asian countries in 1950 and 1990 and the ratio of the 1990 population to the 1950 population |

Country	1950	1990	Ratio of 1990 population to 1950 population
Bangladesh	41 783 000	109 820 000	2.63
Bhutan	734 000	1 433 000	1.95
Burma	17 832 000	41 825 000	2.35
Cambodia	4 346 000	8 610 000	1.98
China	554 760 000	1 122 683 000	2.04
India	357 561 000	849 514 000	2.38
Indonesia	79 538 000	178 232 000	2.24
Japan	83 625 000	123 537 000	1.48
Korea, DPR	9 726 000	21 771 000	2.24
Korea, Republic of	20 357 000	42 869 000	2.11
Laos	1 755 000	4 140 000	2.36
Malaysia	6 110 000	17 763 000	2.91
Nepal	8 182 000	18 916 000	2.31
Pakistan	39 513 000	112 351 000	2.84
Papua New Guinea	1 613 000	3 875 000	2.40
Philippines	20 988 000	61 480 000	2.93
Sri Lanka	7 678 000	16 993 000	2.21
Thailand	20 010 000	56 303 000	2.81
Vietnam	29 954 000	66 233 000	2.21

Source: Sanderson and Tan 1996.

in Sub-Saharan Africa, is underway in China and has already taken place in Western Europe. While this transition may bring with it some painful social consequences, the ecological consequences and resultant human suffering of continued rapid population growth are far more serious.

Because there is a link between population size and the use of natural resources, harvesting natural resources has also increased rapidly over the last two centuries. However, resource use is not simply related to population size. Per capita resource use is much higher in developed countries than it is in developing countries. There is also a link between population size and environmental degradation but, again, the relationship is not simple, as section 13.5 will demonstrate. The rapid increase in the world's human population has increased the need for food production, enhanced natural resource use and increased the rate at which pollutants are produced. Clearly there must be some limit to this population growth, and, ever since Malthus in 1798 con-

cluded that 'the power of population is indefinitely greater than the power in the earth to produce subsistence for man', ecologists have attempted to answer the question: What is the earth's human carrying capacity (see section 4.7.5)?

An early computer model of the impact of increasing human populations on industrial output, food production, pollution and resource use is shown in Figure 13.7. This model predicted that the earth's human carrying capacity would be exceeded before the end of the twentieth century. These models did not adequately incorporate the cultural capacities of human societies to change and innovate, and the predictions have, in gross terms, not come to fruition. For example, the use of copper as a raw material has declined following the development of fibre-optic cables, aluminium has been used in place of steel, energy sources now include wind, nuclear and tidal power and food production per unit input (land area, labour, energy) has increased. However, the

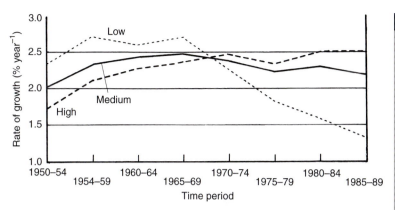

Figure 13.6 Population growth rates in Asian countries (see Table 13.1) from 1950–54 to 1985–89 grouped according to human population fertility in the period 1985–89. Low fertility: China, North and South Korea, Sri Lanka and Thailand; medium fertility: India, Indonesia, Malaysia, Burma, the Philippines and Vietnam; and high fertility: Bangladesh, Cambodia, Laos, Nepal and Papua New Guinea (after Sanderson and Tan 1996 with kind permission from Ashgate Publishing Limited).

underlying message that these early models conveyed remains pertinent: supplies of natural resources have limits.

The Global 2000 report produced for United States President Carter and published in 1980 also predicted dire environmental consequences largely stemming from rising oil prices. This report indicated that energy costs would increase by 150% between 1975 and 2000 and this would cause similar increases in the price of fertilisers derived from oil. However, these predictions, too, have not come to fruition, with oil prices in the latter part of the twentieth century actually declining in real terms.

The quotation from George Bush at the start of this chapter embodies a positive outlook. Certainly additional people can work towards finding solutions, producing more food and raising living standards. However, those people also contribute to waste generation, resource use, biodiversity loss and land degradation (see Cohen 1995). Furthermore, population numbers do not, as Cohen points out, provide the cultural, environmental and economic resources necessary to make additional hands productive. Ehrlich and Ehrlich (1998) provide a thorough analysis of how scientific issues have been misconstrued by people wishing to downplay the seriousness of human impacts on the environment.

In 1992, just 15% of people living in the wealthiest nations enjoyed 79% of the world's income. Among 4.4 billion people in developing countries, almost 60% lack basic sanitation and one-third have no safe drinking water. There are only 5–10 cars per 1000 people in many countries

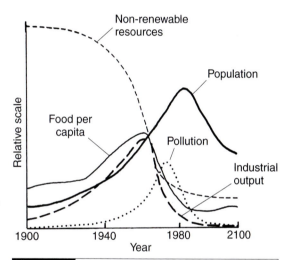

Figure 13.7 Computer model of the growth in the human population and its impact on resource availability, pollution, per capita food supply and per capita industrial output. This model was produced by a group of scientists, economists, social scientists, political scientists and industrialists who met in 1968 (after Meadows *et al.* 1972).

of South-East Asia and Sub-Saharan Africa, but 450 cars per 1000 people in industrialised countries (United Nations 1998). Owing to these inequalities in income and resource use, humans in different regions of the world affect the environment in different ways: an average North American or European uses far more resources and generates more waste than people living in Sub-Saharan Africa or on an island in the tropical Pacific.

Human choice must also be factored into the

equation. For example, each day people over the world may be faced with choices about what to eat, whether to use a private car or public transport, or whether to support designation of a national park or development of a timber or mining project. In many parts of the world, options and choices are few and the stark reality is reduced to a search for the next meal. The human carrying capacity of the earth is, therefore, not easy to predict, since it is not simply determined by a combination of limiting resource supply and other natural constraints. We certainly can not easily apply to human populations the carrying capacity concept described in section 4.7.5 for animal populations. However, we can look at how food production, natural resource use and levels of pollution have changed with increasing human populations.

13.4 | Food production

Although humans utilise a wide variety of organisms to provide their food and other needs, the number of domesticated species is relatively small. Humans feed on fungi, algae, plants (seeds, fruits, leaves, roots, stems), and a wide range of animals from insects to snails, frogs to rats and bats, snakes, ungulates and primates. They also use micro-organisms to produce dairy products and beverages. It has been estimated that humans have monopolised 40% of the world's primary production to meet their needs (Vitousek *et al.* 1986).

Food production per capita has actually increased despite the growth of human populations. In 1998, there was a 20% surplus in world food production, although this may vary quite markedly from year to year. However, food supplies are not regionally uniform; in some regions food is stockpiled or even destroyed while in other parts of the world people are dying from starvation. Famines are usually caused through a combination of low food production owing to poor growing conditions (inadequate rainfall and degraded soils), poor distribution networks and political instability and war. Food is produced either though cultivation (agriculture, aquaculture and mariculture) or through the direct

exploitation of natural populations (harvesting fruits and vegetables, hunting and capture fisheries). No matter how food is produced, its production comes at some cost to the environment.

13.4.1 Agriculture

In an ecological context, agriculture involves the replacement of natural communities with deliberately selected crop plants and livestock animals. This has resulted in significant modification of landscapes in many parts of the world. In Europe and North America, few natural landscapes remain and this has led to a loss of wildlife, deforestation and drainage of wetlands. Intensive agricultural production has also led to nutrient enrichment of water bodies and their pollution with pesticide and herbicide residues, loss of topsoil through erosion and salinisation of soils through irrigation. Clearing natural vegetation for agriculture leads to a reduction in soil organic matter and hence lower nutrient storage, cation-exchange and water storage capacities (see section 2.9). These changes also lead to reduced diversity of soil organisms.

The intensity of human intervention varies from the slash-and-burn and nomadic pastoralist type of agriculture described in section 13.2.1 to the very intensive farming that involves crop rotations, plantations and high-density animal rearing in carefully controlled environments. In **subsistence agriculture**, production is generally geared towards supplying the needs of a family or local community. The Pawaia practice **shifting cultivation**, growing crops on one piece of cleared land for a few years before moving to another. They may return to the original land later but, in the interval, natural vegetation can reclaim the land (Figure 13.8).

As populations increase, shifting cultivation gives way to some form of land ownership and a more settled existence. This type of agriculture sustains the great majority of rural populations in the developing world. These small farms aim to produce enough food to meet the needs of the family and also to produce either an excess or a cash crop such as coffee or cocoa for sale. As urban populations grow, more intensive agriculture is required to provide the needs of people living in

Figure 13.8 Slash-and-burn agriculture being practiced in a remote highland area of Papua New Guinea (Photo: Patrick Osborne).

cities who lack the capacity to produce their food. Plantation agriculture may also provide commodities for international trade with nations unable to produce sufficient food to feed their residents.

In India, grain production increased almost fourfold between 1950 and 1990; this was achieved through increasing the land area being farmed, irrigation, fertiliser application and through the development of higher-yielding crop varieties. This **green revolution** not only made India self-sufficient in food, but also a net exporter of grains. However, as with Europe and North America, these achievements have come at a cost. Natural habitats have been converted into farmland, nutrient run-off has enriched lakes and streams and agricultural chemicals have entered food chains (see section 13.5.1). Poor farming practices have led to soil erosion and nutrient depletion. Soil losses throughout the world range from 20–300 t ha^{-1} and topsoil is being lost at 16–300

times faster than it can be replaced (see Kendall and Pimentel 1994). About 16% of the world's croplands are under irrigation and these fields produce around one-third of all crops. Irrigation has resulted in raised water tables and increasing soil salinities. The shift from manual labour to machines has increased consumption of fossil fuels.

Globally, the land available for effective agriculture is unlikely to increase. It has been estimated that as much as 10^7 ha of formerly productive farmland may be lost each year owing to poor farming practices. New farmlands are being created, but these are often in areas that have only short-term potential owing to poor soil fertility. Global grain yields increased throughout most of the latter half of the twentieth century, but have now reached a plateau. This translates into a decline in the per capita availability of grain produce. On a regional basis, owing to differences in human population growth and grain yields, North America, Australia and New Zealand have become net grain exporters while Europe, Africa and Asia are net importers of grains. Tropical countries are able to counterbalance some of these imports through exports of tropical crops such as coffee, cocoa, sugar, palm oil, fruits, spices and nuts. However, many countries, particularly in Sub-Saharan Africa, remain short of food, with mean per capita calorific food intake leading to widespread **malnutrition** (lack of essential minerals, amino acids and vitamins) and **undernutrition** (inadequate food energy).

A quarter of the crops produced are not fed to humans but are used as livestock feeds. Even in developing countries where food is scarce, farmers are switching from crop production to livestock rearing to meet the growing demand for meat and other animal products. This demand is driving the conversion of tropical rain forests to cattle pastures, and overstocking results in land degradation through overgrazing leading to soil erosion. Intensive animal-rearing units result in problems with manure disposal, and livestock production is responsible for significant inputs of greenhouse gases (methane and carbon dioxide) to the atmosphere (see section 14.4).

Globally, human success can be largely attributed to the domestication of crops and animals, but we also harvest significant food and other resources from natural populations and this, too, is having devastating effects.

13.4.2 Exploitation of natural populations for food

The Pawaia people in Papua New Guinea harvest natural resources not only for food, but also to provide shelter, firewood, tools, fibres and medicines (see section 13.2.1). With small human populations operating in large areas, the use of these natural resources might have minimal effects and could be sustained through natural replacement. However, human harvest of natural populations, even at low levels, can impact not only the species being utilised but also the ecosystem in which they occur. Larger individuals tend to be selected for harvest, and this can affect both age and sex structure (see section 4.14). Hunting has exterminated many animal species, and those on islands have been particularly susceptible (see section 12.7). Where wildlife harvesting is conducted with suitable controls, it not only produces food, but also may serve to conserve wildlife populations and justify their protection in wildlife preserves (see section 14.3.3) In carefully managed programmes, harvesting the diverse mammalian fauna of the African savanna can produce greater yields of meat and animal products than turning the same area over to cattle ranching. Further revenue can be gleaned through hunting and wildlife-viewing safaris.

Aquatic systems have always provided an important source of food, particularly protein-rich items. Fish and other aquatic organisms are harvested from the sea, lakes and rivers in **capture fisheries**, and from ponds and marine enclosures in **culture fisheries**.

13.4.3 Capture fisheries

Capture fisheries can be divided into three categories:

1 subsistence fisheries: fish are caught using simple techniques and consumed by the local community. The catch is usually not bartered or sold.

2 artisanal fisheries: small commercial operations, usually not focused on a particular species, with a multi-species catch that is almost entirely utilised. This type of fishery is particularly prevalent in developing countries (Figure 13.9). Overfishing (see Box 13.1) may result in smaller populations of the most desirable fish species, but the fishery may be sustained by switching to less desirable species.

3 industrial fisheries: operations utilising sophisticated fishing vessels and modern technology that are often highly focused on catching particular fish species. Many of the world's largest and oldest fisheries are overfished; this has come about through excessive fishing using techniques that provide short-term profits.

Capture fisheries harvested 91×10^6 tonnes in 1995; only a little more than the annual catches made in the late 1980s (Figure 13.10; Postel 1998). However, owing to the growth of the human population, the global fish catch per capita was down nearly 8% from its 1988 peak. Many of the

Figure 13.9 A beach seine net operation on Lake Chilwa, Malawi. Some of the catch will be sold in local markets (Photo: Patrick Osborne).

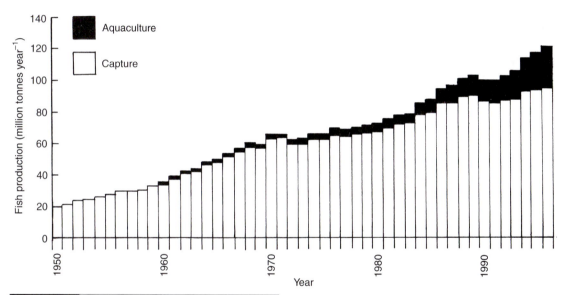

Figure 13.10 Global fish production from aquaculture and capture fisheries from 1950 to 1996 (Grainger 1998 with permission of the Food and Agricultural Organization of the United Nations).

world's fisheries are overfished, with the harvest exceeding the maximum sustainable yield (see Box 13.1). In temperate oceans, stocks of cod, halibut and other prime fish are declining, and in the North Atlantic off Canada the previously productive cod fishery in 1992 was closed by government decree. The Food and Agriculture Organisation has indicated that 25% of the world's fisheries are now either overexploited or have already crashed, with too many fishing boats

with advanced capture techniques chasing too few fish. Tuna fisheries in the late 1990s were close to being fully fished or overfished, and quota systems are in place in many areas. In the Indian Ocean, where tuna were abundant in the 1980s, fish catches in the 1990s contained few big yellowfin tuna. Skipjack tuna harvests were still viable in the Western Pacific in the late 1990s.

Fewer of the larger predatory (high-demand) fish are being caught, and more fish lower down the food chain are being harvested (Pauly *et al.* 1998). A temporary dip in this global trend was recorded in the 1960s as fishing fleets discovered the rich anchovy (low in food chain) fishery off the coast of Peru which was soon overfished and remains commercially non-viable. Catching species lower down the food chain has helped to sustain fish catches, but this trade-off is not sustainable. Furthermore, techniques to catch these smaller species also net juvenile predators and, therefore, recovery of the preferred fishery is impeded. Fishery biologists are now recommending that fishing be banned entirely in some areas so that stocks of all species may recover. Fish consumption is being sustained through expansion and innovation in aquaculture.

Box 13.1 | How many fish in the sea? The maximum sustainable yield concept

From the standpoint of fisheries production, more important than the number of fish in the sea is the rate at which populations of each species can grow. Through reproduction, fish replace individuals lost through natural causes and those harvested by humans. Fishery managers need to know the maximum yield that can be sustained from one year to the next. This yield is equivalent to the increase in fish biomass resulting from the recruitment of new individuals plus the increase in body mass of those remaining in the population. This yield depends on the size of the population (also known as the **stock**) and body growth rates. If the fish population is small, the number of offspring will be small. If the population is very large, population growth slows owing to competition for food and through overcrowding. In between these two extremes, population growth is highest (see Figures 4.12 and 4.13). Therefore the population size determines the growth rate and the sustainable yield.

The largest catch that should be taken each year is known as the **maximum sustainable yield**. This is indicated on Figure 13.11 and is equivalent to the fish biomass produced each year without reducing the fish stock. The maximum sustainable yield is not a constant as it will vary with environmental conditions from year to year, and this variation adds to the challenge faced by fisheries managers. If harvests exceed the maximum sustainable yield, fish populations decline and fishermen go out of business. This happened with the Peruvian anchovy fishery which collapsed in 1972 as a result of the combined effects of overfishing and an El Niño year (see section 1.2.6). The economic repercussions of this collapse were indeed large, and it is important to note that the cause can be attributed to both natural and human influences.

Fisheries can be managed using mathematical models, which predict the maximum sustainable yield each year, based not only on the population size of the commercial species, but also on the environmental conditions that might influence population growth. Where this is feasible and adequate data are available, overfishing can be prevented by reducing catch effort. This can be done by instituting a quota system or through restricting the type or design of fishing gear used, but this requires the co-operation of all involved in this economic activity.

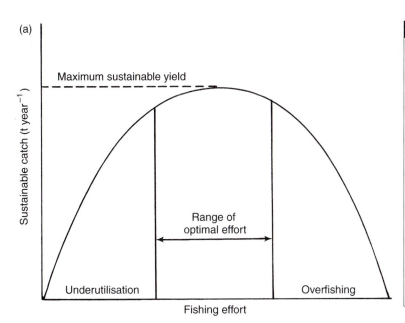

(a)

Maximum sustainable yield

Sustainable catch (t year^{-1})

Range of optimal effort

Underutilisation

Overfishing

Fishing effort

Figure 13.11 (a) Theoretical curve relating fish catch to effort indicating range of optimal effort to sustain the fishery. (b) General relationship between the fishing effort and yield of a fishery (curved line) and the cost of the fishing effort (straight line). The maximum sustainable yield (MSY) is indicated. The maximum economic yield (MEY) is a compromise between the intensity of fishing effort (economic cost) and the yield. It is important to note that MSY and MEY are not constants and will vary, from year to year, with environmental and ecological conditions that affect the population growth of the species under consideration.

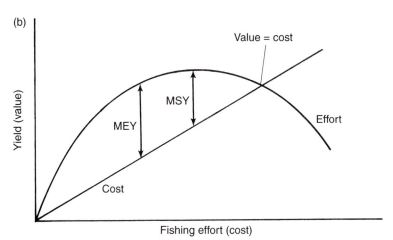

(b)

Yield (value)

Value = cost

MSY

MEY

Effort

Cost

Fishing effort (cost)

13.4.4 Aquaculture and mariculture

One in every five fish consumed is now produced in ponds or enclosures in lakes or the sea (Figure 13.10). This growth industry (**blue revolution**) is very productive, but it, too, has some major drawbacks and problems. Much effort in aquaculture is directed towards producing species that can command a high price rather than towards those species that will provide protein to more people. For example, shrimp farming in India is growing by about 15% per year. Many of the cultured species are at the top of the food chain and therefore their culture requires a high-protein diet.

This is provided as fish meal made from so-called 'trash species' such as anchovies and sardines. In effect, this leads to a net loss of fish: more, low-value fish are used to produce fewer high-value fish.

Aquaculture also exacerbates some environmental problems. Culture of freshwater and brackish species requires inputs of freshwater, and in many countries this is already scarce (see Box 6.2). Nutrient enrichment, leading to eutrophication of the waterways downstream of culture ponds, is another problem (see section 5.15). In these densely stocked systems, fish diseases can spread rapidly and disease-causing organisms can spread through stock transfers and water movements from one pond to another. For example, disease problems are hindering the growth in production of cultured shrimp.

In many developing countries, aquaculture has been used effectively to provide food for local rather than overseas markets. Many farmers in China raise carp, and this low-technology process provides protein, but these ponds are often built on land that was already used to produce food and therefore may not represent a net gain in food production. Ponds constructed in coastal zones can lead to significant loss of natural habitats such as mangroves, and the resultant offshore pollution can degrade coral reefs and reduce water quality. These environmental impacts affect the productivity of natural fisheries as these coastal waters are important breeding grounds for many fish, shellfish and crustaceans.

13.4.5 Food in the future

Providing enough food for the human population in the first half of the twenty-first century presents an enormous challenge. Dwindling fish stocks, land degradation, declining water availability, pollution and the desire to conserve some natural habitats all conspire against increasing food production.

Recent developments in molecular and cellular biology have opened the way to the production of genetically engineered organisms. Using this technique it is now possible to produce crops which are more resistant to drought, salinity, pests or to herbicides. It is quite feasible that genetic engineering might enable production of crops such as wheat, rice or corn capable of nitrogen fixation. These are exciting developments, but public health, socio-economic and environmental issues remain to be resolved.

We need to develop novel ways to manage soil, water, pests, diseases and weeds that rely more on our knowledge of community and ecosystem ecology and less on chemical solutions. Application of integrated pest-management techniques has been successful in controlling rice pests in South-East Asia. Similar gains could be made through improved cropping systems and rangeland management systems that mimic more closely those employed by natural herbivore populations.

13.5 | Industrialisation, natural resource use and pollution

Industrialisation in Europe and North America was accompanied by a slowing in the growth of human populations (see section 13.3). Some demographers have used this trend to suggest that similar social and economic advances in countries which still have high population growth rates will slow these rates. However, some ecologists such as Paul and Anne Ehrlich (Ehrlich and Ehrlich 1991) have suggested that rapid environmental degradation and natural resource depletion in these densely populated countries will preclude the economic advances necessary to stimulate this transition.

Some of these problems would be resolved as populations growth declines, but, as described above, population decline is a slow process. Sanderson and Tan (1996) provide the following example for the Philippines. With a per capita income growth of 5% and current projected population growth, the level of pollution in the Philippines in 2030 would be 12 times 1990 levels. If fertility levels were reduced immediately to replacement levels in 1990, pollution in 2030 would still be 10 times the 1990 level. Clearly, the three processes of industrialisation, resource use and pollution levels are linked with both human population growth and urbanisation.

The living resources utilised by humans as described in section 13.4 are known as **renewable resources**. While these resources are renewable, they are often overused and their utilisation leads to environmental damage through, for example, pollution and habitat destruction. Other natural resources, such as minerals (copper, gold, zinc) occur in a finite supply and are referred to as **non-renewable resources**. Consumption of resources (and waste generation) is far from uniform globally. Resource consumption is much higher in developed countries than it is in those of the Third World. Therefore, opportunities to reduce, reuse and recycle resources are greater in countries with the highest rates of resource use.

Resource utilisation also influences pollution levels, but the economic capacity to treat waste products is also important. Economically strong countries can enforce more stringent environmental standards. Therefore, even though greater quantities of pollutants may be produced by industry in these countries, application of pollution removal technologies, reduces pollutant disposal to the environment.

13.5.1 Pollution

Pollutants are defined as substances that are in the wrong place and harmful to organisms. Many of these compounds are manufactured and are slow to breakdown once they enter natural systems. Compounds that breakdown through natural processes are called **biodegradable** and, if breakdown is both complete and rapid, are significantly less harmful to the environment than those resistant to these natural processes.

Heavy metals, such as mercury, lead, copper, cadmium, nickel and zinc enter the environment in a number of ways but particularly from mine wastes and ore-smelting plants (see Box 13.2). Lead enters the environment from vehicles that run on petrol with lead additives. These additives have been banned in some countries, but many, particularly in the developing world, still have numerous cars that use leaded fuels. Heavy metals are readily absorbed into the body of organisms where, even in very low concentrations, they interfere with specific, vital enzyme reactions with severe consequences. In humans, for example, lead poisoning causes mental retardation and mercury poisoning leads to birth defects and insanity. Some plants have evolved a high degree of tolerance to growing in soils contaminated with heavy metals. These plants provide an opportunity for ecological restoration of mine dumps, and their presence on waste dumps, at least, reduces erosion and movement of contaminated materials into surrounding ecosystems.

Box 13.2.	**Money or your life: mining revenues or pristine ecosystems?**

The Ok Tedi gold and copper deposit is located on Mount Fubilan in the far west of Papua New Guinea, and the mine developed to extract the resource is one of the largest in the world (Figure 13.12). Waste rock and tailings are dumped directly into the upper reaches of the Ok Tedi, a tributary of the Fly River. The impact of mine waste discharges has been characterised by increasing suspended solid levels and concomitant increases in dissolved and particulate heavy metals, particularly copper in the streams draining the mine site.

Biologists working for the mining company monitored fish populations at sites in the Ok Tedi and Fly River (Smith and Hortle 1991; Smith and Morris 1992). They found that, in the upper Ok Tedi, catches were reduced to low levels shortly after mine operations commenced. In the lower Ok Tedi, distinct changes in the fish assemblage during the different phases of mine operation were detected. Below the Ok Tedi–Fly River junction, mine contaminants were considerably diluted by the waters of the Fly River. The fish stocks below the junction were also greater and more diverse than those of the lower Ok Tedi. Change in the fish assemblages was more gradual, except for a dramatic reduction in herring (*Nematalosa* spp.) abundance. Smith and Morris (1992) attributed the reduction in herrings to a massive, accidental disposal of cyanide into the river, which occurred on 13–14 October 1986, from which herring populations failed to recover. Recovery of the fishery following the cessation of mining will depend on the rate of erosion of accumulated mine wastes in the bed of the Ok Tedi and at the mine site, and on the availability of recruits from fish stocks in water bodies less seriously affected by mine discharges.

The enormous wetland system associated with the Fly and Strickland Rivers is of high conservation value, providing a refuge during drought years for waterfowl from Australia. More importantly, over 40000 people are sustained by the natural resources of the Ok Tedi and Fly River. Consequently, the environmental impacts on these wetlands resulting from the construction and operation of the Ok Tedi mine have been a cause for some concern (Rosenbaum and Krockenberger 1993). Recovery may take 20 years and, given a 30-year mine life, this represents, at least, a 50-year disruption to the ecology of the Fly River system and potentially to the traditional life styles of the local inhabitants. Is this disruption to the environment and lives of the local people worth the revenue produced by the mine? How has the mine development benefited local communities? What are the costs and benefits to the nation? What is the value of a pristine stream and the life in it? These are, indeed, challenging questions and ones ecologists and other specialists need to answer.

Figure 13.12 The Ok Tedi mine in the remote western highlands of Papua New Guinea (Photo: Patrick Osborne).

Harmful chemicals enter the environment through myriad pathways. Some of these breakdown rapidly into benign compounds or are diluted to levels below which they are no longer harmful. Other compounds are more intransigent and, worse still, are concentrated in organisms through a process known as **bioaccumulation**. Chemicals that are resistant to biological breakdown and toxins such as heavy metals may be stored in the tissues of animals that absorb them. These animals form the diet of others, and the stored chemicals become concentrated in the tissues of the predators and so on up the food chain.

In this way, very high concentrations can develop in animals, such as birds of prey and crocodiles, at the top of the food chain. Bioaccumulation is particularly serious with heavy metals and a range of synthetic organic compounds such as pesticides.

Many plants and animals produce toxins as compounds of either defence or offence. Humans have utilised some of these compounds to produce herbicides and pesticides. Pyrethrum, for example, is a naturally occurring compound which is toxic to many insects. These naturally occurring compounds are biodegradable and therefore do not have a lasting effect on the environment. This can not be said for some of the novel agricultural chemicals manufactured in the laboratory. Chlorinated hydrocarbons (e.g. DDT, lindane and dieldrin) and organophosphorus compounds (e.g. malathion) are highly effective pesticides, but they remain in the environment and enter food chains with concentrations being magnified with each link in the chain (Figure 13.13). These compounds kill by disrupting a basic physiological process. Therefore they not only kill the target pest, but may also harm or kill all organisms that rely on the physiological process disrupted by the pesticide or herbicide.

The use of compounds such as DDT has been banned in many countries, but DDT remains one of the most effective chemicals in malarial mosquito control and therefore is still widely used in many tropical countries. The environmental impact of pesticides has been reduced through education programmes which have encouraged more judicious use and proper application. Newly developed pesticides are more pest-specific, and their application can be timed to prevent a pest outbreak and have less effect on non-target organisms. These newer pesticides act quickly and then breakdown to less harmful substances.

Another problem with the use of pesticides is the evolution of **resistance** to them by successive generations of the pest they were originally designed to harm. Pest species evolve and their tolerance to a particular chemical may increase. This can be countered either by increasing the amount of pesticide applied or by developing new pesticides that are either more potent or to which the pest has little or no resistance.

13.6 | Human population growth: consequences and solutions

Some of the consequences of population growth include an increase in disease outbreaks with increasing density of human populations. As populations grow, so there is also an increase in resource use, waste generation, land degradation and the rate of destruction of natural habitats. Solutions to these problems include reducing human fertility, conserving resources through reduced consumption, re-use and recycling and novel ways to reduce waste production and to convert wastes into a resource. We have already covered issues regarding resource use, and will look at conservation of natural habitats in chapter 14. The growth in human populations is regulated by birth and death rates. Solving the population crisis by allowing an increase in death rates is morally unpalatable, and human nature directs efforts to do the reverse. A more acceptable way to reduce populations is through a reduction in human fertility. However, some methods to achieve this are regarded as immoral by some religions.

13.6.1 Human diseases

From the plagues that infested the early human settlements along the River Nile to the outbreaks of bubonic plague in Europe during the Middle Ages and the HIV (Human Immunodeficiency Virus) that causes AIDS (Acquired Immune Deficiency Syndrome) epidemic of today, disease has been an important cause of human mortality. **Endemic diseases** are present in a population all the time at an approximately constant level of infection. **Epidemic diseases** are those such as bubonic plague, that arise suddenly, spread quickly, infecting many people and then largely dissipate.

Pathogens that infest humans can be divided into three groups: **metazoan parasitoids**, **micro-parasites** and **macro-parasites** (Hassell and May 1989). Parasitoids lay their eggs or larvae in or on hosts and these feed directly on the tissues of the host. Micro-parasites include viruses, bacteria, protozoa and fungi that reproduce within their

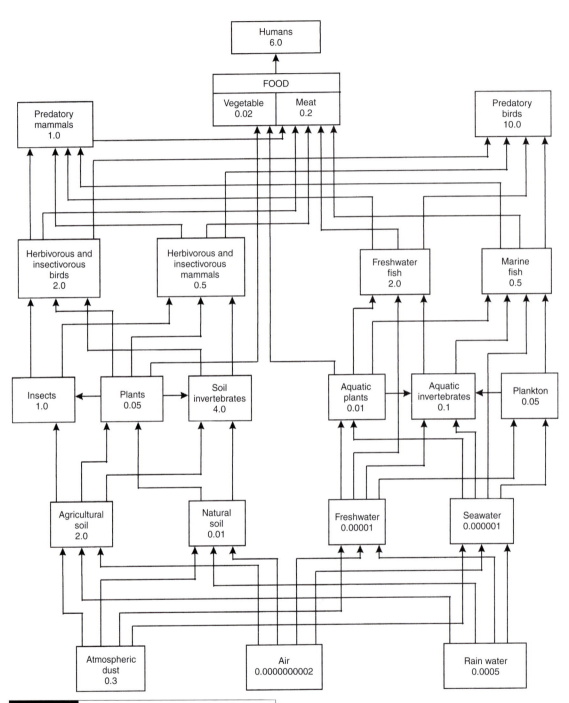

Figure 13.13 Some toxic compounds absorbed by organisms are not excreted but accumulated as a way of neutralising their effect. For example, some animals store pesticides in fat bodies where the impact of the pesticide on the animal's metabolism is minimised. Through a process known as bioaccumulation, these toxins can become concentrated as they pass up the food chain (after Edwards 1975, reprinted with kind permission of © CRC Press, Boca Raton, Florida).

hosts. They are characterised by small size, rapid rates of reproduction, a short duration of infection and the production of an immune response by the host. Macro-parasites (parasitic nematodes, platyhelminths, ticks, fleas) are usually large enough to be seen by the naked eye, live longer and do not complete their reproduction within or on their host. Macro-parasites produce infective stages that are released from the host. Some diseases spread directly from one human host to another, others require the intervention of an intermediate host or **vector**. Malaria is spread by female anopheline mosquitoes, schistosomiasis by snails (see Box 5.7) and trypanosomiasis by the tsetse fly (see Box 4.2).

Human hosts can be divided into individuals that are susceptible to infection, already infected or recovered with, or without, immunity to further infection. Many mathematical models have been developed to describe the population dynamics of parasites and their hosts. Clearly, host population density is critical in determining whether a parasite can survive and continue to infest a population. Early humans were probably infested with parasites such as hepatitis B and herpes that exhibit high transmission rates and stimulate low immunity responses (Dobson and Carper 1996).

As humans started to congregate in settlements, infestations with macro-parasites such as round-worms probably increased and water supplies became contaminated with bacterial and protozoan parasites. Accompanying this more settled existence was a change in diet from the mixed diet of meat, fruit and grains gleaned by hunter–gatherers to one dominated by grains. Some archaeological evidence suggests that these early settlements faced increased child mortality and higher levels of disease owing to the effects of malnutrition (Dobson and Carper 1996).

It was not until the first large cities developed that bacterial and viral infections increased in human populations. Early city dwellers lived in close association with their animals, and many of these early diseases evolved from diseases of domestic stock. Measles is closely related to canine distemper and rinderpest (see section 4.5); smallpox probably evolved from cowpox. Cities

also provide a breeding ground for disease reservoirs such as rats, as well as disease vectors such as mosquitoes.

These aggregated human populations facilitated the spread of diseases and, because these human populations had not been previously exposed to these novel diseases, immunological resistance to them was low. As disease resistance increased, mortalities from successive disease outbreaks declined. European colonisation of the New World introduced novel diseases to the people that already lived in North, Central and South America. The introduction of diseases such as smallpox, measles and typhus to these populations with no natural immunity had devastating effects. Successive outbreaks of these new diseases led to a reduction in the human population of Mexico from 20 million to 3 million in just 50 years in the sixteenth century (Dobson and Carper 1996).

The development of vaccines to provide immunity to many of these diseases was a major contributor to reducing rates of child mortality. The complete elimination of smallpox provides a classic example of disease control through implementation of a rigorous vaccination programme. Complete control occurred first in countries with low population densities of susceptible individuals (people not vaccinated). As the percentage of individuals not vaccinated declines, disease prevalence decreases, even amongst these non-vaccinated individuals. Smallpox infections persisted in countries such as Nigeria, India and Pakistan with high population densities. In these countries, reducing the population of susceptible people to below ten per square kilometre required vaccination rates of around 98% of the population (Dobson and Carper 1996).

Disease-causing organisms are highly specialised, exhibiting a range of adaptations that ensure effective transmission from one host to another and their survival within the host's body following infection. The parasite benefits if host life span is not curtailed, and many parasites have evolved so that they have little impact on the health of their host. Host defences against infection and immunological responses also evolve to suppress the impact a parasite might have on the host. Host–parasite interactions provide another example of **co-evolution** (see section 8.8). This capacity to evolve and change has provided a significant challenge to our attempts to control the spread of diseases.

Disease control has focused on sanitation, water purification, vaccinations, drug prophylaxis and treatment, and vector control. Successful programmes usually entail an integrated approach of treatment, prevention and vector control. Smallpox has been eliminated and other diseases have been successfully constrained at low levels. However, malaria control in many tropical countries has so far been unsuccessful with its vector, anopheline mosquitoes, developing resistance to DDT, and the malarial parasite itself developing resistance to drugs such as chloroquin used both as a prophylactic and to treat infected patients. Research to find effective techniques to reduce the incidence of malaria continues, but far more funds have been committed to finding a cure for HIV. The number of AIDS cases (around 500000 in 1990) is lower than recorded cases of malaria (around 100 million) but then AIDS is almost 100% fatal with a long period of infectivity requiring significant health care. Furthermore, recent evidence suggests that HIV infection rates in some African countries are significantly higher than first thought. In Zimbabwe, 26% of the adult population are believed to carry the virus, and infection rates may be at a similar level in other countries in southern Africa (Brown and Flavin 1998). If these infection rates are correct, population stability in these countries could be achieved very early in the twenty-first century.

HIV belongs to a family of viruses called retroviruses, and it was first isolated in 1983. This virus developed as a result of an infection of a human with a monkey virus (SIV, simian immunodeficiency virus) which then evolved into HIV. The growth and spread of human populations into forests may increase contact between humans and animal reservoirs of viral diseases such as SIV, Ebola and Lassa fever, and this may facilitate interspecific transfers. HIV is characterised by extensive genetic variability and distinct subtypes have been recognised. By early 1990, cases of AIDS had been reported from 150 countries. It soon became clear that transmission modes differed in different parts of the world. In North America and Europe, risk of infection was greatest amongst homosexual men, bisexuals, intravenous drug users, their sexual partners and children born to infected mothers. In developing countries, heterosexual transmission predominates (FitzSimons 1990).

In many tropical countries, the impact of disease is compounded by malnutrition. Around 1 billion people do not have a diet that is adequate to support normal daily activity, and about half of these are slowly starving (see Daily and Ehrlich 1996). These two scourges, disease and malnutrition, affect not only human well-being, but also the capacity these populations have to enhance economic activity and pass through the demographic transition described in section 13.3.

13.6.2 Human fertility

Human fertility has been reduced through a desire for smaller families and this has been facilitated by increased availability and use of birth control techniques. India was the first country to promote an official policy to reduce population growth. This was implemented through enhanced availability of contraceptive methods such as the birth control pill and intra-uterine devices and condoms, and education programmes that promoted their use. Most developing countries now have family planning programmes, although these are opposed by some religions (most notably the Catholic Church) and this has impeded their progress where these religions predominate. The Chinese government implemented controversial legislation limiting family size to one child. The impact of these programmes can be seen in the reduction in family size in developing countries from 6.1 in the mid 1960s to 3.8 in 1990 (see Bongaarts 1994).

The most rapid changes have taken place in Asia, where fertility has declined to 2.3 births per woman with contraceptive use at around 80%. Fertility reductions are also now accelerating in some African countries, with significant declines in the birth rates in Botswana, South Africa, Kenya and Zimbabwe. Reduction in human population growth rates is linked to both economic development (improvements in human health, education and social services) and the availability of birth control methods and the opportunity they provide to regulate family size. Consequently, family planning programmes need to focus on both the provision of birth control methods and human development through education, health and the empowerment required to make choices that will result in smaller families.

13.7 | Conclusions

Attempts to expand per capita food availability will require greater application of programmes that will reduce human population growth, reduce land degradation, enhance energy inputs derived from renewable sources and ensure more efficient use and re-use of water resources. Failure to implement these programmes will result in an increase in the number of malnourished humans. Implementation of these programmes will require a global effort, the like of which there is no precedent. People, and their governments, will need to establish programmes with long-term aims that benefit not only their nationals, but also those who live beyond their borders. This will require a significant change in attitudes with people being less concerned about national aspirations and more concerned about global issues. We will discuss some of these global issues in the next chapter.

13.8 | Chapter summary

1. The world's human population is predicted to continue growing, and by 2030 will have increased to around 9.5 billion. The proportion of people living in developing countries will increase from 78% in 1990 to 86% in 2030. All populations will contain a higher proportion of elderly people.

2. In developed countries, 80% of the population now live in cities and, while this contrasts with only 30% in developing countries, worldwide human populations are becoming more concentrated through urbanisation.

3. Early humans developed an effective social organisation, had a strong capacity to learn, store and pass on information to successive generations and, through bipedalism, which freed the hands, and possession of an opposable thumb, had fine manipulative skills.

4. 10 000 years ago, following the end of the last ice age, human societies became more settled and began to domesticate plants and animals. By 5000 years ago, humans established cities in the Middle East, Egyptian Nile Valley and Central America. During the Iron Age, humans began to convert forests into pastures and arable lands.

5. Following the industrial revolution, mortality rate declined through a more assured food supply and medical advances, and the human population grew from approximately 1 billion in 1850 to 2 billion in 1930 and to over 6 billion in 2000.

6. In Europe and North America, human population growth has slowed through falling birth rates and increased longevity, a change characterised as a demographic transition. This transition is underway in many countries in South-East Asia but has yet to occur in most African countries. Countries with a younger population will sustain population growth for a number of years after fertility rates have declined (population momentum).

7. In shifting agriculture, humans clear an area of forest to grow crops, use the land for a few years and then move on. Produce from subsistence agriculture supplies the needs of a family or local community settled on land they own. Plantation agriculture is geared to commercial sale of the produce.

8. Fish are caught from natural populations (capture fisheries) or harvested from ponds or enclosures (culture fisheries). To maintain natural fish stocks, catches should be limited to the fish biomass produced each year (maximum sustainable yield).

9. Food availability per capita has increased despite the growth of human populations, although fish harvests have declined. Food supplies are not regionally uniform and famines occur in parts of the world with dense populations, low food production, poor distribution systems and political instability.

10. Resources produced by living organisms are renewable, other resources (minerals, fossil fuels) utilised by humans have a finite supply and are non-renewable.

11. Pollutants are substances that are harmful to organisms. Some pollutants break down naturally (biodegradable), others enter the food chain and become concentrated in organisms at the top of the chain (bioaccumulation).

12. Human population growth has been regulated by disease. Endemic diseases are present in populations all the time; epidemic diseases arise suddenly, spread quickly and then dissipate.

13. Human fertility has declined in many countries through the desire for smaller families and the increased availability of birth control techniques.

Chapter 14

Global ecology:
biodiversity conservation, climate change and sustainable development

The world is warming. Climatic zones are shifting. Glaciers are melting. Sea level is rising.

Houghton and Woodwell 1989.

We have seen in the last chapter that the growth in the human population is leading to depletion of food stocks and that efforts to enhance food production often result in significant environmental degradation. Agricultural expansion and intensive resource extraction activities are also converting natural habitats into simpler, human-dominated landscapes. Some of these human-induced environmental changes have a global dimension. Before we look at some of the global environmental challenges, first let us look at some of the differences between tropical and temperate ecosystems.

14.1 | Temperate and tropical environments

In chapter 1, we defined the tropical region as lying between the tropics of Cancer and Capricorn. Having looked at tropical ecosystems, what can we conclude about them that makes them distinct from those found in parts of the world at higher latitudes? How are tropical and temperate regions linked? Why should people living in one of these regions be concerned about biological conservation efforts in the other?

The most obvious difference between tropical and temperate areas is climate. Tropical lowlands are warm throughout the year with daily variation often exceeding seasonal changes in temperature. There is no winter in the tropical lowlands.

At higher altitudes, diurnal temperature variations are even more marked and are far more significant than seasonal changes. This contrasts with temperate mountains where climate is markedly seasonal. Seasonality in the tropics is more strongly imparted through variation in rainfall, and this contrasts with temperate areas where rainfall is often more uniformly spread throughout the year and temperature is the key seasonal factor.

Surviving a temperate winter is a challenge to many organisms, and mechanisms to do this include physiological and behavioural adaptations (losing leaves, sequestering food), hibernation or a life history that includes an overwintering, dormant stage. Another strategy for mobile organisms such as birds is to migrate to a warmer climate. Most bird species that breed in the tropics remain there throughout the year and are able to survive even in areas with a pronounced dry season. Many birds which breed in temperate areas migrate to the tropics to avoid low winter temperatures and poor food availability. These birds require suitable habitats in both the temperate and tropical expanses of their ecological range as well as along their migration route. These species provide an excellent example of a link between tropical and temperate regions, and their conservation will require co-operative efforts between temperate and tropical countries. Numerous migrants move from the vast area of North America and congregate in much smaller areas in Central America and the Caribbean. This influx exerts considerable pressure on food supplies in these areas and disrupts the resource partitioning patterns (see section 4.9.5) established when the migrants were absent.

Rainfall seasonality in the tropics drives many of the life history strategies of tropical organisms and we have discussed examples throughout this book (wildebeest migration in the Serengeti, reproduction and resource allocation in savanna grasses, breeding in riverine fish, mangrove leaf production). This seasonality in rainfall also has significant consequences for aquatic organisms inhabiting rivers, particularly those living in smaller tributaries. These streams may be reduced to a series of small pools, or even dry up completely during the dry season. In the wet season they are transformed into raging torrents with each major rainfall event. Riverine organisms inhabiting these streams must be adapted to deal with these extremes.

In the wet, tropical lowlands, plant growth is more uniform and trees tend not to exhibit the annual growth rings found in their temperate counterparts. Fruit production by tropical trees is less seasonal and therefore specialist frugivores are more common in the tropics. Leaves on tropical trees tend towards a more uniform shape and are heavier than those on trees in temperate areas. As tropical trees retain their leaves for longer, it is worth investing resources in them and to protect those resources from herbivores. Trees in temperate regions produce thin leaves that can be shed in the autumn with less loss of resources.

One feature of tropical ecosystems that distinguishes them from those in temperate areas is their extraordinary diversity of species. Lowland tropical rain forests constitute the most diverse communities, but coral reefs are also impressively diverse and the mammalian fauna of the African savanna is renowned for its diversity. Since tropical ecosystems generally harbour such a wealth of species, conservation biologists have focused on these systems in order to stem the rate at which species are becoming extinct.

14.2 | Biodiversity loss

We have seen, in chapter 8, that there are links between the diversity of species (biological diversity or biodiversity) and the way ecosystems function. There are many other reasons why humans should be concerned with biodiversity conservation. Organisms provide a wealth of resources and ecological services that benefit humans. Biotic resources include food, building materials, firewood and medicines. Ecological services that rely on diverse ecological communities include: soil formation, nutrient cycling, nitrogen fixation, bioremediation of polluted sites, biological pest control, pollination and biological processes that control the concentration of gases in the atmosphere, particularly carbon dioxide. Other reasons to conserve biodiversity may be less practical but are none the less compelling. Many organisms bring significant pleasure and humans also have a moral and ethical responsibility to care for the environment and the variety of life it supports.

As we saw in chapter 8, we do not know how many species live on earth. Estimates vary from 5 to 50 million, with perhaps 80% of terrestrial species occurring in the tropics. The diversity of organisms on earth has been increasing since the origin of life some 4 billion years ago. This increase in species has not occurred at a steady rate but has been punctuated by periods of rapid speciation (see section 12.6) and mass extinctions (see section 12.7). The demise of the dinosaurs in the Cretaceous is the best-known example of five identified mass extinction events. However, currently, with the growth of the human population, we are in the midst of a sixth major extinction event (Leakey and Lewin 1996).

Like determining the number of extant species, it is also difficult to determine the number of species going extinct each year. If there are, say, 30 million species, the extinction rate is likely to be higher than if there are only 5 million species. Extinction rates are best known for organisms such as fish, birds and mammals, since these are relatively large, conspicuous and well studied. We discussed the decline in fish stocks in section 13.4.3. Bird populations, except for a few species, are declining on every continent as a result of habitat degradation (deforestation, wetland drainage, pollution) and, in some cases, through hunting. Hunting for meat and deforestation are the greatest threats to primate populations (Spinney 1998). Other threats include the introduction of exotic species, the spread of exotic and endemic diseases and the incidental capture of aquatic reptiles and mammals in fishing nets.

Using information from the well-known vertebrate groups and by considering rates of habitat destruction (particularly of tropical rain forests where very diverse communities reside) scientists have estimated species losses to be between 20 000–100 000 per year (Wilson 1992; Ehrlich and Ehrlich 1992). At these rates we could lose 20% of all species by 2025.

14.2.1 Habitat destruction and biodiversity loss

Significant areas of natural habitat have been replaced by human-dominated systems, and this process of habitat destruction is probably the major cause of biodiversity loss. This process is escalating owing to the growth in human populations, the desire to enhance living standards and our ever-increasing capacity to exploit natural resources. It has been estimated that only 90 million km², roughly 52%, of largely undisturbed land remains on earth (Hannah et al. 1994). If we exclude inhospitable land (rock, ice, deserts), the proportion of human-impacted land rises to 75%.

Tropical forests are being cleared at the rate of 1–2% per year with 40% of their original extent already lost (Myers 1992). Destruction of these forests reduces total habitat area and leads to habitat fragmentation, the creation of isolated patches that may not be large enough to support the variety of species that live within them. Some forest species will not cross even short distances of treeless vegetation and therefore are effectively restricted to one forest patch. This may limit their capacity to find mates and will also reduce gene flow between populations isolated in these fragmented habitats.

Tilman et al. (1994) described a mathematical model that demonstrated that even moderate habitat destruction would eventually lead to the extirpation of the dominant competitors within the remnant patch. This model showed that the most abundant species in these isolated fragments were also the most susceptible to disappearing from them. Habitat fragmentation reduces the effective colonisation rates of all species (see section 12.5 and the role of island size on colonisation rates). However, species with lower colonisation rates, usually the dominant competitors in a habitat, will be more affected than those with good dispersal and colonisation capacities. Tilman et al. (1994) warned that habitat destruction may lead to the loss of the strongest competitors which are the species that make the most efficient use of resources and play key roles in ecosystem function. Their model also showed that species loss from forest fragments only occurred some generations after fragmentation, which explains the slow loss of species that occurs from recently isolated habitats.

14.3 | Biodiversity conservation

What can be done to stem the loss of species? Once we have recognised the importance of biodiversity, we need to identify those areas that are particularly species-rich (diversity 'hot spots', see Box 14.1). We then need to develop strategies that will reduce rates of species loss, and this requires a sound understanding of the role biodiversity plays in ecosystem dynamics. As many of the world's most diverse habitats are tropical and concentrated in economically challenged countries, biodiversity conservation requires significant international co-operation with economic assistance flowing from developed nations to those of the developing world.

Biodiversity conservation is being tackled on a number of fronts. The first of these is a species by species approach. International agreements have been signed which limit harvests and trade in species that are in danger of extinction. Conservation agencies are investigating ways to conserve selected species that are in danger of extinction. Another approach is directed more towards habitat conservation with the aim of conserving the whole suite of species that inhabit an area.

| **Box 14.1** | Conservation International and its 'hot-spot' Rapid Assessment Programme |

Conservation International (CI) was formed in 1987 with a mission that is focused on the protection and sustainable use of biologically diverse ecosystems. CI has developed a technique of priority setting that uses the best scientific information available, in order to put its resources to the best possible use. CI has utilised the hot-spot concept developed by Myers (1988) to select areas that harbour diverse biological communities and contain a high proportion of endemic species. It soon became apparent that there were significant gaps in knowledge about these megadiverse areas, and CI developed the Rapid Assessment Programme (RAP) in 1989.

RAP is a biological inventory programme designed to provide information necessary to develop a rational conservation management strategy for a particular area. In this programme, a small team of local and international biologists is assembled to assess the species diversity, degree of endemism and the threats and opportunities for the successful conservation of the area. The RAP technique is designed to provide scientific information more rapidly (and at a lower cost) than that produced through longer-term ecological field studies. CI recognises the importance of long-term studies and RAP is not designed to replace them. RAP, however, does provide a technique that reflects the urgency underlying the conservation of biodiverse regions. RAP also couples the assessment of the biological value of a site with the threat from environmental degradation under which it exists.

14.3.1 International agreements

The Convention on Biological Diversity was negotiated before the United Nations Conference on Environment and Development (UNCED) held in Río de Janeiro in 1992. Over 175 countries are now party to this convention which aims to conserve biodiversity through its sustainable and equitable use. Signatory countries have indicated that they are aware of the general lack of information regarding biological diversity and have agreed to enhance scientific and technological studies to provide the basic knowledge required to implement biodiversity conservation strategies.

14.3.2 Endangered species conservation

The Convention on International Trade in Endangered Species (CITES) was established in 1973 under the auspices of the United Nations Environmental Programme (UNEP). Over 140 countries have signed this convention in which endangered species are listed on either Appendix I (all trade prohibited) or Appendix II (trade is regulated). CITES is administered from offices in Geneva, Switzerland, and member countries meet regularly to add or remove species from the Appendices.

The World Conservation Union (WCU) is a private organisation that publishes Red Data Books which list endangered species and provides information on their distribution, ecology, threats to survival and conservation measures that have been implemented. The WCU defines an **endangered** species as one that is in danger of extinction if threats to its survival persist. **Vulnerable** species are those that are likely to become endangered if their population continues to decline through overexploitation or habitat destruction. **Rare** species exist in small populations that are neither vulnerable nor endangered but are none the less at risk because of their small population size. Countries with the highest numbers of threatened mammals include Madagascar, Indonesia and Brazil. Indonesia and Brazil also have the highest number of threatened birds. These tropical countries are at the top of these lists not only because they have high mammal and bird diversity, but also because they have high rates of habitat destruction.

Many conservation organisations have, as their focus, the protection of endangered populations and their habitat. For example, World Wildlife Fund is active in panda and tiger conservation. A species-by-species approach to biodiversity conservation in tropical ecosystems faces a major hurdle: we simply do not know enough about the species that make up these complex systems. We have not identified most of them, let alone determined whether they are either keystone or endangered species. Endangered species lists are generally heavily biased: most are animals, and many are either charismatic species or those that provide humans with a desirable resource and are, therefore, avidly hunted. However, while many protected areas have been established to protect charismatic species, this has also provided protection to the many species that coexist with them.

The loss of species is occurring faster than we can identify the species that live in tropical systems and, therefore, it is difficult to select those with high conservation priority. One way to overcome this problem is to focus on habitat conservation through the establishment of protected areas in which plant and animal populations are maintained in a setting that, at the very least, approximates natural conditions.

14.3.3 Protected areas

The global network of protected areas larger than 1000 km^2 grew from none in 1900 to nearly 10 000 at the end of the century, with some 3% of the earth's surface protected (at least on paper). Ideally, protected areas should be established to ensure that representative habitats and species are conserved. Protected areas should be established according to three criteria relating to the communities they aim to protect: distinctiveness, endangerment and utility. A rare, endemic species has a higher intrinsic conservation value than one that is widespread and common. Similarly, a species that is under some threat of extinction should have a higher conservation

priority than one that is less threatened. Species that have an obvious use or value to people are also more highly valued.

However, in most cases the designation and design of protected areas has been haphazard. Larger parks are generally located in remote areas in landscapes that are not readily convertible to other human uses. Smaller protected areas are often set aside nearer towns and cities. In Africa, and other parts of the world, many protected areas were established by colonial governments with little or no consultation with the local inhabitants. Rarely have protected areas been established and designed on the basis of sound ecological concepts which relate to the species or habitats that are to be protected. A number of basic principles of reserve design have been established and attempts are now being made to follow some of these principles by adding to or redesigning the borders of protected areas established many years ago.

14.3.4 Reserve design

From a consideration of island biogeography (see chapter 12), Diamond (1975b) proposed that nature reserves could be considered as islands surrounded by a sea of human-altered habitat. Nature reserves need to be designed so that the suite of plants and animals contained within them can continue to live and thrive there. According to the theory of island biogeography, extirpation rates are related to island size. Diamond (1975b) proposed that extirpation rates within nature reserves could be reduced if reserves were designed according to the following criteria: (1) larger reserves are preferable to smaller ones; (2) a single large reserve is preferable to a similar area divided into several reserves; (3) if reserves are divided, then having them close to each other is better than having them more widely spaced; (4) separate reserves are better if clumped than arranged in a line; (5) circular reserves are better than elongate ones; and (6) reserves connected by corridors are better than unconnected reserves. This concept was extended by Shafer (1997) (Figure 14.1).

Within a protected area, activities can be zoned so that sensitive areas receive maximum

		Worse	Better	
Figure 14.1 Principles of protected area design based on considerations of theories of island biogeography. Very few reserves in tropical countries have been designed according to these principles. Concept developed by Diamond (1975b) and further adapted by Shafer (1997 with kind permission from Kluwer Academic Publishers and Elsevier Science).	Ecosystem partially protected			Protect complete ecosystem
	Smaller fragmented reserves			Larger reserve
	Fewer reserves			More reserves
	Isolated reserves			Corridor between reserves
	Isolated reserves			Reserves linked by 'stepping-stone'
	Uniform habitat			Diverse habitats
	Irregular-shaped reserve			Reserve close to round with buffer area surrounding core area
	Only large reserves			Mix of large and small reserves
	Reserves managed individually			Regional management of reserves

Figure 14.1 Principles of protected area design based on considerations of theories of island biogeography. Very few reserves in tropical countries have been designed according to these principles. Concept developed by Diamond (1975b) and further adapted by Shafer (1997 with kind permission from Kluwer Academic Publishers and Elsevier Science).

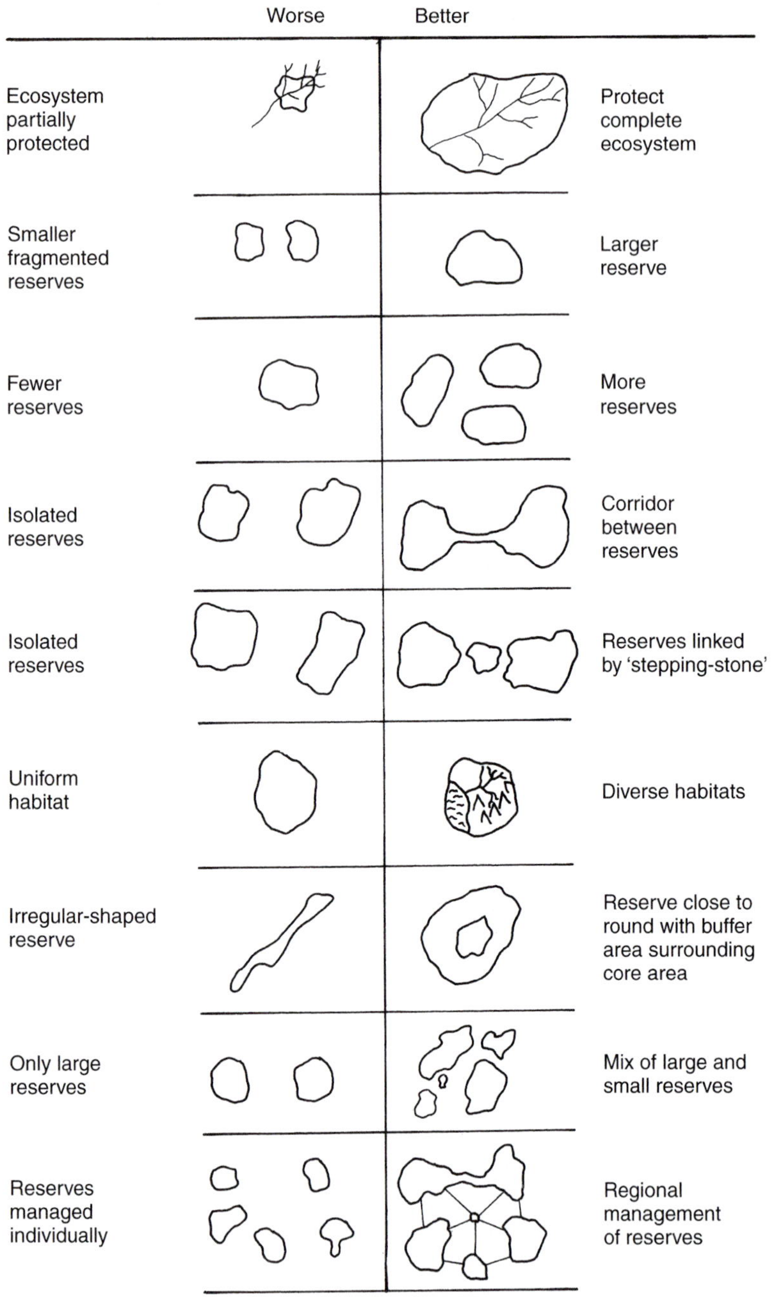

protection and visitors are directed towards less sensitive areas. For example, a central core of a protected area could be off-limits to the general public. Other areas may be accessible only on foot. More intensive use of the protected area could be limited to areas near the entrances. Through careful design of roads and trails, visitors can be guided through the area so that disturbance is kept at a low level. A buffer zone should be maintained around the area and, within this zone, activities such as controlled hunting, grazing domestic stock and firewood harvesting for personal use may be permitted.

Many conservation biologists now feel that

even well-managed biological reserves will not adequately conserve biodiversity. Too little area has been set aside and many reserves, particularly in tropical countries, are poorly managed or under threat from large human populations settled along their boundaries. In some tropical countries, protected areas lack financial support and adequately trained personnel to manage them and, therefore, they have little more than legal status. For these reasons, conservation practices have to be applied to areas outside reserves, and economic development programmes need to be integrated with conservation strategies.

14.3.5 Reserves, buffer zones and parks beyond parks

Few parks are large enough to constrain the fauna they were designed to protect. For example, over 1.5 million wildebeest make seasonal migrations outside the Serengeti National Park boundaries and this brings them into contact with the 40 000 people who live near the park. The most frequently reported problem with wildlife is crop damage and predation on livestock. Through a questionnaire, Newmark *et al.* (1994) found that 71% of local people living near wildlife areas in Tanzania reported problems with wildlife. People affected by wildlife must be compensated for their losses; this can be done by using revenues from gate receipts, tourism and controlled sale of wildlife products.

Integrated management is based on local participation from the start, and resources in the area are assessed for their economic potential. Animals may be harvested for their meat, skins and trophies, and revenue from the sale of these natural assets remains within the community. Two excellent examples of where this type of management has been applied successfully are described in Box 14.2.

Box 14.2 | **Parks beyond parks: a vision for wildlife conservation in Kenya and Zimbabwe**

The Kenya Wildlife Service has developed a policy of wildlife conservation – Parks beyond Parks – that is not solely focused on the protected areas under its direct control. In this policy, local community participation in the development of conservation strategies has been given a very high priority. Furthermore, local people have been encouraged to accept wildlife on their land and to play a role in wildlife management. In return, the community has rights to utilise wildlife for their own needs and to establish enterprises that cater for tourists. People who live on the borders of National Parks receive a share of park revenues from the Kenya Wildlife Service in return for their tolerance of wildlife that strays outside the park. In other areas, wildlife–human conflicts are reduced by constructing fences along the park boundary, but the preferred option is one in which wildlife comes to be viewed, in the eyes of the local people, as an asset rather than a liability.

In Zimbabwe, the Department of National Parks and Wildlife has established a Communal Areas Management Programme for Indigenous Resources (CAMPFIRE). Through this programme, responsibility for the management of wildlife resources has been effectively transferred to local communities. Local communities, working with government agencies, sell hunting rights to safari companies, provide ecotourism opportunities and control wildlife poaching. Decisions to allocate areas for crop production, cattle raising and wildlife are also taken at the local level. Conflicts that arise, such as between farmers and crop-raiding wildlife, are also handled locally. Revenue that is generated does not go to the central government, but is used to fund local development projects such as providing water, schools, health services and other community facilities. Again, this programme has altered the view local people have of wildlife being a nuisance to one of it being an economic asset.

Few studies have been undertaken to compare the effect on mammal populations of the complete exclusion of human activity versus the more integrated approach described above. However, Caro (1999) showed that two partially protected areas in Tanzania contained lower densities of large mammals than a more fully protected National Park adjacent to them. The principal cause of this difference was attributed to illegal hunting; densities of prized meat species increased with distance from urban areas. However, upgrading the level of protection in these areas may not necessarily result in increased wildlife populations. More long-term monitoring of animal populations is required to assess the efficacy of various conservation strategies.

While the rate of biodiversity loss may be reduced through the careful management of protected areas, their design and management is directed towards maintaining the assemblage of species they contain. Management principles are based on the assumption that the environment to which these species are adapted will stay much the same. Scientists have now accumulated striking evidence which suggests that the earth's climate is undergoing significant warming and that these changes are having significant impacts on biological communities.

In a detailed study of a $30 \, km^2$ site in the cloud forest at Monteverde, Costa Rica, scientists have related changes in biological communities to changes in dry-season mist frequencies (Pounds *et al.* 1999). Twenty of the fifty species of anurans (frogs and toads) in the study area, including the locally endemic golden toad (*Bufo periglenes*), disappeared following synchronous population crashes in 1987. Other changes have been detected in the altitudinal distribution of birds with colonisation of the study site by species from lower altitudes. Anoline lizard populations in the study area have also declined. These diverse biological changes correlate with declines in dry-season mist frequency, and mist frequency is negatively correlated with sea surface temperature in the equatorial Pacific. These scientists concluded that the biological and climatic patterns indicate that atmospheric warming has raised the average altitude of the clouds that hang over the forests and is responsible for the biological changes observed.

While some threats to biodiversity are more immediate than this process of climate change, established links between biodiversity decline and climate change provide us with an opportunity to plan ahead. In the next section we review the causes and consequences of this global change in climate.

14.4 | Global climate change

14.4.1 The greenhouse effect

Carbon emissions from oxidation of fossil fuels have elevated CO_2 concentrations in the atmosphere. The carbon dioxide concentration in the atmosphere fluctuates seasonally, declining during the northern hemisphere summer and increasing through the winter. During northern hemisphere spring and summer, photosynthesis markedly exceeds the rate of respiration, but, in the autumn and winter, respiration predominates as plants lose foliage and litter decomposition is promoted. However, the underlying increasing trend (around 1.8 ppm per year) is clearly shown in the measurements that have been made at Mauna Loa in Hawaii since the late 1950s (Figure 14.2). These seasonal trends are driven by the seasonal cycles in the northern hemisphere because surface area of land is larger in this hemisphere.

We can relate this increase in atmospheric CO_2 concentration to the start of the industrial revolution in the nineteenth century through analysis of gas bubbles trapped in Arctic ice sheets.

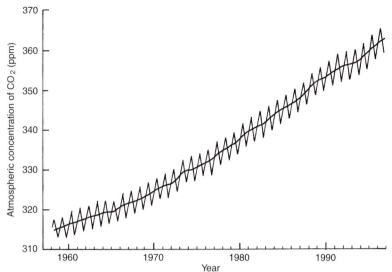

Figure 14.2 The concentration of atmospheric carbon dioxide measured at Mauna Loa Observatory, Hawaii, showing the seasonal cycle (resulting from changes in photosynthetic and decomposition rates) and the long-term increase that is due largely to increased burning of fossil fuels. Data prior to May 1974 are from the Scripps Institution of Oceanography and data since May 1974 are from the National Oceanic and Atmospheric Administration.

Atmospheric concentrations of other gases (methane (CH_4), chloroflurocarbons (CFCs) and nitrous oxide (N_2O)) have also increased. All these gases contribute to a global warming process called the **greenhouse effect**, so-called because these gases operate in much the same way as glass in a greenhouse.

The radiation that reaches the earth is mostly in the visible region of the spectrum (400–700 nm). This short-wavelength radiation warms the surface of the earth. Some of this thermal energy is radiated back into the atmosphere with a spectrum that is richer in long-wavelength radiation. Absorption of this radiation in the infra-red region of the spectrum is a property of the greenhouse gases listed above. The radiation that these molecules absorb results in higher temperatures. Without these gases in the atmosphere, the mean temperature of the earth would be more than 30 °C colder. The earth's atmosphere, with its composition of greenhouse gases, lets through the short-wave ultraviolet and visible light, but traps infra-red radiation that is radiated from the earth. In this way, the atmosphere acts as an insulator, trapping heat that would otherwise be lost to space.

The concentration of these heat-trapping gases in the atmosphere is increasing and, since their concentration in the atmosphere is small, their concentrations are easily changed by a large per-centage. An increase in the concentration of any of these gases enhances the capacity of the atmosphere to retain heat. Carbon dioxide is the most important greenhouse gas because of its higher concentration in the atmosphere and its effectiveness as a radiation trap. Methane is produced through anaerobic respiration in the stomachs of animals, particularly ruminants, in wetlands and in the extraction of oil and natural gas. Much of the methane released is converted to carbon dioxide and some is absorbed by soil bacteria, but atmospheric concentrations have none the less increased. Methane is around 20 times as potent as carbon dioxide as a greenhouse gas and is responsible for around 15% of the greenhouse gas effect.

Other gases, such as CFCs are even more potent (10 000–30 000 times more than carbon dioxide), but, because of their much lower concentration in the atmosphere, trap less heat. CFCs are used as propellants in spray cans and as refrigerants in air-conditioners and refrigerators. These compounds not only are potent greenhouse gases, but also they destroy the earth's protective ozone layer. Ozone is also a greenhouse gas and, therefore, its destruction serves to reduce the greenhouse effect. However, ozone also shields the earth from ultraviolet radiation. Lower ozone concentrations in the atmosphere (so-called **ozone holes** which are actually atmospheric expanses with reduced ozone concentrations, rather than actual 'holes') have been detected over Antarctica and the Arctic. Increased ultraviolet light results in increased incidences of skin cancer and also damages the photosynthetic apparatus in plants. Because of these serious impacts, nations have agreed to phase out use of CFCs and their concentration in the atmosphere is likely to fall following adoption of the Montreal Protocol in 1987.

14.4.2 Impacts of global warming on climate

Owing to the complexity of the world's climate, predicting the effects of enhanced concentrations of greenhouse gases in the atmosphere on global climate is an enormous challenge. Using computers, scientists have produced global circulation models (GCMs) and used these to predict a mean rise in global temperature of 2 °C from 1990 to 2100 (Inter-governmental Panel on Climate Change 1995). This warming trend is clearly apparent: 1988, 1987, 1983, 1981 and 1986, in that order, were each recorded as the warmest years since the beginning of the century. In the 1990s, 1998, boosted by El Niño (see section 1.2.6), was the warmest year on record, surpassing 1997 as the previous record holder. It has also been shown that the average temperature in Canadian lakes has increased, the extent of sea ice surrounding Antarctica and in the Arctic Sea has declined and glaciers throughout the world are receding (see Box 9.1).

How these warmer temperatures will affect climate is more difficult to predict. Some of the climate changes will enhance greenhouse effects. These changes include: less snow cover in the northern hemisphere reducing the earth's **albedo**, release of the greenhouse gas methane as the permafrost of the Arctic melts, increases in the rates of both respiration and decomposition releasing even more carbon dioxide, and greater evaporation leading to an increase in the water vapour (another greenhouse gas) content of the atmosphere. Some changes will decrease the greenhouse effect: greater cloud cover will increase albedo, increased polar precipitation (from the enhanced water content of the atmos-

phere) will enhance snow cover and also increase albedo, and higher concentrations of carbon dioxide in the atmosphere should stimulate photosynthesis and removal of carbon dioxide from the atmosphere (Graves and Reavey 1996).

Climate change is not occurring uniformly over the earth. The greatest degree of warming has occurred at higher latitudes. The deciduous forests of North America will need to migrate 500–1000 km northward over the next century if they are to keep pace with the predicted warming of 2–6 °C. It is likely that this required rate is far too great for tree species to attain.

At lower latitudes, precipitation and soil moisture have declined owing to a cooler upper and warmer lower atmosphere. The impact of even small changes in temperature, total rainfall and the timing of rainfall may be considerable by affecting reproduction, species composition and fire frequency. Species that migrate between the temperate regions and the tropics will have to accommodate the changes in climate across their migratory ranges. These mobile species will be able to alter their ranges easily but in doing so will affect the species that live in the extremities of their current range.

Apart from changes in mean climate figures, global warming may also result in a change in the frequency of extreme events, and predicting these changes is proving to be very difficult. Some parts of the world are predicted to become drier, others wetter. Either way, these changes will cause disruption to the type of agriculture that is practiced in particular regions. Let us now look at some of the environmental impacts that are likely to occur as global warming progresses.

14.4.3 Environmental impacts of climate change

Perhaps the most dramatic impact of global warming is a rise in mean sea level. This will occur largely as a result of thermal expansion as water temperature rises. Ice-cap melting and glacier retreat will play a lesser role in this process. However, recent measurements of the thickness of Arctic ice caps have indicated significant thinning of the ice at rates that exceed those predicted simply by a rise in temperature. It has been hypothesised that melt water is lubricating the interface between the ice and underlying land, and that the rate of ice movement into the sea has, therefore, increased.

The Inter-governmental Panel on Climate Change (1995) predicted a rise in sea level of about 50 cm (range: 15–95 cm) by 2100. The upper limit of this prediction, a sea level rise of around 1 m, would flood 17% of Bangladesh and 12–15% of the arable land in Egypt, and would almost entirely destroy the island nations of the Maldives and Kiribati. Coastal flooding will be accompanied by coastline erosion, and salinisation of coastal soils and ground water. Over the last century, mean sea level has risen by 15 cm.

Changes in sea level will affect the distribution of littoral vegetation (mangroves and sea grasses). Coral species have precise depth requirements for their growth and they may be unable to grow quickly enough to keep up with rising water levels. Abnormally high water temperatures have affected coral growth through the death of the coral zooxanthellae (coral bleaching, see Box 11.1) and therefore coral growth in a warmed world may be slower than it is today.

Climate change will significantly affect agriculture, altering both production and the current range where particular crops can be grown. In the temperate zone, with elevated temperature and extended growing season, plant production may increase as a result of global warming. In the tropics, plant production may decline through increased heat and drought stress. Those organisms living at the environmental extremes of their range will be particularly affected. The vegetation of temperate zones will be more affected than that in the tropics because the increase in temperature is predicted to be greater at temperate latitudes than at those near the equator. Global warming will also result in the expansion of the geographic range – both altitude and latitude – of tropical diseases such as malaria, yellow fever and dengue fever.

Some organisms will have the dispersal capability to keep up with climate change, leaving formerly favourable areas for those with a similar climate under the new climatic regime. This progression will be facilitated by a smooth, gradual change in the climate. However, if climate change occurs more suddenly, some species will be unable to respond fast enough and may face extirpation or even extinction. Some organisms will be particularly sensitive to this process. In crocodiles and turtles, sex is determined by the temperature at which eggs are incubated. For example, a 2 °C rise in sand temperature would result in all green and leatherback turtle hatchlings being female. This will have obvious impacts on the population dynamics of these species, particularly as they are faithful, year after year, to their nest sites. Therefore, extirpation of these species is likely to occur in areas experiencing a significant rise in mean temperature during the egg incubation period.

14.4.4 The global carbon balance and the missing sink

We discussed the carbon cycle in section 5.13.1. If we are to control the supply of carbon dioxide to the atmosphere it is important to be able to identify and quantify the global sources and sinks of this gas. Eight billion tonnes of carbon enter the atmosphere each year from fossil fuel burning and as a result of deforestation. Nearly half of this amount remains in the atmosphere. Around 2 billion tons is absorbed by the oceans and 0.5 billion tonnes by northern forests. What happens to the other 1.5 billion tonnes is unclear, and scientists are actively engaged in attempting to identify the missing carbon sink (Lawler 1998). Possible sinks that may be absorbing more carbon than attributed by current estimates include the northern forests, tropical rain forests and deep ocean waters.

Quantifying the carbon cycle is not purely an academic exercise. These numbers are needed to remove the scientific uncertainty that underpins the climate change treaty that was signed by 174 nations in Kyoto, Japan in 1997. By this agreement, developed countries must produce an assessment of 1990 greenhouse gas emissions from all sources. They have also agreed to reduce these emissions by a certain amount or to increase the amount of carbon stored in forests through afforestation (new forest plantations). Nations can now trade in carbon credits. Costa Rica, for example, is selling carbon credits to countries that have high rates of carbon emissions. In return, Costa Rica guarantees to plant and maintain forests which will provide the sink for the carbon produced by the purchaser of the carbon credits (Pearce 1998a).

14.4.5 Measures to reduce greenhouse gas emissions

The largest producers of greenhouse gases are those countries with the biggest use of fossil fuels (the industrialised countries of North America, Europe and the Pacific Rim) and the populous countries of China and India. Global carbon emissions from fossil fuel burning alone have increased from around 540 million tonnes in 1900 to 5.9 billion tonnes in 1993 (Brown *et al.* 1994). Greenhouse gas emissions have slowed in the developed nations through gains in fuel efficiency, but output rates continue to increase in the newly industrialised nations of South-East Asia and Eastern Europe. While carbon output in the United States grew by 8% between 1990 and 1996, emissions in Brazil, India and Indonesia grew by 20%, 28% and 40% respectively over the same period (Brown *et al.* 1997). Owing to its large human population and rapid economic growth, China is expected to become the largest source of carbon emissions early in the twenty-first century. Fossil fuel combustion is now the primary source of atmospheric carbon dioxide. However, in the 1960s deforestation was the major cause of increasing levels of atmospheric carbon dioxide.

Deforestation releases the carbon fixed in the tree biomass to the atmosphere either directly when the wood is burned (to clear the land or as a fuel), or more slowly through decomposition. Deforestation may also enhance soil erosion, and the humus in the soil is exposed and more readily oxidised, releasing its carbon to the atmosphere. This loss of soil humus is important in two ways. First, it contributes directly to the concentration of carbon dioxide in the atmosphere, and, second, its loss impoverishes the soil making reforestation more difficult.

The countries responsible for the carbon dioxide inputs from land-use management are tropical countries with large forest reserves undergoing significant deforestation. Brazil and Indonesia are the largest producers of carbon from land-use changes. The relationship between deforestation and climate change is not straightforward and there is considerable uncertainty attached to the general conclusion that deforestation leads to a warmer and drier climate (see O'Brien 1996). Reducing fossil fuel use is another way to reduce greenhouse gas emissions. Notice, however, that reducing deforestation and fossil fuel use will affect the capacity humans have to increase food production (see section 13.4).

The rise in carbon emissions can be related to the growth in the human population (see section 13.3) and economic and technological developments by:

$$\text{Carbon emissions } (C) = P \times A \times T$$

where P is the size of the human population, A is a measure of the affluence of that human population and can be expressed in terms of the amount of energy used per capita and T assesses the technology or amount of carbon released per unit of energy, a measure of energy use efficiency (Meyerson 1998).

We have seen in sections throughout this book that humans are having an immense impact on the environment. The human population is so large that we utilise some 40% of all primary produce (Vitousek *et al.* 1986). We utilise 35% of the land area to produce crops and raise animals, and even then half the world's population has an inadequate diet. Forests have been destroyed over much of Europe and North America and tropical forests are being destroyed at a rate of 1–2% per year. Fish stocks in many areas of the oceans have been depleted, wetlands have been drained and water resources polluted. We have altered the composition of the atmosphere through burning fossil fuels and deforestation. The wastes we generate accumulate in landfills, soils, rivers, lakes and the oceans and many species have been affected by this litany of change.

This environmental deterioration need not continue, but cessation will require a significant change in human attitudes. We will need to strive for lower rates of human population growth and reduced resource use particularly by those with high rates of consumption. In many cases, with vision and innovation, these can be achieved without a significant decline in human life style. Indeed, a more equitable distribution of resources and fewer people sharing them will actually enhance the life style of the majority of people. These are the aims espoused in the concept of **sustainable development**.

14.5 | Sustainable development

The concept of sustainability is not new. Two hundred years ago, Thomas Malthus, a British economist, recognised that human population growth might exceed the capacity of nature to provide adequate food. He predicted that hunger and disease would lead to increased death rates. That this has not occurred can be attributed to human ingenuity in finding ways to enhance food production and to our utilisation of resources at levels that are not sustainable. We are using resources faster than natural processes can replace them and, using an economics analogy, this can be described as living off nature's capital rather than the interest.

We have discussed in this and the previous chapter the impacts of the burgeoning human population on global climate and biodiversity loss. These provide compelling reasons for looking for novel ways to reduce human influences on ecological systems. As these impacts are global, they need to be addressed at the supra-national level, and the numerous international meetings that have been held to discuss these issues testify to the level of concern that has developed. **Sustainable development** is one concept that has been actively debated at these meetings.

In 1987, the Brundtland Commission published *Our common future* (World Commission on Environment and Development 1987) which warned that the growth in both the human population and resource consumption was not sustainable. This report stimulated a discussion around the question: what is sustainable? and led to the concept of sustainable development. In this report, sustainable development was defined as 'development that meets the needs of the present without compromising the ability of future generations to meet their needs'.

One of the main problems behind the concept of sustainable development is that it promotes economic growth – the cause of much environmental degradation – as a solution to many of these problems. Willers (1994) regarded sustainable development to be an insidious concept because it promotes economic development with few constraints to ensure resource conservation and biodiversity protection. Economic wealth may indeed facilitate nature conservation of those habitats that remain little affected by human activity. In developed nations, this is often a small fraction of the areas that have been modified through human activity that generated the nation's wealth. How can nations that still have expanses of largely unmodified or pristine habitats achieve higher living standards without despoiling the environment and destroying these habitats in the pursuit of economic advancement? How can we link sustainable development with environmental conservation?

Callicott and Mumford (1997) urged that the concept of **ecological sustainability** be distinguished from both the concepts of sustained yield (see Box 13.1) and sustainable development. Ecological sustainability seeks to preserve the normal ecological processes and functions that occur within ecosystems. These authors recommend that this be pursued through the extension of protected areas and through more careful consideration of not only the economic returns, but also the ecological impacts of development projects.

Biodiversity conservation and the pursuit of sustainability are closely linked with economic development and human aspirations. Therefore, solutions to these problems, at a local level, will only be derived through close collaboration between scientists, economists, political scientists, social scientists and the people who live and use resources in the area under consideration. At national, regional and global levels, ecological sustainability can be achieved by visionary world leaders responding to visionary individuals within each nation.

14.6 | Conclusions

The challenge that faces the human race is to provide adequate food and appropriate living conditions for all humankind. Through technology we have the capacity to alter environments at all spatial scales from local to global. We need to use our technological prowess to develop techniques that reduce and repair the environmental damage wrought on ecological systems throughout the world. We need to apply our knowledge to reduce rates of resource consumption and human population growth. We must learn to work with natural processes, to reduce resource use, to recycle wastes, to utilise renewable energy sources and, above all, to work co-operatively at a global level. There is, in this last paragraph, a role for each and every one of us.

14.7 | Chapter summary

1. Tropical lowlands are warm throughout the year with daily variation often exceeding seasonal changes in temperature. Seasonality in the tropics is more strongly imparted through variation in rainfall, and this contrasts with temperate areas where rainfall is often more uniformly spread throughout the year and temperature is the key seasonal factor.

2. Estimates of the number of species vary from 5–50 million, with 80% of terrestrial species occurring in the tropics. Natural habitat replacement by human-dominated systems is the major cause of the current decline in biodiversity and losses are estimated to be between 20 000–100 000 species per year. Biodiversity conservation is now focused on habitat protection through establishment of parks and reserves.

3. Carbon dioxide emissions from burning fossil fuels and increased concentrations of other greenhouse gases are the main cause of global warming. Computer models predict a mean rise in global temperature of 2 °C over the next century. Impacts of this climate change include elevated sea levels and increased frequency of extreme weather events. Measures to reduce global warming rates include efforts to reduce greenhouse gas emissions and slow rates of tropical forest loss.

4. Biodiversity conservation, climate change and the growth in human populations and aspirations are issues that need to be addressed through the pursuit of ecological sustainability.

Glossary

(cf. = compare with; e.g. = for example; pl. = plural)

A-horizon: the uppermost soil layer, the zone of leaching (cf. B-horizon; C-horizon).

abiotic: referring to non-living components of the environment (cf. biotic).

acclimation: reversible and gradual change in an organism's morphology or physiology in response to environmental factors.

acid rain: rain with a low pH resulting from dissolution of atmospheric pollutants such as the oxides of sulfur and nitrogen.

adaptation: (1) evolutionary adaptation: characteristics of an organism evolved as a consequence of natural selection that enhances the ability of an organism to survive within its environment (2) ecological adaptation: changes in the form, physiology or behaviour of an organism during its life time in response to environmental stimuli.

adaptive radiation: the evolution of a variety of forms from a single ancestor.

adiabatic: change in temperature, pressure and volume of air that occurs from the vertical movement of the air without any exchange of energy with the surrounding air.

aerenchyma: a spongy tissue of thin-walled cells with many air spaces, especially common in aquatic plants, that facilitates gas exchange and provides buoyancy.

aerobic: (1) describing an environment with molecular oxygen; (2) describing a form of respiration that uses oxygen (cf. anaerobic).

aestivation: dormancy that occurs in some animals during a period of harsh conditions (cf. hibernation).

age class: individuals within a population within a specified age range; a cohort.

age specific: describing attributes such as fecundity and survival that change with age.

age structure: the number or proportion of individuals within a population in particular age groups.

albedo: percentage of solar radiation that is reflected back from the earth's surface by the tops of clouds and the atmosphere.

allochthonous: organic matter produced in one ecosystem, transferred to another, e.g. leaves falling into a stream (cf. autochthonous).

allogenic succession: successional changes brought about by a change in the abiotic environment (cf. autogenic succession; succession).

allopatric: occurring in different places, usually referring to the geographic isolation of populations (cf. sympatric).

allopatric speciation: speciation that occurs when two or more populations of one species are physically separated such that they can not interbreed (cf. sympatric speciation).

alluvial: referring to material transported by a river or stream and deposited on a floodplain (cf. colluvial).

alpha diversity: the variety of species in a particular area or habitat (cf. beta diversity; gamma diversity; biodiversity; diversity).

ambient: the environmental conditions to which an organism is exposed.

ammonification: production of ammonia (NH_3) from organic nitrogen compounds by decay of detritus and metabolism in living organisms (cf. denitrification; nitrification).

anadromous: migratory behaviour, particularly of fish, exhibited by species which live in the sea but migrate to freshwater to spawn (cf. catadromous).

anaerobic: (1) describing an environment without molecular oxygen; (2) describing a from of respiration that does not require oxygen (cf. aerobic).

annual: a plant that completes its life cycle within one year and then dies (cf. biennial; perennial).

anoxic: an environment in which free oxygen is absent.

aphotic zone: a deep-water zone below the depth of sufficient light penetration for photosynthesis (cf. euphotic zone).

apical: at the apex, top (cf. axillary; lateral)

arborescent: tree-like.

asexual: reproduction without the involvement of fertilisation; propagation by division or the production of bulbils or stolons (cf. sexual; vegetative).

aspect: compass direction to which the plane of a slope faces.

assimilation: absorption of food by an animal's digestive tract.

assimilation efficiency: the percentage of energy ingested by an animal that is absorbed by its digestive tract.

atelomixis: incomplete vertical mixing of a stratified lake resulting in the transfer of nutrients from deeper waters into the euphotic zone, often stimulating phytoplankton production.

atoll: a ring-shaped reef or island that encloses or almost encloses a lagoon, often developed on the collapsed caldera of a volcano.

autecology: the ecological study of a single species; population ecology rather than community ecology (cf. synecology).

autochthonous: organic matter produced within an ecosystem (cf. allochthonous).

autogenic succession: successional change resulting from modification of the environment by the organisms inhabiting it (cf. allogenic succession; succession).

autotroph: an organism which utilises either light (green plants and photosynthetic bacteria) or inorganic compounds (sulfur bacteria) as energy sources to reduce carbon dioxide (cf. heterotroph).

axillary: in the angle between the main stem and a branch or between a leaf petiole and the stem (cf. apical; lateral).

B-horizon: the soil layer which receives leached minerals from the A-horizon above it (cf. A-horizon; C-horizon).

barrier reef: a reef that runs parallel to the shore but is separated from it by a lagoon.

basal metabolic rate: energy expenditure of an animal at rest in an environment that requires no thermal regulatory activity by the animal.

benthic: referring to the bottom zone of lakes and the organisms that inhabit it.

benthos: organisms inhabiting the sediments of aquatic ecosystems.

beta diversity: the variety of organisms within a region arising from turnover of species from habitats (cf. alpha diversity; gamma diversity; biodiversity; diversity).

biennial: an organism that requires two years to complete its life cycle, growing vegetatively in the first and flowering in the second, lives for more than 1 year but less than 2 (cf. annual; perennial).

biodiversity: the diversity of all living organisms (cf. alpha diversity; beta diversity; gamma diversity; diversity).

biogeochemical cycle: the repetitive movement of chemical elements from the environment to organisms and back.

biogeography: the study of the past and present geographical distributions of plants and animals.

biological control: the control of the population size of a pest organism through the introduction of a predator.

biological oxygen demand (BOD): a measure of organic pollution through the reduction in the oxygen concentration of a water sample from the bacterial decomposition of the organic matter present in the sample.

biological spectrum: percentage distribution of plants in a region according to the life-form concept of Raunkiaer (cf. chamaephyte; cryptophyte; hemicryptophyte; phanerophyte; therophyte).

biomanipulation: alteration of an aquatic food chain by the introduction or removal of a predator (top-down control) or by changing the supply of limiting nutrients (bottom-up control).

biomantle: the near-surface soil that is subject to bioturbation.

biomass: the total mass of living plant and animal material in a given area or volume (dry weight per unit area or volume); also known as standing crop.

biome: an extensive grouping of ecosystems, characterised by distinctive plants and animals, such as savanna, tropical rain forest, desert.

biosphere: the part of the earth's environment in which living organisms are found (cf. ecosphere; ecosystem).

biotic: referring to living things (cf. abiotic).

biotroph: organism in a detrital food chain that exploits living organisms (cf. necrotroph; saprotroph).

bioturbation: mixing of soil by soil organisms.

birth rate: the number of offspring produced per individual per unit of time (cf. death rate).

bottom-up processes: regulation of the population structure in an ecosystem (usually aquatic) by the productivity of the autotrophic organisms (cf. top-down processes).

browser: a herbivore that eats twigs and leaves of shrubs and trees (cf. grazer).

C-horizon: the deepest soil layer, composed of parental rock fragments (cf. A-horizon; B-horizon).

C_3 plants: plants with a photosynthetic strategy in which carbon dioxide fixation first occurs to form a three carbon compound, phosphoglyceric acid (PGA), typical of temperate plants and plants growing at medium to high altitudes in the tropics (cf. C_4 plants; CAM plants).

C_4 plants: plants with a photosynthetic strategy in which carbon dioxide fixation first occurs to form a four carbon compound (oxaloacetic acid) which is transported to cells forming a vascular bundle sheath where the carbon dioxide is released and fixed by the C_3 pathway, commonly found in tropical grasses adapted to high temperature, strong light and low carbon dioxide concentrations (cf. C_3 plants; CAM plants).

caatinga: thorn forest of semi-arid, tropical Brazil.

caldera: a collapsed volcanic crater; caldera lakes may occur within the basin created (cf. atoll).

Calvin cycle: photosynthetic fixation of carbon dioxide into a three carbon compound and subsequent synthesis into a wide range of organic compounds; the C_3 cycle.

CAM plants: Crassulacean Acid Metabolism; plants

with a photosynthetic strategy in which CO_2 is absorbed at night and fixed temporarily as organic acids. The next day the acids break down and the CO_2 released is fixed by C_3 photosynthesis. Stomatal closure during the day reduces water loss; common in Crassulaceae and other xerophytic, succulent plants (cf. C_3 plants; C_4 plants).

carbon dioxide compensation point: the carbon dioxide concentration at which the rate of carbon fixation through photosynthesis equals that lost through respiration.

carbon fixation: reduction of carbon dioxide into organic compounds utilising the energy from the light reaction in photosynthesis.

carnivore: an animal that feeds on other animals (cf. detritivore; herbivore; omnivore).

carrying capacity: the maximum number of individuals of a population that can be sustained in a particular habitat (symbol: K).

catadromous: migratory behaviour of fish that spend most of their life in freshwater but travel to the sea to breed (cf. anadromous).

catchment area: area drained by a river or stream (cf. watershed).

catena: a sequence of soil types from top to bottom of a slope, developed in similar positions in similar circumstances.

cation exchange capacity: the capacity of a soil to release a cation (an ion with a positive charge) in exchange for a proton.

cauliferous: borne on the trunk; applied to tropical trees in which flowers grow from the main trunk.

chamaephyte: a life-from category of a plant in which the perennating bud or shoot apices are borne very close to the ground (cf. cryptophyte; hemicryptophyte; phanerophyte; therophyte).

chemoautotroph: a prokaryote that obtains energy from chemical reactions (without photosynthesis) and obtains its carbon from carbon dioxide (cf. photoautotroph).

chemocline: a distinct change in the chemical composition with depth in an aquatic ecosystem (cf. thermocline).

circadian rhythm: an endogenous rhythm with a periodicity of approximately 24 hours, such as the opening and closing of stomata.

clay: a constituent of soil comprising mineral particles less than 0.002 mm in diameter, a class of soil texture containing at least 30% by weight of clay particles (cf. sand; silt).

climate: the average weather conditions experienced at a particular place.

climax: the final stage in a plant succession in which the plant community becomes more or less self-perpetuating.

climax species: species which occur in the later stages of succession (cf. pioneer species).

cline: a gradual change in some environmental feature.

clumped distribution: a distribution of organisms in space in which they occur in groups (cf. random distribution; uniform distribution).

co-evolution: evolution in which two species become increasingly adapted to each other.

cohort: a group of individuals within a population of a similar age (cf. age class).

colloid: molecules of a solute grouped together in a mobile state (sol) or stable state (gel).

colluvial: referring to material that has moved down a slope by creep or surface wash (cf. alluvial).

colonisation: establishment of an invading species in a new habitat.

commensalism: an interaction between two species in which one species, the commensal, benefits, but the other is unaffected (cf. mutualism; parasitism; symbiosis).

comminution: the physical breakdown of litter into smaller particles.

community: a group of interacting species in a particular area.

compensation point: the level of intensity of some environmental factor such as carbon dioxide concentration or light at which the amount of carbon fixed by a plant in photosynthesis equals that lost in respiration.

competition: an interaction, such as resource use or defence, between organisms that is harmful to one or both (cf. interspecific competition; intraspecific competition).

competitive exclusion principle: a principle which states that two or more species can not coexist on a resource which is in short supply relative to demand.

competitor: a plant species which is highly adapted to survive under intense competition from other species (cf. ruderal; stress-tolerator).

conformer: a term applied to estuarine animals that exhibit little control over the osmotic concentration of their body fluids (cf. regulator).

connectance: a measure of the number of links in a food web.

conservation: the maintenance of environmental quality, resources and species composition of a particular area.

consumer: an organism which utilises the energy fixed through photosynthesis by eating either a plant direct or an animal that has fed on plants (cf. producer).

continental drift: the mechanism which describes the relative movement of continent-sized land masses over the surface of the earth (cf. Gondwana; Laurasia; Pangaea).

continuum: a gradual change in the composition of vegetation in response to environmental factors which makes it difficult to classify into distinct types.

convergent evolution: evolution of two, often taxonomically unrelated, species such that they resemble each other through response to similar selection pressures.

coral reef: a massive biogenic structure found in shallow, tropical seas consisting of the live corals, their skeletal remains and other organisms, particularly coralline algae.

Coriolis force: a force acting on moving objects as a result of the earth's rotation, causing oceanic and atmospheric currents to be deflected to the right in the northern hemisphere and to the left in the southern hemisphere.

cosmopolitan: having a world-wide distribution.

cotyledon: the seed leaf (cf. dicotyledon; monocotyledon).

cryptobiosis: a form of dormancy in which an organism shows no sign of life for an extended period (cf. diapause; dormancy).

cryptogam: plants reproducing by spores and not seeds, *e.g.* algae, mosses, ferns (cf. phanerogam).

cryptophyte: a life-form category of a plant in which the perennating bud or shoot apices lie below the ground or water surface (cf. chamaephyte; hemicryptophyte; phanerophyte; therophyte).

Cyanobacteria: a group of photosynthetic bacteria which possess chlorophyll *a*, commonly called blue-green bacteria or, previously, blue-green algae.

death rate: the number of deaths per unit of population per unit of time (cf. birth rate).

deciduous: falling off at maturity, often referring to the loss of leaves in response to seasonal variations (cf. evergreen).

decomposer: organisms involved in the breakdown of organic matter into simpler molecules and eventually inorganic molecules.

deforestation: the destruction of an area of forest by cutting down the trees.

demersal: referring to fish that live close to the sea floor.

demography: the study of populations.

denitrification: microbial production of N_2 and N_2O from nitrites and nitrates, usually anaerobic (cf. ammonification; nitrification).

density: (1) mass per unit volume; (2) the number of organisms in a defined area or volume.

density dependent: describing a population in which the size is regulated by its density (degree of crowding) (cf. density independent).

density independent: describing a population in which the size is not regulated by its density (degree of crowding), population size is controlled by some environmental factor (cf. density dependent).

desert: a land area where the rates of evaporation and transpiration exceed the rate of precipitation for most of the time.

desertification: a process of land degradation in arid areas, often occurring through inappropriate agricultural practices.

deterministic: describing a mathematical model in which relationships are fixed, a given input always produces the same result (cf. stochastic).

detritivore: an organism that feeds on detritus (cf. carnivore; herbivore; omnivore).

detritus: dead organic matter.

diapause: a quiescent, physiologically inactive stage that is regularly a part of an organism's life cycle (cf. cryptobiosis; dormancy).

diatoms: microscopic algae with a silica cell wall belonging to the Division Bacillariophyta.

dicotyledon: a plant in which the seed has two cotyledons (cf. monocotyledon).

diffusion: the random motion of particles from regions of higher concentration to regions of lower concentration.

dimictic: referring to a lake which has two circulation or mixing periods per year, one in the spring and one in the autumn (cf. meromictic; monomictic; oligomictic; polymictic).

dioecious: having unisexual flowers with the male and female flowers on separate plants (cf. monoecious).

discharge: a measure of water flow expressed as volume per unit time at a particular point along a river system.

disjunct: a geographically isolated population or one that exists outside the characteristic range for the species.

dispersal: the movement of an organism away from its birth place or centre of high density, resulting in an increase in the geographical spread of the species (cf. dispersion).

dispersion: the spatial distribution pattern of a population, often classified into three types: random, clumped or regular (cf. dispersal).

distribution: the geographic extent within which a taxon or other group of organisms occurs.

diurnal: daily, applied to the rhythms related to the 24 hour, day–night cycle, organisms active during daylight (cf. nocturnal).

diversity: the species richness of a particular area or community (cf. biodiversity; diversity index; alpha diversity; beta diversity; gamma diversity).

diversity index: a mathematical measure of the diversity in a particular area that takes into consideration the relative abundance of the species present (cf. diversity).

doldrums: an oceanic, equatorial region with low pressure and light, variable winds.

dominant: the species having the greatest influence on community form and function.

dormancy: a resting condition found in seeds and buds in which germination or growth is temporarily suspended (cf. cryptobiosis; diapause).

dystrophic: referring to a lake that is rich in humus giving the water a brown colour; deeper waters are often anoxic.

ecocline: a gradient from one community to another often associated with a gradual change in environmental conditions.

ecological amplitude: the tolerance range of a species with respect to environmental factors.

ecological efficiency: the amount of energy, expressed as a per cent, captured by one trophic level from the one beneath it.

ecological energetics: the study of energy flow within an ecosystem.

ecological pyramid: a graphical representation of the trophic structure (numbers, biomass or energy content) of a community with producers forming the base of the pyramid and successive trophic levels leading to the apex.

ecological release: expansion of resource or habitat use by a species when interspecific competition is low or absent.

ecology: the scientific study of the relationships between organisms and all aspects of their environment.

ecosphere: the entire atmosphere, lithosphere and hydrosphere of the earth within which organisms live or influence (cf. biosphere; ecosystem).

ecosystem: an integrated system in which living organisms interact with the environment resulting in energy flow from the sun through producers to consumers and in the cycling of nutrients (cf. ecosphere).

ecotone: a narrow and clearly defined transitional zone between two communities or habitats; an edge habitat.

ecotype: a genetically adapted population of a widespread species that is often restricted to a particular habitat.

ectotherm: an animal that maintains its body temperature within narrow limits by behaviour (cf. endotherm).

ectotrophic mycorrhiza: mycorrhiza in which the fungal hyphae do not penetrate the root cells but grow between them (cf. endotrophic mycorrhiza).

edaphic: pertaining to, or influenced by, the soil.

egestion: elimination of undigested food material (faeces).

El Niño: a warm water current that periodically flows southwards along the west coast of South America. This change in ocean currents is accompanied by large-scale changes in the normal weather patterns in the Pacific as well as other parts of the world.

eluviation: the downward movement of dissolved substances within a soil profile, usually from the A-horizon to the B-horizon (cf. illuviation).

emergent: (1) plant parts raised above the water surface; (2) a forest tree whose crown stands above the level of the canopy.

emigration: movement of individuals out of a population (cf. immigration; migration).

endemic: an organism, or taxonomic group of organisms, confined to a defined region.

endorheic: referring to a lake basin with no outflow (cf. exorheic).

endotherm: an animal that maintains its body temperature within narrow limits by means of internal, physiological mechanisms (cf. ectotherm).

endotrophic mycorrhiza: mycorrhiza in which the fungal hyphae penetrate the tree root cells, found in numerous plant families, also known as vesicular arbuscular mycorrhiza (VAM) (cf. ectotrophic mycorrhiza).

energy: the capacity to do work.

energy flow: the passage and dissipation of energy along a food chain.

environment: the physical, chemical and biological surroundings in which an organism lives.

environmental impact assessment: a report assessing the environmental consequences, both positive and negative, and the options available to reduce the impacts and enhance the benefits of development projects.

enzyme: a protein-based molecule which acts as a biological catalyst.

ephemeral: short-lived.

epilimnion: the upper, well-mixed, zone of a stratified lake (cf. hypolimnion; metalimnion; thermocline).

epiphyte: a plant which grows on another, but which takes no nutrients from the supporting plant; not parasitic (cf. phorophyte).

erosion: the movement of soil by wind and water.

estuary: the mouth of a river where the fresh, river

water mixes with seawater; estuaries are often tidal and may exhibit wide fluctuations in salinity.

eukaryote: organisms with cells possessing membrane-bound organelles (e.g. nucleus, mitochondrion, chloroplast), all organisms belonging to the kingdoms Protista, Fungi, Plantae and Animalia (cf. prokaryote).

euphotic zone: the upper, illuminated zone of a lake or the sea (cf. aphotic zone).

eury-: a prefix meaning wide and used in ecology to describe the breadth of tolerance a species exhibits to particular environmental factor; hence eurythermal (wide temperature range), euryhaline (wide salinity range) (cf. steno-).

eutrophic: describing a nutrient-enriched lake with high primary production; also used to describe soils rich in nutrients (cf. mesotrophic; oligotrophic).

eutrophication: nutrient enrichment of a lake often from the disposal of sewage effluent within its catchment area, resulting in high primary production in the epilimnion and oxygen depletion of the hypolimnion. The process may be reversed through a reduction in the phosphorus and nitrogen inflow to the lake.

evapotranspiration: the combined loss of water from surfaces and by transpiration from plants.

evergreen: applied to a tree or shrub that always retains some leaves (cf. deciduous).

evolution: change in the heritable characteristics of an organism.

excretion: the elimination from the body of nitrogenous wastes, excess salts and other unwanted compounds.

exorheic: referring to a lake basin with a distinct, surface outflow (cf. endorheic).

exotic species: an introduced species; not native to a particular area.

exploitation: removal of individuals or biomass from a population by consumers.

exponential growth: continuous change in the size of a population in which the rate of growth changes with the size of the population at any given time (cf. geometric growth; logistic growth equation).

extant: applied to a taxon with living members (cf. extinction; extirpation).

external loading: input of nutrients to a lake or stream from the catchment area (cf. internal loading).

extinction: the complete elimination of a taxon (cf. extant; extirpation).

extirpation: the demise of a species in a particular part of its range (cf. extant; extinction).

facilitation: a process in which the activities of one species results in the enhancement of conditions which favour other species (e.g. grazing or forage facilitation).

fauna: the animal life in a particular region or geological period (cf. flora).

fecundity: rate at which an individual produces offspring.

fertile: (1) producing seeds, spores or pollen capable of germination; (2) of a plant with reproductive organs (cf. sterile; vegetative).

field capacity: the amount of water a soil can hold against the pull of gravity.

flagship species: a species with significant appeal to humans that can be used to draw attention to issues of habitat conservation (cf. keystone species).

floodplain: part of a river valley with river-borne sediment deposits that is periodically flooded.

flora: the plant life in a particular region or geological period (cf. fauna).

flux: the flow of energy or nutrients into, or out of, an area or system.

folivore: a leaf eater.

food chain: an abstract representation of the passage of energy through a series of consumers, e.g. from primary producer to herbivore, and from herbivore to carnivore. With each transfer much energy is lost, a fact that limits the number of steps in a chain to four or five.

food chain efficiency: ratio between the energy value of the prey consumed by a predator and the energy value of the food eaten by that prey.

food web: a diagrammatic representation of the feeding relationships of organisms in a community.

foraging: finding food.

founders: individuals of a species that establish a population in a new habitat, the new population usually possesses less genetic variation than the parent population.

front: a meeting of two water (or air) masses with different characteristics.

frugivore: a fruit eater.

gamete: a haploid sex cell, such as an egg or sperm, that fuses with a gamete of the opposite sex to form a diploid zygote.

gamma diversity: regional diversity, inclusive of all habitat types (cf. alpha diversity; beta diversity; biodiversity; diversity).

gap phase: the early colonisation of an opening in the canopy of a forest.

gene flow: the movement of genetic information between and within populations of a species by transfer of gametes or spores or movement of individuals.

gene pool: the total population of all alleles in all the sex cells of the individuals making up a population.

general circulation model: a mathematical model used to predict climate change from global warming.

generalist: a species with a broad range of habitat and/or food preferences (cf. specialist).

generation time: average age at which a female produces offspring; the time for a population to increase by a factor equal to the net reproductive rate.

geometric growth: increase or decrease in a population in which the increment is proportional to the number of individuals present at the beginning of the period, often the breeding season (cf. exponential growth; logistic growth equation).

geometric rate of increase: factor by which the size of a population changes over a time period (λ).

gestation period: duration of pregnancy, from conception to birth.

global warming: a process resulting from the increased retention of terrestrial radiation by certain atmospheric gases ('greenhouse gases') leading to a warmer global climate (cf. greenhouse effect).

Gondwana: southern portion of the ancient continent of Pangaea (cf. continental drift; Laurasia; Pangaea).

gravitational water: water that moves through the soil under the influence of gravity.

grazer: a herbivore that eats grasses and herbs (cf. browser).

greenhouse effect: solar radiation entering a greenhouse (glasshouse) is reflected as long wavelengths which can not pass through the glass and so the greenhouse heats up. Carbon dioxide, methane, and other so-called greenhouse gases in the lower atmosphere behave in the same way as the glass in a greenhouse. As the concentration of these gases in the atmosphere increases so does the amount of trapped radiation. This leads to climatic warming (cf. global warming).

gross primary production: the total energy assimilated by a photosynthetic organism, a population, or a community, including losses to respiration; net production plus respiration (cf. net primary production; primary production).

guard cell: a pair of epidermal cells bordering a stomata which are able to adjust the size of the stomatal aperture.

guild: a group of species occupying a similar ecological position within the same habitat.

guttation: the exudation of water as a liquid by plant leaves.

habit: the general appearance of a plant.

habitat: the place where an organism lives.

habitat selection: an organism's preference for a certain habitat.

halocline: a zone in which there is a marked change in salinity with depth in the sea or a lake.

hectare: an area 100 m by 100 m.

heliophyte: a sun-loving plant (cf. sciophyte).

hemicryptophyte: a life-form category of a plant in which the perennating bud or shoot are at ground level (cf. chamaephyte; cryptophyte; phanerophyte; therophyte).

herb: a vascular plant that is not woody; lacking secondary tissues.

herbivore: an animal which eats plants (cf. carnivore; detritivore; omnivore).

hermaphrodite: having both sexes.

hermatypic coral: a reef-building coral.

heterotroph: an organism which utilises organic matter as an energy source (cf. autotroph).

hibernation: a strategy in which the metabolic rate is reduced and an animal enters a period of deep sleep in order to survive cold winters (cf. aestivation).

holomixis: complete, vertical circulation of a lake.

home range: the area within which an animal normally lives (cf. territory).

homeostasis: maintenance of constant internal conditions even in a variable environment.

homeotherm: an animal with the ability to maintain its body temperature within a narrow range (cf. poikilotherm).

homoiohydric: referring to an organism that has the capacity to maintain a constant internal water content (cf. poikilohydric).

horizon: a characteristic layer within a soil profile.

humidity: a measure of the moisture content of the atmosphere.

humus: material produced through the decomposition and oxidation of organic matter on, or near the surface of soils.

hurricane: an intense tropical cyclone that occurs in the Caribbean region and on the north-eastern coast of Australia (cf. typhoon).

hydrological cycle: the water cycle within the ecosphere.

hydrolysis: the breaking of a chemical bond by the addition of water to it, with a proton being added to one product and a hydroxylion to the other.

hydrophyte: a plant living in water or on very wet soils (cf. mesophyte; xerophyte).

hydrosere: a successive series of plant communities developing as a result of shallowing of a water body, eventually leading to the replacement of the water body with dry land (cf. xerosere).

hydrosphere: all the water that exists on or close to the surface of the earth.

hypertonic: having a salt concentration in the body

fluids or cell cytoplasm that is greater than the surrounding medium (cf. hypotonic; isotonic).

hypolimnion: the cooler, often oxygen-depleted layer in a stratified lake that lies beneath the metalimnion and epilimnion (cf. epilimnion; metalimnion; thermocline).

hypotonic: having a salt concentration in the body fluids or cell cytoplasm that is less than the surrounding medium (cf. hypertonic; isotonic).

igapó: an Amazonian open forest type which is flooded by whitewater (silt-laden) rivers, usually annually (cf. *terra firme; várzea*).

illuviation: the accumulation of dissolved substances within layers of a soil profile, usually the B-horizon (cf. eluviation).

immigration: movement of individuals into a population (cf. emigration; migration).

infauna: aquatic animals that burrow in the sediment (cf. meiofauna).

inflorescence: the arrangement of flowers.

infra-red radiation: electromagnetic radiation having a wavelength longer than about 700 nm (cf. ultraviolet radiation).

innate capacity for increase (r_0): the intrinsic growth rate of a population given ideal conditions.

insectivore: an insect eater.

insolation: the amount of incoming solar radiation that is received over a unit area of the earth.

instar: a stage in the life history of an insect larva, between one moult of its exoskeleton and the next.

interception: the capture of rain water by vegetation from which it evaporates and therefore never reaches the ground (cf. throughflow).

interference competition: competition between two organisms in which one excludes the other from access to resources or a part of a habitat.

interflow: the lateral movement of water in the soil, common after heavy rainfall.

internal loading: recycling of nutrients within a lake or stream, particularly the release of nutrients from the sediment (cf. external loading).

interspecific competition: competition between individuals of different species (cf. competition; intraspecific competition).

Inter-Tropical Convergence Zone (ITCZ): a low-latitude zone of convergence between air masses at the boundary between the north-easterly and south-easterly trade winds. The zone moves latitudinally with the seasons.

intraspecific competition: competition between individuals of the same species (cf. competition; interspecific competition).

intrinsic rate of increase (r_m): exponential growth rate of a population with a stable age distribution.

island biogeography: the study and interpretation of the distribution of species on islands or in areas that are sufficiently isolated as to resemble islands (mountain tops, lakes).

island hopping: the colonisation of islands by organisms from nearby islands or land masses.

isohyet: a line connecting points of equal rainfall.

isothermal: having the same temperature.

isotonic: having a salt concentration in the body fluids or cell cytoplasm that is the same as that in the surrounding medium (cf. hypertonic; hypotonic).

iteroparous: referring to an organism in which reproduction occurs repeatedly during a lifetime (cf. semelparous).

key factor: an environmental factor that plays a major role in population regulation.

key factor analysis: an analytical technique undertaken to identify the important factors in the regulation of population size.

keystone species: a species which has a dominant influence on the composition and function of a community (cf. flagship species).

Kranz anatomy: the vascular bundle sheath found in C_4 plants.

K-selection: selection of life history traits for competitive ability: large size, low birth rate, high survival rates of offspring, production of few but large offspring, parental care and prolonged development (cf. *r*-selection).

labile: referring to organic matter that is easily broken down by decomposers (cf. refractory).

latent heat: the heat absorbed or emitted when a unit mass changes from one physical state (gas, liquid, solid) to another.

lateral: to the side (cf. apical; axillary).

laterite: a residual soil rich in hydrated oxides and hydroxides of iron and aluminium, commonly found in tropical soils subjected to weathering under alkaline conditions.

Laurasia: northern portion of the ancient continent of Pangaea (cf. continental drift; Gondwana; Pangaea).

leaching: removal of soil materials in solution by water percolating through the soil matrix.

leaf area index: a ratio of the total leaf area of a plant to the ground area beneath the plant; a measure of the number of complete leaf layers.

lentic: referring to lakes and other bodies of standing water (cf. lotic).

Liebig's law of the minimum: the growth of an individual or a population is limited by the substance supplied in the lowest amount relative to requirements.

life expectancy (e_x): the mean remaining lifetime of an individual in a population.

life history: an organism's lifetime pattern of growth and reproduction.

life table: an analytical technique to study the survivorship and fecundity of individuals in a population.

light compensation point: the light intensity at which the rate of carbon fixation through photosynthesis equals that lost through respiration.

limiting factor: an environmental factor which limits the growth of an individual or population.

limnology: the scientific study of lakes, rivers and wetlands.

lithosphere: the upper layer of the solid earth, comprising crustal rocks and the uppermost part of the mantle.

litter: dead organic matter on the soil surface.

littoral: the shoreline and shallow, inshore waters of a lake or sea (cf. pelagic).

logistic growth equation: a mathematical equation describing the growth rate of a single-species population in a defined space with limited resources (cf. exponential growth; geometric growth).

lotic: referring to running waters, rivers, streams (cf. lentic).

luxury consumption: uptake of a nutrient in excess of its need by an organism; usually undertaken when the nutrient is abundant.

mark–release–recapture method: a technique of estimating the size of a population through the analysis of the proportion of marked to unmarked individuals recaptured.

mast flowering: the production, in some years, of prodigious quantities of flowers by some trees and shrubs.

matric potential: a measure of the effect of a matrix on a substance's ability to absorb or donate water; a component of water potential (cf. osmotic potential; pressure potential; water potential).

maximum sustained yield: the maximum rate at which individuals may be harvested from a population without reducing its size in the long-term.

meiofauna: microscopic aquatic animals that live on the bottom (cf. infauna).

meristem: a localised group of cells in plants specialised for the production of new cells.

meromictic: referring to the partial circulation of a lake, the lower denser layer never, or rarely, mixing with the upper layer (cf. dimictic; monomictic; oligomictic; polymictic).

mesophyte: a plant living in a moderately wet environment (cf. hydrophyte; xerophyte).

mesotrophic: describing a lake which is moderately enriched with nutrients and is, therefore, moderately productive (cf. eutrophic; oligotrophic).

metabolism: the sum of all chemical reactions occurring in an organism.

metalimnion: the water layer in a lake between the epilimnion and the hypolimnion; the region occupied by the thermocline (cf. epilimnion; hypolimnion; thermocline).

metapopulation: a population that is divided into subpopulations between which interchange of individuals may occur facilitating gene flow.

micro-climate: the physical conditions, particularly temperature and humidity, prevailing within a small space that might be occupied by an organism.

micro-habitat: parts of a habitat that provide specialised conditions for the survival of an organism, e.g., cracks and crevices with higher humidity, zones of low current velocities around a boulder in a fast-flowing stream.

migration: movement of organisms from one place to another and back, usually undertaken on a seasonal basis (cf. emigration; immigration).

mineralisation: the conversion of an element from organic to inorganic form.

monimolimnion: the permanently stagnant layer in meromictic lakes.

monocarpus: referring to plants that flower once, prolifically, and then die.

monocotyledon: a plant in which the seed has one cotyledon (cf. dicotyledon).

monoecious: having unisexual flowers with the male and female flowers on the same plant (cf. dioecious).

monomictic: referring to a lake that has one mixing event each year (cf. dimictic; meromictic; oligomictic; polymictic).

monsoon: a seasonal change in wind direction particularly affecting the climate of the Indian subcontinent resulting in distinct wet (monsoonal) and dry seasons. The climate of South-East Asia, West Africa and Northern Australia is also monsoonal.

monsoonal forest: seasonal (wet–dry) forest in Asia.

montane forest: high-altitude forest characterised by moss-laden, stunted, contorted trees and a floristic composition often having affinities with forests found in lowland areas at higher latitudes.

morphogenic: related to the evolution of specific landforms.

mortality (m_x): proportion of individuals of a particular age group that die within that age class (cf. natality).

mutualism: interaction of two species that benefits both (cf. commensalism; parasitism; symbiosis).

mycorrhiza: close association between a fungus and

the roots of a plant (cf. ectotrophic mycorrhiza; endo-trophic mycorrhiza).

natality: birth rate (cf. mortality).

natural selection: the preferential survival, under natural conditions, of those individuals with alleles that favour their survival over other individuals with different alleles.

neap tide: a tide with a small tidal range (cf. spring tide).

necrotroph: organism in a detrital food chain that kills its food (cf. biotroph; saprotroph).

nekton: large invertebrates and fish, organisms capable of swimming (cf. plankton).

Neotropics: New World (American) tropics (cf. Palaeotropics).

net primary production: energy accumulated by auto-trophs through photosynthesis after some has been used in plant respiration; gross primary production minus respiration (cf. gross primary production; primary production).

net production efficiency: the percentage of assimi-lated food used for growth and reproduction by an organism.

net reproductive rate (R_0) the expected total number of offspring of a female throughout her life.

niche: the functional position of an organism in a community.

nitrification: the process of oxidising NH_3 to NO_2 and NO_2 to NO_3 (cf. ammonification; denitrification).

nitrogen fixation: the conversion of nitrogen into organic, nitrogen-containing compounds, a process accomplished only by some bacteria and Cyanobacteria which possess the nitrogenase enzyme complex.

nocturnal: referring to organisms active at night (cf. diurnal).

nutrient: any substance required by an organism for normal growth and development.

nutrient cycle: the possible pathways a nutrient element can follow from the soil, air or water into living organisms and its subsequent regeneration in inorganic form through decomposition.

nutrient spiral: an imaginary spiral followed by a nutrient as it cycles in a river while being carried downstream.

oligomictic: referring to a lake in which stratification breakdown occurs rarely and irregularly (cf. dimictic; meromictic; monomictic; polymictic).

oligotrophic: referring to a nutrient-poor lake with low primary production; also referring to soils poor in nutrients (cf. eutrophic; mesotrophic).

omnivore: an animal with a broad diet, including both plant and animal tissues; an animal that feeds on more than one trophic level (cf. carnivore; detriti-vore; herbivore).

optimal foraging: a feeding strategy that maximises the net rate of food intake, reduces the time spent feeding and reduces the risk of predation.

osmoconformer: an organism that allows the concentration of its body fluids to vary with the salin-ity of its surroundings (cf. osmoregulator).

osmoregulation: regulation of the salt and water content in cells and body fluids.

osmoregulator: an organism with strong capacity to control the salt content of its body fluids (cf. osmo-conformer).

osmosis: diffusion of a substance from a high concentration to a low concentration across a differ-entially permeable membrane.

osmotic potential: a measure of the effect of the concentration of solute particles on the substance's ability to absorb or donate water; a component of water potential (cf. matric potential; pressure poten-tial; water potential).

overturn: the vertical mixing process that occurs with the breakdown of thermal stratification in lakes.

oxidation: removal of electrons from an atom, ion, or molecule; addition of oxygen (cf. reduction).

ozone hole: a region in the upper atmosphere with reduced ozone (O_3) concentrations, usually found at high latitudes.

ozone layer: the atmospheric layer at 15–30 km alti-tude in which ozone (O_3) is concentrated that limits the amount of ultraviolet radiation that reaches the earth's surface.

palaeolimnology: the study of the history and ecolog-ical development of lakes, mostly undertaken through the analysis of features of dated sediment cores.

Palaeotropics: Old World (Africa, Asia) tropics (cf. Neotropics).

Pangaea: the ancient single continent consisting of practically all the earth's land mass which existed at the end of the Palaeozoic Era; the future continents of Gondwana and Laurasia combined (cf. continental drift; Gondwana; Laurasia).

pantropical: throughout the tropics.

PAR: photosynthetically active radiation.

parallel evolution: the similar evolution of systematic groups that have been isolated geographically.

parasitism: interaction between two organisms in which one obtains its nutrients from the other and harms, but does not usually (or at least immediately) kill it (cf. commensalism; mutualism; symbiosis).

ped: an aggregate of soil, crumb structure.

pedogenesis: the natural process of soil formation.

pelagic: referring to the open water areas of a lake or sea (cf. littoral).

perennial: an organism with a life cycle lasting two or more years (cf. annual; biennial).

perhumid: a climate with no dry season.

periphyton: aquatic plants and animals living attached to surfaces.

pH: a measure of the alkalinity or acidity; the logarithm of the concentration of hydrogen ions.

phanerogam: a plant that reproduces by seeds (cf. cryptogam).

phanerophyte: a life-form category of a plant in which the perennating bud or shoot are borne on aerial shoots (cf. chamaephyte; cryptophyte; hemicryptophyte; therophyte).

phenology: the study of the periodicity of leaf, flower and fruit production and development.

phloem: the part of a plant's vascular system involved in conducting sugars and other organic compounds (cf. xylem).

phorophyte: a plant providing support to an epiphyte.

photic zone: the illuminated zone in aquatic environments, the zone in which net photosynthesis can occur.

photoautotroph: an organism that obtains its energy through photosynthesis (cf. chemoautotroph).

photorespiration: the oxidation of carbohydrates which occurs when ribulose biphosphate carboxylase adds oxygen and not carbon dioxide to ribulose biphosphate; a process which effectively reduces the rate of carbon fixation; prevalent in C_3 plants photosynthesising at high temperatures and in high light intensities.

photosynthate: the products of photosynthesis.

photosynthesis: the conversion of carbon dioxide and water into organic compounds utilising energy from sunlight (cf. C_3 plants; C_4 plants; CAM plants).

photosynthetic efficiency: percentage of light energy assimilated by plants.

phyllode: a flattened stem that resembles a leaf.

phytoplankton: microscopic, photosynthetic organisms belonging to the Protista growing in the pelagic zones of lakes and marine systems (cf. plankton; zooplankton).

pioneer species: the first organisms to colonise an area; the species which occur in the early stages of succession (cf. climax species).

plankton: microscopic aquatic organisms (cf. nekton; phytoplankton; zooplankton).

podsol: a soil formed by leaching under acidic conditions resulting in a silica-rich, upper horizon and a darker, lower horizon enriched with bases and sesquioxides (podsolisation).

poikilohydric: referring to an organism that lacks the capacity to maintain a constant internal water content, so that its water content varies with that of its surroundings (cf. homoiohydric).

poikilotherm: an animal with little ability to control its body temperature (cf. homeotherm).

pollen: the microspores or the dust-like fertilising cells of flowering plants and gymnosperms.

polymictic: referring to a lake with many circulation events per year (cf. dimictic; meromictic; monomictic; oligomictic).

population: individuals of a species that live in a particular area at the same time and can interact with each other.

potamon: that part of a river in which the water is typically deep and slow-moving (cf. rithron).

predator: an animal that kills and eats animals (cf. prey).

pressure potential: a measure of the effect of pressure on a substance's ability to absorb or donate water; a component of water potential (cf. matric potential; osmotic potential; water potential).

prey: an animal killed and eaten by a predator.

primary consumer: a herbivore (cf. secondary consumer).

primary forest: forest which has not been subject to severe disturbance (cf. secondary forest).

primary production: the autotroph biomass produced by photosynthetic and chemosynthetic organisms (cf. secondary production).

primary productivity: the rate at which primary production accumulates (cf. secondary productivity).

primary succession: sequential change in the vegetation commencing with the colonisation of a site not previously occupied by organisms such as a larva flow, newly formed sand dune or bare rock (cf. secondary succession).

producer: an organism with the capacity to manufacture food from simple, inorganic compounds and an external energy source (cf. consumer).

production: accumulation of energy or biomass.

profundal: the deep area of a lake or sea lying beneath the level of light penetration.

prokaryote: organisms with cells that lack membrane-bound organelles, the bacteria and Cyanobacteria belonging to the kingdom Prokaryota (cf. eukaryote).

protoplasm: the fluid filling the cells of living organisms.

proximate factor: an environmental factor that an organism uses as a cue to alter behaviour or begin a development stage (e.g. flowering and day-length) (cf. ultimate factor).

pyramid of biomass: a diagram, in the shape of a

pyramid, showing the biomass (usually expressed as dry weight) of each trophic level, with the producers forming the base.

pyramid of energy: a diagram, in the shape of a pyramid, showing the energy content of each trophic level, with the producers forming the base.

pyramid of numbers: a diagram, in the shape of a pyramid, showing the number of organisms in each trophic level, with the producers forming the base.

quadrat: a sampling unit used to assess density or biomass of organisms per unit area.

rain shadow: dry area on the leeward side of a mountain range.

random distribution: the distribution of organisms in space with no obvious pattern (cf. clumped distribution; uniform distribution).

recruitment: addition of new individuals to a population.

redox potential: the tendency of a molecule to accept or donate electrons during a chemical reaction.

reduction: addition of electrons to an atom, ion, or molecule; removal of oxygen (cf. oxidation).

refractory: referring to organic matter that is difficult to break down (cf. labile).

refugia: isolated areas where extensive changes have not occurred, providing organisms with protection from unfavourable conditions and allowing them to persist.

regulator: a term applied to estuarine animals that exhibit tight control over the osmotic concentration of their body fluids (cf. conformer).

relative humidity: the water vapour content of the air at a given temperature.

renewable resource: a resource continuously produced by a natural system at a rate comparable with its consumption.

reproductive effort: the proportion of resources expended by an organism on reproduction.

residence time: the average time that a substance remains in a particular compartment of its biogeochemical cycle, expressed as the ratio of the size of the compartment and the flux through it.

resource: a substance, object or space that is required by an organism for its normal growth, development and reproduction.

respiration: the breakdown of organic, energy-rich molecules to produce ATP. Oxygen is required for aerobic respiration but not needed in anaerobic respiration (fermentation).

rhizome: a modified underground stem, usually growing horizontally, the stem of ferns.

rithron: that part of a river in which the water is typically shallow, fast-moving and turbulent (cf. potamon).

riparian: referring to the streamside; the edge of rivers and streams.

r-selection: selection of life history traits for maximising the intrinsic rate of growth (r): small size, high birth rate, low survival rates of offspring, production of many and small offspring, little or no parental care and rapid development (cf. K-selection).

RuBP carboxylase: the enzyme, also known as RUBISCO, in photosynthesis that carboxylates (addition of carbon dioxide) ribulose biphosphate.

ruderal: a plant adapted to inhabiting frequently disturbed sites, usually exhibiting a capacity for rapid reproduction and growth (cf. competitor; stress-tolerator).

salinity: the total inorganic salts dissolved in water.

sand: a constituent of soil comprising mineral particles 0.05–2 mm in diameter; a class of soil texture containing at least 80% by weight of sand particles (cf. clay; silt).

saprophyte: an organisms deriving energy and nutrients from decaying organic matter.

saprotroph: organism in a detrital food chain that utilises dead material (cf. biotroph; necrotroph).

sciophyte: a shade-loving plant (cf. heliophyte).

sclerophyll: a plant with leaf cell walls thickened and lignified to give rigidity and reduce water loss.

Secchi disc: a disc 20 cm in diameter, painted in black and white quadrants, lowered into the lakes and seas to measure water transparency on the basis of visibility.

secondary consumer: a carnivore or omnivore (cf. primary consumer).

secondary forest: a forest re-establishing on an area cleared of primary forest and usually containing a high proportion of pioneer species (cf. primary forest).

secondary production: the accumulation of biomass by heterotrophs (cf. primary production).

secondary productivity: the rate at which secondary production accumulates (cf. primary productivity).

secondary succession: sequential change in the vegetation recolonising a site previously occupied by organisms, such as a gap created in the canopy of a forest, an abandoned field (cf. primary succession).

semelparous: referring to an organism in which reproduction occurs only once during a lifetime (cf. iteroparous).

senescence: gradual deterioration in the function of an organism or organ with age.

sere: a characteristic stage in a primary or secondary succession.

sesquioxide: compound in which two metallic atoms are combined with three oxygen atoms, e.g. Fe_2O_3 and Al_2O_3.

sex ratio: the relative number of males and females in a population.

sexual: concerned with reproduction through the union of male and female gametes to form a zygote which develops into a new plant (cf. asexual; vegetative).

Shannon–Weaver index: a species diversity index weighted by the relative abundance of each species.

shifting cultivation: an agricultural system employed by nomadic people in which a small area of forest is cleared (slash-and-burn), cultivated for a few years and then abandoned as soil fertility declines.

silt: a constituent of soil comprising mineral particles 0.002–0.05 mm in diameter; a class of soil texture containing at least 50% by weight of clay particles (cf. clay, sand).

Simpson's index: a measure of species diversity weighted by the relative abundance of each species.

soil: the mineral and organic matter, and the organisms that live within it, occurring at the surface of the earth.

soil horizon: a layer of soil of variable depth with properties differing from the soil above and beneath.

soil profile: the vertical structure of a soil into its horizons.

soil seed bank: the store of ungerminated, viable seeds present in a soil.

soil texture: the proportions of sand, silt and clay in a soil sample.

solar equator: the latitude that lies directly under the sun at any given season.

specialist: a species with a narrow range of habitat and/or food preferences (cf. generalist).

speciation: the development of new species.

species: a group of individuals capable of interbreeding that are reproductively isolated from other species.

species diversity: see diversity.

species richness: the number of species in a defined area.

spore: a single, vegetative, reproductive cell that does not contain an embryo; in cryptogams.

spring tide: a tide with a large tidal range (cf. neap tide).

standing crop: see biomass.

static life table: a life table constructed from the age structure of a population at a single moment in time.

steady state: a situation in which opposing fluxes are balanced.

steno-: a prefix meaning narrow and used in ecology to describe the breadth of tolerance a species exhibits to a particular environmental factor, hence stenothermal (narrow temperature range), stenohaline (narrow salinity range), stenotopic (narrow range of habitats) (cf. eury-).

sterile: (1) unable to procreate; (2) without reproductive organs (cf. fertile; vegetative).

stochastic: describing a mathematical model in which relationships are probabilistic and random; a given input will produce a number of possible results (cf. deterministic).

stomata: the intercellular space and pore bounded by guard cells in the epidermis of leaves through which carbon dioxide and water are exchanged with the atmosphere.

stream order: a numbering system of stream and river tributaries, the higher the order the more tributaries a river has; a stream without tributaries has a stream order of one.

stress: a physiological condition caused by extreme environmental conditions.

stress-tolerator: a plant species which is highly adapted to survive in a stressful environment (cf. competitor; ruderal).

succession: a non-seasonal, sequential change in the species composition of a site in response to either an environmental change or to one induced by the organisms themselves (cf. allogenic succession; autogenic succession).

survivorship: the probability of an organism surviving to a particular age.

symbiosis: a close association between two different organisms (cf. commensalism; parasitism; mutualism).

sympatric: occurrence of species together in the same area (cf. allopatric).

sympatric speciation: speciation that occurs within a limited geographic range; populations separated by reproductive, rather than physical barriers (cf. allopatric speciation).

synecology: the study of communities (cf. autecology).

taxon: any taxonomic group: species, genus, family, order, phylum, division, kingdom (pl. taxa).

taxonomy: the science of naming, describing and classifying organisms.

tectonic: referring to all types of activities within the earth's crust.

temperature inversion: an increase in temperature with altitude.

terra firme: an Amazonian forest type that is not flooded (cf. igapó; várzea).

territory: the area defended by one or more individuals against invasion by others of the same or different species (cf. home range).

thallus: a simple plant body which lacks vascular tissue.

thermal stratification: layering in lakes established as a result of temperature-induced density difference with a layer of warmer water overlying colder (cf. thermocline).

thermocline: a density gradient resulting from temperature change (cf. chemocline; epilimnion; hypolimnion; metalimnion).

therophyte: a life-form category of a plant which completes its life history rapidly during favourable periods and survives unfavourable conditions as a seed (cf. chamaephyte; cryptophyte; hemicryptophyte; phanerophyte).

throughfall: rainfall intercepted by vegetation that subsequently falls to the ground (cf. interception).

tidal range: the difference in height between consecutive high and low waters.

tide: the predictable, periodic rise and fall of the oceans caused by the relative gravitational attraction of the sun, moon and earth.

top-down processes: regulation of the population structure in an ecosystem (usually aquatic) by the predation intensity of the top carnivore (cf. bottom-up processes).

topsoil: the surface soil used in agriculture.

trade winds: persistent prevailing winds, generally north-easterlies in the northern hemisphere and south-easterlies in the southern hemisphere.

transpiration: evaporation of water from plants, mainly from the leaves.

trophic: pertaining to food or nutrition.

trophic cascade: impact that results from predator introduction or removal on the biomass of trophic levels on which the predator depends either directly or indirectly.

trophic level: position of an organism in a food chain, determined by the number of energy transfer steps to that level.

tropical cyclone: an intense, low-pressure system that develops over tropical oceans.

turnover time: a measure of the movement of an element in a biogeochemical cycle: the quantity of the element in a reservoir divided by the flux rate for that element into and out of the reservoir.

typhoon: a powerful, tropical cyclone that occurs in the western Pacific (cf. hurricane).

ultimate factor: an environmental factor that is of direct importance to an organism (cf. proximate factor).

ultraviolet radiation: electromagnetic radiation at wavelengths between 10 and 400 nm (cf. infra-red radiation).

uniform distribution: a distribution of organisms in which they are evenly spaced (cf. clumped distribution; random distribution).

upwelling: an upward movement of water in oceans and lakes which brings colder, nutrient-rich water to the surface.

várzea: an Amazonian forest type that is flooded by blackwater rivers, usually annually (cf. *igapó; terra firme*).

vascular: of tissue containing the conducting elements of the plant: xylem and phloem.

vegetative: of a plant lacking reproductive organs, not involving sexual reproduction (cf. fertile; sterile).

vesicular arbuscular mycorrhiza: see endotrophic mycorrhiza.

Wallace's line: a line which separates the Oriental and Australasian zoogeographical regions. The line passes east of Java, north through the Makasar Strait separating Borneo and Sulawesi and then east to south of Mindanao in the Philippines.

water potential: a measure of the ability of a substance, soil or cell to absorb or donate water (cf. matric potential; osmotic potential; pressure potential).

watershed: the boundary between two adjacent catchment areas (cf. catchment area).

weathering: the physical and chemical breakdown of rocks and minerals to form soil.

weed: a plant growing where it is a nuisance.

xerophyte: a plant adapted to living in a dry environment (cf. hydrophyte; mesophyte).

xerosere: successional sequence of communities in an arid environment (cf. hydrosere).

xylem: the part of a plant's vascular system involved in conducting water and mineral salts from the roots to all parts of the plant (cf. phloem).

zonation: the distribution of species into distinct bands along an environmental gradient.

zooplankton: small aquatic animals.

zooxanthellae: unicellular algae that live symbiotically with corals and other reef organisms.

References

Alcala, A.C. (1988). Effects of marine reserves on coral fish abundances and yields of Philippine coral reefs. *Ambio* 17, 194–199.

Allee, W.C., Emerson, A.E., Park, O., Park, T. and Schmidt, K.P. (1949). *Principles of animal ecology*. Saunders, Philadelphia.

Alongi, D.M. (1994). The role of bacteria in nutrient recycling in tropical mangrove and other coastal benthic ecosystems. *Hydrobiologia* 285, 19–32.

Ambler, J.W., Alcala-Herrera, J. and Burke, R. (1994). Trophic roles of particle feeders and detritus in a mangrove island prop root ecosystem. *Hydrobiologia* 292–293, 437–446.

Anderson, J.A.R. (1961). The destruction of *Shorea albida* forest by an unidentified insect. *Empire Forestry Review* 40, 19–29.

Anderson, J.A.R. (1964). The structure and development of the peat swamps of Sarawak and Brunei. *Journal of Tropical Geography* 18, 7–16.

Archibold, O.W. (1995). *Ecology of world vegetation*. Chapman and Hall, London.

Ashton, P.S. (1964). Ecological studies in the mixed dipterocarp forests of Brunei State. *Oxford Forestry Memoirs* 25.

Attwell, C.A.M. (1982). Population ecology of the blue wildebeest *Connochaetes taurinus taurinus* in Zululand, South Africa. *African Journal of Ecology* 20, 147–168.

Babcock, R. (1995). Synchronous multispecific spawning on coral reefs: Potential for hybridization and roles of gamete recognition. *Reproduction, Fertility and Development* 7, 943–950.

Ball, E. and Glucksman, J. (1978). Limnological studies of Lake Wisdom, a large New Guinea caldera lake with a simple fauna. *Freshwater Biology* 8, 455–468.

Barbault, R. (1992). *Ecologie des peuplements. Structure, dynamique et évolution*. Editions Masson, Paris.

Barbault, R. and Sastrapradja, S. (1995). Generation, maintenance and loss of biodiversity. In: Heywood, V.H. (ed.), *Global biodiversity assessment*, pp. 193–274. Cambridge University Press, Cambridge.

Barnes, D.J. and Chalker, B.E. (1990). Calcification and photosynthesis in reef-building corals and algae. In: Dubinsky, Z. (ed.), *Coral reefs. Ecosystems of the world 25*, pp. 109–131. Elsevier, Amsterdam.

Barnes, R.S.K. (1974). *Estuarine biology*. Studies in Biology 49. Edward Arnold, London.

Bayley, P.B. (1995). Understanding large river-floodplain ecosystems. *BioScience* 45, 153–158.

Bayly, I.E.A., Peterson, J. and St. John, V.P. (1970). Notes on Lake Kutubu, Southern Highlands of the Territory of Papua New Guinea. *Bulletin of the Australian Society of Limnology* 3, 30–47.

Beadle, L.C. (1981). *The inland waters of tropical Africa*. 2nd edition. Longman, London.

Beard, J.S. (1946). The *Mora* forests of Trinidad, British West Indies. *Journal of Ecology* 33, 173–192.

Beck, E. (1994). Cold tolerance in tropical alpine plants. In: Rundel, P.W., Smith, A.P. and Meinzer, F.C. (eds.), *Tropical alpine environments: Plant form and function*, pp. 77–110. Cambridge University Press, Cambridge.

Beck, E., Scheibe, R. and Senser, M. (1983). The vegetation of the Shira Plateau and the western slopes of Kibo (Mount Kilimanjaro, Tanzania). *Phytocoenologia* 11, 1–30.

Belk, D. and Cole, G.A. (1975). Adaptational biology of desert temporary-pond inhabitants. In: Hadley, N.F. (ed.), *Environmental physiology of desert organisms*, pp. 207–226. Dowden, Hutchinson and Ross, Stroudsbury.

Bell, R.H.V. (1970). The use of the herb layer by grazing ungulates in the Serengeti. In: Watson, A, (ed.), *Animal populations in relation to their food resources*, pp. 111–123. Blackwell, Oxford.

Belsky, A.J. (1984). Role of small browsing mammals in preventing woodland regeneration in the Serengeti National Park, Tanzania. *African Journal of Ecology* 22, 271–279.

Belsky, A.J. (1994). Influences of trees on savanna productivity: Tests of shade, nutrients, and tree–grass competition. *Ecology* 75, 922–932.

Belsky, A.J. and Canham, C.D. (1994). Forest gaps and isolated savanna trees. *BioScience* 44, 77–87.

Belsky, A.J., Amundson, R.G., Duxbury, J.M., Riha, S.J., Ali, A.R. and Mwonga, S.M. (1989). The effects of trees on their physical, chemical and biological environments in a semi-arid savanna in Kenya. *Journal of Applied Ecology* 26, 1005–1024.

Belsky, A.J., Mwonga, S.M., Amundson, R.G., Duxbury, J.M. and Ali, A.R. (1993). Relative effects of trees on their understorey environments in high-rainfall versus low-rainfall savannas. *Journal of Applied Ecology* 30, 143–155.

Benzing, D.H. (1990). *Vascular epiphytes: General biology and related biota*. Cambridge University Press, Cambridge.

Bierregaard, R.O. and Lovejoy, T.E. (1988). Birds in Amazonian forest fragments: Effects of insularization. In: Ouellet, H. (ed.), *Acta XIX Congressus Internationalis Ornithologici II*, pp. 1564–1579. University of Ottawa Press, Ottawa.

Bierregaard, R.O. and Lovejoy, T.E. (1989). Effects of

forest fragmentation on Amazonian understory bird communities. *Acta Amazônica* 19, 215–241.

Bierregaard, R.O., Lovejoy, T.E., Kapos, V., Augusto dos Santos, A. and Hutchings, R.W. (1992). The biological dynamics of tropical rainforest fragments. *BioScience* 42, 859–866.

Black, C.C. (1971). Ecological implications of dividing plants into groups with distinct photosynthetic production capacities. *Advances in Ecological Research* 7, 87–114.

Blake, J.G., Stiles, F.G. and Loiselle, B.A. (1990). Birds of La Selva Biological Station: Habitat use, trophic composition, and migrants. In: Gentry, A. (ed.), *Four Neotropical rainforests*, pp. 161–182. Yale University Press, New Haven.

Bond, W.J. (1993). Keystone species. In: Schulze, E.D. and Mooney, H.A. (eds.), *Biodiversity and ecosystem function*, pp. 237–253. Springer-Verlag, Berlin.

Bongaarts, J. (1994). Population policy options in the developing world. *Science* 263, 771–776.

Bootsma, H. and Hecky, R.E. (1993). Conservation of the African Great Lakes: A limnological perspective. *Conservation Biology* 7, 644–656.

Bourlière, F. (1973). The comparative ecology of rain forest mammals in Africa and tropical America: Some introductory remarks. In: Meggers, B.J., Ayensu, E.S. and Duckworth, D. (eds.), *Tropical forest ecosystems in Africa and South America: A comparative review*, pp. 279–292. Smithsonian Institution, Washington D.C.

Bourlière, F. (ed.). (1983). *Tropical savannas*. Ecosystems of the World 13. Elsevier, Amsterdam.

Briand, F. (1983). Environmental control of food web structure. *Ecology* 64, 253–263.

Briggs, S.V. (1977). Estimates of biomass in a temperate mangrove community. *Australian Journal of Ecology* 2, 369–373.

Brokaw, N.V.L. (1985). Gap-phase regeneration in a tropical forest. *Ecology* 66, 682–687.

Brookfield, H.C. (1964). The ecology of highland settlement: Some suggestions. *American Anthropologist* 66, 20–38.

Brouns, J.J.W.M. (1986). Seagrasses in Papua New Guinea, with notes on their ecology. *Science in New Guinea* 12, 66–92.

Brown, L.R. and Flavin, C. (1998). *State of the world 1999*. W.W. Norton and Worldwatch Institute, Washington D.C.

Brown, L.R., Kane, H. and Roodman, M. (1994). *Vital signs: The trends that are shaping our future*. Worldwatch Institute, Washington D.C.

Brown, L.R., Renner, M. and Flavin, C. (1997). *Vital signs 1997: The environmental trends that are shaping our future*. W.W. Norton and Company, New York.

Brylinski, M. (1980). Estimating the productivity of lakes and reservoirs. In: Le Cren, E.D. and Lowe-McConnell, R.H. (eds.), *The functioning of freshwater ecosystems*, pp. 411–453. Cambridge University Press, Cambridge.

Brylinski, M. and Mann, K.H. (1973). An analysis of factors governing productivity in lakes and reservoirs. *Limnology and Oceanography* 18, 1–14.

Buckley, R.C. (1982). The habitat-unit model of island biogeography. *Journal of Biogeography* 9, 339–344.

Budowski, G. (1965). Distribution of tropical American rain forest species in the light of successional processes. *Turrialba* 15, 40–42.

Bullock, A. (1993). Perspectives on the hydrology and water resource management of natural freshwater wetlands and lakes in the humid tropics. In: Bonnell, M., Hufschmidt, M.M. and Gladwell, J.S. (eds.), *Hydrology and water management in the humid tropics*, pp. 274–300. International Hydrology Series. Cambridge University Press, Cambridge.

Bunt, J.S. (1982). Studies of mangrove litter fall in tropical Australia. In: Clough, B.F. (ed.), *Mangrove ecosystems in Australia – structure, function and management*, pp. 223–239. Australian Institute of Marine Sciences, Townsville and Australian National University Press, Canberra.

Bunt, J.S. (1995). Continental scale patterns in mangrove litter fall. *Hydrobiologia* 295, 135–140.

Burgis, M.J. (1978). The Lake George ecosystem. *Verhandlungen Internationale Vereinigung für theoretische und angewandte Limnologie* 20, 1139–1152.

Burrows, R. (1995). Demographic changes and social consequences in wild dogs, 1964–1992. In: Sinclair, A.R.E. and Arcese, P. (eds.), *Serengeti II: Dynamics, management, and conservation of an ecosystem*, pp. 400–420. University of Chicago Press, Chicago.

Caley, M.J. (1993). Predation, recruitment and the dynamics of communities of coral-reef fish. *Marine Biology (Berlin)* 117, 33–43.

Callicott, J.B. and Mumford, K. (1997). Ecological sustainability as a conservation concept. *Conservation Biology* 11, 32–40.

Cane, M.A., Eshel, G. and Buckland, R.W. (1994). Forecasting Zimbabwean maize yield using eastern equatorial Pacific sea surface temperature. *Nature* 370, 204–205.

Carlquist, S. (1974). *Island life*. American Museum of Natural History, New York.

Carmouze, J.P., Durand, J.R. and Lévêque, C. (1983). *Lake Chad, ecology and productivity of a shallow tropical ecosystem*. Dr W. Junk, The Hague.

Caro, T. (1999). Densities of mammals in partially protected areas: The Katavi ecosystem of western Tanzania. *Journal of Applied Ecology* 36, 205–217.

Carpenter, S.R., Kitchell, J.F. and Hodgson, J.R. (1985).

Cascading trophic interactions and lake productivity. *BioScience* 35, 634–639.

Castro, P. and Huber, M.E. (1992). *Marine Biology*, Mosby, St. Louis.

Chale, F.M.M. (1996). Litter production in an *Avicennia germinans* (L.) Stearn forest in Guyana, South America. *Hydrobiologia* 330, 47–53.

Chambers, M.R., Kyle, J., Leach, G.J., Osborne, P.L. and Leach, D. (1987). A limnological study of seven high-land lakes in Papua New Guinea. *Science in New Guinea* 13, 51–81.

Chan, H.T. and Appanah, S. (1980). Reproductive biology of some Malaysian dipterocarps. I. Flowering biology. *The Malaysian Forester* 43, 132–143.

Chapman, S.B. (1976). *Methods in plant ecology.* Blackwell, Oxford.

Clements, F.E. (1916). *Plant succession: Analysis of the development of vegetation.* Publication 242, Carnegie Institute of Washington, Washington D.C.

Cloudsley-Thompson, J.L. (1977). *Man and the biology of arid zones.* Edward Arnold, London.

Cloudsley-Thompson, J.L. (1991). *Ecophysiology of desert arthropods and reptiles.* Springer-Verlag, Berlin.

Cloudsley-Thompson, J.L. (1994). The Sahara Desert – life without water. *Biologist* 41, 72–75.

Cloudsley-Thompson, J.L. and Chadwick, M.J. (1964). *Life in deserts.* G.T. Foulis, London.

Clough, B.F., Boto, K.G. and Attiwill, P.M. (1983). Mangroves and sewage: A re-evaluation. In: Teas, H.J. (ed.), *Tasks for vegetation science*, pp. 151–161. Dr W. Junk, The Hague.

Coates, D. (1983). Notes on the miscellaneous fish species from the Sepik River, roundwaters and flood-plain. Report 83-20, Department of Primary Industry, Port Moresby.

Coche, A.G. (1968). Description of physico-chemical aspects of Lake Kariba, an impoundment in Zambia-Rhodesia. *Fisheries Research Bulletin of Zambia* 5, 200–267.

Coe, M.J. (1967). *The ecology of the alpine zone of Mount Kenya.* Dr W. Junk, The Hague.

Coe, M.J. (1969). Microclimate and animal life in the equatorial mountains. *Zoologica Africana* 4, 101–128.

Coe, M.J., Cumming, D.H. and Phillipson, J. (1976). Biomass and production of large African herbivores in relation to rainfall and primary production. *Oecologia* 22, 341–354.

Cohen, J.E. (1995). Population growth and Earth's human carrying capacity. *Science* 269, 341–346.

Cole, M.M. (1963). Vegetation nomenclature and classification with particular reference to the savan-nas. *South African Geographical Journal* 55, 3–14.

Cole, M.M. (1986). *The savannas: Biogeography and geo-botany.* Academic Press, London.

Colinvaux, P. (1986). *Ecology.* John Wiley and Sons, New York.

Commonwealth Science Council (1986). *Coral island hydrology: A training guide for field practice.* CSC Technical Publication Series 214, Commonwealth Science Council, London.

Connell, J.H. (1978). Diversity of tropical rain forests and coral reefs. *Science* 199, 1302–1310.

Connell, J.H. and Lowman, M.D. (1989). Low-diversity tropical rain forests: Some possible mechanisms for their existence. *American Naturalist* 134, 88–119.

Connell, J.H., Hughes, T.P. and Wallace, C.C. (1997). A 30-year study of coral abundance, recruitment, and disturbance at several scales in space and time. *Ecological Monographs* 67, 461–488.

Corfield, T.F. (1973). Elephant mortality in Tsavo National Park, Kenya. *East African Wildlife Journal* 11, 339–368.

Corlett, R.T. (1987). Post-fire succession on Mount Wilhelm, Papua New Guinea. *Biotropica* 19, 157–160.

Corner, E.J.H. (1964). *The life of plants.* Weidenfeld and Nicolson, London.

Coupland, R.T. (1979). *Grassland ecosystems of the world: Analysis of grasslands and their uses.* International Biological Programme, Cambridge University Press, Cambridge.

Cox, G.W. and Ricklefs, R.E. (1977). Species diversity, ecological release, and community structuring in Caribbean land bird faunas. *Oikos* 29, 60–66.

Cracraft, J. (1983). Species concepts and speciation analysis. In: Johnston, R.F. (ed.), *Current ornithology*, volume 1, pp. 159–187. Plenum Press, New York.

Crane, J. (1975). *Fiddler crabs of the world (Ocypodidae: genus Uca).* Princeton University Press, Princeton.

Cummins, K.W. (1992). Catchment characteristics and river ecosystems. In: Boon, P.J., Calow, P. and Petts, G.E. (eds.), *River conservation and management*, pp. 125–135. John Wiley and Sons, Chichester.

Currie, D.J. (1991). Energy and large-scale patterns of animal- and plant-species richness. *American Naturalist* 137, 27–49.

Daily, G.C. and Ehrlich, P.R. (1996). Global change and human susceptibility to disease. *Annual Review of Energy and Environment* 21, 125–144.

Davies, B.R. and Walker, K.F. (1986). River systems as ecological units. An introduction to the ecology of large river systems. In: Davies, B.R. and Walker, K.F. (eds.), *The ecology of river systems*, pp. 1–8. Dr W. Junk, Dordrecht.

Davis, L.C. (1964). The Amazon's rate of flow. *Natural History* 73, 14–19.

Day, J.W., Coronado, M.C., Vera, H.F.R., Twilley, R., Rivera, M.V.H., Alvarez, G.H., Day, R. and Conner, W. (1996). A 7-year record of above-ground net primary production in a southeastern Mexican mangrove forest. *Aquatic Botany* 55, 39–60.

Day, T.A. and Detling, J.K. (1990). Grassland patch dynamics and herbivore grazing preference following urine deposition. *Ecology* 71, 180–188.

Delany, M.J. and Happold, D.C.D. (1979). *Ecology of African mammals*. Longman, London.

Dempster, J.P. (1963). The population dynamics of grasshoppers and locusts. *Biological Reviews* 38, 490–529.

Denny, P. (1985). Emergent plants of permanent and seasonally-flooded wetlands. In: Denny, P. (ed.), *The ecology and management of African wetland vegetation*, pp.43–107. Dr W. Junk, Dordrecht.

Diamond, J. (1974). Colonization of exploded volcanic islands by birds: The supertramp strategy. *Science* 184, 803–806.

Diamond, J. (1975a). Assembly of species communities. In: Cody, M.L. and Diamond, J.M. (eds.), *Ecology and evolution of communities*, pp. 343–344. Harvard University Press, Cambridge, MA.

Diamond, J. (1975b). The island dilemma: Lessons of modern biogeographic studies for the design of nature preserves. *Biological Conservation* 7, 129–146.

Diamond, J., Bishop, K.D. and Van Balen, S. (1987). Bird survival in an isolated Javan woodland: Island or mirror? *Conservation Biology* 1, 132–142.

Dobson, A.P. and Carper, E.R. (1996). Infectious diseases and human population history. *BioScience* 46, 115–126.

Doherty, P.J. (1983). Some effects of density on two species of tropical, territorial damselfish. *Journal of Experimental Marine Biology and Ecology* 65, 249–261.

Dollar, S.J. and Tribble, G.W. (1993). Recurrent storm disturbance and recovery: A long-term study of coral communities in Hawaii. *Coral Reefs* 12, 223–233.

Drake, C. (1997). Water resource conflicts in the Middle East. *Journal of Geography* 96, 4–12.

Dubinsky, Z. and Jokiel, P. (1994). The ratio of energy and nutrient fluxes regulates the symbiosis between zooxanthellae and corals. *Pacific Science* 48, 313–324.

Dublin, H.T. (1986). Decline of the Mara woodlands: The role of fire and elephants. Ph.D. dissertation, University of British Columbia, Vancouver.

Dublin, H.T. (1995). Vegetation dynamics in the Serengeti–Mara ecosystem: The role of elephants, fire, and other factors. In: Sinclair, A.R.E. and Arcese, P. (eds.), *Serengeti II: Dynamics, management, and conservation of an ecosystem*, pp. 71–90. University of Chicago Press, Chicago.

Dublin, H.T., Sinclair, A.R.E., Boutin, S., Anderson, E., Jago, M. and Arcese, P. (1990). Does competition regulate ungulate populations? Further evidence from Serengeti, Tanzania. *Oecologia* 82, 283–288.

Dudgeon, D. (1984). Longitudinal and temporal changes in functional organization of macro-invertebrate communities in the Lam Tsuen River, Hong Kong. *Hydrobiologia* 111, 207–217.

Dudgeon, D. (1994). The influence of riparian vegetation on macroinvertebrate community structure and functional organization in six New Guinea streams. *Hydrobiologia* 294, 65–85.

Dudgeon, D. and Bretschko, G. (1996). Allochthonous inputs and land–water interactions in seasonal streams: Tropical Asia and temperate Europe. In: Schiemer, F. and Boland, K.T. (eds.), *Perspectives in tropical limnology*, pp. 161–179. SPB Academic Publishing, Amsterdam.

Dumont, H.J. (1986). The Nile River system. In: Davies, B.R. and Walker, K.F. (eds.), *The ecology of river systems*, pp. 61–74. Dr W. Junk, Dordrecht.

Eccles, D.H. (1974). An outline of the physical limnology of Lake Malawi (Lake Nyasa). *Limnology and Oceanography* 19, 730–742.

Eccles, D.H. (1985). Lake flies and sardines – A cautionary note. *Conservation Biology* 33, 309–333.

Edmondson, W.T. (1970). Phosphorus, nitrogen, and algae in Lake Washington after diversion of sewage. *Science* 169, 690–691.

Edwards, C.A. (1975). *Persistent pesticides in the environment*. CRC Press, Cleveland.

Edwards, P.J. (1982). Studies of mineral cycling in a montane rain forest in New Guinea. V. Rates of cycling in throughfall and litterfall. *Journal of Ecology* 70, 807–827.

Ehrlich, P.R. and Ehrlich, A.H. (1991). *The population bomb*. Ballantine Books, New York.

Ehrlich, P.R. and Ehrlich, A.H. (1992). The value of biodiversity. *Ambio* 21, 219–226.

Ehrlich, P.R. and Ehrlich, A.H. (1998). *Betrayal of science and reason*. Island Press, Washington, D.C.

Elewa, A.S. (1985). Effect of flood water on the salt content of Aswan High Dam Reservoir. *Hydrobiologia* 128, 249–254.

Elmqvist, T. and Cox, P.A. (1996). The evolution of vivipary in flowering plants. *Oikos* 77, 3–9.

Elton, C.S. (1927). *Animal ecology*. Sidgwick and Jackson, London.

Engelhardt, U. and Lassig, B.R. (1996). *A review of the possible causes and consequences of outbreaks of the crown-of-thorns starfish (Acanthaster planci) on the Great Barrier Reef – an Australian perspective*. CRC Reef Research Centre and Great Barrier Reef Marine Park Authority, Queensland.

Ennos, A.R. (1993). The function and formation of buttresses. *Trends in Ecology and Evolution* 8, 350–351.

Erwin, T.L. (1983). Beetles and other insects of tropical forest canopies at Manaus, Brazil, sampled by insecticidal fogging. In: Sutton, S.L., Whitmore, T.C. and Chadwick, A.C. (eds.), *Tropical rain forest: Ecology and management*, pp. 59–75. Blackwell Scientific Publications, Oxford.

Etherington, J.R. (1982). *Environment and plant ecology*. 2nd edition. Wiley, London.

Ewer, D.W. and Hall, J.B. (1972). *Ecologial biology 1*. Longman, London.

Ewer, D.W. and Hall, J.B. (1978). *Ecological biology 2*. Longman, London.

Falkowski, P.G., Dubinsky, Z., Muscatine, L. and Porter, J. (1984). Light and the bioenergetics of a symbiotic coral. *BioScience* 34, 705–709.

Faust, M.A. and Gulledge, R.A. (1996). Associations of microalgae and meiofauna in floating detritus at a mangrove island, Twin Cays, Belize. *Journal of Experimental Marine Biology and Ecology* 197, 159–175.

Fearnside, P.M. (1986). Spatial concentration of deforestation in the Brazilian Amazon. *Ambio* 15, 74–81.

FitzSimons, D.W. (1990). AIDS. *Biologist* 37, 97–99.

Flohn, H. (1969). *Climate and weather*. McGraw-Hill, New York.

Folke, C., Jansson, A., Larsson, J. and Costanza, R. (1997). Ecosystem appropriation by cities. *Ambio* 26, 167–172.

Fortes, M.D. (1988). Mangrove and seagrass beds of East Asia: Habitats under stress. *Ambio* 17, 207–213.

Foster, R.B. (1977). *Tachygalia versicolor* is a suicidal Neotropical tree. *Nature* 268, 624–626.

Frankie, G.W., Baker, H.G. and Opler, P.A. (1974). Comparative phenological studies of trees in tropical wet and dry forests in the lowlands of Costa Rica. *Journal of Ecology* 62, 881–919.

Fraser, R.H. and Currie, D.J. (1996). The species richness–energy hypothesis in a system where historical factors are thought to prevail: Coral reefs. *American Naturalist* 148, 138–159.

Freeth, S. (1992). The deadly cloud hanging over Cameroon. *New Scientist* 15 August 1992, 23–27.

Frost, P.G.H. and Robertson, F. (1987). The ecological effects of fire in savannas. In: Walker, B.H. (ed.), *Determinants of tropical savannas*, pp. 93–140. IRL Press, Oxford.

Frusher, S.D. (1983). The ecology of juvenile penaeid prawns, mangrove crab (*Scylla serrata*) and the giant freshwater prawn (*Macrobrachium rosenbergii*) in the Purari Delta. In: Petr, T. (ed.), *The Purari – tropical environment of a high rainfall river basin*, pp. 341–353. Dr W. Junk, The Hague.

Fry, B. and Parker, P.L. (1979). Animal diet in Texas seagrass meadows: ^{13}C evidence for the importance of benthic plants. *Estuarine, Coastal and Marine Science* 8, 499–509.

Fryer, G. (1960). Concerning the proposed introduction of Nile perch into Lake Victoria. *East African Journal of Agriculture* 25, 267–270.

Fryer, G. and Iles, T.D. (1972). *The cichlid fish of the Great Lakes of Africa*. Oliver and Boyd, Edinburgh.

Ganf, G.G. (1975). Photosynthetic production and irradiance–photosynthesis relationships of the phytoplankton from a shallow equatorial lake (Lake George, Uganda). *Oecologia (Berlin)* 18, 165–183.

Ganf, G.G. and Blazka, P. (1974). Oxygen uptake, ammonia and phosphate excretion by zooplankton of a shallow equatorial lake (Lake George, Uganda). *Limnology and Oceanography* 19, 313–326.

Gaudet, J.J. (1977). Natural drawdown on Lake Naivasha, Kenya, and the formation of papyrus swamps. *Aquatic Botany* 3, 1–47.

Gentry, A.H. (1974). Flowering phenology and diversity in tropical Bignoniaceae. *Biotropica* 6, 64–68.

Gentry, A.H. (1988). Tree species richness of upper Amazonian forests. *Proceedings of the National Academy of Sciences* 85, 156–159.

Gentry, A.H. and Dodson, C. (1987). Contributions of nontrees to species richness of a tropical forest. *Biotropica* 19, 149–156.

Ghiold, J. (1990). White death – the fate of a deserted coral. *New Scientist* 2 June 1990, 28.

Gibson, A.C. (1998). Photosynthetic organs of desert plants. *BioScience* 48, 911–920.

Gill, A.M. and Tomlinson, P.B. (1971). Studies on the growth of red mangrove (*Rhizophora mangle* L.). 3. Phenology of the shoot. *Biotropica* 3, 109–124.

Gill, F.B. and Wolf, L.L. (1975a). Foraging strategies and energetics of East African sunbirds at mistletoe flowers. *American Naturalist* 109, 491–510.

Gill, F.B. and Wolf, L.L. (1975b). Economics of feeding territoriality in the golden-winged sunbird. *Ecology* 56, 333–345.

Gleason, H.A. (1926). The individualistic concept of the plant association. *Torrey Botanical Club Bulletin* 53, 7–26.

Goldschmidt, T., Witte, F. and Wanink, J.H. (1993). Cascading effects of the introduced Nile Perch on the detritivorous/planktivorous species in the sublittoral areas of Lake Victoria. *Conservation Biology* 7, 686–700.

Golley, F.B., Odum, H.T., Wilson, R.F. (1962). The structure and reproduction of a Puerto Rican red mangrove forest in May. *Ecology* 43, 9–19.

Golterman, H.L. (1969). *Methods for chemical analysis of fresh waters*. IBP Handbook 8. Blackwell Scientific Publications, Oxford.

Goss, H. (1995). Meltdown warning as tropical glaciers trickle away. *New Scientist* 24 June 1995, 18.

Goulding, M. (1980). *The fishes of the forest. Explorations in*

Amazonian natural history. University of California Press, Berkeley.

Grainger, R. (1998). *Recent trends in global fishery production*. FAO Fisheries Department, Food and Agriculture Organization, Rome.

Graves, J. and Reavey, D. (1996). *Global environmental change: Plants, animals and communities*. Longman, London.

Green, G.M. and Sussman, R.W. (1990). Deforestation history of the eastern rain forests of Madagascar from satellite images. *Science* 248, 212–215.

Green, J., Corbet, S.A., Watts, E. and Lan, O.B. (1976). Ecological studies on Indonesian lakes. Overturn and restratification of Ranu Lamongan. *Journal of Zoology (London)* 180, 315–354.

Greenway, P. (undated). Survival strategies in desert crabs. In: Cogger, H.G. and Cameron, E.E. (eds.), *Arid Australia*, pp. 145–152. Australian Museum, Sydney.

Griffiths, J.F. (1972). *World survey of climatology, volume 10. Climates of Africa* (ed. Landsberg, H.E.). Elsevier, Amsterdam.

Grime, J.P. (1979). *Plant strategies and vegetation processes*. Wiley, Chichester.

Grubb, P.J. (1977). Control of forest growth and distribution on wet tropical mountains: With specific reference to mineral nutrition. *Annual Review of Ecology and Systematics* 8, 83–107.

Haberyan, K.A. and Hecky, R.E. (1987). The late Pleistocene and Holocene stratigraphy and paleolimnology of Lakes Kivu and Tanganyika. *Palaeogeography, Palaeoclimatology, Palaeoecology* 51, 161–197.

Hadiwinoto, S. and Leitman, J. (1994). Jakarta. *Cities* 11, 153–157.

Haines, A.K. (1983). Fish fauna and ecology. In: Petr, T. (ed.), *The Purari, tropical environment of a high rainfall river basin*, pp. 141–177. Dr W. Junk, The Hague.

Hairston, N.G. and Hairston, J.G. (1993). Cause–effect relationships in energy flow, trophic structure and interspecific interactions. *American Naturalist* 142, 379–411.

Hall, D.O. and Whatley, F.R. (1967). The chloroplasts. In: Roodyn, D.B. (ed.), *Enzyme cytology*. Academic Press, London.

Hanby, J.P., Bygott, J.D. and Packer, C. (1995). Ecology, demography, and behavior of lions in two contrasting habitats: Ngorongoro Crater and the Serengeti plains. In: Sinclair, A.R.E. and Arcese, P. (eds.), *Serengeti II: Dynamics, management, and conservation of an ecosystem*, pp. 315–331. University of Chicago Press, Chicago.

Hanks, J. (1973). The population explosion in Rhodesia and the consequences of unlimited growth. *The Rhodesia Science News* 7, 249–256.

Hannah, L., Lohse, D., Hutchinson, C., Carr, J.L. and Lankerani, A. (1994). A preliminary inventory of human disturbance of world ecosystems. *Ambio* 23, 246–250.

Hardin, G. (1960). The competitive exclusion principle. *Science* 131, 1292–1297.

Harper, D. and Mavuti, K. (1996). Freshwater wetlands and marshes. In: McClanahan, T.R. and Young, T.P. (eds.), *East African ecosystems and their conservation*, pp. 217–239, Oxford University Press, Oxford.

Hassell, M.P. and May, R.M. (1989). The population biology of host–parasite and host–parasitoid associations. In: Roughgarden, J., May, R.M. and Levin, S.A. (eds.), *Perspectives in ecological theory*, pp. 319–347. Princeton University Press, Princeton, New Jersey.

Hastenrath, S. and Kruss, P.D. (1992). The dramatic retreat of Mount Kenya's glaciers between 1963 and 1987: Greenhouse forcing. *Annals of Glaciology* 16, 127–133.

Heald, E.J. and Odum, W.E. (1970). The contribution of mangrove swamps to Florida fisheries. *Proceedings of the Gulf Caribbean Fisheries Institute* 22, 720–735.

Hecky, R.E. (1984). African lakes and their trophic efficiencies: A temporal perspective. In: Meyers, D.G. and Strickler, J.R. (eds.), *Trophic interactions within aquatic ecosystems*, pp. 405–448. American Association for the Advancement of Science, Rome.

Hecky, R.E. (1991). The pelagic ecosystem. In: Coulter, G.W. (ed.), *Lake Tanganyika and its life*, pp. 90–110. Oxford University Press, Oxford.

Hecky, R.E. (1993). The eutrophication of Lake Victoria. *Verhandlungen Internationale Vereinigung für theoretische und angewandte Limnologie* 25, 39–48.

Hecky, R.E., Spigel, R.H. and Coulter, G.W. (1991). The nutrient regime. In: Coulter, G.W. (ed.), *Lake Tanganyika and its life*, pp. 76–89. Oxford University Press, Oxford.

Hedberg, O. (1964). Features of Afro-alpine plant ecology. *Acta Phytogeographica Suecica* 49, 1–144.

Hellden, U. (1984). *Drought impact monitoring*. Lund University Naturrgeografiska Institute, Lund.

Henty, E. (1969). *A manual of the grasses of New Guinea*. Division of Botany, Lae, Papua New Guinea.

Hilborn, R. and Sinclair, A.R.E. (1979). A simulation of the wildebeest population, other ungulates, and their predators. In: Sinclair, A.R.E. and Norton-Griffiths, M. (eds.), *Serengeti: Dynamics of an ecosystem*, pp. 287–309. University of Chicago Press, Chicago.

Hilborn, R., Georgiadis, N. and Lazarus, J. et al. (1995). A model to evaluate alternative management policies for the Serengeti-Mara ecosystem. In: Sinclair, A.R.E. and Arcese, P. (eds.), *Serengeti II: Dynamics, management, and conservation of an ecosystem*, pp. 617–637. University of Chicago Press, Chicago.

Hnatiuk, R.J. (1994). Plant form and function in alpine New Guinea. In: Rundel, P.W., Smith, A.P. and Meinzer, F.C. (eds.), *Tropical alpine environments: Plant form and function*, pp. 307–318. Cambridge University Press, Cambridge.

Hoegh-Guldberg, O., Berkelmans, R. and Oliver, J. (1996). *Coral bleaching: Implications for the Great Barrier Reef Marine Park*. CRC Reef Research Centre and the Great Barrier Reef Marine Park Authority, Townsville, Queensland.

Horn, H.S. (1971). *The adaptive geometry of trees*. Princeton University Press, Princeton.

Houghton, R.A. and Woodwell, G.M. (1989). Global climatic change. *Scientific American* 260, 36–44.

Howard-Williams, C. (1977). Swamp ecosystems. *The Malayan Nature Journal* 31, 113–125.

Howard-Williams, C. (1979). The distribution of aquatic macrophytes in Lake Chilwa: Annual and long-term environmental fluctuations. In: Kalk, M., McLachlan, A.J. and Howard-Williams, C. (eds.), *Lake Chilwa: studies of change of a tropical ecosystem*, pp. 105–122. Dr W. Junk, The Hague.

Howard-Williams, C. and Gaudet, J.J. (1985). The structure and functioning of African swamps. In: Denny, P. (ed.), *The ecology and management of African wetland vegetation*, pp. 152–175. Dr W. Junk, The Hague.

Howard-Williams, C. and Lenton, G.M. (1975). The role of the littoral zone in the functioning of a shallow tropical lake ecosystem. *Freshwater Biology* 5, 445–459.

Hubbell, S.P., Foster, R.B., O'Brien, S.T., Harms, K.E., Condit, R., Wechsler, B., Wright, S.J. and Loo de Lao, S. (1999). Light-gap disturbances, recruitment limitation, and tree diversity in a Neotropical forest. *Science* 283, 554–557.

Hughes, T.P. (1994). Catastrophes, phase shifts, and large-scale degradation of a Caribbean coral reef. *Science* 265, 1547–1551.

Humphreys, W.F. (1979). Production and respiration in animal populations. *Journal of Animal Ecology* 48, 427–453.

Hunter, C.L. and Evans, C.W. (1995). Coral reefs in Kaneohe Bay, Hawaii: Two centuries of western influence and two decades of data. *Bulletin of Marine Science* 57, 501–515.

Huntley, B.J. and Walker, B.H. (1982). *Ecology of tropical savannas*. Ecological Studies 42. Springer-Verlag, Berlin.

Huston, M.A. (1985). Patterns of species diversity on coral reefs. *Annual Review of Ecology and Systematics* 16, 149–177.

Hutchings, P. and Saenger, P. (1987). *Ecology of mangroves*. University of Queensland Press, St. Lucia, Queensland.

Hutchinson, G.E. (1957). Concluding remarks. *Cold Spring Harbor Symposia on Quantitative Biology* 22, 415–427.

Hutchinson, G.E. (1959). Homage to Santa Rosalia, or why are there so many kinds of animals? *American Naturalist* 93, 145–159.

Hutchinson, G.E. and Löffler, H. (1956). The thermal classification of lakes. *Proceedings of the National Academy of Sciences* 42, 84–86.

Inter-governmental Panel on Climate Change (1995). *IPCC working group I: Summary for policymakers*. Cambridge University Press, Cambridge.

Jacobs, M. (1988). *The tropical rain forest. A first encounter*. Springer-Verlag, Berlin.

Janzen, D.H. (1967a). Interaction of the bull's horn acacia (*Acacia cornigera* L.) with an ant inhabitant (*Pseudomyrmex ferruginea* F. Smith) in Eastern Mexico. *University of Kansas Science Bulletin* 47, 315–558.

Janzen, D.H. (1967b). Why mountain passes are higher in the tropics? *American Naturalist* 101, 233–249.

Janzen, D.H. (1973). Rate of regeneration after a tropical high elevation fire. *Biotropica* 5, 117–122.

Janzen, D.H. (1976). Why do bamboos wait so long to flower? In: Burley, J. and Styles, B.T. (eds.), *Tropical trees: Variation in breeding and conservation*, pp. 135–139. Academic Press, London.

Janzen, D.H. (1981). Digestive seed predation by a Costa Rican Baird's tapir. *Biotropica* 13 (suppl.), 59–63.

Janzen, D.H. (1983). Food webs: Who eats what, why, how, and with what effects in a tropical forest. In: Golley, F.B. (ed.), *Tropical rain forests: Structure and function*, pp. 167–182. Elsevier, New York.

Jarman, P.J. (1974). The social organization of antelope in relation to their ecology. *Behaviour* 48, 215–266.

Johns, R.J. (1982). Plant zonation. In: Gressitt, J.L. (ed.), *Biogeography and ecology of New Guinea*, pp. 309–330. Dr W. Junk, Dordrecht.

Johns, R.J. (1986). The instability of the tropical ecosystems in New Guinea. *Blumea* 31, 341–371.

Johnston, B. L., Richardson, W. B. and Naimo, T. J. (1995). Past, present and future concepts in large river ecology. *Bioscience* 45, 134–141.

Johnstone, I.M. (1981). Consumption of leaves by herbivores in mixed mangrove stands. *Biotropica* 13, 252–259.

Johnstone, I.M. (1983). Succession in zoned mangrove communities: Where is the climax? In: Teas, H.J. (ed.), *Tasks for vegetation science*, pp. 131–140. Dr W. Junk, The Hague.

Jokiel, P. and Martinelli, F.J. (1992). The vortex model of coral reef biogeography. *Journal of Biogeography* 19, 449–458.

Jordan, C.F. (1986). Shifting cultivation. In: Jordan, C.F.

(ed.), *Amazonian rain forests: Ecosystem disturbance and recovery. Case studies of ecosystem dynamics under a spectrum of land-use intensities*, pp. 9–23. Springer-Verlag, New York.

Junk, W.J. (1984). Ecology of the varzea, floodplain of Amazonian white-water rivers. In: Sioli, H. (ed.), *The Amazon: Limnology and landscape ecology of a mighty tropical river and its basin*, pp. 215–243. Dr W. Junk, Dordrecht.

Junk, W.J. and Howard-Williams, C. (1984). Ecology of aquatic macrophytes in Amazonia. In Sioli, H. (ed.), *The Amazon: Limnology and landscape ecology of a mighty tropical river and its basin*, pp. 269–293. Dr W. Junk, Dordrecht.

Junk, W.J. and Piedade, M.T.F. (1994). Species diversity and distribution of herbaceous plants in the floodplain of the middle Amazon. *Verhandlungen Internationale Vereinigung für theoretische und angewandte Limnologie* 25, 1862–1865.

Junk, W.J., Bayley, P.B. and Sparks, R.E. (1989). The flood pulse concept in river-floodplain systems. In: Dodge, D.P. (ed.), *Proceedings of the international large river symposium. Canadian Special Publications of Fisheries and Aquatic Sciences* 106, 110–127.

Kalk, M. (1979). Introduction: Perspectives of research at Lake Chilwa. In: Kalk, M., McLachlan, A.J. and Howard-Williams, C. (eds.), *Lake Chilwa: studies of change in a tropical ecosystem*, pp. 3–16. Dr W. Junk, The Hague.

Kalk, M., McLachlan, A.J. and Howard-Williams, C. (1979). *Lake Chilwa: studies of change in a tropical ecosystem*. Dr W. Junk, The Hague.

Kaufman, L. (1992). Catastrophic change in species-rich freshwater ecosystems. *BioScience* 42, 846–858.

Keddy, P.A. (1989). *Competition*. Population and Community Biology Series. Chapman and Hall, New York.

Keeley, J.E. (1988). Photosynthesis in quillworts, or why are some aquatic plants similar to cacti? *Plants Today* 1, 127–132.

Kendall, H.W. and Pimentel, D. (1994). Constraints on the expansion of the global food supply. *Ambio* 23, 198–204.

Kilham, P., Kilham, S.S. and Hecky, R.E. (1986). Hypothesized resource relationships among African planktonic diatoms. *Limnology and Oceanography* 31, 1169–1181.

Kira, T. (1978). Community architecture and organic matter dynamics in tropical lowland rain forests of Southeast Asia with special reference to Pasoh forest, West Malaysia. In: Tomlinson, P.B. and Zimmermann, M.H. (eds.), *Tropical trees as living systems*, pp. 561–590. Cambridge University Press, Cambridge.

Knowlton, N. and Jackson, J.B.C. (1994). New taxonomy and niche partitioning on coral reefs: Jack of all trades or master of some? *Trends in Ecology and Evolution* 9, 7–9.

Kohlmeyer, J., Bebout, B. and Volkmann-Kohlmeyer, B. (1995). Decomposition of mangrove wood by marine fungi and teredinids in Belize. *Marine Ecology* 16, 27–39.

Kohyama (1993). Size-structured tree populations in gap-dynamic forest – the forest architecture hypothesis for the stable coexistence of species. *Journal of Ecology* 81, 131–143.

Kok, O.V. and Nel, J.A.J. (1996). The Kuiseb River as a linear oasis in the Namib Desert. *African Journal of Ecology* 34, 39–47.

Köppen, W. (1884). Die Warmezonen der Erde, nach der Dauer der Heissen, Gemassigten und Kalten Zeit, und nach der Wirkung der Warme auf die Organische Welt betrachter. *Meteorologische Zeitschrift* 1, 215–226,

Köppen, W. (1931). *Grundrisse der Klimatunde*. Borntraeger, Berlin.

Krebs, C.J. (1978). *Ecology: The experimental analysis of distribution and abundance*. 2nd edition. HarperCollins, New York.

Krebs, C.J. (1994). *Ecology: The experimental analysis of distribution and abundance*. 4th edition. HarperCollins, New York.

Krog, J.O., Zachariassen, K.E., Larsen, B. and Smidsrod, O. (1979). Thermal buffering in Afro-alpine plants due to nucleating agent-induced water freezing. *Nature* 282, 300–301.

Krohne, D.T. (1998). *General ecology*. Wadsworth Publishing, Albany, New York.

Kruuk, H. (1972). *The spotted hyena: A study of predation and social behavior*. University of Chicago Press, Chicago.

Kyle, J.H. and Ghani, N. (1982). Methylmercury in ten species of fish from Lake Murray. *Science in New Guinea* 9, 48–59.

Lack, D. (1947). *Darwin's finches*. Cambridge University Press, Cambridge.

Lamprey, H.F. (1963). Ecological separation of the large mammal species in the Tarangire Game Reserve, Tanganyika. *East African Wildlife Journal* 1, 63–92.

Lamprey, H.F. (1988). Report on the desert encroachment reconnaissance in Northern Sudan. *Desertification Control Bulletin* 41, 1.

Lamprey, H.F., Glover, P.E., Turner, M.I.M. and Bell, R.H.V. (1967). Invasion of the Serengeti National Park by elephants. *East African Wildlife Journal* 5, 151–166.

Langer, R.H.M. (1979). *How grasses grow*. Edward Arnold, London.

Latif, A.F.A. (1984). Lake Nasser – The new man-made

lake in Egypt (with reference to Lake Nubia). In: Taub, F.B. (ed.), *Lakes and reservoirs. Ecosystems of the world 23*, pp. 385–410. Elsevier, Amsterdam.

Laurenson, M.K. (1995). Implications of high offspring mortality for cheetah population dynamics. In: Sinclair, A.R.E. and Arcese, P. (eds.). *Serengeti II: Dynamics, management, and conservation of an ecosystem*, pp. 385–399. University of Chicago Press, Chicago.

Lawler, A. (1998). Global change fights off a chill. *Science* 280, 1682–1684.

Laws, R.M. (1970). Elephants as agents of habitat and landscape change in East Africa. *Oikos* 21, 1–15.

Leach, G.J. and Osborne, P.L. (1985). *Freshwater plants of Papua New Guinea*. University of Papua New Guinea Press, Port Moresby.

Leakey, R. and Lewin, R. (1996). *The sixth extinction: Patterns of life and the future of humankind*. Doubleday, New York.

Lee, S.Y. (1995). Mangrove outwelling: A review. *Hydrobiologia* 295, 203–212.

Le Houérou, H.N. (1986). The desert and arid zones of northern Africa. In: Evenari, M., Noy-Meir, I. and Goodall, D.W. (eds.), *Hot deserts and arid shrublands, Ecosystems of the world 12B*, pp. 101–147. Elsevier, Amsterdam.

Leith, H. (1978). *Patterns of primary productivity in the biosphere*. Hutchinson Ross, Stroudsberg.

Lerdau, M., Whitbeck, J. and Holbrook, N.M. (1991). Tropical deciduous forests: Death of a biome. *Trends in Ecology and Evolution* 6, 201–202.

Lewis, S.M. (1985). Herbivory on coral reefs: Algal susceptibility to herbivorous fish. *Oecologia* (Berlin) 65, 370–375.

Lewis, S.M. (1986). The role of herbivorous fish in the organization of a Caribbean reef community. *Ecological Monographs* 56, 183–200.

Lewis, W.M. (1973). The thermal regime of Lake Lanao (Philippines) and its theoretical implications for tropical lakes. *Limnology and Oceanography* 18, 200–217.

Lewis, W.M. (1974). Primary production in the plankton community of a tropical lake. *Ecological Monographs* 44, 377–409.

Lewis, W.M. (1978). Dynamics and succession of the phytoplankton in a tropical lake: Lake Lanao, Philippines. *Journal of Ecology* 66, 849–880.

Lewis, W.M. (1986). Phytoplankton succession in Lake Valencia, Venezuela. *Hydrobiologia* 138, 189–203.

Lewis, W.M. (1996). Tropical lakes: How latitude makes a difference. In: Schiemer, F. and Boland, K.T. (eds.), *Perspectives in tropical limnology*, pp. 43–64. SPB Academic Publishing, Amsterdam.

Liebig, J. (1840). *Chemistry in its application to agriculture and physiology*. Taylor and Walton, London.

Lindeman, R.L. (1942). The trophic dynamic aspects of ecology. *Ecology* 23, 137–139.

List, R.J. (1971). *Smithsonian meteorological tables*. 6th edition. Smithsonian Institution Press, Washington D.C.

Löffler, H. (1973). Tropical high mountain lakes of New Guinea and their zoogeographical relationship compared with other high mountain lakes. *Arctic and Alpine Research* 5, 193–198.

Long, S.P. and Jones, M.B. (1992). Introduction, aims, goals and general methods. In: Long, S.P., Jones, M.B. and Roberts, M.J. (eds.), *Primary productivity of grass ecosystems of the tropics and sub-tropics*, pp. 1–24. Chapman and Hall, London.

Longman, K.A. (1985). Tropical forest trees. In Halevy, A.H. (ed), *CRC Handbook of flowering*, vol. 1, pp. 23–39. CRC Press, Baton Rouge.

Longman, K.A. and Jeník, J. (1987). *Tropical forest and its environment*, 2nd edition. Longman, London.

Lotka, A.J. (1925). *Elements of physical biology*. (Reprinted in 1956 by Dover Publications, New York.)

Louw, G. and Seely, M. (1982). *Ecology of desert organisms*. Longman, London.

Lowe-McConnell, R.H. (1975). *Fish communities in tropical freshwaters: Their distribution, ecology and evolution*. Longman, London.

Lowe-McConnell, R.H. (1987). *Ecological studies in tropical fish communities*. Cambridge Tropical Biology Series, Cambridge University Press, Cambridge.

Lowe-McConnell, R.H. (1993). Fish faunas of the African Great Lakes: Origins, diversity, and vulnerability. *Conservation Biology* 7, 634–643.

Lowe-McConnell, R.H. (1996). Fish communities in the African Great Lakes. *Environmental Biology of Fishes* 45, 219–235.

Lugo, A.E. and Snedaker, S.C. (1974). The ecology of mangroves. *Annual Review of Ecology and Systematics* 5, 39–64.

Lund, J.W.G. (1950). Studies on *Asterionella formosa* Hass. II. Nutrient depletion and the spring maximum. *Journal of Ecology* 38, 1–35.

Mabberley, D.J. (1992). *Tropical rain forest ecology*. 2nd edition. Blackie, Glasgow.

MacArthur, R.H. (1972). *Geographical ecology: Patterns in the distribution of species*. Harper and Row, New York.

MacArthur, R.H. and Wilson, E.O. (1967). *Theory of island biogeography*. Princeton University Press, Princeton.

Mackey, A.P. and Smail, G. (1995). Spatial and temporal variation in litter fall of *Avicennia marina* (Forssk.) Vierh. in the Brisbane River, Queensland, Australia. *Aquatic Botany* 52, 133–142.

Mackey, A.P. and Smail, G. (1996). The decomposition of

mangrove litter in a subtropical mangrove forest. *Hydrobiologia* 332, 93–98.

MacLulich, D.A. (1937). Fluctuations in the numbers of the varying hare (*Lepus americanus*). *University of Toronto Studies in Biology Series* 43, 1–136.

MacNae, W. (1966). Mangroves in eastern and southern Australia. *Australian Journal of Botany* 14, 67–104.

MacNae, W. (1968). A general account of the fauna and flora of mangrove swamps and forests in the Indo-West Pacific region. *Advances in Marine Biology* 6, 73–270.

Maddock, L. (1979). The "migration" and grazing succession. In: Sinclair, A.R.E. and Norton-Griffiths, M. (eds.), *Serengeti: Dynamics of an ecosystem*, pp. 104–129. University of Chicago Press, Chicago.

May, R.M. (1979). Production and respiration in animal communities. *Nature* 282, 443–444.

May, R.M. (1992). Past efforts and future prospects towards understanding how many species there are. In: Solbrig, O.T., van Emden, H.M. and van Oort, P.G.W.J. (eds.), *Biodiversity and global change*, pp. 71–81. The International Union of Biological Sciences, Paris.

McClanahan, T.R. and Obura, D.O. (1996). Coral reefs and nearshore fisheries. In: McClanahan, T.R. and Young, T.P. (eds.), *East African ecosystems and their conservation*, pp. 67–99. Oxford University Press, Oxford.

McGinnies, W.G. (1979). Arid-land ecosystems – common features throughout the world. In: Goodall, D.W., Perry, R.A. and Howes, K.M.W. (eds.), *Arid-land ecosystems: structure, functioning and management*, volume 1, pp. 299–316. Cambridge University Press, Cambridge.

McIvor, C.C. and Smith, T.J. (1995). Differences in the crab fauna of mangrove areas at a Southwest Florida and a Northeast Australia location: Implications for leaf litter processing. *Estuaries* 18, 591–597.

McNaughton, S.J. (1976). Serengeti migratory wildebeest: Facilitation of energy flow by grazing. *Science* 191, 92–94.

McNaughton, S.J. (1985). Ecology of a grazing system: The Serengeti. *Ecological Monographs* 53, 291–320.

McNaughton, S.J. and Banyikwa, F.F. (1995). Plant communities and herbivory. In: Sinclair, A.R.E. and Arcese, P. (eds.), *Serengeti II: Dynamics, management, and conservation of an ecosystem*, pp. 49–70. University of Chicago Press, Chicago.

McNaughton, S.J., Banyikwa, F.F. and McNaughton, M.M. (1997). Promotion of the cycling of diet-enhancing nutrients by African grazers. *Science* 278, 1798–1800.

McNaughton, S.J., Ruess, R.W. and Seagle, S.W. (1988). Large mammals and process dynamics in African ecosystems. *BioScience* 38, 794–800.

McNeely, J.A., Gadgil, M., Leveque, C., Padoch, C. and Redford, K. (1995). Human influences on biodiversity. In: Heywood, V. (ed.), *Global biodiversity assessment*, pp. 715–821. Cambridge University Press, Cambridge.

Meade, R.H. (1985). *Suspended sediment in the Amazon River and its tributaries in Brazil during 1982–84*. United States Geological Survey Open-File Report 85–492, Denver, Colorado.

Meade, R.H. (1994). Suspended sediments of the modern Amazon and Orinoco Rivers. *Quaternary International* 21, 29–39.

Meade, R.H. (1996). River-sediment inputs to major deltas. In: Milliman, J.D. and Haq, B.U. (eds.), *Sea-level rise and coastal subsidence: Causes, consequences and strategies*, pp. 63–85. Kluwer Academic Publishers, Dordrecht.

Meadows, D., Meadows, D., Randers, J. and Behrens, W. (1972). *Limits to growth*. Universe Books, New York.

Medway, L. (1972). Phenology of a tropical rain forest in Malaya. *Biological Journal of the Linnean Society* 4, 117–146.

Melack, J.M. (1979). Temporal variability of phytoplankton in tropical lakes. *Oecologia (Berlin)* 44, 1–7.

Melack, J.M. (1996). Recent developments in tropical limnology. *Verhandlungen Internationale Vereinigung für theoretische und angewandte Limnologie* 26, 211–217.

Mepham, R.H. and Mepham, J.S. (1984). The flora of tidal forests – a rationalization of the use of the term 'mangrove'. *South African Journal of Botany* 51, 77–99.

Meyerson, F.A.B. (1998). Population, development and global warming: Averting the tragedy of the climate commons. *Population and Environment* 19, 443–463.

Miller, D.J. (1989). Introductions and extinctions of fish in the African Great Lakes. *Trends in Ecology and Evolution* 4, 56–59.

Miller, K.M. (1994). Serengeti lions fall prey to distemper. *New Scientist* 11 June 1994, 8.

Minshall, G.W., Petersen, R.C., Cummins, K.W., Bott, T.L., Sedell, T.L., Cushing, C.E. and Vannote, R.L. (1983). Interbiome comparison of stream ecosystem dynamics. *Ecological Monographs* 53, 1–25.

Minter, R. (1991). Muddy waters: The quagmire of wetlands regulation. *Policy Review* 56, 70–77.

Mitchell, D.S. and Rose, D.J.W. (1979). Factors affecting fluctuations in extent of *Salvinia molesta* on Lake Kariba. *PANS* 25, 171–177.

Mitsch, W.J. (1994). *Global wetlands: Old World and New*. Elsevier, Amsterdam.

Mitsch, W.J. and Gosselink, J.G. (1986). *Wetlands*. Van Nostrand Reinhold, New York.

Mitsch, W.J., Mitsch, R,H. and Turner, R.E. (1994). Wetlands of the Old and New Worlds: Ecology and management. In: Mitsch, W.J. (ed.), *Global wetlands: Old World and New*, pp. 3–56. Elsevier, Amsterdam.

Mittermeier, R.A., Tattersall, I., Konstant, W.R., Meyers, D.M. and Mast, R.B. (1994). *Lemurs of Madagascar.* Conservation International, Washington D.C.

Money, D.C. (1980). *Tropical savannas.* Evans Brothers, London.

Montgomery, W.L. (1990). Zoogeography, behavior and ecology of coral-reef fish. In: Dubinsky, Z. (ed.), *Coral reefs. Ecosystems of the world 25*, pp. 329–364. Elsevier, Amsterdam.

Moore, R. and Reynolds, L.F. (1982). Migration patterns of Barramundi *Lates calcarifer* (Bloch) in Papua New Guinea. *Australian Journal of Marine and Freshwater Research* 33, 671–682.

Moriarty, D.J.W., Darlington, J.P.E.C., Dunn, I.C., Moriarty, C.M. and Telvin, M.P. (1973). Feeding and grazing in Lake George, Uganda. *Proceedings of the Royal Society (London)* B 184, 299–319.

Moss, B. (1988). *Ecology of freshwaters: Man and medium.* Blackwell Scientific Publications, Oxford.

Mugidde, R. (1993). The increase in phytoplankton primary productivity and biomass in Lake Victoria (Uganda). *Verhandlungen Internationale Vereinigung für theoretische und angewandte Limnologie* 25, 846–849.

Mulkey, S.S., Smith, A.P. and Young, T.P. (1984). Predation by elephants on *Senecio keniodendron* (Compositae) in the alpine zone of Mount Kenya. *Biotropica* 16, 246–248.

Murcia, C. (1995). Edge effects in fragmented forests: Implications for conservation. *Trends in Ecology and Evolution* 10, 58–62.

Myers, A.A. (1994). Biogeographic patterns in shallow-water marine systems and the controlling processes at different scales. In: Giller, P.S., Hildrew, A.G. and Raffaelli, D.G. (eds.), *Aquatic ecology, scale, pattern and process*, pp. 547–574. British Ecological Society Symposium, Blackwell Scientific Publications, Oxford.

Myers, A.A. (1997). Biogeographic barriers and the development of marine biodiversity. *Estuarine, Coastal and Shelf Science* 44, 241–248.

Myers, N. (1980). *Conversion of tropical moist forests.* National Research Council, Washington D.C.

Myers, N. (1988). Tropical forests: Much more than stocks of wood. *Journal of Tropical Ecology* 4, 209–221.

Myers, N. (1992). *The primary source: Tropical forests and our future.* W.W. Norton, New York.

Natural Systems Research (1988). *Porgera gold project environmental plan, Volume C.* Porgera Joint Venture, Report CR 257/13, Melbourne.

Newmark, W.D., Manyanza, D.N., Gamassa, D.M. and Sariko, H. I. (1994). The conflict between wildlife and local people living adjacent to protected areas in Tanzania: Human density as a predictor. *Conservation Biology* 8, 249–255.

Nicholson, S.E., Tucker, C.J. and Ba, M.B. (1998). Desertification, drought, and surface vegetation: An example from the West African Sahel. *Bulletin of the American Meteorological Society* 79, 815–829.

Norton, I.O. and Sclater, J.G. (1979). A model for the evolution of the Indian Ocean and the breakup of Gondwanaland. *Journal of Geophysics Research* 84, 6803–6830.

Norton-Griffiths, M. (1979). The influence of grazing, browsing, and fire on the vegetation dynamics of the Serengeti. In: Sinclair, A.R.E. and Norton-Griffiths, M. (eds.), *Serengeti: Dynamics of an ecosystem*, pp. 310–352. University of Chicago Press, Chicago.

Noy-Meir, I. (1974). Desert ecosystems: Higher trophic levels. *Annual Review of Ecology and Systematics* 5, 195–213.

O'Brien, K.L. (1996). Tropical deforestation and climate change. *Progress in Physical Geography* 20, 311–335.

Oldfield, F. (1977). Lakes and their drainage basins as units of sediment-based ecological study. *Progress in Physical Geography* 1, 460–504.

Orians, G.H. (1969). The number of bird species in some tropical forests. *Ecology* 50, 783–801.

Osborne, P.L. (1995). Limnology in the wet tropics. In: Gopal, B. and Wetzel, R.G. (eds.), *Limnology in developing countries*, pp. 121–160. International Association of Theoretical and Applied Limnology, International Scientific Publications, New Delhi.

Osborne, P.L. and Leach, G.J. (1983). Changes in the distribution of aquatic plants in a tropical swamp. *Environmental Conservation* 4, 323–329.

Osborne, P.L. and Polunin, N.V.C. (1986). From swamp to lake: Recent changes in the aquatic flora of a lowland Papuan swamp. *Journal of Ecology* 74, 197–210.

Osborne, P.L. and Totome, R.G. (1992a). Water column stability and stratification breakdown in oligomictic Lake Kutubu, Papua New Guinea. *Archiv für Hydrobiologie* 124, 427–449.

Osborne, P.L. and Totome, R.G. (1992b). Long-term impacts of sewage effluent disposal on a tropical wetland. *Water Science and Technology* 29, 111–117.

Owen, R.B., Crossley, R., Johnson, T.C., Tweddle, D., Kornfield, I., Davison, S., Eccles, D.H. and Engstrom, D.E. (1990). Major low levels of Lake Malawi and their implications for speciation rates in cichlid fish. *Proceedings of the Royal Society (London)* B 240, 519–553.

Page, S.E. and Rieley, J. (1998). Conservation of tropical peat swamp forests: A peatland catchment in Central Kalimantan. In: Harper, D. and Brown, A.G. (eds.), *The sustainable management of tropical catchments*, pp. 165–186. John Wiley and Sons, New York.

Paine, R.T. (1969). The *Pisaster–Tegula* interaction: Prey patches, predator food preferences, and intertidal community structure. *Ecology* 50, 950–961.

Paine, S. (1997). Swimming for dear life. *New Scientist* 13 September 1997, 28–32.

Pauly, D., Christensen, V., Dalsgaard, J., Froese, R. and Torres, F. (1998). Fishing down marine food webs. *Science* 279, 860–863.

Payne, A.I. (1986). *The ecology of tropical lakes and rivers*. Wiley, Chichester.

Pearce, F. (1998a). Growing pains. *New Scientist* 24 October 1998, 20–21.

Pearce, F. (1998b). Population bombshell. *Inside Science* 112, *New Scientist* 11 July 1998, 1–4.

Petr, T. (1983a). Introduction. In: Petr, T. (ed.), *The Purari – tropical environment of a high rainfall river basin*, pp. xiii–xvi. Dr W. Junk, The Hague.

Petr, T. (1983b). Limnology of the Purari basin. Part 1. The catchment above the delta. In: Petr, T. (ed.), *The Purari – tropical environment of a high rainfall river basin*, pp. 141–177. Dr W. Junk, The Hague.

Petr, T. (1983c). Limnology of the Purari basin. Part 2. The delta. In: Petr, T. (ed.), *The Purari – tropical environment of a high rainfall river basin*, pp. 179–203. Dr W. Junk, The Hague.

Pianka, E.R. (1970). On r- and K-selection. *American Naturalist* 104, 592–597.

Piedade, M.T.F., Junk, W.J. and Long, S.P. (1991). The productivity of the C_4 grass *Echinochloa polystachya* on the Amazon floodplain. *Ecology* 72, 1456–1463.

Pilskaln, C.H. and Johnson, T.C. (1991). Seasonal signals in Lake Malawi sediments. *Limnology and Oceanography* 36, 544–557.

Pimentel, D., Levin, S.A. and Soans, A.B. (1975). On the evolution of energy balance in some exploiter–victim systems. *Ecology* 56, 381–390.

Pimm, S.L. (1982). *Food webs*. Chapman and Hall, London.

Polunin, N.V.C. (1988). Efficient uptake of algal production by a single resident herbivorous fish on the reef. *Journal of Experimental Marine Biology and Ecology* 123, 61–76.

Pomeroy, D.E. and Service, M.W. (1986). *Tropical ecology*. Longman, London.

Poore, M.E.D. (1968). Studies in Malaysian rain forest. I. The forest of the Triassic sediments in Jengka Forest Reserve. *Journal of Ecology* 56, 143–196.

Postel, S.L. (1998). Water for food production: Will there be enough in 2025? *BioScience* 48, 629–637.

Pounds, J.A., Fogden, M.P.L. and Campbell, J.H. (1999). Biological response to climate change on a tropical mountain. *Nature* 398, 611–615.

Powell, A.H. and Powell, G.V.N. (1987). Population dynamics of male euglossine bees in Amazonian forest fragments. *Biotropica* 19, 176–179.

Preen, A. and Marsh, H. (1995). Response of dugongs to large-scale loss of seagrass from Hervey Bay, Queensland, Australia. *Wildlife Research* 22, 507–519.

Primack, R.B. (1998). *Essentials of conservation biology*. 2nd edition. Sinauer, Sunderland.

Pringle, C.M., Naiman, R.J., Bretschko, G., Karr, J.R., Oswood, M.W., Webster, J.R., Welcomme, R.L. and Winterbourn, M.J. (1988). Patch dynamics in lotic ecosystems: The stream as a mosaic. *Journal of the North American Benthological Society* 7, 503–524.

Ramadan, F.M. (1978). The effect of the Aswan High Dam on the Nile water quality. In: *Proceedings of the international symposium: Environmental effects of hydraulic engineering works*. Tennessee Valley Authority, Knoxville.

Raunkiaer, C. (1934). *The life form of plants*. Oxford University Press, Oxford.

Reich, P.B. and Borchert, R. (1984). Water stress and tree phenology in a tropical dry forest in the lowlands of Costa Rica. *Journal of Ecology* 72, 61–74.

Richards, P.W. (1952). *The tropical rain forest: An ecological study*. First edition. Cambridge University Press, Cambridge.

Richards, P.W. (1996). *The tropical rain forest: An ecological study*. Second edition. Cambridge University Press, Cambridge.

Ricklefs, R.E. (1973). *Ecology*. Chiron Press, Newton, Massachusetts.

Ricklefs, R.E. (1997). *The economy of nature*. 4th edition. Freeman, New York.

Roberts, C.M. (1993). Coral reefs: Health, hazards and history. *Trends in Ecology and Evolution* 8, 425–427.

Roberts, C.M. (1997). Connectivity and management of Caribbean coral reefs. *Science* 278, 1454–1457.

Roberts, C.M. and Polunin, N.V.C. (1993). Marine reserves: Simple solutions to managing complex fisheries? *Ambio* 22, 363–368.

Rogers, C.S. (1993). Hurricanes and coral reefs: The intermediate disturbance hypothesis revisited. *Coral Reefs* 12, 127–137.

Rosenbaum, H. and Krockenberger, M. (1993). *Report on the impacts of the Ok Tedi Mine in Papua New Guinea*. Australian Conservation Foundation, Fitzroy.

Rowe, S. (1991). *Ecosphere, environment and ecosystem: Three critical terms*. Discussion Paper R.57 UN/ECE Seminar on ecosystems approach to water management, Oslo.

Rundel, P.W. (1980). The ecological distribution of C_4 and C_3 grasses in the Hawaiian Islands. *Oecologia* 45, 354–359.

Rundel, P.W. (1994). Tropical alpine climates. In: Rundel, P.W., Smith, A.P. and Meinzer, F.C. (eds.), *Tropical alpine environments: Plant form and function*, pp. 21–44. Cambridge University Press, Cambridge.

Ruttner, F. (1931). Hydrographische und hydro-chemische Beobacktungen auf Java, Sumatra und Bali. *Archiv für Hydrobiologie* (Supplement) 8, 197–454.

Rzóska, J. (1976). A controversy reviewed, Aswan High Dam. *Nature* 261, 444–445.

Rzóska, J. (1978). *On the nature of rivers*. Dr W. Junk, The Hague.

Sader, S.A. and Joyce, A.T. (1988). Deforestation rates and trends in Costa Rica 1940–1983. *Biotropica* 20, 11–19.

Saenger, P. and Moverley, J. (1985). Vegetative phenology of mangroves along the Queensland coastline. *Proceedings of the Ecology Society of Australia* 13, 257–265.

Salati, E. and Vose, P.D. (1984). Amazon basin: A system in equilibrium. *Science* 225, 129–138.

Saldarriaga, J.G. (1986). Recovery following shifting agriculture. In: Jordan, C.F. (ed.), *Amazonian rain forests: Ecosystem disturbance and recovery. Case studies of ecosystem dynamics under a spectrum of land-use intensities*, pp. 24–33. Springer-Verlag, New York.

Sale, P.F., Forrester, G.E. and Levin, P.S. (1994). The fish of coral reefs – Ecology and management. *National Geographic Research and Exploration* 10, 224–235.

San José, J.J. and Medina, E. (1975). Effect of fire on organic matter production and water balance in a tropical savanna. In: Golley, F.B. and Medina, E. (eds.), *Tropical ecological systems: Trends in terrestrial and aquatic research*, pp. 251–264. Springer-Verlag, New York.

Sanderson, W.C. and Tan, J-P. (1996). *Population in Asia*. Avebury, Aldershot.

Sarmiento, G. (1983). Patterns of specific and phenological diversity in the grass community of the Venezuelan tropical savannas. *Journal of Biogeography* 10, 373–391.

Sarmiento, G. (1984). *The ecology of Neotropical savannas*. Harvard University Press, Cambridge.

Sarmiento, G. (1986). Ecological features of climate in high tropical mountains. In: Vuilleumeir, F. and Monasterio, M. (eds.), *High altitude tropical biogeography*, pp. 11–45. Oxford University Press, Oxford.

Sarmiento, G. (1992). Adaptive strategies of perennial grasses in South American savannas. *Journal of Vegetation Science* 3, 325–336.

Schaller, G.B. (1972). *The Serengeti lion. A study of predator–prey relations*. University of Chicago Press, Chicago.

Scheel, D. and Packer, C. (1995). Variation in predation by lions: Tracking a moveable feast. In: Sinclair, A.R.E. and Arcese, P. (eds.), *Serengeti II: Dynamics, management, and conservation of an ecosystem*, pp. 299–314. University of Chicago Press, Chicago.

Schimper, A.F.W. (1903). *Plant-geography upon a physiological basis*. Clarendon, Oxford.

Schindler, D.W. (1978). Factors regulating phytoplankton production and standing crop in the world's freshwaters. *Limnology and Oceanography* 23, 478–486.

Schindler, D.W. and Fee, E.J. (1974). Experimental lakes area: Whole lake experiments in eutrophication. *Journal of the Fisheries Research Board of Canada* 31, 937–953.

Schmidt-Nielsen, K., Schmidt-Nielsen, B., Jarnum, S.A. and Houpt, T.R. (1957). Body temperature of the camel and its relation to water economy. *American Journal of Physiology* 188, 103–112.

Scholander, P.F. (1968). How mangroves desalinate seawater. *Physiologia Plantarum* 21, 251–261.

Scholes, R.J. and Walker, B.H. (1993). *An African savanna. Synthesis of the Nylsvley Study*. Cambridge University Press, Cambridge.

Schultz, J.P. (1960). Ecological studies on the rain forest of northern Surinam. In: De Hulster, I.A. and Lanjouw, J. (eds.), *The vegetation of Surinam 2*. Van Eedenfonds, Rijksuniversitet, Utrecht.

Sedell, J.R., Richey, J.E. and Swanson, F.J. (1989). The river continuum concept: A basis for the expected ecosystem behavior of very large rivers? In: Dodge, D.P. (ed.), *Proceedings of the international large river symposium* 106, pp. 49–55. Special Publication Canadian Fisheries and Aquatic Sciences, Ottawa.

Seely, M.K. and Louw, G.N. (1980). First approximation of the effects of rainfall on the ecology and energetics of a Namib Desert dune ecosystem. *Journal of Arid Environments* 3, 25–54.

Shafer, C.L. (1997). Terrestrial nature reserve design at the urban/rural interface. In: Schwartz, M.W. (ed.), *Conservation in highly fragmented landscapes*, pp. 345–378. Chapman and Hall, New York.

Shantz, H.L. (1956). History and problems of arid lands development. In: White, G.F. (ed.), *The future of arid lands*, pp. 3–25. American Association for the Advancement of Science, Washington D.C.

Shapiro, J., Lamarra, V. and Lynch, M. (1975). Biomanipulation: An ecosystem approach to lake restoration. In: Brezonik, P.L. and Fox, J.L. (eds.), *Water quality management through biological control*, pp. 85–96. Department of Environmental Engineering Sciences, University of Florida, Gainesville.

Shelford, V.E. (1913). *Animal communities in temperate America*. University of Chicago Press, Chicago.

Sheppe, W. and Osborne, T. (1971). Patterns of use of a flood plain by Zambian mammals. *Ecological Monographs* 41, 179–205.

Shilton, L.A., Altringham, J.D., Compton, S.G. and Whittaker, R.J. (1999). Old World fruit bats can be long distance seed dispersers through extended retention of viable seeds in the gut. *Proceedings of the Royal Society (London)* B 266, 219–223.

Shmida, A., Evenari, M. and Noy-Meir, I. (1986). Hot desert ecosystems: An integrated view. In: Evenari, M., Noy-Meir, I. and Goodall, D.W. (eds.), *Hot deserts and arid shrublands, Ecosystems of the world* 12B, pp. 379–387. Elsevier, Amsterdam.

Simberloff, D.S. (1976). Experimental zoogeography of islands: Effects of island size. *Ecology* 57, 629–648.

Simberloff, D.S. and Wilson, E.O. (1970). Experimental zoogeography of islands: A two-year record of colonization. *Ecology* 51, 934–937.

Sinclair, A.R.E. (1975). The resource limitation of trophic levels in tropical grassland ecosystems. *Journal of Animal Ecology* 44, 497–520.

Sinclair, A.R.E. (1977). *The African buffalo*. University of Chicago Press, Chicago.

Sinclair, A.R.E. (1979a). Dynamics of the Serengeti ecosystem: Process and pattern. In: Sinclair, A.R.E. and Norton-Griffiths, M. (eds.), *Serengeti: Dynamics of an ecosystem*, pp. 1–30. University of Chicago Press, Chicago.

Sinclair, A.R.E. (1979b). The eruption of the ruminants. In: Sinclair, A.R.E. and Norton-Griffiths, M. (eds.), *Serengeti: Dynamics of an ecosystem*, pp. 82–103. University of Chicago Press, Chicago.

Sinclair, A.R.E. (1983). The adaptations of African ungulates and their effects on community function. In: Bourlière, F. (ed.), *Tropical savannas. Ecosystems of the World* 13, pp. 401–426. Elsevier, Amsterdam.

Sinclair, A.R.E. (1995). Serengeti past and present. In: Sinclair, A.R.E. and Arcese, P. (eds.), *Serengeti II: Dynamics, management, and conservation of an ecosystem*, pp. 3–30. University of Chicago Press, Chicago.

Sinclair, A.R.E. and Arcese, P. (1995). *Serengeti II: Dynamics, management, and conservation of an ecosystem*. University of Chicago Press, Chicago.

Sinclair, A.R.E. and Norton-Griffiths, M. (1979). *Serengeti: Dynamics of an ecosystem*. University of Chicago Press, Chicago.

Sinclair, A.R.E., Dublin, H. and Borner, M. (1985). Population regulation of Serengeti wildebeest: A test of the food hypothesis. *Oecologia* 65, 266–268.

Sioli, H. (1984). The Amazon and its main affluents: Hydrography, morphology of the river courses, and river types. In: Sioli, H. (ed.), *The Amazon: Limnology and landscape ecology of a mighty tropical river and its basin*, pp. 127–165. Dr W. Junk, Dordrecht.

Slim, F.J., Hemminga, M.A., De La Moriniere, E.C. and van der Velde, G. (1996). Tidal exchange of macrolitter between a mangrove forest and adjacent seagrass beds (Gazi Bay, Kenya). *Netherlands Journal of Aquatic Ecology* 30, 119–128.

Slud, P. (1960). The birds of Finca "La Selva," Costa Rica: A tropical wet forest locality. *Bulletin of the American Museum of Natural History* 121, 49–148.

Smith, A.P. (1974). Bud temperature in relation to nyctinastic leaf movement in an Andean giant rosette plant. *Biotropica* 6, 263–266.

Smith, J.N.M., Krebs, C.J., Sinclair, A.R.E. and Boonstra, R. (1988). Population biology of snowshoe hares. II. Interactions with winter food plants. *Journal of Animal Ecology* 57, 269–286.

Smith, R.E.W. and Hortle, K.G. (1991). Assessment and predictions of the impacts of the Ok Tedi copper mine on fish catches in the Fly River system, Papua New Guinea. *Environmental Monitoring and Assessment* 18, 41–68.

Smith, R.E.W. and Morris, T.F. (1992). The impacts of changing geochemistry on the fish assemblages of the Lower Ok Tedi and Middle Fly River, Papua New Guinea. *The Science of the Total Environment* 125, 321–344.

Smith, S.V. (1978). Coral reef area and the contributions of reefs to processes and resources of the world's oceans. *Nature* 273, 225–226.

Smuts, G.L. (1978). Interrelations between predators, prey and their environment. *BioScience* 28, 316–320.

Soil Survey Staff (1975). *Soil taxonomy*. United States Government Printing Office, Washington D.C.

Solbrig, O., Medina, E. and Silva, J.F. (1996). *Biodiversity and savanna ecosystem processes*. Springer, Berlin.

Sorentino, C. (1979). Mercury in marine and freshwater fish of Papua New Guinea. *Australian Journal of Marine and Freshwater Research* 30, 617–623.

Southwood, T.R.E. (1977). Habitat, the templet for ecological strategies? *Journal of Animal Ecology* 46, 337–365.

Spinney, L. (1998). Monkey business. *New Scientist* 2 May 1998, 18–19.

Springuel, I. and Murphy, K.J. (1990). Euhydrophytes of Egyptian Nubia. *Aquatic Botany* 37, 17–25.

Steinke, T.D., Naidoo, G. and Charles, L.M. (1983). Degradation of mangrove leaf and stem tissues in situ in Mgeni Estuary, South Africa. In: Teas, H.J. (ed.), *Biology and ecology of mangroves*, pp. 141–149. Dr W. Junk, The Hague.

Stiles, F.G. (1983). Birds. In: Janzen, D.H. (ed.), *Costa Rican natural history*, pp. 502–618. University of Chicago Press, Chicago.

Stiles, F.G., Skutch, A.F. and Gardner, D. (1989). *A guide to the birds of Costa Rica*. Cornell University Press, Ithaca.

Stiling, P.D. (1996). *Ecology: Theories and applications*. 2nd edition. Prentice Hall, New Jersey.

Stott, P. (1984). The savanna forests of mainland

Southeast Asia: An ecological survey. *Progress in Physical Geography* 8, 315–335.

Swaine, M.D. and Whitmore, T.C. (1988). On the definition of ecological species groups in tropical rain forests. *Vegetatio* 75, 81–86.

Swift, M.J., Heal, O.W. and Anderson, M.J. (1979). *Decomposition in terrestrial ecosystems*. Blackwell Scientific Publications, Oxford.

Talling, J.F. (1966). The annual cycle of stratification and phytoplankton growth in Lake Victoria, East Africa. *Internationale Revue der gesamten Hydrobiologie* 50, 421–463.

Talling, J.F. (1969). The incidence of vertical mixing, and some biological and chemical consequences, in tropical African lakes. *Verhandlungen Internationale Vereinigung für theoretische und angewandte Limnologie* 17, 998–1012.

Talling, J.F. (1976a). Water characteristics. In: Rzoska, J. (ed.), *The Nile, biology of an ancient river*, pp. 357–384. Dr W. Junk, The Hague.

Talling, J.F. (1976b). Phytoplankton: Composition, development and productivity. In: Rzoska, J. (ed.), *The Nile, biology of an ancient river*, pp. 385–402. Dr W. Junk, The Hague.

Talling, J.F. (1992). Environmental regulation in African shallow lakes and wetlands. *Revue d'Hydrobiologie Tropicale* 25, 87–144.

Talling, J.F., Wood, R.B., Prosser, M.V. and Baxter, R.M. (1973). The upper limit of photosynthetic productivity by phytoplankton: Evidence from Ethiopian soda lakes. *Freshwater Biology* 3, 53–76.

Tamarin, R.H. (1993). *Principles of genetics*, 4th edition. Wm. C. Brown, Dubuque, Iowa.

Terborgh, J. (1992). Maintenance of diversity in tropical forests. *Biotropica* 24 (Supplement), 283–292.

Thomas, P.A. and Room, P.M. (1986). Successful control of the floating weed *Salvinia molesta* in Papua New Guinea: A useful biological invasion neutralizes a disastrous one. *Environmental Conservation* 13, 242–248.

Thompson, B.W. (1966). The mean annual rainfall of Mount Kenya. *Weather* 21, 48–49.

Thompson, K. (1985). Emergent plants of permanent and seasonally flooded wetlands. In: Denny, P. (ed.), *The ecology and management of African wetland vegetation*, pp. 43–107. Dr W. Junk, The Hague.

Thornton, I.W.B. (1984). Krakatau – the development and repair of a tropical ecosystem. *Ambio* 13, 216–225.

Thornton, I.W.B. (1996). *Krakatau*. Harvard University Press, Cambridge, MA.

Tieszen, L.L., Senyimba, M.M., Imbamba, S.K. and Troughton, J.H. (1979). The distribution of C_3 and C_4 grasses and carbon discrimination along altitudinal and moisture gradients in Kenya. *Oecologia* 37, 337–350.

Tilman, D. (1982). *Resource competition and community structure*. Princeton University Press, Princeton.

Tilman, D., May, R.M., Lehman, C.L. and Nowak, M.A. (1994). Habitat destruction and the extinction debt. *Nature* 371, 65–66.

Toft, S. (1983). The Pawaia of the Purari River: Social aspects. In: Petr, T. (ed.), *The Purari – tropical environment of a high rainfall river basin*, pp. 453–474. Dr W. Junk, The Hague.

Tomlinson, P.B. (1986). *The botany of mangroves*. Cambridge University Press, Cambridge.

Tomlinson, P.B., Primack, R.B. and Bunt, J.S. (1979). Preliminary observations on floral biology in mangrove Rhizophoraceae. *Biotropica* 11, 256–277.

Trewartha, G. T. (1969). *A geography of populations: World patterns*. John Wiley, New York.

Turner, J.L. (1982). *Biological studies on the pelagic ecosystem of Lake Malawi*. Fishery Expansion Project, Technical Report F1:DP/MLW/75/019, pp. 165–173, FAO, Malawi.

Twilley, R.R. (1985). The exchange of organic carbon in basin mangrove forests in a Southwest Florida estuary. *Estuarine and Coastal Shelf Science* 20, 543–557.

Uhl, C. and Jordan, C.F. (1984). Succession and nutrient dynamics following forest cutting and burning in Amazonia. *Ecology* 65, 1476–1490.

United Nations (1998). *United Nations Human Development Report*. United Nations, New York.

Uvarov, B. (1961). Quality and quantity in insect populations. *Proceedings of the Royal Entomological Society (London)* 25, 52–59.

Valencia, R., Balslev, H. and Paz y Miño, G. (1994). High tree alpha-diversity in Amazonian Ecuador. *Biodiversity and Conservation* 3, 21–28.

van Beurden, E. (undated). Survival strategies of the Australian water-holding frog, *Cyclorana platycephalus*. In: Cogger, H.G. and Cameron, E.E. (eds.), *Arid Australia*, pp. 223–234. Australian Museum, Sydney.

Van der Ben, D. (1959). La végétation des rives des Lacs Kivu, Édouard et Albert. *Exploration hydrobiologique des Lacs Kivu, Édouard et Albert (1952–1954)*, 4. Institut Royal des Sciences Naturelles de Belgique, Bruxelles.

Vannote, R.L., Minshall, G., Cummins, K.W., Sedell, J.R. and Cushing, C.E. (1980). The river continuum concept. *Canadian Journal of Fisheries and Aquatic Science* 37, 130–137.

Veron, C. (1995). *Corals in space and time: The biogeography and evolution of the Sclearactina*. Comstock, Cornell, Ithaca.

Viner, A.B. and Smith, I.R. (1973). Geographical,

historical and physical aspects of Lake George. *Proceedings of the Royal Society (London)* B 184, 235–270.

Vitousek, P.M. (1984). Litterfall, nutrient cycling and nutrient limitation in tropical forests. *Ecology* 65, 285–298.

Vitousek, P.M., Ehrlich, P.R., Ehrlich, A.H. and Matson, P.A. (1986). Human appropriation of the products of photosynthesis. *BioScience* 36, 368–373.

Vollenweider, R.A. (1975). Input–output models with special reference to the phosphorus loading concept in limnology. *Schweizerische Zeitschrift für Hydrologie* 37, 53–84.

Volterra, V. (1926). Fluctuations in the abundance of a species considered mathematically. *Nature* 118, 558–560.

Wade, L.K. and McVean, D.N. (1969). *Mount Wilhelm studies I: The alpine and subalpine vegetation*. Research School of Pacific Studies, Publication BG/1, Australian National University, Canberra.

Walker, B.H. (1987). *Determinants of tropical savannas*. IRL Press, Oxford.

Walker, B.H. (1992). Biological diversity and ecological redundancy. *Conservation Biology* 6, 18–23.

Walker, B.H. (1995). Conserving biodiversity through ecosystem resilience. *Conservation Biology* 9, 747–752.

Wallace, A.R. (1878). *Tropical nature and other essays*. Macmillan, London.

Walter, H. (1971). *Ecology of tropical and subtropical vegetation*. Oliver and Boyd, New York.

Walter, H. (1973). *Vegetation of the earth and ecological systems of the geo-biosphere*. 3rd edition. Springer-Verlag, New York.

Walter, H. (1986). The Karoo and southern Kalahari. In: Evenari, M., Noy-Meir, I. and Goodall, D.W. (eds.), *Hot deserts and arid shrublands, Ecosystems of the world 12B*, pp. 83–359. Elsevier, Amsterdam.

Walter, H. and Leith, H. (1967). *Klimadiagramm – Weltatlas*. (*The climate diagram world atlas*). VEB Gustav Fischer, Jena.

Welcomme, R.L. (1983). *River basins*. FAO fisheries technical paper 202, FAO, Rome.

Welcomme, R.L., Ryder, R.A. and Sedell, J.A. (1989). Dynamics of fish assemblages in river systems – a synthesis. Special Publication *Canadian Fisheries and Aquatic Sciences* 106, 569–577.

Wetzel, R.G. (1975). *Limnology*. Saunders, Philadelphia.

White, I.D., Mottershead, D.N. and Harrison, S.J. (1993). *Environmental systems: An introductory text*. Chapman and Hall, London.

Whitmore, T.C. (1984). *Tropical rain forests of the Far East*. Clarendon Press, Oxford.

Whitmore, T.C. (1989). Canopy gaps and the two major groups of forest trees. *Ecology* 70, 536–538.

Whitmore, T.C. (1993). *An introduction to tropical rain forests*. Clarendon Press, Oxford.

Whittaker, R.H. (1972). Evolution and measurement of species diversity. *Taxon* 21, 213–251.

Whittaker, R.H. (1975). *Communities and ecosystems*. 2nd edition. Macmillan, London.

Whittaker, R.J. and Flenley, J.R. (1982). The flora of Krakatau. In: Flenley, J.R. and Richards, K. (ed.), *The Krakatoa Centenary Expedition. Final Report*, pp. 9–54. Department of Geography Miscellaneous Series 25, University of Hull, England.

Whittaker, R.J., Bush, M.B., Partomihardjo, T., Asquith, N.M. and Richards, K. (1992). Ecological aspects of plant colonization of the Krakatau Islands. In: Thornton, I.W.B. (ed.), *Krakatau – A century of change. GeoJournal* 28, 81–302.

Wiebes, J.T. (1979). Co-evolution of figs and their insect pollinators. *Annual Review of Ecology and Systematics* 10, 1–12.

Wiens, J.A. (1989). *The ecology of bird communities*, volumes 1 and 2. Cambridge University Press, Cambridge.

Wilkinson, C.R. and Buddemeier, R.W. (1994). *Global climate change and coral reefs: Implications for people and reefs*. Report of the UNEP-IOC-ASPEI-IUCN Global Task Team on the implications of climate change on coral reefs. IUCN, Gland, Switzerland.

Willers, B. (1994). Sustainable development: A new world deception. *Conservation Biology* 8, 1146–1148.

Williams, O.B. (1979). Ecosystems of Australia. In: Goodall, D.W., Perry, R.A. and Howes, K.M.W. (eds.), *Arid-land ecosystems: Structure, functioning and management*, volume 1, pp. 145–212. Cambridge University Press, Cambridge.

Williams, W.D. (1995). Inland lakes of brine: Living worlds within themselves. *Biologist* 42, 57–60.

Wilson, E.O. (1992). *The diversity of life*. Harvard University Press, Cambridge, MA.

World Commission on Environment and Development (1987). *Our common future*. World Commission on Environment and Development (Gro Harlem Brundtland, chair). Oxford University Press, Oxford.

World Conservation Monitoring Centre (1992). *Global biodiversity: Status of the Earth's living resources*. Chapman and Hall, London.

Young, H.J. and Young, T.P. (1983). Local distribution of C_3 and C_4 grasses on Mount Kenya. *Oecologia* 58, 373–377.

Young, T.P. (1996). High montane forest and Afro-alpine ecosystems. In: McClanahan, T.R. and Young, T.P. (eds.), *East African ecosystems and their conservation*, pp. 401–424. Oxford University Press, Oxford.

Young, T.P. and Van Orden Robe, S. (1986). Microenvironmental role of a secreted aqueous solution in the afro-alpine plant *Lobelia keniensis*. *Biotropica* 18, 267–269.

Zaret, T.M. and Paine, R.T. (1973). Species introduction in a tropical lake. *Science* 182, 449–455.

Index